Louis Marshall and the Rise of Jewish Ethnicity in America

Modern Jewish History
Henry Feingold, *Series Editor*

OTHER TITLES IN MODERN JEWISH HISTORY

The "Bergson Boys" and the Origins of Contemporary Zionist Militancy
Judith Tydor Baumel

Bundist Counterculture in Interwar Poland
Jack Jacobs

Contemporary Sephardic Identity in the America: An Interdisciplinary Approach
Margalit Bejarano and Edna Aizenberg, eds.

Jewish High Society in Old Regime Berlin
Deborah Hertz

Judah L. Magnes: An American Jewish Nonconformist
Daniel P. Kotzin

New York Jews and the Decline of Urban Ethnicity, 1950–1970
Eli Lederhendler

"Silent No More": Saving the Jews of Russia, the American Jewish Effort, 1967–1989
Henry L. Feingold

An Uneasy Relationship: American Jewish Leadership and Israel, 1948–1957
Zvi Ganin

We Are Many: Reflections on American Jewish History and Identity
Edward S. Shapiro

Will to Freedom: A Perilous Journey Through Fascism and Communism
Egon Balas

M. M. Silver

Louis MARSHALL

and the Rise of Jewish Ethnicity in America

A Biography

Syracuse University Press

First Edition 2013

13 14 15 16 17 18 6 5 4 3 2 1

A portion of Chapter 6 is taken from "Louis Marshall and the Democratization of Jewish Identity," American Jewish History Volume 94, Numbers 1–2, March–June 2008, reprinted here with permission.

∞ The paper used in this publication meets the minimum requirements of the American National Standard for Information Sciences—Permanence of Paper for Printed Library Materials, ANSI Z39.48-1992.

For a listing of books published and distributed by Syracuse University Press, visit our website at SyracuseUniversityPress.syr.edu.

ISBN: 978-0-8156-1000-7

Library of Congress Cataloging-in-Publication Data

Available upon request from publisher.

Manufactured in the United States of America

For David Silver

M. M. Silver teaches modern Jewish history at the Max Stern College of Emek Yezreel. A graduate of Cornell University, he earned his doctorate in Jewish history at the Hebrew University of Jerusalem. His English and Hebrew publications include *Our Exodus: Leon Uris and the Americanization of Israel's Founding Story*. He has worked as a visiting scholar in several US universities and lives in the Galilee.

Contents

List of Illustrations ix
Introduction xi

PART ONE: From Upstate to Uptown

1. Syracuse 3
2. Manhattan and Moral Reform 25

PART TWO: A National Organization for the Jews

3. The Origins of Organized Activism 79
4. Abrogation 135
5. Avoiding the Guillotine of Immigration Restriction 222

PART THREE: War and Peace

6. World War I 249
7. Paris and Haiti 345

PART FOUR: Marshall Law

8. Ford 381
9. Jews and Birds 402
10. Ethnic Affairs in the 1920s 444
11. Crimea and Eretz Israel 490
12. Epilogue: Massena, Zurich, Emanu-El 526

Acknowledgments 537
Notes 541
Bibliography 615
Index 629

Illustrations

1. Portrait of the lawyer as a young man ~ *16*

2. Louis Marshall and Florence Lowenstein Marshall on their wedding day ~ *31*

3. Portrait of Marshall ~ *122*

4. The Protocol of Peace ending the cloakmakers strike, September 1910 ~ *190*

5. Portrait of Marshall ~ *244*

6. Florence and the four children ~ *289*

7. Magnes as Marshall's puppet ~ *295*

8. Knollwood country home, facade ~ *416*

9. Knollwood country home, interior ~ *417*

10. Marshall resting with Adirondack guide Herb Clark ~ *419*

11. Bob Marshall in his element ~ *430*

12. Louis Marshall Memorial Hall ~ *436*

13. Marshall with grandchildren Florence Billikopf and David Billikopf ~ *439*

14. New York delegation in favor of a bill to unite separated families ~ *454*

15. Marshall in the mid-1920s ~ *524*

Introduction

The life of Louis Marshall (1856–1929) encapsulates the political history of the Jews in the United States during the first three decades of the twentieth century, up to the Great Depression. Born in Syracuse to immigrant parents of middle European ancestry, Marshall made his mark in Upstate New York as a successful lawyer with a special flair for constitutional issues. When he moved to Manhattan at the age of thirty-eight, nothing in his past necessarily foreshadowed the stature he would attain in the twentieth century: the premier figure in organized Jewish efforts in the United States whose name after World War I also became inextricably linked to the rights of Jewish communities overseas, and a lawyer of renown who is said to have argued more cases before the Supreme Court than any private attorney of his time.

Marshall catapulted to prominence partly as a result of his association, as an insider-outsider, with Manhattan's elite circle of German Jews, whose undisputed chief until his death in 1920 was the wealthy banker Jacob Schiff. Although Marshall's Jewish leadership position and influence was made possible by this access to the resources of New York's powerful Uptown Jews, he became a figure of preeminent authority in Jewish affairs as a result of hard work, discerning intelligence, and compelling devotion to issues of concern to all Jews. By the 1920s, Jews in America were even said to be living under the rule of "Marshall law." This association between an era of communal endeavor and the mostly beneficent, though sometimes imperious, wisdom and activity of one experienced organizational leader had no precedent in American Jewish history, nor could it possibly have been recapitulated in subsequent eras. Marshall's peak period of impact in American Jewish affairs also has few parallels in the ethnic history of the United States as a whole.

Marshall was the man who, for twenty years, led the fight to keep America's doors of immigration open. In the absence of his legislative lobbying and the help of predecessors and colleagues in this immigration sphere, Hitler and the Nazis would have killed several hundred thousand more Jews. Marshall was the man to whom Henry Ford capitulated and apologized, after sponsoring a vitriolic hate campaign against the Jews for several years in the 1920s. During the first decade of British Mandatory control in Palestine, Marshall was the man to whom the pioneer Zionists turned, seeking make-or-break support for their heroic attempt to re-create a Jewish national home. And Marshall was the man who drew up the papers, ironed out guidelines of structure and policy, and almost single-handedly orchestrated the signature public campaigns of leading Jewish organizations and institutions of his day. Marshall's energetic vision was the prime component distinguishing the first quarter century of the American Jewish Committee (AJC), the first organization in the history of the United States to be formed by an ethnoreligious group for the purpose of defending its rights and those of its brethren overseas. His intelligence and impassioned commitment left indelible marks as well on several other key Jewish religious, cultural, and philanthropic institutions; some, like the Jewish Theological Seminary (JTS) and the Joint Distribution Committee (JDC), continue to thrive today.

In American affairs, Marshall's major contributions toward what the country's twenty-first-century citizens cherish most about its recent past and guard most vigilantly with a worried eye toward its future are stunningly underappreciated. Upon his death, the country's leading African American advocacy organization, the National Association for the Advancement of Colored People (NAACP), noted that every single case of "any constitutional importance" it had handled for several years had been personally litigated by Marshall or carefully supervised and directed by him. One NAACP spokesman said simply, "no man has done more for the Negro."[1] Concurrently, Native American empowerment groups posthumously honored Marshall for the "great service" he had rendered to their cause in his final years. Marshall's legal briefs and advocacy for Native American rights, they said, "had the quality of a trumpet challenge to the imagination and conscience."[2]

Such encomia would dignify any American's résumé. However, it is important to note that, apart from his ongoing work as the leader of the country's Jewish community, Marshall's most abiding interest as an advocate of rights did not attach to any human group. An impassioned conservationist, Marshall and his son Robert (a legendary figure in American environmental history) were crucially instrumental in the conceptualization of wilderness protection as a matter of moral and legal right. Marshall was the driving force in the complex, tightrope-walking establishment and administration of what may have been America's first degree-conferring institution for environmental studies, the New York State College of Forestry at Syracuse University (today the SUNY College of Environmental Science and Forestry). The forestry school was one jewel in an array of efforts he undertook, not just in environmental spheres but for general public improvement in New York State. For instance, Marshall took special pride in having been selected to serve in three New York State Constitutional Conventions.

All of the phases of Marshall's robust career, even those that apply to nonsectarian issues such as the environment, are discernibly part of a Jewish story of self-preservation, adaptation, and settlement in the United States. This is a biography of Marshall and also a study of Jewish peoplehood, an admittedly ethereal concept that refers to the way Jewish continuity is achieved via a series of interlocked interactions. These include the interaction between various Jewish subgroups, the interaction between religious and ethnically secular components of Jewish identity, and the interaction between a Diaspora Jewish group and its host (in this case, American) national society.

Particularly as a result of Jewish continuity concerns precipitated by the Holocaust, a significant amount of philosophical and public discussion has been devoted in past decades to ideas of Jewish peoplehood. While suggestive, such inquiry, I believe, is at risk of sliding toward blithering incoherence in the absence of a conscientious demonstration of how Jewish interactions actually unfold in richly complicated historical contexts. By monitoring the life of one precociously active ethnic leader and its interplay with existing Jewish networks and outlying American contexts, we can gain precious insight about Jewish peoplehood, perhaps not as a phenomenon consecrated by divinely provident *hasgacha* but rather as the product of intelligent mediation between elite classes and hard-working masses of Jews, as well as thoughtful negotiation between Jewish values and American norms. Close study of one authoritative life that became dedicated to the ideal of Jewish peoplehood can be of value both to readers with interests in Jewish affairs and Jewish life, and to those curious about an important facet of twentieth-century American ethnic history.

More specifically, while trying to provide a reliably accurate biographical account of Marshall's life, this book tells the story of the rise of a discernible form of American Jewish ethnicity in a period stretching between the latter part of the Gilded Age and the eve of the Great Depression. Resulting from the creative (and often tense) interaction between a settled "German" Jewish elite and a mass of "Russian" Jewish immigrants in New York City,[3] a fusion of conservative patrician and radical populist outlooks expressed itself in a recognizably liberal American Jewish ethnic style in the 1930s and afterward. No single figure, organization, or episode could possibly reflect all of the variants and components in the evolution of this ethnicity; but more than any other individual in the community, Louis Marshall consciously and conscientiously experimented with an array of organizational and identity formulas that would bring this union of Uptown and Downtown Jews, the classes and the masses, to a successful American and Jewish conclusion.

A few attempts have been made to rate the importance of Marshall's experience in comparison to other prominent American Jewish lives,[4] but they appear grounded on unsatisfactorily inchoate standards of judgment. In fact, wondering whether Louis Marshall was America's "most important" Jew of his era or in general is probably meaningless, and possibly disingenuous. On the achievement level, such judgments are entirely context specific—in other words, if you are looking for the most important American Jew with regard to Zionism, try Louis Brandeis, whereas if your interest is baseball, try Sandy Koufax; then again, if your context of interest is American Jewry's twentieth-century organizational history, Marshall would probably be the premier figure. Ethnicity, however, is not a specific context but rather an evolving communal state of feeling, and so its main contributors are surely best examined on a scale where achievement is not the main measurement.

In ethnic identity, expressiveness would appear to be the premier standard. Regarding key facets of American Jewish life—for instance religion—it is not difficult to think of many figures more articulately expressive than Louis Marshall, who was not a theologian; yet, no figure in the history of the community has ever expressed so much, by words and deeds, about the prevailing questions of duty in American Jewish life. His life was a continuing deliberation about the cardinal questions of what Jews owe to one another in America, what they owe to their newfound land and its non-Jewish inhabitants (and what its non-Jews owe to them), and what American Jews owe to Jews of other lands. If no individual could have produced resolutely conclusive solutions to any of these questions, no American Jew has ever been more expressively robust than Marshall in the endeavor to reconfigure the confusing chaos of daily life pragmatically as a coherent pattern of American Jewish identity.

Developments in Marshall's own style and habits reflect key transitions in American Jewish communal life over a three-decade period, some of which have been overlooked by scholars who focused on the Uptown German/Downtown Russian rivalry in terms of binary polarization, rather than on constant flux, internal ambivalence, and continually shifting responses to outside events both in America and overseas. As the chapters of this biography attempt to demonstrate, Marshall's life, and his community's, went through a series of overlapping phases: the patrician stage, wherein the Uptown elite fashioned model programs for vulnerable immigrants virtually as exercises in small-scale colonization, moved into the organizational stage, wherein the elite established nationwide institutions by fiat, basically excluding the presumed mass Jewish beneficiaries of the new organizations. In the World War I period, Marshall's life (and American Jewish affairs) developed a much more populist ethos, and finally, in the 1920s, American Jewish affairs pivoted uniquely around the judgments and doings of one leader, Louis Marshall, in a phase that has been, and still can be, called (not entirely facetiously) "Marshall law." Examined in critical detail in the chapters of this volume, the contents of such transitions need not be spelled out here.

At this stage, it suffices to point out that beneath the boisterous infighting between the Downtown Russian and Uptown German groups, there remained always remarkable congruency between the shifts in Marshall's own public and private Jewish persona and those of the community he served. Owing to this congruence, the rationale of this biography of Louis Marshall, the first attempt to provide a systematic and scholarly account of his life, can be summarized in brief. As an examination of Louis Marshall's richly complicated life, this book bears witness to the rise of American Jewish ethnicity in pre-Holocaust America.

Louis Marshall and the Rise of Jewish Ethnicity in America

PART ONE

From Upstate to Uptown

1

Syracuse

The first phase of Marshall's life appears as an immigrant success story, featuring the rise of the child of struggling German Jewish immigrants in provincial Upstate New York and his transition to professional success in New York City. Compared to the voluminous records of Marshall's subsequent career as a lawyer and Jewish communal leader based in Manhattan, documentation of this first phase of his life is relatively scant, and our knowledge of his Syracuse years has relied almost exclusively on nostalgic reminiscence colored by subsequent knowledge of the sort of "Uptown" personality Marshall would become.

In fact, Marshall could never have been fully Uptown. His unprecedented success as a mediator between wealthy Jewish philanthropists of Manhattan and East European immigrants owed much to his own background, to the fact that he himself was rather closer to the grinding poverty and vulnerability of the immigrant experience than the Downtown activists (as well as overseas Jews, Zionists, and zealots of other persuasions) usually realized. The passion and persistence of the key commitments of his later life—lobbying for open immigration being one obvious example—can be fully understood only in view of his early years in Syracuse.

Part One of this biography therefore explores Marshall's Syracuse years and the transition to New York City in some detail, seeking to understand how his personality became endowed with traits and tendencies suited for the fundamental roles of his career. His labors in creative mediation between elite and immigrant Jews in the United States and around the globe, his advocacy of Jewish interests in Gentile society, his impassioned pleas for environmental protection, and his defense of civil rights for Americans of all races, religions, and beliefs always bore an imprint of his Syracuse youth and of the "rags to riches" dynamic of his resettlement as a successful New York City professional.

By the end of the first phase of his career, Marshall had compiled considerable experience in Jewish communal affairs, acting as the leading administrator, lobbyist, or publicist in a number of patrician Uptown endeavors to Americanize the East European Jewish immigrants. The benevolent paternalism of these efforts was destined to be overwhelmed by the mass energy of the immigrants. That is, broad historical and cultural circumstances compelled Jacob Schiff, Marshall, and other Uptown cohorts to abandon this blatant, almost colonialist, brand of paternalism and to experiment with more inclusive forms of communal endeavor. The establishment of a national Jewish organization, the American Jewish Committee, was a milestone marking a new stage in the consolidation of American Jewish ethnic identity, and its early, defining endeavors constituted a new phase (see Part Two) in Marshall's biography.

Of course, a transformation in spirit and organizational tactics in a growing community of hundreds of thousands of immigrant and settled Jews could not be directed by any single individual. In a society scrupulously observant of the separation of religion and state, where the activity of any religious-based community proceeded exclusively on a volunteer basis, communal leadership necessarily retained an ambiguous character. And if any single individual "governed" aspects of Jewish communal life in the era of the late nineteenth and early twentieth centuries, it would have been Jacob Schiff, not Louis Marshall (who, in various contexts, became Schiff's protégé, manager, and lawyer).

Nonetheless, even in this early period that precedes his prominence in American and world Jewish life, Marshall, as much as anyone in the vibrant Jewish communities of the Empire State, appears as a miniature embodiment of the creative crosscurrents that produced twentieth-century American Jewish ethnic identity. Just as the condescending ethos of the early communal experiments examined here in Part One was inevitably cast aside by a mass of energetic and increasingly articulate Jewish immigrants, the late nineteenth-century patrician methods of moral reform sponsored by his adopted Uptown peers could not be sustained for a prolonged period in the spirit and deeds of Louis Marshall. That was because his own background kept him attuned to the sensitivities and needs of the immigrants. The search for a communal formula that would combine the better parts of the Uptown philanthropists' intentions with the democratizing populist energy of Downtown Jewry belongs both to Marshall's biography and to the story of the rise of American Jewish ethnicity.

First Years

The fate of the Union weighed heavily on the minds of many in the year of Marshall's birth, and their anxieties were inscribed on the landscape of his hometown, Syracuse, New York. Marshall was born on December 14, 1856, nine years after Syracuse's formal establishment as a city. The summer before his birth, renegade New York Democrats, outraged that their party was being abused as the "tool of a slaveholding oligarchy," convened in Syracuse, where they held a Democratic Republican state convention and resolved to throw their support to the candidate of the recently formed Republican Party, John Frémont, because his election would "make Kansas a free state."[1] Eight years later, during the Civil War, the spirit of these renegade Democrats would be renewed in Syracuse in a National Equal Rights League meeting convened by Northern blacks, including Frederick Douglass, who were pondering ways states ought to promote civil rights struggles. Such events bequeathed to Syracuse something of a reputation for liberal idealism. Meantime, the city grew steadily. In 1850, Syracuse was a midsize upstate town of 20,000 inhabitants. Solidly networked by the Erie Canal and railroads, its population would triple during the next thirty years. The town's first street railway began operation in 1860; ten years later came the founding charter of Syracuse University.

On the American Jewish timeline, late 1856 is notable for the births of the two lawyers named Louis. In Louisville, Kentucky, just a month before Marshall's birth, Louis Brandeis was also born to Central European Jewish parents. Each Louis was destined to leave an indelible mark in American law and in Jewish politics, though the differences separating their philosophies and purposes in these two fields appear no less significant than their similarities, and the comparison between the two men continues to intrigue scholars of Jewish history.[2]

Louis Marshall was the eldest child of Jacob Marshall and Zilli Strauss. At the time of their son's birth, neither had been in the country for longer than seven years. Making his way from Bavaria, Jacob arrived in New York in 1849, at the age of nineteen. His surname was originally "Marschall"—late in his life, Louis joked that after a fifty-day sailing voyage, his father was seasick by the time he reached America and thus favorably disposed to striking the "c" ("sea") from his name.[3] Jacob had five francs, less than a dollar, upon arrival, which he promptly squandered on peaches. Jacob peddled, had goods stolen by thieves, caught typhoid fever and recuperated, and worked for a spell in the construction of a stretch of the Northern Central Railroad until a swindling contractor withheld his wages. The hapless immigrant tried his luck at work on the Erie Canal and also found employment as a porter in a hamlet in New York State's west-central Livingstone County.[4] Surviving as a peddler and porter, Jacob worked his way up through the Mohawk Valley, between the Adirondacks and the Catskills, before settling in Syracuse. He worked unsuccessfully as a pack peddler and then opened a fruit stand in the Granger Block. The twenty-six-year-old boarded at a residence on East Jefferson Street.[5]

In one generation, Syracuse's Jewish population grew from the bare minyan prayer circle of ten men who founded the Society of Concord congregation in 1839 to around 1,000 persons. A city directory published just months after Jacob's arrival indicates that most of the Jews dwelled around Genesee and Mulberry streets, in the city center's fifteenth ward, and worked as peddlers or in dry good and grocery stores. Most were of Central European origin and, like Jacob Marshall, felt comfortable putting down roots where Syracuse's growing immigrant Jewish population was quartered. In September 1851, when Syracuse's Jewish community consecrated the new building of the Temple of Concord, on the corner of Mulberry and Harrison streets, the ceremony's guest of honor, Rabbi Isaac Leeser of Philadelphia, noted in his periodical, the *Occident,* that the congregation's president Jacob Stone addressed the proud worshippers in German; however, the young boys who formed a procession as part of the ceremony carried a banner with an English inscription.[6] This was, in short, a hard-working community of Americanizing German Jews. Not fully arrived economically (in his article, Leeser noted that of the eighty-six Concord members, only ten could "be styled comparatively rich"), the Jews nonetheless had enough confidence and ambition to build a new house of worship that would put them on a par with the city's other religious groups.

On Sunday, December 14, 1856, the day of Louis Marshall's birth, the steeple of this proud Temple of Concord was blown off by a windy hailstorm and crashed next to the Marshall home.[7] The *Syracuse Daily Standard* reported that the "spire of the Synagogue was entirely demolished, and a brood of doves which made the steeple their meeting place was killed."[8] The steeple was never replaced, leaving the temple with the appearance of a "hen minus its head."[9]

Zilli Strauss, of Württemberg, Germany, made her way to Syracuse two years after her arrival in the United States in 1853. Marshall spoke of his father in a properly respectful, though somewhat reserved, voice, as though he were an advocate representing the memory of the patriarch of the American branch of his family;[10] his closest relationship was with his mother, and his scattered references to her are effusively laudatory. It was Zilli who inspired Marshall's prodigious industriousness, his love of learning, and his disciplined approach to challenges. Toward the end of his life he recalled his mother with unguarded affection and admiration, attesting: "I can say without qualification that she was the greatest influence upon my life."[11] He reiterated this sentiment in a letter to Pennsylvania Senator David Reed in 1926, adding that "my mother became the best American that I have ever seen."[12] In such comments, Marshall emphasized the spirit laden within his mother's successful settlement and life in the United States; however, in her cultural bearing, Zilli remained German. Marshall conversed with his mother in that language until her death in 1910 (his own first words were in

German).[13] Zilli had a prodigious memory—Louis recalled that she could recite most of Schiller's poems by heart and had also virtually memorized a German translation of *Ivanhoe*. Memory training she provided, Louis thought, "cut the labor of my later school and law studies in half."[14]

During Louis's childhood years, Jacob struggled to expand a hide and leather business he established in 1861. The work often kept him away for home; two decades after he started his business, Jacob still often found himself on the road, purchasing skins from trappers across New York State and into Pennsylvania. Louis spent some time salting hides and calfskins for his father's business. He also handled his father's business correspondence from his eleventh year until he started law school study (this correspondence extended as far as Cuba[15]), but mostly it was his brother Benjamin who worked at his father's store on 22 James Street. When Louis was born, the young family lived on Mulberry Street, next to the Temple of Concord, but after his father's business started to produce revenue, the family bought a house on Cedar Street. That remained Zilli and Jacob's house for the remainder of their lives. After Zilli's death in 1910, and about a year before Jacob's passing in 1912, Louis held a brief ceremony to donate the home to the Jewish community; he spoke soberly about the facility's future use in the cultivation of "homely virtues of industry and efficiency," but in fact the residence was used more as a social center and by the 1930s functioned as a Young Men's Hebrew Association.[16]

Marshall's New World family roots can thus be traced with some precision, but he did not view his own heritage solely in terms of his parents' sojourn and settlement in Syracuse. At phases in his career as a Jewish intercessor and activist, Marshall searched for evidence indicating that his work had precedent in the spirit and purposes of Jewish ancestors in medieval Europe. One connection was particularly inspiring.

Albert Ottinger, who served as attorney general of New York in the mid-1920s and became the first Jewish gubernatorial candidate in the state's history (a Republican, he lost his 1928 bid to Democrat Franklin Roosevelt), was distantly related to the Marshalls, and he suggested to Louis that their family tree descended from a famed thirteenth-century Jewish scholar, leader, and martyr, Rabbi Meir of Rothenburg.[17] Marshall could not corroborate this claim, but he was intrigued by it, and recalled that his mother had alluded to the line of descent.[18] In some ways, Marshall fashioned himself as a latter-day successor to the example of Jewish leadership and honor set by Rabbi Meir. Just as Marshall himself held formal titles, for instance as president of the American Jewish Committee or chairman of the board of directors at the Jewish Theological Seminary,

Rabbi Meir enjoyed titular designations as the premier rabbi of Germany, but mostly his leadership, like Marshall's own, derived from the "force of his intellectual and moral qualities."

This transposition of Marshall's own self-image as an American Jewish leader onto the medieval past can be found in a lecture he delivered on Rabbi Meir of Rothenburg, at the Jewish Theological Seminary in spring 1906.[19] The lecture demonstrates how Marshall conceptualized his position in the Jewish world not exclusively in terms of the rags-to-riches narrative of German Jewish peddlers opening the door to their families' prosperity in the bountiful democracy of the United States, but also as a link in a much longer chain of Jewish intellectualism, wisdom, courage, and honor.

Marshall's description of the Jewish leadership role played by Rabbi Meir in thirteenth-century Central Europe reads simultaneously as a summary and preview of Marshall's own activities in early twentieth-century America, on behalf of Jews everywhere:

> The subject on which he [Rabbi Meir] passed judgment touched every phase of contemporary life, including those of ritual, of liturgy and of civil and criminal jurisdictional rights of property, rules of commerce, the law of exchange, the marital relation, the right of inheritance, the police power, crimes and punishments.[20]

An authoritative leader, Rabbi Meir set standards regarding the right of communal heads to impose tax requirements upon individuals. In his arduous labors on behalf of captive Jews, Rabbi Meir wrestled with the issue of who could legitimately be asked to shoulder the burden of ransom ("Rabbi Meir insisted that the community was entitled to use the property of the prisoners for their liberation"). Rabbi Meir, Marshall observed, argued that Jewish fencing masters ought to be regarded as teachers. Refracted in such comments on the thirteenth-century rabbi were orientations and possibilities considered by Marshall and colleagues in America's German Jewish, Uptown, elite as they searched for solutions to the plight of indigent East European Jews who sought haven in the United States from economic marginalization and persecution in the Old World. Looking over the career of his reported ancestor, Louis Marshall found inspiration for his efforts in 1906 to accommodate constructively the militant demands of New York's "Downtown" masses of immigrant Jews, who had been seething with anger since the Kishinev pogrom in 1903 and the subsequent anti-Jewish violence in the czar's empire. In this connection, Marshall commented that Rabbi Meir's high regard for Jewish fencers provided "practical authority in support of the contentions of those who favor a defense fund to enable the Russian Jew to procure self-defense weapons."[21] That is to say, Marshall's real or imagined Jewish pedigree sometimes provided leverage for support of unconventional or creative solutions to Jewish problems.

On all accounts, Marshall's childhood in Syracuse was robust and happy. En route to school, he enjoyed stopping at a shoe shop owned by his uncle, Jacob Stolz, who established himself economically by trading in leather during the Civil War and who had married Jacob Marshall's sister, Yetta. Young Louis would read the *Syracuse Daily Courier* aloud to his uncle. Jacob Stolz's brother David, a tailor, married Regina Strauss, Zilli Marshall's sister. David operated a tailor shop on Grape Street in Syracuse for forty years, was the father of Louis's two favorite cousins, and thought of himself as the oldest surviving member of the Odd Fellow fraternal order in New York State[22] (his sons, Louis's lifelong friends, were Benjamin and Joseph; Benjamin remained in Syracuse and became an attorney after working as an assistant to Louis, with the Jenney, Brooks, Ruger, and Marshall law firm; Joseph became a Reform rabbi in Chicago[23]). Louis excelled in the Seventh Ward Public School.

The one sore spot in his public school days was the "exceedingly narrow" and "missionary spirit" of some teachers, "who made it a point to read about the crucifixion of Christ on Good Friday." Morning sessions at school opened with Bible reading and prayer. On the whole, teachers were considerate in the Bible readings, selecting Psalms and Proverbs "that gave offense to nobody." Still, such procedures in public school in Syracuse "tended to mark a classification between the pupils"; looking back on those days sixty years later, Marshall confessed that such "classification" separating Jews and Christians seemed "unjustifiable."[24] Louis's cousin Joseph recalled that they attended German and Hebrew school every afternoon but Friday. Louis Marshall was one of the star pupils. Stolz added that at his Bar Mitzvah, Marshall "recited in temple the whole catechism in German." Saturday mornings, his cousin added, were reserved for "heartily" played games of baseball, a sport Louis loved all his life.[25]

Marshall graduated from Syracuse High School in April 1874.[26] He was apparently one of the first Jews to graduate from the school;[27] Nathan Jacobson, one of the first Syracuse Jews to become a doctor and who later became an instructor of surgery at Syracuse University, graduated in the same high school class.[28] During these years, Marshall and Jacobson honed thinking and presentation skills they later utilized in their respective professional careers by engaging debates in the Progress Club, which met at the basement of the Temple of Concord.[29] Marshall's debating exercises, he later realized, prepared him for a legal career. He recalled that debate subjects related to the Constitution, the Declaration of Independence, and the founding of the country. Preparing for the debates, he studied American history. "I became engrossed in the creation of this new nation, and was eager to learn how its laws had been drawn and its institutions founded. Then I began to talk about them. I suppose it was a natural transition from the debating club to the Bar."[30] The few extant records of Marshall's high school years attest to a strict study routine. In May 1870, he wrote to a young friend, George Brown, about his studies in Latin, French, bookkeeping, literature, and algebra. Every day after school he devoted at least fifteen minutes to each subject.[31]

Following high school, Marshall worked as a factotum in a Syracuse law office headed by Nathaniel Smith, and he was engaged in floor sweeping, mending fires in the winter, and other menial duties. For two years, he supplemented his work as an errand boy by perusing law books in Smith's office and in the Court of Appeals library, which was adjacent to the town hay market. The first break in his legal career was popularized in dramatic form by Marshall's friend and colleague, the Jewish scholar Cyrus Adler. Basing his account on a tribute to Marshall published by the *New York Tribune* in 1924,[32] Adler recapitulated a conference between a Syracuse judge and some attorneys at the Court of Appeals, pertaining to litigation on an Erie Canal issue. The librarian was unable to find a report that conveyed facts germane to the case. A "small, earnest Jewish boy," wearing thick spectacles, suddenly arose from a corner, and, in a trembling voice, informed the judge, "I think I can get what you want." Young Marshall explained that the report was not in the Court of Appeals library, but rather in Nathaniel Smith's office. Incredulous, the conferees waited, as Marshall rushed to obtain the report. When he returned with the document, the judge explained that he was looking for references to stuck juries. "'Oh, yes, sir,' said the boy. 'I've just been looking up stuck juries. I'll write you a list of references. Most of them are here in the library, but they take a little time to find.' He got out his pencil and set to work."[33]

Columbia University Law School

Marshall's legal aptitude and ambition could not be suppressed. He attended Columbia University's Law School for one year, starting in September 1876. Lacking funds to finance a full two-year term of study at the institution, this son of an immigrant tradesman in leather and hides attended first-year classes in the afternoon and second-year classes in the morning.[34] Toward the end of his life, Marshall noted that he technically could not be considered an alumnus of Columbia law school, stating: "I never received a degree because two years actual attendance was required."[35] Though he was not destined to earn a formal undergraduate or graduate degree, Marshall's compressed term of study at Columbia attracted notice, and the twenty-year-old from Syracuse acquitted himself well. In fact, the institution's spirit and methodology aptly suited Marshall's strengths.

Columbia Law School was dominated by Theodore William Dwight, a Catskill, New York, native who, roughly from the time of Marshall's birth, single-handedly developed law instruction at Columbia. When law studies were expanded at Columbia earlier in the 1870s, Dwight became dean and served at that capacity in the law school until 1891. By the time of Marshall's brief but intensive enrollment, the "Dwight method" of legal instruction was fully instituted at Columbia.

Biographical sketches of Marshall have relied on simplified representations of this methodology. These sketches suggest that the Dwight method put a premium on Marshall's two strengths, memorization and debating skills. In his element, Marshall excelled, these portraits emphasize. Adler's insightful tribute to Marshall features an anecdote highlighting the recognition of the Syracuse native's legal "genius" at Columbia, while also depicting legal training in post–Civil War America as memory drill. Professor Dwight, Adler wrote,

> soon came to regard Louis Marshall as a genius. Often, when Professor Dwight recited a principle of law that was referred to in a reported case in this state [New York], he would call on young Marshall to tell the class the name of the case, the book and page where it was to be found, which our young plumed knight always did.[36]

Marshall had a prodigious memory and energetic mind, but such anecdotes draw on hagiographic traditions in Jewish memorials emphasizing the phenomenal intellectual powers of the *ilui,* the Talmudic genius, and also perhaps various hyperbolic strands in American biography. In fact, the passage in Adler's influential short biography of Marshall pertaining to his law school year, which has served as the primary or sole account of Marshall's legal training in subsequent biographical analyses of him,[37] is based on a 1926 *Jewish Tribune* piece about Marshall authored by Henry Wollman, a friend and real estate partner of Marshall's whose credibility as a biographer is questionable. After its publication, Marshall laughed with his sons about passages in Wollman's article and noted that its references to his younger years "should have been carefully edited in order to keep within the facts."[38]

Later in his life, Marshall remarked sparingly about his law school year, but the fragments he left corroborate a common sense supposition of the significant impression it made upon him. Forty years after his enrollment, he corresponded with Ansel Judd Northrup, a county judge from Onondaga County, who dabbled as a writer about nature and political issues. At the start of Marshall's studies, Northrup, a member of the bar in Syracuse, invited him to his house, where he introduced the young prodigy to Dwight. In 1917, Marshall recalled this meeting as "one of the brightest moments in my life" that "marked the beginning of a most pleasant and inspiring relationship with our great teacher." Were he "to attain a century of years," Marshall would never forget the evening.[39]

Since Marshall never provided details about his law school year, Columbia's impact must be measured somewhat speculatively, in terms of the relationship between Dwight's methodology and the character of Marshall's professional activities. Here, the comparison to Brandeis appears suggestive. Both Jewish lawyers named Louis relied heavily on empirical evidence in the preparation and presentation of legal briefs. As discussed by the scholar Jonathan Sarna, the two operated on the basis of differing life outlooks and political ideologies concerning the role of government, the sanctity of contract and property, and the vitality of mass organization as compared to the need for individual protection;[40] ultimately, these differences are rooted in separate life experiences and character tendencies that exceed the issue of the sort of legal training they received and apply to subjects beyond their work as lawyers. Yet they were both lawyers, and an important part of what they became in public life had to have been influenced by the sort of training and socialization to which they were exposed in law school. Moreover, contrasts in descriptions of law school methodologies at Harvard and Columbia are intriguing. The case method at Harvard emphasized the close study of principles in individual cases, whereas Dwight's methodology at Columbia is not believed to have been geared to an elite professional brain trust, as Harvard's case method was, but rather to aspiring men from modest backgrounds who were hungry to pass bar exams and climb the ladder of success. Can different emphases in their legal training be related to the divergence in the course of the two men's careers?

Marshall's year at Columbia prompts questions that go beyond this inveigling comparison to Brandeis. The highly authoritative, occasionally dictatorial, style Marshall maintained in the later, New York City, phases of his life, from his forties and onward, encourages us to overlook how provincial his outlook had to have been when he enrolled in Columbia in 1876. The year he spent at the law school constituted his sole experience as a student on a campus of higher learning; lacking experience, he was apt to absorb messages and methodology transmitted by Columbia.

In a country that faced challenges of industrialization, secession movements, and civil war, the law was a growth industry in the years of Marshall's youth.

There were roughly 24,000 lawyers in the United States in 1850; in 1880, there were more than 64,000.[41] This rise was complemented by the institutionalization of legal study. The concept of a law school was unknown to the country's founders; as was the case in England, the expectation in early periods of US history was that young men read the law in an office (faculties of law on the continent devoted themselves mostly to canon law). On occasion, practitioners, starting with Tapping Reeve in Litchfield, Connecticut, in 1784, calculated that their most promising source of revenue would be formalized training of apprentices, and so private law schools dotted the young nation. By 1860, there were twenty-one law schools in the United States;[42] for the next several years, the country's leader in legal education was the law school at Columbia College. Indisputably, Columbia's premier position was the result of the vision and labors of Theodore Dwight, who was recruited by Columbia from Hamilton College in 1858. One of Marshall's student peers left a vivid description of Dwight, circa 1876: "A man of robust health, of considerably more than ordinary stature, erect and well built. . . . His ruddy face lighted up easily with a smile, altogether giving an impression of benignity and abiding youthfulness."[43]

Believing that legal education of the time constituted a "heterogeneous and ill-balanced jumble of isolated legal rules,"[44] Dwight prepared textbooks that outlined guiding principles and were designed to give students a sense of the law as a whole. Memorization was definitely a key part of the learning process (recalling the very early days of Dwight's tenure at Columbia, a US Circuit Court judge, William Wallace, recalled that two and a half hours of afternoon study were devoted to recitation of memorized passages from the textbooks[45]). Yet the "Dwight method" is misleadingly described as learning by rote; Columbia's pioneer in legal education eschewed mechanical reading of cases and asked students to peruse judicial opinions only inasmuch as they illustrated the principles delineated in his textbooks. Instruction at Columbia catered to the "average" student. Dwight was a gifted, patient, and encouraging teacher who diligently learned the names of all his students in the first days of an academic year. Dwight, one student recalled, "could so cross-question a dunce that the dunce would come off amazed at his own unconscious cerebration."[46]

Dwight loved the law and his work, but his student-friendly disposition was far from sheer altruism. In his legal education sphere, he was at the crux of a national trend favoring the professionalization of training. When he took up the reins at Columbia, the New York Constitution did not require any period of study for admission to the bar. Dwight tried to transport to Columbia an arrangement he had wrested at Hamilton, whereby graduates of his law school would be on a fast track for admission to the bar.[47] By 1860, Dwight secured this "diploma privilege" for Columbia graduates[48]—it was a crucial incentive for students to complete the two-year course at the law school.

These considerations put the so-called Dwight method in perspective as more of a goal than pedagogy. The objective was to attract aspiring legal professionals to a full course of study, and it was a success from the start (twenty-seven of the thirty-five students who enrolled in Dwight's first class in 1858 completed the two-year program[49]). The method worked so well that by the time of Marshall's enrollment, the college's law school was quartered in an impressive new facility, at Great Jones Street and Lafayette Place, and stiffened admissions standards required applicants who lacked a college diploma to furnish proof of knowledge of Latin and of a good academic education.[50] Discussions of extending legal instruction as a three-year program were afoot.

Marshall's curtailment of his studies after one year was not at drastic variance with the norms of his days, which remained suffused with images of self-made practitioners like Abraham Lincoln who never set foot in law school. However, it rubbed against the grain of both the specific procedures and goals of his own institution and also the general professionalization trend of the times.[51]

During the time of Marshall's enrollment, Columbia was losing its reputation to Harvard as the premier institution of legal instruction in the country. The extent to which the case method at Harvard, instituted by Christopher Columbus Langdell when he became dean at the law school in 1870, differed pedagogically from Columbia's Dwight method is open to question.[52] Contrasts between the two institutions can be overdrawn, though a move toward a more intellectually challenging study of law at Harvard can be discerned in the 1870s (beginning with an unsigned attack on the old system authored by Oliver Wendell Holmes, among others). The main difference, in fact, was that at the time the "two lawyers named Louis" enrolled for professional instruction,[53] it was Brandeis who studied at an institution that was starting to conceptualize law study as an academic, rather than a vocational, field. While Dwight was working hard to persuade ambitious young men that his institution promised entry to successful careers, Langdell and Harvard President Charles Eliot were developing the novel notion that law ought to be studied as an academic subject in its own right, at the hands of scholars whose goal was to enlighten students about how to "think like a lawyer," instead of practitioners who volunteered a few hours away from their busy office schedule in order to train students to work like a lawyer. This academic revolution in legal training began at Harvard with the appointment in 1873 of James Barr Ames as assistant professor of law. Harvard's Board of Overseers was "reluctant and dubious" about this appointment, since Ames had never really practiced law, but President Eliot trumpeted Ames's work as harbinger of a time when law school graduates would not necessarily work in court or with a law firm, but would nonetheless contribute to society as "expounders, systematizers and historians."[54] Surviving accounts of Columbia suggest that Marshall's year there was more of a personal encounter with Dwight than the sort of multifaceted graduate school education that later generations of Americans came to expect when they enrolled in advanced degree programs. Thomas Fenton Taylor, a graduate of Columbia's 1877 class of 230 students, recalled that "the entire instruction of both classes for both years, with the exception of the instruction in Torts from Addison's treatise, was [provided] by Professor Dwight himself."[55]

What might possibly have influenced Marshall in a setting so extraordinarily influenced by the outlook and activities of one educator? Dwight was an "outspoken and active" member of the Republican Party who freely encouraged his students to discuss politics;[56] his outlook and party preference probably stimulated Marshall's own keen interest in politics as well as his Republican affiliation. Dwight appears to have kept tabs on religious education and on the use of law in the protection of free thought and speech in religious institutions.[57] In this and other respects, it is possible to trace the impact of the man behind the Dwight method in Marshall's career. Interestingly, an important episode in Dwight's career related to litigation about the use of a charitable trust created by a will. Retained in 1863 by a public philanthropy group, the Rose Beneficent Association, Dwight prepared a lengthy exhaustive analysis that impressed many, even though it did not carry the day in court.[58] As we shall see, a similar dynamic would occur in Marshall's work in litigation regarding a Jewish charitable trust, an episode fraught with consequence regarding his career in American law and as a Jewish leader.

One other contact of consequence distinguished Marshall's law school year. At Columbia he met Samuel Untermyer, a nineteen-year-old who had grown up in Lynchburg, Virginia, as the son of an enterprising dry goods and clothing salesman, Isidor, who immigrated to the United States from Bavaria in 1844.[59] A young child when the Civil War ripped through Virginia, Samuel, who became a liberal Democrat, had the habit in his later life of embellishing tales of his family's connections to the Confederacy. His family was part of a nexus of Swabian Jews in Lynchburg—these were enterprising immigrants who appear to have arrived in the American South from relatively prosperous homes in Bavaria and who were attracted primarily by the political freedom offered by their new country. Samuel's father had business ties with a cousin and another Swabian immigrant, Nathaniel Guggenheimer; Nathaniel's brother Salomon was the father of Randolph, who became an attorney and Tammany Hall politician in New York City, and, in 1882, the founder of the Guggenheimer and Untermyer law firm (which later became Marshall's professional home). Samuel Untermyer's paternal aunt, Adelheid, born in Kriegshaber in 1816, was the grandmother of Florence Lowenstein, Marshall's future wife.

The immigrants in this Lynchburg nexus appear to have experienced economic ups and downs in the antebellum and Reconstruction South. They were involved with Freemasonry and had, according to scholar Richard Hawkins, a "cosmopolitan" outlook, though they maintained strong Jewish ties (Samuel claimed that through his Bar Mitzvah, he was groomed to be a rabbi). The offspring of Samuel's generation were ambitious, fast climbers in American professional and public life.

1. Portrait of the lawyer as a young man. Courtesy of Peter Schweitzer.

Young Lawyer in Syracuse

Marshall returned to Syracuse after his year at Columbia, was admitted to the bar in 1878, and joined the firm of Ruger, Wallace, Brooks, and French. William C. Ruger interviewed Marshall on behalf of the Bar Character Committee and was taken by the precocious young man whose passion for the law had been on display in the law library incident three years before.[60] Ruger was a solid patron. In 1878, Ruger had already practiced law in Syracuse for a quarter century; in 1875–76, he had earned respect in the state for his work as counsel for the defendants in "canal ring" prosecutions initiated by Governor Tilden (subsequently in 1882, Ruger became a judge on the New York Court of Appeals).[61] Marshall was the only Jewish member of the firm,[62] which was the preeminent legal outfit in central New York.[63] The firm's tolerant bearing was due largely to the character and values of one of its main partners, James Byron Brooks. Marshall first met Brooks, a native of Rockingham, Vermont, and a Civil War hero who was wounded at the Battle of the Wilderness, early in 1877;[64] he later attested that he "learned to love and honor" Brooks from the first day of their acquaintance.[65] Brooks dealt with legal matters that "manifested humanity at its worst," but (Marshall recalled) "his faith in his fellow men remained unshaken." Brooks, a Republican who later became dean of Syracuse University's College of Law, was a deeply religious man whose thoughts and life were guided by the Bible. "Though loyal to his own denomination and prepared to make any sacrifice for its advancement," Marshall commented, Brooks was "utterly devoid of narrowness, intolerance or prejudice. He respected the religious and political convictions of others."

Marshall came from Columbia with a firm grounding in legal principles, thanks to Dwight's teaching, but he lacked the detailed grasp of New York case law that would become one of his professional trademarks. His early years at the Ruger firm fixed that. Judge Ruger had a fine professional reputation, but he was not a case lawyer, and he followed a procedure of dictating the main argumentative points of a brief and sending Marshall to the library to support these claims via relevant case precedents.

William Jenney, the son of one of the firm's original partners, trained under Marshall's tutelage for a few years starting in 1889[66] and left a vivid description of his tutor's professional prowess. "I doubt if any lawyer of this or any other time had in his head the knowledge of cases, of both New York State and the United States Supreme Court," the awed Jenney recalled. He remembered Marshall as a rigidly focused attorney who had in Syracuse "little outside interests." Marshall would work in the office from nine in the morning until midnight; he had two breaks, lunch and dinner, taken at home. "His walks from his home, to and from the office, were his only exercise," noted Jenney. Typically Marshall would dictate briefs while seated in his office, "citing cases and quoting from opinions without leaving his desk or looking at a law book."[67] Marshall's erudition and talents of concentration were on display when he defended a priest in a Church tribunal, filing his brief and arguing orally in Latin.[68]

By 1890, Marshall's firm had the most lucrative practice in Syracuse, with an estimated annual income of $40,000.[69] In addition to his virtuoso performance in Latin, Marshall's erudition and oratorical skill raised eyebrows in courtroom debates with renowned personalities of the era, including Agnostic iconoclast Robert Ingersoll. Mostly, however, his reputation grew due to his meticulous mastery of state and federal law; by the age of thirty-five, when he was selected as a delegate for New York's Constitutional Convention (Marshall served two more times in this capacity, at the state's conventions in 1894 and 1915), he was said to have argued more cases before the New York Court of Appeals than had the state's most prestigious lawyers in their entire careers.[70]

Marshall's slavish devotion to his profession did not escape notice in Syracuse, but he was not really known as a bookish oddball. In fact, local newspapers made a point of presenting him as an eligible bachelor. One gossipy 1888 report in the *Syracuse Post-Standard* announced that "the favorite pastime of this young man is gumfuzzling the Court of Appeals, but when he hasn't anything else to do he is not averse to receiving the attentions of the opposite sex."[71] The possessor of a "smooth face and a large erudite head," Marshall could not "tell a story so well" as one of his partners, Colonel Jenny, a Democrat, nor could he "lead a prayer meeting as successfully as J. B. Brooks," his Republican partner, but nobody, this report relayed, could "walk all over a court" with Marshall's lithe expertise, and his meteoric professional rise rendered him a highly desirable catch for any local woman of quality. There had already been "several bids for him," and Marshall was "worth all he asks," the newspaper reported.

Conservative in socioeconomic philosophy, Marshall never joined forces, neither in substance nor in rhetoric, with Progressive spirited crusades to "bust the trusts" that came to dominate American politics in years before World War I. Nonetheless, he balanced his loyalties as a business lawyer against his belief in a state's right to guard public interests, and a portion of his important case work, starting from his Syracuse period, cannot be regarded as being "pro business." His work on behalf of New York State interests, in opposition to various private business entities, was far from altruistic, since Marshall steadily built alliances in Albany and collected IOUs that could be cashed in later, after his move in 1894 to New York City; still, Marshall was serious, even somewhat righteous, about civic duties, and he relished his role as a protector of New York State interests, including environmental ones (see chapter 9). Especially when sound precedent could be found for policy that protected some perceived public interest, Marshall became identified with prominent populist-democratic trends of his era, in defiance of contractual claims prosecuted by private concerns.

For instance, in *Syracuse Water Company v. City of Syracuse,*[72] Marshall reinforced in New York State principles of Jacksonian democracy that had been enshrined half a century earlier in the Supreme Court's landmark *Charles River Bridge v. Warren Bridge*[73] decision. In the *Charles River* case, the controlling interests of an existing bridge argued that the Massachusetts legislature had violated the spirit of its contract by granting franchise rights for the construction of a competitor bridge. Chief Justice Roger Taney, a Jackson appointee to the bench, held that legislative grants should be narrowly construed to protect the public interest. Property rights must be guarded, but if there were no explicit infringement of an existing contract, the state could act for the benefit of its residents by issuing a new grant. "The object and end of all government is to promote the happiness and prosperity of the community," wrote Taney in the court's famous 1837 decision. In 1889, Marshall restated the same principle, upholding the right of New York to issue a grant to a second waterworks company, so long as it did not explicitly infringe the terms of an existing agreement with another water utility. Public grants are to be construed strictly against the grantee, Marshall argued. The New York appellate court ruled in his favor, citing the *Charles River* case.

Marshall lived with his parents in Syracuse on Cedar Street during this phase of his life. Jacob and Zilli kept an Orthodox home (even after he left Syracuse for Manhattan, Louis almost never missed a Passover seder in this beloved home).[74] Evidence of Marshall's public Jewish commitments in this period is spotty. In 1880, he is listed as the co-sponsor of a fund to build a local Jewish orphanage; interestingly, in 1891, he represented Syracuse Jewry as part of a delegation that appealed to Benjamin Harrison for action to alleviate the suffering of Russian Jewry.[75]

When Marshall left Syracuse in his late thirties, he was a man of means, a hard-working professional who enhanced his assets by shrewd but time-consuming investments in real estate. In Manhattan, social ties and Jewish work placed him in the Uptown circle, but as the son of struggling immigrants whose European backgrounds were modest, Marshall's social status in this Uptown world was quite unlike its premier figures, such as Kuhn, Loeb and Company banker Jacob Schiff, who came from elite European Jewish families.[76] Marshall's assets were not nearly on the scale of the Uptown trendsetters; had his resources been more ample, Marshall's disciplined mentality would surely have steered him from the luxurious lifestyles preferred by Uptown figures like Felix Warburg (Schiff's son-in-law).

Along with obvious differences of professional occupation and social background, one interesting point of contrast between Marshall and the Uptown insiders features their attitudes toward real estate. The first generation of New York City Uptown Jews came of age in the years of Marshall's childhood; symbolized by Joseph Seligman, these were financial wizards who had uncanny skill with stocks and bonds and a comparably uncanny reluctance to deal with physical property (this blind spot about dealing with land proved to be a liability for figures like Seligman at the end of the nineteenth century, when railroad-related property investments became the country's prime financial activity).[77] Marshall, in contrast, actively engaged in real estate ventures, mostly in Syracuse but also in Westchester County and elsewhere in New York State, primarily as a means of elevating himself from middle class professional respectability to a higher station of success in America.

Nostalgia supplemented this basic socioeconomic motivation. Marshall initiated real estate investments in Syracuse during the first period of his life when he lived in the city, but he persisted with them during the last decades of his life partly due to a psychological need to cling to some remnant of the quiet challenges and warm communal life of his Syracuse childhood.

Marshall's cousin Benjamin Stolz handled his real estate interests in Syracuse, and Marshall's personal correspondence is flooded with instructions relayed to Stolz over the years about rental and sales terms of the properties. Many of the assets were empty lots in Syracuse, not necessarily of prime value; they had potential for middle class building, and their sale deeds stipulated that purchasers were to build at least a two-story dwelling on the land for no less than $8,000 or $10,000. Marshall took up real estate investments by his thirtieth year; his lifelong Syracuse friend, the physician Henry Elsner, partnered with Marshall in perhaps a quarter of the sales. At the time of his death in 1929, the value of Marshall's estate was estimated, with no clear certitude, as $5 million;[78] the volume of Marshall's real estate dealings (at least twenty-five sales can be identified between 1886 and 1929[79]) indicates that they constituted a fair portion, perhaps 10 percent or 15 percent, of his wealth, but did not really compare to the revenue he generated in his legal work and from other sources. Marshall's extremely prolonged dealings with his cousin Benjamin Stolz about the Syracuse properties probably had motivations beyond sheer business profit—over the years, it had to have crossed Marshall's mind that the number of hours he was investing in Syracuse properties was more than they were worth. Marshall's Syracuse real estate portfolio thus invites speculation about his psychological orientation toward the town of his youth.

Even more palpably than Marshall's prodigious contributions to environmental protection, his land holdings in Syracuse reflected an emotional desire never to leave his home region behind. Despite the wealth of emotionally and financially rewarding activity that New York City provided to him in his mature adulthood, Marshall always felt connected to the upstate idyllic circumstances of his youth. Ever sensible, Marshall put his Syracuse properties on the market whenever he believed he could fetch a good price for them; however, there was also a discernible psychological dynamic governing the periods (1905–7, the early 1920s) when he became most embroiled in Syracuse real estate work. As happened with his periodically intensive work for the New York State College of Forestry at Syracuse University, Marshall reactivated the Upstate New York part of his life with renewed passion whenever the stresses of dealing with Uptown-Downtown Jewish politics in New York, and of American big city life in general, became especially acute. Well into the twentieth century, Marshall thought of Upstate New York as a place where late nineteenth-century life could, or should, simply stand still, in a state of placid good feeling. His business success in Manhattan meant that he was not really dealing with Syracuse real estate because he needed the money. Instead, he held the properties as a way to hold onto Syracuse. Marshall wanted to let go of his past selectively; he hoped to slow down processes of urbanization and social change he deeply distrusted. The fact that most of his Syracuse properties were never developed before their sale reflects this psychology.

Sampson Simson Case

Five years before he left Syracuse, Marshall started work on the Sampson Simson will dispute. This fascinating case set him on the path toward the main chapters of his life in New York City.

In 1889, Adolph Sanger, representing the North American Relief Society, contacted Marshall, asking for his help in the appeal of a Court of Appeals ruling on a contested section in the will of Sampson Simson. The two met in the home of a mutual friend in Syracuse, Simon Rosendale, and Marshall agreed to prepare a brief petitioning the Court of Appeals to reopen the case.[80]

Simson, born in Danbury, Connecticut, in 1780,[81] inherited wealth amassed by his father in prerevolutionary times by ownership of several shipping vessels. He studied at Columbia College and was admitted to the bar in 1802, but never vigorously engaged in the practice of law. Remaining single, he opted for the life of a country gentleman in Yonkers. Simson liked to dress in the old-fashioned way, wearing knee breeches and buckles, and maintained a strict, humorless mien even as he labored in benevolent philanthropic acts. Fastidious about his religious observances—Passover matzos were prepared in his own house—he belonged to the venerable She'arith Israel synagogue.

Simson maintained an ongoing interest in Holy Land affairs. He welcomed *shlichim* emissaries who came from Eretz Israel to New York, including Abraham Nissen (Wolfsohn), who promoted various agricultural and educational projects in the Jewish Yishuv community; also, Simson corresponded with Philadelphia Rabbi Isaac Leeser about Holy Land affairs, and with Philadelphia native Warder Cresson, who was settled in Jerusalem as a convert to Judaism and who in 1853 used Leeser's journal, the *Occident,* to lobby for Jewish agricultural colonies and a Jewish return to Eretz Israel. In the final weeks of 1853, Leeser ran three editorials of his own in the *Occident,* rapturously describing plans for a more productive Palestine and the benefits to be accrued by the modernization of the Yishuv.[82] Generally, from the 1830s, a number of visionary schemes for industrial and agricultural development among Jews in Eretz Israel circulated fairly prominently in Europe and North America, though within the Yishuv nobody appeared to take them very seriously.[83]

Simson was clearly impressed by these pre-Zionist stirrings designed to stimulate productive Jewish work in the Holy Land, in keeping with the disciplined, industrious norms of the Victorian era, and also (in some cases) ideas of Jewish restoration in a revitalized Promised Land. Another Jewish philanthropist of the time, the New Orleans–based Judah Touro, passed away in 1854, leaving in his will a sum of $50,000 to support activities undertaken by Moses Montefiore to aid the indigent Jews of Palestine. Touro clearly had in his mind the vocational, education, and agricultural enterprises that the energetic British Jew, Montefiore, promoted in this era in Ottoman Palestine, and he also associated his bequest with the work of the North American Relief Society.[84] Montefiore maintained frequent contacts with Simson's partner in the establishment of the Relief Society, S. M. Isaacs. Ignoring ambiguous language in Touro's will, the British *shtadlan* intercessor, Montefiore, took full charge of Touro's $50,000 gift, a substantial one by the standards of the time, and his handling of it played a role on his colorful, precedent-setting visit to Palestine in 1855.[85] Simson died in early 1857, and his memory and funds came primarily to be associated with the founding of Mount Sinai Hospital, originally called the "Jews' Hospital in New York." However, Simson was also the founder of the North American Relief Society for Indigent Jews in Jerusalem, Palestine. The circumstances of this organization's founding—that is, its founder's ties with Cresson and Leeser, Touro's approving allusions to it and also to Montefiore's proto-Zionist labors for Jewish economic self-sufficiency and revitalization in the Holy Land—leave no room for doubt as to how Simson conceptualized his $50,000 bequest to the Relief Society. In the Montefiore spirit, his idea was to help Holy Land Jews help themselves.

Myer Isaacs, who had "vivid memories" of Simson, wrote in a biographical sketch of this New York Jewish philanthropist that the Relief Society scrupulously followed the goal of assisting Jews who were on the road to self-sufficiency in Eretz Israel. Support provided by the Relief Society was not just "almsgiving," Isaacs wrote, and sheer charity handouts were to be given only to dependents, to the aged, widows, and orphans.[86] Simson was a lawyer, but (in Isaacs' words) a "very strange blunder" hindered the execution of the provision in his will of a $50,000 bequest for the Palestine Society. After Simson's nephew Moses Isaacs died, the Relief Society claimed that it was entitled to the bequest, since the will referred to payment of the $50,000 "to any responsible corporation in this city [New York]" endowed by its charter for the purpose of "ameliorating the condition of the Jews in Jerusalem"; continuing, the provision described the key term, amelioration, in terms of the promotion of education in "mechanical and agricultural vocations."[87]

Simson's executor, John Riker, became involved in litigation about this provision, due to the discrepancy between its operative term, amelioration, and the language of the Relief Society's incorporation charter describing its purpose as the "relief of the indigent Jews in Jerusalem." A lower court ruled in favor of the Relief Society's argument that no meaningful distinction could be drawn between the Simson will's reference to a corporation charter beckoning the "amelioration" of Jerusalem Jews through work programs and the Relief Society's charter allusion to charity "relief." The Court of Appeals, however, ruled that the Relief Society was chartered to provide immediate charity relief in a way inconsistent with the deceased's intention to support work rehabilitation programs for the Jerusalem poor.

After securing the court's authorization to reopen the case, Marshall forcefully argued that Biblical, Talmudic, and ethical conceptions followed by the Jews are founded on "two fundamental principles." Aid, Marshall explained, is to be given in a way that allows the recipient to maintain self-respect, and aid is "bestowed as to enable the recipient to become self-supporting." He lavished the brief with citations from the Old Testament,[88] as well as codifications contributed by Maimonides and the Shulchan Aruch, in support of the idea that charity activity in Jewish life had always been undertaken with the aim of preventing recipients from becoming dependent upon their fellows. Simson could therefore have never consciously intended to distinguish between "amelioration" and "relief," Marshall argued. Jewish charity traditionally went to recipients not as mere handouts, but rather as means of self-support.

In his brief, Marshall called on two authorities, Richard Gottheil, professor of Semitic Languages and Rabbinic Literature at Columbia University, and Rabbi Alexander Kohut, the author of an exhaustive, multivolume project on the Talmud, *Aruch Completum*. Kohut put his hefty reputation fully at the disposal of Marshall's defense of the Relief Society's claim. Marshall inserted in his brief Kohut's claim that "according to the Talmud, a truly meritorious act of charity is that which anticipates the necessities of the distressed, and endeavors to enable them to provide for themselves."[89]

In April 1892, the Court of Appeals narrowly ruled against Marshall's argument on behalf of the Relief Society, in a four to three vote (Marshall believed that victory was missed only because of recent changes in the court's composition).[90] The Simson will case had, the *New York Times* reported,[91] "excited considerable interest in legal circles," and Marshall's robust defense, his creative presentation of Jewish traditions in an American courtroom, caught the attention of influential American Jewish figures who were involved in the representation of Jewish concerns in a variety of contexts. While doing research in Philadelphia regarding Simson's testamentary intentions, Marshall made contact with Judge Mayer Sulzberger; Sulzberger was connected to New York attorney Randolph Guggenheimer; the sequence of contacts led ultimately to Marshall's departure from Syracuse,[92] and the unfolding of the main phases of his life as a New York City business lawyer and public Jewish advocate.

The Simson case essentially initiated Marshall to Jewish advocacy, and its place in the arc of his public career merits attention. Marshall was, first and last, an American Jew, but poetic truth can be adduced from the fact that he began and ended an adult lifetime of Jewish communal labors in advocacy relating to the welfare of Jews in Eretz Israel. In Albany in 1892 on the Simson case, and in Zurich in summer 1929, where he died while attending meetings inaugurating the "Pact of Glory" to include wealthy American Jewish philanthropists in an expanded Jewish Agency, Marshall worked on the same issue: what were the rightful terms of American Jewish support for Jewish revitalization in the Holy Land? What, really, did American Jews owe to the Yishuv, to the proto-state community in the Jews' historic homeland?

2

Manhattan and Moral Reform

New Partner at Guggenheimer and Untermyer

In late 1893, Untermyer invited Marshall to join the Guggenheimer and Untermyer firm in New York City, and the Syracuse native moved to Manhattan in February 1894, staying for the first several weeks with the Untermyers.[1] From the start, Untermyer treated Marshall as a junior, rather naïve, partner who was not suitably appreciative of the firm's arduous early ascendance to prosperity.[2] "When you consider our small beginnings and rapid rise, you will understand with what horror I contemplate any retrograde step or even a standstill," Untermyer preached to Marshall. He also served as Marshall's social mentor, coaxing the thirty-eight-year-old legal wizard from Upstate New York toward the Manhattan dating circle. "You couldn't do anything that would please us better except to get married, provided always that all of us are thoroughly satisfied with the girl," Untermyer told Marshall soon after the latter joined the Manhattan firm. Marshall was pushing forty, and in all respects it was time for him to settle into married life. Just a few months after his arrival in Manhattan, he met at the opera his future wife, Florence Lowenstein, who (it will be recalled) was related to Untermyer.

Unlike Marshall, a conservative purist from Upstate New York, a region known for ideological zeal, Untermyer, a son of the social rough and tumble of the American South, never seemed overly judgmental or moralistic about New York City's patchwork society of immigrant communities and machine politics. Untermyer embraced social realities in Manhattan that were derided as profanity by most members of Marshall's Uptown group. From the moment Marshall embarked on a professional partnership with him, Untermyer insisted that Jews in New York City would best be served by cooperation with Tammany Hall. "Between the Irish leaders of Tammany and the high-toned Jew hating Presbyterians on the other side, I consider Tammany the lesser evil for those of our race," he explained to Marshall.[3] Untermyer evolved politically as a liberal Democrat; his views on key local and national issues were often unlike Marshall's, and the political differences between the two men became especially pronounced in years before World War I, when Untermyer formally left the firm.

When Marshall joined the firm, Untermyer lectured solemnly about the outfit's lawyerly integrity. "I would rather make nothing and feel that our prestige and reputation were on the increase than double our income and have the reverse feeling," Untermyer told Marshall.[4] In fact, there was little danger that the driven lawyers on the firm would be content to earn nothing. As months passed by, Untermyer, an aggressive business lawyer, made clear to Marshall that prestige and reputation were not exactly goals that could be separated from moneymaking. A year into their partnership, he seemed cognizant that Marshall no longer genuflected after each sermon and was carving out his own spheres of independence on the firm. "I have often wondered whether with your good practical business mind you appreciate the fact that people in our busy city judge others *solely* by results, and that risks which one can seriously take with litigation in smaller cities are dangerous to our reputation," Untermyer lectured to Marshall in autumn 1895. His new partner did not appear to be listening in rapt deference. "I am afraid that you think me a 'crank' on this subject and that you are inclined to treat me good naturedly rather than seriously," moaned Untermyer to Marshall.[5]

Marshall's advancement in the Guggenheimer and Untermyer firm was delayed at the start by his participation in the 1894 New York Constitutional Convention,[6] but he advanced quickly at work, and immersed himself deeply in it during his first five or six years in New York City. His public Jewish commitments during this period were not preempted by his commitment to business law, but they were sporadic and not intimately connected to the circumstances and sensitivities of the East Side's burgeoning Jewish immigrant community.

At the turn of the twentieth century, his most conspicuous Jewish advocacy work involved firing off appeals to high authorities, including the president of the United States, on behalf of young Jewish men of his own, or his Uptown associates', acquaintance who desired entry as cadets at West Point. In the period of the Spanish-American War and Rough Rider Theodore Roosevelt, American culture admired and rewarded muscular patriotism, and so Marshall took some steps on behalf of the West Point candidacy of young "co-religionists," such as Jacob Goldstein of Rochester or Louis Blumenthal. In his petition on Goldstein's behalf to President McKinley, Marshall explained the rationale:

> I am not one who believes in distinctions of race, creed or nationality. We are all American citizens who know no allegiance other than that which we owe to the Flag. But in view of the oft-repeated slander that the Jew is no patriot, our people have become actuated by an intense desire to convince their fellow

citizens of the falsity of such a charge, and that they are ready to serve their country whenever it calls.[7]

Jewish participation in the armed forces exhibited American patriotism, and in the next three decades Marshall would in various ways highlight and encourage such Jewish military involvement, yet this 1900 appeal to the president does not exactly presage these future lobbying efforts. The petition, in fact, was backward looking. It was motivated by slurs to the honor of a previous generation of American Jewish immigrants (that is, Jews who came from Central European lands in the mid–nineteenth century) that were expressed in the 1880s and 1890s about the Civil War and its aftermath by anti-Semites, such as Cornell University Professor Goldwin Smith.[8] Thus, in another 1900 petition for an aspiring Jewish West Point candidate, Marshall noted that the young man's acceptance would dispel the slander about Jews not wanting to fight for their own country. "In view of the statements made a few years ago by Goldwin Smith and others, I think that it should be our endeavor to demonstrate the utter falsity of the vile slander [about unpatriotic and draft-shirking Jews]," Marshall wrote in his appeal for Louis Blumenthal.[9]

Throughout these early New York years, Marshall operated on the assumption that the Jews' greatest protection in America was the Constitution and that Jewish advocacy should therefore focus upon the strengthening of constitutional norms of religious toleration and free speech. Detached from the strivings, sensitivities, and daily circumstances of New York's Jewish immigrant community, Marshall wrote about Jewish interests in the generic idiom of constitutional freedom and saw no urgent need to design novel approaches and institutions to uphold the particular needs of immigrants and others in America's Jewish community.

Strong evidence of his analytically cogent, but emotionally detached, Jewish orientation in the late nineteenth-century years is provided by Marshall's 1896 *Menorah* article "Is Ours a Christian Government?"[10] Marshall's brief cited legal precedents and statements in support of the thesis that the historic development of American society and government was toward full separation of church and state. The impetus for his rather abstract argumentation was not the day-to-day concerns of Jewish immigrants, who wondered whether they were staking roots in a coercively Christian milieu, but rather tendentious comments about America's status as a "Christian nation" made by jurists such as Supreme Court Justice David Brewer.[11]

Arguing that colonial government closely wedded religion and state and that the principle of separation was subsequently woven into the Constitution by the founding fathers, Marshall closely followed the timeline and turnstiles of the George Bancroft school of historiography.[12] By suggesting that demographic heterogeneity encouraged the founders to think in terms of toleration, Marshall offered an oblique defense of immigration, but his phrasing in this respect was abstract ("by the slow process of evolution which builds homogeneous states and nations out of the most heterogeneous elements, a new era was ushered in during the French and Indian War, which was later stimulated by the American Revolution"). Marshall inserted a few statements affirming the democratic openness of the American system to citizens of all creeds, but these catchy declarations ("A Mohammedan born in this country may become President, a Buddhist may become Governor of the State") conveyed little practical advice to East Side pushcart peddlers and sweatshop workers who wanted to know whether discrimination in higher education and professions would prevent their children from climbing upward in a country that had a firm Christian majority.

The article's key passage discussed whether the country's majority had a normative or practical right to press a Christian stamp on its political and social arenas. Citing sources such as Madison's 1785 *Memorial and Remonstrance Against Religious Assessments,* which was directed toward the legislature of Virginia, Marshall argued eloquently that the country's founders recognized that the conferral of legislative authority on religious issues to the majority was in nobody's interest, because the majority was liable to change. In effect, this type of argumentation said to Jewish immigrants that they ought to feel protected at the end of the nineteenth century because the country's liberal founders had a century earlier fought for religious toleration.

Marshall's article offered little guidance to an immigrant who was wondering whether the resurgence of antiforeigner nativism on the eve of the twentieth century represented a substantive challenge to the country's traditions of open immigration and constitutional liberty. His article contained only glancing, perfunctory references to neo-Know-Nothing groups such as the anti-Catholic American Protective Association. Moreover, a portion of Marshall's legalistic argumentation was inconsistent and unpersuasive, particularly in passages that related to Sunday laws in New York State as mere economic and police regulations entirely devoid of religious motivation.

Ultimately, his article contended that America was definitely not a Christian country in constitutional theory, nor was its public sphere fundamentally Christian in practice. Regarding areas where religious imposition or coercion remained in force, Marshall's sole prescriptive recommendation was respect for the Constitution. This message to the immigrants was profoundly conservative. America's constitutional system was perfect and ought not to be changed "one jot":

> Sustain your constitutions, state and national, as they have been framed by the fathers of the Republic. Do not permit them to be disturbed one jot. Let not one word be added nor one syllable be taken away, to the end that they may continue to stand, as they have stood for more than a century, the hope, the refuge and the beacon-light of all the world.[13]

Marshall's early years of work at the Guggenheimer and Untermyer firm were not in sync with his future activities as a leading American and global advocate of Jewish rights. During these early Manhattan years, he combined in his professional work an earnest devotion to constitutional principles and an unflinching commitment to property rights. At times, he projected the legal conservatism of late nineteenth-century America right into the eye of the storm of mass Jewish immigration from Eastern Europe, and he defended principles of free enterprise and property rights that were at variance, implicitly or explicitly, with widespread concerns and sentiments in New York's East Side Jewish immigrant community.

A conspicuous example of this late nineteenth-century divergence between Marshall's priorities as a business lawyer and his evolving understanding of the needs and vulnerabilities of Jewish immigrants is his victory in an 1898 New York appellate court decision, *People of the State of New York ex rel. George Tyroler v. Warden of City Prison of New York*.[14] Scholarship has cast a positive light on Marshall's involvement in this case as an extension of his principled constitutionalism,[15] and his arguments were, in fact, far from unethical or illogical. Nonetheless, this Tyroler case should be viewed as an early signpost in Marshall's development as a Jewish leader. Early in his New York career, Marshall gave precedence to business principles as compared to immigrant needs and sensitivities; as years went by, his priorities were colored much more prominently by Jewish concerns.

The facts in the Tyroler case were relatively simple. In 1897, the New York legislature passed a law mandating that the sale of passage tickets by railroad and steamship to immigrants must be limited to authorized carriers. Marshall's client, a broker, had been convicted under the law for selling tickets of passage without requisite authorization to do so. Marshall, partnered with Samuel Untermyer, claimed that the state illegitimately used its police power under the ticket broker law to create a small monopoly of agents that was, in fact, a combination in restraint of trade.

Marshall's brief cited a familiar array of conservative-tempered case law condemning legislative regulation as a violation of Fourteenth Amendment guarantees of equal protection and due process. His specific argument appealed to common sense: it was unfair to put a slew of ticket brokers out of work because a few of them were committing fraud, at the expense of hapless immigrants. Of course, Marshall's free enterprise outlook could be countered by arguments relating to the acute vulnerability of the relevant class of consumers, overworked immigrants who had limited English-language skills. The regulatory protection offered by the 1897 law to a defenseless class of consumers, immigration seekers, could be perceived as a legitimate counterweight to the free enterprise considerations that Marshall upheld. The immigrant community was rife with heartbreaking stories of newcomers who toiled day and night in sweatshops to save pennies needed to bring their loved ones to New York and who then had their hopes cruelly shattered by ruthless brokers who sold worthless tickets.

Following Marshall's argument, the court ruled that this Jewish welfare concern was not determinative. Ruling for Marshall, the New York court opined that to "cut up, root and branch, a business that may be honestly conducted to the convenience of the public and the profit of the persons engaged in it is beyond the legislative power."[16]

Marriage

Marshall's legal work in these early New York years was interrupted by his engagement to Florence Lowenstein, a striking young woman sixteen years his junior, who hailed from a prominent German Jewish family that had a business interest in Memphis, Tennessee. Florence had grown up largely in the absence of parents; her father Benedict died when she was just eight, and her mother Sophie passed away at the age of thirty-seven, when Florence was thirteen.[17] Remembered by her siblings as a beautiful, graceful, and gracious girl, Florence was raised for a few years by a bachelor uncle, Bernard Lowenstein, who kept his nieces in comfort in a Fifth Avenue dwelling, located close to the prestigious Reform Congregation Emanu-El. Later in her teenage years, Florence took charge of her younger sisters Elsie and the irrepressible Beatrice (Judah Magnes's future wife). There is a record of Florence's confirmation at Emanu-El on Sunday, June 5, 1887,[18] but her sister Beatrice recalled that their Jewish observances were rather attenuated, not going beyond Saturday morning services at Emanu-El (this Lowenstein sister did not recall Passover, Sukkot, or Hanukkah celebrations in their home).[19]

Smitten, Marshall conducted an impassioned, no-time-to-wait courtship, firing off letter after letter to Florence in February and March 1895. "You can scarcely surmise my feelings while seated by your side at the theatre," the ardent, and somewhat self-involved, suitor wrote to Florence. "There was the sense of

2. Louis Marshall and Florence Lowenstein Marshall on their wedding day, May 6, 1895. Courtesy of Peter Schweitzer.

pride and pleasure of having you with me, a feeling of triumph at having won the great victory, an avalanche of satisfaction at having accomplished the great feat which I had set out to do."[20] In mid-March, Marshall took the fateful step of introducing Florence to his Syracuse family. Obviously relieved, he reported the results of this meeting to his beloved:

> You were placed in a most difficult position—for the first time you were to meet my parents, relatives and friends, all of whom in their partiality for me, naturally expected much of you, and although wishing to criticize you favorably, almost by the law of centuries were strongly tempted to be severe in their judgment. With infinite tact, with admirable sweetness, with your frank, truthful manner you solved all difficulties.[21]

Florence charmed Marshall's family, and he delightedly reported that the "crises have been successfully passed, and the horizon is clear." The wedding was set for Florence's birthday, May 6, 1895. The powerfully expressive Marshall believed that he had a poetic side, and so he composed a series of effusive love letters to Florence. For a man who conducted a lifelong partnership with words, his engagement to a beautiful younger woman could be no exception to his communicative habits; Marshall pedantically explained to Florence why they should keep sending romantic letters back and forth up to their wedding (the letters, he explained, "preserve the atmosphere of halcyon days of courtship, and however deficient in style, they contain the essence of poetic and spiritual feelings; they are a mere thank you offering of love"[22]). A week before the wedding, Florence was clearly looking forward to the end of their Victorian-style courtship. "Last night I awoke peacefully, I had just dreamed that I was lying in your arms, that we were one at last," she confessed to Louis on April 30. "As the days advance I approach our wedding day calmly, with the one thought to do all in my power to bring happiness to the best, the finest, the noblest, yes, even the most godlike of beings."[23] This reverentially admiring and devoted tone would characterize Florence's attitude toward Louis in two decades of married life—she clearly believed she was wedded to a uniquely gifted personality.

"Louis and I were married at home by Dr. Gottheil at 6:15 PM," Florence recorded in her diary on May 6, referring to the same Temple Emanu-El rabbi who had officiated at her confirmation eight years before. "We left home near midnight and went to the Waldorf Hotel."[24] "The momentous day has come," Louis wrote the same day to his bride. His wedding wishes contained surprisingly critical allusions to the "sickly and fetid" superficiality of New York's Uptown society. Marshall expressed "resolve that the atmosphere of the house which we are to establish shall be pure, cheerful, warm and intellectual, that it shall not be the sickly and fetid air in which our mindless social life revolves."[25] A day after their wedding ceremony, the newlyweds sailed to Europe aboard the SS *Teutonic;* after two days at sea, they both fell ill (the seasickness left its scars; Marshall infrequently traveled overseas after his honeymoon). They toured England, France, Germany, Italy, and Belgium, and sailed back to New York at the end of July.[26]

Their eldest child, James, was born the following year; a daughter, Ruth, and two sons, Robert and George, completed the family circle.

Educational Alliance

Following five years of settling into professional and family life in New York City, Marshall emerged as one of the country's Jewish leaders. Before the 1920s period of "Marshall law," when he stood out as the preeminent figure in American Jewish affairs and also an unusually prominent character in American ethnic history, Marshall's activity in Jewish life over two decades divided into a series of overlapping yet distinctive phases.

The first phase of moral reform lasted several years and featured Marshall's role as a key player, though not leader, of relatively small-scale initiatives, such as a reformatory for troubled Jewish youth (called the protectory) and the Jewish Theological Seminary, which utilized religious, educational, media, or social welfare organizations and outlets to reach the hearts and minds of troubled or promising immigrants, and turn them into good Americans loyal to their Jewish faith.

This approach drew upon nineteenth-century romantic streams in American culture that identified connections between individual feeling and a universal God, or Oversoul in Ralph Waldo Emerson's formulation. Moral improvement of the individual, through the enrichment of his or her surroundings and by physical exercise and sympathetic education, was seen as a quasi-religious endeavor undertaken to uplift immigrants and sanctify their inclusion in a new, blessed country. In spirit, this approach shared more with causes like Temperance that, as the nineteenth century passed into the twentieth, came to be associated with conservative politics; with its emphasis on moral amelioration and its exhortative appeals for individual discipline, this approach was unlike America's "left" Progressive streams that focused on ideals of scientific expertise and rationalized reorganization of social effort.

These "left-right" tags can be misleading, however. Insofar as it drew upon sources outside of Jewish experience and tradition, this moral regeneration phase, which lasted until a tumult in New York Jewish affairs in 1903 to 1905 arose largely in response to pogroms in Russia, drew from European liberals who were positioned between romanticism and socialism. One was Thomas Davidson, an itinerant, idealistic educator who was born in Scotland and relocated in North America in the 1860s under the spell of the New England Transcendentalists (at one stage, Davidson taught summer school with Emerson). Experimenting with various educational initiatives in America, Davidson began to distance himself both from the Transcendentalists and Hegelianism, believing that both had ignored the cultivation of individual feeling as a means of reaching God. "I am a feeling or sensibility, modified in innumerable ways by influences which I do not originate . . . and these modifications, when grouped are what I call the world, or *my* world, for I know no other," declared Davidson.[27] Teaming with Bronson Alcott on experiments involving communalism and education, Davidson drew the consummate Romantic conclusion that a new moral order could be created not via a radical realignment of social institutions, but rather through the correct education of each individual: the good society was to be built out of harmonious individual worlds.[28]

This was the philosophy that Davidson infused in moral reform efforts engaged by the Jewish Uptown elite in the late 1890s through 1905. It won some Downtown converts. Morris Raphael Cohen, a young immigrant leader of the Marx Circle at City College, greeted Davidson with hostile skepticism when the peripatetic Scottish educational reformer delivered lectures at the Educational Alliance (hereafter referred to as Educational Alliance or simply as alliance) in 1898. "I was not favorably impressed by his [Davidson's] gospel of salvation by education," Cohen recalled. "I was convinced that no substantial improvement of our human lot was possible without a radical change in our economic set-up." Cohen admitted that he heckled Davidson during question and answer periods following the latter's Educational Alliance lectures. He was impressed when the moralist "responded to my attacks in the friendliest way."[29] Unfazed, Davidson lectured on "The Problems Which the Nineteenth Century Hands Over, for Solution, to the Twentieth Century" and gradually began to persuade skeptics like Cohen about the viability of education as a means of individual and social regeneration. Astounding everyone with his commitment to the education of Jewish and other immigrants, Davidson devoted one night a week in the last years of his life to their education at the Breadwinners' College, an initiative connected to the Educational Alliance and supported financially by Joseph Pulitzer. Davidson's influence was recognized by the Uptown leaders; a few years after his death in 1900, Marshall recalled in a note to Morris Raphael Cohen that Davidson's "influence was a most inspiring one, and its lasting effect is evidenced at the Educational Alliance."[30]

Davidson's work at the Educational Alliance and its impact on Downtown Jewish immigrant intellectuals, such as City College's Morris Raphael Cohen, highlight levels of complexity in Marshall's activity in this moral reform phase. The phase's purpose was largely the Americanization of the immigrant, and it was tied, in ethos and method, to early twentieth-century American movements that brimmed with conservative reservations about features of urban modernity. Yet this phase also drew from European sources and had links to left-wing politics, both in America's Settlement House movement[31] and on the European continent (for instance, figures like Davidson contributed to the "ethical tone" of British socialism[32]).

More obviously, this moral reform phase consolidated as a result of pressures and hierarchies in the relationship between acculturated and economically prospering Uptown Jews and indigent, ambitious immigrant Downtown Jews. Uptown Jews fashioned the approach out of economic class and social status considerations. In the eyes of a Jewish patron such as the banker Jacob Schiff, moral reform was unthreatening and a far more attractive agenda than any formula fashioned with an implicit or explicit purpose of economic reorganization. As the philosopher Morris Raphael Cohen's reminiscence about Davidson implies, Downtown liberals and radicals suspected that talk of educational or religious salvation masked class interests by persuading immigrants that their own moral character was the problem, rather than the exploitation of their labor in the needle trades and other low-income occupations.

Along with class interest, social status concerns helped mold this approach. Using media, educational, and religious institutions and mechanisms, Uptown elites sought to eradicate "foreign" appearances and discourses on the East Side and thereby persuade Gentiles in the country that Jews were morally worthy and well-mannered Americans.

By the end of this phase, when Downtown critics caustically satirized the moral-educational patronage of Schiff, Marshall, and others in such forums as Yiddish theater genius Jacob Gordin's well-known 1903 play *The Benefactors of the East Side,*[33] many immigrant Jews doubted whether Uptown's efforts really ought to be respected as an idealistic, Jewish variant of aristocratic noblesse oblige. It all smacked too much of self-interest, as though the hard-won reputation of the German Jew was to be protected by the moral reform of the Russian Jew.

Such criticism was a subjective element in the volatile Uptown-Downtown nexus of the period, but the suspicions about class and social status fears of elite stewards like Schiff and Marshall pointed to one undeniably objective feature of this phase. Even though projects such as Marshall's *Jewish World* newspaper potentially reached thousands of Jews, the Uptown leaders in this phase were basically trying to limit the focus of Jewish politics. Sometimes this limited focus appeared self-defeating, since projects such as the protectory were designed to benefit a mere several dozen Jewish immigrant youths, and yet their establishment and operation exhaustively tested the energies and resources of its Uptown patrons. But the key point is that the sensible, orderly bankers, businessmen, and lawyers in the Uptown elite remained wary throughout this moral reform phase of taking on more than they could handle. Counterparts in organized parts of American Jewry, such as the president of B'nai B'rith, Leo N. Levi of Texas, found peace with the idea that perhaps *all* of East European Jewry could or should find its way to North America. In 1902, in the middle of his five-year tenure as B'nai B'rith president, Levi spoke expansively about Jewish immigration, declaring that "in a few years we shall see on this continent a re-born, rehabilitated, virile, powerful Jewry."[34] Such exclamations envisioned a mass scope of American Jewish politics that, at this stage, intimidated figures like Schiff and Marshall, who, unlike the Texan Levi, happened to live in New York City, the port of entry and settlement for the immigrant Jewish masses.

Jewish idealism in this moral reform phase was limited to the agenda of Americanizing the East Side immigrant already in the United States. It was not about Americanizing the Jew. The difference between these two operations could be counted as the millions of Jews in Central and Eastern Europe who had yet to embark on a journey to the New World.

Much as the Downtown Yidden occasionally chided the Uptown Yahudim for acting out of perceived self-interest, this phase of moral reform lasted so long as the Downtown immigrants themselves remained relatively preoccupied with their own problems, wheeling pushcarts on Hester Street and attending night classes in English at the Educational Alliance on the corner of East Broadway and Jefferson Street. The Kishinev trauma and pogroms elsewhere in Russia from 1903 to 1905 destroyed temporary patterns of self-focus on both sides of Jewish New York, both in the "German" Uptown and the "Russian" Downtown. Once the Uptown elite formed a new organization, the American Jewish Committee, whose purposes went beyond moral exhortation, and once this elite group shifted its emphasis from reprogramming newly settled immigrants to keeping the door open for new masses of immigrants, Marshall and his peers entered a new phase of Jewish politics in America (discussed in Part Two of this biography); this subsequent phase lasted a decade, up to World War I.

The expiration date on this moral reform phase's limit was a product of Downtown-Uptown self-absorption. Though figures like Schiff and Marshall were far from universally popular Downtown, their moral reform efforts were condoned or (in cases like the Educational Alliance) widely utilized during a transitional period when the immigrant newcomers themselves were emotionally and practically invested in Americanization routines. The phase lasted as long as the immigrants felt at liberty to focus on their own lives and families; once everyone had reason to worry about the survival of brethren overseas, the phase was finished. This meant that the scope and character of Marshall's work was dictated not just by Downtown temperament, but also by the czar's policies, and so as Jewish politics in this prewar period transitioned from one phase to the next, it was no surprise that Marshall's patron and partner, Jacob Schiff, began to personalize Uptown's engagement with the czar.[35]

In the heyday of the moral reform work, Marshall recognized that the success of any particular project depended upon the recruitment of a capable, driven Downtown leader whose involvement would persuade fellow East Side immigrants that the work in question was a shared Jewish interest, and not a selfish byproduct of Uptown needs and desires. In line with this insight, David Blaustein of the Educational Alliance became an emblematic figure in this moral reform phase of American Jewish history.

Born in Lida in 1866,[36] Blaustein slipped out of czarist Russia into Memel, Prussia, as a seventeen-year-old. There he studied in a Beit Midrash for a few years until he left for America, due to reasons his widow affixed loosely to Otto von Bismarck's discrimination. An ambitious young man, Blaustein enrolled in Harvard in 1889 as a special student in semiotics and attained a BA from the university, with honors, in 1893. At Harvard, he befriended Jesse Straus, son of Macy's co-owner Isidor Straus, a key figure in Uptown's moral reform campaign, and the connection helped bring Blaustein a few years later to the Educational Alliance. Before his arrival in New York, Blaustein worked for six years as a rabbi employed by the Congregation Sons of Israel and David in Providence, Rhode Island; in this early professional experience, he excelled in social welfare work, serving as a board member of public charities in Rhode Island (while also teaching Semitic languages at Brown University and attaining a graduate degree from that institution). In 1898, this energetic thirty-two-year-old was hired as superintendent of the Educational Alliance, located in New York City's Lower East Side, whose president was Isidor Straus.

The Educational Alliance had been founded nine years earlier, in 1889, with a budget of $125,000, as an amalgam of three existing institutions, the Hebrew School Free Association, the Aguilar Free Library Society, and the Young Men's Hebrew Association.[37] The institution lagged for its first few years; it reorganized in 1893, when Straus became president, and a year or two thereafter it started to offer a well-organized routine of educational classes, physical activities, and singing and social clubs. From the start, its purpose was understood by all board members, including Jacob Schiff, as Americanization of immigrants; with that goal in mind, Educational Alliance work put a premium on English instruction. Blaustein's tenure (1898–1905) as the alliance's director is recalled as a high point in the institution's history. While a tribute to Blaustein's selfless labors (he "had no private life," his wife recalled[38]), the Educational Alliance's success in this period stemmed largely from loose ends in the New York City public school system: until the passage of the 1904 Compulsory Education Law, the city schools largely ignored immigrant children who could not speak English. Up to 1899, the Baron de Hirsch Fund had worked unsystematically to fill this gap among immigrant Jewish children; soon after he took the reins at the Educational Alliance, Blaustein took steps to ensure that it assumed responsibility for English instruction in Downtown New York. For the next five years, until the passage of the 1904 law, day classes in English for children of less than two years' residence in America, along with night classes for adults of less than two years' residence, became the staple of the Educational Alliance's work and put the institution on the map of Jewish New York. Along with educators and philosophers like Davidson, prominent labor figures, such as Samuel Gompers, gave lectures at the alliance. The building facility teemed during the week with sports activities, English and citizenship classes, lectures, and more.

In mid-1897, not long before Blaustein's recruitment, Marshall was invited by Straus to serve on the Educational Alliance's Committee on Moral Work,[39] which was at the time chaired by Henry Leipziger, an upright, England-born librarian affiliated with the Aguilar Free Library Society. Marshall immediately took up various tax matters for the alliance and handled the finalization of its consolidation with the Hebrew Free School Association.[40] By 1899, his leadership role was formally recognized when he became chairman of the Moral Work Committee (Leipziger remained a member, along with education activist Julia Richman).

Marshall's work with the Educational Alliance produced fewer substantive results than did his involvement with other projects, such as the Jewish Theological Seminary, in this moral reform phase. Yet, along with its role in creating links with personalities such as Zvi Hirsch Masliansky, this Educational Alliance activity warrants mention in Marshall's biography as a weathervane pointing explicitly to what was in his heart and mind at this early stage of his career in Jewish politics.

Taken up in earnest some five years after his arrival in Uptown Manhattan from Upstate Syracuse, Marshall's activity at the Educational Alliance allows us to identify the Jewish leader he was and was becoming. After mechanically referring to constitutional liberty as a panacea for all Jewish issues, he was at this stage adopting a more activist, hands-on orientation of religious education. This emphasis is interesting—if, as one scholar has maintained, American Jewish affairs were transformed "between 1900 and 1915 [by] the transfer of Jewish legal authority from rabbis to lawyers,[41] this moral reform phase served an intermediary function in the transition. A lawyer like Marshall was using not the law, but rather religious education, to promote the Americanization of the Jewish immigrant.

Though Marshall sometimes wrote haughtily about "idleness, vice and immorality" in East Side areas, he was unmistakably perturbed by the way work at the Educational Alliance reinforced hierarchical patterns in American Jewish affairs. Alone among the Uptown elite, he came to recognize that a project like the alliance could rightfully be designated as a form of colonialism, so long as Downtown leaders were not involved in its management; in fact, his admonitions about this issue of colonialism were arrestingly explicit.[42] The moral reform and Americanization of the Jewish immigrant was the purpose of Marshall's activity throughout this 1894–1904 phase, but its problem was the abiding concern of his life: could the Jews really become a cohesive ethnic presence in America when their empowering institutions remained undemocratic?

In November 1899, Marshall, as head of the Moral Culture Committee, authored a revealing report that was circulated to the alliance's directors.[43] He opened by transposing his conservative fears onto New York's Jewish scene. Moral reform work was imperative, he suggested, lest East Side Jewry transmogrify as a menacing mob:

> The great Russian exodus, which has been in progress during the last fifteen years, has brought to this municipality nearly a quarter million unfortunates, who have taken up residence within the contracted limits of the New York ghetto, where medieval orthodoxy and anarchistic license are struggling for mastery. A people whose political surroundings have entirely changed, who are apt to become intoxicated with the liberty of action which has been suddenly vouchsafed to them, who are tempted to break through the restraints of religion as soon as they begin to sneer at the ceremonies which they have held in superstitious dread, is apt to depart from its moorings, and to become a moral menace.

The "overwhelming majority" of immigrants were Americanizing on the road toward model citizenship, yet the Jews' salutary progress in the United States had a "reverse side" on the immigrant East Side, where "idleness, vice and immorality are painted in dark and lurid coloring." Marshall referred specifically to existing maladies of gambling, prostitution, and "anarchy and unbelief seeking to destroy government."

The remedy was religion, "the strongest factor of civilization." Marshall called for the expansion of the alliance's People's Synagogue and for development of lectures on Friday evenings and Saturdays "in which the duties of citizenship will be treated as religious obligations."

This missionary work to Americanize the Jewish immigrant could not be administered and supervised exclusively by the Uptown elite, Marshall warned.

In a series of hard-hitting, revealing sentences, Marshall contended that the Educational Alliance, as then structured, was becoming a form of Jewish colonialism. "It is undoubtedly unfortunate that our Board of Directors is composed entirely of members who have but little knowledge of the inner life of the people for whose welfare we are struggling," Marshall wrote. He posed the issue of Jewish democratization with pungent, provocative analogies. "We are attempting to legislate for a community of whose thoughts we are profoundly ignorant, entirely from our standpoint," Marshall continued. "One might as well expect the Municipal Assembly of New York to properly govern Cuba or the Philippines."[44]

The alliance's moral culture work centered on the People's Synagogue services as well as public lectures, mostly delivered by Masliansky. Marshall sought to introduce the dignified Reform decorum of Temple Emanu-El to the immigrant East Side, via the alliance's Shabbat services. In a subsequent committee annual report, he ascribed Reform-like features to the People's Synagogue, saying: "The conduct of the people is more orderly; decorum is better observed; the dignity of the services is above that which prevails in the other synagogues of the East Side."[45] Yet Marshall was finding that only the relatively acculturated immigrants attended the alliance's religious services; Friday nights, immigrants who were "too Orthodox to be attracted by our regular synagogue service" preferred to listen to Rev. Masliansky's discourses on everyday social and political topics.[46]

Significantly, this Friday night routine was occurring in a 1900–1901 interval, a time when (as we will see) Marshall reluctantly abandoned the dream of uniting the Reform Hebrew Union College (HUC) and the Jewish Theological Seminary (JTS) and set out to reorganize the latter institution with an efficiency and vision that would eventually help lead to the creation of a new Jewish religious stream in America, the Conservative movement. Thus, at the beginning of the new century, as social workers working in settlement houses in Chicago, New York, and elsewhere were learning about the need to modify preexisting ideas about immigrant adaptation in the melting pot,[47] the Educational Alliance appears to have provided a weekly demonstration to Marshall and others about the inevitability of differentiation in Jewish religious structures in America, due to the unsuitability of the assertively modernized Reform service for traditional-minded immigrants.

Masliansky immigrated to America in 1895 at the age of twenty-nine, after having acquired some fame in Jewish circles in Russia, Germany, and England as a Zionist *maggid* teacher-preacher who dipped liberally into the Bible and Midrash while expounding Jewish nationalist ideas (born in the Minsk area, he had studied as a youth in the Mir and Volozhin yeshivas).[48] Early in 1900, Marshall identified a groundswell of support for Masliansky's regular employment at the Educational Alliance, and (fatefully) he believed that Masliansky exercised hypnotic effects on the Yiddish press, because the immigrant newspapers had started to report more favorably on the alliance since Masliansky began lecturing at the institution.[49] Blaustein reported to Marshall about the way Masliansky artfully extracted Americanization cues from the Torah, as exemplified by a lecture on *Yitro,* in which the preacher observed, in a vein reminiscent of the counsel given by Moses's father-in-law Jethro, that immigrant Jews in their new Promised Land had a good work spirit but were not systematically organized. The moral of this lecture, Blaustein explained, was that the immigrant Jew "should not lose sight" of his traditional ideals but "should also learn from America to be orderly and systematic in whatever he does."[50] In his own energetically disciplined way, Marshall engaged Masliansky extensively at the Educational Alliance—the "national preacher" delivered fifty-two lectures at the alliance during 1900 and 1901 as well as a roughly equal number elsewhere in New York and along the East Coast.[51] This was a busy warm-up to Masliansky efforts as owner and publisher of the *Jewish World,* a media initiative known to posterity as "Louis Marshall's Yiddish newspaper."

Although the alliance was not affiliated formally with any political party, its moral reform work had a clear association with city reform movements that consolidated in this period as Citizens Union and Fusion tickets, sending Columbia University's scrupulous, respected president, Seth Low, to City Hall in 1901. A persevering yet reserved personality, Low took exception to explanations that attributed early twentieth-century urban morass to the alleged character traits of immigrant groups (and he endeared himself to Citizens Union backers like Jacob Schiff by adamantly resisting anti-Semitism at Columbia[52]). Instead of catering to or baiting ethnic groups, Low explained with patient optimism that urban realities would improve steadily once city officials learned to fashion appropriately responsive institutions and services.[53]

Low's good government message could be a bit bland, but it had the utterly redeeming feature of not being Tammany Hall. While Uptown recoil from Tammany was partly governed by religious and ethnic tensions between Jews and Irish Catholics (tensions that, as we will see, exploded a year after Low's election, during the riots that occurred during Rabbi Jacob Joseph's funeral procession),[54] it also had a clear basis in the poor record of municipal governance accumulated over the years by Tammany mayors, including Robert Van Wyck, who bested Low in New York City's 1897 mayoralty race. Deficiencies in city management spawned ignorance, despair, and vice—precisely the evils that Jewish moral reform workers sought to rectify at the Educational Alliance. On the eve of Low's autumn 1901 election, 5,269 children were denied admission to public schools in Manhattan, due to lack of accommodations, and 58,123 were enrolled in limited, half-day programs.[55] Yet more notoriously, Tammany patronage and corruption seeped through the city's police force (police shakedowns of Jewish pushcart peddlers were one widely known abuse), and Low's police reform platform in the 1901 municipal elections sparked hopes among moral reformers.[56]

In the 1900–1901 period, Marshal did not disguise his contempt for Tammany's "control of the Police Department, the Health Department, [and] the charities." He complained about Tammany in exchanges with Felix Adler, the founder of the Ethical Cultural Society, an outspoken Fusionist who publicly lauded Low as "the last, best hope of earth." "I am and have always been a Republican and have no sympathy with Tammany Hall," Marshall declared to Adler.[57] Throughout the 1901 mayoralty campaign, Marshall kept contact with Blaustein, hoping that alliance activities would, one way or another, keep the immigrants out of Tammany's clutches. Blaustein shared this antipathy; although Downtown voting for Fusion was not quite as large as he had anticipated, the alliance director was gratified by Low's election, and Blaustein announced to Marshall that "this was the first time that a word of truth was spoken through the Voice of Ghetto."[58] This was an indirect, but unmistakable, indication that the moral reform phase of Marshall's activity unfolded within a broader movement of anti-Tammany city reform. The anti-Tammany motivation would become much more pronounced in Marshall's activities with the *Jewish World*.

Jewish Theological Seminary

The JTS had been in operation for close to fifteen years before it was reorganized under Marshall's administrative leadership. Founded in 1887, its New York City campus was wedged between the modernist radicalism of the Reform movement, symbolized by the HUC's infamous nonkosher 1883 trefa banquet, and the movement's 1885 Pittsburgh Platform[59] and Orthodox traditionalism, symbolized by the founding in 1886 of the Etz Chaim Yeshiva.[60] Appealing to "Jews of America faithful to Mosaic law and ancestral tradition," the new seminary's constitution deliberately staked out middle ground between the antitraditional radicalism of Reform and rigid Orthodox observance, but divisions of outlook and temperament separated Sephardic rabbinical leaders (Sabato Morais, Henry Pereira Mendes) and American-born, German-trained rabbis (Henry Schneeberger, Bernard Drachman) who were involved in the JTS founding.[61] In fact, scholars continue to debate whether this embryonic moment in what was to become the Conservative movement should be viewed more as a response to "Orthodox" traditionalism or Reform innovation[62] (just as, more broadly, the question of when exactly a "Conservative" stream came into being remains open to question[63]).

Before its reorganization in the early twentieth century, the JTS was plagued by administrative, financial, and ideological difficulties. However, its reputation as a largely dysfunctional institution might have been exaggerated by the "conspirators" (as Cyrus Adler half-facetiously described his own group) responsible for the JTS reorganization, an event described critically by one scholar as a "coup d'etat."[64] In its first years, the JTS migrated between borrowed rooms at Congregation Shearith Israel and Cooper Union, before Jacob Schiff housed it in a "large and commodious brownstone" on Lexington Avenue near 59th Street. Schiff provided some additional financial support in years preceding the JTS reorganization, as did a few other philanthropists, but the institution's finances remained, in Hasia Diner's description, "shaky." Its most important rabbinical leader, Mikveh Israel's Reverend Sabato Morias, resided in Philadelphia and was in failing health; the most important JTS lay leader, Joseph Blumenthal, died in 1901 (he was effectively replaced by Marshall in the reorganized JTS, though technically Marshall was only a member of the new JTS board until 1905, when he replaced Cyrus Adler as its chairman). In other words, the original seminary lacked strong leadership. Lay supporters of this original JTS were troubled by a confused administrative amalgam of rabbis and secular figures. In Philadelphia, Judge Mayer Sulzberger, who, with Adler, was instrumental in the recruitment of Solomon Schechter to revitalize the JTS and who was responsible for the institution's remarkable library, was particularly incensed about the meddling of rabbis in the management of the original institution. The new JTS, insisted the ordinarily moderate-tempered Sulzberger, had to be reorganized "on a basis of entire secularity."[65]

Crucially, as the nineteenth century turned into the twentieth, the JTS seemed ill-equipped to meet the challenges posed by the influx of thousands of East European immigrant Jews in New York. Its students had in the 1890s come mostly from poor immigrant homes,[66] but they were far too few in number to serve as influential models on the East Side (in fifteen years, a paltry total of fourteen rabbis graduated from the JTS[67]). The original JTS had developed "no substantial constituency" on the East Side, neither among observant immigrants nor among modernizing newcomers,[68] and its administrators were apt to draw insensitive distinctions between its "English speaking" and immigrant students.[69] Circumstances were ripe for reorganizing the seminary.

Colorful myth mingles with fact in the sequence leading to the Uptown group's wholesale reorganization of the JTS. Cyrus Adler marked the start of the reorganization at a 1901 social gathering hosted by Macy's co-owner Isidor Straus. On Adler's telling, he lamented how New York, soon to be the home of the world's largest Jewish community, was allowing its sole Jewish institution of learning to perish. Listening to this peroration, Schiff, "a man of quick decisions," exclaimed suddenly, "Dr. Adler is right," and within a few weeks the banker had assembled an Uptown philanthropic group, featuring Schiff himself, Daniel and Simon Guggenheim, and Leonard Lewisohn, to revamp the JTS. The group organized an endowment of over half a million dollars that enabled the JTS to invite Solomon Schechter and, "with the powerful help of Louis Marshall," reorganize and save itself.[70] This somewhat self-serving account abridges circumstances leading to the JTS reorganization, but precise details are not germane, since the seminary's financial, administrative, and student shortcomings were widely recognized in 1901, and there was also a swell of opinion favoring the recruitment of Solomon Schechter as a panacea for the JTS.

Schechter was wooed by the JTS for a dozen years, beginning in 1890 when Sabato Morais invited him to join the new institution.[71] Romanian born and raised in a Hassidic family, Schechter had been ordained as a rabbi in Vienna, studied in Berlin, and authored well-received books on early rabbinic Judaism.[72] He made his way to England, where he analyzed Hebrew texts in the British Museum and the Bodleian Library, and he joined the faculty at Cambridge University in a lonely and underpaid position. He gained world renown for his part in the uncovering of the Cairo Genizah, an invaluable repository of discarded Jewish books and sacred materials, some of them a thousand years old.

Despite his well-earned fame, Schechter never settled comfortably in England. He complained about the lack of spiritual life in the country and about how "I lose my life among Christians" in Cambridge, where there was "no [Jewish] community and no synagogue."[73] Schechter pined for America, "the greatest and best nation," where there might even be a "place for Torah."[74] Owing to the friendly help of Adler and Sulzberger, he made a debut visit to America in February 1895, delivering six lectures and solidifying ties in the country.[75] His move to America was subsequently a much-discussed topic, and by the end of the century periodicals like the *Jewish Exponent* and the *American Hebrew* issued calls for the eminent rabbi to come revitalize Judaism in North America. Though it stalled for several years, Schechter's arrival struck the powerful stewards in Marshall's crowd as a perfectly natural occurrence. Why shouldn't a world-famous Jewish scholar who had learned to write and teach in English (thanks to the help of his wife, Mathilde Schechter) work in America? For Schiff, recruiting Schechter to the JTS to revitalize Judaism in the country was the American thing to do: "We in the United States, who are ever striving to secure the best, were not long in the discovery of Solomon Schechter," Schiff reflected.[76]

Marshall discovered Schechter later than his Uptown peers. His role as the central administrator in the emergence of Conservative Judaism was marked by irony and unintended consequence. This deeply significant chapter of his life begins not with Solomon Schechter's arrival in America, as the savior of the JTS and progenitor of a yet unnamed branch of American Judaism, the Conservative movement, but rather with the death of the leader of the Reform movement, Isaac Mayer Wise.

A few weeks after Isaac Mayer Wise's death in 1900, Marshall headed the HUC's soliciting committee for a fund memorializing the patriarch of Reform Judaism in America. For the next several months, Marshall acted on the assumption that a seminary run under Reform auspices would satisfy the theological needs of American Jewry as a whole, and, in a mix of wishful thinking and psychological denial, he vowed that no schism between branches of Judaism was brewing in America. Strengthening Reform Judaism would help solidify the status of Jews in America in the new century. As the twentieth century opened, the focus was on carving a place for the Jews in the country rather than modifying their existing religious and social institutions to accommodate subdivisions between "Russians" and "Germans" or between "modernists" and "traditionalists" in the community. Marshall was not at this point delving into fine points of religious ideology. Had he done so, he would have been conscious of the irony of his position at the forefront of a memorial campaign for Isaac Mayer Wise, since Wise, as symbolized by his *Minhag America* prayer book, emphasized the singularity of Jewish experience in the United States,[77] whereas Marshall consistently viewed religion as the sphere where Jews of all times and places became united by spirit and tradition, and he attached his reverent enthusiasm for American uniqueness to political (i.e., nonreligious) matters.

Starting in spring 1900, Marshall worked hard to raise funds for a Reform theological seminary in Wise's memory. Now that Jews were prospering in America, he wrote to prospective funders, how could they allow it to be said of them that "while the feeblest of religious sects in our nation is able to maintain a theological seminary . . . Judaism, the mother of all religions, has, in its American home, so degenerated and become so indifferent to its mission, as to allow this noble work to perish from the earth?"[78] Jacob Schiff contributed $5,000 to the Isaac Mayer Wise Memorial Fund, but as was happening with other moral reform crusades Schiff and Marshall promoted in this period, Jews did not reach very deep into their pockets during the Wise memorial campaign. Frustrated,

Marshall complained to his cousin Joe Stolz, the Chicago rabbi-in-the-making who had an HUC background, that "the average man is willing to subscribe to a hospital" but is "entirely apathetic when asked to assist an educational institution." The potential for Jewish charity, Marshall estimated, was $2.5 million a year, but a project like the Educational Alliance, which helped acclimatize hundreds of immigrant Jews, had barely received $140,000 in donations, despite Marshall's energetic campaigning; in contrast, Mount Sinai Hospital had raised $1.4 million over the previous year. Marshall was aiming to raise $50,000 among New York Jews for the Wise fund.[79]

Within a year, the Uptown elite shifted direction, no longer viewing Reform as a viable mechanism to promote unity in America's Jewish life or as a means to solidify the Jewish community's presence on the country's landscape. The focus was now on finding a practical way to reach the masses of East European Jews in Downtown New York. The general faith in religion as an ameliorating influence had not dissipated, but Schiff in particular seemed to doubt whether Reform really had any meaning for the Russian Jews. Pushing hard, Schiff by April 1901 promoted the plan to reorganize the JTS and utilize its more traditional ethos as a means of reaching the Russians.

In addition to recruiting Schechter, Schiff had promising ideas about the JTS reorganization. He pledged to purchase land near Columbia University on Morningside Heights as the new seminary's site. This was an inspiring decision for a Jewish place of learning to take root as an "Acropolis on the Hill," alongside Columbia; abandoning the casual spirit of the Lexington Avenue residence, the new JTS would become "Judaism's Home of Science on West 123rd street."[80] The relocation probably aimed at the moral uplift of JTS immigrant students; leaving their Lower East Side and Brooklyn homes, they were to travel to the area of a distinguished American university, in a commute that symbolized American acculturation.[81]

As an integral part of this reorganization that was in step with Sulzberger's call for "entire secularity" in the seminary's management board, Schiff counted on Marshall to take the lead in the seminary's rebirth by handling its legal and administrative aspects and articulating its purposes. Schiff is "anxious that I become Chairman of the Executive Committee of the Jewish Theological Seminary," Marshall confided to Judge Mayer Sulzberger.[82]

He was wary of this assignment for personal and public reasons. A business lawyer, Marshall was not punctilious in his observance of Jewish ritual, and he wondered whether he was qualified to negotiate a delicate balance between tradition and change at the JTS. He therefore told Schiff that he would serve on a reorganized JTS board but could not accept its chairmanship, since he was not a "Shulchan Aruch Jew."[83] Continuing, Marshall returned to the message he had delivered privately to his cousin a year earlier, as a frustrated Reform fund-raiser: when it came to furnishing support, neither the immigrants nor the well-established members of the community really had Judaism on their minds, and so Marshall was loath to become "prominently identified with an institution which would constantly languish."

Making an offer that Marshall could not refuse, Schiff nullified his reservations on the spot.[84] He asked Marshall how much money would be needed to revitalize the JTS; the attorney replied, $100,000. Schiff pledged a quarter of that sum, promised that Adolph Lewisohn would donate $50,000, and observed that recruiting the remainder would not be a problem.[85] Marshall demurred, but after some pro forma consultation with Sulzberger and Leonard Lewisohn, he succumbed to Schiff's requests. His association with the JTS would have profound impact on his thinking and activity for the next three decades, continuing up to his final hours, when in what unwittingly became a final testament (and, perhaps fittingly, also a fund-raising appeal), he wrote to Sears, Roebuck magnate Julius Rosenwald about how the seminary had "performed miracles" but continued to receive "scant support from the Jewish Community."[86]

Though in 1901 Marshall was not fully cognizant of what might be termed the denominational consequences of this turn of events, he was a little uncomfortable about raising funds one year for a modernist spirited Reform cause and then campaigning the following year for a more traditional JTS. The switch happened because priorities had shifted from showcasing Judaism as a symbol of Jewish arrival in America, to using a moderately conservative variant of Judaism to Americanize the Downtown Jewish immigrants.

Initially a reluctant founder of the new JTS, Marshall took up Schiff's latest pet project in the hope that it would become a Conservative flank complementing the Reform movement's position at the more radical side of one unified cause, Judaism in the United States. He was thinking not about the emergence of distinctive branches of the religion, but rather in terms of internal differentiation analogous to the way a cohesive political party might host sub-factions in America.

Here in clear relief was a leading dilemma of Marshall's career: he had a deep romantic commitment to the ideal of unity, but frequently found that under the modernizing pressures of the twentieth-century world, his most meaningful contribution to Jewish affairs would be to rationalize, and effectively institutionalize, its divisions and differences. At first glance, Marshall's work on the JTS reorganization and his advocacy almost two decades later at the Paris Peace Conference after World War I for Jewish minority rights appear as disparate sorts of contributions to Jewish life, but the underlying dynamic in such activities was strikingly consistent. Jewish rights were conceptualized differently in Western democracies and Central and East European monarchies; although Marshall traveled to Paris after World War I as a proud diplomatic proponent of one global solution for Jewish politics, as things ended up he had to negotiate compromises that essentially recognized and perpetuated two, "West" and "East," brands of Jewish politics, one based on individual rights and the other on group rights. Similar dynamics are recognizable in other Marshall campaigns in Jewish politics, including his negotiations for dual formal recognition of Zionists and non-Zionists on the expanded Jewish Agency. Always, a clean but rather misplaced dream of unity was followed by a messy but pragmatically endorsed reality of political or religious denominationalism. Marshall's work on the JTS illustrates how theology fit into this career pattern.

Had Marshall had his way, he would have preempted Schiff's JTS maneuvers and amalgamated the JTS and HUC in an American Judaism melting pot. A year before Schiff commissioned him as chief JTS reorganizer, Marshall had argued that Isaac Mayer Wise's death was an "opportune time to consider the consolidation" of the JTS and the HUC. This HUC-JTS consolidation plan was proposed in the *Jewish Messenger* in late April 1900.[87] As far as Marshall was concerned, theological or temperamental differences between the two institutions related "to matters of form only." Modernist Reform theologians and traditionalist JTS teachers could operate together in one seminary, in the same way that a political science department might offer courses on contrary, liberal and conservative, political ideologies. An "investigation into the history of Israel," declared Marshall, "requires alike a consideration of the conservative and the more radical elements." His idea that theology could be studied in an ecumenical spirit comparable to dispassionate academic study in a university displayed considerable naïveté, but also demonstrated the pull exerted by the ideal of unity in Marshall's thinking:

> Just as in the study of political science, the principles of monarchical and republican forms of government, the policies of the free trader and the protectionist, the views of the bimetallist and of the monometallist, are taught in the same college, so, likewise, the contrasted doctrines of the orthodox and of the reformed Jews may be elucidated and developed, possibly by different professors but yet in the same seminary.[88]

Remarkably, Marshall persisted with this vision of a unified, pluralistic seminary a year later, after he acceded to Schiff's demands. In this moralistic phase of his career, Marshall's Jewish activities had been dedicated to ideals of decorum and harmony, and this vision of Jewish wholeness prohibited him from drawing the simple conclusion, based on the experience of Christianity in America, that religion in the country tended toward institutionalized differentiation. "While I see many difficulties in the way of a consolidation of the Hebrew Union College and the Jewish Theological Seminary, I believe that it is entirely feasible," Marshall declared in spring 1901. Schiff gave him no choice but to head the JTS effort, but Marshall was skeptical that the seminary could provide a cure-all in American Jewish life. Hoping that "consolidation" might someday become a reality, he would continue in the interim to work for both the HUC and the JTS. The latter was "important for the conservative interests," but since the "majority of our Jewish population is drifting toward radicalism" the HUC still had to be supported. The HUC, in fact, "served a much greater proportion of the community."[89]

As months passed by, Marshall recruited Schechter to head the JTS, handled the legal work for the seminary's reorganization, and tirelessly raised funds for the institution. Ironically, his efficiency in the reorganization merely aggravated the dilemma. While he and Schiff were prominent members of New York's elite Reform congregation, Emanu-El, they were setting up the JTS as the linchpin of a new Conservative stream of Judaism in America. Such a denominational alignment appeared to reinforce popular images of the Jews as a divisive and divided race, which Marshall abhorred on a moral and aesthetic level and also knew to be potentially pernicious in important spheres such as immigration. Thus, in private correspondence and public acts he searched for phrases and schemes that might forestall the evolving reality of Jewish denominationalism.

In June 1903, Marshall resigned from his role on the Isaac Mayer Wise Memorial Fund, complaining that Reform men of the cloth had been "insinuating" that his vision of One Judaism was "erroneous." Emotionally, however, he remained drawn to that vision.[90] In spring 1904, when his cousin Joseph Stolz was ordained as a rabbi by HUC, Marshall sent heartfelt congratulations.[91] The one substantive message Marshall imparted was that Stolz ought to distance himself from all the "American rabbis" who regarded differentiation into branches as a fact of nature. "There is but one Judaism," Marshall insisted, even if "there are various roads by which an appreciation of its beauties and of its lessons may be attained." Marshall groused about the way Reform leaders attacked his efforts for the JTS ("the cause of religion cannot be furthered by attacking the motives, or the ideals, or the methods of those who in their own way are seeking to advance it"). Even as he praised his cousin and exhorted him to do "untold good," Marshall could not disguise his anxiety about how the establishment of a rival seminary to HUC provided an institutional basis for internal bickering and contentiousness in Jewish affairs.

For years, Marshall viewed the JTS as an agency of unifying power in Jewish affairs, and he wrestled emotionally and rhetorically with the senses in which it appeared to be endowing a new division in Jewish life, Conservative Judaism. For instance, halfway through 1907, Marshall devised a plan to connect the JTS with a large number of Orthodox Jews on the East Side. He persuaded the JTS Finance Committee to apply to several Orthodox synagogues in the city and ask them "to induce their members to contribute a sum of one dollar annually."[92] He explained to Educational Alliance veteran David Blaustein that the scheme's purpose was to alter the "attitude" of Orthodox congregations toward the JTS: "Thus far they have contributed nothing to it."[93]

This plan unsettled Schechter, who tactfully articulated concerns about preserving the seminary's prestige and dignity. Marshall dismissed such reservations. "I believe that the [Orthodox] congregations" on the East Side "should be stirred up into affiliation with our cause," he told Schechter. Tellingly, he chose an analogy that underscored theological unity, rather than Protestant-style denominationalism—Catholic seminaries were supported by laymen, not priests, Marshall observed. Once a popular base Downtown was forged for the JTS, he explained, the seminary would be a force of unity, not division, in Jewish affairs. The JTS belonged neither to a separate branch of Judaism nor to the Uptown elite. It belonged to the Jewish people in America:

> We must create a constituency. We have none. We are injured by the popular notion that we are endowed and supported by a few millionaires. It will not detract from the dignity of institution if it is known that this is not the fact, [that this] institution is one in which Jews have a part.[94]

Marshall pitched his plan for Orthodox Jewish support for the JTS at a meeting held on June 19 at the Educational Alliance. Though the gathering was not largely attended, the idea was received sympathetically[95] and sparked discussion in the Downtown press. Not in intention, but in effect, Marshall's plan was designed to draw traditional-minded immigrant Jews and their children away from Old World Orthodox synagogues on the East Side and toward a Americanized and somewhat less traditional institutional setting of the embryonic Conservative movement. In this transitional moment, such designations ("Conservative") were lacking, and Marshall could not give his unqualified blessing to all the implications of his own labors. Yet he had a keen grasp of their rationale and necessity. When one newspaper asked him to summarize his presentation at the Educational Alliance, Marshall sat down at his summer Adirondack home, Knollwood, and composed the most cogent explanation yet offered of the work he, Schiff, and Schechter were doing at the JTS. This was, in fact, Marshall's first and best exposition on the rise of Conservative Judaism in America.

Younger Jewish immigrants and children of Russian Jewish immigrants, Marshall explained,[96] were falling away from synagogues, largely because "they have become accustomed to the orderly and decorous methods" of school gatherings and other public assemblies in the United States. The chaotic appearance of Orthodox prayer instills among them "a sense of shame" and "impels them to abstain from further attendance" in synagogues. This sense of alienation from the Orthodox synagogue rendered young generations of American Jews "agnostics, and adherents to the latest fads in so-called religion, economics or ethics." The worst was yet to come, because once a majority of the community's Jews were American-born, there would be an overwhelming trend of Jewish children "scoffing at what their parents held sacred."

The "time has come," declared Marshall, to create a "model synagogue" that would bring young American Jews back to the religion and help them realize what Judaism meant for ancestors "who were ready to suffer martyrdom" for it. To accomplish this aim of revitalizing faith among young Jews, "it is not necessary to inculcate reformed Judaism, or to depart from any of the principles of Orthodoxy."

Such description of a "model synagogue" positioned between Reform and Orthodoxy enshrined Conservative Judaism in all but name. As an unnamed evocation of a new brand of American Judaism, Marshall's description of this model synagogue warrants quotation:

> All that is necessary is to make the service attractive; to eliminate that which is improper to American mind, to introduce congregational singing, to give the worshipper an opportunity to take part in a service he understands, to include as part of the service an English sermon on a religious topic, and to cast out that which is grotesque and uncongenial to a mind influenced by American culture.[97]

Marshall played deputy to Schiff through the key phases of the JTS reorganization. At Schiff's bidding, he drew up papers consolidating the JTS through a "rather novel scheme of reorganization."[98]

Mel Scult's careful scholarship exposes aspects in which this reorganization was an Uptown power play carried out to the detriment of the seminary's original association. While Scult's negative characterization of the reorganization as a "coup d'état" is not very persuasive, because it ignores overlap between the seminary's old and new boards (symbolized by the fact that Schiff himself built the facilities of the old and the new JTS) and attributes an exaggerated sense of vitality to the old JTS, which graduated rabbis at the phlegmatic pace of one per year, it nevertheless points cogently to a pattern of minimal, yet real, self-interested promotion by the Uptown elite.

By any objective measure, the German Jewish elite in New York compiled an impressive record of achievement in the early twentieth century, but it also tended to minimize the way its flagship organizations and institutions inherited the resources or accumulated experience of preexisting initiatives. Just as several members of the "Our Crowd" German Jewish elite were not quite the rags-to-riches economic success stories they claimed to be (though many did, in fact, start out in America as peddlers), they or their heirs tended to project their philanthropic and Jewish communal successes as entirely original creations that arose, ex nihilo, as absolutely necessary correctives to the unregulated chaos of Jewish life on the East Side. Typically, however, they were, on a larger and more efficient scale, carrying out work that had been done by predecessor organizations, institutions, and individuals. Such Uptown takeovers were an inevitable consequence of Schiff's ample resources, of Marshall's potent energy and lawyerly skills, and, more broadly, of the shift in the Jewish demographic balance to New York City, away from Midwestern locales where important organizations like B'nai B'rith or HUC were based. They tended, however, to be executed with less than perfect tact and were resented by ousted and ill-appreciated predecessors. The JTS reorganization fits this pattern.

Marshall reassured Schiff that the purpose of the JTS legal work, which wove its way through the New York assembly in 1902 and won the governor's final approval in May 1903, was to "keep control of the seminary in our hands."[99] Control was attained by creating a bicameral directorship (class A and class B directors) that would be submitted to the directors of the old JTS as a fait accompli.[100] Polishing rough edges on the plan, Marshall explained at length to New York State legislators that Jewish leadership of the seminary was needed. "It would be contrary to the spirit of our constitution if such an institution [JTS] were to be . . . supervised by anybody other than one composed exclusively of Jews," Marshall argued.[101] In these legislative lobbying efforts, Marshall trumpeted Schiff's philosophy of Jewish noblesse oblige and emphasized the JTS contribution toward the moral improvement of immigrants. Quoting Schiff, Marshall told the New York State senators that "the solution of the Jewish question in this country depends largely on the success of the Educational Alliance and of this [Jewish Theological] Seminary."[102]

New York legislators approved the plan with little resistance, but the old JTS directors resented the Schiff-Marshall power play. In a meeting held at the end of March 1902 at the Baron de Hirsch Trade School on East 64th Street, heated debate preceded a vote to merge the "A" and "B" boards in a reorganized JTS.[103] Rabbi Henry Morais, son of Sabato Morais, opined that the merger ought "not be decided upon in fifteen minutes," but he was powerless to forestall the reorganization.[104] Marshall was gratified by this result because he viewed the fusion of JTS former and present directors as an aesthetic and substantive necessity. "There should really be but one Jewish Theological Seminary in this country as there is but one Judaism," he counseled Schiff.[105] Not surprisingly, he found it difficult to rally the enthusiasm of directors from the old JTS board who had been hijacked onto the reorganized directorate. When he turned to one of them, Moses Ottinger, in an appeal for funds, the resentful New York real estate dealer disputed Marshall's contention that the seminary's reorganization had proceeded with the unanimous consent of all its supporters, and he accused Marshall's group of presenting an overly rosy assessment of the financial foundation of the newly reorganized JTS.[106]

Marshall was Schiff's compliant lawyer and administrator, but he also advised the banker about key aspects of the seminary's development. As also happened with the Educational Alliance, Marshall was concerned about the public relations and substantive implications of elite Uptown control of the JTS. "I am of the belief that there should always be on the Board those who shall represent the popular element," he wrote to Schiff, adding bluntly that Downtown representation on the JTS managing board would signify that "the institution is not one which is the plaything of a few individuals, but [instead] gives expression to the ideas and aspirations of Judaism in America."[107]

In a period when Marshall and his associates were mopping up cash losses leaked ceaselessly by another initiative in Jewish immigrant edification, the *Jewish World* newspaper, Schiff pressured Marshall to find subscribers for a campaign to cover the seminary's administrative costs and supplement the $200,000 contributed by Schiff himself and some Uptown philanthropic associates (Schiff, it will be recalled, also purchased land near Columbia College for the project). Marshall labored frenetically to arrange five-year pledges from donors, all on a small scale of $200 or $300 annually, and meet the $70,000 target figure.[108] Removing one stone of worry, he reported to Schiff at the end of 1902 that the subscription target had been met for this campaign.[109] This sigh of relief, however, did not last long. A combination of factors such as faculty expansion and the socioeconomic profile of JTS students created chronic funding worries at the JTS, and in the prewar years Marshall sent repeated pleas to friends and philanthropists to fund JTS needs such as student scholarships.

Schiff's patronage "worked miracles" with the JTS, Marshall observed, but he was often frustrated when prominent associates assumed that the seminary had no worries because of this Uptown support. "It is erroneously assumed that our Seminary is adequately endowed," Marshall complained in one 1908 pitch for scholarship funds that emphasized the burden of JTS students from low-income homes who had no time to work as tutors, owing to their rigorous studies at JTS and course obligation at Columbia and other universities.[110]

The seminary's impressive development deeply satisfied Marshall, though by the end of his life he was noticeably exhausted by its endless fund-raising challenges. "We have been compelled to make bricks without straw" at JTS, he lamented days before his death, "simply because the majority of our people have not possessed the vision to appreciate that the perpetuation of Judaism depends upon an educated body of rabbis and teachers."[111]

Marshall was rewarded for these JTS labors by his work with Schechter. The relationship developed its own independent dynamics, divorced from the onerous pressures occasionally exerted by Schiff. Schechter exerted a uniquely powerful educational and spiritual influence on Marshall's adult life.

Marshall's respect for Schechter preceded their acquaintance and stemmed from his knowledge of the famous Jewish rabbi and scholar's extraordinary work with the Cairo Genizah, as well as from Judge Mayer Sulzberger's effusive endorsements of Schechter. Before he had met the famous scholar, Marshall conditioned his involvement with JTS upon Dr. Schechter's recruitment.[112]

Almost instantly, Schechter's arrival in America attained quasi-mythic proportions. Described as a "large, lumbering man who exuded warmth with his grandfatherly white hair and long handsome beard,"[113] Schechter's scholarly achievements thrilled admirers in America, and his personal background and inclusive theological vision of "Catholic Israel" rendered him well suited for work bridging the community's Uptown German and Downtown Russia subparts. At his November 1902 inaugural address at JTS, Schechter, dressed majestically in scarlet doctoral robes, unfurled his inviting vision of Jewish unity in cadences that resembled the message of One Judaism that Marshall had been advocating for months. When Schechter invited all types of Jews, "the mystic and the rationalist, the traditional and the critical,"[114] to train and study at the seminary, he hit all the right notes, as far as Marshall was concerned.

After Schechter's arrival, Marshall shielded and supported the Moldavian-born rabbi whose years at Cambridge University had not completely prepared him for the rough and tumble of Jewish life in New York. For months, Marshall took steps to downplay Schechter's positive interests in the Zionist movement,[115] fearing that their raw presentation could compromise the newcomer's status in the eyes of an Uptown elite that flinched whenever Jewish nationalism was mentioned. A variety of accounts regarding Schiff's sensitivity about pro-Zionist pronouncements justify Marshall's early cautiousness on the subject. For reasons that await clarification, but are apparently related to his emotional revulsion from the pogroms in Russia,[116] Schechter decided in 1906 to no longer suppress his support for Zionism, which he called the "Declaration of Jewish Independence from all kinds of slavery, material or spiritual." A perturbed Schiff promptly wrote a chastising letter to the JTS president. "Speaking as an American," Schiff lectured Schechter, "I cannot for a moment concede that one can be at the same time a true American and an honest adherent of the Zionist movement."[117] This may not have been mere tongue-lashing: Mordecai Kaplan asserted that as a consequence of Schechter's open embrace of Zionism, Schiff directed his funds away from the JTS and toward Jewish medical and senior citizen facilities.[118]

Over the years, as Schechter became more assertive in America about Zionism, Marshall literally found himself caught in the middle between the antipathetic and sympathetic attitudes held by his organizational and spiritual patrons toward Jewish nationalism. Marshall endured this awkward circumstance with varying degrees of success. One JTS student and future Conservative rabbi recalled an episode when Marshall arrived at the seminary to deliver Schiff's message to Schechter, prohibiting the use of its student lounge for Zionist gatherings. "The money bags are not going to rule the Seminary," an enraged Schechter yelled.[119] Perhaps in the aftermath of this little seminary drama, Marshall regrouped at Knollwood, in summer 1907, to write a tactful defense of Schechter's Zionism, as a diplomatic reply to Schiff's published attacks on Jewish nationalism. His words entranced two visitors to the Lake Saranac summer home, his sister-in-law Beatrice Lowenstein and Reform Temple Emanu-El's Zionist rabbi, Judah Magnes. According to Beatrice's charming recollection,[120] her relationship to her husband Judah began at this moment, in the pair's lakeside admiration for Marshall's defense of Schechter's Zionism, a heartfelt and courageous act, given Schiff's attitude.

During Schechter's early days in America, Marshall attended to prosaic details, not matters of romantic nationalism. Among other administrative errands, he finessed Schechter's oscillating salary demands, no small accomplishment in light of the fact that the rabbi's arrival in America was delayed for years after his mini-lecture circuit in 1895, partly due to this subject (in his first weeks in the United States, the new JTS president stiffened his demands when he heard about salary terms negotiated at HUC by its new president, Rabbi Kaufmann Kohler).[121]

Marshall shared with Schechter the experience of rebuilding the JTS from scratch. Fairly or unfairly, both had little regard for the institution's existing class of rabbinical candidates. "They do not seem to possess the requisite intelligence," Marshall wrote in June 1902, describing JTS students after accompanying Schechter on one of the newcomer rabbi's first visits to an institution that would become indelibly associated with his name and spirit. "Dr. Schechter is very much disgusted with the exhibition," he added. "They are a body of mental and physical cripples."[122]

Schechter's work at the JTS reversed this unkind estimate of its student body. Within three years, Marshall staunchly defended JTS student scholars as "earnest, intelligent and ambitious." When the *New Era* magazine, prompted by Isidore Singer, published in autumn 1904 a critical article about the seminary, Marshall replied indignantly. In Schechter's two and a half years, the institution had been "reorganized from bottom up," Marshall announced. Its first class of four had recently graduated, been ordained, and called to prestigious pulpits around the country, and their progress was a credit to "one of the greatest Jews who has ever lived in America," Dr. Schechter.[123]

A still more revealing estimate of Schechter's influence and of Marshall's appreciation of what the JTS was becoming came in response to private and published criticisms of the seminary issued by a talented but spiritually troubled JTS student and English instructor, Eugene Lehman. After distinguishing himself as an undergraduate at Yale, Lehman became one of America's first Rhodes scholars to study at Oxford. Lehman quickly became disenchanted at JTS and involved Marshall and other trustees for months in meandering correspondence about his resignation and return to the institution, sometimes allowing his disparaging remarks about "benighted Talmudists" to reach the newspapers.[124] Marshall regarded Lehman as a promising young man who had been misled by bad advice, and he attempted in a series of letters to throw perspective on Lehman's disparaging assessments of Downtown students at JTS. Marshall had not entirely relinquished his own skeptical feelings about the comportment of East Side religious scholars: during his first visit to the seminary he had caustically referred to them as "cripples," whereas in early 1905 he conceded that Schechter's pupils "may lack polish, fluency of speech, refinement of manner or even cleanliness."[125] However, in this phase of his career when Marshall conceptualized Jewish work as a quasi-colonial endeavor to ameliorate the perceived educational, moral, and physical defects of Jewish immigrants, he came to see JTS, under Schechter's leadership, as the standard-bearing institution in the Jewish world. Under JTS training, "all these outward defects" displayed by immigrant students "will in time be obviated," Marshall predicted.

Marshall confessed to this troubled young instructor that he spoke so highly about Schechter's influence on the basis of his own personal experience. "For years my mind has run to the law," he wrote. "Yet as a result of my intercourse with Dr. Schechter I have been led, in my leisure moments, to pursue studies relating to Jewish literature, and I feel that I have personally profited."[126] Marshall was referring specifically to a lecture he had delivered and published, at Schechter's prompting, on Wissenschaft des Judenthums (Science of Judaism) founder Leopold Zunz, but he was also alluding more generally to the spiritually restorative impact of his relationship with Solomon Schechter.

In early 1905, when Marshall exchanged these letters with the disgruntled JTS student-scholar dropout, his own Jewish career was in transition. Up to this point, his Jewish work had been tied almost exclusively to exercises in the public education and moral amelioration of Jewish immigrants via shelters, schools, and media outlets like the protectory, *Jewish World,* and JTS. Now, with Downtown agitated by (among other things) reports of political unrest and continuing pogroms in Russia, his own Uptown elite faced new challenges and was developing new methods. Marshall, in fact, had just filed a petition against Melvil Dewey, New York's anti-Semitic state librarian, in a bold move that symbolized his adoption of a rather different orientation of antidefamation and Jewish self-defense work. The former approach of moral reformation had its pros and cons, some of which remained, for some time, opaque to Marshall, but he was broadly aware that moral amelioration of immigrants typically came down to the agenda of rapid and radical Americanization. Immigrants were uprooted from the traditional ways of their former worlds and thrust headlong into an urban modernity whose early twentieth-century symbols in areas of transportation, entertainment, media, and politics were not always perfectly suited to Marshall's own conservative outlook. Judaism promised continuity and moral anchoring in an Americanization process laden with the threat of anarchically limitless change.

Originally, Marshall had believed that Reform Judaism could serve as such an anchor and that it might be best suited to the immigrant's quest for something new in America. But, under Schechter's tutelage at JTS, Marshall grasped that many of the Reform rabbis had attempted to modernize and Americanize the religion in ways that subverted its power as a source of continuity. At the turn of the century, newly immersed in a program for Jewish moral amelioration, Marshall headed a campaign in Isaac Mayer Wise's memory; a few years after Schechter's arrival, he negated the thrust of Wise's legacy, the project of creating a newly American form of Judaism. "There is no such thing as American Judaism,"[127] Marshall declared in the climax of these letters of advice to the troubled JTS student. Judaism is a permanent, immutable system of beliefs and doctrines. "It is the same in Palestine as in New York, as in Russia, as in Chicago, as in England, as in San Francisco." No theory of Americanization could legitimately brand some Jewish students and scholars as being inferior to any other class of Jews. "The most orthodox, conservative Jews" in America were just as "good as the so-called Reform Jew."

The JTS was a crucial link in a chain, but its work had to be viewed in a broad Jewish perspective, bereft of faddish American expectations of instant progress. "Systems of theology are not established in fifteen minutes,"[128] Marshall had remarked pungently to Isidor Lewi, the editor responsible for publishing the critical magazine piece about the JTS. In a similar vein, Marshall counseled Eugene Lehman to seek wise teachers, not prophets, at the seminary. "The Jewish rabbi in America will be obliged to serve a congregation of constantly increasing numbers, drawn from various communities of the Old World, forming new relations in a new country, and subjected to new cultural influences," Marshall wrote.[129] As one of the patrons of Conservative Judaism, he then gave his blessing to the leaders of a new movement he had sponsored, ironically, in the name of Jewish unity: "Whoever does his task conscientiously, in an endeavor to serve his brethren and glorify God, and to preserve the principles which have made Judaism a world force, will have done his duty, even though he may not rank among the prophets."

The moral reform phase of Marshall's career yielded mixed results. Some projects (as we shall see presently, in the example of "Marshall's Yiddish newspaper") failed outright, but assumptions and insights in their temporary implementation serve as useful measures of Marshall's intentions, character, and evolution as a Jewish leader. Other projects, such as the Educational Alliance, were fraught with patronizing, even colonialist, expectations and procedures, but nonetheless served extremely useful temporary purposes in the provision of requisite skills to needful immigrants. In the moral reform phase's intriguing array of effort, the JTS stands out as a project that has had an enduring, vital impact upon Jewish life, religion, and culture in the United States. After the reorganization, the JTS founders were able to reevaluate its purposes in a practical, constructive spirit; they abandoned messianic expectations regarding the perfect uplift of immigrants and of Jewish life and came to expect practically that JTS staff members function as wise teachers, not prophets. A full explanation of the seminary's unusual talent for adaptation and revitalization exceeds the scope of this study, but for our purposes it has sufficed to highlight ways Marshall's energy, lawyerly skills, and power of expression contributed indelibly to the crucial phase of the institution's rebirth. A strong hint of Marshall's own appreciation of the seminary's place in his career, and in American Jewish life, can be found in his will. Ten percent of his estate was donated to various charities, and one-half of this contribution went to the JTS.[130]

Marshall's Yiddish Newspaper

The moral amelioration phase hit its limit with Marshall's supervision of a Yiddish newspaper, *Di Yidishe Velt* (*The Jewish World*). This publication, known to posterity as Louis Marshall's Yiddish newspaper,[131] failed in every practical sense and was based upon a fallacious premise.

The Yiddish press, Marshall and his Uptown cohorts feared, inculcated among its East Side readers a foreign, radicalized viewpoint and inhibited their integration in American society. This apprehension was exactly wrong. By the mid-1920s it had become readily apparent to dispassionate observers that in contradistinction to a widespread idea holding that foreign language print media in the United States functioned primarily to keep its immigrant readers abreast of events in their former countries, the Jewish Downtown newspapers were (as one study put it) essentially "American newspapers printed in Yiddish."[132] Belatedly, after World War I, Marshall's elite group grasped this fact,[133] but at the turn of the twentieth century, Marshall related to the Yiddish newspapers as pernicious forces, as "decidedly yellow" and often "socialistic" outlets that "lacked character"[134] and impeded the immigrants' evolution as worthy American citizens. His most ambitious project in immigrant moral edification, the *World,* would be "clean, wholesome, [and] religious in tone." It would be "the advocate of all that makes good citizenship."[135]

The Yiddish press took root in America in the early days of the East European immigration, during the Syracuse period of Marshall's life.[136] Probably the first Yiddish daily in the world, the *Yiddishes Tageblatt* (*Jewish Daily News*) was founded in New York City in 1885 by Kasriel Sarasohn. Published in a Germanic Yiddish, this pioneering Jewish newspaper was conservative in politics, and catered mostly to religiously Orthodox readers. Propounding a secular-socialist viewpoint, the *Vorwaerts* (*Jewish Daily Forward*) began circulating in 1897, and before long it became the most profitable foreign-language newspaper in America. Another important Yiddish newspaper, *Yiddisher Morgen Journal* (*Jewish Morning Journal*) was established by Jacob Saperstein in 1901 to fill a specific need—its want ads were anxiously scanned each morning by unemployed immigrant readers.

At the turn of the twentieth century, five Yiddish newspapers in the United States had a combined circulation of 62,000. Median reader age was forty-five to fifty, but the papers were known to have many young readers, and at least 35 percent of the Yiddish readers were women. The newspapers' Yiddish became less Germanic and more Americanized after 1900. Though two major New York papers (*Tageblatt* and *Morgen Journal*) shared Marshall's Republican political sensibilities, he distrusted their editors and cited examples of the newspapers' eleventh-hour political turnabouts on election eve.[137] On the whole, when Marshall thought about Yiddish newspaper politics, he had in mind the *Forward's* pro-labor, socialist viewpoint.

Marshall toyed with the idea of supervising a Yiddish newspaper in early 1902, and he consulted about possible pros and cons with *New York Times* mogul Adolph Ochs.[138] As Marshall mulled publishing possibilities, Z. H. Masliansky was taking steps to transform his lecturing for immigrant moral improvement at the Educational Alliance into a daily Yiddish publishing effort. Teaming in mid-March with Yiddish journalist Max Bucans and some Downtown acquaintances, Masliansky purchased for $9,000 the presses of the defunct *Abendblatt*.[139] His group turned to Marshall for additional finances; Marshall complied with this appeal, contingent on the condition that "the people whom I represent" would have "control of the newspaper and are to dictate its policy."[140] By June he announced to prospective investors that the newspaper would soon find its way to press. The newspaper initiative, Marshall explained, was a direct outgrowth of "the performance of my duties as Chairman of the Committee on Moral Culture of the Educational Alliance."[141] Rather than edifying several dozen immigrants through lectures at the Educational Alliance, a Yiddish journal "speaks to a community of 350,000 souls." Immigrant readers were "impressionable people, of great natural intelligence," Marshall explained. With "proper guidance," Yiddish newspaper readers would become "exemplary citizens," and a carefully produced newspaper was needed to divert the immigrants from the "pernicious theories" of "demagogues."

The original investment group for the *Jewish World* was comprised of twenty-five subscribers. On Lucy Dawidowicz's estimate, at least half of these Uptown investors were millionaires, but their contributions were relatively small (Jacob Schiff, Felix Warburg, and Adolph Lewisohn contributed about $5,000 apiece). Marshall allotted $2,000 of his own funds to the experiment.[142] The capital at stake was negligible, but Marshall handled its public presentation in an unusually stealthy and clumsy manner that contrasted sharply with his adroit handling of other moral and religious uplift experiments in this period, such as the JTS.

Badly underestimating the ability of perceptive immigrants to read between the lines and discern the character of a Yiddish newspaper's controlling interests, Marshall believed that the newspaper's credibility would be preserved so long as the true identities of its owners and directors were hidden from the public. Hatching his plan in consultation with Ochs, Marshall nominated five directors for the *World*, with Masliansky and Israel Wolf representing the "Downtown element," and the names of the three Uptown directors remaining a "profound secret."[143]

To keep the names of wealthy investors like Schiff and Warburg under wraps, he transferred control of the investment group's stock to his brother-in-law, Paul Herzog, a name lacking volatile associations on the East Side. Marshall imagined that he could pull strings as an invisible puppeteer of the Yiddish Fourth Estate. Everything depended upon hiding his control. "The usefulness of the paper will depend upon our concealing the fact that it is anything other than what it purports to be, the enterprise of Mr. Maslianski," Marshall explained to Isidor Lewi, an editorialist with the *New York Tribune*.[144] To Schiff and other investors who worried that funding a Yiddish newspaper was like putting explosive powder in a loose cannon, Marshall offered lawyerly assurances that they were assuming no individual liability.[145]

His tactic of shadow newspaper management cast ill effect. By 1902–3, Downtown Jews approached new initiatives with considerable suspicion, expecting that they derived from self-interested calculations of the German Jewish elite. Any item that conveyed moral exhortation was branded "made in Uptown" and met with little patience on the East Side.

This impatient mood was perceptively chronicled by Isaac Max Rubinow, an Americanized Russian Jew who had a distinguished career in medicine, social science, and political activism.[146] Lambasting religious propaganda emanating from Uptown sources, Rubinow noted in 1903 that "the enlightened people of the East Side became sick of that tendency, which was so crude."[147] Just imagine, Rubinow recorded, "the German and American Jews have . . . decided to spread religion among the Polish, Lithuanian and Galician Jews. Doesn't it sound ridiculous?"[148] Precisely at the moment when Marshall organized his shadow supervision of a Yiddish newspaper, Downtown Jews had grown weary of what Rubinow sarcastically decried as the "Renaissance of Morals." Facts of Jewish life in this period, Rubinow noted, "caused the people of New York to talk about an existing conflict between the Russian and German Jews."[149] The "underlying cause," of this conflict, explained Rubinow, was the Uptown Jew's blithe misunderstanding of the Downtown immigrant's "spiritual and intellectual aspirations." He continued:

> The methods which the German used led to an outcry, emanating from the East Side. "We do not want your money and free us of your compassion." The growing East Side began to show signs of independence.[150]

With animosity toward Uptown moralizing reaching a crescendo on the East Side, there was no hope of disguising management circumstances in the *World's* media missionary crusade. In fact, the cultural life of Jewish New York at the time was dominated by theatrical unmasking of the patronizing intents and operations of Uptown benefactors. Most famously, Yiddish playwright Jacob Gordin's one-act parody of Uptown moralizing, *The Benefactors of the East Side,* which was staged to a large, approving audience of 2,000 or 3,000 Jews about a year after Masliansky's group made their down payment for the *Abendblatt* plant, displayed Downtown's emphatic rejection of the moralistic information campaign Marshall was heading with the *World.*[151] The play lampooned philanthropist and lawyer characters transparently based on Schiff and Marshall. The drama's benefactors sententiously lamented that Downtown immigrants "are not prepared to be good, loyal citizens." It was all too easy, the benefactors insisted, "to propagandize all kinds of anarchistic and demagogic theories" among the Russian Jewish immigrants.[152]

The condescending analysis of Gordin's fictional benefactors rather uncannily reproduced Marshall's real-life descriptions of Yiddish newspaper readers as "impressionable people" who easily "come under the influence of demagogues." Observers contended that the large audience for Gordin's play registered an "open protest against the patronizing air which some of the wealthy Jews of the West Side assume towards their less fortunate brethren of the East Side."[153] In fact, the play reflected an attitude of Downtown anger and resentment that was not likely to be credulously receptive to the propagandistic manipulations of Marshall's Yiddish newspaper.

For a spell, the maneuvers seemed to produce results. The sheer fact that thousands of *World* newspapers were circulating on the East Side and conveying moral messages about good citizenship enforced a sense that the work of the Educational Alliance had gone up a level and expanded exponentially. "This is one of the most important achievements for the amelioration of conditions on the East Side which has thus far been accomplished," Marshall gushed to Educational Alliance director David Blaustein shortly after the *World*'s debut.[154] The *Jewish World* is "destined to become the leading paper published in the United States,"[155] he assured New York State assemblymen over the summer, succumbing to high hopes and wishful thinking.

Marshall meddled incessantly with the Yiddish newspaper's copy, partly to promote his own work for Jewish causes and also the pet projects sponsored by Schiff and his Uptown partners. Marshall asked, for instance, that Bucans publicize protests he lodged with the New York appellate courts when their opinions extraneously noted that defendants in larceny cases were Jewish.[156] He was anxious that the *World* provide ample coverage to the JTS, partly to disseminate Schechter's Jewish wisdom in the East Side and also more broadly to describe the variant of Judaism that was evolving at JTS and distinguish it from the attenuated rituals and observances of Reform Judaism.

In her article on Louis Marshall's Yiddish newspaper, Lucy Dawidowicz exaggerated when she portrayed the *World's* coerced coverage of the JTS as an acutely vainglorious and futile aspect of this whole newspaper initiative ("The East Side was not interested in the Seminary," she bluntly concluded).[157] Quixotic in essence and limited in circulation, the *World* was nonetheless a reputable public forum that reached thousands, and it was hoisted in its early period by great expectations. Due to the didactic character of the publication, Marshall found himself spelling out rules and norms in the Yiddish newspaper with an explicitness he found prudent to avoid in most other spheres. Far from pointless futility, these facts produced a palpable result whenever the *World* conveyed information about a project such as the JTS: by experimenting with newspaper publicity, Marshall and his peers were forced to use simple language to explain to themselves, and to thousands of readers, what exactly they wanted and were trying to do. In the case of the JTS, this clarification process seems significant. In August 1902, the heyday of *World* expectations, Marshall instructed the newspaper's editorial staff to act as the "earnest champion" of "the great movement" that was consolidating at the JTS.[158] In every way other than bestowing the name "Conservative Judaism," he dictated through the editors behavioral and ritual requirements for the new religious stream. The *World*, for instance, was to make clear that young men who enrolled at JTS "with the idea of becoming a rabbi must conform strictly to the laws pertaining to the Jewish Sabbath and Jewish dietary laws."[159]

In this moral education phase of Marshall's Jewish career, the *World* played a kind of labeling role, bringing into words and formalizing the dimensions of ideas, beliefs, and pedagogical performances that were being played out at projects such as the Educational Alliance and the JTS. The total effect was paradoxical. All the time, Marshall preached the gospel of Jewish unity, but publications in the *World* on a topic like the JTS acknowledged the reality of ever-increasing differentiation in Jewish communities. When this phase braked to a halt, largely as a result of violent events in New York City (such as Rabbi Jacob Joseph's funeral, which occurred in the *World's* early days) and, more dramatically, in czarist Russia, Marshall continued to view this differentiation as a dire threat symptomatic of the immigrant Jews' undisciplined fractiousness. Even as his own labors institutionalized forms of Jewish diversity, he resisted understandings of pluralistic identity as an inevitable and potentially empowering result of Jewish adaptation in an open democratic society.

The shadow editorializing in the *World* had motivational sources apart from the understandable desire to publicize Jewish projects in which Marshall's group had invested time and money. Marshall inveighed constantly against immigrant parochialism. Americanization enjoined a spirit of ecumenical harmony. In practical terms, this meant that Marshall had to act as though his own recoil from Tammany in New York had nothing to do with the ethnoreligious aspects of machine politics and was based entirely on principles of good government. The immigrant Jews of New York City, he believed, had absolutely no reason to voice complaints about their Irish Catholic neighbors, even after the Rabbi Joseph altercations where (as we shall see) Irish policemen corrupted by the Tammany system were widely perceived as culprits in anti-Jewish violence. Speaking with the authority of a member of the public committee appointed by Mayor Low to investigate the brutal events of the rabbi's funeral, Marshall cajoled the *World* for weeks to "stop printing slurring remarks about other religious denominations and nationalities."[160]

Such counsel displayed the disparity of concerns that riddled the entire newspaper effort. Livid, Downtown Jews viewed police brutality at the Rabbi Joseph funeral in late July 1902 as the continuation of patterns of Irish bullying that included police shakedowns of pushcart peddlers; from his different standpoint, Marshall understood that Jewish interests would be promoted in the city via bridge-building with elites from various power and ethnic groups. Marshall was therefore mortified when his partner on the Rabbi Joseph funeral commission, Thomas M. Mulry, from the St. Vincent de Paul Society, complained about "slurs" in the Yiddish newspapers about Irish policemen.[161] Marshall used his Yiddish newspaper to tell enraged immigrant Jews to turn the other cheek. When Downtown emotions stayed heated in the last weeks of summer 1902, after the funeral altercation, Marshall kept pounding this moral message in the *World*, insisting to the editors that the golden rule of melting pot tolerance was a fitter Jewish prescription than ethnic baiting. "I do not know of any subject by which more good could be done than to urge the people to be free from bigotry and intolerance, to give to Protestants and Catholics the same treatment as they the Jews desire to have meted to them," Marshall observed.[162]

This exercise in moralistic media also had political motivations. The paper was to be a Republican outlet, this being the political party Marshall and Uptown colleagues associated with good government and economic and social stability. At the time of the newspaper's founding, Marshall was specifically concerned to disseminate information in favor of Republican candidates in 1902 gubernatorial and congressional elections.[163] A few days before the 1902 balloting, when Joseph Jacobs, a distinguished Jewish scholar and author who had been recruited to handle the *World*'s English page, objected that the newspaper had been turned outright into a partisan tribune, Marshall disingenuously indulged semantic pilpul in defense of the *World*'s Republican slant ("The newspaper is to be independent in politics, but not of politics," claimed Marshall; the *World*'s "board has decided that during the present campaign the public interest would best be promoted by supporting candidates of the Republican party, though this will not be a Republican organ"[164]). Dismayed by such nondenial denials about the newspaper's partisanship, Jacobs resigned after a few turbulent months bickering with Marshall at the *World*.[165]

The *World*'s politics kept in step with Republican party-related power alignments in New York City whose names shifted in the late nineteenth and early twentieth centuries (e.g., Fusion, Citizens Union). Members of these alignments were well-educated bankers, lawyers, and businessmen who harnessed their energies to Seth Low, trying to steer a middle course between the socialist dispositions of reformers like "single tax" advocate Henry George (a mayoral candidate in 1897) and the Democrats' Tammany machine that was notorious for cronyism and dubious uses of public funds. Low, it will be recalled, evinced an inclusive attitude toward the city's immigrants and spoke about a "civic virtue" platform of moderate reforms in the police force and the school system; his backers included premier members of America's financial elite, including Schiff, J. P. Morgan, Andrew Carnegie, and John D. Rockefeller.[166]

Marshall linked the *World* to this financial elite, soliciting at one point a $1,000 donation for the Yiddish newspaper from Henry Huttleston Rogers, a major financier of the Republican Party and an associate of Rockefeller and E. H. Harriman.[167] During the 1903 municipal campaign, when Low ran an unsuccessful reelection campaign on the Fusion ticket, the *World* was racked by financial debt, but Marshall nonetheless mustered all his resources for a full frontal attack against Tammany and for Seth Low (who lost handily). From September 9 until election day on November 3, the *World* published pro–Fusion stories and editorials day after day.[168]

As a shadow editor, Marshall's operating principle was that Downtown's ethnocentric politics could be construed as being un-American. His preaching in this respect provides a crucial yardstick for measuring his own evolution as a Jewish leader and the rise of Jewish ethnicity in America in general. During this early phase in his career, Marshall's abiding message to the immigrants was that they must stifle their Jewish sensibilities, lest they interfere too strongly with their patriotic allegiances as new or as soon-to-be Americans. When Downtown Jews rallied together in assertive responses to anti-Semitic occurrences of the 1903–5 period, Marshall began to doubt the premise he had circulated in his Yiddish newspaper; it became difficult for him to persist in the self-denying belief there was something fundamentally American about not being too Jewish. Those inchoate doubts propelled him toward a new phase of ethnic politics.

The *World* ought to desist from pressuring the Roosevelt administration for further action on behalf of Romanian Jewry, Marshall told Masliansky in October 1902. "We must be very guarded in our action toward the government," he explained. "If we are constantly making demands we will forfeit the confidence we have at length succeeded in inspiring."[169] For months after the April 1903 Kishinev pogrom, Marshall persisted in this campaign for ethnic self-restraint. It was enough, he told the *World*'s new editor, that President Roosevelt had "indicated his sympathy for persecuted Jews." Downtown needed to understand that "Jews form but a very small fraction of the people of this country." What America's democratic government could do to assuage Jewish concerns was therefore limited. "We have no more right to embroil ourselves as a nation with regard to the treatment of the Jews in Russia that we would have to interfere with domestic affairs in Greece, Turkey or Italy."[170] Striking a similar chord in a letter to Masliansky, Marshall argued that *World* criticism of Roosevelt administration policy after Kishinev "has the vicious tendency of promoting discontent against the government with regard to a subject as to which the government is practically powerless to act."[171]

Marshall reinforced in the *World* class divisions between Uptown and Downtown Jewries. His Yiddish newspaper was the tribunal of the propertied classes, and he used it as a soapbox to agitate against East Side union militancy and socialist politics. No doubt, Marxist-oriented readers Downtown dismissed the *World*'s moralistic messages about unity and Americanization as the ideology of class interest. A convenient catch-all concept for Marshall's Uptown group, the pliable idea of patriotism could be twisted in ways that stifled the legitimate desires of laborers in the needle trades and other pursuits to oppose exploitative work circumstances.

Thousands of Downtown immigrants—the constituency of Abe Cahan's left-wing *Forward*—never became sufficiently engaged with Marshall's conservative economic propagandizing in the *World* to develop a cohesive analysis of its character and purposes. In economics, no less than other realms, Marshall's shadow editorializing simply talked past the East European Jewish immigrants whose practical circumstances and identity needs were at this stage qualitatively unlike the socioeconomic situation and political perspective of settled, Uptown American Jews. As one recent study forcefully argues,[172] Jews immigrated to New York after enduring searing processes of socioeconomic marginalization in the Pale of Settlement. Crowding into the East Side tenements and the sweatshops, they were an acutely vulnerable social group who had in the Old World lacked the anchor of belonging to any class whatsoever. Motivated by objective socioeconomic realities, Downtown's left-wing stirrings in the trade unions and the *Forward* expressed an existentially vital process of identity reconstruction, what the historian Eli Lederhendler calls the "recovery of class." Thus, while Marshall and his group fretted about how Downtown socialism would be viewed suspiciously by America's Gentile elites as evidence of the lack of assimilability of inveterate Jewish subversives, the Jewish immigrants who fought in the unions for the closed shop, and who devoutly read the *Forward*, were acting out of necessity—they literally had nowhere left to go other than to their own reinvention as a working class. Founded on his expertise about their sanction in American law, Marshall's preaching in the *World* about property rights had undeniable authority, but it was entirely irrelevant to immigrants who clung to socialist métier as a precious first possession in a struggle to gain a foothold of any sort in modern life.

For months, Marshall persisted in his belief that dignified Yiddish argumentation would exorcise the socialist dibbuk from the souls of Downtown immigrants. While public discussion in the early twentieth century concentrated on issues of economic monopolization, he sternly told the *World*'s editors to avoid any rhetoric about trust-busting. Marshall believed that Theodore Roosevelt's economic policies were fundamentally conservative, and he instructed his newspaper's editors to write enthusiastically about White House policies that were based on "sound reason and common sense."[173] In autumn 1902, Marshall was enraged when the *World* criticized the Roosevelt-brokered settlement reached to end the much-discussed strike in the anthracite coal fields of eastern Pennsylvania, on the grounds that the settlement did not proffer recognition to the relevant union, the United Mine Workers of America. "It should be our object to encourage industrial peace," Marshall wrote to Max Bucans, "to dissuade the working people from striking and from attempting to create imaginary differences with their employers."[174] Paraphrasing Roosevelt's dictum that there are three parties to any strike, the employer, the employee, and the public, he claimed that the *World* should "always take the middle ground" between these groups. In economics, as elsewhere, his gospel was unity, but here its conservative capitalist motivations were unmistakable:

> The people on the East Side must learn to appreciate the importance to the entire community of the maintenance of a friendly relation between employer and employed. The continuance of friction can only result in serious injury to both.[175]

Marshall monitored the *World*'s socioeconomic commentary more closely than its reporting on specific items of Jewish affairs. Zionists manned the *World*'s staff—Masliansky had for years been interested in Jewish nationalism, dating from his preaching in Eastern and Western Europe on behalf of the Hovevei Zion pioneering efforts in Ottoman Palestine,[176] and Jacob De Haas, a journalist and American Zionist organizer, replaced Jacobs as editor of the *World*'s English page.[177] Though the nationalist predilections of the newspaper's staff members were known to Marshall, Zionist lobbying was not really condoned on the printed page; one scholarly estimate holding that "Marshall and Masliansky probably had an understanding that Zionism would be advocated on the Yiddish pages"[178] is not entirely accurate. Marshall explicitly instructed the newspaper's editors "not to allow any sympathy for Zionism to color the views of this paper,"[179] but he did so not really from personal reservations (his own views on the subject were mixed) but out of deference to the fact that the newspaper's Jewish investors served as trustees in Jewish colonization efforts outside of Palestine and were likely to object to Zionist propaganda in the *World*.[180]

Marshall's activities in this moral reform phase featured continuing contact with the Downtown immigrants in forums such as the Educational Alliance, and he stood out among his "German" peers as an Uptown communal leader uniquely connected to Jewish immigrant life, via (among many things) his acquired knowledge of Yiddish and use of the language as a means of contact in this *Jewish World* venture. Yet if the main tune was practical contact with Downtown, the flip side was a continuing dynamic of denial—Marshall ignored quantifiable indications that the East Side Jews were simply not listening to the *World*'s political and moral messages.[181] This denial extended to the most basic nomenclature relevant to immigrant Jewish life in New York.

Marshall conceptualized the *World* as an American newspaper that happened to be written in Yiddish, circulated among American citizens who belonged to the country's public sphere and who had absolutely no ties to a Jewish "ghetto." In the first years of the twentieth century, reports about vice and theft on the East Side eventually led, as we will see, to semiofficial (and highly controversial) claims about Jewish responsibility for a disproportionate share of the city's crime. Some sympathetic onlookers sought to preempt perceptions of the East Side as a ghetto ridden by prostitution and poverty by producing a counterimage of a downtown gilded ghetto enriched by authentic Jewish spirituality and creativity. For instance, in 1902, the year of the short-lived *World*'s debut, Hutchins Hapgood published his upbeat *Spirit of the Ghetto*,[182] a volume that recast the "ghetto" as an urban frontier in which American democracy would revitalize in the twentieth century, thanks to the inspired creativity of Yiddish writers, theater personalities, and journalists.

This strategy of idealizing East Side life had little appeal to Marshall, who opted for a strategy of denying that Jews anywhere in Manhattan were living in a ghetto. In spring 1904, he moved effectively to erase the very term "ghetto" from the pages of the *New York Times.* He urged Adolph Ochs,[183] the energetic and heavily burdened owner of the newspaper (which moved during the year to Longacre Square, soon to be known as Times Square) to "adopt a rule banning the word" ghetto. The mere fact that "a lot of Jewish citizens live in a certain portion of the city is not a sufficient reason for applying to them a word which in history has been identified with contumely, oppression, ridicule and hatred," Marshall explained. Were the *New York Times* to persist in the use of the term, both in reference to an uptown gilded ghetto and a downtown impoverished ghetto, Marshall added, "it will not be long before every Jewish citizen of this city will have attached to him a sort of moral yellow badge in place of the physical badge which our forefathers were obliged to wear at the time when Ghettos existed in reality." A few days later, Ochs consented to this act of conceptual denial. "I have given instructions to prohibit the use of the word Ghetto with reference to the Jewish quarters on the East Side," he informed Marshall.[184]

In this period when Ochs and Marshall designated the term "ghetto" unfit to print in the *New York Times,* the *Jewish World*'s failure, in financial and all other practical aspects, was manifest. For many months, Marshall, under orders from Schiff, had consulted with Ochs about the *World's* present and future prospects; at one stage, the *New York Times* owner sent his number crunchers to examine the Yiddish newspaper's books and make financial suggestions.[185] In April 1904 Marshall informed the *World's* managing staff that the newspaper's fate is "most uncertain";[186] a month later, he stage-managed the newspaper's sale through his brother-in-law, telling Herzog "let us get rid of this incubus as quickly as possible."[187] On May 11 the paper's ownership was transferred to Ezekiel Sarasohn.[188]

The sale's ugly aftermath merits mention because of its influence as a cautionary tale whose lessons Marshall scrupulously upheld later in his career. Never again would he allow himself to become mired with messy control responsibilities reminiscent of the *World* debacle.

Marshall found himself coercively manipulating the *World's* copy for many months after he had transferred control to Sarasohn, and he also tried to limit the personnel wreckage left by the paper's lack of success. After the *World*'s sale, its recently hired editor, D. M. Hermalin, was unceremoniously dismissed; all Marshall could do for him was to offer a financial loan.[189] The *World*'s financial tailspin continued after its sale. Cutting his losses, Sarasohn tried to turn the publication into a weekly, but Marshall pointedly warned him that such a switch would infringe the terms of the newspaper's purchasing agreement. He also reminded the hapless editor that this agreement required the *World* to "actively support and advocate the national and state platforms of the Republican party" throughout the 1904 elections.[190] Facing a penalty of $25,000 for an infringement of the purchasing agreement,[191] Sarasohn grudgingly complied with the political requirements.

Weeks before the 1904 elections, Marshall realized that he would lose his political leverage at the *World* since the purchasing agreement obliged the newspaper's pro-Republican orientation only through November. He prepared surveys of New York's Yiddish newspaper scene and sent them to Republican leaders in the state.[192] Candidly disclosing his failures with the *World* ("I was the unfortunate founder of this paper and succeeded in losing $50,000 of my own and friends' money"), he noted the imminent expiration date of the newspaper's Republican slant and then tossed out a novel idea: Sarasohn, Marshall divulged, was prepared to sell his controlling interest in the *World* and the *Tageblatt,* along with his shares in the *Abend Post* and the *Morgen Journal* (newspapers nominally owned by Jacob Saperstein), to buyers in the Republican Party! Sarasohn's newspapers had, at this time, a circulation of 75,000. Fancifully, Marshall was proposing a Republican Party takeover of Yiddish media on the East End. "Speaking entirely from a party standpoint, it would be an excellent investment were Sarasohn and his papers captured body, soul and breeches," by the party, Marshall declared, and proceeded to offer his help in negotiating a deal.[193] The proposal went nowhere, but its outlandish extremism betrays Marshall's lingering anxieties about radical political orientations on the East Side and about the *Forward*'s role as their purveyor. His failed experiment with a Yiddish newspaper taught that he had no tangible way to control those orientations; by imagining that he could persuade New York Republicans to co-opt them once and for all, Marshall reached the acme of denial in this early phase of his career as a Jewish leader.

The Jewish Protectory

The campaign for moral amelioration of the Jewish immigrant community was relatively short-lived. Beginning with the revamping of model institutions like the Educational Alliance and the JTS at the end of the nineteenth century or the early twentieth century, the phase lasted several years, giving way around 1905 to organized initiatives in Jewish lobbying and defense, a newly assertive attitude in the confrontation with anti-Semitism, and a concentrated lobbying campaign to keep the doors of immigration open to masses of East European

Jewish newcomers. Despite its short duration, the phase spawned lasting institutions, such as the JTS, even though some of its experiments, such as the Yiddish *Jewish World,* crash-landed and disappeared. Despite its quixotic, narrowly pro-business and condescendingly missionary characteristics, this moral amelioration campaign can rightly be considered a *force* in American Jewish history. It brought new institutions and new communal self-definitions and self-perceptions into being in ways that have too often escaped the notice of historians, just as researchers chronically overlook the central contribution made by Louis Marshall in an early phase of his career when several of his views on Jewish life were still unrefined.

The Jewish Protectory, a reformatory for delinquent Jewish youth known subsequently as the Hawthorne School, offers a powerful example of the need to revisit this early twentieth century moralistic brand of Jewish philanthropy and to recognize its role as an empowering causal agent in American Jewish life. In her study of Jewish communal responses to the problem of East Side criminality in the first decades of the twentieth century, Jenna Weissman Joselit presents the Hawthorne School's dedication in Westchester County in May 1907 as a groundbreaking event symbolizing the American Jewish community's sudden recognition that something had to be done about the unexpected problem of Jewish criminality.[194]

Chronologically and conceptually, her interpretation places the Hawthorne School alongside initiatives and experiments such as the New York Kehillah (an intriguing effort to organize certain educational, social welfare, and religious activities along semiautonomous lines) that consolidated in years before World War I, primarily in response to sensational allegations of Downtown Jewish criminality, most notoriously New York Police Commissioner Theodore Bingham's 1908 charge that half of the city's criminals were Jews.[195] At the Hawthorne School's 1907 opening, its building committee chairman, Henry Solomon, identified Jewish crime as an "absolutely new problem" and (Joselit explains) expounded upon "how ill prepared most New York Jews were to recognize its seriousness." In her study, Louis Marshall appears once or twice in cameo, as a detached analytic voice reinforcing the idea that well-to-do Jews built a facility for Jewish juvenile delinquents that sprawled on an impressive tract of land overlooking the Hudson River and that featured sports fields and garden plots, as a kind of knee-jerk protective reflex to the unanticipated challenge of Jewish criminality. Marshall, on this account, justifies the initiative in terms of simple self-interest. Young Jewish criminals constituted a mark of Cain for the Jewish community as a whole. When a Jewish criminal is arrested, Marshall opines, "discredit attaches to us whether we do or do not recognize him,"[196] and so the Jewish community opened the Hawthorne reformatory in 1907 in order to preempt or minimize this communal ignominy caused by young Jewish criminals.

Joselit's informative account is not, of course, incorrect to point out that the Jewish reformatory, the Hawthorne School, was established as a response to the issue of Downtown criminality, but by overlooking the project's long gestation period she dismisses outright the possibility that some facts in Jewish communal life arise out of the moral vision and stamina of elite groups. The point is not the elitist recommendation that history ought to be viewed primarily "from above," solely in terms of the purposes of communal stewards. Instead, it is fair to suggest that a narrowed motivational focus on sheer self-interest—along with the suggestion that even a relatively small-scale project like the Hawthorne School can arise suddenly, virtually ex nihilo, in a panic response to sensationalized reports of Jewish gangsters, prostitutes, and juvenile delinquents—unrealistically truncates complicated legislative and organizational processes, just as it unfairly reduces the complicated motivations of elite stewards who invest hours of volunteer time and considerable personal resources in a project's making.

Louis Marshall lobbied in Albany for years to get the Jewish Protectory project off the ground. He sent dozens of solicitation letters to Uptown associates to gather funds for the project and sometimes insultingly goaded them into reaching deeper into their pockets; on one or two occasions he leapfrogged over his own generally unflinching party loyalty to the Republicans and privately berated the widely respected New York Mayor Seth Low, in order to push the protectory project forward.

Certainly the broader motivations of noblesse oblige and immigrant Americanization and reform he shared with Schiff and other Uptown patrons can be faulted on various ethical grounds as a patronizing form of Jewish narcissism or even colonization. For Marshall and others, moral reform of the immigrants typically meant refashioning them to act and look like the stewards themselves. All the same, in this moral reform phase, the stewards were setting standards of communal responsibility that could, and would, become a foundation of a new form of ethnic politics, and they were doing so in a relatively systematic and reflective fashion, very much *not* in response to passing sensationalized episodes.

Of course, in their day, the stewards could not really have foreseen the unfolding and amplification of this ethnic politics. In retrospect, however, these ethnic dynamics are manifest. What started with a handful of Uptown stewards trying to help a few hundred troubled Jewish teenagers—because the youngsters were making a mess of their own lives and impugning the reputation of their own community—proceeded to delegates of Downtown and Uptown organizations and institutions, elected semidemocratically in the novel American Jewish Congress framework, who were trying to attain rights for Jews in Eastern European countries threatened by the rise of anti-Semitism after World War I—and then ended up in highly sophisticated (and unprecedented, in American ethnic terms) forms of community mobilization to furnish funds and diplomatic support for a Jewish state troubled by Arab aggression after its establishment in 1948. While such later events were never precisely in view, the range and energy of the stewards' programming initiatives in this moral reform phase can only be understood in terms of their consciousness that important examples were being set. An expression of the rise of twentieth-century Jewish ethnic politics, the tenacious commitment Marshall displayed on behalf of a project like the protectory has been unjustifiably ignored by historical scholarship.

In early 1902, Marshall monitored the New York legislature's act incorporating the Jewish Protectory and Aid Society. In his lobbying efforts, he explained to New York City Mayor Seth Low that "unfortunate conditions which prevail on the Lower East Side" had resulted in the "commitment of several hundred Jewish boys and girls" to various penal institutions. "Jewish citizens who have given thought to the subject" had decided that "better results can be obtained if these juvenile delinquents were committed to an institution conducted under Jewish auspices, where moral and religious training can be afforded."[197] Marshall was appalled when Low refused to commit city funds to the protectory and attributed the mayor's reluctance to "bigotry;" he asked Schiff, one of Low's leading supporters, to write a few lines to the mayor, endorsing the project.[198] Double standards in city allocations rankled Marshall: reform institutions sponsored by other ethnoreligious groups won city support "as a matter of right," and so it was intolerable that Jews were being "relegated to the backyard to receive a bone."[199]

Two years later, Marshall had taken legislative steps to rectify such iniquitous double standards in city allocations. He asked Low's Democratic successor in City Hall, George McClellan, to affix his signature to a bill that placed the Jewish Protectory on "precisely the same footing as . . . the Catholic Protectory."[200] By this time, Marshall had full throttle control of the protectory fund-raising effort. He reiterated the project's rationale to prospective donors: "An institution conducted under Jewish auspices" was more likely to rehabilitate troubled Jewish youngsters, he argued. Marshall outlined the project's remedial rationale and activity schedule, declaring "it is the purpose of this institution to teach those committed to its care useful trades, to encourage agricultural and horticultural work."[201] His fund-raising goal was $250,000, and Schiff had already contributed 10 percent of this target.[202] His arguments for the project combined humanitarian concern for the troubled teenagers, a sense of Jewish duty compounded by the shame of watching dozens of Jewish juvenile delinquents being sent to Randall's Island or the Catholic Protectory, and also self-interest. "Who do you think will be charged with this criminality?" he asked Isaac Guggenheim, implying that settled Jews would be convicted in the court of American public opinion as abettors of Downtown hoodlums. "Who will wince when he sees in the newspapers [reports] of another Jewish burglar, pickpocket or robber arrested?"[203] He shamed Uptown notables, such as Macy's co-owner Isidor Straus, who balked about contributing to the project. "Let me say that although financially I do not belong to the class of which you are a prominent member, and have a young and helpless family dependent upon me, I have agreed to subscribe $5000," he wrote to Straus.[204] Months later, Marshall approached the target subscription figure by persuading Schiff to raise his contribution to $100,000, and by enlisting $25,000 from Adolph Lewisohn.[205]

Some basic project parameters were settled as early as 1904. The protectory would be located within forty miles of New York City and feature "pursuits of agriculture, horticulture, mechanical and technical work."[206] To correct miscues that had complicated the management of other reform projects, such as the Educational Alliance, Marshall recruited East Side delegates for the protectory board. "You are the first person identified with the East End to show interest in the Protectory," he told Abraham Leo Wolbarst, a New York physician.[207] "We are most desirous of having the Russian Jewish element represented on our board," Marshall added, asking Wolbarst to propose some names. Diligently, Marshall reported to Schiff that he was recruiting "three or four good men from the East Side" to serve on the protectory board.[208]

In months before and after the facility's 1907 transformation[209] as a fully functioning Hawthorne School facility with several hundred young people quartered in groups of thirty in appealing cottages that (observers claimed) "resembled summer homes,"[210] Marshall personally handled a bewildering array of minute technical and broad ideological details. Marshall never obtained confirmation of the facility's tax-exemption status and then suddenly in 1908 and 1909 he received foreclosure notices due to the school's unpaid property taxes. He paid the debt out of his own pocket; after months of inquiry and petition, Westchester County's Board of Supervisors reimbursed the sum, accepting the argument that the reformatory had been eligible for property tax exemption from the start. Marshall donated the reimbursement to the facility.[211] As he did with the other projects in this phase of Jewish communal endeavor, Marshall sternly insisted that the protectory emphasize spiritual reform work. In June 1907, shortly after the Uptown elite gathered in Hawthorne for the facility's dedication ceremony, he ordered the reformatory's superintendent to start immediately with religious work. "Our institution is not for agnostics," Marshall explained. Its purpose was "to bring up the children who are committed to us as Jews."[212]

Hawthorne, the historian Joselit comments, "was a rigorously controlled environment."[213] The youths' regimen started early in the day with religious services, conducted (observers recorded) "as a sort of compromise between the reform and orthodox forms of service."[214] At least in its early days, the protectory emerged as one of the more popular projects fashioned by the Marshall and his Uptown cohorts, in this moral reform mode. Praised widely as a "splendid institution,"[215] we may leave it as a perfect symbol of the intents, limits, and accomplishments of Marshall and his peers during this moral reform phase of his biography.

PART TWO

A National Organization for the Jews

3

The Origins of Organized Activism

The founding of the American Jewish Committee (AJC; also hereafter referred to as the committee) in 1906 marked a turning point in Marshall's career and created new options for the organized life and identity of the American Jewish community. To be sure, habits and assumptions of the previous moral reform phase lingered in this new stage of Marshall's life. In administrative and communicative (though not financial) senses, he took charge of affairs for an Uptown elite that continued to demand a large share of control of Jewish affairs in America and that deeply distrusted radical or foreign-seeming currents of Jewish life in Manhattan's Downtown neighborhoods. Indeed, in the perspective of the East European immigrants, presumed differences between the earlier stage of Marshall's career and the new era symbolized by the birth of the AJC were specious. From one year to the next, Marshall and his Uptown associates kept telling them what they had to do to become real Americans.

Downtown objections to Uptown's heavy-handed paternalism certainly remained discernible throughout this new second stage in Marshall's career, but his confrontation with them did not become the primary component of his Jewish work until the volatile World War I years, analyzed in Part Three of this study. In ways that remained mostly opaque to the Downtown immigrants, he took steps in this second transitional phase of his career that dramatically transformed the organized capabilities of American Jews. These moves did not exactly promote unity between settled elite and poor immigrant Jewish groups (the romantic ideal of unity was, and would remain, chimerical), but they provided a steady lever for coordinated action between disparate Jewish subgroups on issues of obvious, overwhelming concern to all Jews.

Given the mindset of the German Jewish Uptown group, establishing a national Jewish organization posed a formidable conceptual challenge. Potentially, such an organization belied Uptown's endlessly repeated incantations about the American loyalty of Jews, about how Jews had no distinctive issues or concerns of their own in the public domain. For Uptown, it was unmistakably Marshall who grabbed these conceptual reins and who was entrusted with the task of explaining how the advent of a new national Jewish organization, the AJC, did not contradict all that generations of Jews in the United States had said about themselves. His job was to explain that the birth of the committee reinforced rather than undermined the existential requirement holding that members of the community were Americans in public and Jews privately in the religious worship of their homes and synagogues.

From the start, there was no doubt the articulate Marshall would find some rhetorical formula that would effectively allay loyalty concerns attendant to the formation of the AJC, certainly among members of his own Uptown group and also among many in outlying Jewish and non-Jewish circles. Verbal formulas were not the problem, however. Instead, the issues related both to daily activity and internalized self-perception. The new organization needed to set a work agenda whose items constituted credible concerns to a sufficient portion of America's Jewish community and whose handling enhanced whatever hard-won status the struggling immigrant Jews and their comfortably settled peers had attained. A survey of Marshall's activity in this period provides a fascinating glimpse of how this agenda materialized for the AJC—and since the committee was a groundbreaking endeavor both for American Jews, and for ethnic groups in the United States on the whole, this portion of his biography warrants close scrutiny.

No less significant than the AJC's agenda is the issue of how its founding members felt about setting it. How did this precedent-setting organizational occurrence affect their evolving internal perceptions of what it meant to be Jewish in the open democracy of the United States? However they looked at it, the committee's founders had to admit—at least to themselves—that they shed a layer of inhibition about being "too Jewish" in America when they established a national Jewish organization to deal with matters that had obvious social and political, as opposed to religious, characteristics. But what did this internal identity transition really mean?

For Louis Marshall, it meant that the personally fulfilling journey from Upstate to Uptown in the first phase of his career had not satisfied his sense of public responsibility. Heretofore he had preached the gospel of American constitutionalism to the immigrants and printed messages of moral reform and political conservatism to them in the Yiddish press. Now he was beginning to learn what it meant to be their advocate, first in America and then on the global stage.

Some parameters of this advocacy remained in flux throughout this second stage and even after it, and ways in which Marshall challenged key patrician sensibilities of his Uptown crowd typically remained unappreciated by the Downtown beneficiaries of his representation. For instance, nobody knew or remembered that Marshall had insisted in the early days that the AJC be a democratic organization (that this important point was overlooked cast considerable irony upon his situation throughout the tumultuous Uptown-Downtown debates about Zionism and the AJC during World War I, when Marshall figured in the imagination of the immigrants as the veritable symbol of the antidemocratic elitism of the German Jews).

Fluctuation and misunderstanding in the way Marshall was shaping his identity as a Jewish advocate did not mitigate the efficacy of his advocacy about specific, critical items of Jewish interest. Among many other things, during this second phase of his career, Marshall began years of concerted effort to keep the doors of immigration open to Jews and others, a campaign of real import in the reduction of the massive scope of the Nazis' future crime. Despite ongoing debates about core issues such as communal stewardship versus communal democratization, this was the period when the range, intensity, and shrewdness of Marshall's work on Jewish affairs came into focus.

The patrician Uptown style was too deeply resented by the East Side immigrants for anyone at the time (or, indeed, for future generations of Jews and non-Jews) to fully appreciate what was happening to Marshall's persona, as it was shaped by a truly staggering investment of volunteer hours for common Jewish interests. This was a period when the Progressive volunteer idealism of "the other lawyer named Louis," that is, Brandeis, justifiably endowed him the title of "attorney for the people." Marshall, always a staunch American patriot who (as we shall see) frustratingly lost a bid for the Supreme Court bench, emerged during these years as an ethnicized counterpart to this other Louis. In Jewish affairs, his administrative, lobbying, legal, and communal work was indefatigable and displayed acumen regarding the country's power structure and Jewish communal patterns and needs. In effect, Louis Marshall became the "attorney for the Jewish people."

Tellingly, the transitions in the style and substance of Marshall's role as an American Jewish leader, and in the spirit and content of American Jewish communal affairs, unfolded in part as responses to a series of violent events in the backyard—in the backyard of their new homes in New York City and in the backyard of their abandoned homes in czarist Russia's Pale of Settlement. Immigrant Jewish politics took on the character of globalized locality in this pre–World War I era. Marshall was called upon to represent masses of Jews who felt that their own future, present, and past homes were, or were about to be, dangerously violated.

More than anything else, this sense of urgency changed the scale of Marshall's, and Uptown's, efforts. Members of the Jewish elite had worked energetically on the pet projects of the previous moral reform phase, but the scale of endeavor could be limited so long as its temperamental inheritance was the abundant optimism of the Gilded Age. Much changed when a sense of mass emergency rifled through the Jewish community. Louis Marshall's evolution as a Jewish leader turned on an axis rotated roughly by the doings of Irish factory workers and policemen on Grand and Broome streets on New York's East Side and by the Russian pogrom makers of Kishinev in the Old World.

The Jacob Joseph Funeral Riot

The worst anti-Semitic riot in American history erupted on July 30, 1902, around Grand and Broome streets on Manhattan's Lower East Side, during the funeral procession of Jacob Joseph, the Kovno-born rabbi who had been brought to New York from Vilna by a federation of synagogues in 1888 and crowned chief rabbi. That title commanded little authority, and the hapless immigrant rabbi spent the last years of his life in misery and isolation, but the rabbi's passing stirred an unexpectedly massive wave of mourning among downtown Jews.[1] Police on the scene "went berserk," joining with fellow Irish workers at the Hoe and Company printing press factory on Grand Street in violent attacks on Jews.[2]

Since New York's police force was indelibly associated in the public mind with the Tammany regime that had governed the city for decades, victims of the bloody events of the day were apt to think that they carried an element of government endorsement. It mattered little that city Mayor Seth Low was anti-Tammany and had campaigned in 1901 on a platform of police reform. Inevitably, the cruel brutality of Irish Catholic laborers and cops was perceived in a prism of analogy by vulnerable and harassed Russian Jewish immigrants, for whom memories and images of pillaging Cossacks were acute. This was, for many, a made-in-America pogrom, a sensational occurrence that belied an entire community's confidence in the idea of New World exceptionalism, the notion that "America is different."

The melee transpired as a bizarre, chaotic medley of primitivism and turn-of-the century modern innovation. In full view of the soon-to-be finished Williamsburg bridge—a symbol of the aspiring city's reaching for modernity, as the longest suspension bridge on earth—Catholics hosed and clubbed Jews in tribal fury. Once what "could not happen here," a pogrom, appeared to occur in the backyard of the Downtown masses, New York Jewry mobilized in the direction of a new type of ethnic politics. In the middle of this vortex was Marshall. In his mind, he was standing his ground, upholding his lifelong principles of moderation, law, and rational, systematic opposition to mob violence. In actual fact, he was being swept up by New York Jewry's newly militant mood and hurled toward a noticeably more assertive brand of Jewish advocacy, toward a new biographical phase of organized activism.

By summer 1902, Jews had been streaming in to make new lives on the East Side at a huge annual rate of approximately 60,000, a mind-boggling number whose sole precedent in the annals of American immigration was set in the nineteenth century by the Irish Catholics, who themselves had been subjected to the depredations of Know Nothing anti-immigrant hostility. When a mood hit it, these Jewish immigrants, who lived and worked together in close and crowded quarters, were liable to act en masse, yet the New York police were manifestly unprepared for the swelling throng of 50,000 or 100,000 bereaved Jews who trailed the 200 carriages in the Jacob Joseph procession around Sheriff, Cannon, and Broome streets. The carriages headed toward the Grand Street ferry (the pious rabbi was buried in Brooklyn); in minutes before the coffin was moved to the ferry, the Jewish mourners were pounded by a fusillade of iron belts, blocks of wood, screws, melon rinds, and sheets of water from buckets and hoses.

Some Yiddish speakers sought refuge inside the Hoe and Company plant on Grand Street. This action appears to have been the decisive trigger in the riot, since the "Irish boys" in the factory (97 percent of the Hoe plant's labor force was comprised of Irish Catholics) had been involved in altercations with Jews in preceding months and bore grudges. Fighting and chaos disrupted the factory. About two hundred police reinforcements who were called to the scene could rationalize their part in the anti-Jewish spree by claiming that their mission was to restore order and protect property in a legitimate business operation whose production had been stopped by Jewish trespassers. Eyewitness accounts, however, exposed such explanations as cynical pretext. Witnesses depicted a ranking officer (Inspector Cross) crying out "kill those sheenies" and police underlings swinging clubs with sadistic abandon. For thirty minutes, Jews with bloodied heads and bruised bodies fled from uniformed officers "who had apparently gone crazy."[3] Two hundred Jewish victims needed medical attention. Adding insult to injury, eleven Jews were arrested and taken to Essex Market Court; some were slapped with fines.

Enraged, frightened immigrant Jews on the East Side wondered how far they had really journeyed when they settled in New York tenements. The pogrom analogy was on everyone's mind. "This was a thing that even a Russian would have been ashamed of," lamented one immigrant. When Inspector Cross, vilified on the East Side as the riot's main culprit, was transferred to the Bronx, the

Forward's Abraham Cahan quipped to a crowd of protestors that he should have been exiled to Siberia.[4]

Having highlighted Tammany police corruption in his city reform campaign, Mayor Low necessarily related to this gruesome Jacob Joseph riot as a test of his administration's raison d'etre. The initial police report on the event, orchestrated by Cross, was a laughable whitewash that blamed the mourners for coming armed with stones, nuts, and bolts to the funeral. Needing a blue ribbon investigation commission, the mayor tapped an impressive five-man panel—William Baldwin of the Long Island Railroad, a long-time foe of Tammany, Thomas Mulry, a Catholic banker and philanthropist, attorney Edward Whitney, and, as Jewish delegates, Nathan Bijur and Marshall. The East Side press was satisfied with these Jewish delegates, opining that the mayor could not have found two more qualified men had he scrutinized every Jew in the city.[5] Beginning on August 12, the committee met for a week in the heart of the East Side, on Rivington Street, and made mincemeat of the aggressors' excuses. Responding to Hoe employees who abjured responsibility for violence on the technical grounds that no bolts or scalding water could have been found in the factory, Marshall and Mulry visited the plant and uncovered hundreds of bolts that fit the victims' description, along with no lack of boiling water.[6]

The committee report exonerated the Jewish mourners, holding "it is universally conceded that those who actually took part in the funeral procession are entirely without fault." The culpability of the Hoe employees had been erased in a cover-up, Marshall and his committee members suggested ("to us, there seems to be every indication of a concerted effort to hush up the affair and protect inmates of the factory").[7] The report identified police brutality in rather mild, restrained language, commenting that "through the day, the mourners and spectators were treated by the police with marked incivility and roughness."[8] Mayor Low took this as a cue and ordered that responsible parties on the police force be brought to justice; however, police chief Colonel John Partridge stonewalled and eventually dismissed charges against his accused underlings. Partridge then left the scene, resigning at the end of 1902.

Marshall hoped that the committee's report would frame the funeral riot in proper American perspective and stifle murmuring on the East Side about a New World pogrom. "I do not wish to create a feeling that there is such a thing as anti-Semitism" in America, he explained to the *World*'s editor,[9] the day the report was submitted to Mayor Low. Downtown Jews remained angry about the hostile disposition of City Magistrate Robert C. Cornell in the Essex Market Court, so Marshall allowed the *World* to continue its exposé of unfair dealings in the police court, but he clarified that Cornell was "mentally unfit by reason of impatience and indifference" and did not act out of religious prejudice. By no means should the *World* confine its coverage of unfair justice at Essex Market to the "purely Jewish aspect of this question."[10]

As far as Yiddish newspaper readers were concerned, everything about Essex was unfair to accused Jews, and so Marshall's media instructions typified the attitude of denial that colored his work with the *World*. Still, something was changing.

Downtown had its eyes wide open and would not be fooled by facile explanations of affairs of direct concern to it. For his part, Marshall was accustomed to handling legislative and business matters over protracted periods, but seldom before had the implications of any isolated political or social event of Jewish interest occupied his energies for a prolonged period. Much as he continued with his posture of denial, Marshall began to understand that big events in Jewish politics would not come and go in a minute, because the Downtown immigrants were increasingly discerning and adamant in their perceptions and demands. How long could Marshall in good conscience continue to dismiss their reasons for believing that the municipal system could not really be trusted? Moreover, exactly in this period when Marshall and Ochs contrived the *New York Times*' denial of the very existence of a ghetto, it was becoming increasingly evident that the mass of energy and striving on the East Side was, under dramatic circumstances, an item of national interest. America on the whole took note when the ghetto was truly aggrieved. In these senses—the immigrants' unrelenting demands for justice and the fact that American public opinion was making some room for Jewish matters—Marshall and his group had reason to grasp that Jewish politics in America was climbing in scale well above the tightly confined dimensions of several dozen seminary students and a few hundred at-risk youths that had characterized their endeavors in the moral reform phase.

Unlike his work on the Jewish Theological Seminary (JTS), the Educational Alliance, and the Jewish Protectory, whose parameters of moral rebirth, neotraditionalism, decorum, and Americanization pertained to internal Jewish communal dynamics, Marshall was starting to relate to Jewish matters in the recognition that the world was closely watching them. Thus, in the late months of 1902, when Downtown Jews pressured him about the way Colonel Partridge stonewalled the prosecution of the riot's offenders, Marshall issued the usual denials and tepid assurances, but there was something new in his focus. He admitted to the *Jewish Gazette* in the final days of 1902[11] to being "somewhat disappointed" by Partridge's refusal to allow convictions, but he insisted that the effect of the Rabbi Joseph investigation "has been wholesome." There is, he declared, "no occasion to fear a repetition of the offenses which so greatly moved the whole community last summer." His commission's main contribution, Marshall implied, involved not necessarily its refutation of the "infamous charge" that "Jews were the aggressors," but rather the adoption of its findings by the national media. Once the commission told the truth in its report, the "press of the entire country with remarkable unanimity condemned those who were responsible for the wanton attack on the funeral procession." Under some circumstances, Jewish matters needed to be public and national in scope, because "in this country public opinion is the greatest power for good." One layer of inhibition about being Jewish in the public sphere was peeled away by the events and aftermath of Rabbi Jacob Joseph's funeral.

Kishinev and New York Jewry

Nine months after Rabbi Jacob Joseph was buried in Brooklyn, an anti-Semitic melee in Bessarabia convulsed Jewish politics around the globe. The pogrom in Kishinev erupted on Easter Sunday, April 19, 1903, the last day of Passover.[12] What started with a few boys hurling rocks at windows of Jewish homes and shops and continued with two days of plunder, rape, and butchery, including forty-seven murdered Jews and three million rubles of damage to property, ended with new political alignments in Eastern Europe, Palestine, Europe, and North America.

While the level of complicity for Kishinev and subsequent pogroms borne by high czarist officials and local bureaucrats remains in dispute, there is no question that the overall anti-Semitic orientation was dictated from the top, since Nicholas II's closest associates consistently branded the Jews enemies of the state. "There is no revolutionary movement in Russia, there are only Jews who are the true enemies of the government," declared Minister of the Interior V. I. Pleve in 1902.[13] In Kishinev, where a third of the 150,000 residents were Jews, a variety of factors led to the pogrom, including the incendiary propaganda in the local *Bessarabets* newspaper, the persistence of ritual murder beliefs among superstitious peasants and hostile clergy, and the prejudicial attitudes of empowered local officials, such as the head of the military garrison, V. A. Bekman. Nuances and complexity in the sequence of religious, social, and political determinants of violence were overlooked in the pogrom's aftermath, because Nicholas' government unsubtly propounded the view that the Jews were ultimately to blame. It appointed an anti-Semitic contributor to *Bessarabets,* M. Davidovich, as investigating magistrate of the Kishinev affair. Interviewed by the *New York Times,* Count Arthur Cassini, Russia's ambassador to the United States, cynically ruminated "the Jews ruin the peasants with the result that conflicts occur."[14]

Viewing Kishinev as the horrifying consequence of Jewish traditional inertia and religious stupor in the *galut* (exile), many Zionists were privy to this theory that reasons could be found for blaming the Jewish victims of Kishinev. "Your deaths are without reason; your lives are without cause," cried H. N. Bialik's provocative "In the City of Slaughter," a poem commissioned as an elegy for Kishinev's victims that reconceptualized the tragedy as a call for new forms of Jewish national activism. Meantime, non-Zionist Jewish nationalists, particularly members of the Bund, were mobilizing to arrange for Jewish self-defense in future pogroms. In Zhitomir in May 1905, when organized Jews wielded revolvers, primitive bombs, and daggers to ward off attackers, a Bund legend was born and inscribed in the slogan "If not for self-defense, Zhitomir would have been another Kishinev." Jews around the world were responding to Kishinev on the understanding that what happened in spring 1903 in Bessarabia was the start of a new round of anti-Jewish wave of violence, a recapitulation of the horrific pogroms of the early 1880s.

This premise was entirely correct. Between 1903 and 1906, three successive phases of pogroms ravaged Jewish life in czarist Russia. In the first wave, a pogrom in Gomel, in the Mogilev province, followed Kishinev in September 1903—ten Jews were murdered, though local administrators were more positively responsive to Jewish victims in this pogrom, probably because the proportion of Jewish residents (50 percent) in Gomel was greater than in Kishinev. The second pogrom wave continued through 1904, synchronized with Russia's setbacks in its disastrous war against the Japanese. More than half of the 43 pogroms during the year were related to the war, scholars estimate; Jews were targeted generally as a unpatriotic element in the period of the frustrating war, and on occasion Jewish villagers were accosted as a result of specific, outlandish allegations about Jewish collusion with the Japanese (in actual fact, a large number of Jews, 30,000, fought for the czar in Manchuria[15]). During these two successive waves of pogroms in 1903 and 1904, close to one hundred Jews were murdered, and some four thousand were injured.

Despite Kishinev's notoriety, these first two phases were a dress rehearsal for a far more devastating spree of pogroms in 1905 and 1906 that were precipitated by political change in the empire (highlighted by the October 1905 Manifesto creating, nominally, a constitutional monarchy). The broad causal dynamic in this wave was the widespread belief that Jews spearheaded revolutionary unrest that led to the October Manifesto; this idea emanated from the highest authority in the empire, since Nicholas II endorsed it (accounting for the manifesto in a letter to his mother, the czar wrote that "because nine-tenths of the troublemakers are Jews, the people's whole anger turned against them"[16]). Whatever the theory motivating the pogroms, they were spearheaded by right-wing political groups (e.g., the Union of the Russian People) and militias (e.g., the Black Hundreds) that came into being in this period, in loose association with the czarist bureaucracy, and concentrated their energies in 1905 and 1906 on anti-Jewish attacks before turning to other matters in the decade preceding the empire's collapse. This combination of emotion and administration—of reactionary anger and anxiety about constitutional change in Russia and the organization of right-wing radicalism in political parties and armed groups—proved lethal. The 1905–6 years, a period when American Jews were commemorating 250 years of experience in a democracy based on triumphant constitutionalism, was an interval of horror for Russian Jews. The number of pogroms leapt exponentially, from several dozen in 1903–4 to several hundred in 1905–6 (the Zionist Leo Motzkin claimed in his survey of this latter period, *Die Judenpogrome in Russland,* that 690 pogroms occurred in the two-year period that followed the issuance of the manifesto). The 1905 death toll was excruciating—800 Jewish dead in Odessa, 100 Jews killed in Kiev, and another 100 murdered both in Minsk and Kalarash (Bessarabia), and 200 dead in Belostok.

The historian Jonathan Frankel, who devoted much of his career to investigating how Russian Jewish politics in the Pale permeated beyond it, identified this 1905 era as the point where modern Jewish politics can be regarded as a "single subsystem with a two-way feedback linking Russia to the West in many ways." Citing the example of relief fund mobilization sponsored by Judah Magnes and supported by Louis Marshall in late 1905, Frankel insightfully observed that this period was significant for the way it made "broader circles . . . conscious of the urgency of the Jewish problem."[17]

This was the international background that propelled American Jewish affairs into a new, more assertive phase. Many Downtown Jews had found freedom in America after escaping from earlier rounds of anti-Jewish violence in the late nineteenth-century Russian empire. Their feelings of empathy for Russian Jewish sufferers from 1903 to 1906 were potent, and their special sense of responsibility toward the persecuted Jews of the Pale flowed upward to Marshall's group, where it was understood that nobody in Jewish New York would become reconciled to Nativist maneuvers to limit immigration to Ellis Island. The czar's Jews were fighting for their lives, and everyone in New York City knew where they were likely to turn for help or for sanctuary.

Questions being asked in this 1903–6 period were not detached ideological musings. Downtown Jews anxiously monitored the fates of thousands of imperiled friends and family in Russia, and they were also looking Uptown, to Marshall's group, for tangible proof of leadership. On a serpentine but discernible course, the violent anti-Semitism fomented in Kishinev by the hateful *Bessarabets* pushed Marshall toward a confrontation with the physically harmless but insulting anti-Semitism of a famous librarian at Lake Placid, New York. Removing Melvil Dewey from a senior public post because of private anti-Jewish snobbery became Marshall's first proactive endeavor in Jewish self-defense in the new phase of his career. It led to larger campaigns in Jewish advocacy.

For months after Kishinev, Marshall was paralyzed by an obsolete mode of operation. Downtown Jews wanted action to protect their kind in Russia, or at least to protest the criminal pogroms and isolate the czarist regime for its predatory lawlessness on Jewish issues. Meantime, Marshall was still trying to edify the immigrants and Americanize them. This moral reform agenda mandated stifling any East Side expression that could be construed as being antigovernment and anti-American. As 1903 drew to a close, Marshall was dipping deeply and disingenuously into his reservoir of legal argumentation to explain to Downtown's Russian Jews why they should not demand substantive responses to hellish Kishinev from the Roosevelt administration. "If we should attempt to interfere with the domestic affairs of a foreign nation," he queried through the proxy editors of the *World,* "Russia might ask about our treatment of Negroes, Chinese or Indians."[18]

Such rhetoric was becoming a liability in a period when America's Russian Jews had compelling reasons to be fixated with models of Jewish self-defense. So long as there was no obvious way for American Jews to develop those models overseas, Marshall's efforts began to pivot around the models' adaptation at home. To be sure, his group chose an issue—anti-Jewish exclusion in the Adirondacks—of particular concern to its own social climbing instincts and a part of its own agenda since Joseph Seligman was denied entry to the Grand Union Hotel in Saratoga in 1877;[19] that is, nothing in the campaign against Melvil Dewey could possibly furnish palpable assistance to persecuted Jews in Russia. But Marshall enforced a prosecution of Dewey's anti-Jewish policies at his Lake Placid Club in a combative spirit characteristic of Jewish life of the time, and the Lake Placid campaign was designed to tie together some loose ends left by the Rabbi Jacob Joseph committee investigation and inculcate a message of American exceptionalism as an antidote to the confusions engendered by Kishinev. The point was to prove that the country's laws and democratic system provided the means to guarantee that Jew hatred had no place in America.

Melvil Dewey and Anti-Semitism at Lake Placid

In terms of place and time of birth, Melvil Kossuth Dewey and Louis Marshall were compatriots.[20] Born five years before Marshall, Dewey hailed from the "burned-over" Jefferson County district of Upstate New York, some sixty miles from Syracuse. His native area was a powder keg of religious revivalism, including Mormonism and Millerism, as well as various political and social reform movements running the gamut from temperance to abolitionism. Dewey was raised as a Baptist in a region rife with theological disputation and schism—members of his family attended two of the three Baptist churches in Adams Center, a small hamlet that expanded somewhat at the time of Dewey's birth due to the advent of a railroad line. Dewey's interest in education and libraries can be associated with the reformist temper of his native milieu.

During his years at Amherst College, 1870–74, Dewey devised his revolutionary decimal system. This system was destined to save librarians and library patrons "millions of dollars and countless hours of confusion."[21] Along with the rise of the middle class and the patronage of Andrew Carnegie, the Dewey Decimal System is considered one of the crucial factors in the rise of the library movement, a palpable achievement of pre–World War I America (America had less than two hundred public libraries at the time when Dewey thought to use decimals in book classification; in 1913, it housed 3,562 libraries). Dewey's influence was not limited to the decimal system. During the last decade of the nineteenth century, he was a driving force in the reform of secondary and higher education in New York State. Additionally, Dewey's leadership at the Lake Placid Club set style and fashion standards in twentieth-century America and, incidentally, set the stage for Lake Placid's subsequent hosting of two Winter Olympic competitions, in 1932 and 1980.

Dewey and his wife Annie broke ground in the Adirondacks in 1893. They created the Lake Placid Club from a blueprint depiction of this Adirondack idyll as therapeutic relief from urban stress and taxing "brain work." Professional city labor, many believed, posed grave health risks.[22] Motivated by similar concerns and calculations, Jews built their own restorative camps on the other side of Adirondack lakes. At Knollwood on Saranac Lake, as we shall see, Marshall and his family and friends temporarily left behind the frenetic tumult of modern life; at Lake Placid, the Deweys added the insidious principle of social exclusion to this same conception of romantic retreat.

As would happen in the dramatic clash with Henry Ford in the 1920s, Marshall's confidence in his prosecution of Dewey's anti-Semitism stemmed largely from psychological insight: in both cases, he knew something about his antagonist's antimodern, romantic impulses. Yet motoring Ford's hate-mongering in the *Dearborn Independent* was an inscrutable mix of ignorance and business calculation, whereas the contest with Melvil Dewey boiled down to an unusually discernible, almost "rational" difference of opinion between the Gentile and the Jew. Because his professional obligations in modern life obliged Dewey to provide equal library services to immigrants and workers he really did not like, he felt entitled to enforce exclusion in his private world at Lake Placid.[23] Marshall's counterpoint was that public service is a trust that prohibits any individual from ostentatiously parading this invidious distinction between nondiscrimination at work and discrimination at play.

In 1903, seven years after Dewey first drafted his club's exclusive membership rules, Henry Leipziger sauntered happily around the Lake Placid Club grounds as an invited guest of the New York Library Association's "Library Week." A 50-year-old, Manchester-born single man with a distinguished record of academic and professional achievement (a doctorate from Columbia and a stint as assistant superintendent of New York Public Schools), Leipziger was a familiar figure in Uptown circles, and Marshall (it will be recalled) knew him as a somewhat stiff-mannered colleague on the Educational Alliance's Moral Culture Committee. Browsing through the club's 1901 catalogue, Leipziger discovered to his chagrin that he was not at liberty to seek membership in the attractive club. The circular stated, "No one shall be received as member or guest, against whom there is physical, moral, social or race objection . . . It is found impracticable to make exceptions to Jews or others excluded, even when of unusual personal qualifications."[24] Well respected for his work with the Aguilar Free Library and a distinguished member of the New York Public Library Circulation Committee, Leipziger was appalled that being Jewish negatively trumped such "unusual personal qualifications."

For years Leipziger had inquired about membership possibilities at the club, but before he stumbled across this circular, he had never grasped the reason for Dewey's evasive answers. Leipziger summered in 1904 in the Lake Placid area but pointedly told acquaintances that he would boycott the upcoming Library Week. During that year a Jew, Edward Lauterbach, joined the Board of Regents of the University of the State of New York, and Leipziger sensed that the appointment provided leverage for action against the Lake Placid Club, since Dewey was employed as state librarian of New York under the aegis of the regents. He brought the grievance to Marshall's attention in the fall.

In late November, Marshall asked a Gentile friend, William Taylor, to write to Dewey's club as though he were inquiring about membership requirements.[25] Once he had collected materials confirming anti-Jewish exclusion at the Lake Placid Club, Dewey's stewardship of that policy, and the abusive use of Dewey's public title in advertisements circulated by the discriminatory social club, he prepared a formal petition to the board of regents.[26]

The petition demanded Dewey's removal as state librarian. Leading lights of Uptown, Jacob Schiff, Adolph Lewisohn, Daniel Guggenheim, and Isidor Straus, co-signed the petition with Marshall, who submitted it to the regents on December 20, 1904.

"The intolerable spirit" of anti-Jewish exclusion in Dewey's Lake Placid Club circular, Marshall wrote, "is the far-off echo of the ignorant brutality of medieval times."[27] The same discriminatory spirit, Marshall conceded, emanated from other social clubs in the state, but Lake Placid's situation was different because Dewey was a high public official appointed by the regents "at the head of an important branch of the education system of the state, one to whom the youth of the State are accustomed to look for instruction and guidance." This public office was supported by taxpayers of New York, a state that included 750,000 law-abiding Jews. These Jewish citizens had "sought to advance the cause of education to as great an extent as any part of the citizenship of this Commonwealth"; they therefore had a right to demand that a public servant whose salary came from the public treasury show appropriate consideration to all groups of citizens in the state. If Dewey were allowed to impose obloquy to the Jews today, tomorrow he could attack the Catholic, and the next day the Methodist. As far as Marshall's group was concerned, Dewey could be allowed to do what he wanted in his private club, but it demanded his dismissal as state librarian.

Marshall's argument had holes, since Dewey could claim that he was scrupulously tolerant in the performance of his public responsibilities and could also promise changes in membership policies at the Lake Placid Club. The regents were by no means unanimously resolved to dismiss Dewey, whose qualifications for the state's top library post were unquestionable. Unwisely, Dewey issued ambiguous explanations and apologies while concurrently launching counterattacks against Marshall; he proved to be far more adroit at classifying library arrangements than arranging his own professional defense.

By mid-January 1905, the petition's contents had been disclosed publicly, but the regents were keeping mum. Dewey started to fire off explanations to the press, saying on January 23 that his club's circular had done the Jews a favor by preempting the embarrassment of their nonacceptance. He passed himself off as a victim, saying he had been threatened due to the sour grapes of a New York Jew, meaning Leipziger. Actually, what sounded sour was such pleading—one rabbi, Bernard Drachman, stated in the *New York Times* that Dewey's statement constituted "as painful a bit of reading as it has been my misfortune to peruse," and Marshall correctly estimated "Dewey has played into my hands."[28] Specious apologies would not suffice in this matter; a combative Marshall announced to a relative, "Dewey has presented his apologetic answer, and I shall not rest until I have his scalp dangling at my belt."[29]

Dewey's behavior was infuriating, but by the end of January Marshall was thinking about the petition generally as a trial run for antidefamation work in the United States. Should the petition succeed, it would demonstrate that the Jews had a substantive part to play in shaping the rules of democratic conduct in the public sphere. High public officials had standards to keep, even in their private lives; it was wrong for such officials to incorporate the prestige of their publicly funded positions in the discriminatory policies of a private establishment. "I am interested in making a public lesson of Mr. Dewey," Marshall confided to one acquaintance.[30] "He is a state official, and he has an international reputation; if the proceedings against him succeed, and I think they will, the effects will be salutary." One of those effects would be to establish Marshall's leadership status in an ethnic community whose anxious immigrant members were searching feverishly for viable models of Jewish self-defense.

Dewey continued to fight back, selecting a peculiar duo of allies: I. K. Funk, a prominent Protestant publisher, and Isidore Singer, editor-in-chief of the *Jewish Encyclopedia*, then under Funk and Wagnalls production.[31] Singer's part in the Dewey controversy was particularly confounding. Born in Moravia, Singer had been influenced by the Science of Judaism (Wissenschaft des Judentums) movement and had worked on various media and cultural projects in France before becoming embroiled in disputes with wealthy French Jews (in what would become a recurring pattern in his career, Singer was upset by his inability to find local patrons for his Jewish cultural plans).[32] In America, Singer renewed his reputation as the concocter of wildly ambitious plans and the possessor of a volatile personality, but he established a working relationship with Funk, whose company published Singer's 1904 memorial to Kishinev, *Russia at the Bar of the American People*.[33] Singer's work on the *Jewish Encyclopedia* project preceded this volume, and it was accompanied from the start by heated discussions between Singer and his publisher, with the former periodically accusing Funk of anti-Semitism. Funk, for his part, appears to have held evolving ideas about Jews and was prone to issuing unctuously patronizing statements on the subject. "To non-Jews as well as to many Jews, it will be an interesting surprise to turn over the pages of the *Jewish Encyclopedia*," Funk declared in the project's promotions. "It must be admitted that Jews have much to be proud of."[34]

This high-charged pair, Funk and Singer, found agreement in their objection to the Marshall group's effort to oust the celebrated librarian, Melvil Dewey. Funk issued public statements promising that Marshall's petition would backfire as a "defeat for the Jews," because it would aggravate anti-Semitism.[35] Singer chimed in, calling Marshall the "evil genius of New York Judaism," informing petition co-signer Isidor Straus that Marshall is a "stiff lawyer and a bitter hater who would compound Jewish suffering" and declaring in New York newspapers that "a dozen Jewish individuals do not represent 75,000 New York Jews."[36] The *Sun* provided an ample platform for Singer's fulminations. He swore in this newspaper that he could compile a counterpetition in Dewey's behalf signed by 11,000 "Hebrews" from all the states in the Union. The *Sun* corroborated the Funk and Singer admonitions and attacks, its editorials branding the Marshall group's petition "ill advised and unfortunate."[37]

Marshall's furious, pugnacious letter to I. K. Funk,[38] written in mid-February 1905 when various New York State University committees were considering the fate of the Dewey petition, inaugurated this new phase of advocacy and self-defense in Marshall's career. One of its concluding phrases, couched both in the machismo rhetoric of the Theodore Roosevelt era and the Bundist spirit of militant self-defense, as though Jewish Rough Riders were warding the Cossacks from the shores of Lake Placid and the New World as a whole, can be regarded as the first fully articulated statement of Louis Marshall's credo as a figure of note in modern Jewish politics. "You forget that the glory of American citizenship has aroused the consciousness of manhood," Marshall pugnaciously told Funk. The half-empty results of the Rabbi Jacob Joseph funeral investigation, followed by the shattering pogrom of Kishinev, dislodged Marshall from the idea that teaching immigrants to be deferential about their Jewish concerns was the highest purpose of Jewish work. After Kishinev, vigilance was the watchword—not, at first, for the protection of persecuted Jews, but rather in the guarding of the exceptionalist principle that America, for Jews and all other freedom seekers, was different.

Using scare tactics, Funk had described to Marshall a dinner held in New York involving seventy-five clergymen at which the Dewey petition was discussed, and the participants found cause to resurrect "old stories against the Jews." Marshall lampooned these creepy warnings: "Were the old stories that your clerical dinner companions 'resurrected' at that memorable feast, the shameful superstitions of medieval bigotry, stories of the Black Death, of poisoned wells, of the horrible blood accusation?" Marshall sarcastically queried. Demanding that Marshall's group withdraw its petition against Dewey, Funk had not even addressed the substantive matter at hand, the issue of whether a "paid official of the State may, while he is drawing a salary out of the State treasury, to which Jews as well as Christians contribute, disseminate documents of anti-Semitic tendencies." Instead, by indulging innuendo and attempting to exploit dark fears, Funk was defending the proposition that Jews, in the democratic civilization of North America, were "once more to assume our wonted attitude" and "kiss the hand that strikes the blow." To this, Marshall clarified the purpose of the Dewey petition: advocacy would drive a wedge between Old and New worlds of Jewish experience. Marshall seemed to be taking post-Kishinev vows of Jewish activism and of allegiance to American exceptionalism when he mocked Funk's "disclosure" about the clergymen and their old stories. When he declared that "he who would be free, himself must strike the blow," Marshall was preaching Bund ideology to a leading American publisher and also taking a giant step away from the moralistic messages of accommodation he had disseminated in the *World*:

> Your disclosure is most valuable. It tells us where we stand. It warns us, that we cannot afford to loll at our ease, and permit the establishment of a dangerous, and nefarious, precedent. It teaches us the oft-told, but too often forgotten precept, that "he who would be free, himself must strike the blow."[39]

The fate of the Dewey petition was decided by New York University at a series of February 1905 meetings. At the first, held by the university's Library Committee, Dewey latched on to Singer's *Sun* editorializing for support and hinted about intentions to sever his connection to the Lake Placid Club. He opportunistically abjured having any personal feelings of anti-Semitism but also delivered glimpses of his true attitudes in his belabored discussion of the way Marshall collected evidence about the club's discrimination through the services of his "decoy," William Taylor. "You have hit me hard. It was cleverly done and I give you all the credit. I have always said that the Jewish race was the smartest on earth," he declared[40]—one wonders where in the Dewey Decimal System Marshall privately contemplated filing his antagonist's cant. In public, Marshall tried to summarize this February 2 meeting judiciously, telling the *New York Times* that Dewey had said "he really liked Jews and would reconsider his connection with the Lake Placid Club." Dewey, however, was recalcitrant and employed the services of the grudge-bearing Isidore Singer to disseminate a self-serving forty-page pamphlet devoid of the contrite poses he had struck at the Library Committee meeting. However transparent his duplicitous behavior, Dewey was an empowered individual with a track record enshrined by the development of the American public library system; whether the snake charmer was his public achievements or his private anti-Semitism, he rallied an impressive mass of support as his case headed for a showdown at the regents' mid-February meeting. Marshall and his co-petitioners watched nervously as the Dewey controversy was debated in New York for weeks. Coming to Dewey's side were editorialists and commentators in the *New York Sun,* the *Saratoga Sun,* the *Brooklyn Eagle,* and *Harper's Weekly;* Herbert Putnam defended Dewey in a letter to the university regent Whitelaw Reid, and the nation's library science journals were, naturally, in Dewey's camp.[41]

Arranging this newspaper commentary was Dewey's sole successful maneuver in his own defense. The regents could not entirely overlook a hefty compilation of published opinion holding that what Dewey did at his private club was not the university's business. At their February 15 meeting,[42] the regents therefore adopted the formal position that no tangible connection could be identified between the Lake Placid Club actions described in Marshall's petition and Dewey's public duties as state librarian. Nonetheless, the regents publicly censured Dewey for his part in the club's 1901 circulation and held that "further control" by Dewey of this private club would be "incompatible" with his public position in the service of the educational interests of the state. In effect, the regents argued that they lacked the authority to apply Marshall's novel argument to the past, but they accepted it as a guiding standard for the future.

For the time being, Marshall could live with the regents' decision. By questioning the propriety of Dewey's continued association with the discriminatory club, the regents had established an "important principle relative to the status of American citizenship." He wrote to Whitelaw Reid to thank the regents for their "satisfying and gratifying disposition of the matter."[43] In a letter to a relative,[44] Marshall claimed that censure was the optimal solution, because dismissal would have encouraged Dewey's supporters to cast him as a holy martyr. This was not entirely truthful, since just a month earlier Marshall had promised the same uncle that he would have Dewey's "scalp"; but Marshall was nonetheless relieved that his argument about the duties of a public official had been partially sanctioned by the regents, and his confidence as a Jewish leader was clearly on the rise. "I have contributed something to the welfare of the Jews for years to come," he boasted.[45] Meantime, he continued to monitor Dewey, who already had a proven tendency to backtrack on his promises and expressions of contrition. Sure enough, Dewey disseminated counterattacks in the spring, claiming that the regents had overstepped when they publicly rebuked him. Marshall fired off a series of complaints to Edward Lauterbach, informing the regent that Dewey was "trying to make capital out of his own disgrace" and arguing that the librarian was guilty of "insubordination" by branding the university's proceedings in his case as "preposterous" and motivated by "petty spite."[46]

The Marshall group's petition, the subsequent monitoring, and the demons in Dewey's own character had created an irreparable breach between the regents and the state librarian. The book was shut on Melvil Dewey when he resigned from his public post in summer 1905. It was Marshall's first major victory in Jewish advocacy.[47]

Characteristics of Marshall's Law Career

In this moment when Marshall's assertiveness as an advocate of Jewish interests was rising in intensity and transforming in quality, he took on in his professional work litigation of a noticeably public-spirited character. Marshall could never quite promote himself as a "people's attorney." In fact, as one scholar has observed, one reason why his counterpart Louis Brandeis acquired such a reputation, whereas Marshall remained identified as a business lawyer, was that Brandeis deliberately relegated an increasing share of his legal work as pro bono activity done free of charge for the public interest, whereas Marshall (as we shall see) insisted on receiving legal fees commensurate with the quality of his contribution, even in cases such as an important 1904 action about New York's corporation tax where his work should justifiably have been seen as an idealistic act of citizenship.[48] On occasion, Marshall bitterly complained that his legal work for regulation or restraint on business activity received little public recognition;[49] since some of his trial work, in particular this 1904 corporate tax litigation, really set significant limits on free enterprise and private profit, we might pause briefly to consider reasons why none of the people's attorney luster rubbed off on Marshall in the years before World War I.

Differences in social orientation and self-perception separating the "two lawyers named Louis"[50] are appreciable. Brandeis remained identified with a relatively austere New England Brahmin lifestyle and Progressive reform politics, whereas Marshall became tied to the far more affluent "Our Crowd" lifestyle of the German Jewish Manhattan elite, and also, as a conservative, he generally had no interest in claiming credit in public for making a contribution toward campaigns for social change. However, rich as it is in contrasts, the ambiguities of Marshall's public persona ought not to be viewed solely in terms of the comparison with Brandeis. The categories affixed to the social orientation of both men can be misleading: just as Brandeis was probably not quite as integrated in the New England Brahmin elite as he would have been liked,[51] Marshall could never have become a true insider in New York's Jewish Uptown elite. To be sure, before World War I the two Louis lawyers crossed paths in high-profile settings, especially (as we will see) in the Protocols of Peace arbitration of the 1910 cloakmakers strike; nonetheless, in the period preceding Brandeis's nomination to the Supreme Court, Marshall had no compelling reason to fashion his own public persona in a pro or con response to Brandeis's emergence as the people's attorney.

Associates much closer to him than Brandeis became highly visible figures in political reform campaigns, often advocating liberal positions that were antithetical to Marshall's own worldview and also potentially problematic in terms of his interests as a business lawyer responsible to clients who were leading bankers, financiers, and businessmen. We will, for instance, note later that the involvement of his law partner, Samuel Untermyer, in the 1912–13 congressional subcommittee (the Pujo Committee) investigation of the banking "money trust" raised extraordinarily complicated issues regarding the way a business lawyer could, or should, balance professional obligations to clients against political philosophies advocating regulation or breakup of big banking structures or corporate monopolies. Though the motivations and effects of Brandeis's famous critique of the banks (*Other People's Money, and How the Bankers Use It*) have not been assessed by scholars in light of Western civilization's long-standing association of the Jew with usury and banking malfeasance, Untermyer was, in his Pujo work (which directly influenced Brandeis),[52] acutely conscious of its Jewish implications, stemming largely from his firm's strong connections with Jacob Schiff, one of the wealthiest men in America and a Jewish banker. From the point of view of a Gentile businessman, the Pujo Committee might have been seen through a jaded prism of anti-Semitism as an instance of a Jewish lawyer like Untermyer playing on both sides of the court, as a corporate attorney and as a social crusader, to expose crooked Jewish and Christian bankers.

These professional and ethnoreligious considerations suggestively hint about why Marshall never chose to develop a persona as a people's attorney. Yet there were several other, more prosaic, reasons. He had four children to support, and, apart from his volunteer work on Jewish causes, he had no emotional reservations about being compensated for hard work.

Dating from his work on the Sampson Simson case (litigation, it will be recalled, that became the springboard for his professional success as a New York City lawyer), Marshall retained a large, mostly unstated, emotional attachment to the perception of Jewish charity as a personal identity imperative and as an expression of justice. For three decades in the twentieth century, he invested an extraordinary, even staggering, amount of entirely uncompensated labor for an array of Jewish causes, the protectory, the Jewish Theological Seminary, the AJC, innumerable antidefamation cases, the East Europe minority rights campaign, the Jewish Agency, and more. When an occasional note of resentment surfaces in his letters relating to Brandeis's celebrated public persona as a people's attorney, Marshall was undeniably jealous, but he was also semiconsciously pointing to an objective truth: Marshall's pro bono labors as a Jewish people's attorney might be inadequately recognized in his own time or by posterity, due to the contentiously ideological rough and tumble of the Jewish socioeconomic world, whereas Brandeis's pro bono efforts for the American Progressive movement were immediately appreciated and retrospectively honored by large circles of liberal Americans.

For whatever reason, Marshall's substantive contributions to America's evolving pre–World War I discussions about business regulation and corporate responsibility have been overlooked. His leading effort in this regard occurred in 1904.

That year, the New York legislature imposed a corporate tax on all government-granted franchises, including utilities in water, gas, and oil, piers, bridges, telephones, and surface railway systems in New York City.[53] Eight trolley and railroad lines refused to pay the tax, arguing that the law was "nothing but a mere arbitrary exercise of power" that violated existing property law precedents regarding equal protection and due process. The railroads hired the best corporate attorneys money could buy. One, Elihu Root, who was in transition between terms as secretary of war and secretary of state, fashioned himself as a paragon of the early twentieth-century business lawyer—in 1904, the year this litigation in *Metropolitan Street Railway Company v. New York Board of Tax Commissioners*[54] reached the Supreme Court, Root winked at the graduating class of Yale Law School, assuring its members that "some prize of business law" awaited them.[55] Another Marshall antagonist in this case, William D. Guthrie, thrilled business lawyers in early twentieth-century America as the subject of sensational reports about his $1 million annual income.[56] Intimidated by the railroad plaintiffs' all-star cast of lawyers, New York Attorney General Julius Meyer engaged Marshall as special counsel for the state in the *Metropolitan* litigation; the two men were friends and failed to spell out the terms of Marshall's retainer, an oversight that caused subsequent friction.[57]

In his argument to the Supreme Court, Marshall noted that the New York franchises, being vendible and transferable, had all the attributes of property and that the authority of every state to tax all property is "axiomatic."[58] Reiterating his successful argument in the 1889 Syracuse Water Company case, and the principle grounded in the Supreme Court's famous Charles River Bridge ruling, Marshall claimed that in the conferral of franchises, a state surrenders no sovereign power other than what is explicitly demarcated in the franchise agreement. Since the railway and trolley plaintiffs had never been granted corporate tax exemption in their franchise agreements with New York, they had no right to argue for exemption by inference, and their claims, as public grantees, about due process property violations had no merit, in light of existing precedents. The court followed Marshall's argument to the letter, holding that New York had granted privileges to the franchisees "in the construction, operation and maintenance of a street railroad." These were "all [the privileges] that were granted . . . there was no express relinquishment of the right of taxation," and the plaintiffs' claims about due process infringement were without merit.

For New York State, this was a tremendous triumph, enabling it to collect what Marshall estimated as $25 million in piled up tax collection and add hundreds of millions of tax revenue to its public coffers in years to come. In the name of public welfare, the ruling imposed significant financial responsibilities upon transportation and other corporations.

The Metropolitan Street Railway ruling was, for Marshall, an impressive personal victory in a taxing struggle against the heftily compensated and well-staffed legal team assembled by the railroad companies. He wanted to be paid for it. Meyer, however, claimed for months that he had no funds left in his department. Marshall lost patience, and in 1907 he fired off three emphatic requests to New York lawmakers, asking for a fee of $10,000 and noting (not unreasonably) that his work had accrued millions for the state and that he would have earned five times the requested fee as a private litigant.[59] The wrangling continued, with Marshall implying that New York's evasiveness had become personally insulting (any compromise about the fee, Marshall said in one letter, "would be inconsistent with my dignity"[60]); as the correspondence meandered, Marshall shifted gears as to whether he would be willing to redefine his work as a pro bono service or compromise with a fee of $5,000.[61] A bittersweet dénouement to one of the finest moments of his legal career, the episode also suggests that Marshall's constructive ties with Albany legislators, while an important source of strength in his labors on behalf of an array of professional, Jewish, and environmental matters, had their limits.

American Jewry's 250th Anniversary

Under the pressure of circumstances, the thrust of the elaborately planned celebrations of the 250th anniversary of Jewish arrival in North America in 1654 (expelled from Recife, twenty-three pioneering Jews arrived in New Amsterdam aboard the *Sainte Catherine* that year) shifted from commemoration to advocacy.

In a poignant irony, the keynote 250th celebration was scheduled for Thanksgiving Day at Carnegie Hall. In his insightful article on the 250th pageantry, the historian Arthur Goren understates the situation when he writes that "November 1905 was not a good month for festivities."[62] Out of the traumatic 1903–6 pogrom period in czarist Russia, American Jews unwittingly chose by far the bloodiest stretch to celebrate their own 250-year experience with democratic freedom. Over 80 percent of the pogroms in the calamitous 1905–6 period transpired in Russia in the six weeks following the issuance of the October Manifesto.[63] With friends and family under attack in Russia, masses of Jews who had immigrated to New York and elsewhere in the preceding quarter century were in no mood to celebrate lavishly their good fortune, and so a number of communities (Chicago, Philadelphia, Cincinnati, Milwaukee) abandoned plans for large-scale 250th celebrations, either by scaling them down and relocating them in synagogues or by sponsoring large protest gatherings in lieu of festivities.[64]

In a way, such developments accentuated the uniqueness of Jewish experience in America: in North America, Jewish well-being had increased during 250 years of democratic development, whereas the October Manifesto advent of constitutional democracy in Russia spelled disaster for the Jews, because empowered reactionary forces held them responsible for the affront to autocratic tradition. The unstated implication of this contrast was that the Jews had no real future in Russia. This thought was not publicly articulated for many reasons. One was that some Uptown Jews, particularly Schiff, believed in this period that Russia's defeat in the Japan war might weaken and shock the czarist regime and thereby radically transform Jewish realities in Eastern Europe.[65] Not stated in words, the understanding that life in the Jewish Pale had become insufferable found expression in actions supportive of future large-scale Russian Jewish immigration to the United States. Marshall, in fact, came to think of the 250th celebration primarily in terms of this purpose, as though the elaborate demonstration of past Jewish contributions to American democracy were to be included in a brief he was preparing against Nativist lobbying for immigration restriction. Yesterday's American Jewish accomplishments constituted the strongest evidence he could marshal about the likely benefits of Russian Jewish immigration tomorrow. Marshall revealed his thinking lucidly in one private letter:

> The sole purpose of this celebration is to point out to the people of this country that the Jews are here as of right, that they are not interlopers; that they were among the earliest of the colonists, and consequently, that the agitation against Jewish immigration, which has been smoldering for a number of years and which threatens to burst into a serious flame, is un-American.[66]

A member of the 250th executive committee, Marshall dominated the anniversary's organization and set its tone, even though the highest ranking committee titles went to the bankers, Schiff (chairman) and Isaac Seligman (treasurer).[67] He articulated the celebration's purpose for the executive committee in a piece on "The Jews as Elements in the Population, Past and Present."[68] The anniversary's goal was to depict the Jews as a group that "should be classed as American pioneers, not as interlopers, not as exploiters, but as active participants in the building of the nation."

In the 250th preparations, Marshall's increasing concern about immigration issues was symbolized by the presence of his administrative deputy, Max Kohler, a Washington attorney with an august Jewish pedigree (as the son of preeminent Reform Rabbi Kaufmann Kohler) and a wealth of experience in immigration law; destined to invest countless volunteer hours as Marshall's sidekick in crucial lobbying fights for open immigration, Kohler served as secretary to the anniversary's main organizing committee, probably because he had worked in a similar capacity with the American Jewish Historical Society since its inception in 1892. With Kohler's reliable help, Marshall attended to every detail, large and small, of the 250th celebrations.

From the start, Marshall opposed plans to erect a grandiose stone or brass monument, arguing that a fund in support of immigrant issues would be more appropriate.[69] Consulting with Schiff, he complained about President Roosevelt's reluctance to attend the Carnegie Hall event. "In a moral sense," Marshall wrote, the Jewish 250th "is fully as important as the celebration of the Louisiana Purchase, the settlement of Jamestown," or other anniversaries favored by the president's participation, so Marshall urged Schiff to "bend every energy to persuade Roosevelt to attend."[70]

Marshall was also the mouthpiece of the patriarchal executive committee that decided to disqualify women from participation on any of the 250th organizing committees. "Owing to the great likelihood that jealousies might arise if every woman who is ambitious to appear on a committee should not actually be appointed, harm rather than good would result by making the women a factor," declaimed Marshall, after the executive committee "carefully considered" the issue.[71]

For months, Marshall stroked the ego of Simon Wolf, the veteran American Jewish intercessor who felt neglected and upstaged by the way the 250th celebration was organized.[72] In what was now the routine with any new Jewish organizational endeavor, Marshall exhorted his Uptown colleagues to recruit Downtown Jews for membership on the 250th executive committee[73] (in the end, no Russian Jews were included on this body, though eight Downtown delegates joined the lower-ranking general committee[74]). An appropriately inclusive formula for Russian Jewish participation was never really found—looking back at the 250th celebrations from the standpoint of the 350th anniversary, one commentator concludes broadly that the 1905 events "failed to acknowledge the ever broadening significance and contributions of the massive influx of East European Jews" who had arrived since the 1880s.[75]

Increasingly, Marshall found himself caught between the habitual paternalism of the Uptown elite and the Downtown Jewish demands for power sharing. The 250th anniversary would be a sham, Marshall believed, if it did not project compelling images of Jewish unity. Not everyone agreed. In early October, just days before the czar's constitutional concession and ensuing reactionary violence utterly deflected New York Jewry attentions, Marshall negotiated with David Blaustein, hoping that the Downtown communal leader would exert his influence to preempt the immigrants' plans to erect a 250th monument of their own in the heart of the East European Jewish neighborhoods on the East Side. "Why should there be a division of counsel in this," Marshall pled, explaining that the 250th executive committee had already commissioned a Jewish sculptor, Isidore Konti, to produce a memorial statue for the community as a whole. "We are all immigrant Jews in one sense of the word," exclaimed Marshall. "For heaven's sake, stop such destructive" separatist movements, Marshall implored Blaustein. "This constant stirring up of jealousies, this perpetual differentiation of Jews into classes, this unwillingness to become a party to any organized movement, will in the end only lead to injury."[76]

Interestingly, no less than anxieties and grief elicited by the pogroms in Russia, the threat of sectarianism nullified plans to erect a grand memorial for the 250th anniversary of Jewish settlement in North America. Marshall had never been happy about the plan, and he was frustrated by his discussions with Blaustein. In the end he put a new twist on his reservations, explaining to H. Pereira Mendes that the executive committee had abandoned plans for the monument because building one "would establish a most dangerous precedent." A Jewish 250th statue would be followed in New York City public places "with monuments commemorated by Catholics, Presbyterians, Episcopalians and Christian Scientists."[77] In the end, the 250th national organizers reallocated money raised for the memorial to relief for the persecuted Jews of czarist Russia.[78]

President Roosevelt remained a no-show, and Kohler and Marshall managed to obtain only a "most disappointing" letter from the White House to be read at the main 250th event in Carnegie Hall.[79] The president expressed his "deep sympathy" for persecuted Jews overseas and praised the "fine qualities of citizenship" displayed by Jews in the United States.[80] Former president Grover Cleveland became the keynote speaker. The event was impressive.[81] Led by Jacob Schiff, the executive committee members filed into the hall to the accompaniment of Mendelssohn's "March of the Priests" played by the New York Symphony Orchestra. The hall, packed with 5,000 enthused attendees, was draped lavishly by flags and coats of arms of the states in the Union, along with green hangings "embossed with golden bucklers emblematic of Jerusalem." Oscar Straus and other speakers portrayed the 1654 entry of the twenty-three pioneers aboard the *Sainte Catherine* as the Jewish analogue of the arrival of the Pilgrims at Plymouth Rock. The ceremony closed with dignified singing of "Adon Olam" by the Downtown Cantors, whose participation was organized by event handlers as a symbol of immigrant inclusion and Jewish unity.

Not everyone heard "Adon Olam," and the event's recitations on the whole, in that spirit. Persisting in the attitude of resentment and suspicion described by Blaustein in his reports to Marshall before the celebration, Downtown's feisty left-wing *Forward* declared that the Carnegie Hall event was not a celebration of the Jewish people. Instead, "it was a festival for wealthy Jews who gathered to praise God for his benevolence to them."[82] In contrast, the conservative *Tageblatt* praised the jubilee celebration as the "most magnificent and radiant gathering ever held by Jews in America."[83] Similarly, the *New York Times* wagered that the splendid celebration would be long remembered in "the annals of that famous meeting place," Carnegie Hall.[84]

Marshall, naturally, shared the enthusiasm. "This was the greatest meeting in the history of Judaism since the beginning of the world," he gushingly informed Nathan Straus.[85] While exultant, he was not resting on his laurels. In Marshall's mind, the 250th celebrations had not been about the past; instead, in a period of tremendous peril overseas, Carnegie Hall had provided a dramatic platform upon which a case could be built for America's continuing role as a haven for oppressed Jews. Ruminating on the event's meaning, Marshall promised its "effect will be beneficial, not only to the Jews in this country, but also to our unfortunate brethren in Russia."[86]

The pressures of planning for the celebration, along with the ongoing emergency in Russia, precluded a broad view of the interaction of the American Jewish past, present, and future. That vision was unfurled belatedly, in spring 1906, a few months after the keynote event in Carnegie Hall, and at a juncture when the pogroms overseas were subsiding. Invited to speak at Philadelphia's Congregation Rodeph Shalom in a coda to the 250th celebrations, Marshall delivered the most fascinatingly complex, and autobiographical, statement on Jewish leadership he ever composed.

Here, all the contrasts that welded together creatively in his character appeared in a lecture on a historical figure, Asser Levy, who was presented as a kind of work-in-progress reflection of Marshall himself. Tracing a timeline that ran between New Amsterdam and Kishinev, and then projected into the future with uncannily precise forecasts of Marshall's contributions to the abrogation of the Russian treaty before World War I and the drafting of minority rights accords for East European Jews after the Great War, Marshall validated contrasting sets of values and images—the conservative protection of property and the militant struggle for new ideas of freedom; the bold assertion of Jewish interests in a Darwinian reality of survival of the fittest and a tactful reserve about Jewish needs in an ethnically and religiously neutral public sphere; America as a land of exceptional freedom and opportunity where the Jew could be content with his good fortune and an American Jewish mission of exporting democratic norms and cultivating constitutional rights for Jews everywhere in the world. With his shifting frames of reference, from a patriotic ideal of American citizenship to a globalized sense of Jewish responsibility, Marshall previewed his career to come.

American Jewish history, Marshall explained, afforded a "unique spectacle."[87] For centuries "despised, condemned, derided and oppressed," the Jew in America had become a fully accepted citizen, owing to his continuing "vigorous assertion of rights." This "glorious story" began 250 years before with the arrival in New Amsterdam of Asser Levy, "the protagonist of Jewish rights and liberties in America."

Hurdling past discriminatory restrictions contemplated by Peter Stuyvesant, Levy became the "first Jewish owner of real property within the United States." As he had done in the acquisition of property, Levy bypassed Stuyvesant's desire to exclude the Jews from municipal defense. Refusing to pay a special tax imposed on residents who did not bear arms in the colony's defense, Levy demanded the right to stand guard. In so doing, Asser Levy "became the first Jewish citizen in America, acquiring the priceless badge of manhood."

Continuing, Marshall reviewed the Jewish experience in colonial time with an eye to the early twentieth-century needs and dilemmas of Jewish immigrants on the East Side and also to arguments he was fashioning for soon-to-come fights in favor of open immigration. Jewish immigrants were Americans even before they were obviously acculturated as such, Marshall claimed. "The Jew, transplanted to this country, became an American in sentiment before he became an American in speech, or outward appearance." Laden within the address's high rhetoric ("A new being has been born into the world—the American Jew, the spiritual heir of all the ages, the deathless messenger of monotheism") were rebuttals Marshall would hurl at the restrictionists when they maneuvered via literacy tests and fitness standards to shut the doors to Jews who looked foreign and who read foreign language newspapers. Jewish newcomers were deeply ethical beings whose heritage of "revelations of human equality" was obviously compatible with American democracy.

Marshall's description of his heroic model, Asser Levy, led him toward an intriguingly phrased self-portrait:

> He must be aggressive in the assertion of his rights, but he must not be offensive in the methods which he pursues in their assertion. He must fight, with discretion, with reasons, but he must not be vulgar or hysterical. He must be calm and judicial, not bumptious or egotistical.

This job description of an early twentieth-century American Jewish leader was not offered in a vacuum. Surveying 250 years of American Jewish experience, Marshall was simultaneously spelling out the platform of the AJC, which was at the time in process of formation. "What is needed above all things is organization," Marshall declared.

Telegraphically, Marshall cited the ideas and premises he had been refining in his mind for weeks as the rationale for this novel endeavor, the establishment of a national Jewish organization with substantive powers to work on sociopolitical issues of some sort. "If the Jews of the US, acting as a religious body, shall unite in the effort to secure the civil and religious rights of Jews in all countries where such rights are denied or endangered, they will not speak in vain," Marshall explained. In a glancing but unmistakable fashion, he promised that the new organization would fight for the right of American Jewish holders of US passports to enter czarist Russia—securing this right, we shall see, would become the defining issue for the new AJC. In an increasingly globalized world, American Jews had the requisite means, along with the moral responsibility, to bring their democratic freedom to oppressed Jews overseas. Above all else, it was their mission to emancipate the Russian Jews from the tyrannical depredations of the czar, the modern Pharaoh. With great optimistic flair, Marshall traced this arc of freedom, from the liberation of the American Jew 250 years before in the entry to New Amsterdam to the liberation of Russian Jewry after Kishinev, thanks to the support of a newly united American Jewry represented by a viable American Jewish organization:

> In these days, when a girdle can be placed around the earth in 40 minutes, and commerce has obliterated the boundaries of nations, when American statesman can silence the thunders of artillery and the hell-fire of musketry in Manchuria, and cause peace to emerge from among the contending nations in Morocco, 1,500,000 Jews, who are at the same time loyal American citizens, will, if they act as one man, be able to prepare the way for a third miracle—the softening of the heart of the modern Pharaoh.

The American Jewish Committee in Historical Perspective

The American Jewish Committee, the first organization in the history of the United States to be formed by an ethnoreligious group for the purpose of defending its rights and those of its brethren overseas,[88] was born without a blueprint. It arose as a means of producing rational responses to Jewish passions and concerns shared by the Uptown elite German Jews and the Downtown masses of Russian Jews and for the minimization of debilitating tensions between these two groups, whose members were, by and large, separated by class and social mores. It materialized not exactly by accident and not exactly by design: just as the AJC's makers had urgent, immediate concerns, mostly relating to the fate of Russian Jewry, they had a long-standing anxiety about how organization along Jewish lines could be regarded suspiciously by Gentile society as disloyal maneuvering to create a "state within a state."

Prior to the AJC's creation, its elite Jewish founders sometimes knew *what* they wanted to do without knowing *how* to achieve their goal, whereas other times they had strong ideas about *how* Jews ought to go about things in an open democratic society without really grasping *what* the masses of Jews in the country wanted (or, at least, why Downtown Jewry pursued its ideological purposes with such intensity). Given these fluctuating emphases on means and ends, it can hardly be surprising that discussions in the AJC's period of formation shifted back and forth between procedural and administrative issues of how a national Jewish organization should operate and be constituted, and action-oriented questions relating to the items and goals designated on its agenda. In a similar way, high moral purpose centered around the Klal Yisrael ethos of worldwide Jewish solidarity blended with prosaic dynamics of ego and power struggle between elite individuals and groups (in this struggle, factors such as regional geography, economic status, and professional expertise held weight, whereas past experience in Jewish communal affairs frequently did not and was sometimes even a liability).

The AJC's establishment could not solve at once these profoundly complicated issues of ideals, communal perceptions, and practical circumstances and challenges. Given the lack of centralized authority in traditional Jewish kehillah community structures in the Diaspora, along with American constitutional and social norms prohibiting state intervention in religious affairs and encouraging dynamics of fragmentation, denominationalism, and volunteerism in the life of ethnoreligious groups, a ground-breaking organization like the AJC was destined to be preoccupied by dilemmas of authority and representative accountability for years. When America entered World War I, a decade after AJC's creation, these dilemmas seemed no less acute than ever before; at that time, the organization became mired in a famous confrontation with a planned rival organization, the American Jewish Congress, in which the ground zero problem of how democratically representative an ethnoreligious organization could, or should, be in the United States was debated with considerable, sometimes ferocious, passion.

The persistence of this debate about ethnic representation in a democracy[89] might misleadingly evoke a sense that the AJC really could get nothing done its first decade of existence, other than ruminate over what it was all about. In fact, born without a blueprint, the AJC was from the start an active, result-oriented organization, and its accomplishments, particularly on immigration issues, should not be downplayed. In fact, the practical consequences of the AJC's founding and the ways its early activities in immigration and other spheres preemptively allayed some of the massive horror of the Holocaust have probably been underestimated by historians.

In the cluster of intention and contingency, high moral purpose and prosaic power play, which congealed with the AJC's founding, we can identity two broad dynamics. First, the organization's founders sought relief from tensions caused by the issue of *control.* By 1905–6, these anxieties were becoming overwhelming and seemed to be reoccurring in an array of what would ordinarily be regarded as disparate spheres, such as synagogue administration, media, fund-raising, and political lobbying. It would be inaccurately reductive to propose that the Uptown founders established the AJC solely to upgrade or protect their power to control communal affairs (obviously, in many contexts and junctions, organization founders did operate with this concern); more accurately, the AJC provided, both in the minds of its makers and the minds of many other Jews in America, a forum for rationalized discussion about this issue of control and for minimizing the dangers and damages that contests about control had already caused or could cause in the future. Second, and no less obviously, the AJC was established as a means to streamline responses to the dire emergency faced by Russian Jewry in the hours of the organization's formation; and, along with this reflex dynamic, the organization was established out of the recognition that the topic of Russia and its Jews was not going to reach a happy ending anytime soon.

The establishment of the AJC is a topic of preeminent interest both in American ethnic history and in modern Jewish history; no individual's dealings with these two salient dynamics underlying its establishment, control, and Russian Jewry were nearly as sustained and articulately expressed as Louis Marshall's. The emergence of the AJC is a major item in his biography and in the rise of Jewish ethnicity in America.

The Founding of the American Jewish Committee

In summer 1905, Czar Nicholas II sent Sergius Witte, the president of the empire's Committee of Ministers, to Portsmouth, New Hampshire, to negotiate the end of the Russo-Japanese War. B'nai B'rith head Adolf Kraus initiated a discussion between Witte and a delegation of five American Jewish leaders. Of the five (Kraus, Jacob Schiff, Oscar Straus, Isaac Seligman, Adolph Lewisohn), Schiff was dominant, standing off with Witte about the future of the empire and its Jewish population. Nicholas's envoy urged the stewards to use their resources to encourage Russia's Jews away from revolutionary activity; Schiff, who had helped with Japan's war finances, militantly rebuffed this request, explaining that American Jewish stewards lacked any such power of influence. Besides, Schiff countered, it was natural that "young men became revolutionists in the hope that a republic will grant them just laws which are denied them under the rule of the Emperor."[90]

This was tough talk, and a positive impression of Schiff's principled advocacy of Jewish rights stayed long with Witte.[91] However, as far as Downtown Jews were concerned, the Jewish delegation at Portsmouth lacked a mandate to consort with the enemy. In the socialist *Forward,* Abraham Cahan opined that revolution, not traditional Jewish imploring *shtadlanut* diplomacy, would emancipate Russia's Jews. The *Maccabaean,* an American Zionist journal, complained that the delegation was unrepresentative. Even the *American Hebrew,* a conservative journal normally accommodating of Uptown perspectives, decried the renewal of "medieval practices" inherent in the delegation's self-appointed activity and the lack of a representative Jewish organization.[92]

For his part, Marshall felt left out. A gentleman's agreement among the elite Uptown discussion group, the Wanderers, precluded such a circumstance, in which some members acted on their initiative in diplomacy as though they represented the community as a whole, Marshall groused to Schechter.[93] He "question[ed] the wisdom" of the delegation's work, but ego concern probably muscled aside substantive critique in this complaint. Marshall repeatedly felt underappreciated in this period. Months later, immediately after the 250th celebration, he scolded Adolph Ochs when the *New York Times* mistakenly identified Marcus Marks, not

Marshall himself, as the moderator of the Carnegie Hall celebration who read aloud President Roosevelt's congratulatory letter. "I should have been very glad to have had the newspapers under Jewish ownership not withhold from me the honor," Marshall petulantly wrote.[94]

It did not help Marshall's mood in this December 1905 period when Stephen Wise outmaneuvered him in a much-publicized dispute concerning a rabbinical appointment at Temple Emanu-El.[95] As chairman of the Uptown congregation's board of trustees, Marshall in October invited Wise, a talented thirty-two-year-old rabbi who held the pulpit of Temple Beth Israel in Portland, Oregon, for a series of sermon auditions at Emanu-El. Recruiting Wise, it was believed, would reinforce Emanu-El's position at the forefront of Reform Judaism in America. Much to everyone's surprise, Wise found cause for objection in Emanu-El's recruitment-oriented, welcoming attitude. In employment negotiations, Marshall insisted on the principle that "the pulpit should always be subject to and under the control of the Board of Trustees"; Wise dramatically replied that "no self-respecting minister of religion" could possibly accept such a condition.

Whether this was a spontaneous clash or, on Wise's part, a deliberately planned challenge, Marshall's showdown with Wise highlighted the familiar issue of control of information circulating within, or about, New York's growing Jewish population. To be sure, the topic of trustee review of synagogue sermons had a long pedigree in American Jewish history,[96] so this Emanu-El showdown has roots and dimensions beyond the passions and concerns of New York Jewry in the era of the Russian pogroms and the AJC's formation. As the historian Mark Raider observes, Wise's commitment to the ideal of an independent pulpit, soon to be converted into a reality in the April 1907 founding services of the Free Synagogue, drew upon a mix of free pulpit speaking traditions and models in America. Wise's orientation blended spiritual belief and progressive politics; some examples influencing Wise were non-Jewish (Henry Ward Beecher, William Jennings Bryan), some Jewish (interestingly, before his confrontation at Emanu-El, Wise wrote enthusiastically to Marshall about Z. H. Masliansky's lectures at the Educational Alliance).[97] That is, the determinants and aspects of this Wise-Marshall clash at Emanu-El are by no means identical to the purposes and concerns that governed Marshall-directed experiments with information dissemination and control, such as the publication of the Yiddish newspaper, the *World*. Nonetheless, largely because it became such a highly publicized affair, the Emanu-El pulpit control dispute sharpened in many minds preexisting questions about the legitimacy of Uptown efforts to supervise or monitor public discourse in the Jewish community, and so the controversy can be regarded as one of the turnstiles leading to the formation of the AJC.

Even Marshall ended up saying that the Emanu-El debate was about politics, not theology. At first, he tried to soft-pedal Wise's challenge by relating to it as a point amenable to clarification in a business negotiation. On December 1, 1905, he sent a formal letter to Wise,[98] accounting for his explicit affirmation that the congregation's pulpit "should always be subject to and under the control of the Board of Trustees." Marshall appealed to correct administrative procedure, and legalistically defined the relationship between congregation and rabbi as a contract. It is fair to both the congregation and the rabbi that "both shall understand at the outset, the nature of the contract which exists between them," Marshall explained. The contractual term, Marshall promised Wise, "does not mean that the Board of Trustees will call upon any incumbent of our pulpit to sacrifice or surrender his principles." Wise disagreed in a very fundamental way. Even if a congregation's trustees reliably promised not to assault the rabbi's conscience, acquiescence to any formal insistence that control of the pulpit belonged to the trustees and not the minister was in itself a surrender of principles.

Back in Portland on January 5, Wise read to his congregation his December 3 response to Marshall's letter.[99] Control of the pulpit, Wise declared, is a "question of super-eminent importance." He spoke passionately for the ideal of pulpit freedom. "The chief office of the minister, I take it, is not to represent the views of the congregation, but to proclaim the truth as he sees it," Wise exclaimed. But how could the rabbi "be vital and independent and helpful if he be tethered and muzzled?"

The *New York Times* published Wise's call for a free pulpit on January 7, 1906. The next day, the newspaper quoted Marshall's dismissal of Wise's packaging of the affair as a debate about lofty principles.[100] "The inclination of Dr. Wise to discuss politics" was the reason Emanu-El had not offered him an appointment, alongside Rabbi Joseph Silverman, Marshall said, implying that the congregation had no principled fixation about pulpit control but instead objected to the highly politicized sermonizing characteristic of various Reform synagogues around the country. A few days later, Ochs, a member of Emanu-El, published an editorial accepting Wise's contention that a principle of pulpit control was at stake, while ratifying Marshall's position.[101] "The rabbi [Wise] speaks of 'my pulpit,' but primarily it is not his pulpit," opined the *Times*. Writing that ultimate authority rested with the trustees and contending that a synagogue service ought to be conducted in a spirit of rabbi-congregation unity, Ochs editorialized on this issue with rhythm and formulations characteristic of his friend Marshall's discussion of many aspects of Uptown-Downtown relations. "Religion, on the whole, is likely to be the most vital, to yield the ripest and richest fruit, where the preacher and the congregation are in harmony," concluded the *Times* editorial.

Wise was strong-willed and unpredictable; the late 1905 showdown at Emanu-El would prove to be just the first of several clashes between Marshall and Wise. However, despite the distinctiveness of Wise's personality, Uptown came away from this theatrical standoff at Emanu-El wanting exactly what it had been searching for in the implementation of various moral reform experiments: control and unity. The problem was that Marshall and his colleagues lacked a mechanism for calibrating the optimal integration of these two ends.

Exactly one day before the Emanu-El negotiations with Wise exploded over the issue of pulpit control, Marshall came into contact for the first time with a capable young rabbi, Judah Magnes, who would soon be appointed to the vacant spot at the prestigious 5th Avenue synagogue and also would later become Marshall's brother-in-law. Born in California in 1877, Magnes completed his Reform rabbinical training at the Hebrew Union College and received a doctoral degree in Heidelberg before taking a position as rabbi of Temple Israel in Brooklyn in 1904.[102] In late November 1905, as the spree of pogroms in Russia reached its dolorous peak, Magnes was collecting funds for Jewish self-defense efforts in the Pale. That these two energetic and articulate men, Marshall and Magnes, who developed a relationship of deep friendship and trust despite incredibly stressful moments of ideological disagreement, first came into contact due to mutual support of this Jewish Defense Fund attests to the militant mood of the moment. For better or worse, Magnes' career trajectory in years to come would follow the impassioned arrow of his pacifist belief, and for months after Kishinev, Marshall had been preaching about the imprudence of intervention in internal Russian affairs. However, by the end of 1905, it was obvious to both men that ideals and philosophies had to be subordinated, because Jews in Russia needed the means to fight to survive.

Marshall sent Magnes a $500 check for the Russian Defense Fund and clipped to it an emotional statement he knew the young Reform rabbi would publicize. Whatever doubts he had harbored about efforts to help overseas Jews defend themselves had "disappeared on reading the reports of the unspeakable outrages and the unprecedented murders of innocent men, women and children committed throughout the Pale of Settlement,"[103] Marshall declared. Media reports and private correspondence relating to the latest pogroms, he averred, indicated that "Jews who were armed were able to protect their lives and property." It therefore followed that "the Russian Jew, if afforded the means of self defense, will be able to protect himself." In a few weeks, at Rodeph Shalom, Marshall would claim that the Jew's successful experience with democratic citizenship in America was rooted in Asser Levy's manly insistence on bearing arms in New Amsterdam. This idea was incorporated in Marshall's testimony in favor of the Russian

Defense Fund. Speaking of the Jew in the Pale of Settlement, Marshall argued that "the possession of arms will develop the spirit which is essential to the ultimate working out of his destiny."

Loose ends in the mobilization of support for the pogrom victims and Jewish self-defense were manifest. Magnes was an unknown quantity (so much so that Marshall's check and letter were posted to the wrong Brooklyn address),[104] and many in Marshall's group were troubled by doubts about how exactly relief money for the Jewish Defense Fund could be disbursed under hostile conditions in czarist Russia. Marshall discussed this disbursement subject at length with Schiff; the banker was, for the time being, satisfied that Baron Gunzburg, a prominent Saint Petersburg Jew, could serve as a secure and effective conduit for the relief funds.[105] Still, Marshall and others were unsettled by this issue of administering overseas Jewish assistance in the absence of a properly organized mechanism, and a related problem was disorganization in the flow of basic information about the emergency from Russia to New York. "We have but a slight conception of the destitution which prevails, of the enormous loss of life and limb," Marshall noted to his cousin, Joseph Stolz. "I am sure that if the American Jews would fully appreciate the facts, they would make every sacrifice to aid their stricken brethren."[106] Marshall pressed Magnes for information about the relief disbursement and about the pogroms themselves.

In a whirlwind sequence of days, appreciation of Magnes's passion and capabilities rose rapidly, largely as a consequence of what one historian has described as the highlight of Magnes's long, idealistic (and sometimes controversial) career in Jewish service.[107] On December 4, the rabbi, not yet thirty, led 125,000 immigrant Jews up Broadway to 5th Avenue and Union Square, in a stirring protest against the pogroms. Two days later, just a week after he sent Magnes the relief check, Marshall invited the young rabbi to try out for the Emanu-El pulpit, and even offered Magnes some private tips as he prepared for the audition sermons.[108]

More than any other sphere, immigration piqued Marshall's concerns about Jewry's lack of organization. He thought it would be a grave tactical mistake were well-meaning Jewish individuals or groups to trumpet publicly a truth that was becoming silently obvious to America's Jews in this period of Russian travail: masses of harried immigrant Jews would be streaming toward New York in months to come. Marshall kept in contact with editors of the Downtown press, congratulating them when they urged their "readers to refrain from agitation on the subject of immigration."[109] President Roosevelt had indicated commitment to open immigration, and thus "wild harangues" and "useless agitation" on the subject would backfire, Marshall argued.[110]

Marshall's tactical calculations were genuine. He had a deep belief in the moral rectitude and the practical benefits of open immigration and was about to embark on a monumental twenty-year lobbying effort to protect the flow of immigrant Jews to America. Undeniably, however, this faith was alloyed by ego and power considerations. Unrelentingly, Marshall insisted that agitation for open immigration undertaken in most other sections of the Jewish community, by newspaper pundits, local community leaders, and other interested parties, was unhelpful, amateurish meddling. This position was patronizing but not outlandish. Immigration policy was the product of complicated legislative processes on Capitol Hill, and it made sense that a group of trained lawyers would in the early twentieth-century steward American Jewry's opposition to mounting restrictionist pressure.

If immigration lobbying was for lawyers, it was also a New York matter. In fact, immigration advocacy served as a convenient fulcrum for Marshall's Uptown Manhattan group to assert its primacy in national Jewish affairs. Marshall bristled angrily when he was apprised that B'nai B'rith and the Central Conference of American Rabbis were planning in Chicago a public discussion about immigration. Objecting to this plan, he reiterated the tactical advantage of staying mum about the obvious: "A public discussion of this question . . . would attract attention of Congress and various labor unions to the fact that we expect a large influx of Jewish immigrants from Russia."[111] In this moment when the formation in New York of a national Jewish organization was "in the air,"[112] Marshall pulled the immigration card partly for reasons of power politics. He kept emphasizing that New York Jews had the prerogative on immigration. It was "astonishing," Marshall wrote to a cousin in the Midwest, that the proposed convention "was called at Chicago without first conferring [with] the [New York] community which is most interested in the subject, and which has more at stake in it than the rest of the country put together."[113] The geography had organizational implications. Preparing for the establishment of what became the AJC, Marshall was matching muscles with B'nai B'rith; he was determined that this rival-to-be organization not take the lead on immigration, now the issue of supreme importance to Downtown's agitated Jews. Marshall's power calculations were transparent when he requested that his Midwest cousin, Rabbi Joseph Stolz, use his influence with Adolf Kraus, B'nai B'rith's new president, and with the Reform Central Conference of American Rabbis, to bring the Chicago immigration meeting to a screeching halt.[114]

Established in 1843 as the first secular Jewish organization in the United States, B'nai B'rith functioned in its first decades mostly as a social fraternity for immigrant Jews, but it had worked steadily on immigration issues since the

1890s. This work was facilitated by an interlocking structure agreement between B'nai B'rith and the Board of Delegates on Civil and Religious Rights, a branch of the Reform movement's Union of American Hebrew Congregations. Since B'nai B'rith maintained lodges around the country, the organization provided a logical apparatus for initiatives geared to relocating Jewish immigrants away from the congested ghetto neighborhoods of lower Manhattan to relatively unsettled western areas; reorganized a number of times over the years, this Industrial Removal Office initiative had placed 70,000 men and their families outside of New York by 1914.[115] In organizational terms, immigrant removal westward was far from a B'nai B'rith monopoly (in conjunction with Israel Zangwill's Jewish Territorial Organization, the ITO, Jacob Schiff poured considerable energy and resources into immigration settlement in Galveston, Texas[116]), and the organization's leaders showed authentic commitment to Jewish immigrant needs. In his short tenure as B'nai B'rith president, from 1899 until his death in 1904, Leo Levi developed the organization's work on social reform, and (it will be recalled) seemed to sense, with equanimity, that many, and perhaps most or all, of the czar's Jewish subjects would make their way toward the United States. However, on immigration issues, even a dedicated visionary like Levi faced two challenges. First, with lodges east and west (and also overseas), B'nai B'rith lacked a consolidated office at either of the nerve centers of immigration issues, New York and Washington. As a B'nai B'rith leader, Levi himself moved from Galveston to New York, but his successor, Adolf Kraus, was a Chicagoan. Second, with its roots in nonpolitical social activities, B'nai B'rith lacked experience on legislative matters; over the years, it had delegated legislative lobbying to its partners on the board of delegates.

Under this arrangement, during the last years of the nineteenth century authority for immigration lobbying devolved upon a Washington lawyer, Simon Wolf. A tireless advocate for American Jewish causes, Wolf worked hard on immigration issues until his death in his late eighties in 1923. Chiefly through a network of strong personal ties in the Washington bureaucracy, Wolf's labors yielded impressive (and oft overlooked) results. According to his biographer's eye-popping estimate, Wolf's interventions saved over 100,000 Jewish immigrants from deportation.[117] Yet when Nativist pressures mounted on Capitol Hill in years before World War I, Wolf was not a young man, and he seemed increasingly out of touch with developing twentieth-century legislative processes. As the years went by, his reliance on personal contacts and on the fundamental good-heartedness of key players in Washington's bureaucracy seemed naïve and nonprofessional; tacitly, Wolf acknowledged his own weaknesses by delegating increasing responsibility to his board of delegates' younger associate, Max Kohler, whose work habits and legal orientation were far more compatible with Louis Marshall's group.

At the time of the AJC's formation, Jewish advocacy for open immigration split apart as a contrast between professional, lawyerly constitutionalism and neotraditional Jewish personal *shtadlanut* diplomatic intercession. In Marshall's group, immigration demands were grounded almost exclusively on legal interpretation and precedent; these Jewish advocates were apt to accuse Nativist activist and federal officials of misapplying statutes. Avoiding any hint of antagonism in Washington, Wolf disliked legalistic wrangling and pitched his appeals straight to the hearts of the bureaucrats, relying, as his biographer puts it, "in an old fashioned way . . . on the good faith of the bureaucrat he had to placate."[118] Moreover, Wolf's career was punctuated by political swerving or turnabouts for which critics accused him of sycophantic opportunism. Such accusations were probably unfair, but toward the end of his life, when crucial battles about immigration were fought, Wolf lacked the stamina to repair any temporary miscues. As in the example of his endorsement of a temporary halt to immigration after World War I,[119] Wolf's advocacy in this late period was flawed by tactical retreats and miscalculations, but well before his aged weariness made his weaknesses painfully evident, Marshall and fellow AJC claimants to the mantle of American Jewish leadership considered Wolf a hindrance and a nuisance.

The establishment of America's first ethnoreligious self-defense organization was a Louis Marshall production, first and last. He managed the AJC's constituent meetings, articulated the organization's purposes, and led a significant, albeit exasperatingly irresoluble, discussion about the extent to which it could, or should, be democratically representative.

In the final days of 1905, Marshall conferred with Magnes and persuaded him to forego plans to hold a mass meeting on the Russian question. Marshall argued that it was time to convene a meeting of Jewish leaders "who have for some time past" dealt with sociopolitical issues of Jewish concern; he suggested that the initiative for a national organization come from Uptown elite Jews, and Magnes assented in a "manly" and "excellent" fashion.[120] Reiterating that "there is in the air a general desire for the formation of some central organization," Marshall contacted B'nai B'rith's Kraus, and unfurled his plan of "quietly" inviting twenty to twenty-five prominent American Jews from around the country to decide about the practicability of establishing such a central organization, "whether it be called a Congress or a Committee."[121] Acutely aware of a longstanding communal habit of denying that Jews in America constituted a separate and distinctive ethnonational interest, Marshall counseled crossing the Rubicon with caution. "There are serious perils incident to any organization, especially if it is based on an erroneous theory," Marshall explained to Kraus.[122]

The Uptown elite regarded the organization plan as a dangerous but necessary evil. Troubled by the prospect that any national Jewish organization would provoke "state within a state" loyalty suspicions, the Wanderers group worriedly debated about the pros and cons of forming a new organization; by the end of 1905, the Uptowners decided they had no choice. "Inasmuch as such an organization was in the air, and would undoubtedly be formed by somebody," Marshall explained to Cyrus Adler, the Wanderers decided that "we should take the initiative . . . in order to avoid mischief."[123] Marshall moved quickly to co-opt Magnes. He brought the charismatic young rabbi "into our camp" to guarantee that Downtown would not organize an organization on its own terms (this was amicable co-optation—"the more I see of Magnes, the more I like him," Marshall told a friend in this period[124]). Were its purposes and name to be designated Downtown, the new Jewish organization would likely sound too politically sovereign and national in character, Marshall and his peers believed. Marshall was struggling to find an organizational formula that would not contradict Uptown's long-standing contention that Jews were Americans with no separate political interests of their own. "According to my notion," he wrote to Adler, "it would be most dangerous if we organized on any basis other than that of a religious body."[125]

Marshall talked about religion as the basis of Jewish organization in the United States, but when invitations were sent for what became the constituent meeting of the AJC, the summons appealed to a somewhat different motivational rationale, not religious faith but rather an international sense of Jewish solidarity. The invitation's wording elucidates how Kishinev and the subsequent pogroms prompted this ground-breaking meeting; the phrasing identifies support for overseas Jews, particularly in Russia, as the main purpose of the new organization. "The horrors attending the recent Russian massacres, and the necessity of extending to our brethren a helping hand," warrant the establishment of a nationwide organization, the invitation declared, and the organization would operate so long as Jews were persecuted in Russia and elsewhere ("so long as the objects of our solicitude are subjected to disabilities and persecution, owing to their religious belief").[126]

In his private correspondence, Marshall explicated the new organization's rationale as a search for order.[127] Magnes and two or three other rabbis were proposing the establishment of new organizations, Kraus was insisting that B'nai B'rith affords a panacea for all ills, and the East Side brimmed with organizations, "each national in scope and zero in achievement." "What I am trying to accomplish is to get order out of chaos," Marshall insisted. "More than anything else," the new organization must not appear political, lest it encourage people to believe that the Jews "have interests different from those of other U.S. citizens," he added. Refining his original ideas about religion as the best organizational principle, Marshall conceded that to unite as a religious body implied the adoption of ecclesiastical powers. He played the religion card in another sense: the new organization would assist Jews who "are suffering from discrimination in any part of the world on account of their religious beliefs." The initiative was coming from Uptown, but Marshall was resolute about the new organization's democratic character. "We must, in some way or other, go back to the people and organize on the theory of democracy," he declared to a cousin.[128]

Marshall opened the constituent conference, held on February 3–4, 1906, by submitting a resolution for the formation of a general organization of US Jews, for the purpose of "dealing with problems as affect them as a religious body, and their brethren who suffer from persecution throughout the world."[129] Refusing to chair the meeting, Kraus announced that B'nai B'rith would not be obliged by its decision. Simon Wolf averred that for forty-five years "he had spoken on behalf of oppressed Jews," handling advocacy without any need for a national organization. Magnes candidly cited Downtown skepticism about self-appointed court Jews. Instead of private individuals wielding their personal influence to accomplish communal purposes, delegates on a new organization must have a popular mandate, he affirmed; if nothing else, the new organization would coordinate work with counterpart, Europe-based institutions such as the Hillsverein and the Alliance Israelite Universelle. Schiff simultaneously favored a new organization and feared its implications. He vowed that he would "strenuously oppose the idea of a Jewish Congress as un-American and likely to give rise to a Jewish question." Not surprisingly, on the first day the discussions fizzled as an inconclusive swell of rhetoric, anxiety, and ego.

Marshall appeared to be the only delegate with a detailed plan.[130] The second day opened with his proposal for a representative body drawn mostly from the country's synagogue congregations. In his mind, this congregational formula seemed acceptably American: it sounded nonpolitical and broadly evoked patterns of democratic association in the days of the colonies. "To recognize the Jews on the standpoint of race," not religion, would be "inconsistent with the American conception of government," Marshall explained. The method of selecting delegates from the synagogue congregations had to be democratic; he decried "muzzling anyone" and affirmed that the "proposed committee should be as widely representative as possible."

Many delegates at this constituent meeting had not quite gotten their minds wrapped warmly around the idea of a national Jewish organization of any sort; yet Marshall was racing ahead, saturating this unprecedented conference with details about a fully democratic body. Tipping his hand too early, he recited the proposed details. Any state with a Jewish population of at least 10,000 would be entitled to at least one representative and would be allotted one delegate for each additional 10,000 Jews; to guarantee that New York not dominate the new organization, Marshall proposed that no state be entitled to more than 40 percent of the aggregate delegates.

Just a few years before, Marshall had managed Jewish exercises in noblesse oblige in which benevolent Americanization intentions mingled sometimes with a peremptory paternalism. In some heavy-handed instances, as with the *World*, his Uptown orientation appeared as a form of Jewish colonialism—the Russian Jews were virtually immigrant savages who had to be molded into an American shape by all means available, other than coercive violence. Now he was talking about the democratic election of a coast-to-coast Jewish organization. The minutes of this dramatic conference clearly depict stunned hearers gasping for breath.

The ensuing exchange needs to be set in perspective. The debate over democracy in American Jewish life, notes sociologist Jonathan Woocher, has a "long and honorable history," owing to the community's "voluntary and pluralistic" character.[131] This AJC constituent meeting looms as a crucial signpost in that history. Marshall was telling a gathering of distinguished bankers and jurists and clerics that Jews really could form a democratic, nation-based, organization. Participants responded as though that premise had been, and probably remained, unthinkable.

After Marshall submitted his plan, Cyrus Sulzberger broke the silence by forming an impromptu committee of five (himself, Adler, Kraus, Julian Mack, and J. J. Leucht) to mull the proposal in a separate room.[132] Oscar Straus, former US ambassador to the Ottoman Empire and soon to become America's first Jewish cabinet member (as secretary of commerce and labor in the Roosevelt administration) interjected and demanded that this ad hoc committee of five also contemplate an alternative, elitist organizational body. In terms of representation, Straus explained, the important fact was "not numbers but ability." He proposed that the meeting participants themselves appoint fifteen members to serve as a new organization (as an "Executive Committee"), "to promote the welfare of Jews in general, and aid in securing their civil and religious rights in all countries where these are denied." Sulzberger's committee returned from its consultation recommending the Straus plan.

Enraged, Marshall preached the Downtown gospel to his elite peers. This 1906 philippic stands out ironically in his career, because Marshall accused his Uptown associates of precisely the same wrongs that would be affixed rhetorically to him a decade later, when New York's Downtown insurgents and the Brandeis

Zionists campaigned for an American Jewish Congress. In this 1906 debate, Marshall excoriated the Sulzberger five for its "doubly self-elective" procedure. "The present conference has no mandate to appoint such a representative body, which would undoubtedly be rejected by the Jews of America," he exclaimed. Marshall envisioned the new organization as a means to unify Uptown and Downtown Jews via a cooperative, trusting approach. He was working hard to wiggle out of the paternalist suit. "Confidence should be shown in the men who we are trying to aid," he declared. The precise democratization details were not important. If it were too cumbrous to elect delegates on a state-by-state basis, then elections could be held in the country's nine judicial districts. The crux was to stage "popular elections."

Marshall had few vocal backers in this debate, but one supporter had disproportionate influence. In an arresting display of realism and adaptability, Schiff noted that "a new Jewry had arisen in the U.S. since 1881." No new organization would be workable and effective if it lacked the confidence of the Russian Jews. Since the committee of five's proposal would lack credibility in the eyes of these new American Jews, Schiff endorsed Marshall's plan. Others roundly opposed it. Straus delivered an Aesopian civics lesson, claiming that "the idea of representation by organization was not American." There are "two systems of representation customary among Americans," he explained, "the democratic and gravitational"; under the latter system, the "general weight and authority of individuals" counted as a form of representation. The present case was fit for the gravitational mode.[133] Emil Hirsch, a Reform rabbi from Chicago's Sinai Congregation known for his commitment to liberal and progressive social and political causes, supported Straus's proposal. Marshall's scheme of representative assemblies, Hirsch objected, "would involve much unnecessary trouble." Past experience with congregational-based elections, as in the example of the Reform movement's Union of American Hebrew Congregations, were not encouraging, Hirsch said. "Communal work was done by a small number of real workers," he added. "This was the age of experts."[134]

The meeting vote gave a small, but decisive, victory to Straus's elitist plan, by a tally of 16 to 13. Since this was a relatively close result, Schiff had some leverage to pressure Cyrus Sulzberger; the latter consented to refer the issue of the organization's establishment to another committee, for consultation prior to a follow-up conference in the spring. This, however, was a pro forma concession, since Marshall's democratization plan had lost its momentum. During months of recess before the next conference, the delegates would have too much time to think of all the reasons why democratic elections would be impracticable and fraught with danger.

Somewhat naively, Marshall fine-tuned and promoted his plan through the spring. He consulted regularly with Magnes, inviting the perceptive young rabbi to "exercise the greatest freedom" in revising and critiquing Marshall's democratization plan.[135] In formal compliance with the February 4 conference resolutions, Marshall conferred with a special committee on March 18 to draft a formal proposal.[136] His scheme divided the United States into nine districts and returned to the one delegate per 10,000 residents plan, with the cap of 40 percent placed on the second district, which included New York State. He sent cajoling letters to Uptown peers who seemed particularly resistant to democratization plans. Under his plan, he explained to Cyrus Adler, "No Jew who wishes to affiliate with us is prevented from doing so." Though it appeared "somewhat complicated on paper," his proposed "machinery for election" was, "in reality, very simple."[137]

Scheduled for May 19, 1906, preparation for the second constituent conference was marred by reports of a B'nai B'rith walk-out. Marshall fired off a letter to Simon Wolf, Adolf Kraus, and Emil Hirsch, urging realism.[138] A new national organization was being formed; it was useless for B'nai B'rith to try to flee from the inevitable. "The only problem still requiring solution," Marshall wrote, was "that of representation." Privately, Marshall grumpily identified the B'nai B'rith challenge as petty partisanship. Kraus and Wolf were simply trying to "emphasize that their weak and moribund secret order represents the Jewish people."[139]

The B'nai B'rith boycott held. "We know the temper of our communities," lay leaders from B'nai B'rith, along with Reform notables such as Hirsch, dourly informed Mayer Sulzberger, "and experience teaches us that [Marshall's proposal] will not work in practice."[140] Conservative, prudent figures in each community would be "crowded to the rear," they claimed, and so the new national organization would, under the democratization proposal, "fall into the hands of radical theorists whose vagaries will then be accepted by the American nation as expressive of the views and intentions of the whole Jewish community."

After this protest letter was read at the May constituent conference, Marshall rose in rebuttal, concentrating on B'nai B'rith's barb that his plan "smacked of ecclesiastical pretensions."[141] "We are American citizens, and Jews out of religious convictions," Marshall declared. "The simple and easy thing to do is to come right out without colors and say we are Jews." American Jews could rightfully organize to promote their religion in the same way that "our other fellow citizens and denominations are able to promote their religions." The religious rationale of the plan defused loyalty tensions, Marshall explained. His scheme "would not call into being an 'empire within an empire' any more than have Methodist or Episcopalian organizations."

More than anyone else, Straus nullified Marshall's chances. If adopted, Straus warned, Marshall's plan "will achieve the opposite of what is contemplated—our object will be defeated." Marshall pressed for a vote on his proposal, only to be defeated by a tally of eight to four. He was not overly gracious in defeat. "Every Jew must have the right to vote" for the new organization, he insisted. Were it not based on "democratic representation," he warned, the new committee would not "command respect."

Everything about the founding of America's first ethnic self-defense organization resulted from the relentless energy and pressing circumstances of the Russian Jews, from the incredible ferment of political ideology and creative expression

3. Portrait of Marshall. Courtesy of Peter Schweitzer.

that emanated from the crowded immigrant neighborhoods of New York's East Side and from the Downtown immigrants' unyielding demands for the rescue of their friends and family relations in Russia's torturous Pale of Settlement. Years of managing moral reform projects with Downtown Jews in areas of media, education, and religion left little doubt in Marshall's mind about the orientation of Jewish advocacy in America. The main constituency in that advocacy had to be the masses of Russian Jews. Marshall's Uptown allies, however, formed the AJC in a state of denial about what seems, in retrospect, to have been an elementary demographic and cultural truth.

Mayer Sulzberger, a highly regarded judge of the Court of Common Pleas in Philadelphia,[142] who chaired this series of constituent conferences, ended them with a plea for harmony. He lightly criticized members of his own group by referring to their "assumed superiority" as settled, prospering Jews. At the same time, Sulzberger's summation struck familiar chords of denial. Demographics had no necessary relation to ethnic politics, the Philadelphia judge opined. "The suggestion that mere numbers can give rise to statesmen-like advice in matters affecting the Jewish people is unthinkable," Sulzberger stated. "The arrogant assumption of the so-called East Siders that mere numbers give wisdom ought to be treated as nil," he declared.[143] The lower Manhattan neighborhoods ought not to dominate American Jewish life, Sulzberger explained. "There is a Jewry in the South and the West," he pointed out. The opinions and interests of Jews in these regions "are as important as the somewhat extravagant desires of those who live in the congested quarters" of New York.[144]

The AJC's establishment provoked strong, passing emotions not wholly representative of its founders' deepest beliefs. Pushed into a corner, a steward like Judge Sulzberger intemperately expressed legitimate views.[145] Hailing from Philadelphia, Sulzberger was understandably proud of his own community's substantive contributions to American Jewish society and culture; with Cyrus Adler and a few others (most of them Orthodox Jews), Sulzberger belonged to what scholars have identified as a "Philadelphia group" whose high position in American Jewish life was reflected by the premier positions men like Sulzberger and Adler assumed during the AJC's first years.[146]

During these AJC constituent meetings, Sulzberger was not the only man of experience and wisdom to exhibit anxious befuddlement about the way Jewish circumstances in New York City were impinging on the community as a whole. The formation of a national Jewish organization to handle sociopolitical issues constituted a sea change in American Jewish affairs and had unsettling implications; and the non-New Yorkers involved in the AJC's founding seemed particularly apt to display an array of negative responses, from boycott to resentment.

By and large, these were passing responses and did not reflect indifference to the well-being of Russian Jews in America and the Pale. Men like Sulzberger maintained deep loyalties to their Uptown New York associates and thus heeded the AJC's founding resolutions, even when they had objections of some sort to them. Sulzberger himself served for six distinguished years as the AJC's first president, until Marshall replaced him in 1912.

This quality of Uptown loyalty applied also to Marshall, who had adamantly opposed the AJC's decision in favor of self-appointed representation (in the end, the May 19 meeting adopted Cyrus Adler's formula, by which a self-appointed AJC Executive Committee of fifteen members could eventually increase to fifty, for the purpose of cooperating with various Jewish organizations around the country[147]). Within a few days, Marshall regained his composure, and his communications with Downtown spokesmen conveyed both candor and Uptown discipline. "Much good has been accomplished," he told one Yiddish newspaper editor. Marshall conceded that the AJC's "plan of organization involves defects and is illogical" but contended that "it is the best that could be accomplished under existing conditions."[148]

For months Marshall believed that the reservations of his Uptown associates about democratic representation would ease once the AJC began its work. "It is our design to ultimately make the movement democratic in every sense of the word," he told a banker from St. Louis in early 1907.[149] However, as years passed in the interval before World War I, Marshall abandoned such musings about preferred methods of choosing AJC representatives. He was too busily engaged with the determination of the AJC's action agenda to persist with his thoughts about the necessity of its democratization. By the time the AJC's self-appointed character became a dominant topic in American Jewish affairs, during the WWI debate about the formation of an American Jewish Congress, Marshall's outlook had altered.

The Start of the Immigration Battle

The first item of business on the AJC agenda was immigration. Just three days after the AJC's decisive May 19 constituent conference, William Dillingham, a Republican senator from Vermont, introduced a restrictive immigration bill. His proposal essentially adjusted existing immigrant policies for the purpose of narrowing the influx of newcomers, whose total in the preceding twelve months of 1,100,735 represented a significant immigrant increase of 106,598 over the preceding year.[150] The Dillingham bill recommended raising the immigrant head tax from $2 to $5, adding new varieties of physical and mental disqualification of potential immigrants and stiffening penalties against steamship companies that transported ineligible immigrants.[151] None of these toughened adjustments of existing immigration procedures would have necessitated strategic rethinking of Jewish lobbying approaches on immigration matters that had been deployed prior to the AJC's formation. The new twist was applied by Senator Furnifold M. Simmons, a Democrat from North Carolina, who proposed excluding all would-be immigrant adult males who could not read or write in some language.[152]

This development was a turning point in America's never-ending debate about immigration. "From 1906, when the literacy test reappeared in Congress to the beginning of American involvement in the First World War, the jaunty self-assurance with which America as a whole had greeted the twentieth century was slowly deteriorating. Xenophobia was steadily on the rise," wrote John Higham in his authoritative study on American Nativism, *Strangers in the Land*.[153]

Although Higham identified the 1906 pro-restriction moves in Congress as the start of a new era, he stressed that the new Nativism did not appear with the sudden explosive force of a "second Haymarket riot," but was rather rooted in late nineteenth-century trends. In fact, proposals for literacy test restrictions on immigration had circulated in America's political arena since 1888, when an economics professor, Edward Bemis, first advocated them in the *Andover Review*.[154] Without developing pseudoracist theories, Bemis appealed to prevailing beliefs and popular opinion as he surveyed a long list of immigration issues and problems. "Every one knows that it is our foreign born who indulge in most of the mob violence in time of strikes and industrial depressions," he declared. His major grievance was economic. "A large portion of those now coming to our shores lower the standard of living and wages," Bemis claimed. He advocated the "perfectly practical and exceedingly simple" plan of not admitting to the United States any man over sixteen who could not read and write in his own language. Bemis conceded that literacy is not an exact indicator of capacity for good citizenship, but he argued that the best way of protecting rising standards of living would be to welcome only educated immigrants to the country.[155]

In less than a decade Bemis's proposal seemed so "perfectly practical" that Congress inserted a literacy test provision (mandating an ability to read forty words in any language) in an immigration bill; President Grover Cleveland vetoed the bill in 1897. The literacy test's most dedicated congressional champion in the 1890s was Senator Henry Cabot Lodge, a conservative Republican from Massachusetts. By the time Simmons incorporated the idea in the spring 1906 Dillingham Bill, the literacy test provision posed a substantive threat to immigration, particularly to persons from Southern and Eastern Europe. Between 1899 and 1910 over half (53 percent) of southern Italian immigrants were illiterate, and over a quarter of Jewish immigrants aged fourteen and older were illiterate; literacy figures among English (1 percent), German (5 percent) and other central and Western Europeans in this period were strikingly lower.[156] By 1906, such figures were cited by restrictionists as evidence of racial differences between groups of immigrants; advocates of literacy tests believed they would hold at bay persons of inferior capabilities.

In 1906, Frank Sargent, the country's commissioner-general of immigration, recommended literacy tests, while expounding upon qualitative differences in the immigration of English, Irish, Scandinavian, and German immigrants in earlier days of the Republic and the contemporaneous arrival of "aliens belonging to distinctly different stocks."[157] The "statistics of recent years" on immigration "point unmistakably to the conclusion that we, as a race, are endeavoring to assimilate a large mass of almost if not quite unassimilable material," America's immigration commissioner opined, referring to newcomers from Southern and Eastern Europe. In academia, sociologists such as Edward Ross and economists such as Bemis and John Commons concurred with the commissioner's premises and conclusions.

Motivated by economic considerations, rather than racial theory, organized labor started in the late nineteenth century to lobby for restrictive literacy tests. Some labor leaders, most notably the American Federation of Labor's Samuel Gompers, were themselves immigrants, but the union rank and file regarded immigrants as potential rivals who would work for lower wages and as strike breakers. The 1893 economic slump heightened labor's opposition to mass immigration.[158] In the same period, subgroups in America's socioeconomic elite also mobilized for literacy tests and immigrant restriction. Their most important potent expression was the Immigration Restriction League, an organization founded in 1894 by blue-blooded sons of venerable Anglo-Saxon New England families. As the years passed, the league gained highly influential supporters, including Theodore Roosevelt, Lodge, Harvard University president Abbott Lawrence Lowell, and Stanford University president David Starr Jordan; the most active figures promoting the league's activities were Prescott Hall and Robert DeCourcy Ward.[159] The league kept Charles Edgerton, formerly of the US Industrial Commission, as an official delegate in Washington; he networked among labor unions and urged support for literacy tests as early as 1902.[160] High-ranking supporters of the league lobbied for these tests and other restrictive measures—Henry Cabot Lodge, who pledged full support to the league, advocated literacy tests in 1902, 1903, and 1904.[161]

The Immigration Restriction League's elite membership list seems overpoweringly imposing when compared to its ostensible counterpart, the National

Liberal Immigration League (NLIL). Founded in 1904, the NLIL won some powerful backers (Woodrow Wilson, Andrew Carnegie), mostly among academics, politicians, and manufacturers who had a motivational mix of altruistic and business reasons compelling their support of open immigration. Its ineffectual activities focused mostly on the issuance of antirestriction bulletins and the maintenance of loose ties with ethnic organizations. The NLIL was established by Nissim Behar, a French Jew who served as the US representative of the Alliance Israelite Universelle.[162] Behar was utterly unable to establish productive working ties with the American Jewish leadership. For instance, several years before the establishment of the AJC, he coaxed Marshall into formally joining the Educational Alliance's New York branch. Marshall fumed that Behar was a "very insinuating gentleman" who sponsored activities that were pointless "vocal exercises."[163] Unimpressed with Behar's organizational capabilities, Marshall in 1905 pointedly severed connections with him.[164] In the decade before World War I, the NLIL limped along with financial ailments; in 1914, Gompers delivered a mortal blow, depicting the pro-immigration umbrella organization as a front for business interests.

Restrictionists mobilized in early twentieth-century America to protect a threatened way of life. Furnifold Simmons, the congressional patron of the 1906 literacy test proposal, was not trying to elevate America's educational and cultural levels. He freely admitted that educational achievement was not the factor distinguishing his Southern constituents from immigrants he wanted to keep away. As he put it during the 1906 Senate discussions, "without being educated, without school advantages," his Southern voters embodied a traditional democratic order and naturally exercised the "privileges of citizenship in a country where the people govern."[165]

The restrictionists in Congress were not specially focused on Russian Jewish immigrants, but their maneuvers drew upon decades of stereotypical thinking about Jews. In the Brahmin circles that gave rise to the Immigration Restriction League, the arrival of masses of Russian Jews in the 1880s "provoked interest, comment and judgment."[166] Some New Englanders argued that US policy of admitting the Russian Jews wrongly encouraged "the despotic practices of European countries by receiving their worst classes."[167] The 1890s bequeathed a legacy of precedents useful to anti-Jewish restrictionists; in that decade, influential American officials favored measures to reduce the inflow of the East European Jews. One, Andrew D. White, American minister to Russia, suggested that the admission of East European Jews should be regulated. William Ripley, a professor of economics at MIT in the last years of the nineteenth century, conjured dark imagery of Jewish newcomers as a menace. His manner of conjuring gruesome imagery in the depiction of the Jewish immigrant implied that to merely regulate their inflow might not be enough. Like Germany, Ripley claimed, the United States had a problem: a "great Polish swamp of miserable human beings, terrific in its proportions, threatens to drain itself off into our country as well."[168]

In Congress, different regions of the country converged in favor of restriction measures. Lawmakers from the western states, particularly California, stridently sought to place curbs on immigrants from Asia, just as congressional counterparts from elsewhere in the country found cause to seek restrictions on immigrants from Southern and Eastern Europe. The Capitol Hill restrictionists had a powerful, if somewhat unsteady, ally in the White House. By 1906, President Roosevelt had advocated literacy test restrictions for five years. In his 1901 State of the Union address, the president recommended the tests for an array of reasons, referring darkly to ways "ignorance, malignant passion and hatred" in urban immigrant neighborhoods sometimes engendered "anarchist sentiment." In this speech, Roosevelt reiterated the same economic arguments that had motivated the country's original advocate of literacy tests, Bemis. Massive immigration, declared the president, led to "a lowering of the standard of living and of the standard of wages."[169]

On May 23, 1906, immediately after the Senate incorporated the literacy test in the Dillingham Bill, President Roosevelt launched a determined pro-restriction lobbying effort, concentrating his efforts on Speaker of the House Joseph Cannon, the Illinois Republican of preeminent authority on Capitol Hill. Once again, Roosevelt rehearsed the argument favoring immigration restriction as a means to protect America's standard of living. Literacy standards also promised higher quality immigrants, Roosevelt told the House Speaker. "I want to see immigrants of such a character that we need not be afraid of their grandchildren intermingling with ours as their political, social and industrial equals," declared the president.[170]

In years prior to the AJC's establishment, it will be recalled, projects such as the Galveston Plan and the Industrial Removal Office (IRO) sponsored by B'nai B'rith leaders, Jacob Schiff, and others commingled on some levels with Nativist rhetoric. By redirecting incoming Jews away from New York City, the actions of these Jewish leaders could be taken as acknowledgment that there was something potentially or actually intolerable about the congested East End ghetto. From the Jewish standpoint, Nativists' condoning attitudes toward a project like the IRO could be taken as recognition that immigration itself was not a problem: what needed to be done was to administer its results with an eye on the avoidance of perceived fin de siècle blights, such as urban crowding. This dialogue between pro-immigration advocates, Jewish or non-Jewish, and the Nativists was obviously not a joyful one, but it was a discussion of sorts and even conducive to the betterment of thousands of Jewish and non-Jewish lives. That discussion came to a shrieking halt in the new 1906 era. The turning point in the immigration climate identified by Higham is symbolized by a pamphlet produced in 1905 by Richard M. Bradley, under Immigration Restriction League auspices. Objecting to Russian and Polish Jews being redirected away from New York's lower East Side to other parts of America, Bradley called his publication "Spreading the Slums."[171]

Distracted by the AJC constituent discussions, Marshall lacked experience in immigration legislation and failed to recognize the threat posed by the literacy provision. The vibrancy of Downtown's Yiddish culture misled Marshall and the other stewards, who assumed that immigrants belonging to the People of the Book knew how to read and write. Their estimates of the number of Jewish immigrants who would be adversely affected by a literacy test were tellingly inaccurate: Cyrus Adler, assistant secretary of the Smithsonian Institute and the member of the Uptown group who was most acutely concerned about the literacy test, guessed that the entry of about 10 percent of the East European immigrants might be disqualified under the provision (the actual figure was 26 percent).[172] More than the other Uptown figures, Oscar Straus, the former diplomat from the family that owned Macy's department stores, had close ties with President Roosevelt, so he took responsibility for lobbying in the White House. His approaches were ineffectual and derailed by discussions of whether former president Cleveland had second thoughts about his 1897 decision to veto the literacy test. With mid-term elections still months away, Roosevelt appeared unconcerned about alienating Jewish or other ethnoreligious groups that favored open immigration; the president was holding strong for the test and trying to sway the House Speaker in favor of restrictions.

This was a precarious moment and momentary disorganization in the American Jewish leadership could have proven costly. The Roosevelt White House stands out in this early twentieth-century period as the administration most favorably disposed toward economic, social, and pseudoracial arguments in favor of immigration restriction (Presidents Wilson and Taft vetoed restrictive immigration bills). Anti-Japanese sentiment in California was a harsh gaping fold on the political landscape into which broadly restrictive measures might have been tucked. Had a literacy test been signed into law in 1906, the ensuing history of immigration policy would have been far more detrimental to worldwide Jewish interests.

As it turned out, the literacy test provision was staved off by Uncle Joe Cannon, who exercised his monumental influence in Congress to lower the head tax on immigrants and to reject the literacy test. This was a major triumph for

Jewish interests, but the only discernible contribution made by any Jewish player in the drama was Republican Congressman Lucius Littauer (a friend of Cannon's), who drafted a proposal to grant Russian Jewish immigrants an exemption from possible deportation due to their likelihood of becoming unemployed, destitute "public charges," since they were refugees in flight from religious or political persecution.[173] This suggestion had insignificant practical impact on the June 1906 legislative process, but Littauer's idea of conferring exemption to Jews from restrictive provisions on the grounds of religious persecution would subsequently figure prominently in Marshall's lobbying work on immigration. In the end, no restriction precedents disastrous to Jewish interests were set in May and June 1906 because Joe Cannon decided to defy President Roosevelt's predilections on this issue, as the strong-willed Speaker of the House did on many other matters. Six years later he justified his stance with tobacco-chewing pith, lauding open immigration as a "hell of a success" for the United States.[174]

Soon enough, the Jewish advocates had immigration worries of their own to chew on. After the autumn elections, Roosevelt pushed hard on the Fifty-ninth Congress for restrictive legislation, though he refrained from explicitly espousing a literacy test. With the AJC fully constituted, Marshall began two decades of Olympian lobbying for open immigration in early 1907.

In late January, he contacted Democratic Congressman (and future New York Yankees owner) Colonel Jacob Ruppert, imploring him to keep a new restrictive immigration bill frozen in committee conference.[175] Literacy tests, Marshall contended, were "un-American." Experience showed that subversive anarchist and radical immigrants were highly educated, not illiterate. Particularly objectionable were Nativist proposals to exclude physically ailing immigrants on grounds of "low vitality." That provision would allow immigration inspectors to arbitrarily close doors on worthy asylum seekers who, as a result of inhumane persecution in Russia and other tyrannical lands, "simply appeared not to be in the best condition."

"I understand that the President is very anxious that there shall be legislation on this subject [immigration]," Marshall wrote to associates in early February. Believing that Roosevelt remained a true "friend of the oppressed," Marshall stretched and concluded diplomatically that the Republican president would someday come to regret his policies in this immigration sphere.[176]

Marshall centered his objections to the restrictionist proposals on three issues: (1) the low vitality clause imposed an un-American vicious circle (persecuted people sought a haven in democracy because they had grown physically weary under tyranny); (2) clauses that envisioned the deployment of inspectors overseas as unsupervised immigration "czars" were untenable; and (3) the fallibility of literacy tests. Marshall's argumentation on the third topic, literacy, warrants comment because of its highly personalized character. Though the AJC group was at this juncture developing a honed, professional lobbying method to supplant the old, *shtadlan* personal touch approach favored by Simon Wolf, this did not mean that Marshall's work was devoid of emotion. "I know something about the immigrant," he revealed to Vermont governor Carrol S. Page.[177] Both his parents were immigrants who turned into worthy American citizens. "The entire wealth of my father when he landed was a five franc piece," Marshall recounted. "I am sure that he would not have been able to read fluently the Constitution of the United States in German, and that he would not have understood it." From the start, Marshall was a deeply engaged immigration lobbyist. The combination of his imposing expertise in constitutional law and his personal background rendered him a powerful advocate in this context.

Marshall wrote at length to Governor Page in the hope that the Vermont politician would relay his concerns to his Green Mountain State colleague, Senator Dillingham. Quickly, Dillingham circulated a carefully formulated response to members of the AJC elite (Schiff, Adler, Bijur, and Mayer Sulzberger).[178] He pointed out that the immigration bills he himself sponsored did not have literacy test provisions; these were tacked on by colleagues on the Hill. "Personally I am of the opinion that no good would come from the reading and writing test," Dillingham pled. He differed with Marshall about the low-vitality clause. "Experience has shown that a clause of this kind is absolutely essential to prevent the hospitals and asylums of New York from becoming the dumping place for European subjects," Dillingham explained. He submitted that Marshall's strictures about inspector czars overseas were overblown. The overseas inspection procedure had been proposed only in the House, and it could conceivably apply to no more than half of the European countries, since many states withheld such port-of-departure inspection privileges. Overall, Dillingham observed, immigration was a function of "natural conditions" of economic prosperity or slumps. Numbers of newcomers fluctuated in line with these conditions; the legislative branch's task was "only to insist that those admitted shall be sound physically, mentally and morally."

Careful not to provide Dillingham reason to dig in his heels, Marshall praised the senator's "thoughtful and patriotic" reflections and affirmed that no opponent of restrictive legislation "has the slightest desire to facilitate the immigration of mental or physical incompetents, or criminals or paupers."[179] Yet the AJC lobbyists harbored no illusions. One restrictionist technique, they understood, was to legislate broad provisions that provided unduly wide leeway to anti-immigrant inspectors in the field. Marshall passed along to Dillingham[180] a deferentially phrased brief prepared by Nathan Bijur that made this point. Bijur objected to "the extension of the rule" of low vitality "to a matter not capable of scientific determination"; allowing a "mere opinion" about the "existence of a defect which 'may' affect the ability to earn a living" to dictate policy seemed "rather harsh toward the immigrant," Bijur concluded.

Meantime Marshall networked frenetically to stifle restrictionist maneuvers in this Capitol Hill session. "The American Jewish Committee," he told Daniel Guggenheim, "is moving heaven and earth" to block Nativist legislation on Capitol Hill. Guggenheim, the powerful president of the American Smelting and Refining Corporation, had strong relations with Rhode Island senator Nelson Aldrich, a "great power in the Senate." Marshall hoped that Guggenheim would pressure Aldrich to "prevent the passage of a law which would be most cruel in its operation."[181] The lobbyists crossed party lines. Schiff and Marshall turned to Judge Alton Parker, the 1904 Democratic Party nominee for president, persuading him to pressure Rep. John Sharp Williams of Mississippi to oppose the literacy test.[182] Through back channels, including Judge M. Warley Platzek from the New York Supreme Court, Marshall enlisted the lobbying help of John Fox, president of the National Democratic Club. His instructions to associates in these approaches to Democratic Party power brokers could be Byzantine in detail; as Judith Goldstein observes, Marshall's circuitous, secretive maneuvering with the Democrats can be explained as an attempt not to alienate his most important ally, Congress's Republican strongman, Speaker Joe Cannon.[183] An interesting, incidental feature of this lobbying was the priority given by Marshall and AJC associates to the low vitality proposals, as opposed to the literacy tests. Marshall continued to underestimate the dimensions of the threat posed by the literacy proposals; he told Edward Lauterbach, a New York lawyer who was active with the NLIL,[184] that the literacy provision "does not affect our Russian Jewish immigrants very seriously, since probably 98% of the men can read or write in some language."[185]

Marshall was optimistic. "It seems to me we have killed the bill, yet it may only be scotched," he informed Cyrus Adler in early February.[186] More relaxed, Marshall's thoughts were turning to ways in which the immigrant legislation might be turned to the newcomers' advantage. Probably thinking of the embittering experiences his father endured, as a defenseless immigrant laborer derived of his weekly pay by unscrupulous employers, he gave considerable thought to the meaning of alien vulnerability. Of the various defenseless clients for whose empowerment Marshall fought legal battles in the last decades of his life, his campaign to win rights for immigrants at risk of deportation stands out as a systematic campaign whose outcome remains ambiguous to this day. "There should be an amendment giving to the excluded immigrant a right of appeal to the Department of Commerce and Labor," mused Marshall, as the immigration bill headed for final debate in both houses, in mid-February.[187] Predicting victory in a letter to Schiff, Marshall reiterated his interest in someday winning a right of appeal for unwelcomed immigrants. He also alluded to a last-minute complication in the immigration legislation, the "Japanese imbroglio."[188]

In the first weeks of 1907, President Roosevelt had been doing his utmost for immigrant restriction. His point of reference for policy on the issue was the Immigration Restriction League. The president assured league lobbyist Robert DeCourcy Ward that he was leaving no stone unturned for restriction, but also conceded that the pro-immigration forces were making his task difficult. "You would be astounded at the amount of genuine misconception that exists on the subject, and at the intensity of the hostility aroused among very good people who really ought to be with us," the president wrote to Ward.[189] In February, Roosevelt believed he had found out West a wedge to open the door for restrictive legislation. The president summoned San Francisco Mayor Eugene Schmitz and the city's school board officials to Washington to negotiate a quid pro quo. In autumn 1906, as the city was still emerging from the rubble of the devastating April earthquake, its officials passed an order segregating Japanese schoolchildren, apparently for the purpose of deterring Asian immigration. Anxious to appease the Japanese government, Roosevelt convinced his guests at the White House meeting to revoke the segregation order, but he announced that his administration would work with Congress to deny entry to the country to Japanese immigrants who came from Hawaii and Mexico. This deal appealed strongly to Roosevelt and Secretary of State Elihu Root, who viewed it as a step in the direction of closing the door to Japanese immigration.[190]

For Marshall, this Japanese development was a step backward. In his 250th address on American Jewish leadership, he had hinted about the AJC's plans to contest America's 1832 treaties with Russia, due to the czarist government's discriminatory refusal to allow entrance to American Jews who possessed American passports. The Roosevelt administration's decision to condone, as part of a complicated legislative horse deal on immigration, a related form of discrimination against Japanese passport holders, threatened to preempt what AJC founders were privately regarding as a potential formative campaign for their organization, for the abrogation of the Russian treaties. "I am sorry that the Japanese question has arisen, because it constitutes one more precedent which will make it difficult for our government to agitate for a recognition of its passports in Russia," Marshall wrote to his colleague and AJC president, Mayer Sulzberger.[191] He chided the Roosevelt administration for "pandering to the prejudice, intolerance and bigotry of our citizens." Continuing the thought, Marshall previewed the rationale of his own compelling role in 1920s legal struggles for the rights of Asian aliens in California. Marshall wrote:

> When we are engaged in legislation of a discriminatory character against the subjects of friendly nations . . . any presentation which our government may make to another, on alleged humanitarian grounds, will be rejected with the admonition that we first remove the beam from our own eyes.

On Capitol Hill, that discriminatory beam was cast out in newly restrictive measures in a compromise immigration bill that was worked out in meetings between the Roosevelt administration and House and Senate delegates. Knowing that Cannon's power nullified prospects for a literacy test provision, Root convinced ranking Republicans, including Lodge and Dillingham, to accept the new arrangement on the Japanese question in lieu of the tests. As a result of these consultations, the immigrant head tax went up to $4; though the phrase "low vitality" was scrapped, the new bill excluded immigrants "found to be mentally or physically defective" in ways that affected their ability "to earn a living." The literacy test proposal was dropped, but one significant provision in this compromise bill hinted that the Nativists viewed any concession they were making as an ephemeral tactical maneuver. The bill called for the establishment of an immigration commission (soon to be known as the Dillingham Commission) comprised of three delegates from the Senate, three from the House, and three presidential appointees to study the causes and consequences of recent mass waves of immigration. The Dillingham Commission's establishment and subsequent activities through 1911 put a cap on any sense of relief or triumph felt by Marshall and AJC associates, as this inaugural organizational effort drew to a close, with the successful defeat of restrictionists' literacy test proposal. The restrictionists now had a democratically endowed platform, the Dillingham Commission, through which they could express their outlook and prod for anti-immigration legislation. And the AJC, with Marshall at its nerve center, now had an institutional adversary for a fight on immigration whose outcome could spell life or death for masses of harried Jews in Eastern Europe.

4

Abrogation

The immigration struggle was waged without public demonstrations. Marshall shunned publicity in this sphere, fearing that any trumpeting of gains could cause the restrictionists to dig in their heels. Preemptive in purpose, the lobbying was a protracted and often thankless process. Since their accomplishment was to stave off a catastrophic closure of the doors, it was impossible for Marshall and his American Jewish Committee (AJC) associates to show the Downtown masses that they had attained something new and concrete. The magnitude of their achievement would not be measurable for years, until after the Nativists slammed shut America's immigration doors in the early 1920s and catastrophe engulfed European Jewry. Only at that later date would it be possible to appreciate how many lives were saved because Marshall and the AJC, along with predecessors and associates such as Simon Wolf and the B'nai B'rith–Board of Delegates amalgam, helped stave off restrictive legislation in a way that allowed masses of East European Jews to reach the United States through World War I.

Immigration advocacy appears, in hindsight, as a stellar item in Marshall's personal career résumé and in the organizational record of the AJC, but its impact, and distinctive character in America's early twentieth-century ethnic history, were not at the time apprehensible. Several months after it was founded amid considerable public debate, the AJC remained alienated from its main Jewish constituency, the immigrant masses on the Lower East Side, and it lacked a political action agenda to justify its existence. So long as it lacked an issue that would prove its capability as an ethnically empowering agency, the organization would continue to be defined by its character as a self-appointed body—and that issue of organizational democracy or stewardship was, for Marshall, exasperating from the start.

The five-year period leading up to the eruption of the World War I witnessed changes and triumphs in Marshall's legal career, along with its nadir (his non-selection for the Supreme Court), the circumstances of which have never been understood. His children were growing, and religious and educational reform projects, such as the Jewish Theological Seminary (JTS), to whose origins or rebirth Marshall had invested considerable effort in the previous phase of his Jewish activity, were flourishing. All these developments warrant mention, but they are of secondary import to the story of Marshall's life as a miniature personification of the rise of a new type of ethnic Jewish identity and politics in the United States. From that biographical viewpoint, this phase of his life was dominated by Marshall's search to designate an agenda for the AJC. It was a period when the scope, purposes, and operations of organized ethnic politics came to be better defined. Months into this five-year period, the AJC came to define itself via the struggle to abrogate America's 1832 treaty of commerce and navigation with Russia, due to the czarist empire's discriminatory treatment of Jewish possessors of American passports.

Much in this definitional process can be questioned, both from the point of view of American interests[1] and even the AJC's own needs. Indeed, the historian Naomi Cohen, who published groundbreaking research on the abrogation struggle from a viewpoint largely sympathetic to the AJC, concluded rather dourly that on the eve of WWI, the anti-abrogation predictions that had been articulated months earlier by the Taft administration and the State Department "seemed to come true." Abrogation, Cohen concluded, had brought about "an unfriendly Russia, a decline in trade, and anti-Semitic reprisals in Russia."[2] And, as we shall see, while Marshall and AJC colleagues were absolutely elated after their efforts produced the treaty's abrogation, believing that their organization would now have authority and credibility in the eyes of Downtown immigrants, the relentless challenges leveled against the AJC during the war by the Zionists and the American Jewish Congress proponents would prove that the abrogation triumph did not really render Marshall's organization immune to Downtown criticism.

These points are legitimate, but they are somewhat off the mark. This issue-definition phase is a noteworthy chapter in Marshall's own career, and also, more broadly, in the history of ethnic politics in the United States, because it was, quite simply, *proof of the possible.* Marshall and the AJC proved that an ethnonational group had the right and, in the right circumstances, the wherewithal, to reshape the policy of the entire country on an issue of abiding emotional, and possibly practical, concern to it.

From the start, this brand of demonstrative activity was about identity politics (that is, ethnic pride), rather than about the alteration of practical realities. There is very little in the documentary record of the abrogation campaign to warrant the claim that Marshall, Schiff, and other AJC members really believed that the overturning of the 1832 treaty would necessarily lead to the betterment of Jewish life in the Pale of Settlement. Writing in 1963, Cohen appears to have over-emphasized this aspect in her meticulously researched article—whereas she concluded that the AJC men were drawn to a "simple" logic holding that treaty abrogation would eventually lead to the "emancipation" of Russia's Jews,[3] in reality they evoked this scenario propagandistically, privately understanding that affairs in Russia were bleak, anything but "simple," and invariably resistant to outside pressure. More to the point, by seeking to redress an ethnoreligious insult—the czarist bureaucracy's snubbing of Jewish holders of American passports—the AJC was waging a fight about honor, and the sort of "emancipation" at stake was the Uptown Jewish leaders' understandable desire to liberate themselves from pressures exerted mercilessly by the Downtown Jews, who mocked the *Yahudim* as cowering materialists who had sacrificed their Jewish souls on the altar of American capitalism. A related, no less important, goal, was Uptown's desire to vindicate, on national and international levels, the lesson its social workers, editorialists, and preachers had been inculcating for years at the Educational Alliance, the Hawthorne School, and the *World* newspaper: America really *was* different because it respected its citizens' rights everywhere. While these ethnic pride determinants of the abrogation struggle were abstract, they are more apprehensible a century after their emergence than they were to a historian who wrote half a century after the episode, in a methodological tradition that dismissed as an irrelevant annoyance all nonaltruistic determinants of identity politics.

Abrogation was a fight for Jewish self-respect and for American self-respect. It latched onto the rights of a pitiably small number of overseas American Jews (perhaps a half dozen Jews who had American passports and who were barred entry to Russia) for the purposes of reinforcing the identity needs of hundreds of thousands of insulted Jews in America, and the campaign vindicated the logic of organization, since it altered American foreign policy. In all these respects, the abrogation campaign, and Marshall's decisive role in it, are precursors of many subsequent developments in American Jewish ethnic politics. Some direct spin-offs of the abrogation struggle are mentioned later in this chapter; but, thinking out of the box, we might in passing note less obvious analogues of the AJC's abrogation campaign. One would be the "Who is a Jew" standoffs between American Jewish organizations and Israeli governments. Starting in the 1980s, these Who is a Jew contests related directly to the rights of only a handful of would-be converts or immigrants to the Jewish state, but also expressed deeply rooted recognition needs of hundreds of thousands of Reform and Conservative American Jews; they also, on occasion, changed the policies or even the composition of Israel's government coalitions.[4]

Mobilizing for Abrogation

Essentially the AJC was a political organization masterminded by elite American Jews who insisted that Jews had no political interests in America, or anywhere else.[5] This intrinsic contradiction rendered the task of finding organizationally defining issues no simple feat.

This definitional challenge had implications beyond the need to establish the AJC's credibility in the eyes of the Downtown masses. That the organization faced financial woes eighteen months after its funding is not an indication that it was in jeopardy of collapse (its powerfully wealthy backers would never have allowed that scenario to materialize, of course), but this passing financial shortage can be seen as a sign that its founders were unsure what the organization was supposed to be about, many months after it came into being.

"Funds for the American Jewish Committee are a little short," Marshall wrote to Adolph Lewisohn, at the end of 1907, in a mixed vein of confession and solicitation.[6] Marshall hinted that Schiff would surely pick up the financial slack, but he seemed unable to justify this appeal to Lewisohn beyond referring generically and unimpressively to the considerable time devoted by the AJC to "relieve conditions of Jews in Russia, Rumania and Morocco." Mostly the appeal was phrased in the future tense ("the committee will become a power for good in regard to the broader questions which affect the Jews"). The AJC had nothing by which to define itself.

For that reason, its leaders had little to do throughout 1907 other than to engage nonconstructive turf wars with older organizations. The AJC Executive Committee minutes are almost self-mocking in their description of talks engaged by Marshall, Julian Mack, and Judah Magnes in April 1907 with counterparts from B'nai B'rith and the Union of American Hebrew Congregations, ostensibly for the purpose of demarcating the lines of the various organizations' activities. "In the course of the discussion it became evident that no plan had been prepared and views of the conferees had not crystallized to an extent to make practicable any definition or limitation of powers of the organizations," the AJC recorded.[7] In private communications with his cousin Joe Stolz, a UAHC rabbi, Marshall derided these discussions, and lampooned his would-be partners from rival organizations ("Mr Wolf very naively stated that he saw no reason for any organization, that he had done all the work in the past. . . ."). These talks were just lip service, since the AJC members already regarded their organization as the preeminent entity. "Even though the old and decrepit organizations may issue proclamations, appropriating to themselves the credit of what we have done, we will work silently," Marshall explained, not disguising his disdain.

That disrespect for potential organizational rivals appeared to swell in a period when the AJC men themselves had little constructive activity to call their own. In the one sphere where their contribution was extremely valuable, immigration, they kept bumping inconveniently into Simon Wolf, whose outdated and (in the AJC's eyes) sycophantic methods they abhorred, but who also irritatingly had longer lobbying experience in Washington and proven access to the White House. In fact, in this period of definitional designation, the nadir in the AJC's early history is the way its leaders, ordinarily tough but fair-minded men, tried to hound Wolf out of the arena.

In the ugliest moment, AJC President Mayer Sulzberger took the lead, exploiting one of Wolf's lapses in judgment. Wolf mistakenly believed that an Orthodox synagogue in Boston had denied entry during a High Holy Day service to a uniformed sailor, E. R. Williams, indulged a dubious theory about Jewish tradition barring uniformed persons from religious services, and (quite wrongly) involved the Secretary of the Navy in a discussion about the incident. The AJC pounced upon Wolf's indiscretion, hoping to discredit this rival once and for all. As though in illustration of the theory that the worst turf wars occur when rivals do not know what they are supposed to be doing on their own turfs, the AJC's anti-Wolf actions were overkill (Cyrus Adler even alerted President Roosevelt about Wolf's lapses of judgment).[8] Not the most aggressive AJC member in this attack, Marshall was, at least, candid about its purpose, writing to Sulzberger that "the importance of this episode lies in the fact that it may possibly minimize Wolf's opportunities for doing further mischief."[9]

In early 1908, Marshall found his issue. He fired off an accusingly formulated petition to Secretary of State Elihu Root, protesting a State Department circular Root had signed in May 1907. The circular declared that the department would not issue passports to American-born Jews, or Jewish immigrants who were naturalized American citizens, "unless it has assurance that the Russian government will consent to their admission."[10] Marshall argued that this procedure subjected upwards of a million US citizens to a religious test, in contravention of the country's "time-honored" constitutional commitments to equal protection under the law. Russia had for decades "openly and notoriously" violated its 1832 treaty of commerce and navigation with the United States by subjecting Jewish Americans to discriminatory "humiliation," but now it was America that sought to "to indulge in these inquisitorial practices and to apply an unconstitutional religious test" to its Jewish citizens, thereby "practically justifying Russia in the violation of her treaty obligations, and condoning her contemptuous disregard of the American passport." Marshall respectfully asked the secretary to withdraw the circular.

From the start, Marshall's leadership in the abrogation campaign was about prideful assertion of organized ethnic power, not actual policy. He knew when he penned his petition that it had no practical point, because the State Department had relayed assurances to AJC secretary Herbert Friedenwald that Root's offensive circular was to be withdrawn. Marshall brushed aside Friedenwald's suggestion in favor of patient deference to the department's promises, crying out, "I fear we are getting too damned diplomatic."[11] Here was an opportunity of putting on record the AJC's exposure of the fact that "our government saw fit to issue such a circular." With Marshall's petition, the AJC revealed that "for the first time in our history, American citizens of Jewish antecedents were sought to be segregated from the mass of citizenship." More to the point, for the first time Marshall and his associates had identified a Jewish issue for AJC work that could obviously be associated with American values of justice and equality, and whose resolution could be pursued in an orderly advocacy campaign grounded on constitutional principles. In his February 1908 contacts with the AJC secretary, Marshall very clearly anointed abrogation as the organization's defining issue. Referring to Root's circular and his own petition, he announced: "I feel that by this treatment of the episode, a great opportunity for placing the American Jewish Committee on record with regard to a matter of momentous importance arises."[12]

Marshall was off to the races, energetically prosecuting the abrogation campaign for the AJC. When he received notification from the State Department regarding the withdrawal of Root's 1907 circular (ironically, this circular revocation was dated January 25, 1908, a week before Marshall sent his petition), Marshall promptly sent off objections to the department's new circular.[13] He protested that the second circular denied to Jews the right of expatriation. It stated that an "American citizen, formerly a subject of Russia, who returns to that country, cannot expect immunity from the operation of the Russian law." This declaration that immunity cannot be expected by an American citizen of any sort, native-born or naturalized, constituted "tacit recognition" of Russia's discriminatory practices, which were "at war with our fundamental principles," Marshall argued. At the same time, the restless AJC advocate discussed his dissatisfaction with Root's second circular with a Jewish member of the US Congress, Henry Goldfogle, and announced, "I am very much interested in the debate in Congress in regard to the passport question."[14] Ten days later, when the State Department withdrew Root's second circular, Marshall informed Congressman Goldfogle, "This is very good, but the passport question is still undisposed of."[15] When Julius Rosenwald congratulated Marshall in March upon the withdrawal of the two objectionable State Department circulars, Marshall solidified the link between abrogation and the AJC's organizational well-being. He thanked the Sears, Roebuck executive for his graciousness and reminded him that "the treasury of our organization requires replenishing."[16]

Article 1 of the 1832 Russia-America Treaty promised that persons from the two countries "shall be at liberty to sojourn and reside in all parts" of the two lands, "in order to attend to their affairs," and they shall enjoy "the same security and protection as natives of the country wherein they reside." Adding an ambiguously phrased proviso to this promise of equal treatment, the Article required Americans in Russia, or Russians in America, to "submit to the laws and ordinances there prevailing."[17] In the last decades of the nineteenth century, when American Jews on Russian soil endured economic and residential discrimination, the czar's officials contended that their country was not in violation of the 1832 treaty, owing to this Article 1 proviso rendering this class of Americans subject to the "laws and ordinances" in the empire regarding Jews.[18] The meanings and scope of this proviso were known only to a "few Americans," one scholar argues, adding that "expert opinion" in the State Department remained "uncertain" throughout the abrogation dispute as to whether Russian policy toward Jewish American citizens constituted a breach of Article 1.[19]

Jews and many other American citizens, however, regarded such claims about noninfringement of Article 1 to be sophistic rationalization of blatant discrimination. As Naomi Cohen observed, during the first decade of the twentieth century, a compelling brief against czarist handling of the 1832 treaty centered on a series of understandings:

- that Russia "violated the intention, at the very least" of the accord;
- that Russian inquiries about the beliefs of American citizens who applied for passports constituted a "religious inquisition repugnant to American institutions;"
- that Russia's policy of not honoring the passports of one group of American citizens was an "insult" and an assault upon America's "sacred principle [of] . . . freedom of religion."[20]

Marshall's objection to Root's 1907 circular by no means initiated discussion about the Russian treaty among American Jews. That discussion began as early as 1879, in the *American Israelite* journal, and picked up steam in 1904 when Jacob Schiff conditioned his assent to discussion requests forwarded by Russia's Minister of Interior, Count von Plehve, upon the lifting of restrictions against foreign Jews in the empire. Newly assertive after the Kishinev pogroms, Jewish activists and leaders managed in 1904 to insert in both the Democratic and

Republican platforms clauses pledging equal protection to all American citizens under treaties.[21] It will be recalled that Marshall alluded to Russia's iniquitous treatment of Jewish Americans in his 250th anniversary address. Russia's discrimination against Jewish possessors of American passports prompted these and other responses, but American Jews did not commit themselves to the policy of treaty repeal, abrogation, until spring 1908.

Exactly as he had done in the preparation of the Melvil Dewey petition, when he asked an acquaintance to test the Lake Placid Club's exclusion policies by applying for membership, Marshall in spring 1908 looked for witnesses who could verify that Russia's discriminatory infringement of the 1832 treaty was in continuance. In May, he found a promising example, the case of Louis Horowitz, vice president of the Thompson-Starrett Company, a construction outfit that had already been engaged in major projects in the United States, including one at Washington, DC's Union Station (a few years after his encounter with Marshall, Horowitz would achieve fame in the building of the 792-foot Woolworth building, the highest building in the world at the time[22]). A Russian Jew, Horowitz immigrated to the United States in 1890 at the age of fifteen. In April 1908, on a business trip to Scotland, he reached a spur-of-the-minute decision to proceed to Russia, both to visit his birthplace and to investigate the possibility of Thompson-Starrett work on a proposed railroad station in Saint Petersburg. As he proceeded eastward in Europe, Horowitz asked his firm to prepare passport and papers for the Russian visit; the Russian Embassy in Washington refused to issue Horowitz a visa, since he was a Jew.[23] Horowitz confirmed to Marshall that this discrimination impaired his company's plans to investigate the possibility of doing business in Saint Petersburg, and he agreed to serve on an AJC advisory committee.[24] Concurrently, in order to gain reliable information about the broad sweep of anti-Jewish policies in the czar's empire, Marshall and the AJC supported a visit to Russia paid by the journalist Herman Bernstein;[25] this was a decisive step in a long, productive relationship between Marshall and the Russian-born journalist, whose highpoint would be the exposure of the *Protocols of Zion* and *Dearborn Independent* anti-Semitic fabrications.

Having added to his files information about Russian discriminatory infringement, Marshall necessarily held the abrogation matter in abeyance since the American political system in summer 1908 was dominated by campaigns for the fall elections. In May 1908, the AJC had submitted a formal memorandum to President Roosevelt, surveying Russia's violation of the 1832 treaty and calling for its abrogation, but neither the outgoing president nor the State Department responded to the document.[26]

The Melting Pot and Its Discontents

With abrogation on hold, Marshall applied his energies to an array of Jewish and public causes. Magnes, who married Florence Lowenstein Marshall's sister Beatrice in 1908, alerted Marshall throughout the year about the anomalous situation at City College of New York, whose student body was at least 70 percent Jewish, but offered no courses of study in Hebrew. Marshall feared that Magnes was lobbying too hastily for Hebrew at City College;[27] but when Benno Lewinson, a lawyer who had been active with the Educational Alliance and the Hebrew Orphan Asylum and who was appointed by the mayor to be a City College trustee in 1906, announced that he opposed Hebrew study at the college, Marshall seized the opportunity. He scolded the trustee,[28] accusing him of self-abnegation. "Whenever anything can be done to add to the self-respect of the Jewish people, to develop in them the consciousness of manhood, the strongest opposition is always to be found in the Jewish ranks," Marshall thundered. Such Jewish renegades are "more anti-Semitic than the professed Aryans," he added. When a public trustee like Lewinson opposes Jewish interests in the hope of cultivating respect among Gentile peers, he invariably accomplishes the opposite, Marshall exclaimed. He upbraided Jews of influence who

> would rather bask in the smiles of apparent approval of their Gentile friends, who, in their heart of hearts, have naught but feelings of derision for those who abdicate that sense of dignity, and that devotion to principle, the cultivation of which is the only means of gaining the genuine respect of our fellow-citizens.[29]

Rebutting Lewinson's objection that Hebrew instruction was not ordinarily given at nonuniversity institutions of higher learning, Marshall declared, "I have ascertained that there are more than a dozen college institutions which teach Hebrew." Were it the case that 70 percent of City College's students were French or Italian, would a trustee hesitate to establish a professorship in French or Italian? Marshall pointedly asked. Knowledge of Hebrew provided entry to classics of world culture no less than knowledge of any other ancient or modern language:

> Do you not believe that a student in your college, who is able to read the Pentateuch, or the Psalms, or the Prophets, in the original, will receive as much mental discipline, intellectual culture, and moral advancement, as he would from the reading of the Anabasis, or the Iliad, or a play of Euripides, or of Aristophanes, or, for that matter, from the reading of Ovid, or Horace, or Juvenal?[30]

Marshall's ideas about strategies for Jewish learning in America altered over the years, but this fascinating letter warrants comment as a reflection of a deeply felt response to ascendant ideologies of early twentieth-century America. The letter was written at a time when Jewish activists and literati were preaching the virtues of assimilation in the "melting pot," a term popularized by Israel Zangwill in a famous play first produced in 1908.[31] Opposing this pro-assimilation proselytizing, Marshall developed a conceptualization of City College as a preserver of Jewish tradition and cultivator of Jewish leadership. He contested the college's well-known function as a gateway to professional career endeavor for young Jews who had grown up in poor immigrant homes. Were "the Jewish boys of City College to familiarize themselves sufficiently with Hebrew," Marshall declared, that would "enable them to become teachers of their own people, instead of half-baked lawyers and quack doctors." Hebrew instruction in American higher education could also promote continuity in the country's Jewish culture; at City College, Hebrew study would "prevent the creation of an artificial chasm between the Jewish boy born in America, and his foreign-born parents."[32]

Marshall took on a new public role in this period when he was appointed by New York governor Charles Evans Hughes to head the State Commission of Immigration. Other members of this body included Marcus Marks, Lillian Wald, and Edward Whitney; Frances Kellor, with whom Marshall worked closely and who eventually became the head of the State Immigration Bureau that was formed as a result of recommendations in the commission's April 1909 report,[33] served as secretary. Under Marshall's direction, the commission became a kind of New York, pro-immigration foil to Congress' Nativist-tempered Dillingham Commission.

Marshall was vacationing at Knollwood in August 1908 when Magnes brought to his attention clippings from the *Cincinnati Times-Star,* a newspaper edited by Charles Taft, the Republican presidential nominee's half-brother, that slurred Russian Jews. One piece, an August 18 article relating to the race riot at Springfield, Illinois (a tragic event that left seven dead and led to the formation of the National Association for the Advancement of Colored People), indulged in nasty innuendo, opining, "If it is true that one of the ringleaders of the mob was a Russian Jew who had fled the atrocities of his own country to incite others to violence in his adopted land, that is food for thought." Marshall quickly realized that the insults could be turned to advantage, as leverage in the prosecution of the abrogation campaign.

"As a Jew, I resent these articles," Marshall wrote to Charles Taft at the end of August. Reminding the presidential nominee's brother that "a very large percentage of Russian Jewish immigrants are voters," Marshall got straight to the point:

he suggested that "instead of slurring the Russian Jew, it would be much better political strategy on your part to emphasize . . . the Republican platform which demands the recognition of American passports."[34]

Knollwood that summer was full of bodily knocks. Now over fifty years old, Marshall's frame seemed suddenly combustible. In the Adirondacks, he suffered from a carbuncle on his neck, laryngitis, and muscle ruptures and boils on his legs.[35] His health settled down only after he returned to his office in Manhattan and resumed strategizing for abrogation. He likened Charles Taft's gaffe to the famous "Burchard blunder" in the 1884 presidential elections, when a supporter of candidate James Blaine issued an ill-advised denunciation of "Rum, Romanism and Rebellion," thereby infuriating Catholics who cast ballots for the Democratic rival, Grover Cleveland. Thus far, Marshall explained to AJC President Mayer Sulzberger, William Taft's statements on Russian discrimination and infringement of the 1832 treaty had been "very vague," and thus Charles's "Burchard-like blunder should be utilized to the fullest extent, as a lever to bring about such definite utterance as we have a right to expect."[36]

Not surprisingly, Charles Taft opened his editorial pages to Marshall, who quickly composed a strongly worded article entitled "American Citizenship and Russia," peppering it with ringing pronouncements that were now becoming AJC trademarks ("The time has come for drastic action. American citizenship can no longer be held cheap, disregarded and ignored"). Oscar Straus, Roosevelt's outgoing secretary of commerce and labor, edited the piece; pleased after its publication, Marshall assured the *Cincinnati Times-Star* that "nothing has been done during the present campaign which will so strongly appeal to Jewish citizens."[37]

In September 1908, the Jewish citizens of the Lower East Side were not paying attention to Midwest dailies, however. The Yiddish papers were filled with quizzical, outraged commentary on a sensational allegation leveled by the city's police commissioner, Theodore A. Bingham, who wrote in that month's edition of the *North American Review* about Jewish criminality.[38]

In language couched as a seemingly deliberate slap at years of Jewish lobbying against literacy and physical vitality tests for immigrants, and also as an outright insult aimed straight to the heart of a community proud of its religious and cultural values, New York's police chief declared: "It is not astonishing that with a million Hebrews, mostly Russian, in the city (one-quarter of the population) perhaps half of the criminals should be of that race when we consider that ignorance of the language, more particularly among men not physically fit for hard labor, is conducive to crime." With these stinging words, Commissioner Bingham exploited concerns shared by elite Uptown and immigrant Downtown Jews, since attention-grabbing revelations about immigrant criminality provided fodder for the Nativists,[39] and, more particularly, images of Jewish "burglars, firebugs, pickpockets and highway robbers" (the roster cited by Bingham), along with Jewish prostitutes (a topic of acute sensitivity)[40] belied a community-wide understanding of Americanization as a morally and economically rejuvenating experience. It is hard to find in American Jewish history counterpart examples of one remark prompting so much commotion and action responses in the Jewish community, and that is because Bingham hit New York Jewry where it really hurt.

Worried that mass Downtown protests would merely draw increased attention to Bingham's allegation, Marshall spent the first days of September 1908 counseling communal activists about how it would be "inadvisable to meet his [the police commissioner's] statement by any sensational method."[41] Where discrete or systematic responses seemed possible, Marshall provided encouragement. Thus, to one cleric who worked in the Office of the City Prison and who claimed to have evidentiary refutation of Bingham's contention that half the city's criminals were Jews, Marshall wrote: "If you are entirely sure that your alternative figures are correct, then I would consider it desirable for you to write a letter to *The New York Times*." In collaboration with New York General Sessions Court Judge Otto Rosalsky, Marshall was compiling his own facts and reaching the conclusion that "Mr. Bingham's estimate is grossly exaggerated."[42] Rosalsky and Marshall relied on the research of a Jewish sociologist, Mark Katz, who examined indictment and trial records and concluded that just 16 percent of the city's criminals were Jews.[43]

A week and a half passed after Bingham's allegation first exploded in the Yiddish press, and the apparent inaction of Marshall and the AJC stirred consternation on the Lower East Side. Using a pointed comparison, the *Tageblatt* angrily accused the Schiff-Marshall group of double standards. "When someone refused to allow a [Jewish] aristocrat into a Gentile hotel," this outraged Yiddish paper cried out, "the Jewish four hundred did not rest until the guilty party had been dismissed; and now, they are quiet! Is it because the ones insulted are Russian Jews?"[44] The Federation of American Zionists (FAZ) viewed the AJC's apparent nonresponse as confirmation of its long-standing contention that the Uptown elite had usurped communal authority. The FAZ's journal, the *Maccabaean*, charged that the committee was characteristically ineffectual in dealing with the police commissioner.[45]

Unknown to anyone outside of the AJC Executive Committee, Marshall had in this period engaged talks with New York's assistant police commissioner, Arthur Woods, while Bingham was on vacation.[46] They drafted an agreement based on a public retraction of Bingham's accusation and withdrawal of Jewish demands for the commissioner's resignation. Magnes, who belonged to the AJC

Executive Committee and who had solid ties with Downtown communal leaders, proved invaluable to Marshall in efforts to win recognition for this agreement. Marshall explained to Woods that Magnes would bring their deal to the attention of five East Side "gentleman who have great influence."[47]

"Wrong about Jews, Bingham Admits," triumphantly headlined the *New York Times* in mid-September, as the contrite commissioner returned to his job.[48] "Jewish Citizens Satisfied," claimed the subheadline. Retracting his claim, Commissioner Bingham explained that he had relied on faulty statistics. Mayor George B. McClellan praised Bingham for his "manly" admission of error; Rabbi Magnes of Emanu-El vowed solemnly in this meticulously crafted *New York Times* piece that the "Jewish people is not thirsting for revenge" and knows "how to value a manly admission or error." All these disavowals and reconciliatory pronouncements bore the stamp of Marshall's mediation effort and style of expression. In all probability, Marshall wrote the short paragraphs published as Bingham's apology, which concluded with the commissioner sententiously explaining he had written in the *North American Review* "without the slightest malice, prejudice or unfriendliness." Quoted extensively in the article, Marshall emphatically declared that the Bingham "incident should be considered closed."

It was not. Unlike other Marshall-led crusades against anti-Semitic practices, pronouncements, or personalities, from the Melvil Dewey matter to the Henry Ford crisis in the 1920s, the Bingham affair prompted a lasting institutional response—the organized Jewish community of New York City, the Kehillah, which was led energetically by Judah Magnes and formally connected to the AJC for over a decade after its inception in 1908.[49] In this period of Marshall's career, other anti-Semitic instances featured delusional screed or social snobbery whose main points of reference were the heads, hearts, and habits of the Jew-haters themselves,[50] whereas Bingham pointed, however disproportionately, to a genuine social challenge. Immigrant crime could be viewed as a problem on many different levels: as ammunition for the immigration restrictionists, as a badge of shame for the Jewish people, as personal tragedies affecting hundreds of immigrant families. In whatever moralistic way the matter was judged, in the founding of the Kehillah, communal workers and organizations in New York City acknowledged that there was an urgent need to tackle an array of interconnected facets of the crime issue. Via the Kehillah, they became involved in empirical research about poverty and vice on the Lower East Side, in educational work to preempt juvenile delinquency, and (in what must have been the Kehillah's most daring venture) in the deployment of the Bureau of Social Morals, a "euphemism for a secret service which fought crime and vice in the Jewish quarter," as the Kehillah's historian described it.[51]

Marshall was not shy about receiving credit for the Bingham retraction, but in communications with Downtown representatives he was mercilessly adamant about the need not to take the apology as an acknowledgment that the issue of Jewish criminality did not exist. "Let us not flatter ourselves with the belief that we are entirely Kosher," wrote Marshall to the editor of the *Jewish Daily News*.[52] "Let us assume that not more than 10% of the criminals of New York are Jews—that is 10% too many. What have the Jews of this city done to prevent the increase of criminality?" The uproar regarding Bingham's insult was "trivial" compared to the real challenge confronting New York Jewry. "We have cried because a corn has been trodden upon, and we are entirely indifferent to the cancer gnawing at our vitals."

On this issue, Jewish self-defense work did not end when an empowered Gentile was required to eat his impolitic words. In a tone reminiscent of the earlier, moral reform phase of his career, Marshall preached to the Downtown leaders about the crime issue; the difference was that at this stage, his advocacy was pointing not to a small-scale project like the Protectory, which was initiated and managed by the Uptown elite for the betterment of several dozen Downtown delinquents, but rather to a broad-based organization, the Kehillah, whose administration would depend on an alliance between the adopted Uptown prodigal son, Magnes, and the Downtown activists.

In fact, the Kehillah took root as a multidimensional design for the preservation of Jewish traditional forms in the maelstrom of urban American modernity. As such, it came into being for reasons that went well beyond Bingham's inflammatory article. We can generalize about those reasons by referring to them as the anxiety wrought by mass settlement. In the absence of any unifying agency, wondered the Uptown and Downtown patrons and activists connected to the Kehillah's founding, would it be possible to find anything identifiably Jewish as a common denominator linking the multitudinous labor, cultural, and media institutions of the Lower East Side? This broadly shared tension found specific expressions according to the personal interests and outlooks of any particular Kehillah founder or patron. Since he believed emphatically that the Bingham affair was closed, what (in addition to his personal relationship with Magnes) exactly governed Marshall's relationship to the Kehillah experiment? In Marshall's papers, two answers suggest themselves. First, in 1908, Marshall was momentarily willing to concede that an organizational antidote to pro-assimilation publicity might be warranted. Second, more importantly, the Kehillah caught his attention as a new device for the investigation of the core issue of communal democratization and its limits.

A century after its appearance on the stage in Israel Zangwill's melodramatic production, scholars are now beginning to appreciate the extent to which melting pot assimilation functioned as a fully fledged ideological platform for Jewish life in pre–World War I America, backed by an internationally famous playwright who knew how to catch the attention of political leaders, clergymen, and rank and file readers and theatergoers.[53] Of all the radical responses entertained by immigrant Russian Jews, in their militant mood following the Kishinev-era pogroms, Zangwill presented in his 1908 play *The Melting Pot* an absolute extreme—that is, total Jewish abandonment of the Old World and total fusion with Christian society in the New World, as symbolized by the play's intermarriage union of a pogrom survivor with the daughter of his czarist persecutor. At Temple Emanu-El, this intermarriage prescription hit a raw nerve.

The staged production of Zangwill's intermarriage prescription was roughly synchronized with what the *New York Times* described as the most contentious episode that had occurred in years at Fifth Avenue's elite Temple Emanu-El.[54] In October 1907, Irma Stern, the daughter of banker and merchant Louis Stern, an Emanu-El trustee, was married by the rector of Saint Patrick's Cathedral to Baron Leo de Graffenreid, a Catholic Swiss nobleman. The irrepressible, ethical young Rabbi Magnes transparently addressed this event in a synagogue sermon, arguing that the multiplication of such marriages would spell death for Jewish continuity. A small group of Emanu-El trustees[55] then met in meetings in late January and early February 1908 to discuss the controversy. Essentially alone in his support of Magnes's condemnation of intermarriage, Marshall argued for Stern's resignation as a trustee (Daniel Guggenheim proffered Marshall nominal support). The press caught wind of this trustee dispute and published unspecified reports about contentiously "warm" meetings of the synagogue's board.[56]

Marshall's private correspondence exhibits the extraordinarily emotional and complicated character of discussions staged by affluent, acculturated Jews who belonged to the 43rd Street and 5th Avenue synagogue board at least partly as a matter of social prestige, and who knew that what had happened in Louis Stern's home could possibly come to their own families, this decade or next.[57] As he reported to Schiff, who was in Cairo (on a tour that included a stop in Palestine, where Schiff was surprisingly impressed by the Zionists[58]), Marshall drew a line in the sand during the last meeting about the Stern resignation. Either the board accept Stern's departure, Marshall threatened, or he himself would storm off the panel and return his pews to Emanu-El. That turned the affair around. By a vote of six to two, Stern was forced off the board of the influential Reform synagogue. Marshall's motivations in this episode mixed loyalty to Magnes, a judicially practical sense of how the wider Jewish community viewed the issue, and his own personal commitment to the preservation of Judaism in America. Fascinatingly, Downtown sentiment influenced the way he managed affairs at this archetypal temple of Uptown prosperity—Marshall noted this influence when he wrote in shorthand to Schiff, after Stern's resignation was finally ratified, "Public opinion is almost uniformly in favor of the action of the Board, and concedes the impropriety of Stern being a trustee, under the circumstances." Marshall also had his own feelings to consider. He explained to Schiff: "The more I consider the subject, the stronger I am of the opinion that we adopted the only course possible for the welfare of the congregation, and the promotion of Judaism."[59]

Marshall maintained a warm personal relationship with Zangwill, and at various phases of the playwright's career he helped Zangwill secure advantageous copyright arrangements for his writings. When it came to concrete social and political affairs, however, Marshall deeply distrusted the famous English Jewish writer, who seemed to act on epigrammatic divisions of the world as white and black (one early Zangwill biographer described his subject as the possessor of "violent contraries"[60]), in a way that was anathema to Marshall's predilection for carefully planned, moderate solutions. His innate distrust of Zangwill's political work dates from the playwright's fateful decision to pull away from the Zionist movement and search for an alternative to Eretz Israel as a territorial solution for persecuted Russian Jews. Marshall mockingly referred to the acronym of Zangwill's Jewish Territorial Organization, ITO, as the "Interminable Talking Organization."[61] He scoffed at Zangwill's visionary politics, declaiming "a colonial scheme of the character proposed [by the ITO] has never succeeded since the world began." Expressing himself in an epigrammatic manner worthy of Zangwill himself, Marshall declared that "there is more hope for the occupant of a prison than for a dweller of a poor house,"[62] meaning that Zangwill would transport Russian Jews to sheer destitution in a transplanted colony. These critical sentiments had practical significance (when Jacob Schiff became interested in the Galveston project for Jewish immigrants and joined forces with Zangwill's ITO, he worked outside of the AJC, since AJC associates like Marshall had no interest in Jewish colonization schemes[63]), but they point more broadly to Marshall's ongoing recoil from staged publicity about the "Jewish problem" and extreme solutions to it.

For all these reasons, there was very little chance that Marshall would have sympathy for Zangwill's gospel of intermarriage in *The Melting Pot.* In late October 1908, he enjoyed the company of Zangwill at a social occasion hosted by Daniel Guggenheim. In a private letter thereafter, he confessed to being "very much displeased with Zangwill's theories in *The Melting Pot.*" He worried that the play would yield "mischievous results among those who are destitute of convictions."[64] A year later, Marshall was "inveigled" into attending a production of Zangwill's play. His criticism of *The Melting Pot,* communicated to Solomon Schechter, the head of the JTS, was formulated as though Zangwill belonged to an enemy ideological camp. "From our standpoint, I consider it most mischievous," Marshall declared. "It is the old cry of the assimilationists with new catch words and phrases, which will afford new stock arguments to those who are looking for them to justify their cowardly attitude."[65]

Magnes accompanied Marshall to the production and shared his indignation.[66] In fact, Marshall's brother-in-law promptly brought their shared criticism to the pulpit at Emanu-El, where he cried out that the "Melting Pot is not the highest ideal in America."[67] Referring critically to a moment late in Zangwill's play where the protagonist composes an "American symphony" molding together all the country's social elements homogeneously, Rabbi Magnes preached in the name of what would later be called multiculturalism, declaiming that the country's national symphony "must be written by the various nationalities which keep their individual and characteristic note, and which sound this note in harmony with their sister nationalities."[68] A decade later, toward the end of World War I, Marshall changed metaphors in the *New York Times* while reiterating this critique of the melting pot ideology and upholding the necessity of an immigrant culture's retention of its distinctive voice and identity. Zangwill, he stated, was "guilty of a great mischief" by proposing the melting pot as "the solution of the Jewish problem." Marshall continued:

> It is clear that Zangwill is not a metallurgist or else he would know that in the art of metallurgy the great effort made by those concerned in it, by electrolytic powers, is that the various elements composing the melting pot shall be separated into their constituent parts, so that the copper shall be fused with the copper, the silver with the silver and the gold with the gold.[69]

As much as it was an organized remedy to allegations and realities of Jewish immigrant crime, the Kehillah experiment came into being as an ideological antidote to pro-assimilation, melting pot platforms prescribed in this 1908 period by Zangwill and others. As Marshall later phrased it, the Kehillah's purpose was to organize a kind of counter–melting pot, in which the copper shall be fused with the copper, the silver with the silver, and the gold with the gold. As Arthur Goren observed, for Magnes and his Kehillah associates, the communal experiment "represented a step toward realizing that [alternative melting pot] vision."[70]

As the Kehillah moved forward under Magnes's leadership, Marshall seemed to be stumbling in the blocks over the question of communal representation, the abiding topic associated with his entire career in communal affairs. He would prove to be a supportive ally of Magnes's regarding Kehillah matters, but in the period of the New York Jewish community's formation, Marshall was clearly worried that the Kehillah proponents were co-opting the language of Jewish democratization in a way that accentuated the AJC's status as an unrepresentative, self-appointed body. His thoughts in this respect mixed pettiness, practical experience, and penetrating thinking about the possibilities of ethnic organization in an open, fluid democracy where membership in any ethnoreligious body was purely voluntary.

"As you know," Marshall reminded Magnes in a consultation about plans for the convening of a constituent meeting to establish the Kehillah, at the time of the AJC's founding "I believed . . . that the organization should have for its constituency the Jews of the United States, and should be representative, based on the ideas of democracy."[71] His vision of a democratic AJC was thwarted, and in autumn 1908 Marshall sounded highly skeptical about the possibility of Jewish organizing in the United States on the basis of democratic elections:

> When one considers the many elements of which the Jewish community consists, it is idle to believe that any organization can ever come into being, based on the idea of pure democracy. It would be impossible to get more than a fraction of one percent of the million Jews in this community to act directly in an election. Hence when your notice [of the Kehillah's constituent conference] speaks of an organization that "shall derive its authority from the people" you are merely speaking figuratively.[72]

Marshall's suspicions about an electoral basis for the organization of the New York Kehillah would abate in months ahead; and (as we shall see) during World War I, when the issue of communal democracy flared contentiously in debates about the formation of an American Jewish Congress, Marshall made advantageous use of the democratic aspirations and procedures of the Kehillah—at this later date, when Downtown critics ridiculed the AJC as a patrician, undemocratic institution, Marshall replied that its New York members were chosen democratically through the Kehillah.

These broad bookmark comments are placed at the start and the end of a decade that ensued after the Kehillah's formation in 1908, and they gloss changing shades both in New York communal circumstances and in Marshall's private sentiments and orientations. Nonetheless, such contrasts point to a persuasive way of conceptualizing the meaning of Marshall's life. Given his unflinching loyalty and ideological rigidity on a number of cardinal topics in his life, Marshall was surprisingly inconsistent and experimentally flexible on the issue of Jewish democratization. Sometimes (as in the case of the AJC's founding) he adopted "Downtown" spirited positions in circumstances where his reputation as an elite "Our Crowd" Jew would suggest otherwise. Other times (as in this October 1908 letter to Magnes) Marshall expressed intellectual or emotional disillusionment about democratization plans whose realization he subsequently promoted in good faith and with considerable energy and capability. Marshall is thus situated in American Jewish history as the embodiment of an ongoing discussion about cultural continuity as a function of elite management and of popular participation. In a free and open society, this discussion can probably never be resolved by the ascendance of one principle or the other, and ethnic vitality might actually depend upon the creative tension imposed by the continual intermingling of the principles, elite stewardship, and popular democracy.[73]

Marshall's New York Immigration Commission versus the Dillingham Commission

Meantime, by mid-autumn 1908, Marshall's main concerns attached to America's democratic processes, and he lobbied hard for a Taft victory in the November presidential polling. In previous elections, Marshall's opposition to Democratic candidate William Jennings Bryan had focused on socioeconomic issues, but in 1908 Marshall mostly ignored Bryan's populism. With currency (free silver) issues no longer a staple in the nation's political debates, Bryan stepped up his attacks on socioeconomic privilege per se, running on the slogan "Shall the People Rule"; normally, such electioneering sent shivers down Marshall's politically conservative spine, but in 1908 all he seemed to worry about was "Shall the 1832 Russian Treaty Rule?" Marshall conceded that Bryan had started to speak about the Russian treaty issue, but he objected that the Democrat's "glib" pronouncements about abrogation were nothing more than "glittering generalities."[74] In contrast, Marshall argued that by election day Taft had issued "carefully expressed announcements" in favor of abrogation,[75] and, blatantly exaggerating the significance of a pro-abrogation letter sent by Secretary Root to Schiff, as well as the Roosevelt administration's decision to defer the extradition of a revolutionary, Jan Janoff Pouren, demanded by Russia, Marshall announced publicly that the Republicans in Washington had done "more than any government in the world" on behalf of the rights of citizens in Russia.[76]

Marshall and his Republican AJC confederates might have been fooled by their own campaign rhetoric into believing that the newly elected Taft was firmly committed to the abrogation of the objectionable treaty with Russia. Either for that reason, or because America's ambassador in Saint Petersburg, W. W. Rockhill, warned Cyrus Adler that public agitation for abrogation might dangerously backfire, Marshall and the AJC "for the most part refrained from applying any pressure upon the Taft government"[77] throughout a grace period that lasted into 1910.

Immediately after the elections, Marshall diligently took up his role as chairman of the New York Immigration Commission. He devoted "all my spare time" to the commission work, chairing meetings and taking testimony two or three times a week.[78] After years of vital but wearisome hold-back-the-flood work lobbying against immigration restriction on Capitol Hill, this work on immigration for New York State energized Marshall because it was creative and empowering in spirit. Inviting outgoing Secretary of Commerce Oscar Straus to testify to his commission, Marshall outlined its purposes. "We want to propose the establishment of a permanent bureau to deal with immigrants," Marshall explained to Straus (who in his three-year Cabinet tenure headed the department responsible for immigration). Such a bureau would protect vulnerable immigrants against "exploiters of various kinds, including employment agencies, steamship ticket agents, those who prey upon them at docks, notaries public, so-called bankers and the like."[79] In Washington lobbying, Marshall resorted on occasion to tear-jerker stories of his immigrant father's exploitation at the hands of unscrupulous employers, in the hope of generating sympathy in a way that might shorten the Nativists' legislative reach; in this New York work, the aim was not sympathy and persuasion, but constructive redress and the preemption of similar future travail in the lives of immigrant families.

Another extremely time-consuming but less-rewarding endeavor in this period was Marshall's work as an executor of a contested will left by his wife's relative, Bernard Lowenstein, in Memphis. Litigation over the $1.5 million estate continued for years, with tragicomic soap opera twists endured by Marshall with Olympian patience and as a tribute to his familial loyalty.[80]

During the early months of 1909, Marshall's apprehensions concerning methods of constituting the Kehillah eased, and he became visibly enthusiastic about the organization's potential capacity to promote communal democratization. "Once the Kehillah plan is adopted," he explained, "the result will be that the entire representation of the City of New York on the American Jewish Committee, consisting of more than one-third its members, will be selected by all of the Jews of New

York who are affiliated with the Kehillah."[81] After the Kehillah's Executive Committee was established, Marshall had to placate the offended Solomon Schechter who regarded his noninclusion as a slight. Marshall explained that noncitizens were barred from the executive committee due to concerns about public perception of the experiment in communal self-administration—including foreign-born members on the committee would be "perilous," since the Kehillah "movement would be construed as an attempt to erect an imperium in imperio."[82] Increasingly, he became an enthused advocate of the Kehillah project, recognizing its unique capacity to build bridges across German and Russian, secular and religious, and many other divides in New York's Jewish world, and also appreciating its consolidation as a refutation of stereotypes that sometimes hovered above the Jewish "ghetto" in New York. He was, accordingly, infuriated when the *New York Times* covered the Kehillah's founding convention as though it were a "disorderly and unseemly . . . Donnybrook Fair." Demanding that the newspaper's publisher give the experiment a fair hearing, Marshall insisted to Adolph Ochs that the founding meeting was "dignified" and conducted "on a high plane." Schiff, he reported, "stated it was the most impressive gathering he had attended in many years of communal activity."[83]

Marshall's developing relationship with his brother-in-law, Judah Magnes, brought him closer to the hub of Downtown life, whereas his alliance with Jacob Schiff sometimes left him managing items of special concern and sensitivity to the Uptown elite. At the end of 1908, Schiff seethed with anger about the exclusion of philanthropist Jews from directorships of prestigious educational and cultural institutions in New York City, despite their charitable munificence. His campaign to end this implicit anti-Semitism began at Columbia University, where an evidently frustrated Schiff communicated with Seth Low's successor as president, Nicholas Murray Butler. Schiff was probably aware that Butler was less accommodating to Jews than his predecessor at Columbia,[84] but decided nonetheless to send the university's president an angry letter in January 1907 about how he had tried in vain for fifteen years to secure a Jewish appointee on the board of an institution whose student body was probably a quarter Jewish. The letter's indictment climbed Columbia's walls and lividly attached itself to the leading cultural institutions in the city. "So long as . . . citizens of the Jewish faith are, by a tacit understanding, kept out of the Government of Columbia University, the Metropolitan Museum of Art, the Museum of Natural History, and other leading communal corporations," complained Schiff, "prejudice is being kept alive against the Jewish population."[85]

In spring 1909, Schiff corralled Marshall, and they made the rounds in the offices of New York officials, including Mayor McClellan. Marshall then drafted into a proposed bill an ingenious theory,[86] based upon the argument that the various museums were public institutions at least in the senses that they typically occupied extensive area on city lands for which they paid no rent, and their facilities typically received large contributions for construction or maintenance from the municipality. They were, in fact, taxpayer-supported institutions; under such circumstances, reasoned Marshall, the mayor should have the power to appoint a handful of directors to the boards of the various institutions. Marshall lobbied industriously for the proposed bill, describing to state senators how, "as things stand," institutions like the Metropolitan Museum of Art, the Museum of Natural History, and the New York Public Library were "closed corporations, run by estimable individuals whose slogan is No Catholics or Jews need apply."[87] Endowing the mayor with the right to appoint communal representatives to the semipublic institutions would "add a little red blood to the cerulean-hued fluid which now circulates through these bodies politic." For Schiff, the lobbying with Marshall on such matters was valuable not just for the legislative processes it set in motion, but for the principle it represented. Schiff, his biographer notes, abided by a "private rule": whether or not discrimination could be overturned, it could never be accepted with equanimity, because "self contempt is the lowest degradation to which a human being can sink."[88]

In spring 1909, Marshall's New York State immigration commission submitted its report, following an exhausting investigation that involved twenty-seven hearings and testimony delivered by 193 witnesses. Managing this committee, Marshall penny-pinched and pushed hard, largely because he wanted to present this fundamentally pro-immigration panel as an exhibition of studious civic responsibility, and as a contrast to the profligate, pseudoscientific partisanship of Congress's Dillingham Commission. Thus, disseminating the panel's report to state politicians in Albany, Marshall pointed out that his New York State commission had worked steadily for two years to finish its work, while not utilizing all of the funds in its meager $10,000 allocation, whereas the Dillingham Commission had already burned up $340,000 of public funds, but was still meandering after two years of labor.[89]

The Marshall immigration committee report pointed out that "New York is preeminently the state" in the country "most affected by immigration," and it focused on the vulnerability of the alien newcomer. Its descriptions of alien victimization echoed the embittering experiences endured by Marshall's father in New York State as an itinerant laborer as well as the sympathetic wisdom and professional experiences of Marshall's colleagues on the panel, including social reformer Lillian Wald, whose work at the Henry Street Settlement began around the time of Marshall's arrival in New York City and whose efforts (like Marshall's) on behalf of immigrants in New York were generously supported by Jacob Schiff's philanthropy.[90] The report declared:

> The alien who reaches the city is often permanently held there by poverty, ignorance of conditions, timidity or social attraction, even when his best interests might have led him elsewhere. Not knowing the language of the country and unacquainted with its legal and social institutions, he has often been despoiled, and the records are replete with instances of gross fraud perpetrated against him.[91]

The commission's pro-immigrant orientation was appreciated on the Lower East Side, though some Jewish newspapers worried aloud that Marshall's panel sought to put signal Downtown institutions under the direct control of the State. Marshall explained to the Downtown pundits that Talmud Torah institutions would never be controlled by the government. At worst, his commission had found that some of the religious schools offered no English, in violation of the state's education law ("you and your readers will certainly admit that it is important for all children to become familiar with the English language," Marshall told the Downtown journalists), and also pointed to "deplorable" sanitary conditions in some Talmud Torahs. The Jewish schools had not been singled out by the commission; equivalent issues were raised with regard to parochial Catholic schools.[92]

The commission's chief recommendation was to create in New York State a full-fledged immigration bureau, in order to "best secure for the State the economic advantages derivable from an intelligent utilization of the alien" in the workforce, and to protect the immigrant from "exploitation, fraud and oppression."[93]

Given the ascendance of Nativism in the political climate, Marshall understood that the commission was debarred from openly espousing the virtues of open immigration. Hence, its advocacy was somewhat indirect, focused primarily on the idea that immigrants contribute to the nation's overall prosperity. Diplomatically rejecting the familiar contentions of organized labor groups and restrictionists, the commission concluded that immigrant absorption in the economy does not reduce the employment possibilities or wages of American citizens. Marshall reiterated this point to opinion makers, explaining to the *Globe* in mid-April 1909 that the report's "purpose is to benefit the State, to enable it to utilize the tremendous industrial forces which are placed at its command," and to guarantee that immigration leads to "more profitable employment" for all.[94] Specifically, the commission report led legislatively to two bills: the Parker bill for the creation of the immigration bureau and the Foley bill, featuring many of Marshall's ideas and proposals for the regulation of banks.

Through the immigration commission, Marshall submitted his own plan for moderate bank reform and regulation several months before his law partner Samuel Untermyer formally severed his connection to their firm, Guggenheimer, Untermyer and Marshall, and (as we will see) spearheaded the radical-spirited and extremely intriguing congressional investigation of the "money trust," the Pujo commission. As a result both of its origins in an immigration affairs survey and of Marshall's fundamentally conservative socioeconomic outlook, the Foley bill was much more restrained in scope and spirit than the subsequent Pujo investigation and the public comment and spin-offs Untermyer's panel generated (including Louis Brandeis's famous series of articles, published in 1914 in the volume *Other People's Money and How the Bankers Use It*[95]). Nonetheless, the Foley bank reform faced stiff opposition in Albany among state legislators who viewed its proposals as undue intervention in the state's financial system, and it also was challenged vigorously in the courts, where Marshall encountered surprising opposition from old allies and ultimately found vindication in a Supreme Court ruling. The Foley bill trajectory foreshadowed a dynamic that would become increasingly evident in Marshall's career: starting with an essentially ethnic issue, the protection of vulnerable Jewish immigrants, he became associated with a cause, bank reform, that was clearly identified with the Progressive left politics of the era and whose prescribed remedies seemed to contradict the conservative tenets of his own political outlook.

Among other measures, the Foley bill imposed licensing requirements among small-scale operators who were carrying out banking functions in a chaotic, unregulated environment where the potential for abusive fraud damaging to the interests of unsuspecting, vulnerable immigrants was especially high. The 1910 bill required any individual or partnership that received money deposits for safe keeping or any other purpose to obtain a license in a process that required payment of a $10,000 deposit with the state comptroller and threatened penalties ranging between $10,000 and $50,000. Under the law, any party presenting itself as a "banker" in promotions of any sort, without a license, was guilty of a misdemeanor.[96]

Lobbying for the Foley bill in the media, Marshall arranged a *New York Times* editorial endorsement of it as "well considered" legislation that promised "protection to a class of helpless and trustful aliens who are now exposed to the risk of losing their entire savings."[97]

When New York Bank Superintendent Clark Williams raised objections to the bill, Marshall immediately petitioned Governor Hughes, asking him to convene in May 1909 a special session of the New York legislature to push the measure through.[98] In his lobbying for this small-scale banking reform, Marshall became allied closely with Lillian Wald, who in her settlement house work had observed heartbreaking incidents of immigrant exploitation by unscrupulous, self-described "bankers."[99] Largely due to Williams's opposition to the placement of immigrant banks under the jurisdiction of the state's Banking Department, legislation of the Foley bill dragged on through 1909, and Marshall fired off a series of letters to Albany lawmakers, suggesting that they move ahead with the second measure, the Parker bill, so that a new state immigration bureau might take responsibility for regulating banks that received immigrants' deposits.[100] In early 1910, Governor Hughes issued special endorsement of the immigration and banking measures in his annual message to the legislature, and the governor held a mid-February meeting with Marshall and Williams, who as state comptroller now sought authority for immigrant bank regulation; the meeting culminated with an agreement to transfer responsibility for immigrant bank regulation to the comptroller, in an arrangement Marshall quickly delineated in a new draft proposal.[101]

In April and May 1910, a year after Marshall's immigration commission submitted its report, the revised Parker and Foley bills headed for a final showdown in Albany. Marshall implored assemblymen, reminding them that his commission had exposed extensive fraud committed by steamship ticket agencies, notaries, and private banks; in the banking sphere alone, ignorant immigrants had lost millions of dollars to predators. "Other states are awaiting action in New York" on immigration, Marshall declared; New York "should be in the vanguard, and not await action by other communities."[102] By the end of May, when the bills were finally adopted in Albany, Marshall wrote promptly to the state's commissioner of labor, John Williams, within whose department the immigration bureau was to be housed, and recommended that Frances Kellor, whose dedication to immigrant well-being had been in evidence throughout her work as secretary to Marshall's commission, take charge of the new bureau.[103] Pending court litigation, this was a happy conclusion to a somewhat protracted legislative lobbying effort, one that Marshall personalized as a constructive response to the Nativists' continuing efforts on Capitol Hill to block entry to Jewish and other immigrants, whose expenses he funded out of his own pocket.[104]

Despite its limited scope, the New York banking bill was challenged in the courts almost immediately after its enactment. The plaintiff in *Engel v. O'Malley* presented himself as a banker with two decades of sound communal standing under his belt whose practice was to hold small deposits from immigrants for short periods until the depositors had saved an amount sufficient for transfer to other states or overseas.[105] The banker claimed to lack assets required to meet the new law's licensing requirements, and he also argued that the law unconstitutionally regulated interstate commerce and violated his due process rights. In his briefs on the case, Marshall rebutted these contentions, defending New York's new banking law as a measure "dictated by experience" and enacted "for the protection of those dealing with private bankers." Far from a deprivation of property without due process, the bill had been enacted merely "to regulate the banking business."[106] Reversing his argumentation in the 1898 case, *Tyroler v. Warden of City Prison of New York,* Marshall's reasoning in the Engel banking case strikingly reflected how the passions of ethnic advocacy had transformed his understanding of American society and constitutionalism.

In August 1910, the US Circuit Court upheld Marshall's defense of the New York banking bill,[107] but then, in a surprising and unnerving twist of fate, this experiment in immigrant protection via bank regulation was ruled illegal by an old ally in Jewish affairs, Nathan Bijur. A fellow member on the panel of distinguished New Yorkers appointed by Mayor Low to investigate the Rabbi Jacob Joseph funeral disturbances in 1902, Bijur's 1909 appointment to New York's Supreme Court had been warmly and publicly supported by Marshall ("he is a thorough American and a faithful Jew" whose "heart beats for humanity," declared Marshall in the Yiddish press, urging support for the Bijur appointment).[108] In a move that threatened to nullify a cardinal reform adopted as a result of Marshall's two and a half years of work on New York immigration affairs, Bijur ruled in fall 1910 that the private banking bill was unconstitutional.

Pouring salt into the wound, Adolph Ochs's *New York Times,* which had earlier published paeans of praise for the "well considered" legislation proposed by Marshall's immigration commission, reversed its editorial course after Bijur's ruling. An editorial in the *Times* ridiculed the "ignorant draughtsman" of the banking statute. Since he had personally drafted, financed, and chaperoned the bill and its legislative lobbying, Marshall's apoplectic response to this insulting editorial was inevitable. "All of [my] constructive work is of no consequence to a public newspaper which takes greater delight in destroying reputations than in saying a kindly word for those who, at great personal cost and sacrifice, have sought to perform a public duty in a quiet, unobtrusive manner," Marshall harangued Ochs. He vowed that he would win personal vindication and renew protection for vulnerable immigrant depositors in the Supreme Court. By this period, Marshall's sense of personal honor was so closely intertwined with his commitment to Jewish welfare that the defense of the former would, he assumed, necessarily redound to the benefit of the latter; for this reason, he did not think that he might be putting future Jewish campaigns in jeopardy when he berated the *New York Times* publisher in response to its personally insulting editorial after the Bijur ruling. A Supreme Court ruling favorable to the New York banking bill would, Marshall warned Ochs, "lead the 'ignorant draughtsman' of the statute to reflect on your mental processes."[109]

In January 1911 the Supreme Court unanimously ruled in Marshall's favor in *Engel v. O'Malley* on grounds that twinned Marshall, not for the last time, with the jurisprudence of Oliver Wendell Holmes. In his brief favoring bank regulation, Marshall had departed from conservative traditions in late nineteenth-century law favoring broad protections of property rights via creative interpretations of due process standards. Instead, Marshall's reasoning seemed in line with the "judicial restraint" philosophy developed by Holmes, maintaining that "due process" standards properly applied to fundamental principles of common law rather than economic interests and that courts lacked authority to overturn reform measures deemed necessary as correctives to modern socioeconomic circumstances by democratically elected representatives of a state's population. In the *Engel v. O'Malley* ruling, Holmes wrote that the principle of judicial restraint applied doubly to legislation that applied to immigrant protection: "The quasi-paternal relations shown in the argument [about] the plaintiff's calling and newly-arrived immigrants justifies a supervision more paternal than is needed in ordinary affairs."[110]

Elated by the Supreme Court's decision, Marshall told Wald, "We may congratulate ourselves." Upheld by the highest court in the land, the New York banking law would drive banking "malefactors" who preyed on unsuspecting immigrants "to the wall."[111] Reflecting that Judge Bijur could not have possibly crowded more gaffes into a single ruling, Marshall gloated for a moment about the defeat of his unexpected adversary. But he soon got to the serious work of fine-tuning amendments to the new law to forestall the encroachment of foreign banks that did business in New York. The experience of teaming with Wald to provide legal remedies for the sort of immigrant abuses that had harmed his own father clearly energized Marshall and left him talking like a crusading reformer in a business lawyer's dress. When some Canadian banks offered Marshall a retainer, were he to tone down the foreign bank regulation imposed by his new draft amendment, he scoffed. "I told them that they did not have enough money to retain me," said Marshall.[112]

The Story of Marshall's Lost Bid for the Supreme Court

Louis Marshall reportedly argued more cases before the Supreme Court than any private attorney in American history. In an essay in a volume on nine American champions of law, one legal expert concludes that Marshall's success in "persuading courts to strike down statutes as violative of the federal or state constitutions" had no parallel in his era.[113] "A great lawyer and a great champion of ordered liberty," Supreme Court Justice Benjamin Cardozo called Marshall.[114] Marshall's indisputable qualifications for the Supreme Court, coupled to rumors and evidence of at least one episode in which he lobbied for a spot on the bench, have long intrigued scholars, who have produced a number of largely similar accounts of Marshall's non-nomination for the post, almost always relying on a cryptic, repeatedly misinterpreted, statement made by William Howard Taft, the president who did not choose Marshall.[115]

Other than the fact that Marshall himself deeply believed that he deserved nomination to the land's highest bench and was disappointed when it did not come, there is no irrefutable way to conclude that his non-nomination was really a setback in his career. The author of a dissertation on Marshall hazarded the debatable but not outlandish conclusion that he would have been "frustrated and uncomfortable" on the Supreme Court, in a position that would have precluded leadership on Jewish affairs and prevented him from freely articulating his views on an array of Jewish and American topics.[116] Similarly, it is impossible to measure with certainty how close Marshall really came to winning a nomination during his most determined bid to obtain it, in spring 1910. The only person who could have given an authoritative account in this respect was President Taft, but his personal papers provide only indeterminate hints about his private thinking. If true, one possibility would render moot discussions of Marshall's bid for the Supreme Court bench: possibly, when a spot became available following the death of Justice David Brewer in late March 1910, President Taft favored New York governor Charles Evans Hughes from the start.[117] However, no immediate, clear-cut preference for Hughes is supported by documents in the Taft papers, and the evidence collected later in this chapter about President Taft's laborious equivocations on the abrogation issue conveys hints that he found it difficult to rebuff determined Jewish lobbying, particularly when powerful banker Jacob Schiff had a part in this advocacy (and Schiff championed Marshall's Supreme Court bid). While the question of whether Marshall *almost* won a nomination to the court cannot be resolved with certainty, the reasons why he *could not* have gotten the appointment have, surprisingly, eluded attention, despite the fact that the Supreme Court non-nomination has naturally been one of the most discussed aspects of Marshall's career.

The twists and turns in Marshall's bid for a nomination to the court warrant survey of their own, not simply because they have been obscured by incorrect interpretations of the meaning of the president's explanation of Marshall's non-nomination ("Schiff, if you were President," Taft reportedly asked Marshall's patron, "would you name Sam Untermyer's partner to the Supreme Court?"[118]).

Revelation of the facts in this episode helps us better identify Marshall's status in American society as an accomplished professional and rising ethnic leader, several years before World War I. The episode sheds light on his vulnerability as a successful Jew in the rapidly consolidating field of corporate law, and it discloses crucial information about pros and cons in Marshall's professional partnership with Samuel Untermyer, a subject of interest due to the contrast between Marshall's staunch conservatism and Untermyer's surging liberalism, but a topic clouded by mystery because the pair's firm destroyed most of its records.[119]

Providing a crucial lesson about Marshall's dealings with the mass media of his age, Marshall's failed bid for the court appointment is at one end of his relationship with the most influential journalist of the era, a relationship whose polarities constitute the nadir and acme of Marshall's public career.

Generally, a revised account of Marshall's non-nomination for the court enhances our understanding of the way he calibrated personal ambitions and public commitments in his career. Both the imposing energy and idealism of his volunteer labors for Jewish welfare and rights and his convention-defying defense of African American, Asian American, and other minority group interests in later phases of his career can be understood as mature and practical responses to this episode and to lesser disappointments in Marshall's career. Once he had undeniable evidence of his own vulnerability in the pursuit of personal ambitions, such as a spot on the Supreme Court bench, Marshall won psychological freedom to seek public or ethnic ends like environmental protection or Jewish minority rights in Europe, which offered far less prestige in contemporary American society than a Supreme Court nomination but whose merits were obvious to him.

As it turned out, the white plague, tuberculosis, killed Marshall's chances for the Supreme Court. The one published reference to the role played by the politics of tuberculosis in Marshall's non-nomination to the Supreme Court was offered by the failed aspirant himself, in a bitter 1915 letter sent by Marshall to Hearst newspaper editor Arthur Brisbane.[120] This document, dispatched privately in its day and published in 1957 by Charles Reznikoff,[121] represents Marshall's sole retrospective comment on his bid for a nomination to the court, and it is a mostly accurate assessment of the reason why it was officially quashed. Its meaning has never been explained.

At the end of a long letter, framed as a systematic refutation of the Hearst press's depiction of Marshall as a lawyerly hired gun for business interests, Marshall declared in emphatic and italicized words "this letter is not for publication," and then charged that Arthur Brisbane had borne false witness against him, ruining his chances for the Supreme Court by spreading a "gross" and "grave" lie. Marshall wrote:

> When my name was considered by President Taft for membership in the Supreme Court of the United States, you charged me with unfitness because of my alleged opposition to the Preventorium which Mr. Nathan Straus was seeking to establish at Lakewood, New Jersey. The slightest inquiry would have disclosed that I had nothing to do with that matter. . . . You were not content with making me the victim of a wanton editorial assault, but proceeded to Washington, to oppose my appointment on a false charge. . . . Mr. Straus has frequently expressed his sincere regret that, through your friendship for him, he had been made the innocent cause of inflicting grave wrongs upon me.

The first preventorium in the United States opened in 1909 at Nathan Straus's initiative in Lakewood, New Jersey.[122] The facility initiated a trend of sorts—over the next twenty years, dozens of preventoria operated in several states (most prominently in California) and provided care to thousands of children who were considered at risk of contracting tuberculosis, usually because one or both of their parents suffered from the disease. "'P' is for *prevention,* much better than cure," chanted children in these institutions. One of the movement's leading proponents was a German-born physician named Sigard Adolphus Knopf, who published in 1902 a pamphlet entitled *Tuberculosis as a Disease of the Masses, and How to Combat It;* this publication spurred health professionals and members of New York City's social and business elites to form the Committee for the Prevention of Tuberculosis (CPT). The bacterial basis of the disease had been established by a German scientist (Robert Koch) twenty years before Knopf published his pamphlet, but the focus of the CPT's work was nonbiological aspects of TB epidemiology; factors such as overcrowded, poorly ventilated tenements that had been highlighted in the writings and works of social reformers like Jacob Riis, author of the landmark *How the Other Half Lives,* and Henry Street Settlement House director Lillian Wald (who was deeply interested in the prevention of childhood disease and who had important connections with the city's Jewish elite, particularly Jacob Schiff).

Nathan Straus's commitment to the reduction of childhood mortality and disease stretched back to 1893, when he donated resources accrued via his family's ownership of the Macy's department store chain to sponsor a major campaign for the provision of pure milk to young children in city neighborhoods. Within fifteen years, Straus-sponsored pasteurized milk stations around New York City had virtually halved infant mortality rates, from ninety-six to fifty-one deaths per thousand infants. Part of that dramatic improvement probably involved the reduction of *Mycobacterium bovis,* one of the two forms of bacilli responsible for tuberculosis; ironically, at the time of the founding of the Lakewood preventorium, this aspect of Straus's contribution remained unknown, since scientists were not yet agreed about *M. bovis* infection in cattle and the spread of disease to humans by the drinking of milk from infected cattle.

Straus conceptualized the Lakewood preventorium as a combination of "the best elements of a school, sanatorium and middle-class American home."[123] He put together a blue ribbon board to back the New Jersey project, recruiting Jacob Schiff, Jacob Riis, Isaac Seligman, and steel industrialist Henry Phipps. Early in 1909 he donated his half interest of the Lakewood Hotel, located in a resort town of the same name, for the establishment of the preventorium. The children were to be active in an area known as "Cleveland Cottage," adjacent to the defunct hotel—the name was a tribute to former President Grover Cleveland, who had been a frequent guest at the hotel, with his wife Frances (who in 1909 became an enthusiastic backer of the preventorium project). The first group of ninety-two children arrived at the Lakewood preventorium on July 2, 1909, amid triumphant reportage in the local press about the facility being a "progressive step in the world wide war against consumption" and about Nathan Straus's role as a modern day Santa Claus, owing to his devotion to children's well-being.[124] Speaking for the preventorium board, Marcus Marks announced in the fall that Straus had donated half a million dollars to the project as well as Cleveland Cottage and its surrounding eight acres; other board members had added $200,000 to Straus's gift.[125] Newspapers lavished praise upon Straus, explaining how the philanthropist "who has given so much of his brain and purse to the purification of the world's milk" was now using his resources to "save children whose blood has been touched by the white plague of tuberculosis."[126]

Such laudatory reports were not entirely accurate and were potentially counterproductive, since Straus and his preventorium partners were interested in disease prevention among at-risk youth and had not necessarily brought contagious youth to this exclusive resort area the preceding July. Sure enough, reports of tubercular youth at Lakewood scared elite holders of property in the area, who launched what one scholar has described as an "ugly and personal" antipreventorium campaign that was "rife with subthemes of social class and ethnicity."[127]

By late November 1909, local property owners were holding mass protest meetings to "Save Lakewood" and to express the idea that "the bringing in of several hundred children among us with seeds of the disease already in their system is a serious menace to the health of Lakewood children."[128] The local Lakewood newspaper suggested that a distorted publicity campaign for the preventorium had been funded entirely from Macy's coffers and that the department store's owner was punishing New York newspapers that dared to question the wisdom of locating a tuberculosis facility at low altitude by withdrawing advertisement subscriptions.[129]

Hysterically worried about damage potentially caused by the preventorium to their property investments in the resort area, the Save Lakewood campaigners resorted to still uglier innuendo as late autumn chill overtook New Jersey. The preventorium's Jewish backers, they claimed, were immune in various senses to damages caused by their project. Proof was personified by the medical facility's Jewish director, pediatrician Alfred Hess—he and his family had been exposed to infectious youngsters, but as Jews they had immunologic protection, even though they were apt to spread the disease to others.[130] The preventorium backers issued belated, laconic refutations of such ridiculous, insidious allegations.

Under the thrall of the influential Lakewood property owners, co-opted New Jersey governor John Franklin Fort sent a shameless letter to the preventorium board, upholding the property owners' "rightful opposition" to the facility and bleating about how "we should not permit persons with contagious diseases to endanger the State." Marcus Marks replied to the governor with a brief recitation of the facts ("our attending physician, Dr. Hess, says that no one of the children in the institution has had a cough, or even a temperature of 100 degrees, for the past five months").[131] Encouraged by the state's highest authorities, the resort town's property owners heeded no limits in the Save Lakewood campaign. One week they had the preventorium superintendent and physician Sherburn Wheelwright arrested on charges of unlawfully importing minors into the state; another week, preventorium legal agent Maximilian Rosenberg was arrested on the same charges.[132]

For Nathan Straus this was, understandably, an upsetting sequence of events, but his nerves were utterly shattered when his Lakewood co-owner, Max Nathan, joined forces with the protesting Lakewood property owners and publicly called on the benevolent philanthropist to relocate the facility. Max Nathan was a longstanding member of the New York Jewish elite, and he himself must have been immune to hysterical fears about tuberculosis treatment facilities—a decade earlier, he had been one of the six original owners of the consortium[133] Louis Marshall put together to purchase the Knollwood summer camp, located on Saranac Lake within walking distance of a village founded in the late nineteenth century as a fresh-air center for tuberculosis treatment by the legendary physician E. L. Trudeau, himself a patient. In late 1909, Nathan hired Marshall's firm to handle his demands for the Lakewood preventorium relocation. Samuel Untermyer handled the case; on December 10, 1909, Untermyer dispatched an ultimatum to Straus,[134] threatening legal action should the preventorium board continue the project at its present location; on the other hand, should Straus agree to "remove the preventorium to a place where it will not invade the peace and property rights of others," Nathan promised to donate his half share of the Lakewood Hotel, an investment of over $300,000, to the tuberculosis prevention project, Untermyer wrote. Nathan's lawyer conceded that the community protest had no compelling rational basis ("Mr. Nathan understands your contention that the preventorium does not receive diseased children"), but argued that "no useful purpose can be served by locating [such] an institution in a place which arouses the bitter animosity of neighbors." A few days later the *New York Times* published this letter written by Marshall's partner, Samuel Untermyer,[135] thereby precipitating a mortifyingly ugly public dispute among members of Marshall's social-professional circle that ultimately tarnished his own professional reputation and provided the president of the United States with a pretext not to appoint a viable Jewish candidate to the Supreme Court bench.

New York newspapers ridiculed Untermyer's intervention, depicting Marshall's partner as the greedy advocate of conscienceless property owners whose only worry was that desperately ill children convalesce some place where their precious Lakewood property values would not be jeopardized. "Lakewood Message to Children," screamed Hearst newspaper editor Arthur Brisbane in the *New York Evening Journal*, "Get Out of Here. Live or Die Somewhere Else and We Will Be Very Kind to You."[136] Understanding the demagogic power of such reporting, Untermyer moved quickly to contain public relations damage caused to his client and firm; the day after both were baited publicly as heartless money grubbers by the Hearst newspaper, Untermyer met with the preventorium board and appeared to finalize the proposed settlement whereby Nathan would donate his $300,000 share of the hotel on the condition that the preventorium would be relocated outside of Lakewood.[137] A relieved Governor Fort assumed the Lakewood problem was resolved.

The problem was that the outraged Straus disapproved of the board's pliancy. In his eyes, the preventorium project in Lakewood had become a matter of principle. "I will not voluntarily withdraw these children from Lakewood," exclaimed Straus to New York newspapers,[138] which undoubtedly sensed that readers would be drawn to coverage of a dispute involving estranged Jewish millionaires, Jewish business lawyers, Wasp property owners in a resort town, tuberculosis, and unsuspecting, vulnerable, and possibly afflicted children. Straus taunted Untermyer in the press: "If your clients, the rich men of Lakewood, are able to drive from their neighborhood as lepers these poor children, [who are] not yet even infected with the disease, it will make a precedent marking a step backward in the fight against the white plague."[139]

Depicting Straus's allegations as "wanton and gratuitous insults,"[140] Untermyer did everything he could to evade public stigma as a merciless advocate of property owners. He undoubtedly pressured Nathan to clarify matters publicly, and his client dutifully published in the *New York Times* a statement declaring, "He [Untermyer] took up the struggle most reluctantly, after urging me [Nathan] on account of my age to keep out of it."[141] Straus was demonstrably unimpressed by Untermyer's pleading. Publicly dismissing Nathan's clarifications, the Macy's co-owner, a philanthropist celebrated in early twentieth-century America as a heroic provider of pasteurized milk and protector of childhood health, branded Louis Marshall's business partner of fifteen years with the mark of Cain, essentially calling Untermyer a contemptibly greedy lawyer. "I must state to you that I feel absolutely no friendship toward yourself," Straus wrote to Untermyer, in another letter published promptly by the *New York Times.* "I would rather have ten first-class enemies than one such friend as yourself."[142]

A week later, Straus suffered a nervous collapse. News of the unbearable strain forced upon the beloved champion of childhood health by heartless lawyers and selfish homeowners was national news for days. Setting the tone, Hearst's *New York Evening Journal* reported that "Straus is seriously ill at his home, suffering from a nervous breakdown, surrounded by friends and family who attribute his breakdown to the fight over the Lakewood preventorium, a favorite project of Mr. Straus'." Articles written along these lines appeared in at least eighty newspapers, from coast to coast.[143] Straus remained sufficiently in command of his desires to prosecute his case in court. On January 19, 1910, as New Jersey lawmakers scrambled to placate powerful, land-invested constituents by drafting a proposed bill stipulating that the clearance from the state's Board of Health would hereafter be needed before any consumptive patients could be treated in a facility, Straus obtained a court order requiring Nathan to prove why he could not do whatever he wanted at Cleveland Cottage. Fully persuaded of his moral right to protect at-risk youth at the Lakewood preventorium, the embittered Macy's millionaire overlooked basic legal facts—Nathan, a co-owner at Cleveland Cottage, had never forfeited his share of control of the asset. Dismissing Straus's court petition in early February, a New Jersey Supreme Court judge ruled that finding in favor of the preventorium philanthropist's position in this dispute would require repeal of the entirety of the state's real estate law.[144] Untermyer and his firm had solidly defended Max Nathan's legal rights. "Good men are sometimes wrong," Untermyer announced to the press. He added less delicate words about

Straus: "When a headstrong man gets wrong, he sometimes gets very wrong, and stays so."[145]

The Untermyer firm's legal handling of the case was beyond reproach, and there is nothing in the private records of the dispute to indicate that the lawyers were particularly moralistic about the real estate concerns of Max Nathan's Lakewood cohorts in the dispute. Having built, a decade before, summer cottages in the Adirondacks a short distance from the Saranac Village tuberculosis colony, Nathan and Louis Marshall understood that popular representations of the disease as the white plague were typically infected by hysteria; at Lakewood, on Saranac Lake, they could afford to ignore such irrationality, because the summer camp was for their own use, and not primarily a real estate venture. Property investments, however, had no immunity to popular perception. Evidence proving that Louis Marshall was not morally fastidious about his firm's handling of Nathan's position in the preventorium dispute can be found in a negligible episode that transpired more than two years after the Lakewood affair was forgotten. Marshall and Henry Wollman, a friend and partner in a number of real estate ventures, invested in farmland in Westchester County with the intention of profiting from the development of suburban residences upon the completion of an aqueduct project; when officials in White Plains unexpectedly entertained plans to establish a tuberculosis hospital in this Yorktown Heights area, Marshall fired off a series of petitions that regurgitated precisely the property value arguments that had governed the "Save Lakewood" campaign against Straus's preventorium.[146]

As a practical matter, Untermyer handled Max Nathan's interests at Lakewood, but Marshall was not quite as uninvolved in the dispute as was implied by the downplaying reference in the aforementioned 1915 letter to Arthur Brisbane. At Untermyer's request, in late December 1909, Marshall wrote a long letter to Marcus Marks, outlining what the firm considered to be binding in Untermyer's December 10 letter to Straus, since both Straus and Max Nathan had subsequently altered their feelings and orientations in the affair.[147] One surviving office memorandum from the Guggenheimer, Untermyer firm indicates that Untermyer consulted with Marshall as a matter of course about the Lakewood dispute. On March 7, 1910, Untermyer informed Marshall that he had been in contact with their client, Max Nathan, who was convinced Straus's nervous collapse was a "pure fake"; Untermyer turned to Marshall for advice on the "pertinent question" of how, if circumstances were to warrant it, their firm could serve papers on Straus once the philanthropist sailed to Europe ("it would make us appear ridiculous," were the New Jersey affair to be left on hold indefinitely by a Straus disappearance, wrote Untermyer).[148] Marshall, however, avoided public association with the case, surely because he realized that while his partner's legal advice to Nathan was sound, Untermyer's public presentation of the affair was clumsily impolitic and self-defeating. In the courtroom of public perception—an arena where the tactically systematic and perpetually thoughtful Marshall, and the rapid-fire, impulsively outspoken Untermyer had noticeably different experiences and styles—it was highly questionable to call a respected public benefactor like Straus "headstrong," since any reader unversed in the affair's knockdown legal realities would be disposed to ask what, exactly, was the object of the Lakewood preventorium philanthropist's obstinacy. Ought not the world as a whole be more "headstrong" in the prevention of tuberculosis among children?

Untermyer's intemperate public handling of the Lakewood affair contributed to the drubbing endured by his firm as a whole. The public prosecution of the Guggenheimer, Untermyer and Marshall firm was initiated and aggressively handled by a man who genuinely admired Nathan Straus and who also happened to be America's most influential journalist, Arthur Brisbane. The famous editor of the Hearst newspapers has an ambiguous historical reputation that warrants a capsule summary here, if only because Brisbane played a bookends role in Marshall's life, entering it during this exasperating, low point Lakewood affair and then (as we shall see) reappearing positively many years later, at the moment of Marshall's greatest public triumph, Henry Ford's apology.

Arthur Brisbane (1864–1936), the "Demosthenes of the American barbershops," ranks among the most important journalists of his country's history. He was the son of an intellectual, impractical idealist, Albert Brisbane, who promoted experimental socialist forms in the United States, such as the Fourierist phalanx, which enjoyed brief spells of popularity in pre–Civil War America and captivated leading antebellum literati, including the famed Transcendentalists of Brook Farm. Arthur came of age with practical, rather than intellectual, interests in radical left ideas. As the most prominent figure in the Hearst newspapers, Brisbane liked to hire former radicals, not necessarily because he personally endorsed their politics, but because they knew how to talk to the man on the street.[149] A good example of how ideas Americanized in the two Brisbane generations is provided by Henry George, whose "single tax" plan for land excited radical circles in America at the end of the century. The elder Brisbane was inspired by George's landmark *Progress and Poverty* (1879) and frequently hosted George; at his father's house, the younger Brisbane engaged the political economist in high-spirited discussions about the way property values rise in proportion to population increases. This did nothing for Arthur Brisbane's social outlook, but it inspired his lifelong public gospel about the virtues of real estate investment and his own personal thirst for property. "What I know about real estate and real estate values,

I learned from the teachings of Henry George, though he was opposed to these things and I am in favor of them," Arthur Brisbane once reflected.[150]

Brisbane's politics oscillated left and right over the years, but his preaching about real estate was consistent. "He wrote about it in his column. He spoke of it in his lectures. Friends, acquaintances, even strangers were urged to buy! buy! buy!" notes his biographer.[151] Practicing what he preached, Brisbane, the Hearst editor who by 1910 was the world's highest paid journalist, purchased in 1907 some 600 acres in the deserted village of Allaire, New Jersey, close to his boyhood home, Fanwood. Two years later he boasted about having acquired close to 10,000 acres of land in this area.[152]

Politically, the high point of Hearst-Brisbane radicalism occurred in the early years of the twentieth century, when the newspaper men backed William Jennings Bryan's White House bids, and when Hearst served a brief stint in the US Congress, having campaigned on an antitrust platform that called for public ownership of railroads, telegraphs, and coal mines. Hearst's subsequent squabbling with Democratic bosses of Tammany Hall and his unsuccessful attempts to become mayor of New York City or governor of New York evidently dampened his and Brisbane's left-wing posturing; subsequent allegations about Brisbane's lack of patriotism during World War I (during the period of the Palmer raids and Red Scare, he was questioned about his alleged wartime support of Germany by Lee Overman's Senate committee) appear to have encouraged Brisbane to file away the left-wing idealism of his younger days. During the 1920s, he and Hearst mingled socially with leading businessmen from the era and stridently backed the era's three Republican presidents. One of Brisbane's close social contacts in the postwar era was automobile manufacturer Henry Ford, the American folk hero whose left-to-right outlook on public and political issues traced roughly the same arc as Brisbane's.

Ideology never anchored Brisbane's work, but in key periods of his career he had incentive to publicize ideas and proposals that might appeal to a mass audience. The profit-driven Hearst papers catered to immigrants and workers in crowded urban locales. "Writing good editorials is chiefly telling people what they think, not what you think," Brisbane famously quipped. His biographer concurs, describing Brisbane's decades of newspaper work as a "jungle of half-digested and half-remembered fact and fiction . . . that mirrored the mind of the average man."[153] To describe Arthur Brisbane as a harmless populist simplifies matters, however. He was a standard setter in the history of yellow journalism, honing that title at Hearst's *Evening Journal* by shamelessly publishing allegations of Spanish atrocities in Cuba to drum up public opinion for the Spanish-American War. In the new century, Hearst and Brisbane pushed their lurid sensationalism to an abysmal low that could never again be repeated in American history. Avowed proponents of trust busting, the pair grew so impatient with the relatively conservative outlook of the McKinley administration that they splashed their newspapers with insidious, incendiary discussions inviting readers to consider the advantages of the assassination of the president of the United States. "We Invite Our Readers to Think over This Question," Brisbane's *Journal* exclaimed. It added, shockingly, "If bad men cannot be got rid of except by killing, then the killing must be done."[154] After McKinley's assassination in September 1901, rival publishers mentioned in their newspapers' coverage that the culprit, Leon Czolgosz, had a copy of a Hearst paper in his pocket at the time of the murder.

An editor of unprecedented influence whose orientation toward ideas and public initiatives was more self-interested than idealistic, Brisbane's track record before World War I contained disturbing evidence of ways the unbridled populism of the Hearst papers he edited could be damaging and dangerous. As it turned out, however, the Lakewood dispute tapped the better aspects of Arthur Brisbane's heritage and character. His contribution to its resolution was commendable in all public respects and left behind only one casualty: Louis Marshall's most cherished professional ambition.

In early February 1910, Brisbane contacted Marcus Marks of the Lakewood preventorium board, proposing that the facility be relocated on 100 acres of "wooded upland, the healthiest for living purposes," in Monmouth County, six miles from Cleveland Cottage.[155] With no strings attached, the Hearst editor proposed that his real estate become "the absolute property of your [the preventorium board's] charity." Brisbane asked for nothing in exchange for this gift and subsequently contributed equipment and staff support for the newly relocated preventorium. Asking to remain anonymous, he clarified to Marks that "my interest in the matter is based upon my admiration and affection for Mr. Nathan Straus, whom I believe to be one of the best citizens of this country."[156] After New Jersey newspapers revealed Brisbane's land gift,[157] the newspaperman asked the preventorium board to credit his father in its announcements, as though the property's new location was due to a "fund established by the late Albert Brisbane."[158]

Justice Brewer passed away on March 28, 1910, just days after Brisbane finalized arrangements for the preventorium's relocation on his lands. When Marshall turned to his powerful allies, Mayer Sulzberger and Jacob Schiff, asking them to submit his candidacy for the bench to President Taft, it was not his first bid for the Supreme Court—after the death of Rufus Wheeler Peckham in mid-autumn 1909, Marshall had conferred hopefully with Schiff about his possible eligibility for a nomination and delivered to the banker documentary "information as to my experience in litigation of the character which comes before the Supreme Court."[159] This earlier bid, however, was not seriously pursued—Taft ended up appointing an old friend, Federal Circuit Judge Horace Lurton, and rumors suggesting that Judge Sulzberger himself, a veteran of fourteen years of experience as a judge on Philadelphia's Court of Common Pleas, was on the president's mind at this stage as a possible appointee[160] probably compromised Marshall's ability to rally his friends in support of his own ambition. The effort after Brewer's death was decidedly more assertive and began when Marshall approached Schiff to "discuss the propriety" of his "again" championing Marshall's aspirations for the Supreme Court bench after Justice Brewer's death. Schiff "did not think" that his associate's chances for the nomination were "very great," but he agreed to help and confidentially enlisted Mayer Sulzberger for a joint effort.[161] Sulzberger, the AJC president, and a judicious, respected Republican who "struck responsive chords with Taft,"[162] sent a handwritten note to the president on March 30, asking whether he could come to the White House with Schiff to advocate the appointment of Marshall to the Supreme Court.[163] The president replied on April 1, cordially scheduling an appointment with Sulzberger and Schiff for noon on April 7 (he asked Isaac Ullman, a prominent Jewish Connecticut Republican to join the meeting[164]). Taft did not hint about a preference for Hughes in this initial contact with Marshall's supporters; at most, the president's papers indicate that in late March, on the very day when Taft composed a condolence letter to David Brewer's wife, he sent a cordial note to the wife of New York governor Hughes, thanking her for her hospitality on a recent visit and vowing that he would "always treasure the friendship" he had with the governor and his wife. The admiringly warm, respectful tone Taft evinced toward Charles Evans Hughes contrasted sharply with the bristling innuendo about Louis Marshall as an enemy of sick children, which Arthur Brisbane was during this nominee selection period publishing in the Hearst newspapers. Brisbane conveyed characterizations of presumptive court candidates directly to the president, dispatching a letter to Taft on April 7,[165] the day Schiff, Sulzberger, and Ullman arrived at the White House to lobby for Marshall's nomination. This was the interview where President Taft angered Schiff by asking the banker, "Schiff, if you were President, would you name Sam Untermyer's partner to the Supreme Court?"[166]

Close to forty years after this episode, Marshall's old rival, Rabbi Stephen Wise, wrote bitingly in his memoir that Taft already had Hughes's acceptance letter for the court spot in his pocket during this meeting with Schiff, Sulzberger, and Ullman. Wise's account is not reliable. Taft offered the nomination to Hughes three weeks after the meeting with Marshall's advocates, and the president's flatteringly entreating, and somewhat unctuous, letter to New York's governor on April 22, a document that conveyed assurances that Hughes himself would someday make it to the White House and tried to allay Hughes's practical reservations about the court appointment by (among other things) citing specific figures about expected salary hikes for the bench's occupants,[167] irrefutably proves that the appointment was far from a clinched arrangement until the end of April. Before that time, President Taft received approaches from politicians and public figures who proposed an array of names as promising candidates for the Supreme Court position,[168] and as late as April 18, he candidly assured petitioners, such as Iowa governor B. F. Carrol (who lobbied for his state's Supreme Court Chief Justice) that he had yet "to take up the subject" of the nomination in earnest. Whatever the president's private inclinations on the subject, Louis Marshall's candidacy for the Supreme Court during Taft's deliberation period was wiped out by Arthur Brisbane.

In this period, the Hearst newspapers had much to say about Sam Untermyer's partner, as evidenced by this editorial:

Mr. Marshall for Supreme Court—We Hope Not

It would be a sudden jump from fighting weak, sick children to handing down Supreme Court decisions.

Jacob Schiff and Judge Mayer Sulzberger of Philadelphia have called at the White House and urged the appointment of Louis Marshall of New York to the vacancy on the Supreme Court bench caused by the death of Justice Brewer . . . It is also stated that Mr. Taft declares that he has Mr. Marshall on the list of eligibles.

Without any wish to hurt Mr. Marshall's feelings, or to reflect on his profound legal ability, we suggest to Pres. Taft that he REMOVE Mr. Marshall from the list of eligibles.

Mr. Marshall is a member of the law firm that distinguished itself in a very savage and effective fight against a refuge for poor children at Lakewood. Kind-hearted men and women had arranged to take from New Jersey a certain number of half-starved children living under dangerous conditions and build them up at Lakewood.

But this didn't suit the aristocratic and selfish instincts of some other individuals at Lakewood. THEY didn't want the sickly children around them. They wanted them to go somewhere else. In short, they wanted to kick them out of Lakewood. AND THE FIRM OF WHICH MR MARSHALL IS A MEMBER WAS ENGAGED TO DO THE KICKING OUT.

It was done successfully. And the aristocratic atmosphere of Lakewood is not to be contaminated with the presence of friendly, sickly children.

> We beg to suggest to Mr. Taft that a law firm able and willing to keep the wretched poor of the big cities from finding a refuge from disease anywhere in the country near the rich and prosperous WILL PROBABLY HAVE PLENTY OF IMPORTANT LUCRATIVE WORK ON ITS HANDS FOR MANY YEARS TO COME!
>
> The fact that these children were put out of Lakewood, the fact that Mr. Marshall's law firm was successful in its contention that the poor have no rights when their presence interferes with the delicate sensibilities of the rich, will cause many prosperous neighborhoods to engage Mr. Marshall's firm for similar work. . . .
>
> We believe that Mr. Taft, in his appointments, considers the opinions of those who elect him.
>
> And we believe that he will find for the Supreme bench some lawyers in a firm that has never been distinguished by the energy and success of its attack upon unfortunate children.[169]

Naturally, Marshall's supporters were alarmed by such inflammatory reports in the Hearst press and worried about the scope of the damage they caused to Marshall's professional ambitions. Marshall rebuffed advice that written rebuttals to Brisbane's accusations be arranged and published—evincing his abiding tactical perspective, Marshall judged that published rebuttals "would only tend to give emphasis to that which is on its face not only unjust but absurd."[170] Ideally, a confidential approach to Brisbane could have worked, but Marshall understood as a practical matter that the Hearst editor was unlikely to be dissuaded from his campaign. Referring to the head of the preventorium board and his associates, Marshall wrote wanly: "If Mr. Marks with other friends of Nathan Straus can induce Mr. Brisbane to take back editorially what he has said—well and good."[171] Such retraction was not a possibility, however. Late in the month, after the Hughes nomination, Marshall's exacting sense of personal honor prevented him from elaborating upon his acute disappointment. He exhibited just a small trace of his innermost feelings in one note, written to Thomas Mulry, an ally from Marshall's debut appearance in public adjudication on the Rabbi Jacob Joseph funeral disturbance panel. "The kindly expressions of friendship which I have received at every hand," Marshall confided to Mulry, "afford me compensation for whatever disappointment I may have sustained in not receiving the appointment."[172]

President Taft could never have given a direct account of the extent to which the prejudicial innuendo and jaundiced characterizations of Marshall's legal work in the Hearst newspapers impinged upon his thinking for the Supreme Court nomination. A hint in this respect can, perhaps, be gleaned from a line Taft inserted in a polite reply to one of the pro-Marshall petitioners, Albany politician Samuel Koenig, who wrote to the president in praise of Marshall on April 4. Replying a few days later, Taft carefully emphasized that the candidate's Jewish identity was not an issue—"I can not appoint anybody because he is a Jew, and I certainly shall not decline to appoint anybody because he is a Jew," wrote Taft.[173] The next line in this reply can possibly be interpreted as a complying nod to the Hearst newspaper's vituperative campaign against Marshall, since Taft implies that Marshall, at least in the public mind, cannot be identified as a "gentleman" who is "competent" for a Supreme Court appointment in "every respect." Taft wrote: "It would give me gratification should I find a gentleman competent for the place in every respect if he were a Jew, because by my appointment it would be made emphatically to appear that no man is denied the highest place in the Republic because of his race."[174]

Encounter with the Halutz Zionist Prototype: Aaronsohn and Atlit

In the years before World War I, Americans energetically debated about the promises and risks of life in a newly urbanized, technologically capable modern landscape, and these ongoing discussions were taken up with acute wonderment and intensity in Jewish New York, where the encounter of settled elite privilege and mass immigrant ambition provoked considerable insight about what, exactly, was new and worthwhile in twentieth-century life. Far from being unnerved by personal setbacks, like his failed Supreme Court bid, or by public challenges posed by anti-immigrant Nativists, Marshall remained unflinchingly committed to the American values and dynamics he held responsible for the extraordinary success of his own career, as the son of immigrants from Upstate New York whose law practice kept him in touch with the cardinal socioeconomic and constitutional questions of his day and whose work on Jewish matters inspired a deep, perhaps spiritual, inward sense of satisfaction. His success was inarguable, but it was possible to debate whether the late nineteenth-century dynamics that had accounted for it were becoming obsolete in an urban milieu in which young Jewish and Christian Americans were now racing to the same goals in motorized vehicles and professional education programs.

In fact, by the end of the first decade in the new century, Marshall was beginning to look back nostalgically to the slower, more self-reliant methods that had transported him to wealth and professional success. New York was becoming crowded by ambition and narrowed by shortcuts. During the first years of the decade, Marshall contributed to projects like the Educational Alliance due to the feeling that the Jewish immigrants could not Americanize quickly enough; by 1910, he was wondering whether these Jewish youngsters were Americanizing too fast. More than the preservation of their Jewish identities seemed to be at stake. Marshall was having trouble identifying the steady core of what subsequent generations would call "the American way."

Several revealing letters from this period exhibited his doubts about newly modern ways of thinking about success in America. One was written to Professor E. R. A. Seligman, a Columbia economist who had for years experimented with novel ideas like progressive taxation and who asked Marshall whether the provision of public assistance to Jewish immigrant graduate students would have moral and practical merit. Marshall doubted that tuition scholarships to Jewish students in law or medical schools would be wise. "It is very desirable to stimulate ambition among these young men," he told Seligman, "but I doubt the policy of presenting them with crutches."[175] Marshall referred to the value of making "personal sacrifices" as a means of satisfying personal ambition, and he offered variants of his own route as a collectivized prescription for success when he noted that "there have been men who have risen in the [legal] profession, who never went to law school" (or who never finished law school). However, he wondered whether his own professional story remained pertinent to rising generations. Seldom shy about the pertinence of his advocacy, Marshall tellingly admitted to Seligman his personal views about pathways to twentieth-century success probably should "not be foisted on anybody."

Marshall was ambivalent about ways his ancient people was endeavoring to become very new. In particular, he was struggling inwardly about the purposes and implications of the Zionist movement. The issue had abstract and practical dimensions, but for a number of years, all its aspects seemed to converge in the body of one individual, a mesmerizingly talented agronomist from the northern regions of Ottoman–controlled Palestine, Aaron Aaronsohn, who in 1906 had impressed the world scientific community by discovering near Rosh Pina a promising wild strain of wheat, *Triticum dicoccoides*.[176]

Aaronsohn called on Marshall in mid-November 1909, and in one meeting enlisted the energies of the shrewd, ordinarily circumspect business lawyer. As happened with several other figures in elite American Jewish circles, Marshall came away from his initial encounter with the agronomist wondering whether a new type of pioneer Renaissance man was taking shape in Eretz Israel. Technically not a made in the Land of Israel Sabra (Aaronsohn was six when he left Romania with his parents, who were among the founders of Zichron Ya'akov), Aaronsohn's electrifying effect upon figures like Marshall, Julius Rosenwald, and Louis Brandeis can nonetheless be explained by the spell he cast as a new

Jewish prototype that fused pioneering élan readily appreciable in America and cutting edge twentieth-century scientific capability. Marshall excitedly exclaimed to his confidante Cyrus Adler, "I am much interested in his [Aaronsohn's] plans," and he vowed to take the "first opportunity" to recruit Schiff and Rosenwald as patrons for Aaronsohn's proposed agricultural experimental station. Aaronsohn, Marshall noted, "has made a great discovery," wild wheat, "which promises well, not only for agriculture in Palestine, but all arid regions."[177]

Within days, Marshall and Aaronsohn had raised a total donation of $20,000 from Schiff and Rosenwald, a sum estimated as the initial cost of the experimental station. Marshall was drafting documents to incorporate this Eretz Israel research project in the state of New York. Aaronsohn needed subscriptions for a fund guaranteeing an annual research allocation of $10,000 for five years; to this end, Marshall sent fund-raising appeals to wealthy associates such as Adolph Lewisohn and Dan Guggenheim. "Aaronsohn has certainly made a conquest of me," Marshall told these potential patrons, and he recited the roster of the Palestine agronomist's scientific backers, from Europe (including German botanist Georg Schweinfurth) and in the US Department of Agriculture.[178]

This alliance with Aaronsohn was loaded from the start with two combustible elements. First, as a paragon of a new immigration process (the First Aliyah) to a self-sufficient, modern Jewish community in Eretz Israel, the "New Yishuv," Aaronsohn embodied an ideal of Jewish pioneering independence that contrasted with the religious dependents of the "Old Yishuv," who had relied everlastingly on *halukah* charity handouts. This value of halutz pioneering self-sufficiency was becoming a staple in the developing ideology of Zionism, and it rendered characters like Aaronsohn fundamentally problematic to patrons in the Jewish Diaspora. Since Ottoman–controlled Palestine was desperately short on infrastructure, reality dictated that the new Zionist pioneers needed outside funds for their development projects; simultaneously, their own nationalist ideology dictated that these new Jewish pioneers had to forge their own destiny in the land, because any dependency upon Diaspora largesse would dilute the existential line in the sand that was being drawn between the traditional Old Yishuv and the modernizing New Yishuv. The conundrum applied generally to proto-Zionists or Zionists who appealed ambivalently to Diaspora donors for an array of cultural, educational, and economic development projects in the Yishuv, but Aaronsohn posed a special challenge, since this likeable but volatile agronomist had an unpredictable temperament and was liable at every juncture to transform an established relationship with an overseas patron into a brawling power struggle. Had highly enthused patrons like Marshall and Rosenwald been apprised of the facts of Aaronsohn's turbulent relationship with Baron Edmond de Rothschild's

Jewish Colonization Association during the first phase of his activities as a Palestine agronomist,[179] it is doubtful that they would have thrown caution to the wind as they did in offering Aaronsohn support.

Second, support for an ambitious Eretz Israel personality like Aaronsohn forced Marshall and his circle to face the practical limits of their outlook on the Holy Land. Marshall, Schiff, and many others came to be identified ideologically as "non-Zionists," meaning that they had strong emotional ties to a land cherished more than any other by Jewish religion and tradition but chose to devote their energies and resources to the development of "nonpolitical" scientific and cultural projects in the Yishuv. The non-Zionists feared that support for the Zionists' political Jewish statehood program could in various ways jeopardize the status of Diaspora Jews, and they often objected formally that political Zionism contradicted their own Reform Jewish belief that Jewish identity in the modern world was entirely religious, and so no Jewish national entity could exist. The Zionists, however, were far from meticulous about separating cultural and economic aspects of their work from political dimensions. In fact, in their minds, support for the Yishuv's economic, educational, and scientific infrastructure was not separate from their Jewish statehood program, but was instead a necessary prerequisite for its realization. During World War I, Aaronsohn's creation of the pro-British Nili spy ring proved that as he saw it, his efforts in experimental science could not reasonably be distinguished from the question of Palestine's political future. This World War I revelation of the agronomist's highly politicized orientation rattled the tidy non-Zionist formulas held in Marshall's German Jewish circle; as we shall see, Marshall spent the 1920s recovering from this shock and looking for constructive responses to it.

Previews of the perplexities imposed by these two issues arose in the early months of Marshall's partnership with Aaron Aaronsohn. In early January 1910, less than two months after Marshall's rhapsodic initial encounter with the agronomist, the aura was lost in his writing about Aaronsohn. He wrote to Aaronsohn to establish "a clear understanding": Marshall had never himself taken on fund-raising responsibility for the experimental station, and he would file incorporation papers for it on his own, not Aaronsohn's, discretion. "I am overwhelmed with my work," Marshall complained to the persistently demanding visitor from Eretz Israel, "and I must repel the thought that the present period of inaction in your [Aaronsohn's] affair is due to me, directly or indirectly."[180] The Holy Land pioneer managed to make Marshall feel guilty. "Aaronsohn seems to lie down on me, as though I were the guarantor of his scheme," Marshall moaned to Adler. "I would be glad to finance the entire enterprise, but inasmuch as I have not [the money], I must depend upon the moods and humors and foibles of the millionaires."[181]

Wolf was positioned haplessly at the eye of the storm. He brought to his Dillingham testimony a long-standing opposition to the classification of immigrants by their Jewish faith. As he saw it, identifying newcomers on a religious basis was a constitutional violation. Wolf also decided, fatefully, to deny outright that there was any justification for classifying Jewish immigrants on a racial basis. "A Jew coming from Russia is a Russian," Wolf explained to the committee, "from Roumania a Roumanian, from France a Frenchman." As the historian Eric Goldstein has pointed out, this approach bewildered his congressional questioners "who were sharply focused on race as a central factor in immigration policy."[192] In what became a notoriously famous colloquy, Senator Lodge ran circles around the immigration advocate by using the example of Disraeli, whom Wolf insisted on regarding as a Jew, even though he was baptized as a Christian. Obviously contradicting his denials of a Jewish racial identity, the outwitted Wolf stammered about how Disraeli, Heine, and others could be considered Jews, "born of their blood," even though "they ceased to be Jews from the standpoint of religion."

"Poor old Simon Wolf," American Zionist Bernard Richards wrote scathingly, in the *Hebrew Standard*.[193] "Thousands of years as a distinct race and nationality" had "no meaning for his little group of Reform Jews." Richards declared that "the time has come to speak plain words" and excoriate advocates like Wolf "who have been spreading a great falsehood [in their denial] of the Jewish race." Richards dropped a series of rank insults about the German Jewish advocates' "blundering" and "bungling," but he developed one substantive claim: the effort to protect Jewish interests and oppose immigration restriction was liable to achieve the opposite when it denied obvious empirical realities and stirred contempt among Gentiles for Jewish lobbying sophistry. The Gentiles on the Dillingham Commission who listened incredulously to Wolf's specious extemporizing about Disraeli "knew more about the Jews" than did the misguided Jewish lobbyists.

Marshall might have countenanced this blistering polemic had it been directed against Wolf alone, but Richards also included in his diatribe Julian Mack,[194] an associate whom Marshall believed "had done much to elevate the Jews in this country."[195] Beyond such personal loyalty, Marshall objected to Richards' right, as the secretary of the New York Kehillah, to dismiss the "German Jews'" preference for conceptualizing Jewish identity in religious, rather than racial terms. That was an interesting, but indeterminate, accusation, since the New York Kehillah's founding convention had considered establishing the experiment on religious lines, but opted in the end for neutral constituent formulations referring blandly to the representation of the "Jews of New York City," without taking a stand on whether this constituency was a race or a religious group.[196] In fact, the preference for the religious classification was Marshall's own, not the Kehillah's. His complaint to Magnes about Richards's article left little room for doubt about that point: "I take more interest in a religious Jew than in an Atheist who, for ulterior reasons, may find it convenient to be classified as a Hebrew, on the theory that he belongs to a race of that name," Marshall testily declared.[197] He also had legitimate concerns that a Jewish recognition of race as a standard of immigrant classification could backfire, since the Jews might find themselves classified outside of the entitlements offered to the white race. "Every day I find more reason for scenting danger in this [racial] classification," Marshall explained. "Within the last few days a bill has been introduced in Congress which is intended to prohibit both naturalization and immigration by others than 'white persons of the Caucasian race.'"[198]

Marshall's worry about immigration doors closing to the Jews due to their classification as nonwhites jibed with a rising community sentiment. By 1909, Goldstein observes, there were "increasing fears" among Jewish leaders "that Jews' status as whites was in danger."[199] And well into the fall of 1910, Marshall was deeply involved in court litigation and legislative lobbying whose purpose was to guarantee that "Asiatic Jews," along with Armenians, Turks, and other groups, were "white persons" as defined by naturalization laws.[200] Yet Marshall's ire in this debate about Jews as a race or religion did not necessarily exhibit a shared feeling in the Jewish leadership elite or arise out of tactical-practical calculations. "All this fighting about names and words is, to my mind, utterly trivial," he declared, in sheer despair.[201] As a result of several factors, Marshall was undergoing a period of doubt in Jewish affairs. His mother's death in late January 1910 deprived him of what had been the surest anchor in the development of his own identity. With the abrogation campaign held in abeyance, the AJC still lacked tangible proof of its utility. Zionist initiatives and theorizing stirred in him an irritating ambivalence. Later in the spring, the failed bid for the Supreme Court nomination further demoralized Marshall. All told, Marshall was becoming increasingly ill disposed to new Jewish plans or familiar debates about Jewish life and destiny.

The AJC's chiefs were, in this period, restless, irritable, and visibly concerned about the organization's viability in the eyes of Downtown's immigrant masses. Schiff set the tone at AJC Executive Committee meetings, arguing that the organization had been misled by the Taft administration's promises of action on the Russian treaty question.[202] It was the same old story, Schiff angrily told his peers. "We have been fed on similar promises and assurances for many years, that everything was being done to reach an understanding with Russia, but nothing has ever come of it." In this private organizational sanctum, Schiff was speaking about the AJC in a caustic fashion reminiscent of the way America's Russian Jews talked about it. "We [have] simply [been] licking the hands of the President," cried the banker. "We do not respect ourselves sufficiently to come out boldly and demand our rights." Continuing, Schiff pinpointed the rationale of the abrogation campaign and why it could not remain stalled. As a warrant of the AJC's organizational credibility, and as a proof to the immigrant Russian Jews of the accountability of the American political system, abrogation would guard a social order America's German Jewish elite could not live without. "Unless the President is made to understand what it is we want and that we want it very much, there will be a revolt on the part of Russian-Jewish citizens which could not be checked," Schiff predicted.[203] Marshall reiterated that abrogation must remain the goal. "Bullying was all right, if it was the right kind of bullying," Marshall told his AJC associates, adding that unfocused speeches in Congress were pointless.[204] In such private meetings, Marshall cried out for abrogation, but the problem was that neither he nor the AJC as a whole had at this moment a workable plan for real action.

In March 1910, Israel Friedlander, a thoughtful, respected JTS scholar, approached Marshall, asking whether he would consider taking an active interest in the newly formed Zionist youth organization, Young Judaea. Marshall's vehemently negative reply, filled with non sequiturs and embittered surveys of Russian Jewish ingratitude toward Uptown leadership, undoubtedly shocked Friedlander. Marshall was in an angry passing mood, but his sarcastic words warrant citation, since they reflect authentic doubt about the salient issues of American Jewish life at the time. On the basis of considerable personal investment of time and emotional resources, Marshall was wondering whether anything could be organizationally workable in American Jewish affairs and whether tensions between the East European immigrants and the settled Central European stewards would prove, in the end, to be mutually debilitating, rather than mutually empowering:

> Whenever any individual conceives what he considers to be a good idea, he at once forms an organization around it. A mass meeting is held, glittering speeches are delivered, officers are elected, and then subscription papers are passed around to the same handful of individuals who are called upon to support every kind of communal work that is conceived by the mind of man and who, as a reward for their contributions, are immediately attacked, reviled and insulted by the very organizations which they are called upon to support. Their motives are misconstrued, they are not given the credit of having ordinary intelligence, nor are they recognized as having the right to entertain opinions of their own. The very acme of hate and contempt is injected into the words

> "philanthropists" and "Yahudim" when applied to those who, yielding to the clamorous prayer for contributions, give of their substance with a spirit of good will, which is intentionally misinterpreted.[205]

Apologizing for relating to matters that have "no special reference to Young Judaea," Marshall admitted that he was feeling "more discouraged than ever," largely in response to "intemperate" expressions and recent events, including the ignoble slurs against Judge Mack and the Richards article. Due to the recent death of his mother, he added, he was generally avoiding public meetings.[206]

Jacob Marshall, who was eighty when his wife Zilli died at the age of eighty-four, left Syracuse in this period to live with one of his daughters and her husband. Through the spring and summer, the family pondered ways of memorializing its beloved matriarch. Eventually, a plan took shape to offer the family home on Cedar Street in Syracuse to the city's Jewish communal institutions. Bennie Stolz, the Syracuse attorney who handled Marshall's real estate and other Syracuse affairs, contacted the Young Men's Hebrew Association and the National Council of Jewish Women; in fall 1910, Marshall met in Stolz's office with the organizations' delegates and drafted papers incorporating the Zilli Marshall Memorial Society.[207] The arrangement was conditioned on the house's use for religious, ethical, communal, and charitable purposes for the benefit of Syracuse's Jewish community.[208] "I feel very happy at the thought that the old home is to be devoted to so useful a purpose," Marshall told his father. Its use would preserve "mother's beneficent influence."[209]

The house on Cedar Street was presented to Syracuse's Jewish community on November 24, 1910. At the ceremony, Jacob cut a dignified figure, sitting near the piano, which was draped by an American flag. Louis spoke for him: "My father has been a constant believer in the gospel of hard work; he has always advocated the physical development of young men."[210] As to his mother, he recalled: "She was convinced that so long as the mothers and daughters of Israel devoted themselves to the study of the Bible, to the glorious history of our people and our faith . . . the future would be secure."[211] In a poem he wrote for the occasion, Marshall referred lovingly to his mother's half century in "A simple Jewish home, with blessings filled."[212] For the next thirty-five years, until the end of World War II, Marshall's childhood home became for Syracuse Jews the "Cedar Street Y." Remodeled with club and game rooms and with showers in the old basement, the Y served as a recreation temple for low-income Jewish kids in Syracuse. "From the age of nine, the kids in our neighborhood went to the 'Y' almost every day, except Friday, and not before sunset on Saturday," recalls Herb Alpert, a Syracuse Jewish author and devotee of Marshall.[213]

For Marshall, arranging his mother's memorial society could not be more than bittersweet labor, and, with the Supreme Court bid crushed, he was struggling in this period to find inspiration in new ventures. Some, most particularly the initial petitions for the establishment of the New York State College of Forestry at Syracuse University,[214] got off the ground and became sources of tremendous satisfaction to Marshall. But such solace came later, and he seemed uncharacteristically unfocused when he headed in summer 1910 to the Knollwood retreat. "I am leaving for Knollwood with Florrie and the children," he announced to his partner Samuel Untermyer in late June. "I am not feeling as well as I should, and have never felt the need of rest more than I do at this time."[215] Over the summer, he monitored developments with the private banking law and the Palestine experimental station, not exactly listlessly, but with less energy than usual. The notes he passed back and forth about Aaronsohn's various needs and peeves with Henrietta Szold,[216] who served as secretary for the experimental station's overseas board, prompt reflection. Both figures were in transition phases of their lives (Szold in 1909 paid her first visit to Palestine) and searching for content in organized Jewish endeavor, Marshall in the period before the AJC remobilized in the abrogation fight, and Szold two years before the formation of Hadassah, the Women's Zionist Organization of America.

The Cloakmakers Strike and the Protocol of Peace

Whenever Marshall's involvement with Jewish affairs meandered, Downtown provided direction. This action-response pattern in the rise of American Jewish ethnicity was never more in evidence than in summer 1910.

In a follow-up to New York City's 1909 strike of ladies' garment workers, a massive strike of cloakmakers (three-fourths of the membership of the International Ladies' Garment Workers Union, ILGWU) erupted on July 7, 1910.[217] Representing the ILGWU's Joint Board of Cloakmakers,[218] Meyer London declared that the survival of the fittest had in the cloak industry become the survival of the meanest. The moral justice and work improvements sought by the strikers were greater than the interests of any union, London declared; this was an "irresistible movement of the people" and a "protest against conditions that can no longer be tolerated." Describing strike dynamics, another downtown activist, attorney Morris Hillquit, explained that some 1,800 shops, each with its own semi-independent picket committee, shut down work; a staggering total of 45,000 workers took part in the strike. Three union men were stationed in front of each shop, largely to explain to indecisive workers the strike's purposes and the imperative of labor solidarity.

Preparing for a hard fight, manufacturers, organized in the Cloak, Suit and Skirt Protective Association, with combative Julius Henry Cohen as the association's legal counsel, drew a line in the sand. They balked at granting union recognition in general and were particularly adamant about not consenting to union workforce control via the controversial mechanism of a "closed shop," meaning an enterprise open to union workers alone.

The scale of the strike, and the chasm separating workers' demands and management positions, worried social reformers of various stripes, both full-time social workers and also liberal, moderate-minded industrialists. These peacemakers included Boston social worker Meyer Bloomfield and also Lincoln Filene, owner of the Boston department store Filene's. Two weeks into the strike, these peacemakers were convinced by Cohen and union leaders alike that a "big man" ought to be brought in "to confer with both sides and draw up a fair basis of negotiations," as Bloomfield described it.[219] Accordingly, the call went out to the famed "people's attorney" Louis Brandeis, who had garnered relevant experience as the lawyer for Boston cloak manufacturers during a tumultuous strike.[220] Cohen represented the association, and London was the union's advocate, at an initial meeting held on July 28 to set the stage for Brandeis's mediation. Observers present at this conferral remarked upon the strike's overwhelming sociological fact—participants from both sides were almost entirely Jewish, and they shared background experiences in social reform, labor issues, and various intellectual movements.[221]

During the first days of talks, Brandeis, an able negotiator, focused on wage and hour issues, topics about which gaps seemed bridgeable. As a practical matter, however, his mediation was predestined for failure, owing to Brandeis's refusal to talk about the closed shop mechanism as an industrial remedy. John B. Lennon, American Federation of Labor treasurer and a member of the ILGWU strike committee, pressed Brandeis on that sore point. Brandeis split hairs, claiming that Lennon's reference was really to a "union shop," some future eventuality in which an enterprise "has reached that high degree of perfection in organization that everybody in it is a union man,"[222] but he remained evasive about present-day realities and reminded London and the others that the "closed shop" remedy was taboo in these late July talks. Brandeis's alternative was the "preferential shop," defined as an enterprise in which "union standards prevail and the union man is entitled to preference" over nonunion employees.[223] Downtown workers scoffed at this formula, understanding that it provided no real compliance mechanism to guarantee that manufacturers hire union workers preferentially. The *Forward* ridiculed the preferential shop, branding it "the scab shop with honey and a sugar coated poison pill."[224] In early August, Brandeis's mediation effort failed.

However, the distinguished jurist would subsequently receive credit as the mastermind of the "Protocols of Peace" accord for industrial cooperation that ended the strike.[225]

This reputation justifiably honors the prodigious labors invested generally in this period by the Progressive Brandeis for a rationalized, more equitable workplace. Yet it also falsely casts Brandeis's cloakmakers mediation effort in New York as an unqualified success and reinforces a debatable image of Brandeis as a left-liberal Progressive people's lawyer whose ideas were tailor-made for labor and thus readily adoptable in an agreement to end the massive cloakmakers strike. In fact, Brandeis's summer 1910 mediation broke an initial impasse in this famous strike, and his industrial cooperation formulas exercised a strong public appeal, but he did not solve the problem at hand, and historians have come increasingly to identify aspects of his philosophy conducive to the manufacturers' interests.[226]

In August 1910, the cloakmakers strike, a transformative event both in American labor history and in American Jewish affairs, awaited a settlement that would accomplish two clearly perceptible ends. The union leaders and rank and file needed to be assured that any competent laborers they submitted for hire would truly be granted preference over nonunion men; management needed a formula that avoided outright recognition of the union, and, in particular, would not grant the union monopolistic control of workforce supply. The strike-ending formula that simultaneously met both these requirements was drafted by Louis Marshall, and in this fundamental sense credit for the Protocols of Peace belongs to him. The fact that history overlooked Marshall's significant contribution to industrial relations in early twentieth-century America can be considered in light of two broader dynamics. The first dynamic involves the tendency of Louis Brandeis to rush to and from a scene and then receive adulation as though he had left behind a done deal when in fact Marshall was left picking up the pieces in an incomplete work in progress (the general topic of American Jewry's relation to Zionism really belongs to this dynamic).[227] Second, despite the perception that Louis Marshall, as a conservative Republican, was an odd fit in circumstances associated with social reform, his long-overlooked contributions to an impressive array of left-liberal issues (environmentalism, African American and other minority group rights, Haitian independence, and, in this case, industrial relations and worker rights) were substantive and even, in some instances, determinatively responsible for standards and terms of empowerment that became familiar in American political history.

As days passed in August 1910, the cloakmakers strike veered toward a protracted, perhaps violently confrontational, course. Surprising many, perhaps even its own leadership, the ILGWU collected tens of thousands of dollars for a strike fund to sustain workers who temporarily had no income; in a tribute to Downtown solidarity, a phalanx of worker organizations, political groups, and Yiddish publicists contributed dollars or fund-raising energy for the strike fund, which reached a total of $246,403 by September.[228] Meantime, temperatures Downtown soared feverishly when the manufacturers association announced plans to bring in replacement workers. In mid-August, Cohen filed for an antiunion injunction in New York's Supreme Court. Justice Irving Lehman issued a limited injunction, banning the union from coercing employees to leave their jobs; Lehman also ordered London and the union to show cause why a broader injunction should not be enacted. The union was under pressure, but its militancy remained popular, as evidenced by supportive calls for strike discipline issued in the *Forward* and other Downtown outlets. Judge Lehman's ruling left in a bind not the union but rather the first set of peacemaker mediators. Maneuvering for a broader injunction, Cohen asked Brandeis for documents he believed would prove that the union had operated as a criminal conspiracy. Brandeis as well as Filene and Bloomfield stalled, understandably worried that proactive cooperation with the association, in compliance with a court that seemed determined to break the strike by issuing injunctions, would ruin their credibility with the union and its masses of Downtown supporters.[229] This was, indeed, an impasse.

Three weeks into August, Schiff and Marshall decided to intervene, owing to a mix of direct humanitarian concern about the plight of salary-shorn workers; practical interests, shared in their circle of bankers, lawyers, and businessmen, in favor of the resumption of normal economic activity; and (last but not least) anxieties that a prolonged strike would irk anti-Semitic characterizations of Jews as unreliable and subversive workers and as greedy, heedless employers. Significantly, both the mainstream press (e.g., the *New York Times*) and Yiddish newspapers from all parts of the political spectrum praised the Marshall–Schiff initiative.[230]

Marshall got to work on August 22, meeting separately with the two sides. The problem at this stage was management, since Cohen was convinced that he could break the strike in the courts. Marshall brought in the big guns, Schiff and Joseph Marcus, president of the Lower East Side's Public Bank, to defuse this problem; remembering where they put their money, the manufacturers assented to the bankers' recommendation for renewed negotiations.[231] This was Marshall's moment. The latest attempt to revise the preferential shop formula, submitted by Filene, floundered due to the association's reservations (the Filene compromise formula—"the preferential shop is one which the manufacturers recognize the union"—explicitly proffered recognition to the union, and that was unacceptable to the manufacturers).[232] Though a week of perspiration and continued high

New York, September 2 , 1910.

Louis Marshall, Esq.,
37 Wall Street,
New York City.

Dear Sir:

At a meeting of the Executive Committee of the Cloak, Suit and Skirt Manufacturers Protective Association this day held, the revised Protocol agreed upon between Meyer London, Esq., yourself and myself, was presented and was adopted, and was directed to be delivered to you with the signature of the Chairman of said Committee, to be promulgated, on condition, however, that you shall simultaneously receive from the General Strike Committee of the Unions a like authorization, coupled with a resolution that the strike heretofore existing shall be declared off.

Very truly yours,

Julius Henry Cohen

4. The Protocol of Peace ending the cloakmakers strike, addressed to Louis Marshall, September 1910. Courtesy of Jacob Rader Marcus Center of the American Jewish Archives.

tension still awaited the sides, Marshall's perspicacious choice of words effectively ended the strike. The phrasing enabled the union to believe that as long as it supplied able workers for vacant positions, they had to be employed, and it allowed the association to get out of the strike without formally recognizing the union. Marshall's draft decreed:

> The manufacturers agree that as between union men and non-union men of equal ability to do the job, they will employ the union men . . . the preferential union shop is a shop in which union standards prevail and the union man is

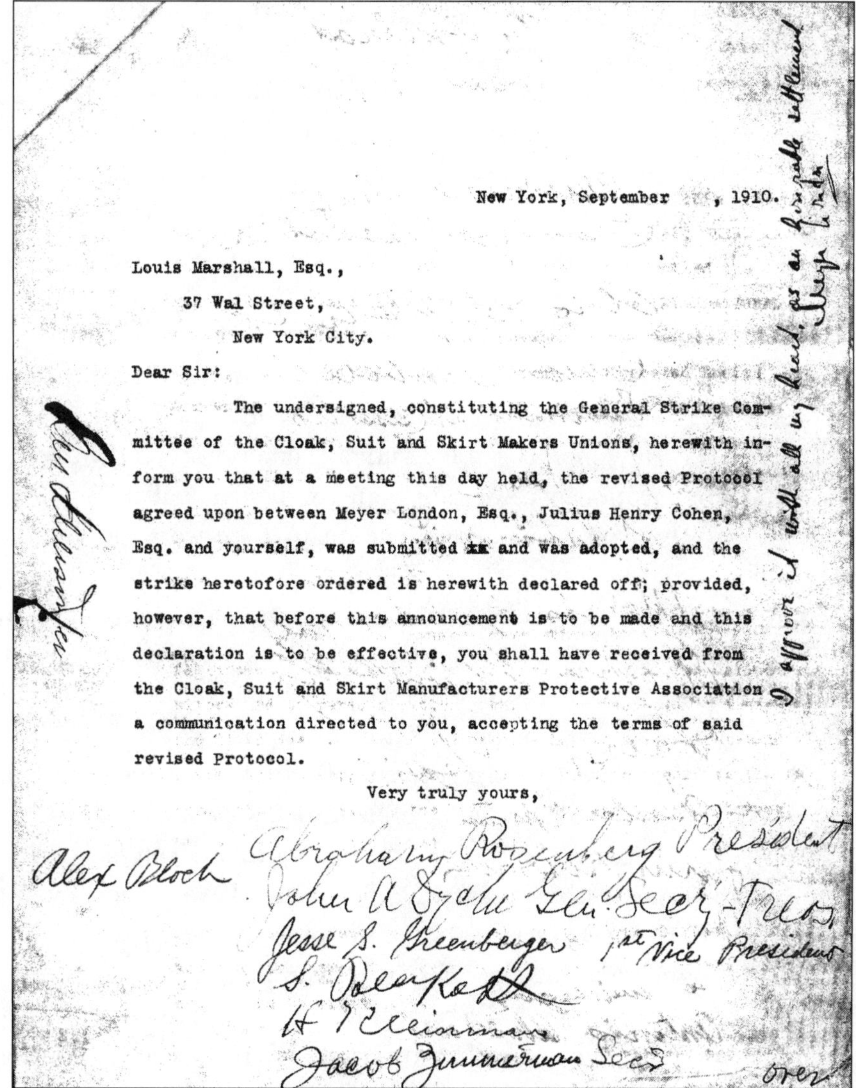
New York, September , 1910.

Louis Marshall, Esq.,
37 Wal Street,
New York City.

Dear Sir:

The undersigned, constituting the General Strike Committee of the Cloak, Suit and Skirt Makers Unions, herewith inform you that at a meeting this day held, the revised Protocol agreed upon between Meyer London, Esq., Julius Henry Cohen, Esq. and yourself, was submitted ~~xx~~ and was adopted, and the strike heretofore ordered is herewith declared off; provided, however, that before this announcement is to be made and this declaration is to be effective, you shall have received from the Cloak, Suit and Skirt Manufacturers Protective Association a communication directed to you, accepting the terms of said revised Protocol.

Very truly yours,

Alex Block Abraham Rosenberg President
John A Dyche Gen. Secy-Treas
Jesse S. Greenberger 1st Vice President
S. Polakoff
H Kleinman
Jacob Zimmerman Secy

over

entitled to preference. This preference shall consist in giving employment to union men as long as they are obtainable.[233]

In ensuing days, the union's strike committee debated heatedly about what was known as the Marshall Compromise and ended up referring the matter to the rank and file for a vote. Concurrently, the association seemed to win a knockdown victory when New York Supreme Court Judge Goff issued a strike-crippling injunction. Though it had been mostly supportive of the association's position throughout the month, the mainstream press responded incredulously in late August to Judge Goff's ruling. Pushed toward the corner, the ILGWU had to reach a decision.

Marshall understood that the sides had run out of time. On September 1, 1910, he sent an ultimatum to Meyer London. After outlining some adjustments relating mostly to hours and wages, Marshall gave the union one day to accept the protocol once and for all. "I cannot close my eyes to all the misery, the suffering, the waste, the disturbance of business conditions and the public injury which are certain to result from a continuance of the deplorable strike which is still in progress after seven weeks of conflict," he wrote, emotively.[234] The union relented, dropping its demand for a closed shop.[235] On September 2, Marshall met with London and Cohen to draft and sign the final settlement. It had three parts, one relating to general hour and wage issues whose terms were relatively generous to labor; a second part covering features specific to the industry, including piece rate, supply costs, and sanitary conditions; and the third part featuring the aforementioned compromise on the preferential union shop.[236] Historians regard the protocol as a precedent-setting framework for "industrial self-government."[237]

Downtown exploded with jubilation after the announcement of the agreement. "That night, the entire city remained awake," ILGWU President Abraham Rosenberg recalled. "It is impossible to describe the spirit of that night. Police estimated that at least one million people filled the streets."[238]

Marshall kept the original protocol agreement (thereby allowing twenty-first-century researchers to unearth it, at the American Jewish Archives in Cincinnati).[239] In retrospect, Marshall commented rather sparingly about his role in the arbitration of this famous labor dispute. No documented explanation about the choice of the term "protocol" appears to be extant; researchers have speculated that Marshall himself chose it, regarding it as neutral nomenclature less likely to fan anxieties among the two sides regarding what they were getting into.[240] In one discursive letter sent more than two years after the strike's resolution, Marshall somewhat petulantly pointed out that Brandeis's mediation did not resolve the impasse.[241] At the time, Marshall correctly grasped that the mechanisms incorporated in the protocol could have general constructive application in industrial relations. "Acting as a mediator, I brought about an adjustment which has proven most satisfactory and which I trust will prevent a recurrence of similar difficulties in the future," Marshall wrote, a week after the deal was signed, to Solomon Schechter, who was in Europe.[242] This contemporary account highlighted the Jewish motivations of Marshall's intervention. Jews constitute about 85 percent of the cloakmaker industry, Marshall explained to Schechter, and "the suffering among our coreligionists was intense." With wage losses totaling close to $1.5 million a week, the "utter bankruptcy of our charitable institutions was threatened," he added.[243]

Marshall's Abrogation Address

By the end of 1910, Marshall traded places with his brother-in-law Judah Magnes. For a spell, the activist became the ruminating planner, and the behind-the-scenes strategist became the militant public activist.

A powerful demonstration of Jewish public assertiveness, the cloakmakers strike showed that Downtown and Uptown activists knew how to put demands on the table and find solutions to them. In all its corners, Jewish life seemed to buzz thereafter with political energy. In fact, it was the Reform Jewish movement, through the Union of American Hebrew Congregations, that triggered the renewed, decisive round in the Russian treaty abrogation campaign when it invited Marshall to speak at its January 1911 convention on the passport question. Regaining direction, Marshall focused effectively for months to come on the abrogation campaign, and his labors strongly enhanced the AJC's credibility and prestige.

Magnes, meantime, was stimulatingly engaged in New York Jewry's public affairs, capably heading the innovative Kehillah. In this period, the experiment in Jewish communal self-administration expanded in creative new directions, one of them being the field of Jewish education, in which Magnes was teaming with Dr. Samson Benderly, a Safed-born idealist who had foregone a career in medicine to prove that Jewish education could modernize and adapt in America as an attractive Hebrew School supplement to public education.[244] Believing that "the Benderly method of Jewish education is well nigh perfect," Marshall joined up with Magnes to work out an arrangement for the Jewish educator to sponsor pilot programs around the city.[245]

His head popping with novel ideas for communal projects, Rabbi Magnes went to synagogue searching for spiritual sustenance, not continued political debate. At Emanu-El, however, he found himself mired in petty disputes, one involving the synagogue's use on Sunday evenings by a Baptist church. Suddenly, he was torn by doubts about the congregation's spiritual commitments. Things came to a head with Magnes's 1910 Passover sermon, in which he decried the spiritual emptiness of Emanu-El style Judaism and called for traditionalist changes in Reform ritual. "Your Judaism is not altogether my Judaism," Magnes boldly told the Uptown congregants at Emanu-El. "Your Jewish ideals are not altogether my Jewish ideals."[246] Soon Magnes left the Emanu-El pulpit, while retaining the respect and affection of powerful supporters, including Felix Warburg, who urged him to take the rabbinical pulpit at Adath Jeshurun, which promised him a freer hand and a substantive salary. Marshall urged his restless brother-in-law to accept the new position, but Magnes spoke indefinitely about organizing a new branch of Judaism. "I am afraid that [Magnes] is deliberating too deeply," Marshall privately reflected.[247] For Marshall, but not for Magnes, the new year, 1911, would be one of action.

For a few days, Marshall pondered the pros and cons of issuing a public call for the abrogation campaign at the UAHC convention. Ochs of the *New York Times* strongly recommended that Marshall seize the opportunity, since it offered the AJC a way to resume work on an issue which would, one way or another, resurrect itself in months to come. Ochs promised Marshall his newspaper's support in publicizing a renewed abrogation campaign. In Washington, Marshall met Oscar Straus and discussed ways of presenting abrogation not as a Jewish issue but as a matter of consequence to the American people. Straus recommended that Marshall deliver the speech. Sulzberger and Adler, however, equivocated, owing to worries that Marshall's speech would be construed as an attack on the Taft administration. They referred him to New Haven's Colonel Ullman, whose ties with the president were well known. Marshall relayed to Ullman the AJC's sense of frustration concerning the "general state of indifference" about Russia's discriminatory infringement of the 1832 treaty, and though he promised Ullman that nothing in his speech would convey an attack on the Taft administration, he confessed that the AJC was disappointed and perplexed by Taft's inaction on the issue in past months.[248]

In discussions with Schiff, Marshall was more explicit and broader in his criticism. A series of presidential administrations had duped Jewish leaders with specious assurances. Negotiations with Russia, Marshall recalled, "have been in progress for 30 years, and will continue for 30 years longer, with the same result, unless our negotiators are brought to a realizing sense that they cannot fool all of the people all of the time." In his despairing earlier letter to Israel Friedlander, Marshall had derided ineffectual Jewish agitators and useless Jewish organizations. In these communications with Schiff, Marshall's point was that the AJC must not become part of this trend of flamboyant impotence. He cried out to Schiff:

> We have been so diplomatic as to hide our light under a bushel. We have during the entire existence of the American Jewish Committee pursued the policy of silence with regard to the passport question. We can point to no triumphs as a result of this policy . . . I am not anxious to act as the 'voice' of the Committee, or the public conscience, but the time in my judgment has come, or will soon arrive, when somebody's voice must be heard on the subject.[249]

Schiff himself was in an assertive mood. While Marshall was being deflected by associates like Julian Mack, who brought up various reservations about the planned speech, Schiff settled the issue in a conference with Charles Norton, the president's secretary. Schiff showed Norton a letter Marshall had written weighing the pros and cons of delivering the speech; Norton confirmed that Marshall's address would usefully set a frame for Taft to forge policy on the Russia issue.[250] Mack had momentarily discouraged Marshall,[251] but Schiff sent him off, resolute and combative, to the UAHC's twenty-second council meeting in New York City to inaugurate the key phase in the AJC's self-defining campaign.

Marshall's impassioned address at the UAHC's January 19, 1911, meeting "set the pattern both in content and tone" for the decisive phase of the AJC's abrogation campaign.[252] "There rests a stain on the honor of our Nation and on the integrity of American citizenship,"[253] he declared, conceptualizing the czarist empire's discriminatory attitude toward Jewish visitors from the United States as an issue of American patriotism. "No man within the hearing of my voice who professes to be a Jew, however eloquent in true Americanism his life has been, can venture within the walls which Russia has erected against the outside world," Marshall challenged his audience. In carefully parsed but ringing words, Marshall articulated the intriguing thought that the experience of American freedom imposed new forms of responsibilities on the Jew, to uphold his rights in a manner cherished by his American countrymen:

> As a Jew he might look down upon his persecutors with pity and contempt, and suffer in silence as his ancestors did for centuries. But he is now more than a Jew—he is also an American citizen, and the hand that smites him inflicts a stain on his citizenship. It is not the Jew who is insulted; it is the American people. And the finding of a proper remedy against this degradation is not a Jewish, but an American question.[254]

Marshall claimed that the 1832 treaty enjoined Russia "to accord to all of our citizens, without distinction, the liberty to sojourn and reside in all parts of her territory." His argumentation became lawyerly, relying on the citation of a series of precedents in American jurisprudence that denied the right of one party to a private contract or treaty to unilaterally exempt one group from the application of the compact's binding provisions. He also cited examples illustrating America's good faith treaty compliance, primarily its agreement to extradite Russian subjects sought by the czar's officials—not all such details were on point regarding the abrogation of the 1832 treaty, but they were inserted because Marshall and the AJC had yet to withdraw their call for repealing the 1887 Extradition Convention with Russia. He reviewed denunciations of Russia's discriminatory policies toward Jewish holders of American passports that had been included routinely in

Republican and Democratic campaign platforms, along with addresses given by President Taft days before the November 1908 elections, and he also cited the editorial he had leveraged into print in September 1908 in the *Cincinnati Times-Star,* an opinion piece that was suffused with pro-abrogation language ("American citizenship can no longer be held so cheap that it can and will be disregarded or ignored").

One attention-grabbing passage toward the end of the address denied emphatically that economic arguments posed against abrogation had merit. Marshall handled these arguments on two levels, first by denying that the economic fall-out of abrogation would be significant. He calculated that the export trade of the United States with Russia stood at $18 million annually and argued that this constituted a negligible portion for a nation "the products of whose soil during the past year amounted to nearly nine billions of dollars." Second, Marshall took the moral high ground, suggesting that inordinate consideration of such materialistic factors would be worthy of a country of "mere shopkeepers." His rhetoric cagily stood a familiar anti-Semitic canard on its head. Arguing for an American Jewish ethnic interest, Marshall implied that anyone who objected to his advocacy was a lowly capitalist who did not care about ideals. "I have a higher opinion of the American people than to believe that they are so destitute of idealism, so devoid of a sense of honor . . . to have it said that our country rates the dollar higher than it does the man, that it esteems the volume of its trade more than its national dignity."

Here, Marshall had his finger on the button of the abrogation campaign's appeal. He understood that many technical and practical arguments could be raised in opposition to his advocacy, but he safeguarded the AJC's campaign by presenting it in a language of national idealism that was readily received by a moralistic public in this prewar period. In the address's most effective flourish, Marshall re-worked a theme Schiff had articulated a few years earlier[255] and lobbied for abrogation as an affirmation of America's highest purposes as a country that afforded equality and protection to all religious groups. His words inspired his Jewish listeners not to accept double standards that degraded their self-worth as Americans:

> If Russia should announce that it would not honor the passport of the United States when held by an Episcopalian or a Presbyterian, a Methodist or a Roman Catholic, our country would not look upon this breach of treaty obligation as a mere insult to the Episcopalians or the Presbyterians, the Methodists or the Roman Catholics of this country, but would justly treat it as a blow inflicted upon every man who holds dear the title of American citizen.[256]

Marshall's references to Russia's discrimination against Christian possessors of American passports ought not to be regarded as a hypothetical complaint about double standards, the AJC argued in accompanying publicity materials. They also referred to a reality. "To hammer home the thesis that theirs was an American cause," observes Naomi Cohen, the AJC "recounted over and over how Russia also refused visas to Catholic priests and Protestant missionaries."[257]

Such AJC clarifications had public relations appeal, but they did not necessarily address substantive policy questions that were left unanswered by Marshall's address. Relying largely on Ambassador Rockhill's dispatches from Russia, the State Department in this period compiled what can be regarded as a counter-brief to Marshall's pro-abrogation address.[258] Its opening premise reversed the AJC presentation of abrogation as an American issue; on the contrary, argued Secretary of State Philander Knox, abrogation would merely serve "the interests of the Jewish population of the United States." Abrogation would cause the czarist empire to dig in its heels, and worsen circumstances for its own Jewish population and American Jews. Some technical elaborations of this point in the State Department brief were a stretch and understandably met with sarcastic incredulity by the AJC. For instance, Article 10 of the 1832 treaty guaranteed to American Jews of Russian origin a right of inheritance in Russia; it was preposterous for the State Department to propose that Downtown Jewish immigrants were concerned about the loss of this entitlement as a result of abrogation, the AJC pointed out. Still, the State Department's general point about the unpredictability of Russian responses to abrogation was apposite.

The State Department had reason to argue that Marshall's depiction of the 1832 treaty as a guarantee of equal treatment to all American visitors to Russia had higher rhetorical than legal cogency. On the department's interpretation, the "national treatment" references in the treaty's Article 1 subjected American Jewish visitors to regulations governing Russia's own Jewish subjects. An intradepartmental memorandum from February 1911 stressed this sticky legal point to undermine the AJC position. "The Department earnestly desires to secure for Americans of Jewish faith or race the rights of free access in Russia," the memo stated, "but it finds its efforts in this direction embarrassed by what it considers an ill-advised agitation based upon the assumption that such rights are guaranteed by the rights of the existing treaty." The memo concluded flatly that "restrictions imposed by Russian law" upon the entry and sojourn in Russia of American and other foreign Jews did not violate the 1832 treaty.

Marshall's argument about abrogation's merits as a means to avoid the double standards infringement of America's constitutional norms reversed the truth, the State Department implied. How could the United States challenge Russia's right to regulate the entry of specific groups of foreigners when it was exercising the same right toward the Chinese and Japanese? The State Department's counter-brief suggested that Marshall had wildly underestimated the potential economic impact of abrogation. It drew from Ambassador Rockhill's assessments of Russia's annual consumption of America's goods as totaling $150,000,000 and American capital investments in Russia as $225,000,000. Finally, the State Department was concerned that anti-Russian measures could upset the Taft administration's policies in Asia: department officials apparently worried that an angered Russia might act against American policies in China and also ignore America's worries about Japanese expansionism. In a self-defeating fashion, Naomi Cohen writes, the State Department failed to articulate these concerns in public.[259]

Replies to these anti-abrogation arguments would not be lacking in the year of AJC action, 1911. Marshall and associates would, for instance, detract from the economic objections by pointing out that treaty abrogation was not the same thing as the cessation of trade; the AJC men would say that restrictive policies toward Chinese and Japanese on the West Coast involved immigration, not travel, issues, and unfolded under agreements not comparable to the 1832 Russian treaty. Such arguments took shape with varying levels of potency, but they were not articulated as part of a direct disputation with the State Department, and honing the content of arguments was not the primary challenge faced by Marshall and other articulate AJC leaders in this pivotal campaign.

Instead, the organization's most impressive leap in this period was procedural and strategic. These were men plagued by enormous existential doubts about the public articulation of anything that could be construed as a separate Jewish political interest, and they had transplanted in America a traditional *shtadlanut* penchant for solving Jewish problems quietly via backroom intercession. Now their keynote organization had come to be identified with a cause, abrogation, whose successful prosecution depended on public appeals to the average American's sense of national honor. Not content-related disputation in private with Ambassador Rockhill, Secretary of State Knox, or President Taft, but the very adoption and engagement of public politics would be the key to success. When things were kept private, the high ground appeals to equal treatment of all American citizens had little traction. Conversely, as Naomi Cohen put it, "when the issue was put before the public in idealistic terms as a stain on America's honor and an affront to a liberal's sense of justice, other considerations became only legal pedantry or crass materialism."[260] For this reason, the momentous impact of Marshall's address at the Reform Jewish meeting and its aftermath on Jewish ethnic politics is not to be found in the words that he used but rather in the fact that he stood up in public as he did.

Following Marshall's address, the UAHC adopted a resolution he had drafted, declaring that the Reform group, "speaking not as a representative of Jews, but as a body of citizens having at heart the preservation of the honor of the nation," urged the president, Congress, and the Department of State to terminate the Russian treaties.[261] "The action at the UAHC has been favorably received throughout the country," Marshall reported to Judge Mack.[262] Charged-up, he quoted Kipling—"there is no truce with Adams-zad, the bear that looks like a man"—when warning about Russian attempts to deflect abrogation pressures via specious promises.[263] He contacted a key Capitol Hill ally, Senator Simon Guggenheim, and asked whether he would speak with President Taft about the UAHC speech.[264] The AJC was at this time, late January, sending copies of the speech to all members of both houses;[265] within two months, it had circulated 32,000 copies of the address to state politicians, journalists, educators, clergymen, and lawyers around the country.[266]

Conferring with congressmen, Marshall tried to intercept anti-abrogation messages circulated on Capitol Hill by Ambassador Rockhill. Russia's position on the treaty issue was intolerably demeaning, Marshall explained, since it was founded on the proposition that trade was more important to Americans than principles. Providing sympathetic cover for this insulting perspective, Rockhill was the "last in a long line of American representatives in Russia . . . who succumbed to the wiles, falsehoods and trickery of Russian diplomacy."[267] He ridiculed Rockhill's and the State Department's solicitude for Russian-born American Jews who could lose their Russian inheritances with the repeal of Article 10 and the rest of the 1832 treaty. "So far as I have absorbed," Marshall noted, for Jews in Russia, "inheritances have consisted only in the infliction of massacres, pillage, rapine, the degradation of manhood and the loss of moral tone."[268]

The Abrogation Meeting with President Taft: "This Means War"

At the end of the first week in February, Marshall had received incomplete reports indicating that his speech had been addressed at two Cabinet discussions.[269] In fact, Taft had on February 3 conferred with six cabinet members late into the night, only to reach the conclusion that he could not, as president, sacrifice the interests of the entire country for a principle of equal treatment that Russia was not likely to honor even after abrogation.[270] Marshall, however, did not know exactly where Taft stood on the issue and thus had to focus on organizing assertive advocacy among a united front of Jewish groups and organizations. After receiving Marshall's address, the president invited delegates from the AJC, the UAHC, and B'nai B'rith to discuss the treaty with him at a mid-February meeting in the White House.[271] As Marshall saw it, the AJC had now engaged a new form of Jewish advocacy founded unyieldingly on principle, and he worried that other organizational partners might poison this new form of lobbying by relying on the old palliative of sycophancy. "The time has passed when sweet words will butter our parsnips," Marshall epigrammatically concluded.[272] Frantically trying to organize a preliminary conference among the Jewish delegates, Marshall explained to Schiff that "the great danger is that some of these gentlemen will feel so flattered by the invitation that they will readily concede that everything has been done that can be done." This time the AJC would lead American Jewry beyond "Mr. Wolf's ordinary policy of say[ing] 'Amen' to anything that our governmental authorities suggest."[273] There could be no retreat from abrogation.

Schiff and Marshall represented the AJC at the February 15, 1911, White House meeting (Mayer Sulzberger was unable to attend), with B'nai B'rith and the UAHC represented by Adolf Kraus, Bernhard Bettman, Philip Stein, Jacob Furth, and J. Walter Freiberg.[274] After a cordial lunch, the group followed President Taft to the old cabinet room on the second floor. The president had prepared a long statement and read it to the Jewish delegation. Taft said that he had given a "great deal of consideration" to Marshall's memorial and the issue had "worried me more than I can tell." As he saw it, the question posed by the Russian treaty involved a "balance of convenience and comparative burden rather than a question of principle." He understood his guests' point of view. "I think perhaps that if I had the same justifiable pride of race that you have and the same sense of outrageous injustice that comes home to a man of that race much more than it can to a man who is not of that race, I should feel as you do," confessed the president. However, he added, "I am the President of the whole country," and "I have to try to look at the subject from all sides."

Taft was sure that "Mr. Marshall, with his profound knowledge of the law," would concur that there was no rule of international law prohibiting a country from excluding any group of American citizens. As to whether the 1832 reciprocal treaty expressly conveyed such a prohibition, Taft said an extensive examination of the records of the State Department showed that several Secretaries of State doubted it did. Marshall's arguments would have "great weight" were they in reference to a new treaty, but the treaty relation between the two countries, formalized during the tenure of Secretary Everett, was of fifty years' standing. Under that relation, "property rights have been acquired, investments have been made, and a status established in respect to a great many things which, if we denounced the treaty, will have no sanction or security at all." The president was impressed by America's huge investments of capital in Russia, as evidenced by Singer Sewing Machines, the agricultural implement business, and life insurance companies. "I do not know what might happen" to this aggregate investment of $50 million or $60 million were "we to take out of our own hands the machinery by which we can intervene to prevent injustice" under an existing commercial treaty. Taft claimed that he would be willing to risk these costs ("I would be willing to take this drastic step and sacrifice the interests that it [abrogation] certainly will sacrifice") were he convinced that upholding the principle of equal treatment of all US citizens would bring practical benefits. However, a "good deal of investigation" had taught him nothing positive would be accomplished by abrogation.

Littered with the president's hints about how abrogation might backfire was his ambivalent attitude toward Jewish immigration. Involving "ourselves in hostility" toward Russia via abrogation would be likely to "change the normal flow of these people from Russia to this country." As things stood, the president was "glad to welcome" Jews who sought refuge in the United States—certainly, he explained, "the more we spread them out in the West, the better I like it." He attested to having endeavored to "widen" the construction of immigration laws, "so that we could help them [Jewish immigrants] directly on to the plains of Texas and in other parts of the western country, where they can have independence and show the industry and ability to build up a country which I have no doubt they possess." But were a Russia maddened by abrogation to emit greater numbers of Jews toward the United States, then would it not be the case that "some of them [would] have to be sent back as is always the case because they cannot satisfy the immigration law requirements." Abrogation would thus place these immigrants "in a worse plight than they are now."

The president indicated that he had just received a communication from Ambassador Rockhill in Saint Petersburg. After Taft tore away some nonrelevant pages, he waited while the Jewish delegation adjourned to a separate room to consider the Ambassador's dispatch. Marshall later recalled that the Ambassador presented "nothing more or less than a pro-Russian argument." The delegates were affronted by the document's suggestions that rights were withheld from Jews in Russia because otherwise they would exploit peasants and that the czar's government had domestic considerations warranting barred entry to foreign Jews from America and other countries. The communiqué referred vaguely to possible change in Russia's discriminatory attitudes after two or three Duma tenures. Infuriated, the Jewish delegates voted to express their displeasure to the president of the United States.

"I never knew Mr. Schiff to be so worked up over anything," Marshall reported to the AJC's Executive Committee a few days after this Rubicon-crossing meeting. Taft evidently thought that his position was well-considered, but Schiff, "very earnestly and strongly" (Marshall recounted) argued "for some time" that the precedence given by the president to material interest rather than principle was un-American. "At the start of the Civil War, the people of the North did not consider the financial aspects of the situation, but the right and wrong of it," Schiff declared, launching the philippic. Marshall joined in, insisting that the issue was not a Jewish but an American question. The president asked Marshall whether, as a lawyer, he believed that abrogation was warranted. "I replied that I unquestionably did," recalled Marshall. The president then asked him about the likely economic effects of abrogation. Marshall replied that abrogation would not render commercial relations impossible. "As a practical proposition, whoever wanted to buy would buy and whoever desired to sell would sell," after abrogation. But, Marshall declared, "whatever the effect might be upon our commerce, it was a negligible matter compared with the great and staunch question of the dignity of American citizenship."

"The President had a most unhappy half an hour," Marshall wryly told the AJC Executive Committee. Taft tried to mollify the delegation, proposing that he issue a statement saying the issue was under advisement. "We said that was entirely indifferent to us, that the President might make any statement he desired, but we were very much disappointed."

The meeting adjourned as a parting of the ways in various senses. Schiff refused to shake hands with the president of the United States of America. "This means war," he exclaimed to Marshall as they headed down the White House stairs. Gone now was the AJC's anxiety about harm to the Taft administration that could come from a public abrogation campaign; in fact, gone was Schiff's, though not Marshall's, unyielding loyalty to the Republican Party (the banker supported Wilson in 1912 and 1916[275]). Schiff authorized Marshall to draw on him up to $25,000 for an abrogation campaign fund. On Marshall's account, the newly militant AJC was now on a path leading away from the engrained traditional cautiousness of other organized American Jewish elements. As the AJC, with Schiff at its lead, marched off to war for abrogation, the Reform and B'nai B'rith delegates retreated back to the passive reticence of *shtadlan* politics. Just after Schiff banged the war drum, Marshall recalled, Bettmen of the UAHC came to him, mumbling "Wir sind in Golus" ("we are in exile").

The following day Jewish delegates testified on Capitol Hill before the House Committee on Foreign Affairs. Horace Stern, a prominent Philadelphia lawyer who in 1920 took a spot on the city's Court of Common Pleas where Mayer Sulzberger had served, remembered Marshall's testimony that day as a highlight of Jewish advocacy in America. For all the AJC's insistence that abrogation was an American issue, Stern wrote years later,[276] abrogation would never have been achieved had the country's politicians been allowed to contemplate the issue as a general matter of citizenship principle. Somebody had to make the insult to the Jews emotionally apprehensible to the lawmakers. Making the chief presentation, Stern recorded, Marshall "amazed not only the Committee but even his own friends by the masterly way in which he handled the question, by his discussion of the principles of international law which were involved, by his passionate invective against Russia's brutalities." In a virtuoso performance, Marshall "was pleading for equality of rights for the Jews and for all others to the protection of the flag under which they dwelt, and this was one of the causes most dear to his heart."

At the time, Marshall was realistic about the effects of his lobbying in Congress. "I can say confidentially that there are several members of Congress who are not sympathetic, and I fear that there are outside influences, set afoot by Russia, who are creating obstacles," he told one confidante the day after his appearance before the Foreign Affairs Committee.[277] Unlike Schiff, a banker accustomed to sealing deals in private meetings, Marshall's lawyerly experience trained him to adjust to less resolute processes in which the key players were constantly recalibrating their own negotiating positions. This difference in professional orientation was at least one of the reasons why Marshall adjusted more practically than Schiff to the president's indefinite behavior at the White House meeting. Marshall, who had his own reasons to be bitter about Taft, correctly assessed the president as a politician who was handicapped by his own indecisiveness but who was also a thoughtful, judicious character who would readjust his views on abrogation once he realized that the Jewish minority's argument of moral principle was appreciated by the American public and thus also carried political weight.

This calculation with Taft illustrates one of the more compelling features of Marshall's personality and a key to his success as a Jewish advocate. Despite his hot temper and fiery style of argumentation, the gentle, understanding, and forgiving sides of his character remained evident even to Marshall's antagonists. His work in difficult negotiation circumstances tended not to result in impasses, since contestants on the other side of a dispute appreciated that it was better to work with an enemy like Marshall, who kept his word, than with friends they could not trust. More specifically, Marshall never burned bridges, not even when he had every earthly reason to do so (as, we shall see, in the Henry Ford case). Thus, when Marshall left Washington after this up and down sequence with the executive and legislative branches, he was not disposed to adopt a self-defeating strategy of full frontal "war" with Taft. The president would come around, he told his acquaintances. "Taft is sympathetic to our attitude. I fear, however, that he is not quite prepared to take action on his own initiative," Marshall concluded.[278]

The Profile of Ethnic Lobbying: William Sulzer and Abrogation

Focusing the abrogation effort on Capitol Hill, Marshall and the AJC chose in this period to work with non-Jewish legislators. During the White House meeting, Taft himself validated this approach when he alluded favorably to the pro-abrogation work undertaken by Herbert Parsons, a Gentile Republican Congressman from New York ("I am glad to recognize that there are others than gentlemen of the Jewish race who take that [pro-abrogation] position," Taft said).[279] Parsons, by the end of February, sponsored an abrogation bill in the House (Texas senator Charles Allen Culberson concurrently submitted a similar bill in the Senate, which was referred to the Foreign Relations Committee). Marshall thought the Parsons bill might make it through the House by the end of its session in March, but he was doubtful about its chances in the Senate.[280] In fact, Parsons' bill stalled in committee, due (the AJC believed) to Secretary Knox's influence.[281]

The rule that Jewish interests are best promoted in the public arena by non-Jewish politicians attained orthodoxy in this period, lasting through the 1912 elections. Marshall could be relentless in its application. When Jewish Congressman Henry Goldfogle waffled somewhat during a House Committee on Foreign Relations hearing on the Parsons resolution in late February, Marshall temporarily severed him from the AJC campaign. "You are right about Goldfogle," he wrote to Parsons. "The passport question has been considered by him as a perpetual lamp to light his way to reelection . . . A great cause has in his handling been taken as a political joke."[282] To Goldfogle, Marshall showed no pity. "To say that I am astounded" he told Goldfogle, referring to the Congressman's refusal to back abrogation resolutely at the Committee hearing, "is to speak with some degree of moderation." From this point, abrogation politics on Capitol Hill really belonged to the Gentiles. "I was glad to see a non-Jew, Mr. Parsons, assume the responsibility of dealing with this American question, rather than one of our own faith," Marshall acidly told Goldfogle.[283]

Out of this suddenly steely rule in ethnic politics, Marshall and his AJC associates forged in spring 1911 an important alliance with NY Congressman William Sulzer, who in April was appointed Chairman of the House Committee on Foreign Affairs.[284] Known as the "Henry Clay of the East Side," due to his resemblance to the famed American nineteenth-century politician, Sulzer was born in New Jersey during the Civil War to a German father and a mother of Scotch-Irish descent, who hoped their son would become a Presbyterian minister. He came up in New York City politics through the patronage of a Tammany Hall boss, John Reilly (on the East Side, his original political moniker was "Reilly's boy spellbinder"). Sulzer was first elected to Congress in 1894 from the Tenth District, whose German and Irish population was rapidly being overtaken by Jewish immigrants. Known as the defender of persecuted peoples around the world, including the Jews in czarist Russia, Sulzer became one of the city's most popular Democrats. Mr. Dooley, the era's indomitable humorist and political commentator, astutely praised the Congressman as a humanitarian and an adroit politician, saying Sulzer "has always been a friend iv th' people. He has lavished his sobs on thim an' has ast nawthin' in return but their votes."[285] Marshall congratulated Sulzer for sponsoring an updated version of the pro-abrogation Parsons bill soon after his appointment as chairman of the Foreign Affairs Committee. "Your resolution is correct in framing this as an American, not a Jewish question," Marshall told Sulzer, and asked for an invitation to testify to his committee for repeal of the 1832 treaty.[286] This was the start of a productive relationship to which Marshall remained absolutely loyal, despite the turbulent future of Sulzer's career in New York politics.

Conservative Jurisprudence: The Case Against Worker Compensation

Marshall's professional career as an American lawyer and his Jewish advocacy work seemed most out of sync during this period. Leapfrogging over self-imposed norms of communal self-restraint, the AJC climbed to new degrees of Jewish assertiveness in the abrogation campaign—the abrogation campaign's message was about challenging the status quo in the name of constitutional rights, and its activist ethos also appealed to Downtown Jewish masses, even though they were not really its direct beneficiaries. Concurrently, in domestic American politics, Marshall defied the activist ethos of Progressive reform proposals such as worker compensation measures, siding with the entrenched conservative legal philosophy that viewed worker protection as a violation of employer property rights.

Marshall's pro-business position in *Ives v. South Buffalo Railway Company* (1911),[287] probably the most archly conservative moment of his career, was a rearguard attempt to stem the tide of what was fast becoming an irresistible item of social reform, that is, worker compensation. The circumstances of this case warrant discussion as a political benchmark in Marshall's career. In contrast to this highly conservative prewar example, Marshall's best known American legal work in the 1920s seems clearly in step with his concerns about civil rights as a Jewish advocate and had a liberal and, in many cases, radically forward-looking, character.

Social insurance started in US history with workers compensation programs. Between 1910 and 1921, all but five states adopted workers compensation plans;

a departure from the idea that private charity was the sole source of support for the disabled and destitute, the advent of workers compensation augured a change in American social philosophy. The question why this shift toward public welfare models began with workers compensation continues to be debated, but scholars suspect that unlike unemployment insurance or social security programs, the idea of compensation for workers already had some roots in common law.[288]

Those roots did not run very deep, however. Through the first decade of the twentieth century, workers had to show proof that injuries were caused by employer negligence. Three common law standards militated against workers' claims for compensation:

• the rule of contributory negligence, under which an injured worker could be faulted for not having exercised reasonable care;

• the "fellow servant" standard exculpating an employer if an injury to one employee was shown to be the responsibility of a fellow employee; and

• the assumption of risk, an especially irksome standard to Progressive reformers, since it lessened a worker's chances for compensation by holding broadly that by taking on a task the worker consented to risks incidental to the job.

In the early years of the twentieth century, the perpetuation of such common law standards under increasingly dangerous conditions of mass industrial production outraged Progressive reformers around the country. In New York, Republican governor Charles Evans Hughes yielded to this public pressure for reform, and convened a special panel to inquire into issues of employer liability for worker disability.[289] Spearheaded by J. Mayhew Wainwright, a state senator from Rye, the commission reviewed 257 instances of worker fatalities in the State in 1908, along with 3,398 reports of injuries. Its fact-filled report, issued in March 1910 (as a kind of moderately pro-labor analogue to the pro-immigration orientation of Marshall's New York immigration committee), featured detailed study of existing liability procedures in New York State and also of evolving systems of worker compensation in Europe.

The Wainwright commission's conclusions did not mince words. "Our present system is fundamentally wrong and unwise and needs radical change," the report concluded, adding that America's laissez-faire attitude toward industrial accidents had been "discarded in almost every other industrial country" and was "inherently unfit to modern industrial conditions." At a minimum, the Wainwright commission called on New York's legislature to compel employers in "intrinsically dangerous trades" to share the accident burden. By adjusting product prices, thereby shifting a portion of the burden of industrial protection to consumers, employers could afford to supply injury compensation. Inspired by the Wainwright recommendations and drawing upon the example of late nineteenth-century labor legislation in England, New York's lawmakers legislated a worker compensation law in 1910.

In its method and conclusions, the Wainwright Commission reflected the Progressive turn of American politics on the eve of World War I. Its energetically empirical procedure implied that opening one's eyes and looking at the facts was all that was needed to prove that decades of conservative jurisprudence in America had become hopelessly antiquated and would, if perpetuated, literally cripple the country. By the time the *Ives v. South Buffalo Railway Company* case reached the New York appellate courts in 1911, worker compensation had gained irreversible momentum around the country.

When, in his *Ives v. South Buffalo* brief, Marshall cast New York's compensation law as being unconstitutional, he relied on a wealth of conservative-tempered precedents holding that such social legislation deprived employers of their property rights, without due process of law. The appellate court ruled in favor of Marshall's familiar argument that conceptualized worker welfare not as an independent concern, but rather as a function of an employer's sovereign right to use his property as he saw fit. "One of the inalienable rights of every citizen is to hold and enjoy his property until it is taken from him by due process," the appellate court concluded, rejecting New York's labor law.[290] The court was not prepared to accept the theory of "judicial restraint" Supreme Court Justice Oliver Wendell Holmes had broached in his 1905 dissent in *Lochner v. New York*—whereas jurists like Holmes and Louis Brandeis believed that courts should defer to policies enacted by popularly elected legislatures,[291] the *Ives* decision insisted that since the right to property "has its foundation in fundamental law," legislatures lack authority to infringe it arbitrarily.

Lurking behind Marshall's arguments and the court's ruling was the fear that employment compensation could be the start of a broader mass assault upon property arrangements. Explicitly noting this concern, the court worriedly speculated that if a "legislature can say to an employer 'you must compensate your employee for an injury not caused by you,'" nothing would stop it in the future from saying to a man of wealth, "you have more property than you need, and your neighbor is poor," so surrender your property. Marshall privately admitted to antiradicalism motivations governing his work on the *Ives* case. "Among the subjects in which I have been interested is to make a fight against the growing tide of socialism, as evidenced by the act passed by the [New York] legislature in 1910, known as the Workmen Compensation Act," Marshall wrote to Syracuse University's chancellor in late March 1911. "I have succeeded in convincing the Court of Appeals of its unconstitutionality."[292] Similarly, Marshall congratulated Appeals Court Judge William Werner, saying his opinion "constitutes a substantial dike against the tide of socialism, and cannot fail to exert a potent influence in the direction of sanity in respect to legislation in which sociology and law conmingle."[293]

Marshall won the case, and conservative contemporaries viewed his work on *Ives* as a highpoint in his legal career. In a well-known essay he published in memorial tribute to his friend Marshall in 1930, Cyrus Adler noted approvingly that many lawyers viewed *Ives* as the "most important brief Marshall ever wrote," and one that "assured his reputation as a constitutional lawyer."[294] This estimate did not age well. In his later years, Marshall witnessed how his *Ives* reasoning on worker compensation lost traction in the courtroom of public opinion and in the adoption of reform measures in states around the country.

Organizing a National Campaign for Abrogation

Meantime, the AJC's agenda featured not workplace reform in state legislation but rather rallying support for abrogation in the state capitals. By the end of winter 1911, AJC Secretary Dr. Herbert Friedenwald reported optimistically that the distribution of Marshall's address had instigated abrogation processes around the country—abrogation resolutions were being adopted by legislatures in New Jersey, Wisconsin, and Arkansas.[295] Eager to launch a nationwide publicity campaign, AJC stewards consulted with leading media moguls, including Ochs of the *New York Times*. The plan was to sponsor a series of magazine articles on the treaty question and to contact editors of leading periodicals in all cities with a population over 100,000 in the hope of obtaining editorials favoring abrogation. The media blitz was to hit its peak in time for the 1912 elections; on this timeline, the AJC's victory in the abrogation campaign actually came prematurely, almost a year before the 1912 polling, but this success was clearly assisted by a deftly managed publicity effort. The article titles pounded home claims and ideas Marshall expressed in his UAHC speech—"Russia Persecutes Christians, too," "Russians Think Only the Dollar Rules in America." Journalists Joseph Chamberlain and James Creelman did most of the writing; politicians, including Sulzer, Champ Clark, and a rejuvenated Henry Goldfogle, added public statements underlining the need to overturn the 1832 treaty.[296] Marshall had hopes that Herman Bernstein could acquire ground level evidence of Russia's discriminatory policies; Bernstein was to stay in contact with trusted correspondents in Russia via cipher codes.[297]

Marshall keenly monitored events on Capitol Hill, the arena where the Russian treaty's fate would finally be decided. "The Jews intend to make a dead set for abrogation," Marshall informed Senator Simon Guggenheim, and so "it is very important to have the right men on the Senate Committee on Foreign Relations."[298] Marshall also consulted with associates from other Jewish organizations about the terms of the debate. "The abrogation of a treaty does not mean the cessation of diplomatic or economic relations," Marshall explained to the UAHC's Julius Walter Freiberg. From a commercial standpoint, the likely effects of abrogation were "not a serious matter," Marshall added. He understood that American trusts like Harvester, the Singer Sewing Machine Company, and Westinghouse were active in Russia, but argued that their business "would not be disrupted by abrogation, because they are carrying out business under protection of charters granted by the Russian government."[299]

Organizing a national campaign for a change in American policy relations toward a major world power was a new, heady experience for Marshall, but events in this period served as sobering reminders of his family responsibilities and professional dependencies. Suddenly, Syracuse ceased to be a warm, steady constant in his private life. In April 1911, for the first time in his life, he celebrated the Passover seder outside of Syracuse. He passed the holiday with Florence, his two oldest children, his father, and his sister's family, at a table set for sixteen in Philadelphia. His father Jacob upset many in the family by announcing his intention of resigning from Syracuse's venerable Reform temple, the Society of Concord, owing to the synagogue's removal that year to a new building. In Louis's private discussions with his siblings about their octogenarian father's grievances, dim echoes of a mild criticism might be heard—Zilli, their mother, had a more harmonious way of melding principle and practicality. Louis had grown weary of the way his father would "become embittered, and reason in a circle, which leads to his considering himself aggrieved." Still, Louis gently excused his father, reminding his siblings "when you get to be over 80 years of age, you probably will feel yourself entitled to ride your own hobbies." The family respected Jacob's decision to attend services elsewhere, realizing that this arrangement was better than "making the whole subject a matter of town talk."[300]

Marshall and Jacob Schiff

On this personal level, the abrogation campaign unfolded with an internal contradiction, a paradox that was not debilitating yet was nonetheless felt in Marshall's internal psyche and also occasionally figured in a public perception of him as Jacob Schiff's lawyer. The ultimate purpose of the abrogation fight was to validate the American Jewry cherished premise that their country was "different"—unlike medieval countries, where Jews depended upon the largesse of princes;

and unlike modern European circumstance where Jews received precious rights of emancipation conditionally, upon the fulfillment of an agenda of personal and communal socioeconomic and religious reforms; Jews lived in America on terms of equality, and under the protection of a democratic Constitution. Yet in some ways, Marshall's rise as a Jewish leader in America replicated dynamics of the premodern court Jew who lived splendidly so long as the prince was pleased—the prince in this case being the Jewish banker, Jacob Schiff. Applied to men of sophisticated discipline like Schiff and Marshall, that analogy can cast a distorted shadow on the noticeably harmonious relationship that developed between the pair. However, the fact that instances of friction between the two were remarkably infrequent does not mean that Marshall advanced in public affairs without a sense of vulnerability bred by his dependence upon Schiff's overpowering resources. This tension abated considerably during World War I,[301] a period when Marshall's political instincts and personal background produced responses that were rather less conflicted than Schiff's—in this later period, Marshall tended increasingly to flatter Schiff's ego with sugar-coated words before implementing courses of action that were rather different in emphasis and direction than Schiff's inclinations. Earlier, Marshall needed to be somewhat more careful.

A revealing instance of his privately kept vulnerability occurred in late 1909 in a trivial matter when a brother of his brother-in-law asked for help obtaining an all-night license for a restaurant in the Tenderloin district, the midtown area which was enjoying its final years of happy notoriety where ladies danced on nightclub tables and there were drinks all around. The petition was incongruous from the start—a teetotaler,[302] Louis preached to the restaurant owner about the immorality of the Tenderloin area (Marshall quoted the old proverb "whoever touches pitch will be defiled"), but out of his abiding sense of family loyalty, Marshall passed the relative's petition along to the *New York Times,* a newspaper whose offices were perched on the northwest corner of the Tenderloin. When the unflappable relative asked for help obtaining Schiff's endorsement for the all-night license, Marshall exploded with anger. He wrote to his brother-in-law: "Leonard has the coolness to ask me to procure the endorsement of Jacob Schiff. What can you think that I am made of? Am I to forfeit my standing in the community, my self respect, to fritter them away in so ridiculous a manner as you suggest?"[303]

In some contexts, Schiff treated Marshall as a business unit manager who had to show quarterly results. The hierarchy between the two men in these specific contexts contrasted oddly with the wide latitude Schiff and the other AJC leaders gave to Marshall in the promotion of national Jewish interests. In years before World War I, as the Uptown elite moved from the earlier moral amelioration orientation to this organizational phase, nobody really gave any serious consideration to imposing checks on the strategies Marshall devised and the practical steps he took on some matters of towering communal importance, particularly immigration. On abrogation, Marshall basically moved into a power vacuum when he delivered the UAHC address. Even though (as Naomi Cohen concluded) credit for the overturning of the treaty in December 1911 belonged to the AJC as a whole,[304] the level of autonomy Marshall exercised in the management of publicity and lobbying resources and the articulation of the Jewish community's grievances and demands is impressive—the biographical point worth emphasizing is how sharply this autonomy contrasted with the lingering, and rather demeaning, dependence Marshall endured as Schiff's assistant and administrator on other issues.

Marshall's fund-raising responsibilities for the JTS well exemplify this lingering subordination. Marshall derived tremendous satisfaction from his work with Schechter and other associates connected with this unique religious institution, but he was also burdened by Schiff's demands concerning the JTS. The seminary was chronically short of funds, and Marshall incessantly and wearily combed the New York elite, seeking donation subscriptions. In May 1910, he realized that the only way he could attain the target goal of a $10,000 annual fund for the JTS would be to turn into a full-time fund-raiser. Marshall took the rare step of protesting this JTS burden to Schiff, reminding the banker that he had his own law firm to attend to, not to mention the abrogation campaign and other ongoing Jewish causes. "I am so busy at this time of year that I cannot without doing great injustice to myself and my partners devote much time to personal solicitations [for the JTS], which I find is the only way to secure substantial contributions," he complained to Schiff. Julius Rosenwald of Chicago loomed as a deus ex machina, but he conditioned his offer of a substantial contribution to the JTS (the first one the institution was to receive outside of the New York area) upon Marshall's obtainment of yet additional subscriptions.

Rosenwald, a visionary philanthropist, had a knack for engaging ethnic minority leaders in cutting-edge discussions about their communities' spirit and future. Just as the Sears, Roebuck millionaire was supportively involved with Booker T. Washington in a fascinating discussion about the purposes of black education (Rosenwald joined the Board of Washington's Tuskegee Institute in 1912 and remained on it for the rest of his life[305]), Rosenwald initiated in this period an illuminating discussion with Marshall about the JTS as a central golden road for Judaism in America, a dialogue that would continue through the very last days of Marshall's life. In May 1911, Rosenwald framed any major philanthropist's perennial question in the JTS context: if the seminary was so vital, why was Marshall so despairingly forlorn about the prospect of finding donors and meeting Schiff's demands? This prompted from Marshall a perspicacious analysis of conditions in Jewish America that would give rise to a new branch of Judaism, the Conservative movement. But the movement's consolidation belonged to the future, Marshall observed:

> You say: if the seminary is so vital, why is it so few people support the institution? The answer is that few people appreciate the importance of educational institutions. Very few seem to realize the necessity of maintaining a theological institute on conservative lines. Jewish men of means are usually members of Reformed congregations, and unable to place themselves in the position of the Jewish masses. The older members of Orthodox congregations look with suspicion at us, because our instruction is conducted in English, with modern methods. Younger members of the Orthodox community are occupied with the problem of earning a living. Hence the institution is confined to a very small public.[306]

For the time being, Marshall confided to Rosenwald in an uncharacteristic vein of unguarded complaint, "there is something wrong in our management" of JTS. Schiff demanded too much from him. "I am the only one who has ever collected a dollar," Marshall noted. "I suppose that if I gave up the practice of the law and devoted myself to the work of collecting for charity. . . . I might bring about better results," Marshall added. "But it is necessary for me to continue in [law] practice in order to earn a livelihood. I sometimes feel like stepping down and out."[307]

Marshall needed a vacation, but his youngest son, seven-year-old George, came down with scarlet fever, and the family's house in Manhattan was put in quarantine for weeks, thereby delaying the annual vacation at Knollwood. Marshall made arrangements with Herb Clark, his children's beloved guide in the Adirondack wilds, to schedule the family's favorite hiking and outdoors activities in a deferred vacation.[308] With the early summer heat sweltering in New York, he escaped whenever he could to baseball games. The sport was in the Marshall blood, particularly ten-year-old Robert's. "You can wake him up in the middle of the night and he can give you the batting average of any man in the league," Marshall told relatives. "I am rapidly becoming a convert" to his children's passion for the sport, he confessed.[309]

"The Little Snowball Becomes an Avalanche"—The Abrogation Triumph

Heading into summer, Marshall and the AJC sustained momentum in the abrogation fight by refuting false reports about easement in the czar's treatment of Jews.

Marshall and others in the AJC were convinced that the Associated Press wire syndicate was responsible for the disinformation. With Marshall, this complaint dated back to the late 1905 period of atrocious pogroms in Russia—when he wrote his check to Magnes for the Jewish Defense Fund, and included a statement for publication, Marshall had inserted a sentence criticizing the AP's noncoverage of the pogroms ("the AP has been silent where it is usually most eloquent, in depicting the horrors of human suffering"), but he subsequently deleted this attack, owing to the worry that it would just create a negative backlash from the powerful news agency.[310]

By May 1911, the AJC had abandoned such reticence regarding the AP. Testifying to a panel headed by the anti-imperialist owner of the *Nation,* Oswald Garrison Villard, AJC Secretary Friedenwald detailed how the AP had distortedly covered Russian affairs in preceding months. The AP's condoning reports of blood libel charges against Russian Jews, the AJC charged, abetted Russian pogrom-makers.[311] Marshall busily explained to politicians and journalists, Jews and non-Jews, that AP reports about the czar's plans to abolish the Pale of Settlement or to extend travel privileges to American Jews "were mere emanations of Russian duplicity." Via the wire service, the Russians were endeavoring to "fool the American people and bring about a suspension of action by Congress on abrogation."[312]

Opposition in public to abrogation was about to collapse like a house of cards, however. On the eve of triumph, Marshall was particularly irritated by close associates like Ochs of the *New York Times,* who momentarily had cold feet about the prudence of an ethnic organization, the AJC, lobbying on the basis of its own minority group's sense of insult for the repeal of a treaty which well served the entire country;[313] but he could not allow such internal Jewish quibbling about tactics and goals to deflect his attention from places where Jews and other immigrant minorities really had antagonists. As the abrogation campaign turned the corner and headed toward a surprisingly swift and sweeping victory, the fight for open immigration renewed in earnest. The AJC was heavily invested in abrogation, but Marshall lacked funds to organize a systematic empirical rebuttal to the findings of the Dillingham Commission, which in 1911 issued its massive forty-one-volume report in support of its operating thesis that immigration from Southern and Eastern Europe, as a threat to America's economy and culture, ought to be curtailed. In June 1911, restriction bills inspired by the Dillingham Commission were pending in Congress; Marshall believed that he had a six-month window, until December 1911, when Congress in its regular session would take up the restriction proposals for legislation. As the centerpiece of its counter-campaign against restriction, the AJC wanted to commission an immigration study by a Russian Jewish statistician, Isaac A. Hourwich. The statistician, who had left Russia in 1890 at the age of thirty and completed a PhD at Columbia, required $6,000 to complete his study. Schiff, with some Philadelphia Jewish associates, had pledged two-thirds of that sum; Marshall spent days in late spring 1911 searching for the remainder, petitioning (among others) Morris Loeb of the New York Foundation.[314]

Hourwich compiled a voluminous 500-page study, *Immigration and Labor*,[315] whose publication in 1912 was delayed a few weeks by the author's diligence, somewhat to the chagrin of Marshall and other open immigration lobbyists, who were hungry for empirical data and racing to stave off restriction maneuvers on Capitol Hill. His volume is a powerfully detailed refutation of the economic arguments for immigration restriction. "There is absolutely no statistical proof of an oversupply of unskilled labor resulting in the displacement of native by immigrant laborers,"[316] Hourwich declared. The effect of immigration on labor, he claimed, was occupational readjustment in the United States. The majority of native-born Americans worked in "farming, in business, in the professions and in clerical pursuits;" immigrants, on the other hand, were industrial wage-owners. Cases of the native or Americanized wage-earner being displaced by the immigrant laborer were "exceptional." Hourwich dissected the internal assumptions of the restrictionists' economic argument: if their analyses were correct, then unemployment should have risen in preceding years, when immigration figures in the United States were high, but his investigation proved that there had been less unemployment during the first seven years of the twentieth century, when immigration crested, than there had been during the preceding decade, when immigration was relatively low.[317] The findings supported the study's main contention, holding that immigration was a consequence and a contributing factor to economic prosperity and not (as the Nativists held) a causal factor responsible for unemployment:

> The relation between immigration and unemployment may thus be summed up in the following propositions: Unemployment and immigration are the effects of economic forces working in opposite directions: those which produce business expansion reduce unemployment and attract immigration; those which produce business depression increase unemployment and reduce immigration.[318]

Hourwich's level of analysis was pertinent insofar as labor union claims about employment loss caused by immigration fanned Nativist sentiment in this pre–World War I era, but his study could be no more than a glancing strike at the Dillingham Commission.[319] The gist of the restriction argument was cultural, founded on propositions about immigrants from Southern and Eastern Europe as a threat to the country's racial fabric. Hourwich, however, had little to say about the cultural contributions, or even economic performance, of ethnoreligious groups and devoted just a few total pages of nonsystematic discussion to Jewish immigrants and scarcely more discussion to Italian or Irish immigrants. His chapters and discussion topics were primarily conceptualized not in racial or ethnic categories but rather in economic terms (unemployment, standard of living) and job sectors (garment workers, iron and steel workers).

Over the summer, Marshall collected resources for a final push on abrogation. Out in Oklahoma on a work trip, he ran across agents who organized Chautauqua events around the country, reaching millions of people; that Marshall considered incorporating abrogation publicity on the Chautauqua circuit says something about how resolved the AJC had become about the popular appeal of its campaign.[320] Once they were told about how some of their fellow passport holders were treated by the czar's officers, Americans would resent Russia's discriminatory policy as an affront to national honor. Marshall admitted that the AJC had no way of influencing Russia's response to an abrogation decision, but he refused to let this issue puncture unity in the campaign. It was a scorching hot summer—in the Adirondacks, Marshall told his sister-in-law Birdie (Beatrice) that he had never known such heat, apart from whenever he read the New York newspapers.[321]

His blood boiled when the *New York Times* published an anti-abrogation op-ed, "The Other Side of the Passport Question,"[322] signed mysteriously by "A Veteran Diplomat," who was, in fact, an avowed Russophile (Cunliffe Owen). This diplomat excused anti-Semitism by alluding to economic factors and exempted Nicholas II from his empire's Jew-hatred. The AJC howled in protest; Ochs, who was in Europe, regretted the piece and scolded his business manager for printing it.[323] On July 16, the *Times* published Marshall's scalding rebuttal,[324] which accused the Veteran Diplomat of being co-opted by the despotic cynicism of the czar's advisors and thereby "swallowing whole the wolf's pretext for his brutality to the lamb." Berating the "acme of blind partisanship" by which the Veteran Diplomat overlooked the way the czar had abusively reneged parliamentary promises, Marshall concluded that the question had nothing to do with whether Nicholas II was the "embodiment of enlightened civilization or not"; the only pertinent fact was that the passports of American citizens were "dishonored, disregarded and flouted by the Russian government."

Quartered at Knollwood, Marshall edited several drafts of the AJC's account of the passport question,[325] monitored happenings in Albany for the bill to establish the College of Forestry at Syracuse, kept in touch with Schiff who was overseas (and who insisted that Kaiser Wilhelm would take suitable action against

Russian anti-Semitism were America to abrogate the 1832 treaty), and followed affairs leading to the Tenth Zionist Congress (though this became known as a "Peace Congress," at which political and cultural streams of Jewish nationalism converged harmoniously in a new form of "synthetic Zionism," Marshall worried that the Jewish nationalists were over-stressing the prospect of a mass Jewish flight from poverty and persecution in Eastern Europe in a way that might be exploited by Nativists in America).[326] He made headway in state legislatures. In Albany, Governor Dix vetoed in 1911 some 300 bills, but signed into law all the banking and forestry proposals that had been drafted or supported by Marshall.[327] The NY immigration bureau was swinging into operation under the able directorship of Frances Kellor, but it was short of funds, and Marshall was embarrassed when Kellor shouldered some of its bills herself; he solicited John D. Rockefeller and Jacob Schiff and raised several hundred dollars to cover Kellor's expenses.[328] In discussions with manufacturers, Marshall reviewed one year later lessons learned from the protocol of peace resolution of the cloakmakers strike. He insisted that industrial relations needed to be put on a new footing of mutual respect. "So long as the manufacturer considers his employees as mere serf and chattel," Marshall warned, "dislike, if not hatred, will be engendered against the employer." If, on the other hand, "the employee feels treated as an equal, and believes that the employer wants to listen patiently to his grievances," the protocol would remain a viable model in industrial relations, Marshall predicted.[329] Marshall corresponded with pro-abrogation advocates from Arkansas and Georgia in order to push abrogation resolutions through governments in those, and other, states.[330]

Meantime, the pro-abrogation energy of counterparts from other Jewish organizations seemed to wilt in the summer heat. Marshall was distinctly unimpressed when some such colleagues pointed to the fact that the president invited several rabbis to his silver wedding anniversary celebration, as though it were evidence of his pro-Jewish inclinations. When Simon Wolf referred anxiously to the possibility of pogroms breaking out in Russia as a consequence of an abrogation resolution, Marshall finally lost his cool. His outburst revealed the militancy of the AJC's commitment to bring abrogation to its conclusion: "If pogroms arise, the whole world will know that they originated at the command of the czar's government," Marshall declared. "If there are to be more martyrs, harsh as it may seem to say so, the eventual result will be a triumph of humanity. The blood of the martyrs is not only the seed of the Church. Through it, Judaism has been preserved through the ages."[331]

Between the end of the summer and the Jewish High Holy Days, Marshall's younger brother Benjamin, who had for years partnered with their father Jacob in the family hide and leather business, passed away due to a cerebral hemorrhage. A gentle-spirited, likeable man, Benjamin had suffered from a nervous disorder for close to two years, but had seemed to be recovering psychologically before his sudden death. He was survived by his wife Ida and two girls; Jacob seemed dazed by the loss, as his other son, Louis, handled arrangements to help Ida in her bereavement. As happened in these periods of family loss, Louis found comfort by working on projects for Syracuse's cultural and educational benefit. Now that Governor Dix had signed the bill creating the New York State College of Forestry at Syracuse, Marshall was honored to be invited to serve as president of its Board of Trustees. Reminding Syracuse University's Chancellor that he could not be identified with an LL.D. title on the institution's letterhead, he proposed that the board meet on weekends, since court arrangements kept him in Manhattan during the week. Throughout this period Marshall creatively juggled the duality of an array of issues by stressing (for example) the need for laborer-manufacturer cooperation in industry or by presenting Jewish demands for abrogation as an American issue. As we will see, Marshall impressively displayed his ability to balance the sensitivities of two different concerns in his extraordinarily energetic labors with the Forestry College board in ensuing months and years: a precedent-setting institution in environmental education in America that would produce 27,000 graduates in the next century, the institution thrived largely due to the way Marshall convinced legislators in Albany to regard it as a New York State project while encouraging administrators at Syracuse University to cultivate it as part of their own institution.

On abrogation, in autumn 1911 there could be no artful negotiation. One member of the Uptown elite, Oscar Straus, disagreed with this premise, and Straus's proposal to resolve the 1832 treaty dispute with Russia via international arbitration set him on a collision course with the Uptown elite. Though not a pacifist, Straus had a deep belief in the feasibility of minimizing violent conflict between states by means of law and arbitration. First winning an appointment from President Roosevelt in 1902, he served for years at the court of arbitration in The Hague, considering it to be his most valuable post in public life. Straus's confidence in arbitration accelerated during the Venezuelan debt dispute in 1902 and was reinforced by developments during the Russo-Japanese war; as a Jew, he believed peaceful arbitration of international disputes paid tribute to the universal ideals of Judaism, and he described the 1913 dedication of the Peace Palace in The Hague as an embodiment of the wisdom of the prophets of Israel.[332] In October 1911, Straus enlisted Theodore Roosevelt's support for arbitration as a means to resolve the impasse over the 1832 Russian treaty. Arguing for arbitration in the *Outlook*, the former president claimed that the arbitration process would expose

Russia's cruel anti-Semitism to the world and also that were arbitration to fail practically, there would still be time to abrogate the treaty.[333] Appalled by this turn of events, Marshall had a terse, unproductive phone conversation with Straus about the arbitration proposal.[334] He then politely rebuffed Roosevelt's recommendation in a published letter to the *Outlook,* claiming that arbitration was superfluous on this matter. Even arbitration advocates like Roosevelt acknowledged that there was no dispute about Russia's infringement of the 1832 treaty, and the only way an international mediating body could rule on Russia's behalf would be if it were staffed by monarchists whose "concepts, traditions and prejudices" were inimical to American constitutional ideas of citizenship and equal protection.[335] "I am sure Roosevelt will not be irritated, because I made sure my article has no sting," Marshall confided to Schiff.[336] He was less diplomatic to Mayer Sulzberger. "I consider Mr. Straus' idea positively dangerous," he confessed. Should an international "tribunal decide against us," the abrogation cause "would be dead as a doornail." Straus, Marshall suspected, operated out of self-interest, with hopes of receiving public recognition on the Russian issue. Straus, Marshall concluded, "has rushed into the situation with a recklessness which is certainly not angelic."[337]

From the start, abrogation was viewed as a defining issue by the AJC, since it punished Russia for its anti-Semitism and had a sweeping, almost radical character in that it required a change in American foreign policy toward a world power. These elements, the AJC reasoned, would appeal to Downtown's immigrant Jews. Protecting the AJC's interests, Marshall emphatically opposed last minute compromise proposals on the Russian issue that threatened to dilute this appeal. When, in late October, Judge Mack aired the thought that the AJC campaign should focus on forcing Russia to admit nonnaturalized Jewish Americans, Marshall gruffly retorted that were "the members of the American Jewish Committee to listen to such a proposal, they might as well prepare to see themselves hung in effigy."[338] About three-fourths of America's two million Jews were of Russian birth or descent. "What account could we give to them of our stewardship if we said that, as a result of our labors, we had succeeded in securing permission to American-born Jews and German Jews to go to Russia, and be accorded rights of American citizens, while as to Russian Jews we conceded that a different rule was applicable," Marshall told Mack, underlining the rationale of the entire campaign.[339]

Marshall and Schiff sent letters in early November to New York's Republican and Democratic Senators, Elihu Root and James A. O'Gorman, asking to bring a delegation of representative citizens to a meeting about Russia's affront to the "honor of our country and to the integrity of American citizenship."[340] Marshall maintained continuing contacts with the two US senators. To Root, he explained that there was no "parallelism" between Russia's infringement of the 1832 treaty and the 1868 Burlingame Treaty with China, which related to most-favored nation status and offered protections to Chinese subjects in the United States but withheld naturalization opportunities; with O'Gorman, Marshall ironed out the composition of the much-awaited meeting, agreeing to invite several judges (Bijur, Greenbaum, and others) who were known to the senator, from his decade on the bench of New York's Supreme Court (Marshall pointedly did not invite Congressman Goldfogle to the meeting).[341]

The conference, held on November 17, opened smoothly, as O'Gorman pronounced himself unqualifiedly in favor of the delegation's pro-abrogation position. Root strained Marshall's patience: "Squirming as usual, Root stated that he agreed entirely with our interpretation of the treaty . . . but he believed that if we continued to exercise patience we might be able, through diplomatic channels, [to] accomplish our purpose," Marshall confidentially reported after the meeting.[342] Root's waffling prompted Schiff to divulge impulsively information about improper influence wielded on the Taft administration by a Russian financial agent, Gregory Wilenkin, who formed a syndicate with engineer John Hays Hammond for the export of American products to Russia. Schiff's revelation stirred, Marshall noted, a "profound sensation,"[343] but the AJC men wondered whether Schiff had played his cards too early, distracting attention toward the scheming wiles of Nicholas's court and relegating the abrogation issue to the background.[344] This fear was excessive, however. At the time of the Manhattan meeting, Rosenwald, Ullman, and B'nai B'rith's Harry Cutler were in Washington, discussing abrogation with the president and Secretary of State Knox. The impression that Taft would not oppose abrogation resolutions passed by Congress circulated excitedly between New York and Washington. Marshall now had no doubt that skeptics like Philander C. Knox were climbing on the bandwagon of a suddenly popular cause. Barely concealing his glee, he told Sulzberger that "our arrows are beginning to penetrate the cuticle of the pachydermatous Secretary of State."[345] "It is very evident that the government is now thoroughly in earnest, and recognizes that the whole country is becoming stirred on this matter," Marshall wrote to Wolf,[346] who felt excluded after not taking part in the Washington meetings.

Eleventh-hour attempts in the Taft administration, spearheaded by Knox, were leveraged on a few accommodating signals made by Russia's new ambassador to the United States, Boris Bakhmetev. In his annual message on December 7, the president referred to progress in talks with the Russians and hinted that Congress should hold the issue in abeyance until it reconvened after Christmas.[347]

Abrogation's momentum, however, proved larger than President Taft's enormous indecisiveness. On December 4, House Foreign Affairs Committee Chairman Sulzer reintroduced his abrogation resolution. Two days later, Sulzer, possessor of a weak character but a lively tongue, outdid himself at a Carnegie Hall, delivering a speech for overturning the 1832 treaty that "meant business and went straight to the point."[348] The rally, an exuberant Marshall reported, "will go down in history." Politicians, he correctly predicted, "will be falling over one another in a few days to vote with us."[349] When, a few days later, the abrogation resolution went to the House floor for discussion, representatives (in Naomi Cohen's words) "could not wait to express their horror of Russian barbaric practices . . . and their insistence upon the inviolability of the rights of American citizens."[350] Sulzer's resolution passed in the House by a vote of 301 to 1. Via some maneuvering in talks with the Russians, Knox managed to block the abrogation avalanche in the Senate for a few days, thereby stirring some anxiety in the AJC, whose members worried that if notice of termination did not go out by January 1, the 1832 treaty would remain in force until January 1, 1914; but on December 19 the Senate unanimously adopted an abrogation resolution phrased in language slightly more moderate than Sulzer's. A day later, the House agreed to these semantic adjustments, and so the United States formally gave Russia notice that on January 1, 1913, the 1832 Treaty of Commerce and Navigation would cease to be.

Formed six years before by American Jews in dumbstruck response to Russia's anti-Semitism, the members of the AJC had changed their nation's negotiated policy with the czar's empire. Abrogation was an inspiring act of redress that lacked precedent both in centuries of Jewish Diaspora powerlessness and decades of ethnic disorganization in the United States endured by Jews and many other immigrant groups.

In months that followed, some portion of the doomsday warnings that had been issued by the anti-abrogation forces found realization in an anti-Jewish and anti-American backlash in Russia. The concession scheme centered around John Hays Hammond fell through; the Russian fleet's planned trip to the United States was cancelled, as was a measure of Russian entente with Japan.[351] A year after abrogation, President Taft privately felt that the Jews had been foolish and that their abstract lobbying for principles of equality had brought harm to themselves, their country, and their coreligionists in Russia.[352]

While the president's skepticism had some empirical grounding in the context of US-Russian relations, it badly missed the mark as an assessment of ethnic politics. In the ethnic sphere, the impact of a campaign like abrogation is to be measured not in terms of practical effects, but rather as an agency of communal unity, and as reinforcement of faith in America as an arena where an ethnoreligious group could rely on democratic process in a march for justice. There is room to wonder what would have happened to American Jewry during World War I had none of its various sub-groups been able to demonstrate the power of nationwide organization and lobbying in years preceding the global conflict. An imperfectly organized entity virtually by necessity, American Jews would rediscover and be inspired by the symbolic logic of the abrogation campaign when they combined organizationally on an array of issues in decades to come. These included causes that had a clear topical affinity to the 1832 treaty struggle, such as the community's support for the Jackson-Vanik amendment withholding most favored nation status to the Soviet Union under the 1974 Trade Act, owing to its policies blocking the emigration of Jews and others.

Ever protective of his loyalties, Marshall had watched Congress adopt the abrogation resolutions with one or two qualms. As a lifetime Republican, he told the president's friend Isaac Ullman, it troubled him that the Taft administration's equivocation had opened a window to the Democrats, who were sure to take "the lion's share of the glory and credit" for what had become a popular cause.[353] He was also wary that the flamboyant public celebrations sponsored by Jewish groups and allied associations "might result in the creation of a reactionary movement, fostered by Russia and her partisans, and even by Americans of anti-Semitic proclivities"; for this reason, Marshall politely dissuaded the National Citizens Committee from arranging a banquet in his honor.[354] As days passed, however, the elated Marshall began to set the abrogation triumph in full perspective. "The little snowball which began to roll from the mountain top, finally became a tremendous avalanche, which swept everything before it," he observed. "I feel as though I had won the greatest law suit in which I have ever been engaged," he told his cousins, Benjamin and Joseph Stolz.[355] For weeks he had argued stridently that abrogation had to be seen as an American issue affecting Jews and Christians alike, but in these private communications Marshall articulated a soaring sense of personal fulfillment due to his contribution to Jewish life and Jewish history. Winning abrogation for the betterment of the Jewish people, Marshall confessed, fulfilled a "boyhood ambition." He added:

> I feel that I have not lived and worked in vain, in that God has enabled me to aid in the solution of at least one of the Jewish problems. It is a source of sorrow to me, that my mother did not live to witness the accomplishment of this result, for which she greatly yearned.[356]

5

Avoiding the Guillotine of Immigration Restriction

Untermyer

The year 1912 opened with a major change in Marshall's professional life when his partner Samuel Untermyer left their firm. "This will keep me very busy," Marshall wrote to his father, in laconic understatement.[1] Samuel Untermyer was a complicated man. A corporate lawyer who built up a thriving business, Untermyer served as guiding spirit and legal counsel on the 1912–13 Pujo Committee investigation of the banking "money trust." While his work on the Pujo panel thrilled Progressives, Untermyer became notorious among members of America's financial elite as a merciless demagogue allegedly responsible for causing J. P. Morgan to die from stress (Morgan's son subsequently referred to Untermyer as "the beast"). All the same, the Jewish business lawyer's social orbit had points of tangency with the house of Morgan (his pedigree collies had once beaten Pierpont's in a dog competition).[2]

Beyond blood ties, the Untermyers and Marshalls were friends—Florence and Louis would greet the Untermyers as they disembarked and returned from ocean journeys. Untermyer liked to laugh at Marshall's neurotic fear of dogs.[3] Actually, the fact that Untermyer trained dogs to compete with the pets of the city's Gentile millionaires, while his partner sidetracked for dozens of blocks on his walks to avoid dogs and moralized about how dog ownership ought to be banned in New York City, perhaps symbolizes something more than just a long-standing running joke between the two professional partners. Marshall was a conservative who sought to preserve nature and Judaism intact, whereas Untermyer was a trainer, adapter, and conqueror who affiliated with the Zionist attempt to revolutionize Jewish life.[4]

Did Marshall feel victimized as "Samuel Untermyer's partner," especially since the President of the United States once mordantly suggested that he ought to? In fact, there is no strong evidence that Marshall regretted his partner's confrontational style. Months after Untermyer's devil-may-care defense of firm client Max Nathan's position in the preventorium dispute damaged the viability of Marshall's candidacy for the Supreme Court nomination, Marshall kindly invited Nathan to rejoin the Knollwood group, since Dan Guggenheim was selling his cottage.[5] In other words, when Marshall traveled to his beloved retreat in the Adirondacks, he had many work pressures to escape from, but he was not fleeing from any reminder of Untermyer's assertive advocacy.

Immigration Politics before World War I

Paradoxically, at the beginning of 1912, the abrogation triumph encouraged Marshall and the AJC to stay in the background in Capitol Hill, lobbying against the restrictionists and their literacy test proposals. "We should not be too much in the foreground" in the campaign against literacy tests, Marshall opined. He held that position "in view of the fact that the passport contest has been so recent, and we do not wish to have the suggestion made that we are trying to run the government."[6]

This position stemmed from a semiformal "Conference on Immigration" Marshall had convened at his own home at the end of 1911, with Max Kohler (representing the Board of Delegates), Leon Sanders (Hebrew Immigrant Aid Society; HIAS), and Jacob Singer (B'nai B'rith). The delegates concurred that "opposition to the restriction of immigration should not emanate solely from the Jews."[7] Throughout 1912, Kohler and AJC member Cyrus Sulzberger would handle public work against immigration restriction via appearances at congressional hearings, publications, and speeches; Marshall, who became president of the AJC in autumn 1912 when Mayer Sulzberger retired, directed the campaign from behind the scenes.[8]

The hard-working Kohler burnished his credentials with potential allies, most importantly Charles Nagel, the secretary of commerce and labor. The son of a doctor who had fled Germany in the 1840s, Nagel won his appointment as a reward for his work on Taft's 1908 campaign, but Schiff and his AJC associates, who had expected a pro-immigration orientation from a second-generation American, were disappointed by Nagel's obstruction of the Galveston project for Jewish immigrants as well as his department's policy of turning away immigrants who had less than $25 at the time of their arrival.[9] Sensing that Nagel might nonetheless be flexible on immigration, Kohler maintained contact with the secretary of commerce and labor from late 1911. "I realize the truth of your statement that persons of my faith are almost necessarily advocates on these [immigration] questions," Kohler confided to Nagel, "but I have tried, personally, to eliminate at least the element of pecuniary interest in shaping my attitude on immigration matters, by refusing to accept one percent of compensation for professional services in these immigration cases."[10]

In spring 1912, Kohler circulated his pamphlet, "Injustice of a Literacy Test for Immigrants," on Capitol Hill, as part of his campaign against restrictionism, a selfless fight that was increasingly appreciated by Schiff and Marshall.[11] Kohler's pamphlet reproduced antirestriction statements made by prominent politicians, including President Cleveland's 1897 veto message regarding the literacy test, and also asserted that the imposition of a literacy test would block more than 25 percent of immigrants who were then streaming into the United States.[12] In tandem, Marshall opened 1912 by trying to engage key congressional leaders in a critical discussion about the restrictionists' guiding concepts. "I am absolutely opposed to any general policy of restriction," Marshall announced to Henry Cabot Lodge. When the senator proposed a restriction standard prohibiting "persons who are not racially eligible to become citizens of the US by naturalization," Marshall complained to Lodge that the word "racially" was "much too general." He explained: "Nobody knows where the expression of such an idea in our legislation might lead. Some 140 years ago Blumenbach divided the world into five races; today, modern anthropologists talk about 150 races."[13]

By early spring 1912, Marshall and AJC colleagues received drafts of restriction proposals that were being worked on by the Senate Committee of Immigration and Naturalization. He was stunned by the way the Nativists had drawn inspiration from Draconian policies that had impeded the immigration of Asians on the West Coast. "The entire bill is framed on the theory that the rules which have heretofore applied to Chinese immigrants are applicable to European immigrants," Marshall explained to Senator Isidor Raynor. "The drastic provisions of the laws pertaining to the Chinese have been made general."[14] Marshall's AJC colleagues were at this moment despondent about circumstances on Capitol Hill. "I fear that we are beaten in the Senate," moaned AJC Secretary Herbert Friedenwald.[15] In fact, in April 1912, the AJC seemed to concede the inevitability of Capitol Hill action mandating literacy tests; for the time being, the organization's focus was on the recognition of Hebrew and Yiddish for the purposes of literacy qualification, and also on the conferral of an exemption from literacy requirements to Jewish immigrants who fled persecution in Russia. Marshall pored through the *Congressional Record* and was relieved to find that Lodge had stated that reading proficiency in Hebrew and Yiddish would count for the proposed literacy test, and also that the existence of religious persecution in Russia would be factored in the conferral of exemptions to illiterate Jewish immigrants.[16]

Lodge, however, was not as firmly committed to recognition of the Hebrew and Yiddish—and religious persecution—standards as Marshall supposed; Lodge and others artfully moved restriction proposals back and forth in committee discussions in a dizzying fashion that confused the AJC's resident lobbyist, Fulton Brylawski, and his colleagues.[17] On the House side, the Committee on Immigration and Naturalization, chaired by Congressman John Burnett of Alabama, drafted a restriction measure based solely on the literacy test, as a contrast to the complicated Dillingham Bill that was being cobbled together in the Senate. Burnett's bill restricted male and female immigrants older than sixteen "physically capable of reading who cannot read the English language, or the language or dialect of some other country, including Hebrew and Yiddish."[18]

Partly because he continued to underestimate the number of Jewish immigrants who could not read in any language, Marshall was not overly alarmed when the Dillingham and Burnett bills marched their way through Capitol Hill. "In my judgment the fear that such a [literacy] test will affect our co-religionists is exaggerated," he privately told a cousin. "But I oppose the test on principle. We have decided to work quietly and not to make this a Jewish question, because that would be decidedly impolitic."[19] In a few limited appearances before civic and church groups in this period, Marshall garnered that their members were weighing the pros and cons of immigration restriction from the point of view of economic costs and benefits. This impression led him to pressure Isaac A. Hourwich to complete his study on immigration and labor—late in the year, the AJC disseminated 25,000 copies of his study's first chapter.[20]

Marshall's continuing discussions with Burnett maneuvered the congressman toward a proposal that was, from the Jewish standpoint, imperfect but not lethal. For weeks in winter–spring 1912, Marshall pressured the Alabama congressman to broaden the persecution exemption for illiterate immigrants from Russia on the grounds that Jews faced onerous political, economic, and social hardships in the Pale, and the justifiable reason for their flight could not always be identified solely as religious persecution. By the time he presented his literacy test bill to his House Committee, Burnett had rejected Marshall's formulations on discrimination exemptions as "too inclusive," but he assured Marshall and Friedenwald in private conversations that his literacy test bill was not designed to decrease the number of Jewish immigrants. He added that illiterate Jewish immigrants would be admitted because of the religious exemption provision, as it was formulated, even without the Marshall modifications.[21]

Marshall kept prodding Burnett, sometimes with ill effect. He called the congressman's attention to the fact that the Alabama state constitution of 1901 declared that "immigration shall be encouraged;" the "Alabama idea is the correct one," trumpeted Marshall.[22] Burnett replied with a testy letter in which he accused Marshall of maintaining an uncompromising attitude on immigration that would ultimately prove self-defeating. The congressman's irritated reply referred generically to Marshall as an overly assertive Jewish lobbyist: "The sooner some of *you* understand that unless conservative legislation is soon adopted that more radical legislation will be demanded, the better it will be for *yourselves* and the country," wrote Burnett.[23] Marshall took umbrage at the way he was lumped together with some unnamed Jewish lobby that had (in Burnett's phrasing) interests separate from those of the country as a whole. "Is it your desire to intimate that those who express the views which I entertain have interests which are distinct from those of other citizens, and that we have not the welfare of the country at heart?" Marshall indignantly queried. Such discussion hinged dubiously on the substantive objective of staving off immigration restriction.

It was not forensics but the 1912 elections that deferred restrictionist legislation until the end of the year. The three-way presidential campaign sparked lively public debate about the trusts, income tax, labor rights, and electoral reform, but immigration restriction figured but little in the electioneering.[24] Though Roosevelt's Progressive Party included social activists who had devoted much thought and energy to immigrant assistance, the Bull Moosers, with the crusading former president at their head, evaded taking a stance on the literacy test during the campaign.[25] In mid-June, Marshall focused on inserting language in the Republican and Democratic platforms proclaiming that no new treaty relations with Russia would be considered so long as the empire persisted with anti-Semitic discrimination; he downplayed the need for immigration planks in the party platforms, reminding Senator Raynor that "thus far we have been able to protect all immigrants who are not objectionable, without any special pronouncement on the subject . . . the wisest course is to leave this subject untouched."[26] The ACJ, represented by Schiff, Adler, and Cyrus Sulzberger, made some approaches to the Democrats, but Wilson refused to issue a public statement against the literacy test and offered only a public letter expressing general sympathy toward immigrants.[27] The AJC asked Marshall, Julius Rosenwald, and Harry Cutler to approach Taft on the literacy test. Two weeks before the balloting, Marshall composed a rather tepid letter that reminded the president that some of America's least desirable immigrants turned out to be highly educated, arguing blandly that any man who comes to the country prepared to work and build up its resources "should not be made the subject of adverse legislation."[28] Taft, whose electoral chances at this late hour were bleak, opted not to say anything about literacy tests.[29]

The *Titanic* and New York Jewry

On April 14, 1912, the *Titanic* passenger liner crashed into an iceberg 400 miles south of the Grand Banks of Newfoundland. Several close friends and acquaintances of the Marshalls were aboard, including Macy's co-owner Isidor Straus and his wife Ida, Edgar Meyer (the youngest son of Eugene Meyer and the brother-in-law of George Blumenthal), and Benjamin Guggenheim. These victims came from Jewish families that were fixtures in Uptown society. "I have never known New York to be under such a pall of grief and sorrow," Marshall wrote privately. At first, he grasped the shipwreck tragedy in his own professional terms, as though he were preparing a civil claim: "The loss of these valuable lives was so inexcusable, the negligence of the steamship company and those in charge of the vessel so glaring in character, that one is left in despair."[30]

When they became known, the heroic circumstances of the Straus couple's passing inspired Marshall to think about the *Titanic* affair beyond such constricting lawyerly frames. Manhattan was amazed by the Straus story—Isidor was told that he could accompany Ida into a lifeboat, but sent his wife's maid, Ellen Bird, in his stead, thereby prompting his wife to refuse to disembark. "I will not be separated from my husband," Ida Straus declared. "As we have lived, so we will die together." This was the end of a thirty-year marriage in which its members wrote to one another any day they were separated; Marshall spoke for many when he admitted, "I have been unable to get out of my mind for a moment the pathos of the end of these two fine exemplars of manhood and womanhood."[31] In a moving letter to Isidor's brother Oscar,[32] the former cabinet minister, Marshall recalled that his acquaintance with the *Titanic* victim dated from his first days in Manhattan, eighteen years earlier. They had worked together on Jewish communal issues on the board of directors of the Educational Alliance and the American Jewish Committee. Straus had belonged to the close-knit Uptown Jewish discussion club, the Wanderers. "He was a leader of men, his philanthropy was of the most intelligent type," Marshall wrote, dazed.

It was not an easy time in Marshall's private life. For the first time, his forty-year-old wife Florence was showing signs of faltering health. In early April she was diagnosed as suffering from neuralgia and confined to bed rest.[33] At the end of the month, Florence remained in her room. "I must confess I am feeling old,"[34] Marshall confided to a cousin. A pall covered this stretch of his life. Moses Weinman, a friend and professional partner who had retired from the Guggenheimer, Untermyer and Marshall firm at the start of the year, collapsed with pneumonia while playing a round of golf and died; his will left tens of thousands of dollars to charity, and his sudden, unexpected death left friends like Marshall gasping that "there was never a finer human being than he."[35]

As always, Marshall's brother-in-law Judah Magnes simultaneously personified and defied prevailing events and trends in the life of Jewish New York. After a tour in Palestine with another Straus brother, Nathan, Magnes and his wife Birdie (Beatrice) had planned on returning to the United States aboard the *Titanic*. At the last moment, however, Birdie decided not to make the journey on a new vessel that had never before crossed the Atlantic.[36] Enormously relieved, Marshall wondered whether to regard Magnes's life as a sequence of miracles, coincidences, or astute intuition (perplexed by, but always loyal to, Magnes, Marshall in this period returned his membership and pew to Madison Avenue's B'nai Jeshurun synagogue, after Magnes left its pulpit when congregation members failed to respond to the crusading rabbi's decision to eliminate organ playing and institute other traditional-spirited modifications in the synagogue's Reform services[37]).

Ida Straus's body was never recovered, but Isidor's was buried at Woodlawn Cemetery in the Bronx. For weeks, New Yorkers paid tribute to the Macy's owner and renowned philanthropist; the most widely publicized memorial was conducted at the Educational Alliance, the immigrant support facility on East Broadway.[38] The service opened in the thronged building with a rendition of "Enosh Kehatzir Yamav" by the People's Synagogue Choir, and then Marshall, on behalf of the alliance's board of directors, delivered an address that featured the reading of a poem, "Life and Death." Marshall had originally circulated his memorial just among friends but then later allowed his poem to be made public. "Strong men were moved to pity," its closing lines announced, and then Marshall melodramatically described the Straus's last embrace:

> Clasped in embrace ecstatic,
> With smile and lustrous eyes,
> Ushered by deeds of goodness,
> They mount unto the skies,
> And in undying grandeur,
> *Titanic* strength impart,
> So long as love and manhood,
> Shall thrill the human heart.[39]

The 1912 New York Gubernatorial Elections

Just months after he composed this heartfelt memorial, Marshall clashed bitterly over politics, during the 1912 elections, with another Straus brother, Oscar.

In Isidor's case, the image of *Titanic* chivalry attained, at the Educational Alliance tribute, an uncannily suitable and stirring cast. Once it turned out that the philanthropic benefactor who had served for many years as president of the alliance was something of a martyred knight, the Americanization norms Straus and his colleagues had tried to inculcate in the institution's educational and cultural programs won enhanced pedigree. Suddenly, the alliance's programs Downtown seemed noble. In the political sphere, however, the question of what constituted honorable service toward the vulnerable immigrants of the East Side remained open to interpretation.

In the 1912 New York gubernatorial elections, Progressive candidate Oscar Straus proposed a platform of reforms aimed at improving the lives of workingmen and immigrants for the Jews of the East Side and for others around the state. Still chagrined by the last-minute impediment Oscar Straus had placed in the way of the abrogation campaign when he recruited Theodore Roosevelt (the 1912 Progressive candidate for president) for support of the international arbitration option, Marshall and his AJC associates were loath to support Oscar Straus for governor of New York. They believed that the Jews owed a debt of support to the Democratic candidate for governor of New York in 1912, William Sulzer, since this "Henry Clay of the East Side" had played a decisive role in Congress by spearheading the passage of the abrogation bill. The 1912 elections thus became a sensationally confusing test of where American Jews owed debts and loyalties in the political arena.

For Marshall, his emotional sequence in relations with one Straus brother and then the other, from poetic eulogy to a mud fight, was incredible. It proved easier to identify a Jewish hero for time immemorial than to support a Jewish candidate for governor of New York.

By late May 1912, Marshall, with the rest of the nation, was speculating about what was destined to be a dramatic presidential race. He recoiled from Roosevelt's socioeconomic proposals, branding them an unconstitutionally radical form of socialism, and he believed the ex-president's attacks on Taft had been "abusive, disgraceful and violent." He reasoned, correctly, that Taft would win the Republican nomination, but he predicted that Wilson had already lost his chances with the rival party and that Democrats would make their "usual blunder" by nominating William Jennings Bryan.[40] In June, Roosevelt's surging bid for the Republican nomination frightened Marshall, who feared that its consummation would "destroy our constitutional form of government." Half facetiously, he asked his cousin Joseph Stolz, a rabbi who had been invited to say a prayer to open a session at the Republican national convention in Chicago, to "insert a whispered prayer for the confusion of Roosevelt and his ilk."[41] After the parties made their nominations, Marshall felt reenergized as a lifelong Republican. "While Taft has many faults, the principal one being his inability to size up the situation until it is too late, politically speaking, to accomplish the best results, he is upright, honest, intelligent and stands for constitutional government," Marshall concluded in mid-July.[42] All that Marshall could say positively about the Democrats' Wilson was that the new nominee was "infinitely better than Bryan." He had little sympathy for the "professedly radical" Wilson.

Jacob Schiff, on the other hand, had irrevocably broken with Taft, due to the president's meandering, unhelpful attitude toward abrogation. In an unusually forthright exchange,[43] Marshall asked Schiff whether his departure from the Republicans after forty years of support, at a time when the party was floundering, might be misinterpreted. In view of Schiff's position in American Jewry, might not the public respond to his switch of political loyalty by charging that "the Jews are not actuated by principle, but instead want to be on the winning team?" Schiff responded by implying that Marshall's continued loyalty to the Republicans displayed a lack of courage. Taft's dilatory administration, Schiff argued, had led the country to the brink of social unrest. However "warranted our dissatisfaction with President Taft, he has made amends," Marshall countered. "The abrogation campaign was won." He denied that impassioned debates in the country about the monopolies or electoral reform were a prelude to revolution. "Ever since Adam and Eve were driven out of Eden, there has been continuous change in social conditions," Marshall wrote back to Schiff. "It is violent change which must be avoided. There is no danger of social revolution, unless Rooseveltism and some of the extreme doctrines advocated recently by Wilson prove successful."

Using his criticism of Wilson's support of Progressive reform trademarks (the initiative, referendum, and recall) as his launching pad, Marshall sent to Schiff his credo of faith as a Republican. Interestingly, his statement shows that Marshall, before World War I, was becoming reconciled to Progressive reforms such as workmen's compensation that he had previously contested with vigor in the courts. His affiliation with the Republican Party, the 1920s would show, was consistent, but Marshall was not zealously absolute in support of its conservative philosophies. He feared rapid change and mass politics because, in his view, they impeded progress and threatened constitutional procedure. He detested the populist style and impatient pace of Progressive politics more than he disputed the worthiness of its goals. Marshall wrote to Schiff:

> Those who are creating a sentiment of distrust of the courts and their judges, who are blindly throwing themselves into the arms of the Socialists, would undermine the magnificent fabric of this country. . . . Never has there been

> greater consideration and solicitude shown to the laborer, to the wage-earner, weak and helpless, and to those who are struggling to better their conditions, than at the present moment. Our statute books are filled with salutary laws having these ends in view, adopted in the usual and ordinary course of legislation and in the natural process of evolution. To have enacted current laws forty years ago would have arrested our industrial development. . . . Whenever needs arise, our legislatures will not hesitate to respond. Hence, during the present administration there has been passed a Workmens' Compensation Act . . . and there have been placed upon the statute books railroad rate regulations, and other similarly beneficent laws. . . . The trouble with this age of publicity and display is, that every demagogue is given a hearing, that no proper discrimination is made between things that are genuine and wild-eyed or half-baked theories, that it has become quite the habit to indulge in a universal hue and cry against existing conditions. . . . I am absolutely convinced that the Republican party presents the only hope against the onslaught which is now in process against our cherished institutions. . . . Harboring these beliefs, as I do, should I now abandon them, my action would be as inexcusable as a departure from my religious convictions.[44]

Schiff and Marshall agreed to disagree about the 1912 presidential elections,[45] but Marshall's well-thought-out pronouncement of his Republican outlook and commitment quickly faced one awkward challenge in New York, when William Sulzer won the Democratic nomination for governor. In early October, Marshall wrote privately to congratulate Sulzer for winning the nomination. "Your record bears no stain," Marshall wrote to Sulzer, and added that his "masterly" handling of the abrogation bill entitled him "to the lasting gratitude of every American citizen." Marshall apologized about his inability to support Sulzer publicly, owing to the fact that he was a "Republican who has taken an active interest in the present campaign."[46] Marshall's tied hands quickly got itchy. The Republican gubernatorial candidate, Job E. Hedges, was a nondescript attorney, but Marshall's ire was raised by the Progressive candidate, Oscar Straus. Sulzer had given the AJC crucial help in its campaign to define itself at a time when "Oscar Straus was trying to sidetrack us by urging arbitration, which would have resulted in our inevitable defeat," Marshall explained to a cousin.[47] In substance, both Straus and Sulzer ran on an anti-Tammany campaign, promising reforms such as direct primaries that would detract from bossism in New York,[48] but for Marshall the commanding factor was the debt owed to Sulzer for his stance in Congress on abrogation.

"I feel very much embarrassed with regard to writing you such a letter, because of my Republicanism . . . and, secondly, because Straus is a candidate and the Straus family regards itself as entitled to the support of every Jew," Marshall apologetically wrote to Schiff. Despite these considerations, he wanted to go on record "as urging upon our Jewish population a sense of obligation to Sulzer."[49] At this mid-October juncture, Sulzer, who had been nominated earlier in the month in Syracuse by a Tammany machine that realized he was the only Democrat in the state who could keep the party's Jewish voters from drifting toward the Progressive Party's Jewish candidate,[50] was issuing assertive, controversial statements about the Jewish vote in the gubernatorial race. He challenged Oscar Straus to "stop prating about Tammany, and tell us what he ever did to aid his race at home or abroad."[51] The Yiddish press criticized Sulzer for baiting Straus in this way. This was the moment when Schiff and Marshall stepped in, publishing pro-Sulzer pieces in *Die Warheit*.[52] "Have our benefactors been so numerous that we can afford to have it said that we have short memories of benefits received?"[53] Marshall wrote in his pro-Sulzer article's most unguarded, emotionally compelling passage. Otherwise, his endorsement read like an energetic semantic callisthenic, and exhibited what the scholar David Dalin identified as Marshall's penchant for denying the existence of a Jewish vote in America while concurrently appealing to it.[54] *Die Warheit,* Marshall explained, chided Sulzer for having had the "bad taste" to refer to his own contributions to Jewish causes. Sulzer, however, was a candidate for political office who sought votes. "A considerable proportion of the voters of this state are Jews. He has a right to present to them reasons why they should support him," Marshall wrote. True, when Sulzer introduced in Congress "his now historic resolutions" for abrogation, he insisted that the question at hand was an American, not a Jewish question. And, Marshall continued, "it is true that every citizen was the beneficiary of his statesmanship. The Jews, however, more than any other class of citizens were directly concerned."[55]

Days before the polling, Marshall and Straus acrimoniously traded barbs in the general and Yiddish press. Appealing to labor interests, Straus underscored the Progressives' support for workplace reform, including worker compensation legislation of the sort Marshall had overturned in his *Ives* litigation. Livid, Marshall diagnosed Straus in the *New York Herald* has a "sufferer of the dread disease, Bullmoosia."[56] Straus had the temerity to condemn as "the enemy of mankind" a lawyer who "presented to a regularly organized tribunal reasons and arguments to show that certain acts of the legislature violate the organic law." In what looked like ineffectual pleading, Marshall argued that substantive workplace legislation focuses on "the actual prevention of accident," whereas the act that was declared unconstitutional in *Ives* "tended to the creation of carelessness." Marshall was on firmer ground when he reminded readers of his own growth and adaptability on labor issues. "The Progressive candidate has denounced me as a foe of the workingman, although as a mediator I settled the strike of the cloakmakers, in which 70,000 workingmen were involved."

The gubernatorial race had turned ugly, and its Jewish dimensions were highly, but not intelligibly, pronounced. Once again, Hearst editor Arthur Brisbane rallied to the side of the Straus family in a public fight, and found cause to slur the motivations and purposes of Straus's Jewish antagonists. In a letter to Straus, Schiff had explained apologetically that his support had been pledged to Sulzer long before the Progressives nominated Straus, and that he could not have done otherwise since the Jews owed Sulzer a debt of gratitude for abrogation. Despite the fact that Hearst was publically committed to Sulzer, Brisbane found cause to ridicule Schiff's explanations. In the *New York Evening Journal,* Brisbane surmised that Woodrow Wilson had secretly promised Schiff that his election as president would lead to financial profit for the banker. For this reason, Brisbane speculated, Schiff crusaded against the Progressive Straus and for the Democrat Sulzer—Schiff was wary that if New York were to be lost to the Democrats in the November polling, he would never reap his rewards from Wilson.[57]

Meantime, Marshall fumed about what he viewed as Straus's efforts to stir "Downtown Jews against the Uptown Jews" by implying that Uptown's "silk stocking millionaires" had "no right to express their views on political questions."[58] Straus, Marshall fulminated privately to Magnes, was a "low, contemptible ignoramus and despicable demagogue." He warned that it "would be the greatest misfortune that could happen to us if he [Straus] should be elected."[59] Straus's electioneering hit two sensitive spots in Marshall's psyche; and days before New Yorkers filed in line at the voting precincts, he protested wildly about this double-edged insult. Deriding his antagonist's work on *Ives,* Straus caused participants in one East Side rally to hiss at the mention of Marshall's name, as though he were a hired gun of capitalist interests. Marshall castigated the editor of the Yiddish *Morgen Journal* for endorsing Straus' jaundiced characterization of him as "an enemy of the workingmen."[60] Second, he was galled at the Progressive candidate's self-presentation as a Jewish leader. Straus had no special claim to Jewish votes because he was no Jewish leader, Marshall argued. "He [Straus] has been preaching assimilation all his life, whereas some of us have been at work day in and day out, to develop among the Jews a feeling of self-respect, to educate the Jewish children in the exalted ethics of their faith," Marshall wrote to the Yiddish editor.[61]

Sulzer was elected governor, receiving 649,559 votes, as compared to 444,105 for the Republican Hedges, and 393,183 for Straus.[62] Marshall was less elated by the national election results. Graciously, he wrote to the defeated

Taft, the president who had chosen not to appoint him to the Supreme Court and whose waffling on the 1832 Russian treaty required the AJC to escalate investments of time and resources in the abrogation campaign. Marshall opined that the election result had been caused by the "malevolence and ungovernable ambition" of the third-party candidate, Roosevelt. "The perpetuation of our constitutional form of government is largely due to your steadfast adherence to fundamental principles," Marshall consoled the vanquished incumbent.[63] At this moment, Sulzer's Democratic backers celebrated his election as governor at New York's Waldorf-Astoria Hotel, while Tammany boss Charles Murphy chose, ominously, not to attend.[64]

Nativism Rising: Literacy Tests and Judicial Setbacks

Weeks after Wilson's election, Congress moved quickly in the adoption of the literacy test. The Burnett Bill passed in the House by a tally of 179 to 52; Marshall's proposal to broaden the persecution exemption was roundly defeated, but Burnett took steps to protect the narrower exemption provision's consideration of Russian Jewish immigrants. On the Senate side, conferees, led by Lodge, Dillingham, and South Carolina Democrat Ellison Smith, incorporated the Burnett bill's literacy test into the broader Dillingham Bill, legislation that now included a provision mandating that an immigrant who arrived from a country that issued certificates relating to a person's lack or possession of a criminal record disclose the certificate to American immigration authorities. Marshall might have been slow in sensing the implications of the restrictionists' maneuvers; he opened the new year, 1913, by petitioning Senator Dillingham to broaden the persecution exemption beyond the religious factor, but he overlooked the new initiatives, including the crippling idea of requiring certificates from immigrants, a device that had appalled him eleven months earlier at the start of the wave of Nativist agitation.[65] Three weeks later, he regrouped and traveled to Washington to bring his objections to the certificate requirement and the literacy test directly to President Taft.[66] Not Marshall but AJC Secretary Friedenwald initiated contacts that led to the excision of new restriction devices like the certificate proposal from the compromise bill; by early February, the bill had passed both houses essentially as a literacy test act (the key figure in the paring down of the Dillingham Bill was Wisconsin Progressive Senator Robert La Follette).[67]

With the literacy test on the president's desk awaiting signature, Marshall and the AJC could no longer remain in the background. On February 6, Marshall headed a hearing with Taft. In his remarks,[68] he disputed the bill's implied connection between illiteracy and political subversion, saying that "the degenerates of foreign birth who come to this country are not to be found among the illiterates. A man may be the master of six languages and yet a villain." Had there been a literacy test before the Civil War, "our country would have been deprived of men who fought valiantly for preservation of the union but were unable to read or write," Marshall noted. He spoke about the hard-working immigrants of the East Side, Russian and Romanian Jews, who crowded night schools and were taking advantage of educational opportunities offered by their new country.[69] As it turned out, this was a winning reference. At the time, Marshall reported that it was a successful hearing, with a large attendance, including representatives of other nationalities whose presence proved that not only Jews opposed the bill.[70]

As a defeated incumbent and lame duck, Taft cut an unusually serene figure, perhaps owing to the vanquishing of Roosevelt's Progressive bid. As he had related to other Jewish matters throughout his troubled term, he procrastinated over the literacy test bill for days in indecisive languor. At the eleventh hour, he conferred with his cabinet and with Nagel separately; the outgoing secretary of commerce and labor characterized the literacy test as an "uncompromising measure aimed at a danger which does not exist." Literacy, Nagel insisted, was not a cultural or racial defect, but rather simply "a denial of the opportunity to acquire reading and writing."[71] His advocacy apparently turned the tide in Taft's thinking. A moderate, judicious man, Taft did not want to leave a legacy on immigration that constituted a breach of the nation's tradition of open doors. Two years after he vetoed the literacy bill, Taft explained that his decision was clinched by memories of a visit he had paid to New York's East Side. He had witnessed among the young immigrants a spirit of patriotic gratitude "that wouldn't hurt some of those whose fathers and great-grandfathers were born in this country."[72]

Attempts to override Taft's veto stalled in the House, but efforts to draft a literacy test into law continued in Congress in 1914 and 1915. In retrospect, these efforts lacked the momentum of the initiatives of the late Taft years because President Wilson was never inclined to sign a literacy test bill, despite the fact that he maintained a public façade of open-mindedness on the issue. For the first time in his administration, he exercised his veto power in early 1915 to reject a restriction bill. In his strongly worded veto message, Wilson stated that he opposed the literacy test because it "excludes those to whom the opportunities of elementary education have been denied without regard to their character, their purposes or their natural capacity,"[73] reflecting a cogently deliberate and firmly held position. For two years, that position closed the book on the Nativists' agenda.[74] In this later, Wilson-era lobbying round against restriction, Marshall's orientation was noticeably more ethnic. The AJC's mandate was to shepherd Jewish interests. Marshall made this point at the onset of the 1914–15 campaign against restriction by declaring it to be "the part of prudence for us to see what we can do for ourselves, rather than to act as the champions of all the world."[75] In day-to-day execution, his orchestration of the 1914–15 effort was not seamless. Among other setbacks, Marshall unfortunately chose Representative A. Mitchell Palmer, a Democrat from Pennsylvania, to sponsor an AJC amendment broadening the persecution exemption of a proposed bill. After communicating with Brylawski for days about the rationale in choosing a prominent Democrat for sponsorship and about the preferred phrasing of the amendment ("all aliens who shall prove to an immigration officer that they are seeking admission to the US to avoid religious or political persecution"), Palmer simply disappeared from Washington before voting on the literacy test bill proceeded.[76] The absence of this would-be congressional sponsor, Marshall admitted, was "most disconcerting." However, such lobbying trials and tribulations had no adverse effect provided that the White House was occupied by a president determined to veto restrictive measures like the literacy test, and so long as popular opinion on immigration was not powerfully prorestriction.

Still, the rising tide of Nativism in American society was reaching all branches of American government before World War I, and Marshall in these prewar years collected sobering evidence about the extent to which anti-immigrant feeling could color constitutional interpretation. Immigration advocacy, it should be noted, was primarily but not solely focused on legislative process and presidential decision; in the courts, the prevailing trend appeared detrimental to the interests of Jews and other immigrant groups.

This restrictive judicial trend was manifest in *Luria v. United States*,[77] a case that reached the Supreme Court in 1913, the same year the high court stymied Marshall's efforts to repeal Leo Frank's conviction. The plaintiff, Luria, was born in Vilna in 1865, immigrated to New York in 1888, attained a medical degree in 1893, and became a naturalized US citizen a year later. He then made his way to South Africa, where he lived until 1910, serving in the Boer War.

America's 1906 immigration act stipulated that a naturalized citizen who demonstrated a lack of intent to live in the United States could be stripped of his or her citizenship. The legal question at issue in *Luria* was whether the 1906 act could be applied retroactively to the case of an immigrant whose naturalized citizenship preceded its enactment. Marshall argued that it could not. Under the naturalization act as it existed at the time citizenship was awarded to Luria, there was no permanent residence requirement; thus, procedures to revoke Luria's citizenship were an unconstitutional ex post facto exercise. Naturalized citizens have exactly the same rights as native-born citizens, with the exception of their ineligibility to become president, Marshall added.

His arguments seemed foolproof, but in a recondite display of reasoning, Justice Van Devanter issued a majority opinion holding essentially that Nativism should enjoy the benefit of the doubt in gray areas of law pertaining to immigrant status. "Citizenship is a membership in a political society and implies a duty of allegiance on the part of the member," the court argued. Though Luria attributed his departure from the country to personal health considerations, his exit after the receipt of citizenship "involved a wrongful use of a beneficent law." The court admitted that relevant, pre-1906 statutes did not mandate the revoking of the plaintiff's citizenship, but inference could be used to the immigrant's detriment. "What is clearly implied is as much a part of a law as what is expressed," ruled the court, in an opinion that elastically interpreted immigration law in a way that previewed the politics of immigrant restriction after World War I.

Sulzer Impeachment

Throughout his political career, William Sulzer's reliance on Tammany Hall was common knowledge. Hence, when he ran for the governorship in 1912, Sulzer's anti-Tammany rhetoric ("the only boss I have ever had is the man under my own hat") was taken by many as typical flimflam—after his election, the self-proclaimed people's governor was expected to take his marching orders from Delmonico's steakhouse on Beaver Street in Manhattan, where Tammany's Boss Murphy held court.[78] To everyone's amazement, perhaps even his own, in spring 1913 Sulzer summoned the resolve to challenge Tammany assertively. His clash with Tammany started with small-scale arguments about appointment spoils, but in April, when the new governor signed a full crew bill that required the railroad companies to employ a specified minimum number of employees in the operation of certain trains, these ongoing arguments about patronage grafted onto what seemed to be a bona fide reform agenda.[79] The governor was challenging the corporations and Tammany alike, in the protection of public interests. In fact, in April, Sulzer crossed the political Rubicon, staking his political life on one reform, the institution of direct primaries for candidates in state elections. He touted direct primaries as an "honest, sincere, comprehensive and practical plan" that would bring an end to the "disgraceful secret alliances between big business interests and crooked and corrupt politics."[80] Within a month, Sulzer's support for direct primaries transmogrified into all-out war against Tammany. Belittling Big Boss Murphy, the governor declared that "such men prevent the will of the people from being carried out by their representatives in the Legislature." Sulzer pledged that he would tame Tammany: "I think I know the Tiger's place. It should be in a cage, and that's where we will put it before we get through."[81] Such pronouncements thrilled veteran Progressives, along with nonaffiliated, self-proclaimed defenders of the common man. William Hearst threw his support behind Sulzer; former President Roosevelt supported direct primaries in a speaking tour around the state and ridiculed the Tammany-favored system of state conventions as "mere devices for registering the decrees of the big and the little bosses."[82] Some of Sulzer's former political rivals, including Oscar Straus, rallied to his side in support of the direct primaries proposal.

Neither the roster of Sulzer's allies, nor really the populist gist of the direct primaries proposal, had commanding appeal for Marshall, but his loyalty to Governor Sulzer remained strongly intact. Sulzer was the congressional champion of the abrogation triumph. Schiff had contributed to Sulzer's campaign—in fact, not through any fault of the banker's, Schiff's $2,500 donation to Sulzer, given on October 14 (the period when Marshall and Schiff were mobilizing to offer the Democrat their public endorsement), figured in the August 1913 impeachment proceedings against Sulzer.[83]

The impeachment, widely understood as a Tammany-instigated reprisal against a turncoat politician who threatened to put it in a "cage," focused on campaign contributions Sulzer had pocketed without issuing disclosure, as required under New York's Corrupt Practices Act. The impeachment would have never gotten off the ground had Sulzer's Tammany antagonists only found evidence pointing to the careless accounting of an exhausted candidate on the stump. However, Tammany's wildest dreams came true when a paper trail led to the sensational revelation that some undeclared campaign contributions had apparently been diverted by Sulzer to the speculative purchase of stocks on the margin, for his own gain.[84] Sulzer had apparently embarked moralistically on a political reform crusade against Tammany after having illicitly used campaign money to make a quick profit on Wall Street.

In summer and fall 1913, opinion around the state divided noisily about the governor's impeachment, with many upstate journals rallying to the governor's defense, largely out of contempt for Tammany and also due to a belief that an elected official ought not to be deposed for offenses allegedly committed before he took power. "The removal of William Sulzer will be greeted with unconcealed joy by every crooked politician, by every grafter in or out of office," sermonized the *Rochester Herald*.[85] Other media outlets, though favorably inclined toward direct primaries and other Sulzer-sponsored reforms, conceded that he had dug his own political grave. "That the proceeding had its origin in political feeling is beyond doubt, but the enemies of the Governor could not invent facts, and they did not," opined the *Buffalo News*. Another disappointed newspaper wrote simply that Governor Sulzer was "not of the material of which heroes and martyrs are made."[86]

Marshall joined Governor Sulzer's defense team for the impeachment trial in a period when public opinion about the affair was agitated and divided, and state government was in turmoil. In Albany, Sulzer quarreled with Lieutenant Governor Martin Glynn about whether, pending the result of the impeachment trial, he had to surrender authority. To prove his point that he did not, Sulzer changed the locks on the door leading from the executive chamber to the governor's private office and held in his possession keys to records of the state's Executive Department.[87] The semifarcical circumstances that paralyzed government in Albany in August and September 1913 seemed distantly removed from the issue of czarist discrimination on which Sulzer and Marshall originally joined forces. Nonetheless, Marshall stayed loyal to his abrogation ally throughout the impeachment trial, addressing broad legal issues for a defense team that included also Cady Herrick, a former Democratic candidate for governor of New York, and a former appeals court judge, Irving Vann.

Unsuccessfully, Marshall challenged the authority of the State Assembly's impeachment decision, arguing that the assembly had exercised power unconstitutionally during a special session. A legislature only had the right to impeach under defined circumstances of its regular session, claimed Marshall. Artfully, he expressed his own long-standing revulsion from Tammany politics and intimated to the court that the entire impeachment proceeding had been rigged by Tammany, when he emphasized this point about the impropriety of an assembly gathering out of session to depose an embattled elected public official. "Of course," Marshall stated, "articles of impeachment could not be presented to the President of the Senate . . . at the Throne Room at Delmonico's."[88]

In his closing argument in the impeachment trial (October 9, 1913), Marshall reviewed and praised Sulzer's long career in politics. With rhetorical flourish, he warned that the proceeding's outcome "will determine whether or not the reign of law has ceased, and that of passion and prejudice has begun."[89] The gist of his attacks on the articles of impeachment was that neither the Corrupt Practices Act nor any other relevant rule required a candidate to act in specified ways when he received "money from his friends as gifts to do with them as he liked."[90] No such arguments, however, could forestall Sulzer's conviction.

Sulzer is one of two elected governors in New York political history whose portrait does not hang in Albany's Hall of Governors leading to the executive chamber (Eliot Spitzer is the other missing face). Not entirely disgraced in his day, William Sulzer was elected to the State Assembly in November 1913, a month after losing the governorship due to his impeachment and conviction. In a sense, his struggle was vindicated, because it left everyone in the state exhausted about Tammany Hall; in the November 1913 elections, anti-Tammany candidates won sweeping victories, including Fusion candidate John Purroy Mitchel in the New York City mayoral race.[91] Never a fan of Tammany, Marshall could be gratified by that result, but while he acted scrupulously on Sulzer's behalf, in recognition of the politician's support of abrogation, the turbulent impeachment affair was not a shining moment in Marshall's career. After the conviction, he bluntly told the deposed governor that there was no hope for a Supreme Court appeal, since the case lacked any federal dimension. The governor is reported to have subsequently derided Marshall in public (though, if Sulzer did so, no evidence of this affront has been found[92]). The defense team haggled with the legislature about fees.[93] In one way or another, the Sulzer impeachment turned into an unsatisfying experience for all its participants, but in historical terms, it appears nonetheless to be an underappreciated turnstile in pre-1920s urban and ethnic politics. Through it, liberal reformers in New York City found a route to bypass Tammany in the rebuilding of the Democratic Party; swiveling in it, Jewish stewards like Schiff and Marshall confronted bewildering or uncomfortable permutations of loyalties forged out of lobbying for an ethnic group concern like abrogation.

The Guillotine of Immigration Restriction

Through the mid-1920s, immigration advocacy was the linchpin of Jewish ethnic politics in America, and after seven years of lobbying on the issue Marshall had sufficient experience on the eve of World War I to set the concerns and ends of this immigration work in historical perspective. His view could never be our own, because neither in 1914, nor at the time of his death fifteen years later, could Marshall have realistically viewed the immigration lobbying, to the extent that it succeeded, as preemptive diminishment of genocide. The achievement of men like Kohler and Marshall in driving a wedge in the door, through World War I, to prevent the restrictionists from closing it in part, or in full, can be appreciated in basic terms, as an ethnic commitment assumed by men who worked for little or no remuneration and who (to this day) have received indefinite communal recognition. Viewed through the prism of the Holocaust, this accomplishment attains imposing dimensions in the rescue of tens or hundreds of thousands of human lives, two decades before the murderous Final Solution was enacted by the Nazis.

While that could not have been in Marshall's field of vision, his career in Jewish politics was consciously responsive to Europe's so-called Jewish question.

From 1906 to 1907 until the early 1920s, his prodigious energy concentrated on open immigration opportunities to the United States as the most viable answer to that question; once the restrictionists blocked that possibility once and for all, Marshall moved on in the 1920s to promote other possible avenues of escape and rebirth for indigent and persecuted Jews, particularly the Agro-Joint's project for Soviet Jewish colonization and also Zionism. These were extraordinary, unforeseeable transitions of Jewish endeavor. In 1914, Marshall would never have been able to anticipate that, instead of worrying about the insertion of the word "political" alongside "religious" to mitigate the effects of proposed immigration restriction, he would, ten years hence, be embroiled in a highly contentious debate about whether priority in the overseas allotment of American Jewish philanthropic resources ought to be given to the Jewish colonies in the Ukraine and Crimea or to the Jewish Yishuv in Palestine, since immigration to America was no longer an option. Just months ahead of World War I, what could he—or did he—understand about the present and future of the main theaters of Jewish politics?

Marshall had, in fact, become a realist. He had entered ethnic politics many years before 1914 in the attitude of noblesse oblige, believing that the object of Jewish work was not to prepare the way for more multitudes of Russian Jews to come to America, but rather to prepare the way for Russian Jews who were already in New York to become better Americans. Subsequently, he and fellow AJC founders embarked on an experiment in national Jewish organization. When it began, the internal dynamics and ultimate purposes of this organizational initiative remained to be clarified. As it proceeded, the AJC experiment functioned as multifaceted validation of the reality of ethnic politics in the United States, of the capabilities and resources of the Jewish Uptown elite, and of an exceptionalist image of America as a democracy that defended principles of equality. Broadly, perceptions of honor governed both these early phases in Marshall's career—just as it would have been dishonorable to enjoy the luxury of Uptown economic affluence while blithely ignoring the distress and deprivation faced by the Jewish masses Downtown, so too would it have been dishonorable to preach the gospel of Americanization to those masses without doing anything to demonstrate how "America is different" due to its guarantee of equal protection to all its citizens.

With World War I just around the corner, much of the romance was already missing in this Jewish politics of honor. Marshall realized he was engaged in a contest that was not about ideals of noble patronage and civic duty. The antagonists were racial supremacists of a sort, who believed that America was their country to protect from newcomers whom they viewed as being innately inferior. The restrictionists would use any device available to them in order to ward away immigrants they deemed to be racially subordinate. All that was missing from Marshall's increasingly realistic viewpoint was an ability to predict the future dimension of this restrictionist movement. By clinging before the World War to the view that Nativism must always be distinctively unrepresentative, and that America's majority would long be accommodating of immigration, Marshall retained one romantic belief in his outlook.

In late February 1914, Marshall delivered an address to the New York University Forum, in reply to a presentation made to the same forum by Senator Dillingham.[94] Congress, he conceded, had the authority to build a "Chinese Wall around our country, to make us an isolated and arbitrary people." For now, however, there was "no direct attempt to bring about the total exclusion of immigrants." Instead, the restrictionists were trying to exclude one large class of immigrants, illiterates. Marshall argued that advocacy for the literacy test, or other restrictionist devices, went against the grain of American experience. The Declaration of Independence presented as one of its grievances the contention that the British crown sought to prevent immigration to the colonies. "Are we materially, morally and intellectually worse off than we would have been if we had confined the privilege of this blessed country to those who were here at the end of the Revolutionary War?" Marshall pointedly asked. He recalled that as a child in Syracuse he had heard of a company in the 149th Regiment of New York volunteers that was comprised entirely of immigrants. The immigrant, in other words, did not stay at home during the Civil War.

"All this talk about race difference means nothing to me," declared Marshall, striking directly at the Dillingham Commission's ideological cornerstone. It was not race but character that had to be the central concern of national policy. "The real test is that of manhood and womanhood. I do not think it makes a bit of difference as to his desirability whether a man is born in Russia, Italy, Scandinavia or Germany." After months of quibbling with restriction-minded legislators about proposed modifications of the exemption provision, Marshall conceded that there had really been no substantive debate about the meaning of the "talismanic" word, "persecution." The Nativists did not really care whether what happened to Jews in the Pale of Settlement was religious or political persecution or some interplay of both; what they cared about was sticking to any phrase or device that shut the door to immigrants. Marshall bitterly exclaimed:

> When the projectors of this legislation are asked to define this world as including persecution, whether accomplished through overt acts or by discriminatory laws or regulations, they balk at the phrase and obstinately decline to add one word, one syllable or one letter to the talismanic phraseology which they have

> adopted. Is not, then, the inference irresistible, that in spite of their fine words they have no other purpose than to keep out of this country all immigrants who happen to be illiterate, irrespective of the reasons which have induced them to come hither?[95]

Marshall disposed of economic arguments for restriction. He recalled lessons he had learned five years earlier, as chairman of the New York State Commission on Immigration. The panel's findings established that immigration did nothing to interfere with the occupations or activities of the native-born Americans. Settled Americans preferred relatively "light and easy" occupations, whereas immigrants crowded in more physically demanding trades; rationally speaking, nothing in this division of labor posed a threat to any settled American group.

Marshall would have been content to end by citing evidence collated by Hourwich in confirmation of these claims about the economic impact of immigration, but he felt compelled to devote a few words to the "novel idea" which Senator Dillingham had recently broached regarding immigration. "With entire frankness," Dillingham seemed to be saying, "we are admitting too many immigrants. There should be some way of cutting down the number." So Dillingham had invented a new quota procedure: he proposed that there "shall not be admitted in any year more than what shall be equal to 10% of the number of each of the several nationalities now constituting the population;" that is, if the country had one million Irishman, no more than 100,000 Irishmen could be admitted in any year.

Not exactly knowing what he was doing, Marshall was forecasting and condemning the shape of things to come in America. Rather than imposing such a cruelly arbitrary quota, Marshall explained, "It would be ten times more honorable to declare that we will not henceforth receive any immigrant from Italy or from Russia or from Hungary or from any other European country south of a certain latitude than to try to accomplish such a result by this indirect and torturous method." Marshall unwittingly commented on the nature of America's immigration laws in the early 1920s when he characterized Dillingham's quota proposal as a procedure "savoring of unfairness and injustice, being dependent upon the accidental operation of an arithmetical rule." Continuing, Marshall evoked a nightmare scenario of would-be immigrants marooned offshore by the cruel vagaries of quota application. In prewar America, he conjured this hellish sequence as something his beloved democracy could never condone:

> How would [the quota system] work? When would this guillotine operate, and on whom? Why, a man sells his household goods in Russia or in Hungary. He

> abandons his home to seek a better and a happier one in America. He buys his tickets and crosses the Atlantic. He arrives at Ellis Island, his soul filled with noble emotions and his mind with high resolves. He is in every way fitted to become a citizen of this blessed country. . . . When he reaches the commissioner's office the books are opened, and it is found that he is too late or too early. He is politely told: "We are very sorry, but yesterday the percentage limit of those entitled to come from your country was passed. You must return whence you came. If you try again early next year, you may come in time. In the meantime you must either anchor outside of Sandy Hook, or do the best you can to find another habitation."[96]

Marshall closed his remarks in a vein of confident optimism, declaring, "I do not believe that our lawmakers are so deaf to considerations of right and wrong" as to regard devices like the immigration quota "with equanimity." Still,

5. Portrait of Marshall. Courtesy of Jacob Rader Marcus Center of the American Jewish Archives.

the thrust of his remarks gave emphasis to a haunting question. Open immigration had for decades been a revolutionary experience in the United States, and it stirred a counter-revolution: that being the case, when would the "guillotine" of immigration restriction fall, "and on whom?" The question was left hanging when Europe started a global war.

PART THREE

War and Peace

6

World War I

The eruption of the war caught Marshall by surprise. At the start of the summer, Florence suggested the family vacation in Europe, but fortunately the children insisted on staying at Knollwood.[1] Marshall was conflicted. As Europe plunged clumsily and cataclysmically to war, he hoped vainly that the fighting would remain a relatively confined affair, pitting Germany and Austria against Russia. In that event, he would "pray for the destruction of Russia." When France and England became embroiled, Marshall's "natural antipathy" toward German autocracy rose quickly, and by the start of August, he was hoping for an outcome "which would mean the destruction of Russia on the one hand, and the humiliation of Germany on the other."[2] This outcome would, of course, materialize but only after interminable years of tension and sorrow, and its challenges and threatening potential would turn out to be nothing like what Marshall could have imagined in the summer of 1914.

Louis Marshall became entangled during the war in contentious disputes involving the actual or possible orientations of American Jewish individuals and groups toward the conflict in Europe. It is difficult in some of these instances to sort out whether his or his adversaries' positions were better vindicated by subsequent events on the Continent and in North America. Overall, however, his wartime activities and policy directions showed a more compelling mix of consistency and pragmatism than those of rivals, and the balance he struck between, on the one hand, protecting the interests of his own American Jewish community in a period of acute political loyalty tensions and, on the other hand, upholding an ethnoreligious sense of obligation toward afflicted Jewish groups in Europe and Palestine is undeniably impressive. Despite, and in some senses because of, the disputes, his leadership accomplishments and skills gained increased appreciation throughout most parts of the American Jewish community during the war.

When the Armistice came, he was positioned in a uniquely authoritative position, one unprecedented in the history of a prospering Diaspora community. Owing to its own choices and to the fluid and free circumstances of American constitutionalism, American Jews had for 260 years of settlement avoided the consolidation of resources and powers, and yet, as the war finally ended, they were under the rule of "Marshall law." More than ever before or since, one man's activities and outlooks would shape American Jewish affairs over an extended, and challenging, period: the Roaring Twenties. Roots of this stretch of unprecedented individual authority can be found in the World War I era. For that reason, this section, Part Three, follows Marshall's wartime and Armistice engagements in some detail while also pointing to ways in which loyalty issues and communal dynamics during the First World War foreshadowed American Jewish processes in subsequent periods.

Marshall's position strengthened during World War I because he never exclusively belonged to one American Jewish subgroup. Undeniably, he was a member of Jewry's Uptown "German" elite by dint of perception and socioeconomic status. Yet many aspects of his own personal background were akin to those of New York's Downtown Jewish masses. He was tied to the Russian Jews in ways his patron Jacob Schiff and many other German Jews could never be. Bereft of the lingering Old World, pro-German sensibilities of men like Schiff, Marshall was free during the war to concentrate his energies, and his ongoing mediation with America's East European Jewish immigrants, on issues of specific American and Jewish communal concern. For all the extraordinary passion it aroused, the community as a whole was well served by his focus on definable issues of loyalty and organization.

When the Armistice came, Marshall's ascendance as the leading mediator and peacemaker in American Jewish affairs took on heretofore unknown global dimensions, just as America's ascendance as the leading mediator and peacemaker in world affairs propelled its highest officials toward unprecedented diplomatic efforts at the Paris Peace Conference. Marshall's diplomacy at that conference, heading an international delegation of Jewish communal leaders and lobbying for a minority rights treaty to protect Jews of Eastern Europe, constitutes one of the most intriguing and difficult to assess endeavors in his career.

Hailed triumphantly on the eve of the 1920s as the Magna Carta of the Jews, the minority rights treaty could be viewed by subsequent generations as a quixotic, even self-defeating, exercise in Jewish advocacy. Colored by retrospective knowledge of the catastrophic events in Europe that culminated a quarter century after the minority rights treaty was negotiated, characterizations of the Paris lobbying invariably run the risk of anachronistically attributing knowledge, options, and authority to Marshall and his delegation cohorts that they did not have at the peace conference. Undeniably, the minority rights treaty failed, yet analysis of its advocacy sheds light not on naïveté but rather on engagingly impressive aspects of Marshall's personality and enduring Jewish commitment.

His situation at the peace conference was extraordinarily complex. Circumstances and honor dictated that he oblige wartime promises to America's Downtown Jews by lobbying forcefully for a better future for their East European brethren. Fulfilling this pledge, he was required to revise or abandon constituent elements of his world outlook as a political conservative in America and as a communal activist beholden to decades-old tenets believed to govern the emancipation of Jews in Europe and North America. Specifically, as a Republican in American politics and as an adopted member of the Uptown elite in American Jewish politics, Marshall brought with him to Paris deep reservations about international mechanisms like the proposed League of Nations and about the conferral of rights to Jews on a group or national basis. The league bristled against his political party's isolationist instincts, and the concept of autonomous group rights for Jews grated against his Uptown elite's belief that Jews were not a national group and instead received rights on an individual basis, as equal citizens of the countries where they lived. That Marshall reworked both of these attitudes in Paris was a determining factor in the Jewish delegation's passing victory and the obtainment of a minority rights treaty; it also was a striking reflection of his capacity for ideological growth.

That is to say, the key to Marshall's 1920s prominence in American Jewish affairs can be found in his war and peace advocacy throughout the grueling five-year-period stretching between the confusing eruption of war in Europe in summer 1914 and his triumphant return from Paris to a Carnegie Hall celebration of the minority rights treaty in summer 1919. Possessor of stern professional discipline and a somewhat dogmatic outward veneer, Marshall had a shrewd ability to forgo rigid adherence to legal and political principles exactly when the dictates of Jewish welfare and communal cohesion dictated flexibility and compromise. As this balancing act between principled consistency and pragmatic adaptation was increasingly appreciated both Uptown and Downtown, by Jewish peers and rivals, he gained communal stature of unusual authority in the ethnic history of his country in the period of Marshall law, examined in Part Four of this biography.

The First Shots of War: Staying Neutral

In summer 1914, while Marshall carefully measured his responses to the outbreak of war in Europe, the Downtown East European Jews exploded with passionate hatred of imperial Russia. Their perception of the war was fixated on the fate of the loathed czar and on the hope that its outcome would speedily bring about regime change in Russia and liberation for its millions of Jews. Not pulling any punches, the Yiddish proletarian poet Morris Rosenfeld declared: "The bleeding of Russia rejoices my heart / May the devil do to her / What she did to me."[3] In the same feverish pitch, one Yiddish daily explained that "the Jews support Germany because Russia bathes in Jewish blood."[4]

The difference between the Downtown attitude and Marshall's was far from absolute. Political beliefs on the Lower East Side were shaped by socialist and other left-wing orientations, unlike Marshall's conservative Republican outlook, but many immigrant Jews had appreciation for democratic systems in England and France and did not necessarily view the defeat of these Allied powers as a positive good in its own right. Whereas Marshall continually balanced his sympathy for Allied democracy against his detestation of czarist anti-Semitic oppression, among Downtown Jews, hatred of imperial Russia and longing for political change in it typically took precedence. The disparate balance in these orientations found innumerable complicated expressions during the war years, but it was ultimately predicated on the sociological difference separating Marshall from the Downtown immigrants. Their experience of Russian tyranny was personal and ideologically determinative. In contrast, the American-born Marshall had genuine, empirically well-grounded concern for Russian Jewry and dislike for the czarist regime, but Marshall's attitude retained some detachment and never became monomaniacal. For instance, Marshall could never countenance the Downtown idea that a day of reckoning would come to England and France because of their unholy alliance with czarist Russia (France deserves to be punished, wrote the Yiddish *Jewish Morning Journal* in early August 1914, because of its "unclean love for Russia"; England, the paper continued, "had no business allying herself with the Asiatic barbarian, and if she will pay dearly for this it will only be a sign that there exists a historical sense of justice"[5]).

Most worrisome, from Marshall's point of view, was the prospect of a slide Downtown from loathing of the czar toward an avowedly pro-German position. Anti-Russian posturing alone might be tolerable during the war, but, in Marshall's understanding, it was imperative that the Downtown masses refrain from an open affiliation with the Central powers in a way that flouted America's policy of neutrality.

Marshall's worries were warranted by developments in key spheres of Downtown life. Not surprisingly, Marshall spent the early years of the war alienated from mass Yiddish tribunals of Downtown opinion. The Downtown press, historians conclude, was pronouncedly pro-German. "Because of its sympathy with the Teutonic camp," wrote one scholar, "the Yiddish press discovered that it had to condemn Russia's allies, though it had no basic antagonism toward them."[6] This survey of Yiddish newspapers during World War I concluded: "The pro-Germanism of America's immigrant Jews was an inevitable consequence of their

Russophobia. The glorification of the Teuton was a negative reaction stemming from the hatred of the Czar."[7]

During the first months of the war, Schiff prodded Marshall to adopt a more pro-German orientation, expressing surprise that, in view of his parents' German origins, the Syracuse-born lawyer displayed "evident unfriendliness to the German government." Marshall firmly replied to the powerful banker that he "imbibed" his outlook from his parents, whose memories of Germany "were little calculated to inspire love or tender recollections."[8]

Throughout the period of America's neutrality, Marshall objected vociferously to any American Jewish public expression of allegiance toward either the Entente or Central powers, but his own inward preference for the democratic nations of Europe solidified quickly. Little time passed after Germany's declaration of war on France before Marshall articulated his orientation toward American Jewish Committee (AJC) confidantes like Cyrus Adler. "I am now anxious that England and France, even though it may mean a victory for Russia as well, shall put an end to the militarism and arrogance of Germany," wrote Marshall days after the war's eruption.[9] He insisted, however, that his own political preferences, or those of anyone else in the Jewish community, should be scrupulously kept under wraps. He feared that public statements of solidarity toward one side could provoke reprisals toward Jewish communities living in lands controlled by the other side, in what was becoming a global conflict. "I do not think that it is desirable or wise, at this time, to discuss in the press or publicly, the attitude of the Jews with regard to political conditions which will arise out of the European war," Marshall wrote confidentially to the *American Hebrew*.[10]

During the period of American neutrality, Jews should eschew politics and focus their energies on the preparation of a list of claims and proposals for postwar Jewish life in Europe to be submitted at some postwar conference, he believed.[11] In addition, Marshall felt that American Jews could legitimately mobilize in public, nonpolitical relief campaigns for relief of overseas Jews, without regard to whether they dwelled in areas under Entente or Central powers' control.[12]

For many American Jews, this distinction between relief work and political pronouncements could not be viably followed in regions engulfed by all-out conflict. B'nai B'rith president Adolf Kraus, for one, fretted that public work of any sort could compromise lodges maintained by his organization in countries like Austria and Germany. Full of disdain for such "arrant cowardice," Marshall persuaded his Jewish organizational colleagues that no ill effect could come from relief work undertaken by American Jews on behalf of overseas coreligionists. Among other arguments, he pointed to the involvement of American citizens with the German Red Cross Society and the Belgium Red Cross Society.[13]

Marshall forcefully argued for relief work, but throughout the early months of the war, his position was not unanimously supported within the community. For many, the logic underlying the traditional German Jewish preference for "neutrality" on political matters was intensified in a period when America as a whole chose to remain neutral about the global conflict.[14] What would the Protestant majority in a country that was not meddling in the war make of Jews who were organized on any level for contacts with counterparts on either of the belligerent sides? In Cincinnati, when Reform rabbi David Philipson made the rounds among Gentile civic leaders to assure them that American Jews were not pro-German, he solemnly promised that American Jews would refrain from involvement of any sort overseas. Infuriated, Marshall countered by claiming that Jewish charity had no political borders. It was rank hypocrisy, he scolded Philipson, for American Reform Jews to speak about the "brotherhood of man" and to involve themselves with "all kinds of ridiculous fads" in American cities at a time when their brethren in Europe faced unprecedented disaster. "Who will look after European Jews?" he asked Philipson. When did "this new idea, that it may be dangerous for Jews to help one another," come into existence?[15]

Political neutrality was not to be confused with apathy. In autumn–winter 1914, Marshall's labors for Jewish wartime relief accelerated feverishly, and he was visibly agitated by colleagues who did not seem to appreciate the gravity of the Jewish emergency, the worst faced in modern times. "Our people have not been confronted by such a calamity since the Crusades," exclaimed Marshall in one letter.[16] By the end of 1914, Marshall was depressed that this sense of urgency was not widely shared. "Our showing thus far is pitiable," he moaned to Schiff, referring to the performance of wartime Jewish relief drives up to that time.[17] A decade earlier, Marshall's Uptown group had closely monitored Downtown's mass, militant responses to the Kishinev violence and subsequent pogroms; now, Marshall longed for the Kishinev era's sense of urgent purpose. Challenging American Jews in early 1915, Marshall used the Kishinev response as his benchmark. In one public appeal, Marshall recalled that a $1.3 million relief fund had quickly been collected after Kishinev and subsequent pogroms to provide relief for some 100,000 Jewish sufferers. Incongruously, no more than one-half of that sum had been raised in many months of relief work on behalf of many millions of European Jews whose lives were imperiled and impoverished by the war during the second half of 1914.[18]

Marshall's assertive lobbying for wartime relief afforded psychological compensation. Apart from providing charity dollars, American Jews lacked the leverage needed to accommodate do-or-die requests that came to them from embattled Europe. In the early months of the war, the AJC fielded requests from prominent

European Jews—Otto Schiff and Walter Rothschild among them—who reported that the East End of London, along with parts of France and Belgium, were teeming with an unending influx of Jewish refugees. Could well-connected New York Jews make "special arrangements with US immigration authorities" and bring in a "fair number" of these refugee Jews? Replying in the spirit of "frankness and candor," Marshall disabused these petitioners of any false hopes. "Our immigration laws are now strictly enforced," he wrote to Lord Rothschild.[19]

In the final months of 1914, Marshall battled in the lobbying trenches of Capitol Hill, trying not to lose traction in the eighth year of a wearying fight to forestall draconian immigrant restriction legislation based on the imposition of a literacy test. As happened at crucial moments in this ongoing fight, Marshall was forced in 1914 to indulge in strained, personal appeals (such new restrictive standards, Marshall wrote plaintively to New York senator Elihu Root, would have slammed the door to his own family—"while my father was able to read and write, with great difficulty, when he came to this country, a strict application of the [literacy] test might have excluded him"[20]). In this climate, American Jews could not offer haven to their European counterparts. Charity help was the best they could do, and Marshall felt honor bound to do what he could.

In the final weeks of 1914, Jewish emotions were beginning to run high, but Marshall remained anchored to the AJC's traditional cautiousness about political demonstrations. "I recognize the natural desires" of American Jews, wrote Marshall in reply to proposals for wartime protest rallies, but the "American Jewish Committee has deliberately avoided threadbare methods of indulging in loud-sounding phrases and seeking publicity."[21] When Marshall chafed in his 1914–15 correspondence about the resort to "threadbare methods" of public demonstration, it was sometimes unclear whether he was thinking about the Great War in Europe or the little war that was being waged in Atlanta to rescue Leo Frank, the Cornell-educated pencil factory superintendent who faced charges of rape and murder in a mob-spirited courtroom in Georgia.[22]

The Leo Frank Case

Marshall's involvement in the Frank ordeal began a year earlier, in September 1913. At that time, he received, as president of the AJC, letters from troubled Atlanta Jews and met with a Reform rabbi from Atlanta, David Marx. The AJC met to discuss these pleas and decided to relate to the Atlanta trial as (in Marshall's words) "a matter of justice" and not as a Jewish issue. Schiff suggested raising a fund in the committee's name for the Frank defense, but his colleagues worried that such Jewish mobilization would reinforce a public perception of the affair as a "Jewish question." Marshall contacted Herbert Haas, the head of Frank's legal team in Atlanta, to explain that the committee would not donate funds, but its members, in their private capacity, would help cover expenses of any new legal proceedings in the Frank case. Though Marshall's response was governed by the tactical consideration that overt Jewish organizational pressure was liable to backfire, especially in light of the volatile climate in Georgia, he clearly understood the gravity of the affair.

Making the rounds in New York, Rabbi Marx found little understanding at the *New York Times*, among other places. Marshall, in contrast, did not soft-pedal the unfolding tragedy in Atlanta. Writing to Irving Lehman, he asserted "the case is almost a second Dreyfus affair."[23] In the final weeks of 1914, Marshall bickered with Frank's attorneys about whether he would assume effective control of appeal proceedings in this excruciating case. To some extent, the discussion was about professional prestige and pride. (Marshall was appalled when Frank attorney Henry Alexander appended his name to an appeal brief that was printed in the *New York Times;* taking umbrage that he was never consulted, Marshall objected that the document contained more concessions than the law warranted.[24]) More broadly, in this period, Marshall was measuring the appropriate extent of Jewish involvement in the Frank ordeal in a way that paralleled his strategizing about the character of American Jewish responses to the trauma of global war.

When Marshall explained to advertising wizard Albert D. Lasker, who had nobly invested his energy and resources in the campaign to exonerate Frank, that "every expression by the Jews is misinterpreted by the mob rulers of Georgia, and only intensifies the feelings of hostility,"[25] he was applying a familiar logic. By the same turn of thought, Marshall and his peers feared that public pronouncements about the mistreatment of thousands of Jews in the czar's Russia, or in any land torn by the war, could provoke "mob rulers" to execute anti-Jewish reprisals.

With his colleagues on the AJC, Marshall decided that "it would be injurious rather than helpful" were the Frank trial to become a "Jewish issue." Although it is true that Frank's Jewish identity "has to some degree" stirred prejudices against him in Atlanta, Marshall informed a prominent Jewish colleague from Baltimore, the main cause for the hysteria and hostility in this case was a malicious and mendacious rumor about Frank as a sexual pervert.[26] At late stages in the Frank case, Marshall decided to take the lead in appeals submitted to the US Supreme Court while remaining far from the affair's battleground. "There is nothing to be gained by my coming to Atlanta," he explained. "The fact that I am a New Yorker, and a Jew, would not help the case there.[27] Being "acquainted with criminology," Marshall professed knowledge of the identity of the culprit in the case, the pencil factory's maintenance man, Jim Conley,[28] but he did not believe that Jews should take part in a counteroffensive on Frank's behalf in the South. "We as Jews had better remain in the background," he explained to Harry Friedenwald. "It is much better if all efforts were concentrated upon securing friendly action from prominent men in the South," both among the Protestant clergy and in the Southern press.[29]

Marshall had faith in the soundness of the constitutional questions about jurisdiction and trial fairness that he was raising in the Frank appeals, but by the end of 1914, he had started to advise confidantes that in all likelihood Frank's fate would rest with "the pardoning power" wielded by Georgia's governor. As it turned out, Georgia governor John Slaton commuted Frank's conviction to a life sentence, but the hapless Jewish businessman was lynched near Marietta in August 1915. The affair was a gruesome landmark in the history of anti-Semitism and precipitated an array of responses, including the formation of the Anti-Defamation League. In terms of Marshall's career, the Frank case has been seen as a poignant illustration of the limits of his Uptown group's cautiousness about being "too Jewish" in public; this interpretation, however, is somewhat unfair. As in the case of Marshall's reservations about public demonstrations of Jewish concern regarding the Great War, his concern that public expressions by the Jews in the Frank case were liable to be manipulatively "misinterpreted by the mob rulers of Georgia" had grounding in reality. As with his arduous fund-raising labors for European Jewry during the war, Marshall exerted considerable effort on Frank's behalf, using tactics he thought would benefit the accused factory manager.

In fact, in both of these contexts, Marshall stands out as the American Jew at the forefront of campaigns waged on behalf of one imperiled individual or of millions of dislocated, impoverished Jews. His apprehension about a Jewish public profile did not limit his activity in these contexts, but he was unyielding in his resolve about the right way to protect Jewish interests in troubled times; and because he often chose to operate behind the scenes and because he saw no choice but to defer some activities until matters like the Frank case or the Great War reached their final stages, his orientation often created the appearance that he and the AJC were acting passively. In a world turned upside down, his leadership style created a vacuum because it offered little emotional comfort to masses of American Jews who demanded that *something, somewhere* be done immediately, who urgently needed to express themselves as Jews.

The Arrival of American Zionism

That vacuum was filled during the war years by the Zionists; the challenge they posed to Marshall and the AJC would change the character of American Jewish life forever.

Prior to World War I, the American Zionist movement was a small-scale operation hampered by budgetary constraints, anxieties about loyalty issues potentially posed by a Jewish statehood program, and the lack of a committed leadership.[30] In general, Zionism, with other nationalist movements, benefited from the World War I–era's focus on the principle of self-determination of small nations. In America, Zionism strengthened during the war because the Jewish national movement was unable to sustain itself organizationally in divided Europe and because new talent, most notably Louis Brandeis, unexpectedly mustered onto the scene.[31]

The rise of American Zionism during World War I triggered a brief but intense power struggle pitting Brandeis and his followers against Marshall and the AJC. Brandeis's Zionist group and Marshall's non-Zionist circle clashed over issues of communal control and prioritization of American Jewish commitments. With his followers mobilizing fervently in support of a plan to establish a new, populist-spirited organization—an American Jewish Congress—Brandeis appealed powerfully both to American democratic values and to the communal instincts of East European immigrant Jews. For his part, Marshall understandably resented that Brandeis's abrupt bid for leadership was not founded upon any actual experience in Jewish communal affairs, and he believed that the American Zionist consolidation under the banner of democratization involved as much ego and expediency as principle.

In historian Jonathan Frankel's detailed survey of the topic, he came to the attention-grabbing conclusion that the struggle over the formation of an American Jewish Congress constituted perhaps the "most remarkable episode" in American Jewish history.[32] Whether it was or not, this colorful confrontation was bred by strengths and weaknesses in the characters of its chief non-Zionist and Zionist protagonists. Just as much as it resulted from the devoted, experienced, and imposingly intelligent Marshall's insensitivity toward the mass emotionalism of America's Jewish community in a period of world upheaval, the clash stemmed from Brandeis's brilliantly empowering but inconsistent assertiveness in Jewish affairs.

Multiple dimensions of Brandeis's contribution to this famous confrontation are sometimes overlooked in flatly hagiographic depictions of his life. Unarguably, Brandeis's contribution to American Jewish life was monumental, primarily because his involvement with Zionism as a prominent attorney (and later as a Supreme Court justice) taught insecure immigrant Jews that they need not repress their Jewish concerns and passions in order to become respectable American citizens. It is also true that within the sphere of organized Jewish life, Brandeis proved to be a divisive figure. Following his group's cantankerous dispute with Marshall and the AJC over the formation of an American Jewish Congress,

Brandeis quarreled fatefully with Chaim Weizmann about the leadership of the World Zionist Organization (WZO). In some striking senses, Brandeis's platform reversed in these two clashes. In the American Jewish Congress campaign, his group pushed for dynamics of consolidation and constructive politicization in American Jewish life; in the Weizmann dispute, Brandeis and his followers called both for a more pluralistic structure of the Zionist movement, whereby the Americans would retain a measure of autonomy, and for the depoliticization of Zionism via a concentration on medical, education, and infrastructure projects in Eretz Israel. The changes in goals and emphases were responses to fluctuating, complicated circumstances in worldwide Jewish politics, and Brandeis earnestly upheld positions that he believed promised maximal benefit to Jewish communities in America, Eretz Israel, and elsewhere. Nevertheless, the inconsistency of Brandeis's positions and the indeterminacy of his Zionist commitments render it impossible to dismiss the skepticism of iconoclastic scholars who suggest that personal ambition and various calculations pertaining to America's power arena (as opposed to Jewish welfare) partially governed Brandeis's moves in the American Jewish Congress debate and in his other confrontations as a Zionist leader.[33]

The Founding of the Joint Distribution Committee

The first rounds in the American Jewish Congress dispute were not fired out of the barrel of differing leadership orientation but rather came as a result of harsh realities on the ground in late Ottoman Palestine. In August 1914, America's ambassador to Turkey, Henry Morgenthau, relayed urgent distress signals to American Jewish leaders, warning of a "deplorable" situation in Jerusalem and the Zionist pioneering colonies, caused by the disruption of items of European assistance that routinely reached the Yishuv.[34] After consulting with Schiff, Marshall contacted Secretary of State Bryan and inquired whether the State Department would organize a relief ship for Palestine.[35] In the final days of August, the AJC decided to allocate $50,000 for relief work in Palestine for causes outlined by Ambassador Morgenthau. Schiff contributed one-quarter of the sum; for the Zionists, Nathan Straus added the same amount, $12,500; and the AJC donated the other half. This decision, a landmark that accelerated American Jewry's philanthropic commitment toward Zionist efforts in Palestine, appears to have been spurred by developments within the American Zionist movement. Marshall and his colleagues reached their decisions about Palestine relief on the very day when Louis Brandeis informed Marshall about the formation of the Provisional Executive Committee for General Zionist Affairs, a mechanism symbolizing America's temporary ascendance as the capital of world Zionism. The sequence suggests an understanding on Marshall's part that were the AJC to allow the American Zionists to take the initiative for any branch of overseas relief work the concession might compromise the committee's ability to control or influence American Jewish communal affairs in general.[36]

Along with gratitude and hope, the Americans' allocation stirred controversy in the Yishuv, owing to Jacob Schiff's insistence that a non-Zionist, Ephraim Cohen, serve with agronomist Aaron Aaronsohn on a Jerusalem-based committee responsible for the disbursement of the $50,000.[37] For some time, this allocation mechanism proceeded placidly with its work, thanks to the supervision of veteran Zionist Dr. Arthur Ruppin and also to Morgenthau's constructive involvement (the ambassador sent his son-in-law, Morris Wertheim, to Jerusalem to help coordinate allocations).[38] Technical problems caused by the wartime chaos temporarily delayed the arrival of the relief money in Palestine, but Schiff and Marshall quickly worked out a satisfactory arrangement for the money's transfer via Standard Oil officials in the region.[39]

Soon enough, however, suspicions between Cohen and his colleagues dogged the philanthropic work. Specific arguments concerned the portion of relief to be allocated to Jerusalem, whose residents at the time made up 53 percent of the Jews in Eretz Israel. The main problem, however, stemmed generally from Cohen's ideological viewpoint and Schiff's support of it. Cohen was affiliated with the Hilfsverein der deutschen Juden (Relief Organization of German Jews), which had in the prewar period antagonized the Zionists due to its support of German-language instruction at the planned Technion in Haifa. Through summer 1915, Schiff insisted that Cohen's ideological orientation was irrelevant and that he was an honorable supervisor of philanthropic allocations; Marshall underscored the importance of designating a delegate on the Jerusalem allocation committee who was seen with favor by officials from the Central powers. In the meantime, Cohen rifled off letters to Marshall, hinting about Zionist machinations and complaining that while the Zionists were not a majority in the Yishuv, they were nonetheless demanding a disproportionate amount of the relief funds. At a summer 1915 AJC meeting, Judah Magnes furnished documents to substantiate allegations that Cohen had divulged compromising information about Zionist activities to the Turks. Schiff did not think that the documents were incriminating, and he alluded to Cohen's responsibilities as a Turkish subject.[40] Controversies persisted, and Schiff eventually withdrew his support of Cohen. With the non-Zionist muscled off the scene, the Jerusalem committee more smoothly handled the American relief support during the war.

In America, the ideal of wartime cooperation between Zionists and non-Zionists symbolized by the $50,000 allocation was comparably tarnished by infighting and suspicion. Marshall's August 31, 1914, announcement to Brandeis about the $50,000 relief fund underscored the AJC's lead role.[41] Brandeis ordered his followers to issue a public call for a conference about Palestine relief work. Marshall immediately took offense, deriding Brandeis and his associates in private correspondence as "self-advertisers" who were "trying to make it appear that the American Jewish Committee is merely a tail to their kite." Moaning petulantly about Brandeis and the other Zionist "fanatics" ("they are entirely destitute of common sense, and entirely regardless of consequences"), he swore that he was so "disgusted" that he might refuse to confer with them.[42]

During a period of European devastation, Marshall found Zionist preoccupation with Palestine indefensible. The Brandeis group regarded the $50,000 allocation as the start of a continuing campaign for the Yishuv, but Marshall argued vociferously that American Jews had to move on to the Continent to focus on much more urgent priorities. On his count, there were 300,000 Jews mobilized in Russia's army, as well as very large numbers of Jews under arms in Austria and Germany; Jewish soldiers' families in such countries were liable to face utter destitution as a result of the war. Validating his dark fears, the Alliance Israelite Universelle informed Marshall that 50,000 indigent Russian Jews streamed into Paris after the war's first months. With 7.5 million Jews adversely affected by the war in Europe, as compared to 50,000 Jews in Palestine, Marshall had little patience for the Zionists' priorities.[43] Moreover, he suspected that an "unduly excited" Morgenthau had provided an exaggeratedly bleak depiction of conditions in Jerusalem.[44]

Once the war's protracted, devastating character became incontestable, Marshall and his associates moved decisively to consolidate support efforts on behalf of Jewish wartime sufferers in Europe. Their efforts created Jewish communal infrastructure where none had existed before. When World War I broke out, the American Jewish community had no mechanism designed specifically for overseas relief.[45] In early autumn 1914, Schiff pushed for a coordinated war relief fund. Marshall initially wavered, wondering whether it was possible to measure the extent of the tragedy or the amount required to alleviate Jewish suffering;[46] but on behalf of the AJC, Marshall soon issued invitations for a national conference to be held on October 25 at Temple Emanu-El to consolidate the collection and distribution of relief funds.

This call was preempted when an Orthodox group, headed by Harry Fischel and Leon Kamaiky, established on October 4 a separate organization, the Central Committee for Relief of Jews Suffering Through the War.[47] In October, Marshall jousted with Fischel, a prominent architect and self-made Russian Jewish immigrant who had become treasurer of the Central Committee. "I had supposed that as a member of the American Jewish Committee, the duty of loyalty was recognized," he scolded, accusing Fischel (and Kamaiky) of destructive renegade behavior and also of a self-interested desire to "see their names in the newspapers."[48] Not intimidated, Fischel replied to Marshall that the AJC collected donations from wealthy contributors, "but there are thousands of Jewish people all over the United States, who are willing to contribute small sums, and such sums are usually given upon reading the Jewish [Yiddish] newspapers."[49] Determined to prove that Orthodox Jewry could provide adequately for its own poor, Fischel and his religious partners persisted in the organization of a separate religious organization.[50]

Concurrently, B'nai B'rith's continuing fear of undertaking any work on behalf of overseas Jews under circumstances of American neutrality flummoxed Marshall. When B'nai B'rith skipped the October 25 meeting, Marshall groused about how he "belong[ed] to another generation, which does not understand the theories, motivations or aspirations of that order [B'nai B'rith]." Furiously, he opined that B'nai B'rith was "timidly" stifled by fears of *ma yomru ha-Goyim*, "what will the Gentiles say."[51]

Despite such frustrations and sidetracking, the October 25 meeting was a resounding success. Appointed to organize an executive committee for the relief campaign, Marshall ecumenically selected, among others, delegates who represented Zionism (Louis Brandeis, Julian Mack), Orthodoxy (Harry Fischel), and the Jewish Socialists (Meyer London).[52] This executive committee then asked one hundred prominent Jewish Americans to organize a consolidated organization for overseas Jewish relief. Marshall chaired this group of one hundred, which formed the American Jewish Relief Committee (AJRC).

To the surprise of many, the Orthodox Central Committee refused to be consolidated into the new Relief Committee. Thus, on November 27, 1914, the Joint Distribution Committee (JDC, or Joint) came into being for the concentrated disbursement of funds collected by these two different bodies; in August 1915, a third group, the socialist People's Relief Committee (PRC), attached itself to the Joint.[53] By the end of 1915, the JDC had raised $1.5 million and organized the departure of a relief ship, the *Vulcan,* for Palestine, but this was only the start. By the end of 1918, the Joint had raised an incredible sum, $16.5 million, for overseas relief.[54] In its tripartite structure the Joint merged the "masses and the classes"; each of the three parts had its own dynamics and funding target groups. The Orthodox Central Committee raised money mainly from middle-class Jews in synagogue settings, whereas the PRC depended on a relatively large staff of volunteer workers to collect funds among Jewish laborers via door-to-door campaigns and tag sales. Marshall's AJRC contributed the lion's share of

Joint funds—from 1916 to 1918, AJRC donations represented about 70 percent of the Joint's total collection[55]—but even though it depended upon large donors, the AJRC had received contributions from more than 7,000 Jews by 1924.

Quite surprisingly, when the Joint's fund-raising campaign reached its peak at the time of America's entry into the war, New York Jewry was not in the philanthropic front seat. Over a decade earlier, during the Kishinev collections, 43 percent of overseas relief funds came from New York Jews, but of the $8,368,000 raised by the JDC between mid-December 1916 and mid-June 1917, just 11 percent came from New York.[56] "I wonder where Mr. Schiff gets the notion that the Jews in New York are asked to do more in proportion to their wealth than Jews in other cities," David Brown, in Detroit, asked Jacob Billikopf (Marshall's future son-in-law) of the AJRC.[57] Personifying this philanthropic shift of gravity away from New York, Julius Rosenwald of Chicago stunned and inspired American Jewry during World War I, promising to add $100,000 for every $1 million raised by the JDC. Jewish newspaper illustrations pictured Rosenwald lifting symbols of European Jewry in his own arms, with captions reading "Must Julius Rosenwald Carry the Burden Alone?"[58]

Somewhat petulantly, Marshall complained for months about the lack of centralization in the Joint's transformative wartime relief campaigns. All the "fuss or feathers" of involving hundreds of small donors to collect a sum that an AJC colleague could have covered by simply writing one check perturbed his sense of efficiency.[59] From a business point of view, it was hard to be enthusiastic about the Joint's tripartite structure, because it allowed for duplicated effort and increased administrative costs. At times, Marshall even suggested that the Orthodox Central Committee and the leftist People's Relief Committee were costing the relief campaign hundreds of thousands of dollars. However, as Zosa Szajkowski, who closely studied American Jewish philanthropy in this period, observed, Marshall scrupulously honored arrangements and agreements forged by the three relief agencies.[60] Months into the war, Marshall colorfully expressed his reconciliation with the emerging JDC structure: "I have told them [the committees] frequently that I would be only too glad to perform the marriage ceremony between these three committees if both the bridegroom and the bride were willing, but I do not believe in forced marriages."[61]

Quantitatively, the Joint's fund-raising performance paid eloquent tribute to the prosperity and communal devotion of American Jewry. In the decade that unfolded after Marshall and his group convened the October 25, 1914, meeting, the JDC distributed $58,195,355 among close to forty countries.[62] The qualitative effects were also transformative. Philanthropy unified and energized the American Jewish community during the wartime and Armistice years. Looking back on what had happened, Marshall's articulate and idealistic brother-in-law Judah Magnes aptly summarized this communal sea change:

> There had been certain Jewish groups who, throughout their existence in this century and by reason of their social tradition, had always been opposed to every kind of charity work. . . . But when this great world catastrophe overtook us and the rest of Europe it was our common, instinctive, fundamental humanity that spoke out; and despite all logic and in the face of social tradition, all kinds of Jews from Right to Left joined together.[63]

Horace Kallen, philosopher and American Zionist, argued that the union of the "masses and the classes" in new structures such as the Joint and the American Jewish Congress democratized the American Jewish community during the war and made available many millions of philanthropic dollars.[64] A related explanation emphasized that the Downtown Russian Jews had come of age during the war in ways that filled the Joint's coffers and also ended the hegemony of the Schiff-Marshall AJC elite. In 1925, Morris Waldman recalled how "the phenomenal commercial opportunities during the war made large numbers of formerly indigent Eastern European settlers in this country wealthy." These newly prospering Downtown Jews seized an opportunity for "communal leadership" during the war, leaving the "German Jewish leadership no longer exclusively in the saddle."[65]

That was overstating the case, since JDC donation tallies in this period clearly establish the dominance of the Uptown AJRC, but Waldman's point was cogent. Unlike causes such as the American Jewish Congress or Zionism, which raised sensitive and complicated issues of communal control, political loyalty, and Jewish identity, overseas relief work mobilized energy and resources in the American Jewish community on behalf of a shared humanitarian goal and a cherished spiritual ethic of Jewish solidarity. As a nonpolitical endeavor, the relief work better accommodated shifting alliances and power alignments in the community; since the work was being done to alleviate the misery of overseas Jews, ego jockeying and power struggles seemed most out of bounds in this philanthropic sphere.

For his part, Marshall perceptively tapped "unity" as the overriding lesson of this wartime relief work. "The one essential thing Jews have to teach the world . . . is *unity, unity* in Israel," Marshall opined in 1921, looking back at the Joint's origins.[66] Though he quibbled in passing about its specific features, the Joint's rise was a consequence of Marshall's insistence from the start of the war that complicated issues of politics and political loyalties need not interfere with Jewish philanthropic work. His towering presence in this revolution in American Jewish philanthropy can be seen on many different levels. For one thing, on-the-ground heroes of the massive fund-raising campaigns—Magnes, Jacob Billikopf—gravitated, sooner or later, toward his own family circle, and Yiddish journals toward the end of the 1920s favorably remarked upon the fund-raisers and activists in Marshall's family as a parable of Downtown-Uptown reconciliation.[67] An anecdote relayed by Szajkowski aptly captures Marshall's dimensions in this context. He was absent during a July 1918 meeting of the JDC Executive Committee, but a subsequent commissioned painting of this gathering puts Marshall at the front, nudging to the back a bearded Central Committee rabbi.[68]

Dimensions of the Jewish Congress Debate

The Jewish congress movement in America was part of a global trend, though it came after a delay and with some twists. In Europe, congress movements mobilized about a decade before World War I; unlike the situation that was to arise in the United States, the impetus for those in Europe was cooperation between Jewish nationalists and non-Zionists. A turning point in the process was the Seventh Zionist Congress's (1905) fateful rejection of the British "Uganda" offer of Jewish settlement in East Africa—many people connected formally or emotionally to the Jewish nationalist movement regarded this deferral as a semiutopian, unrealistic gesture, and discussion began to arise in Jewish circles about the imperative of *Gegenwartsarbeit*—"work in the present"—to allay the suffering of Jews wherever they happened to be found. Zionist and liberal emancipation politics converged at key loci of Jewish life, including czarist Russia, where the "League for the Attainment of Equal Rights for the Jewish People in Russia" was established in Saint Petersburg to lobby for Jewish nationalist rights. Even integrationist liberals in this new League, like Maxim Vinaver, later dubbed the "Louis Marshall of Russia,"[69] were drawn to the aims of Jewish cultural autonomy incorporated in its "Vilna Platform."[70] From this point, during the crucial transition years of 1904–7 through the end of World War I, organized Jewish demands for national rights and Jewish congress movements sprouted in innumerable locales. Some thirty congress movements came to life in world Jewish communities in this period.[71]

The Jewish congress movement congealed in the United States in March 1915 with the formation of a Jewish Congress Organization Committee, staffed by figures such as Gedalye Bublick, editor of the Yiddish daily *Dos yidishestogblat*, and the American Zionist Bernard Richards.[72] One congress proponent, the brilliant socialist Zionist thinker and publicist Nahman Syrkin, immediately conceptualized the proposed organization as a democratic remedy to what he regarded as the oligarchic control of self-appointed Jewish stewards, or *shtadlonim*. In a brochure on the subject published in mid-1915, Syrkin delineated what would remain the congress's primary raison d'être: the new body would lobby at a post-war peace conference for "equal civil rights for Jews in all lands . . . and for a definite number of national rights and freedom for the Jews in Russia, Poland, Rumania, the Balkans and everywhere where Jews had their own national life."[73]

Though Marshall and his AJC colleagues had reservations about the applicability of "national rights" formulas in Jewish circumstances, they had labored for a decade for precisely the ideal Syrkin evoked: the conferral of rights to Jews in all lands. The problem was that congress proponents linked their campaign to the democratization of Jewish life in America. How, asked impassioned spokesman Syrkin, could a *shtadlan* like Marshall, who owed his status in American Jewish affairs to the resources of the Uptown elite and who was not accountable to any constituency other than the AJC oligarchy, reasonably champion the cause of democratic emancipation for the Jews in foreign lands? In Syrkin's words:

> To represent the Jewish people, to speak in its name, to conduct its politics, to organize it, to raise it up, to liberate and restructure its entire life—this cannot be done by self-appointed groups of *shtadlonim,* by a party, by a faction or an organization, but only by the people organized as such, working through its democratically elected representatives and through its own agencies and institutions controlled by the people.[74]

The congress idea lit a spark among populist-spirited Jewish groups. On the Jewish left, the *Forward* announced in early April 1915 the formation of the National Workmen's Committee on Jewish Rights in the Belligerent Lands, which pledged to fight for Jewish rights and freedom in overseas communities. In years to come, this National Workmen's Committee (NWC) flip-flopped more than once on the congress issue, because its internationalist-minded members were never fully persuaded that lobbying for Jewish individual or group rights did not betray ideals of global socialist fraternity; nor were they really at ease working with the capitalists and middle-class professionals who were drawn into the congress campaign. In spring 1915, however, the NWC made its debut as a powerful conglomerate of four Jewish leftist members (the *Forward [Forverts],* the Arbeter Ring, the United Hebrew Trades, and the Jewish Socialist Federation).[75]

Downtown appeared to be mobilizing rapidly to challenge Marshall and the other Uptown stewards in a showdown centered on three issues: the extent of American Jewish responsibility toward overseas Jewish communities, the terms of

Jewish modernization around the globe, and the character of Jewish communal life in the United States.

World War I Politics as Advocacy: Marshall's Assets

The Downtown swell of emotion, concentrated in the drive for a Jewish congress, posed the most serious challenge Marshall had ever faced as a Jewish leader. On a superficial level, the situation would have seemed bizarrely Byzantine to an outsider. Russian Jews in America were accosting German Jews in America for not being sufficiently anti-Russian and pro-German. In this regard, Marshall correctly grasped that explaining to Gentile Americans the true attitudes of immigrant Jews toward their countries of origin would have been too complicated. Beyond such confusing, broad ethnopolitical circumstances of Jewish life, what really caused the contentious congress debate? To what extent was Marshall's alienation from Downtown caused by ego-related concerns about the continuation of the AJC's paramount position? Alternatively, to what extent can his role in this congress controversy be explained in terms of his fear that public manifestations of Downtown Jewry's hatred of Russia, and of its pro-German orientation, could potentially compromise American Jewry's collective interests in a period marked both by official American neutrality and by mounting public sympathy for the Allied Powers?

To sort out these questions fairly, it is important to view world Jewish circumstances in 1914–15 not in terms of our own retrospective understanding but in light of how Marshall himself understood them. Marshall did not anticipate in 1915 that anti-Semitism could ever become a primary determinant of world political affairs. In 1915, not long before his death, Jewish Theological Seminary president Solomon Schechter showed Marshall an article written by Houston Stewart Chamberlain; the AJC president responded by branding the anti-Semite a "mischief maker."[76] In other words, when World War I erupted, Marshall tended to view anti-Semitism through the prism of late nineteenth-century optimism, whereby figures like Vienna's Karl Lueger were seen as foolish opportunists rather than as precursors of a ferocious movement that might arise from the ruins of global warfare. Even as European civilization descended into slaughter and mayhem, Marshall tended to view the world as an extended courtroom wherein professional advocacy, judiciously basing its claims on constitutional rights, could stave off the dark threats of human irrationality. This line of interpretation, I think, provides a persuasive account of motivational questions relating specifically to Marshall's clash with Zionists and others in the congress debate and generally to his complex and robust World War I activities. Marshall acted on the basis of a deep, and partially vindicated, faith in the efficacy of his professional capabilities as an advocate.

Jerold Auerbach, the author of a stimulating and provocative study about the transition in American Jewish leadership from rabbinical figures like Isaac Mayer Wise to lawyers like Marshall and Brandeis, argues with some logic that this change reflected patterns of acculturation and Americanization, whereby American Jews began to replace their faith in Torah and Jewish law with a semireligious commitment to American constitutionalism.[77] His criticism, however, overlooks specific historical circumstances in key periods in American Jewish history. Louis Marshall was rising during World War I to a position of communal preeminence because fundamental challenges and crises facing American Jews *did* involve legislative (e.g., restrictionists' efforts on Capitol Hill to impose literacy tests to block immigration) and trial (e.g., the Leo Frank affair) processes. Thus Marshall's ascent as a leader can readily be explained in terms of the appropriateness of his skills and expertise, along with the credibility he attained in the eyes of members of the community's economic elite, starting with Jacob Schiff.

Marshall's professional orientation as a trained and experienced attorney buttressed his Jewish efforts during this uniquely chaotic period. In fact, one of the keys to understanding why Marshall's status in international Jewish life strengthened coming out of the war years, as compared to the rather exhausted reputation of an overseas counterpart such as the English Jewish leader Lucien Wolf—who was also affiliated with the winning side and who clearly had more experience in international politics than Marshall—was that the American's qualifications as a lawyer offered him some anchoring in an era of near-infinite confusion that a counterpart like Wolf, a journalist, lacked.[78]

In winter–spring 1915, as the impassioned stirrings Downtown and the American Zionist challenge propelled Marshall toward the divisive and potentially debilitating debate about the formation of an American Jewish Congress, he was engaged in Jewish advocacy on issues of tremendous symbolic and practical import. His work on these causes was potentially demoralizing. The appeals process on the Frank case did not reap dividends (though, significantly, Marshall's appeal argument about mob law as an infringement of due process subsequently became a legal standard[79]), and the anti-Semitic Populist and (in C. Vann Woodward's sanitized phrase) "agrarian rebel"[80] Tom Watson was ominously drumming up hatred in Georgia. When the hapless Frank wrote at the end of January 1915 to Marshall, who was now firmly in charge of the appeals process, to ask whether it was advisable for him to plead his innocence by writing in the court of public opinion, his counsel replied, rather pessimistically, "apparently nothing that may be written will, under present conditions, affect public sentiment in Georgia."[81]

Meantime, on Capitol Hill, Marshall and his cohorts were losing ground in their ongoing battle with the restrictionists, who sought to exploit wartime suspicions about foreigners in a renewed offensive to insert a literacy test requirement in an immigration bill. Marshall had no doubts about the character and intents of the literacy test. To former New York governor Martin Glynn, a Catholic, Marshall wrote baldly, "The bill is a Know Nothing measure, and I have reason to know that it is largely anti-Catholic and anti-Jewish in its object."[82]

President Wilson, as it turned out, boldly vetoed the immigration bill, just as Georgian governor John Slaton courageously commuted Frank's death sentence to life imprisonment. In both cases, a tremendously relieved Marshall effusively tendered thanks to the high official who had guarded crucial Jewish interests, defying mob hatred or Nativist hostility. Carefully not identifying himself as a Jewish organizational leader or offering gratitude for Jews, Marshall wrote to Slaton on June 21: "You have saved the honor of your state. You have earned the eternal gratitude of the good people of Georgia and the admiration of every lover of justice in America."[83] To President Wilson, Marshall identified himself as head of the AJC and expressed his gratitude as the child of immigrants. The president's veto of the restrictive immigration bill and his accompanying message, Marshall wrote to Wilson, "writes a new chapter in the glorious chapter of American liberalism." The president's act was appreciated by all who "believe that it is not the right of a nation of immigrations to withhold the sacred privilege of living and striving here."[84]

Both of these positive results were preceded and accompanied by intensive labors on Marshall's part. Throughout January 1915, he pressed aggressively for an interview with Wilson, and then immediately after the president's decision, Marshall endeavored for several tense days to forestall the consolidation of a two-thirds majority in both houses of Congress that was needed to override Wilson's veto. Interestingly, his work on Jewish affairs in this period was hedged on all fronts by his status as a New Yorker embroiled in Southern politics. The day after he told Leo Frank that there was no hope of countering the hateful "vaporings" of Tom Watson and his ilk in the state of Georgia, Marshall informed one congressman that the vetoed immigration bill, "the most brutal piece of legislation that has ever been devised," is "purely a Southern Democratic measure" championed by Alabama's John Burnett in the House and by South Carolina's Ellison D. Smith in the Senate.[85]

In the Frank case, Marshall lobbied arduously behind the scenes, literally flooding colleagues and notables with requests that they petition Governor Slaton for clemency. He contacted Jacob Schiff and Daniel Guggenheim, asking them to mobilize industrialists like Andrew Carnegie and Elbert Gray in this matter; on the other side of the socioeconomic spectrum, Marshall practically begged ("this must be done at once . . . there is no time to lose") East Side Socialist congressman Meyer London to travel to Atlanta to galvanize support for Frank among local labor leaders.[86] Later in May, after Marshall arranged for a number of former governors to petition Slaton, he wrote to Frank's associate counsel: "The machinery which I have set in motion has been in very active operation, with what I believe will prove to be satisfactory results."[87]

These were inconclusive triumphs. Open immigration policy toward Jews would be obliterated seven years after President Wilson's veto,[88] and Frank would be killed by a lynch mob seven weeks after Governor Slaton's commutation. Before these bitter conclusions, Marshall clearly understood that he was facing, at best, an uphill struggle. However elated Frank's backers might have been by Slaton's decision, Marshall did not waste many hours before he reminded Frank's associate counsel, "Nothing short of an absolute pardon will meet requirements" (in the same message, Marshall advised Frank's people in Atlanta to "carefully follow" the movements of the suspected culprit, Jim Conley).[89] The Frank trial had precipitated an outcry, but there was little in the public response that struck Marshall as being particularly prudent and honorable. As far as he was concerned, Albert D. Lasker, the pioneering advertising executive who invested $25,000 of his own funds for Frank and who launched a carefully crafted publicity campaign, was the "only Jew in this country who did his duty" during the Frank ordeal.[90] Just as soon as congressional bids to override Wilson's veto on the restrictive immigration bill were defeated, Marshall looked ahead in a sober, rather lonely, mood of persistence, noticeably similar to his attitude in the aftermath of the Frank commutation decision. Marshall had a consistently low opinion of counterparts in the American Jewish community who had worked hard for years to forestall restrictive immigration bills. Staying in contact with the most prominent of these figures, Simon Wolf, mostly out of deference to the sensibilities and requests of B'nai B'rith leader Adolf Kraus, Marshall wrote in mid-February 1915 that Wilson was committed to his opposition of the restrictive literacy test proposal, but his veto's effect could not be taken for granted. "Even before the 64th Congress convenes, efforts will be made by the restrictionists to secure lacking votes," and reinitiate the literacy test campaign, he warned, perspicaciously.[91]

Marshall's faith in the power of law barred him from anticipating the raw nativist postwar prejudices of what John Higham aptly called the "Tribal Twenties."[92] Since Wilson and Slaton in the immigration and Leo Frank cases could be regarded as ultimate arbiters of justice in courts of last resort, Marshall never really encountered a situation in which legislative or trial processes tailored to his own professional background unequivocally failed. Arguably, when viewed in full historical perspective, the fates of the star-crossed individual, Leo Frank, and of hundreds of thousands of would-be Jewish immigrants of the interwar period, were overtaken by the angry mob, in the literal sense of the term in Frank's case and, more figuratively, in terms of xenophobic and racist mass opinion in the case of draconian restrictive immigration legislation of the early twenties. The conservatively tempered Marshall would never in his life see the twists and turns in his career as a Jewish leader in this light. The law was always his trusted shield against mob rule.

That confidence steadied him. Objectively, he spent an inordinate amount of energy in situations such as the Frank case fending off advocacy possibilities that he believed to be extraneous to an orderly and effective defense—at most stages of the ordeal, Marshall was not, in fact, prepping witnesses for courtroom testimony or preparing appellate briefs, but rather was fighting a desperate battle in public for a mortally imperiled, and innocent, individual. However, as in many other Jewish defense situations, during the Frank case, Marshall shunned forms of public advocacy that were not in harmony with his belief that Jewish problems could be solved according to the rules of law, in a kind of extended courtroom.

Repeatedly, in consultation with Frank's Atlanta-based attorneys, Marshall noted what he had done "to choke off very many ill-advised movements."[93] Fascinatingly, one such "ill-advised" initiative that Marshall nixed, in consultation with his client Leo Frank, were proposals to stage a Yiddish play or to produce a motion picture about the framing of the innocent Jew. (His clout in New York led to the quick nullification of the Yiddish stage idea, whereas his effort to dissuade the Rolands Feature Film Company was more protracted.[94]) Interpreted conventionally, such public relations caution can be attributed to the fear of his German Jewish Uptown elite of appearing "too Jewish" in public, and that interpretation undoubtedly has bearing in the Leo Frank case. However, when circumstances of orderly advocacy warranted the introduction of personal data and an emphasis of specific Jewish concerns, Marshall did not really abide by this German Jewish rule of political "neutrality," certainly not in private contacts.[95] In his advocacy opposing the restrictive literacy test, Marshall had few qualms about sharing with legislators facts about his own Jewish background; he wrote to them revealingly about experiences in his Jewish milieu in Syracuse and how they proved that the children of semiliterate immigrant parents grew up to be fully contributing "Americans in every sense of the word."[96] Far from fearing the exposure of his own or anyone else's Jewishness, the abiding standard was Marshall's sense of appropriately effective forms of advocacy. Whenever they could not be kept formally in a courtroom, those forms hewed as closely as possible to constitutional law and orderly, courtroom-like presentation.

Testimony to Marshall's abiding faith in law-based advocacy was his declaration, "I cannot say there is any pronounced increase of anti-Semitism in America."[97] The statement, made in response to an inquiry posed by a Chicago attorney, Salmon O. Levinson (who would gain increased attention in the interwar period as a peace activist), came in early 1915, a time when circumstances like the Frank trial and the literacy test proposal furnished abundant evidence to contradict Marshall's proposition. Marshall was surely thinking about the South when he conceded that "in some regions," anti-Semitism was "prevalent among certain classes of the community." However, the Jews faced no bugbear in America that the country's laws could not exterminate. Jews who entered American politics sometimes encountered "more or less opposition," Marshall noted, vaguely, but he explained that Jewish candidates were often "objectionable" for reasons that had nothing to do with ethnoreligious identity, and in the recent elections for delegates to the New York Constitutional Convention, he himself received the most votes, 25,000 more than those won by Elihu Root.

This last reference to Root was a pointed example that well reflected the internal psychology of its provider. Overtly, Marshall was in this letter to Levinson, as in innumerable other communications, downplaying anti-Semitism by describing it as an insignificant factor in American life, but much of his language sounded like non-denial denials conveying the message that it was tactically, rather than empirically, incorrect to speak about anti-Semitism in America. "Personally, I believe that it is very unwise to raise the cry of anti-Semitism. No good can come from it," wrote Marshall to Levinson. Marshall also dropped hints about his being vigilantly engaged with anti-Semitism and equipped with all the legal tools needed to defeat it. The Downtown Jewish masses knew to rally to his side when it was necessary. Significantly, a Jewish lawyer had garnered many thousands more votes than Elihu Root, a Republican senator from New York who already had a Nobel Peace Prize under his belt and who, as a Gentile foil from Upstate New York, was regarded by Marshall as an avowed enemy of Jewish mobility in the legal profession. "I have long suspected that he is not a lover of our people," Marshall diplomatically expressed a year later, after writing a scathing rebuttal to Root's contention at a New York State Bar Association dinner that 30 percent of the lawyers in the state were foreign born or had foreign-born parents, and therefore lacked appreciation of the spirit of American institutions.[98] Marshall's besting of Root in the Constitutional Convention vote implied that through vigilant use of their own resources and intelligent exploitation of opportunities, Jews in

America had a formative role to play in its constitutional system and in the defeat of anti-Semitism.

In Marshall's view, the ultimate safeguard against mob rule and rampant anti-Semitism was public commitment to American constitutionalism. "I have found that, when a real question arises which relates to the human rights of the Jew, the people of this country are swift to come to his support," Marshall explained to Levinson.[99] In his experience, the most profound demonstration of this principle had occurred during the campaign for the abrogation of the commercial treaty between the United States and Russia, a struggle for Jewish rights backed by the "whole country," Marshall recalled. Responsible delegates of the American public, including clergy, would never tolerate behavior and policies abusive to the human rights of any American citizens, including Jews.

In this revealing 1915 letter about anti-Semitism in America, Marshall previewed the strengths and weaknesses of his postwar Jewish advocacy. On the one hand, in the crucial phases of his 1920s antidefamation work relating to Henry Ford's *Dearborn Independent* anti-Semitic vitriol, Marshall correctly calculated that American clergy, journalists, and other public spokespeople would not allow the extremely powerful and popular automobile manufacturer to injure Jewish rights. On the other hand, Marshall's viewpoint implied that widespread commitment to constitutional law in America's political culture rather than to constitutional law in the abstract protected the Jews. It can, therefore, be difficult to understand his belief that East European state cultures, founded on historical experiences unlike the American past, would honor constitutional protections for Jews and other minorities. While life experiences firmly guided Marshall's Jewish advocacy in America, wishful thinking led it overseas.

Downtown Versus Uptown: The Congress Debate Crests

The dilemmas and perils of overseas Jewish advocacy would not really become evident until after the war. During the war years, Marshall repeatedly insisted that the particularity of political circumstances in America, as well as the special dimensions of Jewish experiences in the United States, needed to be respected. He articulated this viewpoint most vehemently in contacts with English Jewish spokesmen, who accused American Jewish leaders of pro-German orientations, sometimes baiting them to take openly pro-Allied stances in defiance of American neutrality. Marshall objected strenuously to such English Jewish intervention, declaiming angrily in a private letter to the editor of England's *Jewish Chronicle*, "You have as little knowledge about American Jews as you have of the inhabitants of Mars."[100] Marshall protested that *Chronicle* articles presented America "as a nation of monsters, because we maintain neutrality." English Jews were not on the moral high ground when they demanded that peers in America take a partisan stand. "We can see that this war is the inevitable result of a vicious diplomacy, which has but little regard for right, justice or humanity," Marshall observed in this February 1915 letter. Here and elsewhere, he reiterated that his own sympathies were with the English and French democratic system of government. Caustically, he rejected suggestions about pro-German or self-interested orientations among American Jews. "You say he [the American Jew] is only concerned with lining his pockets with dollars. You charge him with disloyalty to his brethren. . . . Even Houston Stewart Chamberlain would not be more virulent in his denunciation of the American Jew."

Consulting with Richard Gottheil and others, Marshall endeavored for weeks to identify the anonymous *Jewish Chronicle* foreign correspondent who goaded American Jews for not taking a pro-Allied stance, but the English Jewish press was not his principal concern. In Downtown New York, the Yiddish press was bursting with accusations about how Marshall and the other Yahudim (or Jehudin) were betraying their own people precisely because of their pro-English orientation and were also stifling democratization in the community by their opposition to the Jewish congress initiative. "The Yiddish papers are doing infinite mischief," Marshall moaned in a confidential letter to Solomon Schechter.[101] "They have only contempt and contumely for those whom they describe as *Jehudin*." Marshall berated the congress idea as "insanity," saying that "where secret councils are indispensable, they [the Downtown Yiddish newspapers] demand mass meetings and Jewish congresses."

Venting frustration about Downtown Jewry's "insane mischief," Marshall suggested that the warrant for discrete "secret councils" was that his own group had superior experience in American public life and the best chance of quietly formulating positions during the war that would redound to the benefit of Jews in the country and overseas. The fact, however, was that the most prominent figures in world Jewish politics in this period were making calculated guesses about whether it would be better to support one side in the conflict or the other; a long list of personages—among them Chaim Weizmann, Vladimir Jabotinsky, Aaron Aaronsohn, David Ben-Gurion, Yitzhak Ben-Zvi, Chaim Zhitlovsky, Nahman Syrkin, Pinhas Rutenberg[102]—drifted between countries, proposing an array of mechanisms to promote one vision of postwar Jewish life or another; the success or failure of these various schemes (a Jewish congress or a Jewish legion, the Nili espionage ring, and the Balfour Declaration) depended upon the constellation of Jewish and Gentile forces in a host country. More precisely, Jewish politics in this period boiled down to whether a particular Jewish activist hitched his wagon to the right side with the right timing and in a suitably persuasive idiom. In hindsight, it is difficult to say whether a particular individual "won"—in terms of the contemporary acceptance of his proposal and in terms of its long-term impact upon Jewish life—as a result of his preference for secret councils or open congresses. National-ethnic politics in spring 1915 had turned into a guessing game in a violent, bloody, and unpredictable world.

Marshall postured in public as a wise elder whose judgments about the war ought to take precedence in closed, private Jewish conferences, but he himself admitted in private that community policy was relying increasingly on educated guesswork. Not just the Downtown Yiddish papers, but newspapers in England, France, and Germany were filled with lurid, propagandistic information about atrocities in Belgium or against the Jews in ways that obviously served a particular journal's and nation's agenda, and that may or may not have reliably represented facts on the ground. "There has been so much misrepresentation and exaggeration on every side, that one cannot take at face value any of the lurid publications given out by interested parties," Marshall wrote to Mortimer Schiff, Jacob's only child.[103] Refusing to criticize categorically Allied or Central powers, Marshall claimed in this letter that most of the hardship endured by East European Jewry was due to "the machinations of the Poles." Essentially, throughout this early war period, Marshall justified his policy of assertively rejecting the anti-Russian demands of Downtown Jewry as a leap of faith. He had a "feeling" that his, and America's, position of neutrality would, after the war, lead to "improvement" for Russia's Jews. "If I were asked to give my reasons" in support of this feeling, "it would be difficult to point to anything tangible," Marshall admitted. The Russian people, who were "at heart kindly," would in the end confer civil and religious rights to the Jews. "I think that the truth of your father's oft repeated statement, that the Russian-Jewish question must and will be settled in Russia, will soon be vindicated," Marshall wrote to Mortimer Schiff.

This was a subjective assessment of Russian cultural attitudes and political patterns, and Marshall privately confessed that he had no "tangible" proof that neutrality would be better for the Jews in the long term. Yet in public, Marshall opposed calls for an American Jewish Congress by saying that the experienced stewards of the AJC knew more about the present and probable future of European Jewry. The AJC, Marshall told the New York Kehillah Convention in late April, "has carefully observed and studied conditions, for the purpose of taking such action as may be deemed advisable to bring about a new dispensation. . . . Most careful attention has been given to the practical phases of the subject, and to diplomatic methods and procedures which may be invoked."[104]

Such claims about superior information and knowledge were unlikely to intimidate Downtown's East European Jews. They were, as observers on New York's Lower East Side frequently reported during the war, not a pliable and ignorant constituency on war matters.[105] International affairs, these observers noted, were "part of the everyday conversation" of Jewish workers, who had a "far better understanding of foreign relations than the average native American." Editors of the Yiddish newspapers followed the pulse of international affairs, thanks largely to their close relationship with foreign correspondents. Such contemporary observations were, of course, generalizations that could never have applied precisely to all groups of readers and journalists in New York's Yiddish press, whose five dailies had a combined circulation of 406,000 in 1917, but they serve as a reminder that Marshall's rather patronizing Uptown viewpoint on this issue of secret councils versus open congresses was neither realistic nor credible. Why should he have known more than the Russian Jewish immigrants about probable outcomes in their native country?

In ways not entirely discerned by Marshall, the congress campaign created new power alignments among Downtown Jews in spring 1915. About two weeks before the Kehillah Convention, nationalist-oriented Downtown groups had clashed with internationalist socialist delegates at a New York Workmen's Convention for Jewish Rights; the nationalists, called *khaveryim,* had stormed out of the meeting and then lobbied with the *yidn,* East European immigrants, wherever they could find them, arguing that they should join forces to pressure the Yahudim of the AJC to convene the congress. Kehillah leader Judah Magnes rose assertively at the head of this effort to unite the committee and the Downtown groups on the congress plan. Beyond a relationship of friendship and trust with his brother-in-law and other committee members, Magnes had a card up his sleeve—AJC members from the New York City area were elected by the Kehillah, and so, as head of the Kehillah, Magnes was uniquely positioned to argue about ways in which democratization initiatives contemplated under the congress plan might be feasible. Possessor of a strong reputation Downtown, Magnes emerged at this juncture as the figure most likely to persuade Marshall and his colleagues to consent to the congress plan for communal democracy.

In February, the Kehillah, under Magnes's direction, "demanded" publicly that the AJC invite delegates of national Jewish organizations for a discussion about the imperative of forming a congress.[106] From this moment, Magnes, the articulate, charismatic former rabbi of the Reform Temple Emanu-El, walked a precarious tightrope, balancing Downtown's clamoring for full democratization of the American Jewish community and Marshall's objections to the congress plan. As a sop to Lower East Side militancy, he issued "demands" in Downtown's name to the Yahudim of the AJC; in deference to the paramount communal position held by Marshall and his colleagues on the AJC, Magnes insisted that any developments on the congress plan would have to come with the committee's backing. Magnes, whose pacifism transformed him by the end of the war into a highly divisive figure in American Jewish life, labored astutely and forcefully in this period to unify Uptown and Downtown Jewries, but, as Jonathan Frankel observed, "he had underestimated the breadth and the depth" of gaps between the sides.[107]

Marshall's adamant April 1915 Kehillah Convention speech dampened hopes that had soared among Downtown groups thanks to Magnes's mediation. Marshall's most effective moment in the address came when he reminded Downtown Jews that the war's results in various lands remained anyone's guess and that the only thing American Jews could know for sure was that if they were to abandon neutrality and act on a faulty calculation about who would, or should, win the war, their brethren overseas might pay a very steep price. In this Kehillah Convention address, Marshall succinctly formulated this all-important argument for neutrality:

> The Jews, more than any other people, have always been regarded as hostages for each other, and it is therefore incumbent upon the Jews of America to bear that fact in mind, at every instant, lest that, in their zeal, they accomplish the very mischief that they are seeking to prevent.[108]

Marshall argued that an American Jewish Congress would be irrelevant. "It requires no congress to tell the world, that it is the ardent wish, not only of every Jew . . . that equal rights and equal liberties should be possessed by all men."[109] The resolutions reached by such a congress would hardly influence world affairs. "In the cold gray dawn" following the congress's sessions, its decisions would have the effect that "a pebble cast into the Atlantic Ocean would have on the European coast-line," Marshall declared. He was transparently masking the reality that was obvious to everyone in the swiftly intensifying debate about an American Jewish Congress: proponents of the contrasting positions were motivated in large measure by its probable effects upon Jewish communal structure in America, a local, malleable environment to which Marshall's disparaging remarks did not necessarily apply.

Trying to co-opt the congress movement, Marshall announced that the AJC would issue calls for a conference, "at an early day," of leading Jewish national organizations (which he listed), to discuss goals and strategies regarding postwar circumstances of world Jewry. Marshall's group preferred different nomenclature ("conference" as opposed to "congress") due to a concern that the nationalist-oriented congress movement might provoke loyalty accusations about Jews working as a state within a state. Still more importantly, under Marshall's alternative conference proposal, the direction of Jewish communal activity would still be controlled by the AJC and thereby forestall the Zionists' aggressive bid for community power.

Downtown, however, was in no mood to accept this formula. The day following Marshall's address, the Kehillah's resolutions committee defiantly concluded that the congress ought to be convened "subsequent and supplementary" to the conference that Marshall envisioned.[110] In effect, this created what one scholar described as a "constitutional crisis," because although the Kehillah elected a third of the committee's members, it had no authority to impose its position on the congress issue.[111] "I have no fear for anyone but God above and indiscreet men below," Marshall exclaimed impetuously. Personally affronted and genuinely concerned that a congress might compromise Jewish interests, he taunted Kehillah partisans: "If you persist on calling a Congress, I'll have nothing of it." Agitated by the rancorous five-hour debate, Magnes wearily indicated that his brother-in-law had gone too far. "As the people have faith in the American Jewish Committee, so the committee should have faith in the people," Magnes wanly reflected.[112]

Dreams of democratic unity in American Jewish life were ripping apart at the seams. Targeted mercilessly in the Yiddish press as an autocratic oligarch, Marshall bit his tongue. "I am exerting a great deal of self-restraint in view of the outrageous attacks which the *Tageblatt* and *Warheit* are making against the American Jewish Committee," he reflected to a trusted associate.[113] Popular, influential figures in the East European Jewish immigrant world openly rebelled against Marshall and the AJC. One was union leader Joseph Barondess, "King of the Cloakmakers," who flamboyantly quit the AJC in February; Marshall believed that Barondess's "contemptuous and slurring references" to the American Jewish leadership as "Jehudin and moneybags" were "unworthy."[114] Another rebel, Isaac A. Hourwich—a former Russian Marxist who had made his way as an immigrant in the United States as a lawyer and government statistician, and who (it will be recalled) had authored under Marshall's patronage an important prewar study to support the AJC's fight against immigration restriction—openly confronted Marshall at the Kehillah Convention. He berated Marshall's objection to the congress as "the Jews' traditional policy of weakness in matters of grave concern to them."[115] Neither side made headway at this unruly Kehillah Convention. Marshall called it a "drawn battle" and warned colleagues that "the real fight is to come."[116]

Trying to break the stalemate, the Kehillah reconvened in May at Madison Square Garden. Hourwich chaired a committee that produced a compromise formula whereby the much-anticipated democratic gathering would be called a "conference," not a "congress." Delegates to the conference were to be designated not by the heads of national Jewish organizations but instead by a vote of their memberships.[117] Some Kehillah members charged that this arrangement conceded too much to Marshall, because it narrowed the scope of democratic elections in the Jewish community; after another long, heated debate, such reservations were dropped, but congress zealots insisted that the Kehillah's new proposal bind its twenty-five delegates on the AJC. Jacob Schiff, who had consulted cooperatively with the Hourwich committee, objected, maintaining that the Kehillah's AJC delegates must retain freedom of conscience to vote as they pleased. Before Marshall stormed out of the meeting, he joined this criticism. The exasperated Magnes lobbied hard for the Kehillah to repeal its vote in favor of binding the twenty-five delegates; on a series of ballots, the Kehillah decided in favor of the Magnes-Marshall-Schiff "freedom of conscience" position but then reversed itself, deciding to bind the delegates. This May meeting suggested that the capacity of the congress debate to befuddle and demoralize American Jewry's leadership was limitless. "I feel a great deal of my usefulness is at end," lamented Kehillah president Magnes, after the freedom of conscience plank was beaten.[118]

Marshall, who angrily explained to friends about how he left the meeting during the "pandemonium" about the freedom of conscience issue, attested to feeling "sorry for Magnes," who was "undergoing a great disillusionment with regard to the East Side statesmen and his Zionistic coadjutors, who have been plotting against the Kehillah and the American Jewish Committee, all for the purposes of making propaganda for their insane theories."[119] As far as Marshall was concerned, the raucous jockeying at these successive Kehillah meetings "demonstrate[d] the danger, the futility and the fatuity, of holding a Congress."[120] While Downtown impugned Marshall as an "undemocratic and un-American despot," some of his Uptown associates reminded him that they had advised the AJC from the start to turn its back completely on the congress movement. In retrospect, Marshall conceded that they might have been right, but he also realized that the congress movement, conceptualized as a democratization initiative to safeguard Jews in postwar Europe, had gathered too much momentum by spring 1915 to be ignored. "I am beginning to believe, with you, that we should never have attempted to do anything with the great unwashed democracy," Marshall wrote to Cyrus Adler on May 24, following the second Kehillah meeting. "We have, however, taken a position, and we must see it through, and try to save these fools from themselves."[121] Amid the acrimony and anxiety, nobody seemed aware of the situation's poignant irony: alone among his Uptown colleagues at the time of the AJC's founding less than a decade earlier, Marshall (it will be recalled) had lobbied earnestly to organize the instrument on the foundation of democratic elections rather than on self-appointed stewardship.

The particularly strained tenor of this Uptown-Downtown clash over the congress goes beyond insulting ego bickering and beyond the self-interested solicitude displayed by Marshall and his AJC colleagues for their own organization's premier role in American Jewish affairs. In the period between the Kehillah conventions, the *Lusitania* was torpedoed by a German U-boat off the Irish coast. The disaster galvanized American public opinion against Germany. As pro-Allied sentiment surged in the country, never had Downtown Jewry's anti-Russian orientation been so far from the mainstream view. Marshall was almost overcome with worries about how implicit or explicit pro-German posturing at a publicly convened Jewish congress would leave the impression that the country's Jews were an alien, unpatriotic presence.

At an AJC Executive Committee discussion about the congress issue, Oscar Straus, American Jewry's first cabinet minister, indicated that America's entry into the war on the Allied side after the *Lusitania* affair was inevitable. Marshall was not sure that this was the case, but he reiterated that "conditions are such that neither a Congress or a Conference will be of any use."[122] In a private letter to Magnes, he elaborated this point colorfully, contending that the very convening of a Jewish congress would be seen in America as assisting a potential enemy:

> At this juncture, when every American citizen is subordinating every thought to the welfare of his country, when the hyphen has disappeared from every description of American citizenship . . . we are about to enter into a debate with respect to the holding of a Jewish congress, or a Jewish convention, or what not, the very holding of which will give aid and comfort to Germany, a potential enemy of our Government.[123]

On a personal level, the *Lusitania* sinking aggrieved Marshall and exacerbated his enmity toward German autocracy. A cousin, Julius Straus of Ontario, the son of his mother's sister, perished aboard the ocean liner. The loss was acutely distressing because Marshall conversed with this relative the day before the *Lusitania* embarked on its voyage, but he was not aware of dangers posed by German U-boats.[124]

The stress of the congress debate weighed heavily on Marshall. The behavior of Downtown radicals made him almost violently angry—the "insulting and truculent" attitude they displayed toward him and Schiff at a closed meeting held before the second Kehillah Convention left him "disposed to throw some of them out the window . . . if the Adam in me had not been restrained."[125] Under post-*Lusitania* circumstances, the congress plan posed such obvious danger of self-inflicted Jewish communal danger that Marshall wondered in these private communications whether the Downtown "firebrands" had been inspired by a "German agent provocateur," Isaac Straus.[126] The emotionally debilitating character of his Jewish advocacy work at this stage produced one of the stinging ironies of Marshall's career—he was inwardly relieved by the four-month reprieve from the Uptown-Downtown congress war afforded by his work at the New York State Constitutional Convention in Albany, even though in public he challenged the legal propriety of holding the convention.

Intermission: New York Constitutional Convention and Family Matters

Though he garnered the most votes and was elected for a record third time (the first two stints being in 1890 and 1894) as a delegate to the New York Constitutional Convention, Marshall argued that procedural requirements had not been met and that the convention was illegal. Organization for the 1915 convention, Marshall argued in the *New York Times*, had not complied with New York's 1913 election laws, which required the completion of registration procedures ten days before polling. Since this registration obligation was not met, Marshall filed (unsuccessfully) for an injunction to block the convention.[127] This technical appeal for dispersal appears to have been motivated by objections to the event's cost to taxpayers ($750,000), Marshall's partisan Republican concern that its agenda was being rigged by Tammany Hall, and a general unease that the highly charged wartime atmosphere was unsuited to measured constitutional reform. As he told one state senator, New York would be better advised to wait a few years, "when the air will have been cleared and radicalism on the wane."[128]

Marshall dodged repeated newspaper requests to articulate his views on issues slated for discussion at the convention, mentioning only that he favored the appointment (rather than the election) of judges, opposed the granting of public franchises in perpetuity, and would consider measures to prevent the partisan gerrymandering of election districts.[129] He arrived at the convention with a special interest in questions related to the funding and regulation of charitable organizations controlled by religious denominations.[130] In contacts with doubters (like Jacob Schiff), who were not accustomed to outside monitoring of their private charitable enterprises like the Jewish Protectory, Marshall insisted that public regulation and inspection "can prevent mischief."[131] In general, the socially conservative Marshall avoided support of initiatives demanded by labor, including the conferral of collective bargaining rights and of recognition of unions' right to organize.[132] He became combative on environmental issues.[133] In an emotional address on the convention floor for the Adirondack Forest Preserve, Marshall exclaimed that lumber interests in the state were determined to chop down 80 percent of the forest's trees and leave behind "nothing but a howling wilderness of stumps." With moralistic flair, he read out the names of delegates whose only business at the convention was, he charged, to lobby on retainer for the lumber interests. That is how Louis Marshall relaxed during his summer 1915 interlude away from the Downtown-Uptown pyrotechnics of Jewish politics.

In fact, he loved the hard work at the convention. Also on leave from his law practice, Marshall rented a comfortable small house in Albany for $200 a month.[134] "I have never passed a more enjoyable time in my life than at the Constitutional Convention," Marshall wrote to friends and family on the final day of summer. He alluded to arduously long, but productive, eighteen-hour workdays, along with the satisfaction of working with "agreeable associates," high-minded delegates who were the "best men in the State."[135] Marshall played his characteristic role at the convention, acting as an authoritative mediator, as "the fool-killer and the slaughterer of half-baked projects and dangerous innovations, both conservative and radical," he explained to his brother-in-law. As it turned out, his satisfaction at having been a key player in the drafting of the "best Constitution in the country" proved premature because, in November, New York's electorate rejected the constitution. Marshall interpreted that negative result to be the product of Tammany maneuvering and ineffectual Republican leadership, underscoring the last factor in bitter doggerel he penned after the election debacle.[136]

Even though this interlude in New York State politics led to an unsatisfying conclusion, Marshall was thinking of the unflattering contrast to the "firebrands" of Downtown Jewish politics when he praised his high-minded convention colleagues as the finest men in the state. This one-year period, which culminated with the death of his beloved wife Florence in May 1916, was the nadir of his career as a Jewish activist and the only time in his life when he considered abandoning his communal leadership role. "I felt a great sense of relief that for a few months I was absolved from the responsibility of attending to the number of Jewish activities," Marshall confided to Magnes after the Constitutional Convention drew to a close.[137] During the summer, Magnes and his family had moved to a home outside of New York City, and Marshall's congratulations and advice to his brother-in-law were telling. "You have been living on your nerve for several years past," Marshall told Magnes, as though he were speaking about himself as well. "It does not pay to do so." Magnes ought to spend more time with his family and scale back his efforts in the Jewish world from hands-on management to discrete supervision, counseled Marshall. Magnes would do well to "act as a parnass [rather] than as a shamas" and to avoid "cheapening" himself by working too closely with the "rag, tag and bobtail crowd." Marshall confessed to his brother-in-law that "I may to my personal advantage adopt the advice I have just given you."[138]

Congress Debate Continued: The American Jewish Committee Versus the American Zionists

When Marshall was on retreat from Jewish politics at the Constitutional Convention in Albany, the congress debate entered a new, climactic phase caused by the arrival of the American Zionists and their inspiring leader Louis Brandeis. The Zionists' frontal challenge to the AJC's premier role as community steward started on May 9, 1915, when the Provisional Executive Committee for General Zionist Affairs called for the convening, "on a democratic basis," of a congress at an appropriate time.[139] Brandeis and his followers refined the terms of this challenge a month and a half later at the Federation of American Zionists annual conference, held in Boston. The involvement of the People's Attorney electrified Jewish politics; the 8,000-seat Mechanics Hall was filled to the gills, with an estimated 15,000 people outside listening to megaphoned speeches delivered by Zionist politicians from commandeered automobiles.

Compared to the other "Louis," Brandeis personified a strikingly different Jewish political identity. Not religious, and a newcomer to Jewish affairs, Brandeis insisted on making Jewish life in Palestine a priority and promised to democratize Jewish communal life in America.[140] Unlike the strong preference of Marshall's group for discreet handling of Jewish matters, Brandeis promoted an alternative, openly populist orientation in Jewish life, persuasively using his own professional example and his eloquent words to establish that American Jews had nothing to fear when they addressed complicated, seemingly sensitive, topics of Zionism. On the contrary, Brandeis famously insisted, by becoming a Zionist, he became yet a better American, and East European Jews were thrilled by this example of a highly successful attorney catapulting past loyalty anxieties in his dramatically sudden entrance into Jewish politics.

A trusted contributor to President Wilson's New Freedom policies, Brandeis infused cherished values of American democracy and the forward-looking Progressive ideas of his own time into the rough and tumble world of Jewish politics. That Brandeis made his Zionist debut in an adversarial situation—in a contentious dispute about the relative merits of a carefully staged "conference" about postwar Jewish issues as compared to a democratically open "congress" devoted to those topics (with an emphasis on Palestine)—meant that all of the negative attributes his brand of Progressive politics in America imputed to conservatives and city machines like Tammany devolved upon Marshall and the AJC. In American politics, Brandeis attacked the concentration of power—Bigness—in banking and other spheres in the name of Jeffersonian ideals of rights and free democratic competition; he also marshaled norms of scientific administration and expertise, and new techniques of open democracy (the direct primary, the referendum), in a semiholy war against Bigness and governmental corruption. The minute these principles were transposed to the Jewish political context, it naturally appeared to many that Brandeis's antagonists (who happened to be bankers and business lawyers and other professional symbols of consolidated power and Bigness) represented in their opposition to the congress a vision out of step with the highest ideals of their time.

Objectively, Brandeis should have faced a crippling disadvantage as a Zionist newcomer because Marshall and other rivals at the AJC were vastly more experienced in Jewish affairs. Yet thousands of Downtowners were willing to overlook this rather blatant defect. Brandeis symbolized something invaluably precious to acculturating immigrants—his democratic Jewish vision seemed to accord with the loftiest ideals of America. His unexpected presence in Zionist affairs promised East European immigrants that they could have the best of both worlds: unbridled expression of Jewish passion and laudatory American values. Especially during the turbulent, militantly emotional period of the war, this Brandeis formula was intrinsically more popular on the Lower East Side streets than Marshall law, which seemed always to be telling the immigrants that the best way to become successful Americans was to be careful about their Jewishness and sometimes even to hide aspects of it.

In short, the other Louis was, for Marshall's leadership, a serious threat. And in June 1915, the Zionists even seemed to be pulling toward themselves members of Marshall's own German Jewish elite. Macy's co-owner Nathan Straus, whose love for Eretz Israel was clinched on a 1912 visit to the country, impulsively joined the Zionist movement in time for the June 1915 Boston convention, donating his yacht to the cause.

With Brandeis calling the shots at the Boston convention, American Zionist official Louis Lipsky sponsored a motion condemning as undemocratic the AJC plan for a conference of delegates from Jewish organizations. The Lipsky motion called for a democratically organized congress that would consider proposals for the civil status of Jews in all lands and also promote a homeland for the

Jewish people in Palestine.[141] Alarmed at this throwing of the gauntlet against the AJC, Magnes implored Brandeis and his followers to concentrate their efforts on Palestine and to leave all other spheres to the committee, because it had been founded expressly to champion Jewish rights in overseas lands. Brandeis refused to back down[142] (a decision that initiated Magnes's lasting alienation from organized Zionism, even though he would spend the last quarter century of his life in the Yishuv).

With Marshall in Albany, on leave from Jewish politics, it devolved upon Cyrus Adler, the acting chairman of the Executive Committee of the AJC, to cross swords throughout the summer with Louis Brandeis on the "conference or congress" question. With Felix Frankfurter acting as secretary, the two men met at the Astor Hotel on July 12 and then published their contrasting views in the *American Hebrew*.[143] Adler faithfully rehashed Marshall's views that the congress posed dangers of "intemperate speech," that the committee was expressly organized to work on overseas rights issues, and that the committee, as presently constituted, represented "every shade of Jewish opinion without distinction." Countering forcefully, Brandeis maintained that the committee's plan for a conference was undemocratic. Stewards had no right to decide about the arrangements of a national conference. Brandeis declared, "Democracy demands that those representatives of the Jews of America who are to assemble in Conference to take action concerning the problems of the Jewish people shall have some voice in determining the conditions under which the Conference should convene." Also, the committee had no right to predetermine the agenda of conference topics. Continuing in a vein of scarcely concealed ridicule, Brandeis questioned organizational delegate proportions in the conference scheme. The committee proposed giving one organization that had 4,000 members two delegates, whereas it would give another 40,000-member organization just one delegate. Such accusations drew pungently from Progressive political idiom of the time,[144] associating Marshall's conference plan with the manipulative gerrymandering and delegate stacking of machine politics, and tacitly but unmistakably suggesting that its undemocratic character was un-American.

Thus started an incredible sequence in Marshall's fifteen years of stressful, labyrinthine negotiations with the Zionists: in the debate about the American Jewish Congress, his main adversary, American Zionist Louis Brandeis, publicly intimated that Marshall's methods and proposals were insufficiently American, whereas in the 1920s negotiations with Chaim Weizmann about the expanded Jewish Agency, the Zionists would accuse Marshall of being too American.[145] And during the war, the American Zionists accused Marshall's non-Zionist group of being manipulative or duplicitous, whereas Marshall and his non-Zionist allies castigated the world Zionists during the 1920s of the same sins of wily or corrupt politics.

During summer 1915, Marshall gladly allocated to Adler responsibility for sparring with Brandeis and his fellow Zionists, men who had "no practical ideas or common sense." Thanking Adler for stepping in, he noted, correctly, "I am quite sure that I could not have dealt with these men with the patience and self-restraint you manifested."[146] Still more revealingly, Marshall wrote an anguished letter from Albany in August to amiable Baltimore ophthalmologist Dr. Harry Friedenwald, who had held leadership positions in the Federation of American Zionists before Brandeis's arrival.[147] Vituperating about the "deplorable, ridiculous and inept" congress plan, Marshall wrote out of a miserable premonition that Brandeis and the Zionists were about to take control of American Jewish life. The letter reads as a rather self-righteous abdication proclamation, as a passing of the mantle of American Jewish leadership from one Louis to the other Louis.

> It is conceivable that my days of usefulness are at an end, that my vision is too circumscribed, and that practicability too largely guides my thoughts. I have never aspired to leadership, and therefore am surrendering nothing when I indicate my willingness that those who have other theories may be free so far as I am concerned to assume leadership.

Fascinatingly, while Brandeis attacked Marshall's conference plan in the name of progressive American democracy, Marshall attacked Brandeis's and the Zionists' congress initiative in the name of Judaism.[148] Here Marshall was marking the continental divide running between the life philosophies and politics of the two Jewish lawyers named Louis:

> All I can say is. . . . I should be unwilling to follow men who have no sympathy with Judaism and who are avowedly atheists or agnostics, nor can I believe that nationalism can take the place of religion, or of those principles and that spirit which through the darkness of the Middle Ages served to preserve all of Judaism which was most worthy of its preservation, its spiritual relation.[149]

In the end, not religious spirit but the president of the United States restored Marshall's mantle of American Jewish leadership. Wilson appointed Brandeis to the Supreme Court at the end of January 1916, a step that eventually quelled the American Zionists' insurgency on the Jewish congress issue. Any jealousy Marshall might have felt in response to his rival's unprecedented success was placed in perspective by events in the first half of 1916, a period ending with Florence's death. Marshall played no role in the Brandeis appointment because he belonged to the wrong political party; in the first days of 1916, when there was a vacancy on the bench, Marshall and Schiff contemplated appealing to Samuel Untermyer, a Democrat with links to Wilson, in hopes that he might clarify the administration's intents regarding the appointment, but this was idle discussion.[150] Marshall sent Brandeis a perfunctory congratulatory note after the appointment,[151] and within weeks, the two resumed bickering about the congress plan. As Marshall understood it, by mid-February 1916, the AJC and the Zionists had agreed that the congress would convene the moment the war ended, and Marshall consented to the selection of some delegates before the conflict's cessation, so that American Jewry would have delegates promptly in place for any postwar conference.[152] From the final days of 1915, however, a Jewish Congress Organization Committee, spearheaded partly by Poale Zion nationalists, had been gaining steam, preparing to hold an initial congress meeting despite Marshall's and the committee's objections. A month before his nomination to the Supreme Court, Brandeis chaired a Carnegie Hall meeting of this Jewish Congress Organization Committee and hectored Marshall and his colleagues, declaiming "practically all save one of the important national organizations have declared their approval of holding a Congress." Congress committees were active in seventy-two cities across the country, Brandeis noted. Marshall's minority would have to submit to the will of a democratic majority, explained Brandeis, adding that such compliance would be "in accordance with American methods.[153]

By mid-February, Marshall recognized that this Congress Organization Committee was ignoring his demand that the congress not be convened before the cessation of hostilities, and he complained to Brandeis about this breach.[154] When the Congress Organization Committee proceeded to invite delegates from around the country to what it called an "American Jewish Congress" in Philadelphia on March 27, 1916, Marshall naturally cried foul. The AJC, he wrote to the Congress Organization Committee's secretary Bernard Richards, had the unyielding position that the convening of a congress during wartime would be "unwise, impolitic and positively injurious." Turning around what was by now a familiar accusation, Marshall accused the Zionists of trying to "pack" the convention by inviting a disproportionately large number of delegates from small congress committees in cities around the country.[155] Schiff was more outspoken in his criticism of congress moves taken by the new Supreme Court nominee. Addressing participants at a Hebrew Immigrant Aid Society meeting, Schiff declared outright that the convening of a congress would foster anti-Semitism in America. "You will have committed the greatest sin against the Jew in America" if the congress meets, the powerful banker told this audience. "You will once and for all have put [the Jew] in a class by himself, no matter what your new-found, and I believe to a great extent selfish, leaders will tell you."[156]

Ironically, precisely at this moment when the Schiff-Marshall group berated Brandeis as a neophyte and selfish Jewish leader whose impetuousness might bring calamity to American Jewry, they were asked by American media for an opinion regarding the struggle over Brandeis's Supreme Court confirmation. Diplomatically, Marshall thanked journalists who insisted that the nominee's Jewish faith should have no bearing on the confirmation process.[157]

Up to the eve of the Philadelphia meeting, Marshall conferred testily with the congress leaders, wresting from Pinhas Rutenberg and David Pinsky assurances that the event would be described as a conference, not as a congress. Whatever its name, 357 delegates, representing an estimated 1 million Jews, convened in Philadelphia and decided to allow representatives to continue negotiating with the AJC through mid-May; the National Workmen's Committee (the left-labor amalgam) held an alternative conference the same day in New York City. In addition, the conference recommended that the formal congress, to be elected by American Jews via a system of "universal suffrage," meet sometime between September and December 1916, and work on an agenda of its own determination (the conference recommended items such as equal rights and national rights for overseas Jews, Jewish progress in Palestine, and Jewish immigration).

This Philadelphia meeting was a significant show of strength on the part of the congress movement, but its practical effect was questionable. The congress itself had yet to convene, and its backers now found themselves forced to negotiate for unity with a surreal opposition bloc formed by the Uptown bankers and lawyers in the AJC, and the socialists, Bundist nationalists, and laborers of the NWC. What could be more "comic," one congress advocate lamented, than an alliance between "socialists from Eastern Europe who had made 'national rights' their clarion call, and our *yahudim* who have always fought bitterly against the idea that the Jews are a people, with a culture?"[158]

From Marshall's point of view, the ideological maelstrom caused by the congress campaign had a depressing consequence. In the debates, his rivals had a platform upon which they assailed the committee's ten years of hard work and also ridiculed him personally. At the Philadelphia meeting, it was the turn of Rabbi Stephen Wise, a rising star in the congress movement, to take potshots at Marshall. Wise's words were harsh: "We reject no leadership, for we have had no leadership. Policies of inaction and aimlessness and timidity have presumed to erect themselves into leadership."[159]

6. Florence and the four children. Courtesy of Peter Schweitzer.

Florence's Death

As the value of Marshall's Jewish labors was publicly accosted, his private home life veered toward tragedy. Around the time of the Philadelphia conference, Marshall appears to have grasped that his forty-three-year-old wife Florence's condition was terminal. She had been confined to the home at 47 East 72nd Street in New York City since November. For the first weeks, her condition remained undiagnosed, despite the ministrations of several physicians; Louis understood only that his wife kept running a fever and coughing. At first, they discussed trying to leave the city, but Florence was not enthusiastic about traveling to a warmer area or even to Atlantic City.[160] Throughout the winter, on better days, she sat up for a few hours and occasionally took short automobile trips.[161] In the first few days of 1916, Marshall assumed that his wife's condition was amenable to "prompt recovery"; in this optimistic spirit, he consulted with his boyhood friend from Syracuse, Dr. Henry Elsner, about the prospects of remedying problems in Florence's "intestinal tract" and her "consecutive toxemia";[162] Marshall valued his friend's expertise and support, and he was unnerved by Elsner's death in mid-February.[163] From early spring onward, his beloved wife was incapacitated—Marshall described her as being "exceedingly weak and nervous" and glumly told close friends that Florence was making no progress.[164] In mid-May, his wife's condition deteriorated rapidly, and she passed away from cancer on May 27, at the age of forty-three.[165] Three weeks before, she had celebrated her twenty-first anniversary with Louis, who at the age of fifty-nine became a widower with four teenage children. The oldest, James, twenty, was completing studies at the Columbia School of Journalism; Ruth was seventeen and at the start of her studies at Barnard College; Robert (Bob) was fifteen and George twelve.

Florence had loved and admired her husband throughout their marriage. One recollection of their relationship must suffice. Later in his life, her eldest child James recalled his mother's devotion to Louis. "I can remember standing with her [Florence] at Knollwood," James recorded, "when the boat went out and took him [Louis] towards the station for New York, it didn't seem as though I existed. All she was doing was watching that boat with him departing, and he was equally devoted to her."[166]

A few weeks before her death, Florence composed a remarkable list of her parting wishes, asking for a "no fuss" funeral officiated by Magnes. She left her jewelry to her children, asking James in particular to be careful about her engagement ring, since it was her dearest item. To Louis went her Bible, "which contains no thoughts more beautiful than his, no actions more noble."[167]

The distraught widower tried to recover his energies in mid-June by working on declarations to be inserted in the 1916 Republican, Democratic, and Progressive parties' platforms that reaffirmed America's refusal to negotiate a new trade agreement with Russia in the absence of change in the czarist empire's policies on Jewish issues. His energies flagged, however. "I have not been well," he explained to Jacob Schiff, and he told other close friends that he was in "no condition to do business" and was thus spending little time in the office. Toward the end of the month, Marshall's physician ordered him to retreat to the Adirondacks with his children.[168] Knollwood proved to be too full of memories—Marshall spent days in late June writing mordant verse about "groves where now the pine-trees moan / we in reverent mood, clasped in each other's arms, and our eyes shone." His final poem expressed the simple hard fact of the final thirteen years of his private life: "Thou art gone, and I am left alone."[169]

By the standards of her time, Florence enjoyed privileges of education, having attended Normal (Hunter) College and, in the Reform Judaism framework, completing a confirmation process at Emanu-El in 1887.[170] Looking back on her own upbringing and the situation of young Jewish women in the period of her final years, she worried about the future; so Louis resolved after Florence's death to memorialize her by creating a fund to promote the religious education of Jewish women in New York. Marshall donated $150,000 of his funds for purposes he described in conservative terms: whereas in modern life women received in public schools "precisely the same" secular training as male counterparts, "Jewish mothers of tomorrow" were "devoid of that training of their emotions which will best qualify them to perform the sacred duties which are inevitably to devolve on them."[171] In the expression of his deepest passions, Marshall invariably looked to the past, in this case by associating the preservation of traditional Jewish roles with the memory of a woman he had truly loved. In itself, this orientation set him apart from the forward-looking secular nationalists and socialists of Downtown New York during this tumultuous period of American Jewish history.

It was, in fact, sad commentary on the acrimonious Uptown-Downtown rift in the community that the grieving Marshall's effort to preserve Florence's memory was maligned by partisans in the congress fight. One of the trustees designated by Marshall to administer the Florence Marshall Memorial Fund, Judge Irving Lehman, was touched by his friend's gesture and arranged for the publication of Marshall's impassioned explanation of the fund's rationale in the *New York Times*.[172] In the Midwest, one Jewish newspaper published gossip and innuendo suggesting that Marshall's donation was a bribe to the Jewish public motivated by his desire not to lose his position of communal leadership. This occurred just two and a half months after Florence's death.

Marshall's understandably outraged reply to this mean-spirited suggestion provides a rare window to the deep core of his personality and a clue to understanding the psychology of the last phase of his life, a period whose energetic authoritativeness in Jewish communal affairs has few ethnic equivalents in America. Adapting the adversarial orientation of his professional calling as a lawyer to Jewish affairs, Marshall's leadership style was necessarily embattled. His most valued client was Jewish honor. Nothing shook him more surely from his widower's grieving than the misrepresentation of his advocacy for that client:

> My mind was not at the time [of the establishment of the memorial fund] directed to the securing of leadership in American Jewish affairs. In fact, I was rather inclined to retire altogether, particularly in view of conditions which have made it possible for a man's most sacred feelings to be subject to cruel aspersions. . . . You [the Jewish newspaper editor] now characterize me as a political strategist, as a selfish person endowed with political cunning, who to save himself from being deposed, is prepared to sully the memory of her who was dearer to him than all else in the universe. You speak of my being deposed. Deposed from what? From working for the welfare of Judaism? Not all the enemies of Israel, within or without the Jewish fold, can accomplish that result. It is very clear that you do not know me.[173]

Marshall was back in the game by early August. The children remained at Knollwood, but Marshall announced to friends, "I do not feel justified in remaining away from New York City for more than three days at a time at the utmost." He was sleeping again and congratulated himself for not having reached for medication ("I should have felt rather discouraged with myself had it been necessary to resort to drugs," he confided to his cousin).[174] As though mindful of Florence's diplomatically phrased parting request from her ultradisciplined husband—"patience with the children," she noted in her testament[175]—Marshall noticeably relaxed his grip on his children in this period. From his office in New York City, he managed details of his children's late summer stay at Knollwood but only up to a certain point. The tone of his daily letters to his children lightened, and through an amiable style of indirect address, Marshall, a very proud man, was clearly inviting his children to take some share in the way chores and responsibilities were arranged.

As a widower, Marshall for the first time stopped treating his children as clients and started relating to them as junior partners. "Robert is working too hard," he wrote in one letter (August 3) to his children. "He is entitled to more relaxation. I really believe that he should have more than two hours a day for that purpose. All that I expect from him is to work two hours a day. In George's case, I shall be content if he works two hours a day. . . ."[176] He wrote to his seventeen-year-old daughter Ruth about how "it is not good to repress" natural feelings. His words to her focused uncharacteristically on the importance of emotion: "I have noticed for some time that there is a general notion which is becoming prevalent, that to give evidence of grief and sorrow is an indication of weakness. But that is not so."[177]

In the summer of the family's bereavement, a polio epidemic broke out in New York City. It provided a timely reason to keep the children, particularly the younger boys Bob and George, at Knollwood, well into the fall. Nothing could keep that pair still in the Adirondacks, and Marshall knew it. As discussed in greater detail in chapter 9, the boys' hikes and Adirondack activities became local legends—Adirondack rangers would take bets on how long it would take for the boys to bob up and down the hills, and the boys' eventual climbing of all forty-six Adirondack peaks over a height of 4,000 feet inspired later generations of hikers, who call themselves "46ers," often in knowing homage to the Marshall boys' feat (for Bob Marshall, this climbing would be just one item on the outdoors résumé of a quirky yet utterly sympathetic figure of great renown in the American environmental movement). In summer 1916, these outdoor activities were therapeutic, and it was a measure of Marshall's fatherly wisdom that he pled with the two, in a knowingly ineffectual vein, to show some minimal restraint.

"I also expect that you will not swim or go to the lake on Yom Kippur, or engage in sports, but that you will faithfully read the prayer book," Marshall instructed his two youngest sons (the father added a thought that must have left his sons wondering: "as you know I always enjoy Yom Kippur better than any other day in the year").[178]

Marshall was deeply proud of his children's forbearance. "Robert and George would be perfectly willing to become permanent residents of the Adirondack forest," he told his younger sister Ida, adding, "I have never known any children who are so easily contented and whose demands are so few."[179] James had taken up the study of law. In fact, Marshall's oldest child, who was destined to carve an active and successful career of his own in law, was in this period struggling to find his way, and James appears to have been the most direct beneficiary of his father's lightened touch after Florence's death. At the end of 1916, the Marshall child who was cut most closely out of his father's cloth composed a coming-of-age letter, declaring "pop I am in a terribly hard situation."[180] He explained to his father that they had "been reared in different atmospheres" and that he lacked a "moping nature." In fact, James recalled, his tendency to see "the hopeful side of things" had given his mother much comfort during her last months. Getting to the point, he shared with his father his difficulty with observing the traditional year of mourning. "I can see no reason for maintaining a year of exile from those harmless pleasures one has been accustomed to enjoy," wrote James, hoping for his father's blessing. He confided his misgivings about following in his father's professional footsteps. People were saying of his legal aspirations that he had an "easy berth." James exclaimed: "I dislike being known and treated as Louis Marshall's son. I want to be known as James Marshall."

Lovingly, Louis responded to his son's poignant letter by affirming "we must all of us shape our own lives, develop our own individualities, and do our own thinking."[181] He was not the sort of man to chase ambition away from his children, and even in this period when his children most needed his unqualified support, Marshall could not quite find a way to release his children fully from the burden of his own capacious stamina and drive. "It is my daily prayer that my children may be better and rise to nobler heights than I . . . that the standard, such as it is, that I have set, may only serve to influence you, by not falling below it," Louis wrote to his oldest child. These were typically taxing sentences, but James must have sensed that his father understood something when he wrote, "I am glad to have you say that you do not wish to be known as Louis Marshall's son." Most unexpectedly, without putting up any real fight at all, Marshall approved James's request to truncate the mourning for his mother. The one-year mourning period, Louis wrote, is a custom, not a religious precept. "If it really is of sufficient importance to you to go to the opera, or to the theater or to dances before these [next] four months have elapsed, your decision must govern."

Marshall was, in years ahead, to negotiate or dictate the terms of conclusion to the worst anti-Semitic assault that American Jewry ever endured, along with the terms of minority rights for Jews in Eastern Europe, of the enlargement of the Jewish Agency for Palestine, and of civil rights struggles waged by African Americans in the NAACP. Had she lived to see these accomplishments, Florence would have been proud but not necessarily surprised. More certainly, nothing would have meant more to her than to watch the understanding terms her strict, authoritarian husband learned to provide to their children.

Marshall's Ascendance and Resolution of the Congress Controversy

In public debate, Marshall's leadership status was assailed during this tumultuous period of the Jewish congress campaign, and yet his professional expertise and the longevity of his labors on communal issues of primary importance protected his position. The arguments about the congress were not mere performance theater; they expressed vitally important dynamics of immigrant empowerment and compelled Marshall's group to think more realistically about power sharing. And as much as Marshall and his associates groused about Brandeis and his American Zionist associates as pretentious and power-grabbing neophytes, Brandeis, by virtue of his inspiring persona, taught American Jews to think about local and global Jewish concerns not through a narrow prism of zero-sum game Americanization in the melting pot but rather in pluralistic terms of America *and* Zionism, terms that continue to fascinate and intrigue scholars and students in the multicultural twenty-first century. Easily lost in the thicket of egoistic power struggle highlighted by the American Jewish congress debate, we might forget both that standards espoused by the Brandeis Zionists, such as organizational efficiency, were not mere rhetoric but reflected substantive developments in patterns and structures of American Jewish life, and also that Brandeis's own access to the Democratic Wilson administration afforded key advantages in the diplomatic struggle leading up to Britain's promulgation of the Balfour Declaration.[182] All this is true, but it remains a fact that despite the contentious rivalries, or perhaps because of them, Louis Marshall was in this period surging toward a towering position of communal authority, which has suffered considerable neglect in historical research.[183] Heading toward the Jazz Age era renowned for rollicking prosperity, the foundation of his leadership was plain hard work. By the World

7. Magnes as Marshall's puppet. In this June 1916 caricature, American Jewish Committee president Louis Marshall has Kehillah president Judah Magnes recite: "The Kehillah cannot bother itself with the Jewish Congress." Copyright © 1981 Cambridge University Press. Reprinted with the permission of Cambridge University Press.

War I era, key stakeholders in American Jewish life understood the value of Marshall's accumulated experience relating to the community's central challenges. Marshall had become indispensable.

A striking illustration of Marshall's hard-won position arose during a wartime round of the ongoing debate about restrictive immigration schemes, provoked in this case by literacy test proposals in the Burnett Bill. In mid-April 1916, Professor Richard Gottheil, the first president of the Federation of American Zionists, wrote to Marshall out of evident alarm about the way professional associates were insinuating that a mysterious "Jewish lobby" had manipulatively and dubiously arranged for exemptions to literacy test restrictions on Jewish immigrants based on their knowledge of Hebrew and Yiddish. Featuring dozens of daily dictated letters, even in the period of his wife's final days, Marshall's correspondence is so voluminous and intricately detailed that is easy to overlook simple evidence attesting to how extraordinarily authoritative he had become in American Jewish life. Here was the endowed Professor of Semitic Languages and Rabbinical Literature at Columbia University and director of the Oriental Department at the New York Public Library asking a business lawyer why Hebrew and Yiddish could be counted as legitimate languages sufficient to prove the literacy of Jews seeking entry to the United States.[184]

Marshall, of course, dispatched a prompt, persuasive reply. The Burnett Bill, he explained, is the third restrictive measure contemplated by Congress since its reception of the report submitted by the Dillingham Commission, appointed in 1907.[185] After investing hundreds of thousands of dollars, the commission resorted to literacy tests as its sole proposal to restrict the influx of immigrants. Not a "Jewish lobby," Marshall wrote, somewhat disingenuously, but members of congressional committees endorsed Hebrew and Yiddish knowledge as exemptions to the literacy test standard on the unimpeachably logical theory that Jews of Russia and Romania were debarred from attending public schools and thus from learning Russian and Romanian, and their reading and writing skills were therefore limited to Hebrew and Yiddish. If the ability to read thirty or forty words in English "is an indication of intellectual power, and converts an objectionable immigrant into a desirable one," Marshall explained, "then obviously the ability to read the sacred Hebrew language, or Yiddish . . . which is a living tongue and has a fine literature of its own, should be considered as a compliance with that magic test." To authenticate that Yiddish was not a mere "dialect," Marshall referred to the works of Isaac Peretz and also to Leo Wiener's *History of Yiddish Literature in the Nineteenth Century.* He used the same arguments in a letter to the editor of *Harper's Weekly,* who had published criticisms of "political Jews" who lobbied for Hebrew and Yiddish knowledge as an exemption to the literacy test standard. Jews who have fought the literacy test based their contentions on American ideals, insisted Marshall.[186]

The day before Florence's death, Marshall remained active in the fine-tuning of Jewish objections to measures devised by the restrictionists. He wrote to Vermont senator William Dillingham to register his dissent from a clause that would bar entry to persons convicted of offenses in their home countries. The experience of 1848 immigrants from Germany taught that noble persons in periods of historical stress deserved asylum in the United States. More than any prior period, World War I is a time when "it is important to afford a refuge to those who may be regarded in their own lands as traitors, but who are in reality merely the prophets of a better tomorrow."[187] Such a line of argumentation implies much about the lasting power of Marshall's strength as an American Jewish leader. On issues of overwhelming concern to the same radical Jewish leaders who hectored Marshall in the congress debate, he was, in fact, a trustee; his method of reasoning was in line with the sensibilities of Downtown Jewry.

During the period of Marshall's family tragedy, the tide turned in the congress debate, largely due to a decision reached by Jacob Schiff. Worried that his elite could be irreversibly losing traction, Schiff wrote to Marshall in mid-March 1916, asking him to arrange a "very positive and very prompt" AJC response on the congress issue. Downtown, Schiff observed, was worshipping fervently to the golden calf of the congress. It was up to Marshall to forestall a situation wherein the Jewish masses of New York would say, "'This man Moses is dead, these are your Gods, O Israel!,' substituting the American Jewish Committee for Moses, and the proposed congress for 'these are your Gods.'"[188] Marshall mechanically heeded Schiff's request in this, and other matters. During his weeks of private emotional turmoil, Marshall acted more as consigliere than as boss.

In mid-May he contacted Max Goldfarb and arranged an alliance with the left-workers amalgam, the National Workmen's Committee, which had also boycotted the Philadelphia conference. The AJC, Marshall informed Goldfarb, was organizing a conference to consider measures to secure civil and political rights for overseas Jews, including national rights wherever separate group rights were recognized.[189] Symbolizing a union between the masses and the classes against the Zionists, the NWC-AJC alliance electrified Jewish New York. Some leftists howled that the NWC had sold its soul to the Yahudim ("To hob-nob with the great men of the AJC is easier, more pleasant, more acceptable than to devote oneself to such banal subjects as simple Jewish workers," lamented one disillusioned Bundist[190]).

Marshall, for his part, struck an exalted biblical chord as he invited other organization heads to take part in this July conference. "Behold how good and how pleasant it is for brethren to dwell together in unity," he wrote, quoting Psalm 133.[191]

The NWC-AJC alliance produced the climax of the congress controversy at a July 16 conference held at the Astor Hotel, involving delegates from the national Jewish organizations that had boycotted the Philadelphia meeting. The moment, however, was transformative not for Marshall but rather for his brother-in-law. Judah Magnes was an inveterate nonconformist who, in the name of religious and ideological principles, had in the past abandoned the pulpit at Emanu-El and would in the near future sacrifice his position with the New York Kehillah, but his ordeal at the Astor meeting stands out in his iconoclastic career, primarily because it stemmed more evidently from his personal loyalty to Marshall than from any ideological dogma. The moment featured a confrontation between Magnes and Louis Brandeis, who had come to the Astor at the head of a small delegation from the congress organization.

Magnes proposed that the organizations represented at the Astor unite on the basis of parity with Brandeis's Congress Organization Committee. Formalistic in his response, Brandeis, newly confirmed as a Supreme Court justice, replied that his organization was committed by the decisions of the Philadelphia conference in March, meaning that just a few delegates could join the congress from this AJC-NWC led coalition. Magnes bristled at this suggestion that the Zionists were entitled to dictate terms of cooperation to the detriment of delegates from more experienced and better-established national Jewish organizations. In Jewish spheres, Magnes was saying, Marshall and his AJC colleagues could not be treated as junior partners to a Supreme Court justice and his Zionist cohorts. "No, Mr. Brandeis, no Jewish organization at this time can say of representatives of old, established and important institutions of this country, 'you will do as we have laid it down that you shall do, or you cannot cooperate with us,'"[192] exclaimed Magnes.

In this "contest of wills," observed the historian Jonathan Frankel, Magnes basically prevailed, since the Astor conference selected an ideologically diverse executive committee, composed of (among others) Marshall, Goldfarb, Oscar Straus, David Philipson, and Magnes, as a counterweight to offset Zionist domination of the congress movement.[193] Participants at the Astor meeting endorsed the convening of an American Jewish Congress to consider "suitable measures to secure full rights for Jews in all lands," including group rights. Most significantly, Marshall finally relented about the time frame, and the Astor conference did not stipulate that the congress could only be held after an armistice. Though the Astor meeting was conducted in camera, the *New York Times* subsequently editorialized negatively about Brandeis, questioning the propriety of a Supreme

Court justice becoming involved in such a highly contentious and partisan communal matter. Since his nomination at the start of the year, Brandeis had been steadily removing himself from the public spotlight. As would typify his behavior for the next five years, culminating with his dramatic retreat from Zionist affairs during a clash with Chaim Weizmann, Brandeis responded to the insulting *New York Times* editorial as though it were the final straw and an appropriate cause to resign from leadership of the congress movement. In Brandeis's view, the editorial's point was not necessarily incorrect, but it was impolitic and stemmed (as he explained in his confidential letter of resignation as head of the Congress Organization Committee) from Magnes's "malevolent" and "premeditated" actions.

This was a telling moment in the comparison between the "two lawyers named Louis." In contrast to Louis Marshall, Louis Brandeis, after his Zionist conversion, tended to treat Jewish affairs as one case among many, and in a tenable, but strained, fashion, Brandeis found cause to drop his Jewish file whenever he felt that he had lost his leverage, and his efficacy as a Jewish affairs advocate had come to an end. More specifically, his withdrawal as leader of the congress campaign tipped the balance decisively in Marshall's favor. On their own, Brandeis's deputies—Julian Mack, Stephen Wise, and Louis Lipsky—had no choice but to accept a compromise about the congress on terms to be dictated by Marshall.[194]

Acting not out of "malevolent" purpose but rather out of semideferential respect for his brother-in-law's Jewish leadership, Magnes had served Marshall well. The Zionists berated Magnes bitterly as an apostate whose betrayal cost them their most precious asset, the leadership of a Supreme Court justice. Magnes had sacrificed much, out of loyalty. With many others, Judge Mack was alarmed by the anti-Magnes anger in the congress camp, and he induced Marshall to write a conciliatory letter to Brandeis.[195] "When feeling runs high, men too often forget themselves," Marshall wrote to the other Louis, and even added a few lines about his insomnia and new responsibilities toward his children. He also reminded Brandeis that for two years "I have been lampooned and even charged with being a Russian emissary." Since Jewish welfare around the globe was at stake, Marshall asked Brandeis "to consider as unsaid words that should never have been uttered."[196] Before he left for Europe to investigate the disbursement of Jewish relief funds, Magnes also offered apologies to Brandeis.[197]

These, however, were ineffectual gestures. There was little Marshall could do to bridge gaps in priorities and values that surfaced during these congress clashes with Brandeis, even though relations between the two mellowed somewhat after the war.[198] The relationship dynamic between the two brothers-in-law was no less dramatic and significantly more fluid. About a year later, when he protected Magnes from fallout caused by the Kehillah leader's unpopular pacifist stance after America's entry into the war, Marshall would return the favor of personal loyalty.

In an outcome that would have appeared highly improbable just a few months earlier, Marshall now had control of the congress movement. The convening of this much-anticipated forum would occur on his terms. Marshall told Judge Mack in early August that there could be no reliance on tacit understandings or "gentleman's agreements." Were the congress to convene and the Zionists to "present a plan which would be nationalistic in its operation," Marshall would need clearly delineated criteria by which to rule it out of order.[199] Fissures were no longer a likely prospect. In the first days of August, the two main bodies, the Executive Committee for an American Jewish Congress and the Executive Committee of the Conference of National Jewish Organizations, had reached an accord. "There is now every reason to believe that we have succeeded in bringing about peace among the warring factions of American Israel," a confident and relieved Marshall informed B'nai B'rith's Adolf Kraus.[200]

If truth be told, the main reason for the peace in Jewish America was that Marshall had now negotiated a compromise that was essentially similar to the proposal rejected by the AJC in November 1915.[201] The accord circumscribed the scope of the congress's deliberations by prohibiting it from considering resolutions about a "general theory or principle of Jewish life" whose adoption would necessitate the congress's perpetuation. The congress's agenda would be exclusively limited to the topics of civil, religious, and political rights of overseas Jews; of separate group rights in lands where group rights were recognized; and of Jewish rights in Palestine. The accord stipulated that some congress members would be selected via "democratic and universal suffrage," whereas others would be selected by various Jewish national organizations; the proportion of directly elected delegates, as compared to organization representatives, was to be set by future deliberations of an executive committee, whose size was adjustable. The congress was to be held before the cessation of the war.[202]

Immigration Politics in Wartime

Marshall immersed himself in work "in order to forget myself," as he explained to the English Jewish writer Israel Zangwill.[203] "Every day seems an age," he confessed in private correspondence. Months crawled by—at the end of 1916, he observed that the passing of six months since Florence's death felt more like six years. "My only relief is in working as hard as possible, both in the office and in communal affairs," he explained.[204] The presidential elections in autumn 1916 helped focus his attention. Marshall disliked Wilson and thought that the

Democratic president's socioeconomic proposals, such as an eight-hour labor law initiative, stemmed from political self-interest, not social idealism. "My sympathies are with the man who has to work for a living," Marshall insisted, but he branded as "dishonest" Wilsonian liberalism on labor issues. "I would rather walk all the way from Knollwood to New York City than to have placed upon our statute books the infamous eight hour law which the President and his co-partisans have concocted for political purposes," he affirmed.[205] In correspondence with the chairman of the Republican National Committee, Marshall sounded confident about the electoral chances of the GOP candidate, Charles Evans Hughes. About 80 percent of Theodore Roosevelt's Bull Moose followers were returning to the Republican Party, he estimated, meaning that Hughes would win "unless some unexpected contingency arises."[206]

Marshall gnashed his teeth at the way Uptown peers who were Democrats tried to reap dividends of the Brandeis Supreme Court appointment among Jewish voters. When Henry Morgenthau circulated an appeal to Jewish voters suggesting that they owed a special debt of gratitude to the White House incumbent because of his "brilliant appointments," Marshall grumpily objected to this "insult to the intelligence of voters."[207] When the Jewish population of the United States was one-tenth its current level, he wrote in petulant partisanship to one Yiddish newspaper editor, "Republican Presidents appointed Jews to high office."[208] Other associates, such as the journalist Herman Bernstein, tried to rally support for the Democratic candidate in the Yiddish press by arguing that the White House had provided constructive support to the Joint Distribution Committee's overseas relief campaign. Countering, Marshall argued that there was nothing exceptional in this support—"whatever has been done by the administration to assist in relieving Jews in belligerent lands has been in strict accord with the long established policy of our government.[209]

The Republican Marshall had his reasons for supporting Hughes. Marshall applauded the Republican candidate's economic proposals, including support for a protective tariff. Putting aside the uncomfortable fact that Hughes had won a spot on the bench that Marshall himself had coveted, Marshall had been impressed by Hughes's work on the Supreme Court; among other things, Hughes, along with Oliver Wendell Holmes, backed his position in the Leo Frank appeal about mob law interference with due process. Most importantly, Marshall expected that a Hughes White House would stave off the Nativists' campaign for a restrictive immigration bill. When he was governor of New York (it will be recalled), Hughes appointed Marshall to serve in 1908–9 as chairman of the state's Immigration Commission. During the autumn 1916 campaign, Marshall implored GOP heads to advise Hughes to campaign forthrightly for open immigration, even at the risk of alienating labor organizations. The GOP candidate ought to speak with "his accustomed vigor" about immigration, Marshall told the party chairman. "I know that he [Hughes] is the son of an immigrant. I know that he has great sympathy with immigrants."[210]

In the end, Marshall's candidate lost by a razor-thin margin. President Wilson, who lost in his own home state of New Jersey, carried California by a few thousand votes and clinched victory late in the night, after his rival Hughes had gone to sleep thinking he had won the election. Marshall bristled with anger about "damn fools" in the party who had, he believed, misadvised Hughes about when and how to campaign on the West Coast.[211] At any event, this 1916 result did little to frustrate Marshall's concerns and purposes. In the wartime months ahead, he steadily backed Wilson's retreat from neutrality, and in the Armistice period, Marshall grasped, somewhat belatedly, that his herculean labors for Jewish minority rights overseas had to be hitched to Wilson's League of Nations plan rather than to his own party's isolationist orientation.[212] As to immigration, it is doubtful whether Hughes or anyone else in the White House could have done anything during the war other than temporarily derail the increasingly adamant restrictionist movement. Anti-immigrant nativism mounted forcefully in this period; after the war, the US Congress would legislate at its command, much to the detriment of Jewish interests.

A portent of things to come could be seen on the Senate floor shortly after the November elections. Congress was once again at work on a restrictive literacy test, and some delegates were wondering aloud whether special considerations and exemptions had been offered unduly to the Jews. One elderly Republican senator from New Hampshire, Jacob Harold Gallinger, a practitioner of homeopathic medicine, complained that the "Russian Jew is given a preference" in the proposed immigration bill. "Is he [the Russian Jew] an especially desirable citizen?" asked Gallinger, leaving little room for doubt about how he would answer his own question. Gallinger went on the record with this pronouncement: "The Russian Jew does not send his children to the public schools in greater proportion than the colored man does when he is given the opportunity to do so."[213] Gallinger had been active in attempts to improve public schooling in the District of Columbia, but his words sounded more like anti-Semitism than a challenge to American racism.[214] His slurs against Russian Jews were contested strongly in Congress by Senator James Reed, a Democrat from Missouri; "The Russian Jew who has come to this country has been industrious, frugal, and law-abiding."[215]

Marshall applauded Reed's efforts and constantly sent him, and other legislators, facts and figures that could be of use in debates with Nativists. "In the city of New York," Marshall wrote to Reed, "85% of the students at City College are

Jews, most of them of Russian birth or descent."[216] These were standard defense arguments. Because restrictionists couched their proposals implicitly or explicitly on racist suppositions, Marshall and his legislative comrades sometimes had to fashion counter-race arguments, either ascribing innately positive traits to the Jewish "race" or arguing about virtues of Jewish whiteness relative to blacks in America.[217] In the Senate, Reed declaimed how "the Russian Jew comes from a race and a blood that has been civilized for thousands of years. He springs from a race that gave us our religion, and the fundamentals of every one of our laws."[218] Consulting with Reed, Marshall indulged normative comparisons contrasting Jewish whiteness to black natives of Africa. To some extent, his comments reinforce a hypothesis proposed by some scholars that a conscious drive to whiteness, to differentiate Jewish circumstances from those of African Americans, was a leitmotif of twentieth-century Jewish politics.[219] Although this "whiteness" hypothesis has been overworked—Marshall, like other articulate figures in American Jewish politics, had cause to differentiate his vision of American Jewish life from the circumstances and purposes of many groups in the world, including Jewish groups—his comment to Senator Reed warrants citation. Coming from a figure who in a dozen years would win recognition, with Moorfield Storey, as the country's foremost advocate for the NAACP, the following quotation reflects the hobbling pressures exerted on ethnic politics in this wartime era by racist Nativists:

> The difficulty with Senator Gallinger is that he does not understand the Jew, whether he is Russian or otherwise. He regards him as an inferior being. He places him on the same footing as the native of Africa. He forgets what the world has owed to the Jew in the past, and what the Jew is seeking to do in the present.[220]

Geography, rather than the issue of whiteness, was where Marshall waged wartime's immigration battles. Nativists were in this period experimenting with the idea of pinpointing lines of latitude and longitude on the world map to preclude the immigration of various Asian and European groups. In the Senate, Charles Smith of South Carolina explained frankly that geographical coordinates were basically euphemisms adopted because "we do not want to make any invidious comparisons, so we do not refer to any nation."[221] This forced Marshall to quibble with congressmen about whether lines of exclusion were to be drawn on the 110th meridian of longitude east from Greenwich, or anywhere else.[222]

In the last days of American neutrality, long-standing strains of anti-immigrant Nativist sentiment were mobilizing in Washington, and Marshall sensed the danger that the country could "depart from its traditional policy of the open door." "This is a critical period in our national life," he explained to his most influential allies in the fight against the restrictionists. One was Adolph Ochs of the *New York Times,* who published, at Marshall's urging, forceful indictments of restrictive immigration proposals, including the literacy test.[223]

Coming a quarter century before the *New York Times* "buried" reports about the Holocaust in its back pages, owing to the insecure ethnic psychology of its Jewish publishers (one strongly argued study claims[224]), this substantive cooperation between Marshall and Ochs on immigration issues warrants reflection. Not even a tenuous relationship can be proven between the Nazi murder in the later era that buried 6 million Jewish people and the news-reporting policy of any American newspaper. In contrast, Marshall's astute use of his connections with important American media outlets and Ochs's compliance made an irrefutable contribution toward the perpetuation of America's forthcoming immigration policies until the 1920s, policies that reduced the number of Hitler's potential victims by several hundred thousand. When it most counted, America's Jewish community positively utilized its access to important media outlets with an assertive practicality unusual, and perhaps unprecedented, in the country's ethnic history. Marshall's group had an undeniably complicated psychology on many Jewish matters, but it is not clear why the positioning of that psychology in the causal nexus of the Holocaust elucidates historical understanding. When it came to immigration—the matter of most pertinence to Jewish survival in the pre-Holocaust era—Jewish interests were by no means buried in the *New York Times.*

Not limited to the ongoing effort to narrow the portal of immigrant entry at Ellis Island, Nativist pressure in this period meandered into an array of realms, including bids to keep foreigners as far as possible from state government. In spring 1917, the New York State Assembly considered legislation to deny the vote to persons who could not read or write English. Marshall wrote to Assembly Speaker Thaddeus Sweet to clarify that he did not oppose literacy tests for voters, but he objected to the insistence that English fluency be the sole accepted standard of literacy. He was advocating on behalf of "thousands of intelligent men in this State who had no opportunity to learn to read and write English, and who are now too old to learn, and who read each day a newspaper printed in some other language." Marshall attested to being a frequent reader of Yiddish, German, French, and Italian newspapers, and to their laudably public spirited, patriotic contents.[225]

Uptown Responses to the Balfour Declaration and the Russian Revolutions

In the waning months of American neutrality, Marshall sought to set limits on the pro-Allied drift of public debate and politics. With Schiff, he worried that

American businessmen were pressuring Congress and the White House to renegotiate a trade treaty with the Russians in the absence of any change in the czarist empire's treatment of Jews. He complained to Adolph Ochs that "column after column of the *Times* has been devoted to articles distinctly pro-Russian in tone and fact." Everything in the czarist empire was, he declared prophetically, "ripe for revolution," and so it was simply folly for "our great financiers" to exhibit such "love for autocracy."[226]

As the war progressed, lines of communication to Eastern Europe unraveled. Exasperated by the Congress showdown with Brandeis, Magnes traveled to the region to monitor the disbursement of Joint relief funds. Marshall and Beatrice communicated tensely about the lack of information about Magnes's whereabouts—Marshall knew only that the Russians had not allowed Magnes into their country due to his past public denunciations of czarist oppression.[227] Magnes's journey featured characteristic flair and drama—he fell in Vilna, broke three bones in his foot, and recuperated in a Polish nobleman's castle—but little practical insight about how to proceed in Russia. Rather aimlessly, Marshall met with Russian officials who scoured New York financial circles, hoping to find resources for a failing war effort. He assured them that good things would come to Russia were the czarist government to rescind its anti-Jewish policies, but he was not, at this stage, holding out the offer of a loan as a reward for a promise of policy change in Russia.[228]

American Jewish Congress maneuvering ceased to engage much of Marshall's energies in the final months of 1916. Only one Jewish group—the Poale Zion nationalists—evinced dissatisfaction with the summer's Astor compromise agreement, apparently due to the realization that it had lost all influence on the issue.[229] American Zionists such as Lipsky now controlled the nationalist flank of the congress movement; the Poale Zion group had forceful and talented members, most notably David Ben-Gurion (who served as secretary of its Jewish Congress League), but they were mostly mobilizing for a return to the Yishuv in the months ahead by various means, including enlistment in the British army's Jewish Legion. In the meantime, Marshall placidly informed Schiff that there was no danger posed by Downtown worship of the false gods of the congress. "We have solved all the difficulties," he told the banker, outlining the details of the Astor agreement.[230] In successive meetings in November and December, a Jewish Congress Executive Committee (with 140 participants) was chosen to arrange and authorize procedures for elections to the congress, and its long-awaited convening.[231] Marshall endured a minor snub in this congress phase when the Zionist Nathan Straus was selected as permanent chairman of the executive,[232] but this slight had little practical meaning. By the end of 1916, the key issues in contention between the Zionists and the committee were settled; various disputes flared in subsequent weeks, mainly between left-wing Downtown groups, but by March 1917, as revolution engulfed Russia, many of these late contestants in the congress struggle realized that there was nothing left to fight about. For many Jewish socialists, revolution in Russia rendered the congress obsolete, since they had lobbied for a congress to protest the czarist government's treatment of Russian Jews.[233] At long last, congress elections were held over the weekend of June 9–10, 1917. The fact that the congress had become such a protracted and contentious issue did not dampen enthusiasm in these elections: the large voter turnout, about 335,000 (including 125,000 voters in New York City),[234] bears witness impressively to the congress's magnetic pull upon American Jews in a period identified by one historian as the high point of seminational secular culture in American Jewish history.[235]

In the middle of World War I, Marshall's group believed that its work on nonpolitical projects in the Yishuv had been wasted. It pulled away from Palestine affairs exactly at the time Brandeis and his followers mobilized deftly to secure President Wilson's support for developments in Britain that would lead in November 1917 to the Balfour Declaration in support of a Jewish national home in Palestine. Before spring 1917, Justice Brandeis and President Wilson had conferred about general Zionist matters, but in late April, Brandeis received a cable from James de Rothschild requesting an American Zionist effort to win President Wilson's support for policies directed toward creating a Jewish Palestine within a British protectorate. Two weeks later, Justice Brandeis had an encouraging forty-five-minute meeting with the president; Wilson said he was entirely sympathetic to the Zionist movement and thought favorably of the formula of a legally secured homeland for the Jewish people in Palestine. From this point, the American Zionists played an important supporting role in the formation of policy leading to the British Mandate and to the Balfour formula of a Jewish national home.[236]

Marshall's non-Zionist group, in contrast, was greatly unnerved by the abandonment of Aaronsohn's agricultural experimental station at Atlit by the end of 1916. Atlit is "moribund," Marshall learned, and he lamented that his group had been entranced by the charismatic Aaronsohn and persuaded to back wild wheat research and other experiments in unstable Ottoman Palestine. "If we had only acted in accordance with our judgment instead of sentimentality, our work would have been done in California, and we would undoubtedly have something to show at this time," Marshall lamented to Adler in a series of letters in early 1917.[237] News at this time of Atlit's abandonment was the first in a series of disappointments for the non-Zionists regarding Atlit and Aaronsohn. When they eventually learned that the energetic agronomist had organized the Nili covert spy operation with the British, some of Marshall's colleagues, most importantly Sears Roebuck titan Julius Rosenwald, reportedly concluded that philanthropic work in Palestine could never be disentangled from potentially compromising political activity.[238]

Thus stretched in this early 1917 period a visible gap in the attitudes and orientations of American non-Zionists and American Zionists. The former group's disheartening involvement with a scientific project merely exacerbated its long-standing concerns about loyalty problems and political entanglements, whereas members of the latter group were partners in an exciting secret diplomatic initiative that ushered in a new period in the history of Eretz Israel, one promising tremendous opportunity to the Jewish people. It would take Marshall twelve long years to establish that this gap between the Zionists and non-Zionists could be bridged.

In the final stage of American neutrality, there was also a fissure within the country's "German" Jewish elite.[239] Once America entered the war, pro-German figures like Schiff had to recalibrate their orientations in line with their country's war policy and their own American patriotism. Before that shift, Jewish newspaper correspondents questioned Marshall closely, wondering whether Uptown remained unified about the war. Marshall insisted in public that it had. He berated one journalist who speculated about Schiff's involvement in political disagreements about several issues, including Zionism. "Mr. Schiff's relations and mine are warm," Marshall declared, denying that there were disagreements.[240]

With Schiff, Marshall prosecuted American Jewry's claims against czarist Russia until the empire's very last day. Days before the February Revolution toppled Nicholas II, Marshall demanded that all organs and branches of the American government heed the letter and spirit of the Russian treaty abrogation. A circular issued by the US Civil Service Commission on February 20, 1917, caught his eye because it aimed at the recruitment of clerks who knew the Russian language "and who are under no disability as to visiting the Russian empire." The advertisement debarred American Jews from applying to the commission, and Marshall demanded that this "obnoxious clause" be promptly eliminated from the circular.[241] Until the czarist empire took its last breath, Marshall and his colleagues labored to uphold the AJC's most famous achievement, the abrogation of the Russian treaty in 1912, and to forestall the corruption of American constitutional principle by Russian anti-Semitism.

The two American Jewish stewards exploded with joy and relief when news of the czar's demise reached America. "I am filled with gratitude to the Almighty for this wonderful manifestation of His power in driving the Romanoffs from the throne and destroying Russian autocracy," Marshall exclaimed to Schiff, viewing the revolution as vindication of the banker's oft-stated contention that the Russian Jewish question would be solved in Russia. Events in Russia in February–March 1917 were, the two concurred, the most important historic developments since the French Revolution.

Schiff and Marshall immediately pondered how their group might contribute to the fashioning of a liberal constitutional democracy in Russia that would respect Jewish rights. They contemplated sending a supportive cable to Pavel Milyukov, head of the Constitutional Democratic (Kadet) Party; more importantly, they contemplated negotiating a substantial loan with any orderly democratic government that might take shape in Russia. In his exuberance, Marshall judged it appropriate to reformulate phrases in the Passover holiday Haggadah to commemorate the Jewish people's liberation from the Romanov pharaoh. Marshall proposed the following Haggadah insertion: "Thou hast made Thy light to penetrate into the dark recesses where the stiff-necked Pharaoh of the North laid heavy burdens upon us."[242]

Shrewdly, Marshall anticipated one possible complication arising from Russia's February Revolution. Possibly, Nativists in the congress would now challenge "religious persecution" exemptions from restrictive measures,[243] thereby negating formulas carefully negotiated by Marshall, Max Kohler, and others in years of Capitol Hill lobbying. In spring 1917, however, that seemed like a setback worth enduring, were Jewish emancipation really to arise in Russia.

The news from Russia thrilled New York Jews. Salvation was twofold. The immigrant Jews were now spared the prospect of being called to arms on the side of a czarist regime they despised, and rights and liberties were expected to come to Russia's own Jews. For weeks, Downtown and Uptown Jews competed in the fashioning of ingenious demonstrations of support for Russia's revolution. The journalist Herman Bernstein proposed sending to Moscow a replica of the Statue of Liberty. Marshall found that a bit gauche, and he politely pointed out to Bernstein that this symbol would scar the Russian skyline were the Romanovs, "or some equally evil dynasty," to launch a successful counterrevolution.[244] Instead of a statue, the American Jewish Relief Committee came up with a plan to send a complete hospital unit as a "gift to the new Russia from the Jews of America." Schiff was willing to donate $100,000 for this project. Marshall explained to Secretary of State Lansing that the unit would be composed of thirty physicians and forty-five nurses, most of them Jews who were of Russian birth or descent. He added that his eldest son James, who was at the time almost twenty-one and a law student at Columbia, wanted to serve in the unit as assistant director.[245]

The Russian Jewish hospital unit sounded like a good idea, and Marshall promoted it with characteristic energy and persistence, but it never left port. In consultation with the Red Cross in late April, Marshall was discouraged by a daunting list of technical problems and unanticipated costs,[246] and then, unaccountably, two months passed by without anyone in Kerensky's Provisional Government indicating interest in the offer.[247] Finally, on the eve of the Bolshevik ascent to power in Russia, Schiff finally withdrew his offer of $100,000 for the hospital unit. "Unfortunately," Marshall noted wanly, "the unsettled conditions in Russia have made it impossible to organize this unit."[248] This was a wartime preview of the difficulties American Jewry would soon face in efforts to translate its hopes for democratic freedom for the Jews of Eastern Europe into substantive new realities on the ground.

As America fatefully jettisoned its neutrality policy and formally entered the war in early April 1917, Marshall's immediate concern was to establish that neither in Eastern Europe nor on the East Side of New York were Russian Jews a fractious element liable to damage a united Allied effort against German autocracy. As he explained to Schiff, Marshall combed all his contacts among Jewish leftists Downtown to wrest from the Bundists a statement that their party was not seeking a separate peace between Russia and Germany. Through Ochs, he force-fed this statement onto the pages of the *New York Times.* "I have taken considerable interest in this subject because I understand that the government in Washington is concerned with this phase of Russian conditions," he explained to the newspaper's cooperative publisher.

Magnes's Pacifism and the Family Politics of War

This exhibition of Russian Jewish support for the Allied war effort was just one of countless displays to come. In fact, more than at any other phase of his career, Marshall's energies would be concentrated for the next eighteen months on one particular issue, the public demonstration that Jews were fully behind the Allied military effort. This resolve was buoyed by developments in world politics, even as it was challenged by twists and bumps in Marshall's own family circle.

Happily, from Marshall's point of view, the czar's abdication stifled the momentum of the congress movement. The scenario that had terrified Marshall for months—radical delegates of a Jewish parliament, elected democratically as though the congress were a state within a state, issuing pro-German or pacifist proclamations at sharp variance with the orientations of American public sentiment or official government policy—vanished. Marshall could scarcely contain his glee when he forecasted to Cyrus Adler, a yet more adamant critic of the congress idea, that the American Jewish Congress would now be a pitiably futile thing.[249] This was overstating the case, since the staging of an election in America among some 335,000 Jews remains an interesting display of the communal and politicized character of Jewish life in this period. (Almost a century later, trying to designate this event remains a puzzle: what exactly was the American Jewish Congress election, a "national," or an "ethnic," event, or something else?) Insofar as his prediction applied to the political passions of Downtown Jewish radicals, it was apposite, since the Jewish socialists saw little need after February 1917 to convene for the purpose of discussing ways to pressure Russian autocracy for the conferral of rights to Jews and others.[250]

Unhappily, for Marshall, he proved unable in his own family to govern displays of American patriotism exactly the way he wanted. Discussing this aspect of Marshall's wartime labors, historians have naturally focused on the brothers-in-law, Marshall and Magnes, and the various perplexities and complications arising from the latter's iconoclastic decision to act as a pacifist after America's entry into the war. Yet this issue of family discipline and public patriotism is multidimensional; lamentably, it has been reduced to an interesting, but extreme and misleading, hypothesis ventured by one scholar, who, impressed by the tensions engendered by Judah Magnes's idealistically maverick personality, speculated that as soon as they could after the war, Marshall and assimilated Uptown associates exported Magnes to Palestine and to a symbolically inspiring, but far-off, position at the head of the new Hebrew University of Jerusalem.[251] This hypothesis lacks empirical support; the evidence shows that Magnes wandered away from the United States in the early 1920s without any firm idea of what he and his family would do in the decade,[252] and for months after Magnes and family set up a home in Jerusalem, Marshall communicated warmly and supportively with his brother-in-law, largely in the hope that Magnes might return to New York.[253] More significantly, the negative speculations misleadingly narrow the scale of the dilemmas and challenges Marshall faced in his own life and home, as he assembled his case in support of American Jewish patriotism during World War I.

President Wilson presented his case for war against Germany to a joint session of Congress on April 2, 1917, and war was formally declared four days later. Marshall's patriotic passions surged powerfully in that period, but the same could not be said about others in his house. He was a little perturbed by his children's apathy. "James has been a pronounced pacifist," he confessed to his Syracuse cousin Benny Stolz. His eldest child had said nothing about Wilson's war speech. "It is rather curious that my children do not exhibit my fighting blood," stated Marshall, at the onset of a complicated eighteen-month dynamic that featured James's own shifting feelings, Magnes's gadfly patriotism, and Marshall's contradictory position as a protective widower father and as a communal advocate beholden to the feverish patriotism of the moment.

James enlisted as a registrar in the Mount Sinai Hospital Unit. The unit[254] was established as the brainchild of the hospital's president, George Blumenthal, a financier and philanthropist who had contacts with Marshall, sometimes pertaining to American politics.[255] The unit was originally organized under Red Cross auspices, but it was federalized in spring 1917; twenty-four medical officers, sixty-five nurses, five civilian employees, and one hundred fifty-three enlisted men made up its membership. In early February 1918, the unit sailed for France, via Halifax and Liverpool; at Vauclaire, it transformed a Carthusian monastery into a hospital. In autumn 1918, the hospital was overfilled with 2,800 sick and wounded.

Whether it was facilitated by his father's connections, James's mobilization in the unit was somewhat protracted. In early summer 1917, he and his father petitioned New York police officers for a pistol so that James could practice shooting before being called up to active service;[256] by late autumn, he was finally in uniform for Hospital Unit No. 3 and drilling daily;[257] after the dangerous eighteen-day sea journey, in February 1918, Marshall worked as assistant registrar in the unit, with the rank of second lieutenant.[258]

In this sequence, James fulfilled his patriotic obligations as an enlisted soldier in an overseas unit, but he also never reached the western front. His father, who (as we shall see) became in public an unyielding enforcer of American patriotic duty during World War I, was clearly relieved that his son was positioned in an honorable and also relatively safe post. Louis, in fact, took steps in public to protect his son's eligibility for service in the noncombat medical unit.

In early summer 1917, the period when James awaited a summons to train with the Mount Sinai unit, a cloud of doubt passed over the arrangement. There were sudden indications that the government would not allow Americans to serve on Red Cross hospital bases overseas if they came from families that had German ancestry. To be sure, it was not clear whether this directive would have applied to James's Mount Sinai unit or to James himself (the ambiguously formulated Red Cross hospital policy could be construed as applying only to naturalized citizens from Germany or to American-born soldiers whose parents had been born in Germany, neither category applicable to James). Nevertheless, Marshall campaigned aggressively for repeal of the Red Cross policy largely out of concern that it would stigmatize or preclude his own son's participation in the army hospital unit.

Ironically, in opposition to the Red Cross policy, he joined forces with former president Theodore Roosevelt, whose brand of Bull Moose trust-busting politics had, for years, alienated his conservative inclinations. In late June 1917, Colonel Roosevelt published in the *New York Times* a letter condemning the government's policy of stopping naturalized American citizens and native-born Americans from families with German roots from serving at Red Cross hospitals overseas. Marshall followed up with a piece of his own, which the newspaper's editorial board (overriding Ochs's inclination to publish Marshall's piece as an editorial) printed as another letter.[259] Marshall strongly attacked the government's plan to allow ethnic selectivity in the dispatch of soldiers to overseas medical facilities. The planned government policy, Marshall wrote in the *New York Times,* would encourage "one section of our citizens to regard another with suspicion, contumely and hostility at a time when every citizen should be made to feel that one brotherhood unites him and his fellow Americans in striving for a common purpose." Marshall wondered whether such ethnic exclusion reflected a hysterical wartime retreat from the "fundamental principles of Americanism. "Have we lost all sense of humor?" he wondered in the *New York Times.* As he explained to former president Theodore Roosevelt, he signed the piece "A Native American" because he "did not wish to have this question distorted into a Jewish question."[260]

Marshall's query, "have we lost all sense of humor?" rebounded awkwardly and autobiographically in a period of untold personal and communal stress. Two weeks after America's war declaration, Marshall was acutely worried by indications of indifference or dissent among Downtown Jews. On the East Side, some Jewish socialists espoused the theory that conscription violated the Thirteenth Amendment's proscription of involuntary servitude. For Marshall, that creative interpretation was not a laughing matter. Similarly frightened by the implications of a perceived lack of wartime patriotism among Downtown Jews, Marshall's former law partner Samuel Untermyer was organizing a Jewish League of American Patriots for the purpose of persuading Downtown Jews about the imperative to defend American institutions. Marshall had originally opposed this initiative, because it appeared to favor the segregation of Jews or the treatment of them as some sort of special case,[261] but soon after the end of neutrality, he recognized that drastic steps might be necessary to inspire patriotism among the immigrant Jews on the East Side. He reported to Schiff in late April that he had over the past fortnight made a series of inquiries about Jewish responses to the war declaration. "I find that there is a strong undercurrent of indifference," he nervously informed the banker. Quite nonhumorously, Marshall added, "I am prepared to do all that lies in my power to awaken the spirit of American patriotism among our coreligionists."[262]

Marshall meant it. When he referred to "all that lies in my power," he meant summoning the letters and spirit of the US Constitution to instill the fear of death in the hearts and minds of nonacculturated immigrant Jews from Eastern Europe in the crowded city neighborhoods of New York.

Marshall played many roles during World War I, some of them familiar in scholarly research. As Lucy Dawidowicz observed, he functioned for a period as a censor of Jewish radicalism inimical to America's war policies,[263] and as highlighted in Jonathan Frankel's survey,[264] Marshall served as a regulator and container of nationalist ferment in the immigrant community, modifying the aims and even the nomenclature of the congress movement. However, at the height of the crisis caused by the lack of Americanized acculturation among Downtown Jews in a period of patriotic mobilization, Marshall took on the most draconian role of all, as a would-be executioner of recalcitrant brethren, in the enactment of constitutional requirements. Marshall was an extraordinarily generous advocate and patron of Jewish well-being in America and overseas, and so his threatening posture at this juncture cannot, of course, be taken in literal terms, but this moment in his career warrants notice, because it points to an ultimate limit in the optimistic emancipation style of nonnationalist Jewish leadership that evolved between the French Revolution and the Holocaust.

That 150-year spectrum of leadership included moments of severe communal crisis caused by military conscription issues. Toward the end of this continuum of pre-Holocaust Jewish politics, World War I stands out uniquely as a context in which Jewish leaderships in stable democracies, where basic rights and opportunities had mostly, or entirely, been secured, judged that they had to resort to outright coercion to protect vital communal interests.

In England, where wartime stress and suffering was far more severe, the situation faced by Jewish communal leaders was tensely polarized as they latched onto, or opposed, plans to deport immigrant Jewish tailors ("schneiders") in London or elsewhere who shirked conscription (and Zionists like Vladimir Jabotinsky sought to muster them into the ranks of the new Jewish Legion for Palestine).[265] Marshall was aware of circumstances in Jewish neighborhoods in London, and he resisted appeals to oppose British plans to deport the schneiders back to Russia. In America, Jewish stewards never had to deal with government orientations or policies in favor of coercively selective treatment of unpatriotic immigrant Jews. Still, in summer 1917, Marshall and other Uptown Jews (most noticeably, Oscar Straus) used the language of coercion to enforce American patriotism among Downtown Jews who were thinking about the war in terms other than blindly heeding conscription call-ups.

This was an urgent moment in relations between the Uptown classes and the Downtown masses. In a communal standoff, an acculturated group of prosperous American Jews told a non-Americanized group of immigrant Jews that though the newcomers might possibly pay a terrible price for playing by the rules of their new land, they would definitely pay a taxing penalty for disobeying the country's laws. For the Jewish immigrant, if Marshall's words were to be taken seriously, their coercive message was, effectively, this: be a patriot and risk death in the fight against the Germans, or be a radical and risk a comparable result required by the enforcement of the Constitution.

On June 2, 1917, speaking at a Jewish patriotic rally held at the Educational Alliance, Marshall grabbed headlines by declaring that any person who urges a young man not to register for the draft three days later, as required by law, or who advises the young man that the conscription is unconstitutional is guilty of treason and could be executed.[266] Marshall ridiculed the Downtown dissenters who argued that conscription was an unconstitutional violation of the Thirteenth Amendment, saying sarcastically that these immigrants had not read the Constitution and would not understand it if they did. Any person who advises or pursues draft evasion, Marshall continued, deserves an Iron Cross from the kaiser and treasonably aids the enemy. Any man who listens to such draft evasion advice should know that "Uncle Sam has a pretty long arm" and that that arm will make conscription violators pay with their life for treason. "The United States, which opened its arms to all the oppressed persons of the world, to my father and to you and your fathers, will not call on you in vain in this, the hour of her greatest peril."

Marshall supplemented this dire threat of treason execution by citing the story of Asser Levy, the Jew who settled in New Amsterdam in 1655 and insisted on doing his duty by standing guard for the city, defying the suspicious Peter Stuyvesant. It will be recalled that for Marshall the Asser Levy example served as a kind of American Maccabean myth, a symbol of the interaction between political emancipation, communal responsibility, and patriotic duty in New World democracy. He dipped deep into American Jewish history to use this example only at moments of severe identity stress or of communal emergency, and America's entry in the global war was one such time.

Marshall attributed to this archetypal New Amsterdam Jew, Asser Levy, traits he himself cherished, as a fighter for Jewish rights who appreciated the spirit and rules of American democracy. In fact, all the symbols in this feverish address were personal and familial. Essentially, Marshall was projecting his dispute with his pacifist brother-in-law Judah Magnes upon their community as a whole. As a true patriotic American, Marshall's roots went back, at least in his mythologized identification with the Asser Levy story, to the rock bottom of Jewish settlement in the New York of Peter Stuyvesant. Magnes's pacifism, in contrast, was so un-American as to be utterly ignorant of the fundamental precepts of the Constitution and punishable, as treason, by death. Magnes's behavior was the precipitant of this jingoistic Educational Alliance address, but Marshall kept this fact, and his personal concern, secret.

Honorably, Marshall never publicly ostracized his radical brother-in-law, whose pacifist stance during World War I entirely reversed the logic and intents of everything he had done since August 1914. On the contrary, acting out of personal affection, familial loyalty, gratitude for Magnes's recent assistance in the congress debates, and, on some level, respect for his brother-in-law's ideological courage, Marshall protected Magnes and salvaged whatever could be kept of Magnes's professional and communal reputation. Nevertheless, more than an outright threat to Downtown radicals, his Educational Alliance speech was a kind of symbolic purge, or even indirect execution, of his troublesome brother-in-law.

Marshall made this intention explicit in a letter he wrote to Jacob Schiff the day before his Educational Alliance address. Arguing "from the fullness of his omniscience," his Reform rabbi brother-in-law had the presumption to argue that the conscription act is unconstitutional, Marshall sarcastically wrote. "The Yiddish press seems to have adopted Dr. Magnes' line of reasoning," he worried.[267] He was acting out of anger over his brother-in-law's betrayal and out of his practical assessment of Magnes's proven talent for galvanizing emotion among the Jewish immigrants in New York City, an aptitude that had been in abundant display a decade before, during the mass Downtown protests over the Russian pogroms. For Marshall, the issue of Jewish departure from the norms of World War I patriotism centered on Magnes and then became psychologically collectivized.

The day before his Educational Alliance address, Marshall told his brother-in-law exactly what he thought of his participation at pacifist meetings following America's entry in the war:

> I consider that any assemblages such as those in which you have participated go almost to the very verge of sedition and treason. I am speaking with a full realization of what my words mean. You are placing yourself and your family in peril. You are associating with men who are considered, whether rightly or wrongly, as emissaries and representatives of Germany, with men who are discredited and have long been discredited in the eyes of the people. . . . The [pacifist] movement is one which is apt to bestir weak-minded men into hostile demonstrations against the Government. It may occasion riot and the loss of life, and if that should occur those who are at the head of the movement will be held responsible for the consequences by public opinion, which is seldom wrong in matters of this kind.[268]

Continuing, Marshall turned to Magnes as the head of the New York Kehillah and as a leader in Jewish education initiatives. He asserted that Magnes had no right to voice his highly unpopular personal views in a way that knowingly brought injury to great and worthy Jewish causes. "Do you believe that the American people will not attribute to the Jews generally adhesion to a policy which runs counter to that of our government, when you, who are regarded as a leader in Jewry, are at the same time acting as the presiding officer at meetings at which doctrines are avowed which are generally regarded as treasonable?" he asked Magnes. Moments after writing this blistering letter to his brother-in-law, Marshall composed a short note to Magnes's wife Beatrice, his late wife's sister, pleading for her help. "I am trying to keep your husband in check, but I fear I cannot do it without your assistance," he implored.[269]

In August 1917, President Wilson confirmed Marshall's appointment as a member of the New York City District Board of Appeals on the issue of military exemptions. He served with Charles Evans Hughes and Edgar Montgomery Cullen, a Civil War veteran who in the decade before the war had served as chief judge of the New York Court of Appeals. Marshall regarded his appointment as a patriotic duty and as a useful demonstration of Jewish compliance with wartime exigencies. It was also a daunting task—when Marshall took his gavel, an estimated 70 percent of New York City residents who had been deemed physically fit had filed for exemptions, and, in its first round, the committee had accepted close to 30,000 cases for consideration.[270] As a result of his new position and his own complicated relationship with Judah Magnes, during the last weeks of the summer, Marshall followed a peculiar routine of enforcing the country's draft laws in New York City during arduously long workdays and of defending his brother-in-law's public dissent from those laws by night.

Columbia University Semitics scholar Richard Gottheil was one of many prominent communal figures who evinced alarm about Magnes's pacifist actions. Marshall dispatched one letter after another to Gottheil, explaining half-apologetically that his brother-in-law "is a man of very strong views, and not easily influenced." He rebuffed Gottheil's suggestion that he or the AJC issue a public denunciation of Magnes. "I am always ready to fight heretical views, but I do not fight individuals who harbor those ideas," Marshall rationalized. "It would not be wise or prudent for any Jew to attack Magnes," he reiterated in another letter. "That would make a mountain out of a molehill." There was no point in turning Magnes into a martyr to be championed by the Yiddish press, "which looks for sensations."[271] The work on the district board was taxing, but deflecting criticism of Magnes wore Marshall out by the middle of August. "I must have a heart to heart talk with Dr. Magnes," he confided to his children. "I am getting very much alarmed by a growing spirit of hostility which is becoming generally manifested toward him."[272]

In addition to personal loyalty to Magnes, Marshall operated in this period out of dire concern about community welfare. He worried every minute of the day about the implications of displays of lack of patriotism by Magnes, in the Yiddish press, and elsewhere in the Jewish community. At times, these fears overwhelmed him. On one of those rare instances since the Adirondack camp's establishment in 1900, Marshall failed to find Knollwood emotionally restorative. He complained there through July of intercostal rheumatism, of aspirin overdose, of indigestion, and of insomnia.[273] Returning to New York City was helpful, but he remained disturbed; as this wartime chapter in his life wore on, his constant complaining about Downtown was purged of rhetoric and ego, and governed increasingly by fear. In Jewish affairs, Marshall felt unsafe. "I am in a position to know that only a miracle will prevent an anti-Semitic outburst in this country," he wrote to one confidant, showing how rapidly and feverishly his ideas on this issue had developed since the start of the war. The threat was "due to the attitude of the East Side toward the conscription law, the treasonable articles that appear in the Yiddish press, the feeling that many Jews are pro-German, and especially the harmful propaganda of Dr. Magnes."[274]

As summer weeks passed by, the family psychology in this drama subsided, but the acute worries remained. As far as Marshall's Jewish defense efforts were concerned, Magnes ceased to be the enemy of his own people; instead, two other threats from within the Jewish world needed to be defused.

Censoring the *Jewish Daily Forward*

After years of grumbling about the Yiddish press, and his own ill-fated experiment in Yiddish newspaper publishing, Marshall in autumn 1917 assumed the highly unusual role of semiofficial guardian of the socialist *Jewish Daily Forward*. Though the historian Lucy Dawidowicz, writing under the tutelage of the AJC, glossed ongoing dynamics and overstated the case when she concluded that Marshall's monitoring of the *Forward* helped American Jews "transcend class and political differences," and "introduced a measure of harmony in the old feud between Russian Jews and German Jews," she rightly identified Marshall's action, motivated solely out of concern for Jewish well-being, as a "magnificent gesture."[275]

Arguably, this wartime cooperation featured the most representative Uptown German and Downtown Russian Jews of the generation, Louis Marshall and Abraham Cahan, and it bridged significantly different ideological orientations.

After a brief five-year stint with left-Progressive English-language newspapers, Cahan, a Lithuanian-born socialist who immigrated to the United States in flight from the pogroms in Russia in the early 1880s, returned to the helm of the Yiddish-language *Forward* in 1902. Under the leadership of its capable editor, the newspaper had a circulation of 130,000 by the end of World War I, far larger than that of any other Yiddish daily in America and also greater than any other socialist newspaper in the world.[276] Formally, after America's entry in the war, the *Forward* was bound by antiwar resolutions adopted on April 7, 1917, at the American Socialist Party's St. Louis convention—declaring "unalterable opposition" to the war, the party judged it to be the result of "predatory capitalism." Yet the *Forward*'s attitude toward the war had not been consistent since 1914; before the February Revolution in Russia, its news coverage was overtly pro-German, but by spring 1917, Cahan and others seemed enthusiastic about joining forces with the new Russian regime and tilted the paper in a pro-Allied direction, while paying lip service to the St. Louis resolution. Socialist doctrinaires sensed that Jewish communal concerns and Americanization orientations governed shifts in the *Forward*'s politics. Leon Trotsky wrote a few pieces for the *Forward* when he was in the United States but severed his connection with the paper in a huff, branding Cahan an enemy of the Socialist Party (SP) and later fuming in his memoirs about the Yiddish newspaper's "sentimentally philistine socialism."[277]

Exercising its authority under the June 15, 1917, Espionage Act, the US Post Office took steps over the summer and fall to investigate over one hundred media organs for possible subversion and excluded several well-known journals (*American Socialist, Masses*) from the mails. Concurrently, under the Trading with the Enemy Act, foreign-language papers were required to file with the post office translations of all news items, editorials, and articles. On October 5, 1917, officials from the US Post Office notified the *Forward* by registered mail that it had to show cause for why its mail privileges should not be revoked. Acting on advice from the *Forward*'s legal counsel, Alexander Kahn, Cahan turned to Marshall for support. After Cahan briefed him about the facts of the case, at an October 8 meeting held in his office, Marshall assessed the post office's approach as a constitutional infringement. "This is a crime against American freedom," he declared.

"As you know," Marshall told Cahan, "politically and in every other way my views are most divergent from those for which your newspaper has stood."[278] However, he explained, "I am loath to believe that you would consciously act in hostility to our government or advocate doctrines which lead to disloyalty." Thus began a symbolically potent moment of Uptown-Downtown cooperation, as well as a pattern whereby Marshall staunchly protected the constitutional rights of

Jewish and non-Jewish socialists that outlasted the war and produced notably courageous stands by Marshall in the postwar period of the Red Scare.

To be sure, Marshall and Cahan worked out an arrangement that implicitly reinforced hierarchies between the two Jewish subgroups. Marshall asked Cahan to produce a written disavowal of intentions to publish anything that might "encourage disobedience or may be in defiance of the government of the United States." The editor promptly supplied a document (which Marshall apparently edited) that promised 100 percent patriotic compliance with the laws of the United States; he outlined damages that would result from the withdrawal of its second-class mailing privileges to Yiddish readers in the United States. Marshall promised to bring this document to authorities in Washington, stressing in the written record of this meeting with Cahan that he would not accept a retainer for his services and that he was acting entirely out of "loyalty to the Jewish people, whose good name is sacred to me."[279] Within days, Marshall conferred with Postmaster General A. S. Burleson; he was flanked by Julius Rosenwald, who voluntarily served during the war as head of the National Defense Council's Committee on Supplies. Expecting that Burleson and his staff might be intransigent about the *Forward,* Marshall was planning to recruit the American Federation of Labor's powerful president Samuel Gompers for continued lobbying on the *Forward*'s behalf;[280] Socialist John Spargo, who had dissented from the party's St. Louis resolutions and whose patriotic credentials were therefore untarnished, was Marshall's conduit to organized labor during the war, and (as we shall see) this connection proved valuable in the confrontation with anti-Semitism after the Armistice.

As it turned out, Burleson was not swayed by Cahan's written pledge, but he agreed to defer the withdrawal of the *Forward*'s mailing privileges after Louis Marshall promised to serve as a "private censor" and regularly monitor the newspaper's content to guarantee that it was not contrary to the country's wartime interests. This procedure enabled the *Forward* to continue without interruption, although like other foreign-language papers, its editorials and news articles were headed by an English announcement saying that they had been translated and submitted to the postmaster.

The 1917 New York City Mayoral Race

Just days after these arrangements were made for the retention of the *Forward*'s mail privileges, Marshall faced a problem he considered still more threatening to Jewish interests in America. As in his battle with Magnes's pacifism, this was another publicly explosive ideological contest with an idealistic Jewish leader layered over obvious affinities in the background and daily pursuits of Marshall and his antagonist, this time the Jewish Socialist Morris Hillquit.

Before his famous candidacy in New York City's mayoral race in 1917, Hillquit had been involved in an effort identical to Marshall's advocacy for Abraham Cahan and the *Forward*. He applied his lawyerly skills and credentials in efforts to stave off the closure of papers like the *American Socialist*, the *Call*, and the *Milwaukee Leader* by Postmaster General Burleson under the Espionage Act. A socialist with a prominent international reputation, Hillquit was a partly Americanized character (the ambiguity of his situation is reflected by his technical situation; it was widely believed that he ended up in the New York mayoral race because the most natural political option available to him, nomination as the Socialist Party of America's candidate for president of the United States, was precluded because of his foreign birth in Riga). Like Marshall, he was genuinely distressed by the repressively un-American character of the post office's closure policies, and so he represented the threatened socialist media organs as a constitutional matter of civil liberties.[281] Not entirely unlike Marshall's, Hillquit's personal background combined economic success and hardship. His modern-oriented father had owned a prospering factory but lost it in 1884, and brought his family two years later to New York City, where the seventeen-year-old Morris met years of poverty on the East Side. Though he proposed socialist remedies to Downtown suffering, Hillquit's no-nonsense outlook toward East Side life bore resemblance to Marshall's—from their differing standpoints, both men associated success with the ascent out of the Jewish ghetto. Hillquit literally left fellow Jewish socialists gasping for air when he shunned all *Yiddishkeit* in his unromantic and unsparing critiques of Downtown life:

> In no other part of the United States are the social conditions of the inhabitants so pitiable. . . . Our [East Side] district covers a territory of barely one square mile, and it contains a population of over 200,000. It is a cold, cheerless existence that these people lead. The [East Side] is the Home of the Tenements, Pushcarts, Paupers and Consumption.[282]

More inclined to view current circumstances through the prism of socialist ideology than through the lenses of Jewish cultural affection, Hillquit could never be regarded in New York political circles as a fully Jewish candidate, and the extent of his purely ethnic pull among Downtown Jewish voters remains open to question.[283] Marshall, for his part, was a loyal Republican and upholder of conservative principles, but he typically viewed American and world politics in terms of Jewish interests, even as he paradoxically denied the existence of Jewish politics. Hillquit's approach was more eclectic and deliberately unidentifiable when it came to Jewish matters. "I am a Jew, a Socialist, a Russian, an American, a lawyer, a lecturer," Hillquit declared in the year of his election campaign. "As a lawyer I have one sort of interest, as a Jew another, as a Socialist another. As you see, it is not so easy, either for you or me to explain the way one should act."[284]

Hillquit's socialism dated from his teenage days in a Russian-language gymnasium (secondary school) in Riga, and by World War I he had acquired a colorful leftist track record in the United States, having been instrumental in the founding of the Socialist Party of America early in the century, having run unsuccessfully for the US Congress, and having become embroiled in practical and ideological disputes with non-Socialist Progressive reformers and, still more dramatically, with William "Big Bill" Haywood and the International Workers of the World (IWW) over the question of syndicalism.[285] It is difficult to determine whether Hillquit's successful career in America as a lawyer was an asset or liability during his rise as a socialist politician; at any rate, Hillquit passed the New York bar in the period when Marshall began to practice in the city, and by 1897 he had with his brother Jacob established a reputable firm, Hillquit and Hillquit (at 320 Broadway), that was, his biographer reports, "indistinguishable from any nonsocialist's practice."[286]

In the context of his complicated career, Hillquit's opposition to World War I stands out for its consistency and clarity. From its start, he condemned the war on principled socialist terms; his September 6, 1914, article, "The Socialist View of the War and Why They Failed to Stop It," regarded as one of the first published Marxist critiques of World War I, declared emphatically, "the murderous war in Europe is but the inevitable culmination of murderous European capitalism."[287] At the SP's St. Louis convention in April 1917, held immediately after America's entry in the war, Hillquit outmuscled everyone, "out-doing himself," in the words of Theodore Draper.[288] Hillquit berated the viability of a "middle course," and his lobbying and spirit were responsible for the radicalism of the SP's resolutions, which rejected the war as the violent phantom of predatory capitalists and pledged "unyielding opposition" to all American policies of military and industrial mobilization, as well as "vigorous resistance" to all restrictions of freedoms of speech, press, and assembly.[289] Hillquit was from this moment a leading opponent of America's war effort, and to strengthen his pacifist stance, he modified his long-standing reservations about nonsocialist Progressives, joining forces with them (and with Judah Magnes) in the formation of the antiwar People's Council for Democracy and Peace.[290] Clearly, from Marshall's ultrapatriotic point of view, Hillquit's bid in the New York mayoralty race was an issue to be addressed.

That Marshall did. In late October 1917, he circulated an open letter to all the Jewish dailies of New York, predicting apocalypse were Hillquit to make a strong showing in the mayoral race.[291] "A vote by any Jew for Hillquit at the coming election would not only imperil the condition of the Jews throughout the world, but would for generations to come subject civilizations to the incubus of militarism," his letter concluded, in a thunderstorm. In Marshall's view, America was fighting a war for democracy, whereas Hillquit was running for mayor of New York City to do the opposite: "Every vote for Hillquit means a vote for the Kaiser and for the restoration of the Czar to power."

Marshall publicly baited Hillquit as a bourgeois who, for all intents and purposes, was on the payroll of the kaiser. The unfair, ad hominem character of these attacks should be viewed in terms of Marshall's own acute sensitivity about being upbraided in public as a public lawyer who lacked principles and whose work on public issues boiled down to his desire for retainer. Nothing enraged Marshall more than the sully of such injudicious accusations about his own activity, as witnessed by the blistering self-defense in his private letter to Arthur Brisbane, who accused him publicly of having crafted the proposed New York State Constitution in 1915 to protect corporate interests,[292] and his emphatic denials in this period that he was acting as a guardian to the socialist *Forward* because of a retainer. Now Marshall was stooping to the same level, something just short of character assassination, in his excoriation of Morris Hillquit in the Yiddish press: "If this corporation lawyer, who calls himself a Socialist, has actually received a retainer from the Kaiser to help his cause, he could not have earned his money more effectively."

As far as Marshall was concerned, revelations in the past months, such as the Zimmermann Telegram, proved irrefutably that German autocracy was a direct threat to palpable American interests. Hillquit's pacifism was thus "insanely" self-defeating: "No man of intelligence could have studied the disclosures of the past years without appreciating that for more than a decade Germany has been preparing . . . to embroil the US and to destroy the Monroe Doctrine, which for nearly a century has enabled us to prosper," Marshall yelled in his open letter. Had America neglected its recent "opportunity" to "remove the poisonous fangs of the monstrous German military machine," it soon "would have been forced, alone and without preparation, to face that enemy of mankind in bitter and relentless warfare."

This was, in short, a message to Jewish voters that if they supported Hillquit's bid for City Hall, they were casting ballots to destroy America. He asked Henry Morgenthau and Oscar Straus to write similar letters.[293] He also instructed the editors of the Yiddish papers to publish the letter in a way that clearly emphasized how his opposition was not to Hillquit's socialism but rather to his pro-German pacifism; all the editors complied, splashing the letter over three columns. Only Cahan was spared the burden of publishing Marshall's bellicosely formulated appeal; Marshall explained to Judge Mack, who had helped in the arrangement of the *Forward*'s monitoring, that he did not want Cahan to feel he was being unfairly leveraged.[294]

Not willing to be intimidated by the dark prophesies about what his campaign's success would mean, Hillquit refused throughout the election to respond to Marshall's public opposition to him.[295] On the stump, he boldly challenged America's Wilsonian policies, insisting that warfare had little to do with democracy. "Not warfare and terrorism, but Socialism and social justice will make the world safe for democracy," Hillquit exclaimed at a Madison Square Garden rally on September 23.[296]

Hillquit's appeal was not limited to pacifists. His candidacy struck a chord among working-class New Yorkers, Jews, and non-Jews, whose daily worries fixed upon rising wartime prices of consumer necessities, which were reflected in the city's food riots of February and March. The Hillquit Non-Partisan League unfurled banners that read "Hillquit and Five Cents Bread." Since Hillquit fought for domestic causes of immediate concern to Downtown Jews, a left-wing Yiddish paper could, theoretically, throw its support to the Socialist candidate while downplaying his pacifist politics. That might have been the thinking at the *Forward* when it explicitly and proactively supported Hillquit, precisely at the moment when Cahan was enlisting Marshall's services to persuade the US government that his newspaper would absolutely refrain from obstructing the war effort. In late September, the *Forward* launched a $50,000 fund-raising drive to finance Hillquit's campaign, and on October 17, Hillquit spoke, with Magnes, at the *Forward* hall.[297]

Abraham Cahan had an obvious interest in soft-pedaling the pacifist ideology embedded within Hillquit's campaign, but prominent local and national commentators and media outlets were not hesitant to characterize Hillquit's candidacy as an unpatriotic Jewish phenomenon. As the November 6 election approached, with Hillquit putting up a fight against the incumbent Independent, John Purroy Mitchel (who was cast as a reformer), Tammany Hall Democrat John Hylan, and Republican William Bennett, outright anti-Semitic depictions of the Socialist Hillquit as an un-American Jewish leftist gained some prominence, as though to confirm, at least in some measure, Marshall's forebodings. Some of the innuendo was minatory but anonymous in reference. Thus, after Hillquit's fiery Madison Square Garden denial that warfare could make the world safe for democracy, *Leslie's Weekly* wondered whether the spectacle of 12,000 socialists waving red flags and hissing at America's war policy justified Elihu Root's judgment that there were traitors walking the streets and working in newspaper editorial offices who ought to be marched straight to the firing squad. Elsewhere, the media was more blunt about depicting Hillquit's mayoral bid as a symbol of how the Jews were bad for America. One cartoon in the *New York World* showed Hillquit telling a group of repulsive-looking Jews, "We will make of America just what we have made of Russia"; the *New York Herald* showed a hook-nosed politician named "Hillkowitz" or "Hillquitter" waving a "peace at any price" flag at the satisfied kaiser. One well-known author advised Mayor Mitchel to use the two Ks, Kike and Kaiser, as a negative campaign slogan; the German is anxious to save his kin, the Jew to save his skin, quipped Charles Noel Douglas to the incumbent.[298]

Marshall was not alone in worrying about the ill effects of Hillquit's candidacy. On the Tammany side, Samuel Untermyer campaigned for Hylan and reiterated his former law partner's concerns. A Hillquit victory would be a "catastrophe for the Jewish race," announced Untermyer to 2,500 people at a League of American Jewish Patriots rally in the Bronx.[299] Similarly galvanized by the negative, anti-Jewish publicity that was trailing Hillquit's race, a group of nonradical East Side leaders (Joseph Barondess, Herman Bernstein, Bernard Richards), publicly aligned themselves with Mitchel's campaign, as did several prominent Uptown Jews (Schiff, Morgenthau, Oscar Straus, and Marshall).[300]

In Jewish New York at this moment, politics was more local than ever. That was ironic, because in historical perspective, Jewish political destiny was unfolding in places far from City Hall in Lower Manhattan. In the days when Zionists, non-Zionists, and British statesmen were negotiating the terms of the Balfour Declaration, provisionally inviting Jews to establish a national home in Palestine, Downtown and Uptown Jews in New York were preoccupied not by inspiring visions of return to the ancestral homeland but by fears of thuggish anti-Semitism inspired by the principled candidacy of Morris Hillquit.

Exactly as Lord Balfour was publishing his famous declaration, Louis Marshall was composing a scolding letter to his recalcitrant protégé, Abraham Cahan. The *Forward* had galled Marshall by criticizing his appeal to Jewish New Yorkers to desist from supporting Hillquit. "You have misstated my position," Marshall complained to Cahan. He had no quarrel with Hillquit's socialism. Instead, as Marshall saw it, Hillquit's pacifism, his unpatriotic refusal to purchase a Liberty Bond, was liable to "bring about a reaction more horrible than anything that heretofore occurred, even in Russian history." Hillquit's candidacy, Marshall explained to Cahan, menacingly trespassed on 250 years of Jewish endeavor to carve out a prospering, secure home in America. "I am concerned that the

American people will regard the Jews as creating for themselves in the US a ghetto of separatism, of taking themselves out of American life, and of nullifying all that has been done through these many years to prove that the Jew is a loyal, faithful, patriotic American citizen."[301] Marshall ended his letter by warning Cahan to "Beware!" but he was not threatening to withdraw from his role as censor-protector of the *Forward*'s mail privileges. As the mayoral campaign headed for the finish line, Marshall was pleased by the way the *Forward*'s pro-Hillquit lobbying had receded. "I can say that Cahan has been behaving very well," Marshall privately noted to Judge Mack. Nothing published by the *Forward* in the final weeks of the contentious mayoral campaign raised issues of patriotism. By the end of the "exciting campaign," Cahan was acting with "great discretion."[302]

On November 6, Tammany's machine swept Hylan into office, with the Democrat receiving 46 percent of the votes. In an impressive show of strength, the Socialist Hillquit ran neck and neck with the incumbent, taking 22 percent of the vote to Mitchel's 23 percent. Scholars have never established how many of the 145,000 voters who cast ballots for Hillquit were Jews,[303] but the important point, one that largely substantiates Marshall's highly emotive responses to Hillquit's mayoral bid, is that postwar propagators of the "Jewish Bolshevism" characterization of American Jews as subversive elements brought up episodes like this 1917 New York mayoral race as evidence that immigrant Russian Jews were not patriotic. In the best cases, such characterizations regarded Jewish radicalism as an outgrowth of anti-Semitic persecution in Russia and assumed that New York Jews would over time become committed to the norms of American democracy. Thus, a 1919 commission appointed by the National Republican Club to investigate the spread of socialism in New York City reported, "The Jew in America, once he accepts the blessings of liberty and the meaning of our Constitution, will not accept the doctrine of class rule or internationalism."[304] In 1917, the Red Scare and Henry Ford's *Dearborn Independent* hate campaign were down the road, but even as his overwrought emotions subsided in days following Hillquit's defeat, Marshall perspicaciously expressed concerns about ways inchoate images of the Jew in American society were concretizing during the war, sometimes inauspiciously. In one private letter he spoke plainly about empirical realities that governed the entirety of his Jewish defense work during World War I:

> The idea prevails in many quarters that the Jew is disposed to be a slacker and that he is not doing his full duty. There have been covert allusions, and in many instances spoken statements, to that effect in the press. It is whispered in the street; it is the subject of brutal witticism.[305]

Cogently, Marshall grasped that these aspersions were not really evidence of a "Jewish question" in the United States but part of a wider trend of nativism. All ethnic groups were under suspicion of not being full patriotic Americans, and those that had ancestral roots in enemy countries or lands convulsed by socialist revolution were especially vulnerable to incipient rumblings of the xenophobic wave that would become the Tribal Twenties. To counteract allegations of Jewish "slackers," Marshall explained to this interlocutor that he and the AJC were compiling figures to show that America's Jews were "in reality furnishing more than their numerical percentage [of the population] to the army and navy." He explained that this was not a private form of Jewish apologetic. "The Catholics are doing the same," he noted.[306]

The Draft Board

By a combination of chance occurrence and conscious strategizing, Marshall himself embodied an intelligible response to the canard about the wartime Jewish slacker: not only was the Jew not a shirker, he was eminently qualified to monitor and enforce norms of wartime patriotism. In situations like the *Forward* monitoring, this role of patriotism enforcement was not widely known and was susceptible to misunderstanding (Marshall endlessly clarified that he was opposed to Cahan's socialism and that he was not on retainer with the *Forward*).[307] Marshall's work on the draft board was his most visible statement of an American Jew's, his own, unassailable competence to enforce the requirements of American patriotism.

The work drained him. "I have done hard work in the course of my life, but never had such an experience as this with the District Board in military exemption cases. It is a tremendous strain on the nerves," he complained to his children, just a few weeks into the experience. He was obviously distraught by the constant handling of "hard-luck stories"; these cases entailed emotional "pulling and hauling in a hundred different directions."[308] Even this onerous exercise of patriotic duty was not always immune to suspicions about Jewish string pulling. For instance, Marshall asked the committee to grant an exemption to Edmond Guggenheim, a thirty-year-old Yale graduate who had worked hard developing his powerful family's copper interests in Chile; his request was challenged by Senator George B. Agnew, entirely due to "race hostility," in Marshall's judgment. Marshall "pitched into Agnew hammer and tongs," arguing that Guggenheim's part in the management of his family's concerns was "valuable for the defense of the country." His request was accepted; relieved, Marshall confessed to committee partner Charles Evans Hughes that he would have resigned had the Guggenheim application been denied.[309]

Marshall proved to be a rigid reviewer of exemption requests. He fine-tuned provisions of the Conscription Act, proposing ways to foreclose avenues of draft evasion that were evidently being explored by young men in New York. In particular, he worked on the issue of "slacker marriages." As he wrote to the provost general, it was common knowledge in New York State that a "phenomenal number of marriages took place" in the period when the Conscription Act went into effect. Marshall protested War Department interpretations that allowed deferments to men who hastily arranged such marriages proximate to the start of the draft. "We are surrendering to the Kaiser upwards of 100,000 men who would become good American soldiers," he informed Major General Enoch Crowder.[310] After much equivocation, the War Department sided with Marshall's point of view, ruling that marriages performed after May 18, 1917, could not be grounds for exemption. "My associates view this as a triumph for me," Marshall gloated to his daughter Ruth.[311]

Weeks and months of taxing hours on the district board drained Marshall. As ever, he seemed one step behind Charles Evans Hughes, envying him when Hughes's victorious rival in the 1916 presidential election appointed him to head a bipartisan investigation of accusations of financial mismanagement in the Aircraft Board. "I am sure he [Hughes] is delighted to get out of this treadmill," Marshall privately noted.[312] Though unpleasant and tiring, this exercise of enforcing the laws of American patriotism had a sacrosanct character in Marshall's mind as an act of communal obligation. In this Jewish respect, he drew satisfaction from the draft board work, and it provided daily data that boosted his confidence in all the wartime work he did in the protection of Jewish affairs and communal reputation. In late May, Marshall explained to one AJC associate that he had over the past nine months devoted 60 percent of his work time to the district board, and the board had reviewed case files involving tens of thousands of Jews; this work proved incontrovertibly that "so far as loyalty is concerned, the showing of the Jews of New York is equal to that of any part of our population."[313]

Jewish Self-Defense Work During Wartime

During World War I, Marshall's censorship enforcement functions were not limited to the Cahan-*Forward* matter. In spring 1918, he virtually manhandled one of the "Boys from Syracuse," theater mogul Lee Shubert. With his brother Sam, Shubert operated an impressively sprawling theatrical empire, based on Manhattan's Winter Garden and the Schubert Theater, and on their influence in the Independent National Theater Owners' Association, which had outmuscled a rival theatrical syndicate. Lee Shubert had immigrated to Syracuse as an eleven-year-old in the early 1880s, and his family life, marred by an alcoholic father, had been poor and difficult (a sister died of malnutrition during the family's first winter on Grape Street in Syracuse);[314] the rise of these famous theatrical "boys from Syracuse" had started with the operation of theaters in Upstate New York.[315] About a decade before the war, Marshall sometimes did favors for aspiring actors and playwrights in his social circle, asking Schubert whether he would grant an audition or interview to a theater hopeful.[316] During the early years of the war, the Shuberts were probably too engaged in bitingly acrimonious theater turf wars in Philadelphia, Boston, and Chicago to pay much attention to happenings in Europe.[317]

Not a devoted theater patron himself, Marshall was distinctly unimpressed with Lee Shubert when he found out that a Jewish actor (Ed Wynn) was regaling audiences at the Winter Garden with comic monologues about cowardly and disloyal Jewish soldiers. "Some of us are spending our time and every ounce of our strength in trying to maintain for the Jew the respect of his neighbors," Marshall angrily wrote to the theater owner. "Yet you, a Jew, permit your actors, who are Jews, for the purpose of tickling the ears of an undiscriminating mob, to disseminate what I consider to be dynamite." At a time when 60,000 Jewish boys were braving hardship and death in the US army, Shubert should have used the stage to "cause them to be admired and respected." Instead, Shubert was "dragging them and the name of the Jew through the mud and mire, to coin a few dirty shekels." What hurt Marshall "more than anything else," he continued, was that Shubert, "a Syracusan," was staging "this filth and vileness" in his own theater. Marshall threatened the impresario: "You have evidently forgotten the stock from which you sprung, but I have not, and I mean to see to it that if you are unwilling to do so voluntarily, you must honor the race of which you are a member." After the receipt of this fiery letter, the comic monologue was taken off the stage in about the length of time it took for the theater's owner to call out the name "Ed Wynn." Two days after sending his original letter, Marshall wrote back to his fellow Syracusan, acknowledging Shubert's satisfactory handling of the matter.[318]

In the same week when Marshall instructed the Jewish theater mogul how his people ought to be represented on the stage, he instructed the US War Department how Jews ought to be represented in field manuals and in officer commissions. Marshall never missed a beat in this period, operating on the correct assumption that adjustments of ethnic roles and opportunities in American society would occur with much greater speed at a time of war. On March 4, 1918, he wrote to Secretary of War Newton Baker,[319] complaining vociferously that a manual for members of medical advisory boards warned that Jewish petitioners ought to be examined closely, as potential malingerers. Marshall did not rest until this "gross libel" was expunged in every way; within a week, he was contacted by President Wilson's office and assured officially that the manual's Jewish malingerers reference was "absolutely contrary to the views of the Administration" and displayed a "prejudice which ought never to have been expressed or entertained."[320] Wilson's office also called a halt to the manual's publication and ordered that every distributed copy should be recalled by telegram and destroyed.[321] Concurrently, Marshall complained to Secretary Baker about a circular signed by Adjutant General McCain, declaring that no soldier born in an enemy country could receive a commission. "In all the years of my experience, I have never before found in official documents expressions of this character," he wrote to Baker.[322] Employing a tactic he frequently used during the war years, Marshall elaborated on how American patriots must not indulge the prejudicial procedures of their enemy. "A Jew has never been permitted to be an officer in the Prussian army," he recalled. "I trust that the time has not come when commissions are to be withheld from men in the Army because they are Jews."

These were forthright letters[323] couched in a lecturing tone to America's highest war officials, but they reflected gloomy circumstances of social discrimination and snobbery against Jews that seemed to cast a retrospective pall of naïveté upon the antebellum optimism of the Uptown elite. "I greatly regret to say that I am convinced that there is a very strong undercurrent of anti-Semitism in various branches of the army," a discouraged Marshall wrote to Jacob Schiff.[324]

Putting the best foot forward, Marshall threw himself into the organization of the spring Liberty Loan campaign. "It is most desirable in the present exigency that the Jews make a good showing in connection with the Liberty Loan," Marshall explained to Schiff. "It will allay much of the unjust suspicion which our enemies have sought to arouse against the East Side."[325] In early April, Marshall had meetings with East Side newspaper men and activists; the Orthodox seemed a bit underrepresented ("our rabbis never do anything unless they are set in motion by the laity," Marshall reported to Schiff[326]), but otherwise Marshall was gratified by Downtown's demonstration of patriotic loyalty.[327] Resistance among the Russian immigrant Jews about fighting on the czar's side was gone, and as weeks went by, the East Side was seen more demonstrably to be fully on the American side. By the end of the spring, all of Marshall's worries about internal political inclinations in the Jewish community were dispelled. "The Maccabean spirit has been aroused in the Jews of America," an elated Marshall wrote to his colleague Cyrus Adler. "Impelled by the spirit of patriotism which transcends every other emotion, they have dedicated themselves to the cause of liberty."[328]

The Babel Proclamation

Marshall's function as the Jewish People's Attorney consolidated on a daily basis during the period of the country's involvement in World War I. As an Uptown Jew and as an expert on American constitutionalism, he enforced the rules of American patriotism among Downtown's immigrant Jews, sometimes resorting to draconian-sounding (though not particularly viable) threats. Conversely, he championed his community's constitutional rights in strongly phrased petitions to American officials who in their patriotic wartime zeal veered well out of bounds, sometimes tragicomically. This latter function, in which Marshall spoke American truth to American power in the name of Jewish communal interest, is colorfully and unforgettably delineated by his advocacy regarding the Babel Proclamation.

In the 1870s, the Midwestern state of Iowa, eager to expand its population, issued pamphlets in German, Danish, Dutch, and Swedish to attract immigrants.[329] By 1900, Germans were the state's largest immigrant group, being found in all of Iowa's ninety-nine counties. After the country's entry into World War I, officials in Iowa overlooked the state's history of welcoming immigrant ethnic groups and initiated a series of anti-German measures. As a first step, in November 1917, the Iowa State Council of Defense banned the use of German in public schools. Thereafter, in Muscatine, Bismarck Street became Bond Street, and several other German place-names around the state were Americanized; suddenly, children were contracting liberty measles, instead of German measles.

Leading this patriotic surge of feeling in Iowa against all things German was the state's twenty-second governor, William L. Harding, a native of Sibley who was elected in 1917. On May 23, 1918, Governor Harding issued the Babel Proclamation, banning the use of any foreign language in the state, in all schools, over the telephone, in religious services, and generally in public. This assault against the mother tongues of many of his constituents, including native German speakers who had ironically voted for Harding a year earlier due to his opposition to Wilson's pro-Allied leanings, was justifiable, the governor averred, because it would "save the lives of American boys overseas by curbing sedition at home." Clawing for some constitutional basis for his jaw-dropping measure, Harding argued, "Freedom of speech is guaranteed by federal and state constitutions, but this is not a guarantee of the right to use a language other than the language of this country, the English language." The proclamation found its most vigorous enforcement in the monitoring of party-line telephone conversations—at one point, Iowa law enforcement officials raised hackles around the United States by arresting five Scott County farmwives for using German in one such telephone discussion (the women's $225 fine was donated to the Red Cross).

On June 13, Marshall was contacted by the alarmed president of the Des Moines Talmud Torah, who conveyed information about Governor Harding's edict and asked the president of the AJC for advice as to how to proceed. In New York, Marshall was incredulous about what wartime hysteria had wrought in the Midwest. "I cannot conceive the possibility that the people of any state could be guilty of such an absurdity," he exclaimed in his response to the perplexed Jewish Iowan. Yet, before divulging practical advice to the Talmud Torah director, Marshall had to consider the calculation that had, a week earlier, compelled East Side Jewry's Socialist congressman Meyer London to register on the House floor an on-the-record protest against the Babel Proclamation. London had originally been inclined to dismiss Harding's linguistic xenophobia as a "peculiar form of insanity which comes about with war" but then had second thoughts. A labor lawyer, London pointed out in Congress that Harding, as governor, "occupies the position of an executive officer, [and] has the police power of the militia of the state at his disposal." This was the consideration that compelled Marshall to recommend temporary Marranism in the Corn Belt. "It is extremely important that we shall be circumspect and avoid irritation," he told the Talmud Torah president. "My advice to you would be to continue the work of your Talmud Torah quietly and unobtrusively, using the English language in connection with giving of instruction wherever it can be done."[330]

Marshall, of course, did not end the case on this cowering note. While he himself resorted to jingoistic bluster during the war, in the name of community cohesion and well-being, Marshall understood the war to be about the protection of constitutional democracy and not its repeal in the name of some other patriotic ideal; it is, therefore, important not to be misled by his ultrapatriotic rhetoric and to recognize that he was responsible in this period for extraordinary defenses of individual rights that were motivated out of personal and communal loyalty (as in the Magnes case), and an uncompromising devotion to fundamental democratic precepts. Owing to these Jewish and American commitments, Marshall led the fight, from his New York office, against Iowa's Babel law.

Marshall wrote to Governor Harding on June 13 to protest what he flatly characterized as an unconstitutional measure.[331] He shared some facts of life he had learned from his New York Downtown experiences with the Midwestern governor. "There is nothing to which men and women hold more tenaciously than their traditions, including the language of their ancestors," Marshall wrote. He alluded to his recent participation in a Hartford, Connecticut, war rally, in which foreign-born citizens, including Yiddish speakers, issued inspiringly patriotic American statements in various languages. Worst of all, Marshall suggested, Iowa was violating rights of worship. Cuttingly, he wrote, "We have certainly not reached the point when a man can be suspected of treason, sedition and disloyalty because he prays to a God in a language other than English."

Not daunted, Governor Harding fired back to Marshall a stinging letter, rebuking him as a New Yorker who lacked knowledge of local conditions in Iowa and insisting that suspicion was owed to any person who could not comply with his proclamation. Marshall responded to these imputations with a blue ribbon performance, published in Charles Reznikoff's collection,[332] which included an overview of judicial precedents protecting foreign expression and discussion of late nineteenth-century Prussian attempts to suppress the French language; implying that Iowa was evoking patriotism but actually engaging the enemy's autocratic tactics, the brief offered a ringing defense of pluralism as a principle of American constitutionalism. "Americanism is not the product of one but of many civilizations; not of one but of many traditions," Marshall concluded. To say that American citizens "may not preserve the tradition of their ancestors or speak their language is contrary to that spirit of liberality and of freedom upon which our institutions are founded, and which is exemplified in the slogan: *E pluribus unum*."

Marshall's exchanges with Governor Harding were widely published. Iowans who were not persuaded that foreign languages posed a threat to their state and country wrote notes of appreciative gratitude to Marshall.[333] However, through the summer, other patriotic Iowans kept trying to convince East Coast skeptics that they did not understand Midwest conditions. "You are struggling to make Americans out of foreigners, and we are struggling to prevent Americans from being converted into foreigners,"[334] the publisher of the *Des Moines Capital* cried out, in English, to anyone in the East who read his *New York Times* editorial on July 30. Harding kept the Babel Proclamation in effect through the war, repealing it on December 4, 1918.[335]

Downtown Versus Uptown Becomes Personal: Louis Marshall and Abraham Cahan

For many months, Marshall mediated between the clenched patriotic norms of wartime America, on the one hand, and the free-spirited habits of the equally charismatic Judah Magnes and Abraham Cahan, on the other hand. Neither of these situations was truly resolved in amity, and the loose ends they left reflected significant differences in American and Jewish orientations that separated Marshall from the other two men. Magnes was regarded by Marshall as family and more or less as an equal, but the Kehillah director remained a recalcitrant pacifist. Cahan proved to be far more patriotically cooperative than Magnes; however, in contradistinction to images of evolving Downtown-Uptown harmony evoked by Lucy Dawidowicz,[336] whose judgments were tempered by the American "consensus school" historiography of the post–World War II period, Marshall overlooked the Downtown editor and writer's unparalleled knack for recording and guiding Jewish immigrant experience, and articulated a sharply condescending attitude toward Cahan through the end of the war. Ultimately, in the two cases of Magnes and Cahan, he managed to contain his private feelings of consternation and fashioned public responses that protected Jewish interests.

Pressure mounted all the time to excommunicate Magnes effectively by banishing him from all communal roles. Protecting his brother-in-law, Marshall virtually exhausted his stock of defense attorney tactics. When one member of the AJRC demanded Magnes's expulsion from this body, Marshall begged for tolerance: "Let us not become the victims of hysteria, so that we see a spy or traitor behind every bush. There exists the right of free speech,"[337] implored Marshall. He looked for precedents in England that might provide some cushion for his pacifist relative. "Although Lord Landsowne has recently given utterance to views like those of Magnes, nobody in England has suggested that he be expelled from the House of Lords," Marshall noted. When this AJRC associate withdrew his expulsion demand and sent a new check for overseas Jews, Marshall notified Jacob Schiff,[338] who was himself worried about Magnes but who (as his biographer relates) "retained his affection" for the moralistic Magnes, regarding him as a "beloved bad boy."[339] Relieved, Marshall wrote back to the donor, thanking him for ending the "crusade" against Magnes.[340] "I must again express the hope that we Jews should not be chauvinistic. One can be a patriot and yet recognize the fact that there may be a difference of opinion in matters of public policy." Six months earlier, in his impassioned effort to shape Downtown opinion in the war effort, Marshall had raised the specter of treasonable execution of any Jew who followed Magnes's antiwar counsel. Yet, when it came to the practical issue of protecting a relative whose work on the Kehillah was a reservoir of communal pride, not to mention philanthropic investment, Marshall turned from hangman to public defender. Attesting to flexibility of character, that sort of transition can often be found lurking beneath the stiff rhetoric of Marshall's public advocacy.

For Cahan, Marshall repeatedly petitioned senior officials at the US Postal Service, affirming that the *Forward* was in full compliance with its patriotic avowals and asking that it be exempted from the translation requirements of the Trading with the Enemy Act. In September 1918, Marshall informed Post Office Solicitor William Lamar that the *Forward* was urging its readers to contribute heartily to the Fourth Liberty Loan campaign after the newspaper corporation had itself donated a $20,000 subscription to the Third Liberty Loan.[341] Cahan, who had been in frequent conference with Marshall over the past year, freely opened his newspaper's editorial pages to contributions from the AJC president. There was no truth to the rumor that the *Forward* favored the Bolsheviks in Russia, Marshall added. He told the post office official about how Leon Trotsky had feuded with Cahan, bitterly resenting the editor's patriotically American attitude.

Since Marshall and Cahan were archetypal figures of American Jewry's Uptown-Downtown dichotomy, it is important to note that by settling World War I matters between the two on this harmonious note, at variance with the documentary evidence, the Dawidowicz consensus school prematurely telescoped onto the historical record patterns of cultural consolidation whose salience is to be found rather later, after the war. At its best, Marshall's attitude toward Cahan was that of the trial lawyer who is perpetually annoyed that his client is not exactly acting on the witness stand as he has been prepped to behave.

A month after he wrote to the post office solicitor, Marshall testily told Cahan, "I am afraid that I was a little too strong in the expressions which were contained in my letter to Judge Lamar." He was particularly perturbed by the *Forward*'s refusal to editorially advocate the purchase of Liberty Bonds.[342] A week later, Marshall exploded when the *Forward* followed the lead of other periodicals, including the *New York Tribune,* and sensationalized steps Magnes was taking to phase out his involvement in Jewish organizations in light of the controversies generated by his pacifism.[343] This was a touchy subject for Marshall, because he had stretched his philosophy and credibility to protect his brother-in-law's public reputation; understandably, Marshall resented the yellow headlines in reports, "Bolshevik Talk Forces Magnes Out," implying that the AJC had perpetrated an inquisition.

Magnes had resigned on his own volition, Marshall assured Cahan in writing. Though he had never personally demanded gratitude from the *Forward* editor, Marshall insisted that the AJC, "which is dear to me," be "treated with honesty" by Cahan's newspaper. The editor politely asked Marshall for proof that the Magnes had not been hounded into exile by the committee because of his pacifist politics. As Marshall saw it, he had gone to extraordinary lengths to protect Cahan from the consequences of his own political radicalism, and he deeply resented the editor's suspicious, and incorrect, suggestion that he had not done the same for Magnes. "What information do you desire?" he pointedly asked Cahan. "Is my word not sufficient?"[344] By imputing behaviors and motives that could never have crossed into the closely protective family orbits of Uptown Jewry, Cahan had shown how he really did not understand something about the way Marshall and his associates operated, and he had indeed stepped over an invisible line running between the two Jewish worlds of New York.

In a tirade, Marshall articulated the proposition that he would never treat a Downtown Jew as an inferior, as an impertinent immigrant, and then proved exactly the opposite. Ending with a shocking characterization of Cahan—a legendary personality whose autobiographical novel, *The Rise of David Levinsky,* had a year earlier provided American Jewry with its most moving and memorable self-portrait to date—as a "child," Marshall's words warrant quotation, if only as a reminder of the way the complex cultural realities of New York Jewish life in the early twentieth century were sometimes flattened in retrospect by historians as they searched for consensus in research methodologies of the Cold War era. Marshall's words conveyed lingering echoes of prior phases in his Jewish advocacy. Laden within them is the never entirely overcome sense in which his lobbying could be perceived as an internal colonization project. Foreign immigrants in this project were sometimes treated as immature dependents:

> You call my attention twice in your letter to what you regard as the rather strong English that I use in it. I am accustomed to speak plainly. I never beat about the bush. I flatter nobody, not even the editor of a newspaper. I call a spade a spade. What I wrote you was not the result of a slip of the pen. It reflected faithfully a state of mind occasioned by an outrageous injustice. You finally close with the insinuation that the tone of my letter was due to the fact that "after all it was addressed to a mere East Side Jew." That is a form of expression which is as old as the days of Moses and is a statement which comes in very bad part from you or from anybody connected with the East Side. My method of speech to East Side Jews is generally much milder than it is to others because I feel in many respects they are children.[345]

James Marshall Serves in France

Marshall had his own children to worry about during the war. His eldest, James, a sergeant with the Mount Sinai unit, reached France in March 1918. Late in the month, Marshall was thrilled to receive news of the unit's arrival at a monastery; inadvertently, a postmarked letter reached the nervous father, and Marshall quickly found the spot at Vauclaire on a map—his cry of relief in a letter to his cousin, "it is a long distance from the Western front," resonated happily between Manhattan and Syracuse.[346]

Before his enlistment, James had resolved his oedipal worries and taken up the study of law. During his term of service, his proud father encouraged James to make the most of the opportunity to gain a "proper understanding of mankind," for it would make him a better lawyer and person. The world did not end in New York City: "The average man, especially in New York, knows very little of his neighbors, of human nature, he leads a very narrow life."[347] Marshall opened an account for James in Brentano's, so he could acquire books, and even when he was discouraged about the Allies' progress, as in May 1918, when he privately believed that the war would go on for another two years, he cited for James the rhymester wisdom of his high-spirited younger brother Robert, who declared, "All things have to end some way / So the Kaiser must end on a certain day."[348] Marshall wrote to James as though he were a young associate in the office, describing to him some of the intricate and interesting legal work he was doing at the time. Among other things, he had been appointed by Governor Charles Whitman to testify to the Committee on Military Affairs in opposition to the federal government's plan to seize water rights over the Niagara and St. Lawrence rivers, along with all rental fees derived from control of this waterpower. Similarly complicated issues of deciding legitimate compensation for the government's possession of railroads were also on Marshall's work list. "Under normal circumstances, the public would be greatly interested in these issues," he confided to James. "As it is, there is not even a mention now."[349]

In France, James was getting restless. "As a whole," he wrote to his father in May, "the hospital still resembles a community of artisans more than a hospital."[350] Marshall, though relieved that his son was engaged as a hospital registrar far from the front, shared this restive, pre-summer mood. "Why are we waiting?" he wondered aloud to James. "Unless the house of Hohenzollern is defeated, militarism will be rampant and the world bankrupt in every sense of the world."[351] He could not stop sharing with his son anecdotes attesting to the revolting behavior of the enemy. The way Marshall shed every German drop from his identity during World War I hints that, had he lived into the 1930s, his leadership during that latter era's European crisis would have been resolutely watchful and assertive. More certainly, his private musings during World War I render it incongruous to regard Louis Marshall as a "German Jew." He related to James stories of his seasick honeymoon voyage to Europe, and how he and Florence had encountered a brutal, "supposedly educated" German on a visit to Wuerzburg during that trip ("I wanted to resort to blows to teach the wretched brute a lesson in good manners"). France was the only country on the Continent that retained any attraction in his eyes. "I have never thought of Germany without a sense of disgust," the American Jewish leader wrote in June 1918.[352]

Assistant Registrar James thirsted for action. "It is rather difficult for me to quite see the relationship of my wearing out breeches on a hard chair, and saving the world for democracy," he moaned in the first days of July.[353] Such talk made his ultrapatriotic father nervous. Sharing his parental worries with Judge Mayer Sulzberger in August, Marshall sensed that the newly intensive work at the hospital would distract James from such combat-oriented musing. "Every available corner of the hospital, which is three times the size of Mt. Sinai, is occupied by wounded men," James reported, as the summer progressed. Some 600 ailing soldiers arrived at James's facility on one train.[354] Toward the end of July, 1,000 wounded soldiers filled the monastery-hospital.[355]

By September, the end was, at long last, in sight. "These are days of exhilaration. News from the front is most encouraging," Marshall excitedly wrote to his son.[356] He wanted the Allies to press to the end for a total victory, completely obliterating German autocracy. One of Congregation Emanu-El's rabbis, Dr. Enelow, was in Europe, making a "much better impression in uniform than in a frock coat,"[357] James reported to the family, and so Marshall took a turn at the pulpit during the Yom Kippur service. He took advantage of the opportunity to call for the prosecution of the war until it achieved all of its democratization objectives. This was in response to an editorial in the *New York Times,* a newspaper that had acquired a reputation for advocating the relentless continuation of the war, favoring consideration of Austria's diplomatic peace overtures. Marshall's fight-to-the-end sermon was well received.[358] James remained right where his father wanted him to be. In an unwittingly domineering way, Marshall reminded James of that fact right through to the end of the war. "I have been entirely satisfied with the work which you are doing," he wrote to James just several weeks before the Armistice. "I am sure you never cared for a commission. I could easily have secured for you a Lieutenant's commission had I deemed it advisable . . . but my great desire is that you shall continue in the kind of work in which you are engaged."[359]

Appropriately, Marshall shared his elation on November 11 with his soldier son. "Der tag has come! The divine right of kings is now a mere monstrosity on exhibition in historical museums," Marshall wrote at the war's end, adding that he felt proud of his "powers of prophecy." His vision of the war's purposes and possibilities indeed seemed vindicated at the Armistice. "From August 1914 onward I declared that by the time the war was over, the Hohenzollerns, the Hapsburgs and the Romanovs would walk the plank," Marshall recalled. On Armistice Day, Marshall's thoughts about the future of Germany were disturbingly prescient; even at this extremely hopeful time, he had a premonition that a monarchical form of tyranny in Central Europe could be replaced by a modern tyranny of mob rule. He lacked a name for what was coming and could not have predicted the scale of its violence, but Marshall preternaturally understood what could be in store for Germany:

> In the long run, an entirely different Germany will arise, one which may possibly forget the qualities engendered by the militarism and by the greed which was stimulated by the old regime. At all events, if there is to be any tyranny, it will not be that of an oligarchy, but that of the mob.[360]

This was a prophetic but passing instant. During the last decade of his life, whenever Marshall paid attention to Europe, it would be mostly to places east of Germany.

Framing the Non-Zionist Position: The American Jewish Committee's Response to the Balfour Declaration

Conversely, there was one land whose affairs had largely escaped Marshall's notice during the final phases of the war, since the formation of the AJRC, but that was to attract his energies, and sometimes preoccupy them, in years ahead. Belatedly, Louis Marshall addressed the challenges and opportunities posed by the Balfour Declaration of British support for the formation of a Jewish national home in Eretz Israel. Taking shape by the end of the war was a frame for the last, most fateful, mediation effort in Louis Marshall's career in Jewish politics—his protracted, often exasperating, but ultimately successful endeavor to forge an empowering middle ground between the American fixation and loyalty anxieties of the non-Zionists, and the impassioned, monomaniacal labors of the Zionists to create a Jewish state in the ancestral land.

The New York City mayoral election was staged on November 6, 1917, and as long as the pacifist Hillquit remained in the race, running hard, Jewish politics in Marshall's circle went no farther than the city. About a week after the New York elections and two weeks after the Balfour Declaration announcement, Marshall conferred with American Zionists to investigate the possibility of unified action toward future new realities in Palestine. One meeting with Judge Mack and Eugene Meyer lasted well into the late hours of the night, and Marshall came away satisfied that the AJC's position toward Palestine was not hopelessly different than that of the American Zionists. Like Marshall's non-Zionist group, Brandeis and his associates were irretrievably invested in American society and naturally wary of zealously political Zionist rhetoric about the Yishuv being the sole destination of Jews everywhere. Brandeis and his followers also recognized how disproportionate emphasis on the political aspects of Zionism could aggravate loyalty anxieties, as well as anti-Semitism, in America. The Zionists, Marshall reported to Schiff, "appreciate the dangers of the establishment of the Jewish state, to the same degree that we do."[361] He explained to Schiff that his discussions with Brandeis's deputies focused semantically on the term "nation," and he was satisfied that when the Zionists used the term "national home," they were referring to "resettlement in Palestine by Jews as a race or ethnic family, and not as a political society in its sovereign capacity."

For days and weeks after the Balfour Declaration, Marshall pondered how to respond. He wondered whether the semantic taming of the term "nation" arising out of his conversations with the Brandeis Zionists would suffice to ease the anxieties of AJC colleagues like Cyrus Adler, who had vocally opposed Zionism for years.[362] Adler was busily preparing a long manifesto critical of the Zionists and the Balfour Declaration. Marshall implored his friend not to go public with the document, much as he agreed privately with Adler's scathing assessments of behavioral traits and outlooks of the Jewish nationalists. Correct as it might be, the publication of such anti-Zionist criticism, Marshall gently advised Adler, would only "produce bad blood." Between the deep-seated reservations of AJC colleagues like Adler and the buoyant expectancy of the Zionist movement after the conquest of Jerusalem by General Allenby's British forces, Marshall was having trouble finding room to fashion an intelligible reiteration of his readiness to support nonpolitical projects undertaken by the Yishuv. The Zionists "think they have the world by their tail," Marshall explained to Adler. "Drunken with enthusiasm, they are not in a mood to give tolerant consideration to anything which is not entirely laudatory to them and their purposes."[363]

Marshall waited several months for both sides to sober up. He expected the Zionists to withdraw politicized interpretations of the Jewish national home promised by the Balfour Declaration, and he expected that colleagues like Adler would grasp that because realities had changed as a result of the declaration and the British conquest of the Holy Land, the committee could not afford to simply ignore Palestine diplomacy forever. Marshall had a genuinely deep attachment to Eretz Israel as the authoritative core of Judaism, but he was extended arduously in many other directions during World War I; it was probably his keenly alert sense of American Jewish politics rather than his emotional love of the Holy Land that limited his procrastination after the Balfour Declaration. As the American Jewish Congress battle had demonstrated, the American Zionists became a force to be reckoned with during World War I, and they could deliver a mortal blow to any Jewish political figure who brazenly disregarded their excitement after the Balfour Declaration. In 1918, East Side congressman Meyer London defied the Zionists, refusing to introduce a pro-Balfour resolution in Washington. "Let us stop pretending about the Jewish past, and let us stop making fools of ourselves about the Jewish future," declared London. Later that year, London lost his seat in congressional elections.[364]

At last, in early April 1918, Marshall had closed ranks in the committee and drafted an official response in its name on the Balfour Declaration and the future of Palestine. He submitted it to Schiff with an accompanying note clearly demarcating Marshall's adopted role as a key mediator on an issue that was destined to dominate Jewish affairs. The proposed AJC statement, Marshall explained to Schiff, "expresses our sympathy with the aspirations of one part of the community, but avoids giving offense to what I consider to be the most influential part of American Jewry."[365]

The committee's statement was submitted to Secretary of State Robert Lansing on April 15, 1918.[366]

Over the next thirty years, political affairs in Palestine and among the Jews in Europe would, of course, witness momentous or calamitous changes. Heading into the Holocaust years, American Jewish organizations would, on the whole, alter their orientations toward Zionism, becoming reconciled on many levels with its political implications, and in that transition, Marshall's heirs in the AJC, figures such as Maurice Wertheim and Joseph Proskauer, would stand out in their cautiousness while ultimately becoming subsumed within the general, pro-Zionist, trend.[367] Despite the confounding, tragic, or inspiring events of the Holocaust and Israel's establishment, a markedly clear line of consistency runs between the AJC's official 1918 response to the Balfour Declaration and its official response to Israel's establishment in the Blaustein–Ben-Gurion correspondence of 1950.

After the establishment of the Jewish state, AJC President Jacob Blaustein, a Baltimore Jew who, with his father Louis, built up the flourishing American Oil Company,[368] exchanged letters of understanding with Israel's prime minister David Ben-Gurion that have been recognized by scholars as a sustained, formal attempt to place relations between American Jews and Israel on a constructive footing. Among other things, these letters declared that "the Jews of the United States, as a community and as individuals, have only one political attachment, and that is to the United States of America." Blaustein stressed that Israel had, or was becoming, home to hundreds of thousands of Jews from Europe, Africa, and the Middle East; yet, for the overwhelming majority of American Jews, it would not be regarded as an actual home but rather as the inspiration of "pride and admiration" (as well as "passing headaches," Marshall's heir could not resist writing).[369] The contents in these pivotal 1950 documents are essentially the same as the AJC's 1918 statement on "The British Declaration Concerning Palestine";[370] and, in some instances, specific formulations that Marshall used were borrowed and inherited by successors in his organization and by the leader of the state of

Israel, thirty-two years later. The 1918 statement declared it "axiomatic that the Jews of the United States have here established a permanent home for themselves and their children." The Jewish national home in 1918, like the Jewish state after 1948, would be a home for thousands of Jews from lands outside of the United States ("We recognize . . . that a part of the Jewish people would take up their domicile in Palestine," the 1918 statement declared). In other words, if there is a constitutional basis, of sorts, for American Jewry's civil religion attachment to the state of Israel, it was drafted by Louis Marshall in this document, a few months after the Balfour Declaration.

Addressing the specific political circumstances of spring 1918, the committee pledged to support the "realization" of the Balfour Declaration under the auspices of a British "protectorate or suzerainty" in Palestine, the precise nature of which remained to be determined by a postwar peace congress. Flanked on one side of the committee by inveterate opponents of Jewish nationalism like Adler, Marshall was careful not to insert terms like "Zionism" or "national home" in this cornerstone document. The basis of Jewish settlement in Eretz Israel, according to the statement, was not a nationalist program but rather "religious or historic associations," and the Yishuv was defined not as a national home (and, of course, not as an embryonic state) but rather as a "center for Judaism, for the stimulation of our faith, for the pursuit and development of literature, science and art in a Jewish environment, and for the rehabilitation of the land."

Privately, Marshall described the statement as advocating a "middle of the road position." The AJC, he explained, could not conceive of "dual citizenship," of a world where American Jews owed anything but total political allegiance to the United States, but it also wished to sympathize publicly with "those who desire to rebuild the Holy Land."[371] *Medio tutissimus ibis,* he wrote to James. Before going public with the AJC position, he consulted with Secretary of State Lansing, because the issue related to political changes in the vanishing Ottoman Empire, and the United States was not formally at war with Turkey.[372] He was annoyed when the *New York Times* responded to the statement's issuance with indifference, publishing only a "hashed up and inaccurate report in an obscure corner" of the paper.[373]

The statement, in fact, stirred little excitement in a world mired in the last phases of violent fighting in the tragic war. A few months after the announcement, Lionel de Rothschild, president of the League of British Jews, pressed Marshall to clarify the committee's position. "While we sympathize and are willing to aid those who wish *a* home in Palestine, we do not look upon such as *the* home of the Jewish people," replied Marshall. Recognizing that the Balfour Declaration was by this time incorporated into the geopolitical strategy of a wartime ally,

Marshall underscored that the committee had been, and remained, determined not to say or do anything "that might be regarded by your [Rothschild's] government as lacking in appreciation of the exalted statesmanship and humane motives underlying the declaration."[374] For the remainder of the war, that consideration of Allied powers' solidarity became the key lever for Marshall, as he held onto his center position in the face of opposition stirred rather relentlessly by anti-Zionists, including Reform Jewish leaders. The abiding concern of Zionism's foes in America was that the campaign for a Jewish national home, or state, in Palestine would compromise their civil status. Marshall stood this double loyalty fear on its head, insisting that since the Balfour Declaration was a war measure, it was unpatriotic to oppose it. Thus, rejecting an invitation proffered by Cincinnati rabbi David Philipson to take part in an anti-Zionist campaign, Marshall explained sharply that "you do not give due weight to the ideas and circumstances which underlie the Balfour Declaration." He added, "To combat Zionism at this time is to combat the governments of England, France and Italy."[375]

By the end of the war, Marshall had established a noticeably candid, morally engaged dialogue with American Zionist leader Judge Julian Mack. Their discussions about the meaning of the Balfour Declaration were penetrating and bereft of the suspiciousness and euphemistic posturing that often characterized Marshall's contacts with Chaim Weizmann in the 1920s about the expanded Jewish Agency. In fact, perhaps the most revealing statement Marshall ever made about Zionism was conveyed in a private letter to Judge Mack, composed after Marshall's participation in what he described as an "interesting" Carnegie Hall celebration of the Balfour Declaration, held in autumn 1918.

Marshall shared a portion of the loyalty anxiety that governed his elite Uptown group's reservations about Zionism. Ultimately, however, his fear was not that Zionism's progress could compromise his Americanism—nothing would ever do that. Ironically, he was less concerned about political complications that might possibly be stirred by Zionism's triumphs than were avowed secularists in Louis Brandeis's American Zionist group. At rock bottom, his fear, as he explained to Mack, was Zionism's "godlessness." Soon, he would travel to Versailles to negotiate the Jewish delegation's program of minority rights in Eastern Europe—this work was to engage his interest and energy fully because he approached it entirely in a lawyerly mode, with the expectation of applying his professional skills. Zionism never comparably engaged his positive interest because his expectations concerning Eretz Israel were different. In this context, he was a lawyer looking for God, and he felt let down when he found himself surrounded by Zionists who were preoccupied by precisely the issues of rights and obligations that dominated his labors in all other work spheres.

Reluctantly, Marshall engaged with the Zionists on their level and would from this point spend a considerable portion of the rest of his life quarreling with them about levels of representation on commissions and executive bodies, the designation of items on meeting agendas, fund-raising arrangements, and many other topics familiar to him from other facets of his work. He dealt with the Zionists as a lawyer and retreated from them emotionally as though he were a rabbi. Nothing in his tellingly frank criticism to the Carnegie Hall Balfour rally had to do with semantic wrangling about phrases like "national home"; his was a religious critique of the meaning of the Balfour Declaration, and it might have been written not by a political or legal opponent of Justice Brandeis or Chaim Weizmann, but rather by Marshall's close friend and teacher, Solomon Schechter, who had passed away early in the war.[376]

Christians, Marshall explained to Mack,[377] "who are more familiar with the Old Testament than most of the Jews," view the restoration of the Jews to Eretz Israel as a sacred matter. "They regard the Balfour Declaration and the glorious victory of Allenby as a realization of ancient prophecies." To Christians, Zionism is a religious movement—"but, alas, to Jews it is not!" Pointedly, Marshall observed that the rally had been suffused with expressions of gratitude to England, France, Italy, and President Wilson, "but the intervention of God Almighty was entirely ignored." Marshall then proceeded forcefully to detail his religious reservations about Zionism; when read as the foreground to the remainder of Marshall's career, his words attest to the propagandistically hollow character of the lofty terms used to describe his eventual agreements with Weizmann and the Zionists (e.g., the "Pact of Glory" for an expanded Jewish Agency). As Marshall saw it, there was nothing elevating in Zionist accomplishment. His circumscribed support for it stemmed from practical calculations about Jewish well-being and not from his soul. Referring to the godlessness of the Balfour rally, Marshall wrote, "It is just this attitude that has made it impossible for me to become a member of the Zionist organization. I am filled with fear and doubt. I see before me a godless Palestine, whose Jews are forgetting the real glories, the real achievements, and the only reason for the continued existence and preservation of Israel."[378]

Poland

To be sure, God was hard to find anywhere on the battlefields of slaughter left behind by World War I. The ordeal ended, and the next chapter of Marshall's career started soberly—not as a search for the divine but as a mission for Jewish order that would preserve anything precious that could be rescued from the past and also transplant some share of the hopes and dreams of American democracy in the lives of far-away Jewish communities.

The upcoming chapter in his life would most logically focus not on Palestine, where the Yishuv was the home of several thousand idealistic pioneers, but in Poland, also an old-new country in transition that happened to be the home of 3–4 million largely vulnerable and indigent Jews.

Just a few months before the war's end, Marshall dined at the Harvard Club with Julian Mack, Stephen Wise, and the philosopher John Dewey. Marshall was not enthralled by Dewey's reputation for pragmatism. "Philosophers cannot speak in direct terms, but are always groping about for a formula," Marshall bitingly told his children. Marshall was able to garner from the philosophizing Dewey that he had an interest in Polish affairs and opposed the musician Ignace Jan Paderewski, a key figure during the war on the Polish National Committee (and soon to be a leader of independent Poland). Marshall, however, was clearly in no mood for idle chatter about Poland and political rights. He wanted action. Even as the Armistice was announced, and he rapturously watched New York turn into a snowstorm of confetti tossed from the skyscrapers, as a "sight never to be forgotten,"[379] Marshall was holed up in his Manhattan office, strategizing to help the Jews of Poland. He contacted Justice Brandeis, asking him to tap his connections to the White House. "The new Poland will probably contain four million Jews, and [so] the importance of securing the President's interest is obvious," the AJC's Louis wrote to the Supreme Court's Louis.[380]

Marshall, in fact, had already composed a brief on Polish Jewry for President Wilson. Since 1912, he recorded, a "virulent economic boycott" in Poland had been aimed at the "practical destruction of the Jews." The boycott remained in effect. He petitioned the US president to incorporate in the peace agreements a minority rights accord for Poland, based on the principles that "all Polish subjects, without distinction to origin, race or creed, shall enjoy equal civil, political and religious rights," and that "the Jews shall be accorded autonomous management of their own religious, educational, charitable and other cultural institutions."[381]

In the new, postwar reality, the recipient of this letter faced the daunting task of upholding his promises about making the world safe for democracy. In the same reality, the letter's sender was about to head an unprecedented diplomatic effort to make the world safe for the Jews. The limits of what both men would accomplish in Paris proved that the nonfulfillment of the American president's promise spelled untold tragedy for the Jewish diplomat's efforts.

7

Paris and Haiti

Preparing for Paris

Some 335,000 Jewish Americans elected delegates to the American Jewish Congress on June 10, 1917. At the end of June, Stephen Wise met with President Wilson, who indicated sympathy with the congress's purposes but urged that its convening be delayed on account of the "current pressure of general affairs." Much to Marshall's relief, the congress's administrative committee deferred scheduling its sessions until the start of Armistice peace negotiations. The congress thus convened in Philadelphia on December 15–18, 1918.[1]

Serving as congress president, Judge Mack reiterated the peace demand formula that had been outlined in earlier calls to convene the congress: the congress demanded full and equal rights for Jews everywhere and the attainment of "group rights" for Jewish communities in lands where group rights had political recognition.[2] Perhaps the most dramatic moment at the congress occurred when Yiddish enthusiast Chaim Zhitlowsky, not officially a delegate but a prominent early advocate of the Jewish congress movement in America, took the floor and declared that Jews should seek rights on a national basis and not as individuals or as a religious group. His viewpoint, upholding a rigid separation of religion from politics in Jewish national life, antagonized religious Zionists from the Mizrahi movement, which at one point demanded that Zhitlowsky be removed from the rostrum. Intervening, Marshall declared that his own sympathies were on the side of religious delegates at the congress, "but I would consider myself less an American if I could not sit here and listen to anybody express his view" (Zhitlowski concluded his remarks, and Mizrahi leader rabbi Meir Berlin was granted a right of reply).[3]

Marshall's address, "Jewish Rights in Eastern Europe," delivered at the Lu-Lu Temple at the congress's December 15 meeting, essentially became the body's platform and was later disseminated as a pamphlet by the American Jewish

Congress.[4] Having fought tenaciously against the congress advocates for many months during the war, Marshall now emerged as its main spokesman and representative.

"The greatest, the most important, the most difficult of our complications . . . revolve around the new state of Poland which is to be created," declared Marshall. Up to 4 million Jews could live in a new Polish state; meantime, the Poles had for the previous six years enforced a "horrible economic boycott which has threatened the absolute annihilation and extermination of our brethren." Since April, Marshall, along with Schiff, Rosenwald, Mack, Wise, and Oscar Straus, had been in contact with Polish leaders such as Ignace Jan Paderewski and Roman Dmowski. Referring to these inconclusive meetings, Marshall put his best foot forward and declared optimistically that the Polish politicians "have also recognized the fact that at this time they cannot ignore, but must reckon with the Jews." Identifying the "emancipation of our brethren in Poland" as the congress's cardinal objective, Marshall explained that the cautionary precedent was the Berlin Treaty of 1878, which had vacuously referred to the rights to Jews in Romania, only to turn into an unenforceable "Dead Sea apple."

Exactly what mechanism would guarantee the implementation of rights provisions for Jews in Poland and other East European lands? Far from convinced at this stage about the desirability of Wilson's League of Nations program, Marshall believed that the newly constituted states in Eastern Europe would be diligent about minority rights were their very establishment to be predicated upon their acceptance of well-formulated constitutional systems. "The adoption and incorporation into the Constitutions of these new or enlarged States of clauses which will effectuate the will of the Peace Conference must precede and not follow the going into operation of the chartered rights of such States," declared Marshall. In the case of Poland, Marshall suggested that the new state's establishment be conditioned upon its leadership's explicit disavowal of pogroms and boycotts, and its recognition of the "principle that the Jews must have full and equal rights of citizenship" in the country. Throughout his address, Marshall indulged lofty rhetoric in describing what a Jewish delegation might attain at the peace conference (he referred, for instance, to a Jewish "Magna Charta of 1919"), but he studiously avoided the catchphrase cherished by many East European Jews, "national" rights. His words implied that Jews might seek national rights in states that accorded political recognition to national groups, but Marshall avoided associating himself explicitly with Zionists, or Diaspora Yiddish nationalists like Zhitlowski, who thought of Jews as a national entity. Marshall's delicate balancing act can be observed in the address's central affirmation of the congress's purposes:

> Various new or expanded Nations are about to be organized. The Jews constitute but a fraction of each of them. Their lot is with the people among whom they are to live. They can only insist, and I wish to repeat it over and over again, that if these Nations, however few or numerous they may be and however weak or powerful, are formed, then the Jews must be assured by those Nations of rights in every way equal to those of any other inhabitant of the State in which they may dwell. That is the fundamental principle of justice and righteousness for which we must and for which we shall not cease to contend until time shall be no more.[5]

In Marshall's mind, his work as a Jewish diplomat was taking on a familiar mediation dynamic. Just as during the cloakmakers strike, when his protocol formula allowed labor to believe that the workplace was being reconstituted as a union-dominated environment, and manufacturers avoided explicit commitment to dreaded formulas such as the closed shop, he was in this address assuring the Downtown Jewish delegates to the congress that their East European peers would win recognition as a national group in places where other groups were regarded as a political and legal entity. At the same time, however, Marshall did nothing to dislodge his own Uptown peers from their conviction that Jews around the world had a religious, rather than national, identity.

As a lawyer, it was appropriate for Marshall to focus on creative semantic formulations that broke impasses. However, in entering the diplomatic arena, he would be confronted by circumstances that were not necessarily analogous to his previous mediation efforts. In the cloakmakers strike, for instance, power was concentrated mainly in the hands of Jewish employers and employees, whereas the quibbling between Jewish delegates at the congress about national, as compared to individual, rights for East European Jews was liable to become esoteric sophistry insofar as it applied to millions of Jews who dwelled in lands where the main legacy of centuries was the lack of viable rights of any sort.

The work of the congress was undertaken by six committees that dealt with the needs of Jews in Romania, Poland, Russia, Lithuania, the Ukraine, and the new Slavic states. Members of the Romanian committee were especially adamant about the demand of "national" rights for Jews, along with political, civil, and religious rights; when members of the six committees met in joint session, Zhitlowski, along with Hourwich and Syrkin, took this as a cue and pressed hard for national rights formulations. Marshall essentially assented to this pressure when he drafted the "Jewish Bill of Rights" that was unanimously accepted by the congress. A few days after the congress adjourned, Marshall admitted to his old AJC confederate Mayer Sulzberger that national rights formulations were inserted in the resolutions to "avoid a riot" among Downtown delegates to the congress.[6]

The resolutions declared generally that all citizens of a particular land were entitled, "without distinction as to race, nationality or creed," to "equal, civil, political, religious and national rights." The resolutions also adopted the "principle of minority representation" that would guarantee Jewish and other minority groups in a state delegates of their own in the country's parliament, and they stipulated that a minority group "shall be accorded autonomous management of [its] own communal institutions."[7]

Through his sojourn in Paris, Marshall "remained absolutely loyal" to the rights formulas that were hatched by compromise at the congress sessions in Philadelphia.[8] It bears mention, however, that prominent members of his Uptown group were not formally committed to the congress resolutions, and at key phases of the Paris conference, these stewards conveyed directly to American peacemakers their opposition to the idea that Jews could or ought to receive rights on a national group basis in the new or enlarged states of East Europe. One was Henry Morgenthau, who served as an adviser to the American Peace Delegation. A close associate of President Wilson, Morgenthau argued against national rights formulas for Jews while demanding that they receive full civil and political rights.[9] Oscar Straus, who went to Paris as chairman of a committee of the League to Enforce Peace (a group that had since 1915 advocated the formation of a League of Nations), was similarly unreserved about his opposition to Zionists and other Jewish delegates who conceptualized Jewish rights in national terms. Secretary of State Lansing met with Straus for a private lunch on February 27, and mentioned that he was keeping an open mind on the issue of "Jewish nationality" in anticipation of a scheduled meeting with a Zionist delegation. Straus then launched into an attack on "national" formulations of Jewish rights. He announced to Lansing, "I was opposed to dual nationality and to any nationality that might in any way cast a cloud upon my American nationality."[10]

Before he set sail to serve as a Jewish peacemaker in Paris, Marshall had already disavowed this long-standing article of Uptown Jewish belief that Jews in any land ought not to receive rights as a separate nationality. In East Europe, Marshall realized, Jews logically sought rights on some national basis because under local political conditions, recognition had long been granted to national formulations. Thus, when Isaac Landman, the anti-Zionist editor of the *American Hebrew*, objected to the reference in the congress resolutions to the conferral of "civil, political, religious and national rights," Marshall delivered a telling lecture whose point was that American Jews should not blindly impose their own cultural and political sensibilities upon all Diaspora realities.[11] "It is to be borne in mind that we are dealing with Eastern European conditions, not those which prevail in the United States or in England, France and Italy," Marshall explained to Rabbi Landman. In areas such as Galicia, Marshall explained, "it is the belief that the welfare of the State and the happiness of its people will be best promoted by the stimulation of the several racial cultures. It is not for us in the United States to determine the wisdom of that conception. It is one that has entered deeply into the consciousness of the several groups."

The American Jewish Congress selected a Committee of Nine to cooperate in Paris with Jewish representatives from other countries in the adoption of the minority rights resolutions. The nine were Marshall, Mack, Wise, Syrkin, Barondess, Harry Cutler, Jacob De Haas, B. L. Levinthal, and Leopold Benedict.[12] Jacob Schiff and his associates at the American Jewish Committee insisted that Cyrus Adler go to Paris as the AJC's own representative. Adler, who traveled with Marshall to Paris and worked closely with him at the peace conference, was sent with a mandate "to cooperate in respect to securing full rights for the Jews in all lands where such rights are denied."[13]

In Paris, a division of labor developed between the Jewish diplomats, whereby Zionist delegates concentrated on issues relevant to the future of Palestine, and other representatives worked on Jewish minority rights in Diaspora lands.[14] Marshall's American Jewish Congress group became fused in Paris with what had congealed as a "largely self-constituted" Jewish delegation of representatives from Poland, Galicia, Czechoslovakia, Romania, and Italy—this group of Jewish delegates from the United States and Europe, formally constituted on March 25, 1919, came to be known as the Committee of Jewish Delegations (formally, Comité des Délégations Juives auprès de la Conférence de la Paix).[15] Julian Mack was president of this committee, but he left Paris because of professional obligations while the peace conference was still in session. Marshall was vice president but quickly emerged as the group's leading presence.

As Marshall subsequently recalled, a large share of his work was devoted to mediating between the Committee of Jewish Delegations and two imposing Jewish organizations based in France and England, the Alliance Israelite Universelle, and the Joint Foreign Committee of the Jewish Board of Deputies and the Anglo-Jewish Association. The alliance and the Joint Foreign Committee opposed "national" formulations regarding Jewish rights and had filed with the peace conference a separate petition for civil and religious rights for European Jews weeks before the Committee of Jewish Delegations was formed.[16]

In years of contact with Downtown's immigrant Jews, after trying to reform and Americanize them at the Educational Alliance or via propagandistic Yiddish journalism, and after fighting with them bitterly about the congress program,

Marshall had learned one fundamental truth: owing to the differing sociopolitical conditions in their region of origin, East European Jews had views and needs that were not identical to those of their Western compatriots. As he prepared for departure to Paris, Marshall preached passionately in favor of this latitudinarian message. Though he must have been aware that his own quarter-century experience of creative negotiation with Downtown attitudes was unusual, Marshall chided well-settled American Jews for ignoring the backgrounds and orientations of East European brethren. "The difficulty with many of our American Jews is that their views have remained stationary during the past fifty years and they are unable to understand East European conditions," Marshall growled in one private letter, written weeks before his sojourn to Paris. He continued:

> The use of the word "national" which has an entirely different significance in Eastern Europe from what it has with us induces a number of our very good friends to throw fits, merely because they imagine that their own status might be remotely affected by misinterpretation of the word by their fellow citizens of America, when as a matter of fact such misinterpretation is largely the creation of auto-suggestion. It reminds me of the old story of the mother who told her children not to put beans in their ears.[17]

Marshall had personal qualms about traveling to the peace conference. He had not been in Europe for twenty-two years, and he had been wretched with seasickness during his honeymoon journey with Florence.[18] He had hoped that his daughter Ruth might travel with him as a stenographer, but "too much red tape to unwind" precluded her company.[19] After the stress of the war years, including James's stint of service in France, Marshall strongly desired to enjoy the start of the postwar era with his family in New York (at the start, Cyrus Adler, his peace conference companion, was similarly ill-disposed toward the journey[20]). At the end of the congress meetings in Philadelphia, Marshall accounted for his decision to make the journey in tactical terms—he told Sulzberger that he would go to Paris to guarantee that Zionist lobbying on the Palestine question would not "overshadow the essential question of Jewish rights in Eastern Europe."[21]

This explanation simplified his psychology and sense of Jewish honor. Before the Armistice, during months filled with invective and imprecation on the congress issue, Marshall had argued that convening the forum during the war would be destructive of vital Jewish interests. Now, as the congress geared up for the constructive work of lobbying for Jewish security and freedom in Eastern Europe, he could not in good faith withdraw from its work. To do so would have provided retroactive justification to the Downtown accusation charging that Marshall and his AJC colleagues had objected to the congress out of apathy and self-interest, and not (as Marshall had insisted) due to a realistic and responsible assessment of American public sentiment and global circumstances during the war.

In the weeks before his departure, Marshall was caught in an anomalous strategic situation. The effectuation of the congress resolutions he had drafted was obviously dependent upon President Woodrow Wilson's support, but Marshall himself did not have faith in the president's peace program. Before setting off to Paris, he waited patiently for President Wilson to return from his first round of meetings at the peace conference; even as he polished arguments for minority rights accords designed to win Wilson's backing, however, he grumbled that the president's League of Nations scheme was "fraught with infinite peril to our [American] institutions." In a letter to prominent corporate attorney William D. Guthrie, Marshall urged that "lawyers of America retain their sanity" and not support Wilson's program, "which thus far consists merely of rhetorical phrases." He added, "Never has the observance of the warnings against entangling alliances been so important as it is today."[22] American participation in Wilson's league, Marshall warned his son James,[23] would precipitate "conflict after conflict" with the Constitution and also invite the possibility of "European intervention in American affairs." He sensed that the president's quixotic idealism would make America "a catspaw for the purpose of pulling European chestnuts out of the fire." He objected to the way Wilsonian cheerleading about the self-determination of small nations had transmogrified into "an attempt at internationalizing all nations."

Wise arranged for a Jewish delegation to meet with Wilson at the White House on March 2, during the president's intermission between his arduous rounds of diplomacy at the Paris conference. Mack joined Marshall and Wise for the meeting.[24] Marshall resubmitted the two petitions on Poland he had sent to Wilson right at the end of the war[25]—one was an updated list of demands for minority rights in Poland featuring the conferral of autonomous management of Jewish religious, educational, and cultural institutions, recognition of the right to observe the Sabbath on Saturdays and to attend to secular affairs on the other days of the week, and minority representation rights (Marshall added this last request to a similar roster of demands he had previously sent to the president); the second was a request that the president issue a statement hinting that Polish statehood would not be recognized in a peace agreement until the Poles proved that they would end the economic boycott and other anti-Jewish policies. Months before the March meeting, Wilson had replied positively to the first petition, promising that the demand for Jewish and other minority rights in Poland would be "constantly in my thought[s]" at Paris, and negatively to the second request, saying that it would be "unwise" for him to issue an announcement stipulating conditions of Polish statehood ("I think you can hardly realize all the reactions of my attempting leadership in too many ways," Wilson replied to Marshall on November 20, 1918[26]).

"Judge Mack, Stephen Wise and I had an audience with him [President Wilson] at the White House on Sunday evening for nearly an hour," Marshall wrote to his youngest sibling, Ida, after the March meeting. "He was most sympathetic with our program, more so than I am with his League of Nations, which I regard as jeopardizing the future of America."[27]

Arrival at the Peace Conference

Marshall sailed to France on March 12. The trip has been "pleasant," he bravely wrote to his children as the ship approached the Irish coast and simultaneously undermined that characterization by complaining about stretches during which the boat had felt like a "gyroscope." He fasted, stayed in his cabin, and regained his equilibrium ("my inner ear is beginning to find its balance—that's one of the compensations of advancing years," he wrote to his children). Adler's company, at least, was "immensely congenial," Marshall reported. "Had he not been with me this would have been a dreary trip, since I am not so constituted as to make acquaintances easily during these years."[28] Adler and Marshall reached Liverpool on March 23 and headed by train for London, where they quartered comfortably at the Carlton. They were in Paris for Shabbat eve services at the Rue Victoire synagogue on March 28. Hundreds of worshippers rose for the Kaddish mourner's prayer. "The congregation gave me a more forcible idea of what France has suffered than anything I have read," an obviously moved Adler noted in his diary.[29]

Still, peace had come, bringing with it new hopes and the renewed delights of the living. "The Champs Elysees are beautiful," Marshall wrote to his children in early April. "The streets are gay with every imaginable uniform—the boys in khaki are here in large numbers."[30] Marshall at this stage was socializing one night with the nationalists and the next night with the antinationalists; he had dinner one night with "Mack, Weizmann and other Zionist notables" and the next night with Oscar Straus and his wife Sarah.[31]

Seven years after their acrimonious exchanges in the 1912 New York gubernatorial race, Marshall and Straus had let bygones be bygones. In this case, Marshall's aversion to holding grudges paid dividends, because Straus provided him access to Dr. Casimir Dluski, a physician by profession and one of the two Polish delegates to the peace conference. Straus observed privately after the April 8 dinner engagement that unlike his counterpart, Roman Dmowski, Dluski was "not an avowed anti-Semite" and recognized "the necessity of giving the three or more million Jews their fullest religious rights."[32] Lewis Strauss, a young man with (in Cyrus Adler's glowing estimate) "an enormous power of work and a kind heart" who was in Paris as secretary to Herbert Hoover (chairman of the American Relief Administration), brought to this April 8 meeting sobering reports about anti-Semitism in Poland. Sarah Straus translated portions into French for Dluski, who expressed "strong disapproval" of oppression against Jews, while stressing that "there had never before in Poland's long history been any pogroms."[33] Skeptical, Marshall "went fully into the subject" (as Oscar Straus put it) of Poland's recent discrimination against Jews, focusing on the boycott. Marshall reviewed his October 6, 1918, meeting with Dmowski and Paderewski,[34] in which the former unapologetically accounted for the reasons why he and his party instituted a boycott against the Jews. Dluski "spoke disparagingly" of Dmowski's anti-Semitism, Straus noted.[35]

Marshall and the Jewish Delegation in Historical Perspective

Such discussions with foreign leaders were not the focus of Marshall's activity during his first weeks in Paris, however. After sundown on Saturday night, April 5, Marshall chaired an argumentative meeting of forty-five Jewish delegates held on the premises of the Alliance Israelite Universelle. The discussions resumed the next evening and almost culminated in a walkout of East European delegates, who demanded broadly formulated provisions of national autonomy.[36] Organized under the direction of Leo Motzkin, an articulate Zionist from Kiev, the nationalists pressed in this period for provisions, most famously representation for the world's 15 million Jews at the League of Nations, which none of the Western Jewish delegates could readily countenance. Showing exasperation during the April 5 discussion, the alliance's Eugene See exclaimed at one point that "the business of the peace conference is to create a sovereign state for Poland, not for the Jews."[37] On the second night of the discussions, Nahum Sokolow, who had earlier passionately called for unity among delegates of the Jewish delegation, angrily demanded an East European breakaway; "*divorçons! divorçons! divorçons!*" Sokolow cried.[38]

Carole Fink, who surveyed these Jewish debates and the surrounding Paris diplomacy in detail, regards the April 5–6 meetings as a "debacle,"[39] and her harsh judgment is warranted in several ways. Marshall was unable to find common ground for coordinated action between the alliance and Joint Foreign Committee, on the one hand, and the Jewish delegation, on the other; he often ended up lobbying in subsequent weeks at the peace conference at his own discretion, after the Jewish delegation appointed a committee under Motzkin's direction to draft a proposed minority rights treaty. (This committee's work was protracted, and Marshall in 1923 even suggested that the peace conference agreed on terms of a minority rights treaty *before* the Jewish delegation formally submitted its proposal on May 10.[40]) At the time, however, Marshall's own view of the discussions was somewhat more positive. As he phrased it to his children, these were debates staged between the "warring factions of Jewry." These exhausting conferences allowed "all of the steam to be let off," and at the end of the first week in April, Marshall reported confidently, "our work is now making progress."[41] Sharing his friend's cautious optimism, Adler wrote exactly at this time in his diary that "our own affairs here are beginning to take a better turn—at least an approach to unity. . . . I cannot say that harmony is certain, but at least approaches have been made."[42] Marshall had been authorized to appoint a Committee of Seven,[43] and this panel was "accomplishing the impossible"—it was cobbling together formulations and demands in a pragmatic fashion that was "ending all controversies" and would (Marshall hoped) "enable us to present our case before the Peace Conference with a united front." This was no mean feat. "It has been a difficult task, and has required unlimited patience and self-restraint," Marshall privately confided to his children.[44] "God knows this is a time when good understanding and peace are needed in this world," Adler wrote prayerfully in his diary. He was privately pleased that "my traveling companion [Marshall] and I represent the U.S.A. on this committee of seven, so there is no kick coming our way."[45]

The dismal failure of the minority rights accords in the Paris peace treaty in the years preceding the Holocaust obscures our understanding of Marshall's prodigious efforts at the Paris conference to find points of commonality between two distinct—Western and Eastern—modern Jewish political experiences and to forge a coherent platform of Jewish demands acceptable to delegates who spoke two different Jewish political dialects owing to their separate upbringings and allegiances. One dialect spoke about Jewish political integration in Western host societies and Jewish preservation in primarily religious terms, whereas the other dialect discussed Jewish continuity and rebirth in the politicized language of nationalism and stressed not integration but some form of Jewish separatism, either in recognized cultural-social-educational forms of autonomy in states like Poland or in a national home in British-controlled Palestine under the aegis of the Balfour Declaration. These Western and Eastern perspectives, described by historians as emancipation versus nationalist political models, were founded on significantly different premises and pointed to significantly different ends. While a mediator like Marshall might have logically said to Western and Eastern delegates during one of these fiery early April debates in Paris that "we all, as Jews, want the same thing, namely freedom for Jews in Eastern Europe," parties from the two sides would have quickly questioned what was meant by "freedom"—freedom for the Jews of Poland or Romania to become Poles and Romanians, or freedom for them to remain Jews and live in legally safeguarded separate autonomy?

The Jewish delegates at Paris had concrete purposes to accomplish, all relating to the betterment of Jewish life in Eastern Europe and Palestine, but they had compelling historical reasons to speak a bifurcated political babble inexpressive of any realistic diplomatic agenda. That Nazism and other subsequent forces utterly destroyed the platform the delegates had formulated has to do with an array of social, economic, and political factors well exceeding the primary weakness that historians have identified among Jewish delegates like Marshall. Of course, it is true, as scholars have pointed out, that Marshall, Mack, and others in the delegation had limited horizons, since they were trained lawyers who thought about the peace treaty as a kind of binding contract, whereas the treaty's substantive impact was obviously destined to be dependent upon a wealth of factors not related to the words that were legalistically crafted into it.[46] However, Marshall was, in fact, keenly appreciative and adaptable with respect to the political realities surrounding the peace conference (as we shall see, his views regarding Wilson's League of Nations program shifted considerably), and his seminal contribution at the peace conference had more to do with his accumulated experience in Jewish affairs than with his specific training as a lawyer.

Paris in 1919 was an enormously complicated global moment when Jews urgently needed to develop a common vocabulary to articulate their own particular needs. Louis Marshall provided that language of twentieth-century Jewish politics in one of the stellar moments of his career. At the time, his achievement seemed spectacular. In retrospect, his mediation appears clearly as the element that prevented a total breakdown between the two Jewish perspectives at Paris. The author of the most detailed and insightful study of Jewish diplomacy at the peace conference generally emphasizes its fissure between nationalists who "sought protection against a palpable threat to Jewish life in Eastern Europe" and antinationalists who sought protection "against a threat to their hard-won status and influence in the western democracies."[47] Marshall fit somewhere between these camps because, as fundamentally an Uptown antinationalist, he had, over the years, become responsive to the sensitivities and outlooks of Downtown immigrant Jews who remained focused on the fate of their indigent or persecuted brethren in Eastern Europe.

His Paris diplomacy was begotten by the Jewish politics of New York. Marshall's mediation acumen was highly esteemed by everyone who took part in the Jewish delegation at Paris, but their adulatory tributes should not be seen simply as personal accolades. In effect, such adulation honored the complicated but empowering process of Jewish ethnic consolidation in New York City. East-West dynamics are an ongoing, transnational trait of modern Jewish politics, but the experience of early twentieth-century New York featured a unique blend of massive demographics and genuine socioeconomic opportunity. For a quarter century, Marshall had been trading tokens at this New York turnstile of modern Jewish experience, urging the East European immigrants from Downtown to modify some portion of their nationalist orientations while delineating, for the edification of his own Westernized Uptown elite, the moral and practical limits of Americanization schemes. That experience bestowed unique insight into ways Western and Eastern groups of Jews thought about the challenges of communal continuity, the seizure of opportunities, and the attainment of rights. And it was this New York experience that propelled him to the forefront of Jewish diplomacy at the Paris Peace Conference.

A vivid portrait of the emotional climate and substantive circumstances of Marshall's diplomacy was provided by a Galician economist, Joseph Tennenbaum, who served on the Jewish delegation at Paris and later authored, in Yiddish and Hebrew, an important memoir about the experience. The author describes Marshall as "incredibly obstinate" and then proceeds to depict him as being a passionately engaged debater and listener. The implicit appreciation bestowed on Marshall by this Galician delegate at Paris became more pronounced in tributes paid to Marshall in the 1920s by Downtown immigrant Jews in New York, who recognized that within his dogmatic exterior Marshall was uniquely attuned to their sensitivities and perspectives:

> Marshall was an excellent lawyer, but he could also be incredibly obstinate. During hours of exhaustive debate about matters of principle, arguments which lasted for weeks and which featured sparks of rhetorical flair, Marshall would appeal to logic, and also level threats. One after another, the delegates from Eastern Europe would refute his arguments about Jewish integration, displaying their historical bankruptcy. Each delegate would bring examples from his own country whose message was that Western-style acculturation was not consistent with the special circumstances of the Jewish masses. They used parables and anecdotes to show that civil rights without the option of using Yiddish in a country's public sphere would be useless; and that even the principle of "freedom of religion" would be meaningless, were it not to be supplemented by Jewish schools and "Shabbat rest" laws.[48]

Uptown appreciation of Marshall's labors at Paris soared. Later in the experience, toward the end of the peace conference, Cyrus Adler noted privately that

"Marshall has been wonderful, and we never could have accomplished half of what we have without him." In Adler's view, Marshall's profession was, in Paris, a necessity, and he honored it for the benefit of Jewish interests; "this has been largely a lawyer's task," Adler observed, and "in competition with the greatest international lawyers of the world, he [Marshall] has more than held his own."[49] Years later, Lewis Strauss recalled that observing Marshall at work during the conference "surpassed anything I have ever experienced." Also impressed by Adler, Strauss noted in a panegyric vein that "there were giants in those days." Also, essentially rephrasing after thirty-five years the description left by Tennenbaum, Herbert Hoover's secretary at the conference, Lewis Strauss, alluded to Adler's and Marshall's "patience in listening for days on end to long harangues and arguments," their "perseverance in the face of great odds," and "their great force and accompanying gentleness and humanity."[50]

"The Critical Moment in Jewish History": Lobbying for the Minority Rights Treaty

"This is the critical moment in Jewish history," Marshall wrote to his children in mid-April, "and I would deem myself recreant to a sacred trust were I now to desert my post of duty."[51] He was camped at the Hotel de Crillon with Judge Mack, conferring intensely with world diplomats, including Wilson's adviser Colonel House, whose "clear and concise manner of dealing with matters of great complexity"[52] impressed Marshall (ironically, Wilson had at this stage lost confidence in his long-time adviser[53]), and two of House's protégés. One, Manley Hudson, a peace activist who at the time awaited an appointment to the Harvard Law School, was favorably disposed to Jewish minority rights claims and also closely connected to Marshall's circle (Hudson was friendly with Jacob Billikopf, a fundraiser who was deeply respected for his wartime work on the Jewish relief campaigns and would soon marry Marshall's daughter Ruth[54]). The second, David Hunter Miller, legal adviser to the American delegation, responded critically from mid- to late April to Marshall's draft program for minority rights in Eastern Europe. Miller modified references to rights and equal protection, dropped the Sabbath clause, and trimmed the stipulation for minority representation, but did preserve Marshall's arching statement that the Jews in Poland constituted a "national minority."[55] Marshall explained to his children that this drafting and redrafting process was a "most exacting labor." Not Miller's red pencil but the argumentative Jewish delegates complicated the process. "If we had fewer wiseacres to express their views, we would make better progress," Marshall confessed.[56] Exhausted by the speech-making, Marshall was relieved when it became clear that, unlike the Zionists, proponents of minority rights would not have a public hearing before the peace conference.[57]

Even at this high point in the drafting of the minority treaties, Marshall handled other Jewish responsibilities and interests. With Adler, he closely monitored Jewish relief projects—at the end of the first week in April, Adler and Marshall personally supervised the purchase, for $100,000, of army surplus shoes, underwear, socks, and children's clothes for Polish Jews.[58] Marshall and Adler celebrated Passover at a seder sponsored in Paris by the Jewish Welfare Board; 450 of the 500 participants were soldiers, and Marshall's speech after the meal was cabled to Yiddish newspapers in New York.[59] By mid-April, the relief work, Marshall learned, became horrifyingly entangled in anti-Semitic persecution. "There has occurred a shocking series of murders at Pinsk of those engaged in the work of relief distribution, on the pretext that they were Bolshevists," Marshall reported to his children in mid-April.[60]

He was referring to a gruesome event that occurred on April 5, at the Zionist organization's Beit Am (People's House) in Pinsk, a city controlled by the Polish army and where Jews constituted at least half of the 26,000 inhabitants. Following a meeting held at this facility to discuss the distribution of matzo flour provided by the Joint Distribution Committee, a Polish force summarily executed thirty-four of the hundred or so Beit Am occupants and imprisoned many of the others.[61] "The situation created [in Pinsk] is serious," Marshall estimated.[62]

He was right. For weeks, world officials referred to the Beit Am murders to promote points on their diplomatic agenda. Germans, for instance, pointed to Pinsk as evidence that the Poles were incompetent to rule minority groups. Members of the Jewish delegation viewed the Pinsk murders as a grisly reminder that East European Jews had yet to receive protections and rights ("we are presenting this [Pinsk] horror as an object lesson to demonstrate the absolute need of accepting our program," Marshall noted privately at the end of April[63]). For them, Pinsk "also intensified the burden" of defending Jews in Eastern Europe against charges of treachery and Bolshevism.[64] In Carole Fink's analysis, the Pinsk incident was "not literally a pogrom" but rather a "military execution of a small, suspect group of civilians" that exerted disproportionate influence at Paris and was manipulated by victors and losers who held an array of perspectives concerning the disposition of Poland.[65] On the Jewish side, the murderous shootings in Pinsk aggravated differences between the Western integrationist Jewish delegates in Paris and their Eastern nationalist counterparts. For the East European delegates, the Pinsk attack "bolstered the case for the broadest possible national autonomy," whereas for the Western delegates, Pinsk served "as a warning against creating a permanent rift between Poles and Jews."[66]

Marshall, by May, had used whatever leverage could be found to confer with British and American officials, but he had yet to meet with President Wilson in Paris, and he lacked the means to approach the other leaders of the Big Four: David Lloyd George, George Clemenceau, and Vittorio Orlando. In a key gambit, Marshall decided to "stake it all in one card" and follow the "rather risky procedure" of relying on petitions to Wilson. "International politics and the selfish interests of diplomats are shaky reeds," he explained to his children. "Everything will depend on President Wilson."[67]

According to the historian Carole Fink, this was "the great miscalculation" of Marshall's Paris adventure.[68] As a Republican, she points out, Marshall lacked easy entry to Wilson's court. The president believed that as the world rid itself of German imperialism and Russian Bolshevism, his League of Nations would serve as a watchdog of international behavior; hence, Wilson "had no intention of countenancing special privileges for anyone," neither for millions of Germans slated for the new Czechoslovakia nor for Jews.[69] Moreover, before Marshall even reached Paris on his three-month visit, Wilson's all-purpose mechanism for protecting rights around the world, the league, had been constituted in a fashion that did not augur well for vulnerable Jewish communities. To block Japan's demand for a statement on universal racial equality, Wilson omitted from the league covenant a clause requiring all members to grant religious freedom to their inhabitants.[70]

These are, of course, cogent criticisms, but they presuppose that Marshall had other viable options, and they appear to overlook the enormously mesmerizing power Wilson himself projected at Paris, even though the popularity he had enjoyed during his first stint at the conference dissipated somewhat in the spring, as did Wilson's own enthusiasm (the president fell ill in early April and threatened to quit the conference). Americans in Paris in spring 1919 found themselves entirely dependent upon Wilson. For instance, the American Zionists were dealing with the thorny issue of whether holding a plebiscite in Palestine would constitute a fair application of the Wilsonian principle of self-determination, and as the other powers eventually divorced themselves from this plebiscite mechanism, Felix Frankfurter spent his days composing impassioned appeals to Wilson to argue against a use of this machinery that would be rigidly oblivious to Jewish needs.[71] By early May in Paris, both the American Zionist lobbyists and the American proponents of Jewish minority rights had, like delegates from countless other interest groups, hinged their fates entirely upon Wilson.

No less important, in view of the particular circumstances of the American Jewish Congress's formation and the drafting of its resolutions, Marshall had no other place to turn. However acrimonious they had been at stages, his ongoing discussions with the Downtown activists had left Marshall irrevocably committed to various nationalist conceptualizations of minority rights. From the start, this put him at odds with English and French counterparts from the Joint Foreign Committee and the Alliance Israelite Universelle, since (it will be recalled) these two organizations had in February preemptively sent petitions to the peace conference, calling for equal rights in language couched in classically Western, non-nationalist idiom. This meant that, from the start, Marshall lacked counterpart French Jewish or English Jewish intercessors, who might perhaps have helped forge links to the French and British delegations.[72] By choosing to work with East European Jews, both in New York on the American Jewish Congress, and in Paris on the Jewish delegation, Marshall faced a trade-off: he broadened the vocabulary of Jewish political discourse but also burned his bridges to the British and French powers because of the antinationalist dogmatism of representative French- and British-based Jewish organizations at the conference.

As Fink points out, Marshall at one urgent phase of the minority treaty lobbying forged a passing alliance with Lucien Wolf,[73] who was rattled by evidence of pogroms in East Europe that had been forcibly thrust upon him by Felix Frankfurter. This was far from a promising partnership, however. Wolf was well versed in international affairs, whereas Marshall was a novice diplomat in Paris; but Marshall's accumulated experience in Jewish affairs rendered him at least partly accountable to East European sensibilities in favor of Diaspora autonomy and Zionism, whereas Wolf remained fatefully impervious to all nationalist variants in Jewish politics. When, on June 1, 1919, Wolf presented himself as a champion of "the permanent interests of our brethren in Eastern Europe,"[74] he actually demonstrated how inflexibly committed he remained to the battle-worn integrationist models of Jewish politics and how little attuned he would be, despite his considerable diplomatic experience, to the anti-Semitic dynamics of the interwar period. "I look beyond the pogrom-stricken fields," Wolf wrote, "to a time when on the basis of equal rights the Jews of Poland will be full partners in a State in which they will be legitimately proud."[75]

That sort of roseate phrasing, Marshall recognized, was foreign to the nationalist-inflected idiom of the East European Jews. In fact, he believed that Wolf faltered badly at the peace conference in his duties as an advocate of world Jewry, and throughout the 1920s Marshall spoke with disdain about Wolf, observing that the "preponderant majority" of Jews in the world "do not desire his advocacy."[76] This Wolf example illustrates how Marshall's complicated yet authentic loyalties toward Downtown Jews of New York and to their East European counterparts in Paris closed off avenues of European diplomacy. In the end, his only option was to try to affix minority rights formulas to the Wilsonian ideal of self-determination of small nations, exactly as Felix Frankfurter's only option was to attach Zionism to Wilsonian diplomacy.

Marshall's turn to Wilson was not entirely expedient. In a revealing letter written late in 1919 to the English Jewish literary gadfly Israel Zangwill,[77] who had mockingly referred to Wilson's initiative as the "League of Damnations," Marshall detailed his own emotional and ideological transformation in Paris, where he had been "occupied from 16 to 18 hours daily" trying to "create a modus vivendi between [Jews from] Eastern and Western Europe." After describing how most members of the Jewish delegation had become "extremely bitter" toward Wolf and the Alliance Israelite Universelle's Sylvan Levy, Marshall reflected about the way the minority rights program he forged together with his East European counterparts on the delegation became wedded to Wilson's program. "If the League becomes an actuality, I am confident that, in the course of time, the complete emancipation of the Jews will be brought about." Without the league, he feared, "we shall only have obtained paper rights, although even the formulation and adoption of rights of so flimsy a nature as we would then have will be of considerable value." Later, ahead of the 1920 presidential elections, Marshall identified himself with the wing of the Republican Party that, with "reasonable reservations," favored Wilson's program. "I believe in the League of Nations," he declared. "It is not a perfect instrument . . . but unless we desire to convert the whole world into a slaughter-house, we must make up our minds to effectuate the underlying idea of the Covenant of the League of Nations."[78]

Finally, Fink's assessment of Marshall's reliance on Wilson as a crucial miscalculation does not really accord with the record of the president's diplomacy at Paris. The president certainly had considerations at the forefront of his mind that pushed matters of urgency to Jews and other minorities to the rear. However, whatever his priorities and private beliefs, Wilson ended up strongly advocating the minority rights treaty at the May 31 secret plenary meeting he headed (with Lloyd George and Clemenceau), which featured the participation of mostly disgruntled delegates from seventeen states. Speaking at this decisive meeting, Wilson declared that a comprehensive peace agreement must remove all causes of future disorder, including "the treatment meted out to minorities."[79] Essentially, Fink faults Wilson for advocating new diplomatic principles, like minority rights accords, "without having committed himself to the establishment of strong and effective rules" for their enforcement,"[80] but this critique sounds more like a comment on the tragedy of American foreign policy in this era than a valid criticism of Marshall and innumerable other Americans and non-Americans whose agendas depended at this time on the success of the president's program.

The Minority Rights Treaties

Minority rights treaties were hammered out at the Paris peace conference in May by a Committee on New States that included David Hunter Miller and Britain's Sir James Headlam-Morley, who met occasionally with Marshall and Lucien Wolf.[81] As a whole, the committee met in secret and never heard testimony from Poles and Jews. In the middle of the month, the Committee on New States produced a draft inimical to Jewish interests—the blueprint dismissed national claims favored by the East European Jewish delegates, formulated citizenship rights provisions in weak language, and eliminated Shabbat and Sunday trading provisions that Marshall and Wolf regarded as crucial for the future of Polish Jews.

This setback caused Marshall to favor a public lobbying campaign for a stronger minority rights treaty. He seemed more isolated than ever: Judge Mack was returning to the United States, and Zionists and non-Zionists were stunned by news of Aaron Aaronsohn's death in an airplane crash over the English Channel. "This is the time when no relaxation of effort is permissible," Marshall intoned in a letter to his children. "The fate of our people depends on the turn of the hand."[82] In New York, Jews campaigned against pogroms, and at a crowded May 21, 1919, rally held at Madison Square Garden, featuring distinguished speakers such as Supreme Court Justice Charles Evans Hughes, Schiff demanded that Poland not be reconstituted as a state until it provided credible guarantees that it would protect Jews and other minorities.[83] On May 24, Marshall delivered a stirring address to the Ligue des Droits de l'Homme (League of the Rights of Man) at a rally convened to protest violence against Jews in Eastern Europe.[84] "We representatives of the Jews of America have come to Paris to ask for the emancipation of the Jews, and of all minorities," he announced. He emphasized that a minority rights treaty would be a mere "paper constitution" without the backing of the League of Nations. He referred to 150 pogroms that had taken place in Eastern Europe since the end of the war and surveyed the grisly details of the Pinsk murders, adding that 100,000 marks sent by the American Jewish Relief Committee for victimized Jews in the town had been seized by the military. "We have not only to protest against what is past, but also to raise our voices against a continuation of it," Marshall affirmed. "It is for that we are here, to say to the Great Powers, 'Listen to these facts, and notify these people, these governments, that this must not continue and that someone must be punished for these crimes against the human family.'" He called for a specific provision in the minority treaties "that will make pogroms in the future impossible."

As far as Marshall was concerned, the turning point in his three-month diplomatic stint in Paris occurred during his and Adler's "most satisfactory" May 26 meeting with President Wilson.[85] The following day, the "saddest of the year" because it was the third anniversary of Florence's death, Marshall wrote to his children that the "President was exceedingly gracious and at his best."[86] The president's retention of details and arguments cited in Marshall's various petitions amazed the Jewish intercessors. A year and a half later, an admiring Marshall recalled that Wilson "quoted almost literally from the conversation that we had at the White House on March 2cnd. He thoroughly understood the status of the Jews in the several countries."[87] Marshall, Adler, and the president discussed the pogroms, the Bolsheviks, the Poles, the "necessity of protecting minority groups," and "the League of Nations and its functions affording sanctions for the guaranties that are to be given in the constitutions of the new East European governments."[88] The meeting spilled into the president's next scheduled appointment, but Wilson kept the French ambassador waiting as he accompanied Adler and Marshall down part of the staircase. Adler commented that the president seemed to be holding up very well under great strain, and Wilson replied that he was keeping his strength because he had not lost his sense of humor.[89] Adler told Marshall that had anyone told them five years ago that they were to meet the president of the United States in Paris, they would have had to have him locked up as a lunatic; Adler added that this was the first such interview that had been secured at the conference by Jewish American proponents of minority rights.[90] "I am satisfied that with a few exceptions, our entire program is likely to be adopted," an enthusiastic Marshall wrote to his children, after the meeting.[91]

This estimate was somewhat overly optimistic.[92] The drafting and signing of the minority rights treaties was complicated in subsequent weeks by vociferous objections articulated by delegates from Romania, Poland, Czechoslovakia, Yugoslavia, and Greece at a secret plenary meeting on May 31, and then in mid-June, Poland sent a detailed list of criticisms of the minority treaty to the Council of Four.[93] Simultaneously, Polish leaders denied reports of pogroms and suggested that they were circulated maliciously by German and Jewish representatives in order to advance their diplomatic agendas; Polish Prime Minister Ignace Jan Paderewski called for an independent investigation.[94] Hugh Gibson, the new US minister to Poland, similarly cast doubt upon the authenticity of the pogrom reports and leaked insulting characterizations of Polish Jewry to the press. Marshall fought back hard against Gibson, publishing in US newspapers castigations of the envoy's bias.[95] When Wilson asked anti-Zionist Henry Morgenthau to head a Polish inquiry commission, Marshall and colleagues joined with the Zionists in vehement efforts to overturn this appointment; Wilson stood by Morgenthau, however, and when his team's report was issued months later, in autumn 1919, Marshall conceded that it was, "under the circumstances, quite a good document."[96] In the meantime, the Council of Four, eager to wrap things up and naturally focus on the German treaty, struck a bargain with the Poles, allowing their new state to spread into eastern Galicia (thereby adding 700,000 more Jews, not to mention 4 million Ukrainians) in exchange for Dmowski's and Paderewski's assent to the minority rights treaty. Minutes after the Germans signed their treaty on June 28 in the Hall of Mirrors, the Poles put their initials to the "Little Versailles" accord.[97]

"This is a great day in the history of the world, and it is an equally joyous one in the history of the Jewish people," an exultant Marshall wrote to his children.[98] The Polish treaty "confers complete emancipation upon the minorities of that country, and it is to be followed by treaties which are to be written on the same terms with Rumania, Greece, Czechoslovakia, etc." Marshall claimed that the minority treaty "carries out my program in every important feature, and goes further than I had the right to expect." He said the fact that Paderewski and Dmowski signed the treaty was a source of special satisfaction. Marshall was drenched with congratulations. The East European Jewish delegates, he noted, "are the most grateful and appreciative. Although they realize that they still have many obstacles to overcome, they know that they have at least secured a charter of liberty." As he had seven years earlier when the US Congress abrogated the Russian treaty, Marshall spoke reverentially, feeling thankful for the opportunity to contribute to Jewish history: "I feel grateful to the Almighty that he has enabled me to lead in this sacred cause for right, justice and equality."[99]

As in the case of abrogation, however, the obtainment of a minority rights treaty at Paris proved to have symbolic rather than substantive import. Contrary to Marshall's boastful claims to his family about the treaty's fulfillment of his "entire program," one careful scholarly analysis of the treaty's terms reveals that they were insufficient from the start, even before recalcitrant Polish governments chose to ignore them in practice.[100] Article 2 of the Polish treaty guaranteed "full and complete protection of life and liberty" to all inhabitants in the country and included a broad provision for religious freedom. Article 7 stressed that all Polish citizens were to be equal before the law; it established Polish as the official language but protected the use of minority languages in private and public venues. Article 8 furnished forms of legal protection to minorities, allowing them to establish, manage, and control charitable, religious, and educational institutions at their own expense, and to use their own languages and observe their own religious rites in those languages. As Carole Fink notes, this article provided mostly illusory benefits to minorities, and its terms actually paid tribute to the obstinate diplomacy of Polish leaders. By the treaty's terms, neither Jews nor other minority groups won recognition as autonomous or semiautonomous national minorities;

instead, they were referred to as "Polish nationals who belong to racial, religious or linguistic minorities." Furthermore, since Article 8 promised no state support for a minority's self-managed educational, cultural, and religious institutions, it offered little practical benefit to Poland's largely destitute Jewish population. In the months following the signing of this "Little Versailles" minorities accord, Marshall, unlike the wealthy patrons of the AJC and the Joint, appeared to grasp the implications of Article 8. Owing partly to his understanding that the exhausting American Jewish Congress and Paris Jewish delegation discussions about Jewish national autonomy in Poland and elsewhere now meant nothing in the absence of outside budgetary assistance, Marshall unfurled highly ambitious plans for American Jewish funding to aid the reconstruction of Jewish life in Eastern Europe. Unrealistically grandiose from the start, these calls were quickly buried by other priorities and pursuits undertaken by American Jewish philanthropists in the 1920s.[101] Articles 10 and 11, Fink writes, constituted "small victories" for Marshall and his cohorts, attained via hard bargaining that overcame the vehement opposition of Poland's leadership. Article 10 allowed local Jewish committees, "subject to the general control of the state," to disburse funds to religious schools and other institutions, and Article 11 protected Jewish Sabbath observance in civilian life and prohibited the state from holding elections on Saturdays.

Summarizing the Polish treaty and similar accords forced upon other states in the region, Fink writes unsparingly that they "fell far short of Marshall's goals for a Jewish bill of rights." Their citizenship and religious protection clauses "were extremely vague and weak," and "every shred of a Jewish national identity had been omitted from the final text."[102] In a similarly skeptical note, Ezra Mendelsohn, the author of a definitive study of Jewish political and social circumstances in interwar Eastern and Central Europe, wonders why, in view of the treaties' elusive formulations and the obvious difficulty of their enforceability (aggravated by the rejection of Wilson's league program in America), some Jewish groups were so jubilant about the minority treaties, touting them as a Jewish Magna Carta.[103]

Of course, criticisms of the vagueness in formulations of the minority treaties do not necessarily mean that Marshall was manipulated into poor word choices either by the zealous, self-interested Polish nationalists or by skeptical American jurists like David Hunter Miller, who had a world to take care of. It redounds to Marshall's credit that colleagues were deeply impressed by his powers of negotiation and expression in the drafting of the minority treaties; but, historically speaking, that is an incidental rather than substantive evaluation. With regard to such peace conference agreements, the extent of the scribe's expressive tenacity and skill had questionable historical consequence. The terms of the British Mandate were drafted, by and large, at the Paris conference by another gifted American Jewish jurist, Felix Frankfurter;[104] nobody, however, in the voluminous chronicling of the Israeli-Arab dispute, has ever seriously thought to praise or blame Frankfurter for what happened in Palestine under British rule through 1948, and the same should obviously be said about Marshall's treaty draftsmanship and the fate of Jews and other minorities in interwar Poland and other East European states.

The contrasting fates of Jews in North America and Eastern Europe were determined not by the vagueness or sagacity of formulations incorporated in constitutional documents relevant to life in those lands between the world wars but rather by the question of whether historical experience encouraged minority protection and political freedom in the particular region. These are obvious points, but they are too easily overtaken by what the historian E. P. Thompson once called "the enormous condescension of posterity."[105] Issues that can be and have been raised about the merits of Marshall's diplomatic efforts—such as the point that coercively imposing the minority rights treaties upon the Polish nationalists might have aggravated the future course of Polish-Jewish relations[106]—reverse dynamics of causality and unfairly attribute to historical actors options they never had. Marshall had absolutely no warrant to remain cautiously idle in Paris on the theory that an assertion of the principle that Jews ought to have rights might upset the anti-Semites. The formation of the American Jewish Congress, in a milieu of extraordinarily militant ethnic feeling, irrevocably extended to him a duty of Jewish activism. An empiricist, and also never one to be mechanically persuaded by the passions of the crowd, Marshall in Paris scorned a cautiously patient approach, favored by Lucien Wolf (among others), of direct talks with the Polish nationalists because he himself had spoken to Roman Dmowski and others before the end of the war and had witnessed firsthand their hostility to Jewish needs. More than anything, his decision to relate to minority rights after World War I as a constitutional issue, and not in the neotraditional vein of a cowering *shtadlan* obsequiously asking local rulers for favors, derived from an appreciable historical experience of give-and-take between Uptown and Downtown New York, by which both groups searched creatively to fuse American constitutional conceptualizations to considerations of Jewish national pride.

At some point in the process, as Marshall moved from endeavors at the Educational Alliance, the *Jewish World,* the Jewish Theological Seminary, and the American Jewish Committee, he learned to view the Downtown immigrants not as a crowd but as a constituency. And he became their advocate. In Paris, that advocacy internationalized on the grandest stage imaginable and extended to the East Side New Yorkers' East European kin. To suggest that he championed their needs in Poland or Romania because he wanted to keep them out of New York[107] traduces a fifteen-year blue ribbon record of intensive lobbying on Capitol Hill for open immigration; to suggest that his diplomacy at Paris imperiled Jews in Warsaw in any way gives the anti-Semites far too little credit for their ability to dip into a reservoir of pretexts and find causes for action. Needless to say, no vulnerable resident of Eastern Europe became less wary of the rise of Hitler in the 1930s because a long obsolete minority rights treaty was negotiated and signed in 1919.

The actual historical dynamics are in the entirely opposite direction. Marshall, after World War I, became keenly interested in international solutions for Jewish issues because he knew that the clock was ticking on his and the AJC's efforts to keep the doors open to Jewish immigrants. And, as we shall see, postwar anti-Semitism posed a problem to Jewish diplomacy not as a symptom of its success but rather as an impediment to its continuation. Months after his work on the Jewish delegation in Paris, Marshall reasoned that it would be unwise to reassemble an international gathering of Jewish delegates because it would have provided reinforcement to bigoted *Protocols of the Elders of Zion* fantasies that were beginning to circulate in Europe and North America.[108]

Triumphal Rhetoric and Hard Realities: The Reception and Aftermath of the Minority Rights Treaty

The triumphal tone that accompanied the signing of the minority treaty has an undeniably awkward ring, but it reflects an enduring ethnic psychology in the Jewish politics of the era. The truth is that in the Western vocabulary of modern Jewish experience, there were no words for what Marshall, Mack, Adler, and their European counterparts were doing in Paris. Ostensibly, the entire exercise was a contradiction in terms: there was Marshall locked in battle with a Polish nationalist who, by presuming to call a Jew in Warsaw or Cracow a "Pole," was applying precisely the political rule that led Marshall to define himself as an "American" in the New York or Washington public square. There *was,* of course, something fearful in this Paris diplomatic exercise because it had, depending upon the mindset of the observer, more or less proximity to the canard that Jewish concerns crossed borders and were prosecuted by an international cabal that worried about Jewish needs rather than the political interests of the home countries from which the Jewish diplomats came. In Paris, the fears and conceptual confusions were overcome by ethnic ties of Jewish solidarity, but ethnicity is not always a subtly expressive force. The easiest or best way that these ties could find expression was in a rhetoric of triumph that made it seem as though the proponents and objects of Jewish diplomacy had absolutely nothing to fear or be confused about.

This rhetoric proved durable in the 1920s. It helped "non-Zionist" American Jews in Marshall's camp—who often had powerful feelings of empathy for pioneering work being done by the *halutzim* in the Yishuv (particularly in its cultural and educational realms) but who were also deeply wary that the realization of the Jewish state formula might complicate their own citizenship status in the United States—join forces with nationalist-oriented Jews who had no such compunctions about political Zionism. In a manner comparable to the Paris example, an idiom of triumph masked an alliance of non-Zionist and Zionist delegates and activists who possessed significantly different Western or Eastern outlooks regarding the merits or follies of the strategy of Jewish integration in host Christian societies, as opposed to a strategy of Jewish national separation. When, in Paris in 1919, this West-East Jewish confederacy drafted a porous program for minority rights, it was hailed heroically as the Jewish Magna Carta; when, a decade later in Zurich, this West-East makeshift alliance, also forged out of Marshall's strenuous mediation, led to the inclusion of non-Zionists with Zionists on the Jewish Agency, the deal was garnished in elegiac rhetoric as a Pact of Glory. If such lofty rhetoric effectively disguised existential doubts, it had, in historical terms, a very short expiration date—in 1929, for instance, the Glory pact was consummated just days before Arab rioting in Palestine necessitated significant rethinking about Yishuv realities, and just weeks before the US stock market crash rendered useless some of the philanthropic assumptions that had governed Marshall's mediation.

In the case of Marshall's lobbying for Jewish minority rights in Eastern Europe, the gap between the triumphant rhetoric and trying reality can be measured with precision.[109] After the composition of the minority rights agreements in Paris, Marshall returned to a hero's welcome in New York City. While he claimed, disingenuously, that the hoopla came as an unwelcome surprise, he arrived from Paris prepared to address a jubilant crowd that packed into Carnegie Hall on July 28, 1919.[110] Some one thousand ecstatic guests applauded Marshall's efforts. "Stopping the meeting would have been as easy as stopping an avalanche," noted Jacob Schiff in a flattering letter.[111] The program for the banquet, "Mass Welcome to Louis Marshall,"[112] evokes a triptych of themes—traditional notions of Jewish, American, and European emancipation. As cantors sang "Hallelujah," "Hatikvah," and "The Star Spangled Banner," rejoicing Jewish audience members read notes in a printed program that meshed Jewish, European, and American themes. "Among the names of the brave men who have appeared as the champions of the Jewish cause before the assembly of nations in Paris, the name of Louis Marshall will stand out in golden letters," proclaimed the program. "Work accomplished at Paris marks the crowning effort in the movement for Jewish emancipation," it continued. Unlike nineteenth-century Jewish emancipation pacts, which "enfranchised the Jew as a man but frequently led to his disenfranchisement as a Jew," the program explained, the Paris treaty minority rights accords protected the Jews' civil *and* religious rights. It was no accident that this accomplishment was forged via the participation of Marshall and other American delegates at the peace table, since "the Bill of Jewish Rights is a glorious application of the ideals of the American Republic." Marshall, for his part, heralded the minorities' treaties as a Magna Carta for the Jews. "For the first time," Marshall proclaimed, Jews "are accorded the same constitutional rights as are enjoyed by majorities in Western and Eastern Europe."[113]

Less than five years after Marshall's triumphant return to New York, this global vision of Jewish democratization was repealed with cruel finality. The setback to Marshall's expansionist agenda seemed so terrifyingly complete that he could not even play the highly circumscribed role of traditional *shtadlan* intercessor and protect a pocketful of the Old World's most pious Jews. The abject impotence of the Paris minority rights accords in the interwar period was demonstrated by an exchange of letters between Marshall and Mizrachi Zionist rabbi Meir Berlin (later Bar-Ilan) in February 1924.[114]

Berlin notified Marshall that the Lithuanian government, "which is not very favorable to the Jews," had refused to exempt students in the country's yeshivas from army service, even though pupils in other religions' seminaries received such deferrals. The religious Zionist, who had recently moved to Jerusalem, bemoaned the damage caused by this policy, since "the Lithuanian yeshivas are considered the largest and best ones in existence." Marshall's reply acknowledged that the Lithuanian policy was "grossly discriminatory" but offered no remedy. Marshall confessed that American Jews were useless allies: "I am at a loss to know what we here in the US can do to meet such a situation." Elsewhere, a compelling legal argument could be drafted against Lithuania's government, since its policy denying yeshiva student draft exemptions constituted "a serious infraction of the letter and spirit of the Minority Treaty." But that treaty was enforced by the League of Nations and because the United States was not a member of the league, Marshall explained, "our country is not in a position to act." Far from paving the road to unfettered modern citizenship across the lands of Europe, the Magna Carta of the Jews could not even provide minimal protection to the vanguard of Jewish traditionalism in the Old World.

Once we eliminate what one critic has branded an unfair "backshadowing" tendency[115] to examine this minority rights advocacy in view of the calamities that engulfed European Jewry after Marshall's death, how can the level and quality of his commitment be judiciously assessed? The answer, I believe, has two dimensions, one relating to the poignantly yawning gap between Marshall's own capacious energy level and the tightly circumscribed opportunities for improvement of Jewish life in Eastern Europe in the interwar period; the second dimension relates to the interplay between ethnic politics and American liberalism, a fascinating but underappreciated facet of Marshall's career. In terms of the first, Jewish, dimension, there is not much more to say other than that Marshall did all that he could within his power as a conscientious Jewish leader while dealing with preciously few options.

A good illustration is Marshall's work on the Romanian Jewish issue, and his collaboration with a counterpart Romanian Jewish steward, Dr. Wilhelm Filderman.[116] With 800,000 Jews, Romania did not host East Europe's largest Jewish community, but Marshall's interest in the Romanian situation was stimulated by the precedent of minority protections in Romania under Article 44 of the 1878 Treaty of Berlin.[117] Marshall's belief that Romania's noncompliance with Article 44 could be used as diplomatic leverage predated World War I.[118] Throughout 1926, Marshall strenuously lobbied for Romania's compliance with minority protections under the December 9, 1919, treaty. He sent various protests and threats of credit boycotts to Romanian ambassador Nicolas Titulesco.[119]

In March 1926, Marshall diligently supervised the US visit of Dr. Wilhelm Filderman, a former officer in the Romanian army and JDC official who in 1923 became the president of the Union of Rumanian Jews. Marshall told his son Robert that Filderman, "an extraordinarily able lawyer and statesman," was the "only" East European Jew who had really helped him at the Paris conference.[120] Marshall arranged for Filderman's involvement with the American Committee for the Rights of Religious Minorities, and he secured New York governor Al Smith's support for a fund-raising event for Filderman. In April 1926, Marshall asked Herbert Lehman to organize the deposit of funds in a major Romanian bank so that credit would become available to oppressed Romanian Jews (the scheme never materialized).[121] Marshall raised $20,000 for Filderman's activities, paying a quarter of the sum from his own pocket. His support for the Romanian Jewish leader remained steadfast throughout his last years. He persistently endeavored to raise funds to support Filderman's political career, and in May 1928 he discussed with Filderman the pros and cons of American Jews publicly criticizing or supporting the extension of loans to the Romanian government.[122]

The failure of the minority rights treaties was appreciable during Marshall's lifetime, but its impact upon his stature as a Jewish leader cannot be fully assessed separately from his subsequent efforts in Jewish affairs, in the forging of partnerships with the Zionists, in the Jewish colonization experiment in the Soviet

Union, and in the array of antidefamation efforts he spearheaded during America's "Tribal Twenties" era, most importantly his campaign to end Henry Ford's ominous anti-Semitic vitriol. The next, final section of this study, Part Four, relates to Marshall's Jewish work during the last decade of his life, the period when he attained a premier role in American Jewish affairs. First, however, one intriguing permutation of his life endeavors warrants comment, because it points to an overlooked level of symmetry in the interplay between the American and Jewish parts of his ethnic identity. Just as Marshall's intensive advocacy for the protection of Jews in America as a potentially vulnerable minority group broadened, particularly in the 1920s, and inspired his defense of other more vulnerable minority groups, such as African Americans, Asian Americans, and Native Americans, his international work on behalf of Jewish minority rights in Eastern Europe propelled him toward advocacy on behalf of the rights of national groups that had been victimized by colonial processes. Just as Marshall fought first for the constitutional liberties of Jews in America and then also for the constitutional liberties of blacks in America, he fought successively for the constitutional rights of Jews in Eastern Europe and then for the constitutional rights of blacks in the Caribbean. In all cases, he started as a conservative Republican, but his duties and activities as an ethnic champion of Jewish interests propelled him toward the advocacy of oppressed minorities in the United States or within the orbit of America's overseas quasi-colonial expansion, in a métier easily recognizable as cutting-edge left-liberalism of the interwar years.

Minority Rights and Haiti

On May 1, 1922, a crowd of 3,500 gathered at Carnegie Hall in New York to protest American control of Haiti.[123] The rally's lead speaker, Idaho senator William Borah, did not mince words, charging that greed and imperialism had motivated America's seven-year endeavor to gain possession of the Caribbean country. Drawn by Haiti's rich soil and abundant cheap labor, American policy makers had erased the island's sovereignty. Though "it may be true" that Haitians were "not capable of self-government as we understand it," they had sovereign rights, and continued American intervention on the island would destroy America's own moral caliber, declared Borah.

Apart from one passing reference, the *New York Times* projected the rally as a characteristic one-man show performed by Borah, the "Great Opposer" who was known throughout his career for his unyielding isolationist and anti-imperialist views. However, a laconic sentence in the middle of the report noted that the rally was chaired by Louis Marshall, a figure whose professional and organizational affiliations required no identification in this *New York Times* piece. Marshall, it noted, "reviewed the history of the two republics for the past six years, and expressed the opinion that the United States ought to withdraw its troops and control in the island."[124]

Apart from the United States, Haiti is the oldest sovereign nation in the Western Hemisphere.[125] After independence was wrested from France in 1804, a series of constitutions in the republic consistently prohibited foreign ownership of land. That changed in 1915, when the United States effectively took control of the island and its 3 million, largely poor, residents of mixed Catholic and folk vodun faith. America had, at the time, limited economic investments in Haiti ($4 million as compared to $220 million in Cuba), and so, as historian Hans Schmidt argued, America's occupation of the island appears to have been motivated by strategic calculations about stability and control in the Caribbean following the construction of the Panama Canal.

American intervention on the island consolidated with a series of steps in 1914 and 1915, starting with the confiscation by US Marines of $500,000 from the vaults of the National Bank of Haiti, followed by the election of a president (Philippe Dartiguenave) at the behest of US military muscle, and capped by the coerced ratification of a treaty that explicitly placed control of customs, finances, and security matters on the island in the hands of Washington. Haiti escaped the American public's notice during the World War I years, and it became a political issue for the first time during the 1920 presidential election when Republican candidate Warren Harding referred to the "rape of Haiti" and mined the island for political leverage, declaring at one point that he would never "empower an Assistant Secretary of the Navy to draft a constitution for helpless neighbors in the West Indies and jam it down their throats at the point of bayonets borne by U.S. Marines."

Harding was attacking the Democrats' vice presidential candidate Franklin Roosevelt. As assistant secretary of the navy, Roosevelt visited the island in 1917, charmed the Dartiguenave client government by reading speeches in French, and investigated investment opportunities. He had little compunction about the assertion of American power on Haiti and his contribution to it. In fact, on the stump as a vice presidential candidate, Roosevelt declared in August 1920, "you know I have had something to do with the running of a couple of little republics. The facts are that I wrote Haiti's Constitution myself, and if I do say it, I think it's a pretty good Constitution."

By and large, Roosevelt's interventionist attitude reflected mainstream opinion in the United States. Through 1919, forty-nine out of sixty-nine American journals surveyed endorsed American intervention in Haiti and the Dominican Republic.

Harding's outspoken campaign condemnation of America's role in Haiti spurred some activity on Capitol Hill after the Republican candidate's election in 1920. The printed record of one committee's hearings on Haiti sprawled over several thousand pages. Though its chairman, Illinois senator Medill McCormick, publicly bemoaned "our failure in Haiti," his panel's work in autumn 1921 was largely irrelevant, since the Harding administration was locked on a "reorganization" policy toward Haiti, which essentially meant facilitating the control of the country's external debt by American creditors. "In general," wrote Hans Schmidt, "Haiti received little attention in the United States after the 1921–1922 reorganization."

A blip on that screen of apathy flashed in a searing twelve-page brief provocatively entitled *The Seizure of Haiti by the United States: A Report on the Military Occupation of the Republic of Haiti and the History of the Treaty Forced upon Her,*[126] signed by a bipartisan professional group of twenty-four prominent attorneys, including Zechariah Chaffee and Felix Frankfurter from the Harvard Law School, John Grace, mayor of Charleston, South Carolina, William Holly, a constitutional law expert from Chicago, Nelson Spencer, president of the City Club of New York, Moorfield Storey, former president of the American Bar Association, and Louis Marshall. In a way that paralleled his input and composition of documents of paramount significance in American and Jewish history, including the 1910 Protocol of Peace settlement in the New York cloakmakers strike, Marshall took control of advanced stages in the twenty-four-member group's discussions and negotiations, and was responsible for the drafting of the final version of the document.

While Marshall emphasized that the appeal was nonpartisan and written with "great reserve," and relied exclusively on the official records of the McCormick Committee, the document's assertive, combative idiom has the imprimatur of a Marshall brief. Since 1915, Marshall wrote, on behalf of the twenty-four, America has had "virtual control" of Haiti; "our marines have been in military occupation of the country, and the former republic has been stripped by us of every vestige of her sovereignty." As though in obeisance to the goal of maintaining distinguished "reserve," the brief declared that "commentary upon this sad chapter in American history is superfluous." But its indefatigably argumentative author then proceeded to supply the commentary:

> A stain has attached to our national honor which, unless speedily expunged, will become an indelible blot. For this great nation to play the part of a bully toward another, weak in material resources and physically powerless to maintain its sovereign rights against incalculable odds, is nothing short of political immorality.[127]

The group petitioned the White House, asking for an audience with the president. Harding dodged and asked Secretary of State Charles Evans Hughes to receive the twenty-four attorneys and their petition.

On Saturday, April 29, 1922,[128] the twenty-four lawyers were joined in their petition to the Harding administration by Senator Robert Owen, a politician from Oklahoma who was part Cherokee, who had been instrumental in the creation of the Federal Reserve (so much so that there is a park named after him on the Federal Reserve grounds in Washington, DC), and whose name had fleetingly circulated in 1920 when the Democrats chose their candidate for president. Also in attendance were a few members of the Foreign Policy Association (including Lillian Wald and James G. McDonald) who were concerned about Haiti. Hughes stunned the meeting's participants by declaring at the outset that the brief of the twenty-four was "most inadequate" and "one-sided."

Marshall felt betrayed and incensed. The secretary of state had evidently not read the brief and yet pronounced instant judgment. The issue the document raised, Marshall insisted, was nonpartisan, and, besides, nothing in his brief even approached the strident condemnations about the misuse of executive power and unwarranted foreign policy intervention that Harding himself had issued during the 1920 campaign. Marshall had limited himself to the McCormick Committee's publicly recorded facts about Haiti—"to the mind of the lawyer at least," Marshall remonstrated, these facts "demonstrated a disregard of fundamental principles."

When the Sunday papers obligingly publicized the secretary of state's pronouncement of the twenty-four-member group's "one-sided and inadequate" plea for Haitian sovereignty, Marshall was apoplectic. In a lobbying career punctuated by blisteringly phrased communications to public officials on behalf of open immigration and other concerns shared by Jews and many other Americans, his May 2, 1922, letter to Hughes was one of his most ballistic communications.

"I had always fancied that the right of petition existed," Marshall wrote, "that it was the privilege of a citizen to present facts in an orderly and respectful fashion." The only sense in which the brief was inadequate, he furiously explained, was that "it did not begin to state the iniquities that have taken place." The twenty-four had decided not to include information provided by a Baptist missionary and other credible sources who had worked on the island for years and who attested to ways in which America's military had arm-twisted and manipulated ratification of Haiti's constitution through "intimidation and fraud." Nor had the brief mentioned that under America's watch, "the unfortunate blacks have been reduced to a state of peonage, and have been taken miles away from their homes to construct public highways."

During the meeting with the twenty-four, Secretary of State Hughes referred to backwardness and civil strike in Haiti, capping his justification of American intervention by allusion to indolence and successive political assassinations on the island. This provoked acidic sarcasm from Marshall. For the American Jewish leader, it was routine to object to double standards that threatened or hampered his own ethnic group and other minorities. But it was unusual for the patriotically American Marshall to berate a fellow Republican and high public official in harsh words about double standards whose tacit, indicting reference was racism:

> Unfortunately three of our [American] Presidents have been murdered. It is unfortunate that there are indolent people in various parts of the United States, who do not make the most of the resources at their command, and there has been bloodshed in many parts of our country. We have even had a civil war. It is not such facts that have any bearing on the adequacy of the presentation of the fundamental questions of right and wrong.[129]

The petition had nothing to do with supposed indolence or political unfitness on the island of Haiti. The sole germane question was whether America had "tyrannically and despotically" deprived the Haitian people of independence and sovereignty. It could be that some Americans construed the doctrine of manifest destiny as meaning that their country had the right to "exploit the rich lands of Haiti and attend to her finances." Such theory might have constituted "the other side of the question" addressed by his brief. However, Marshall concluded, "I mistake the American people if they will ever accept such doctrines."

The day after the Carnegie Hall rally, Marshall rifled off another appeal to Hughes, explaining that his persistence on the Haiti issue was a "sacred obligation," because he was a believer in the rights of weak nations and of minorities to be protected against oppression.[130] That was a cryptic way of saying that pressuring the United States and other world powers to respect the sovereign rights of autonomous peoples was, under newly established international arrangements, good for the Jews.

Three years after his triumphant appearance at Carnegie Hall to celebrate the conferral of the Magna Carta of Jewish rights in the minority rights treaties, Marshall had returned to Carnegie Hall's center stage, this time to champion the cause of Haitian independence. Connecting the various points in this journey between the Carnegie Hall appearances (Warsaw, Paris, Haiti) was one basic idea: the well-being of millions of Jews in Eastern Europe depended on the extent to which the larger nations regarded internationally negotiated autonomy accords, and the legitimate aspirations of free peoples, as inviolable matters of constitutional duty and human rights. Were Marshall and his peers to condone America's seizure of Haitian independence, how would they have any moral footing to protest attempts made by Poland or any other East European state to perpetrate a seizure of Jewish individual and communal rights?

In Marshall's lifetime and after it, American Jews rallied to the side of blacks in America out of a mixture of authentic empathy for their suffering as victims of racism and also out of an inchoate understanding that consistency in the application of American constitutional principles was a Jewish interest.[131] Now an international version of that motivational mix had shaken Marshall away from the retreating 1920s isolationism of his Republican Party. As abuses continued in the application of the minority rights accords toward the Jews of Poland, how could Marshall voice protests when his own country had compiled a foreign policy track record of substituting Monroe Doctrine imperialism for the constitutional self-development of small peoples and countries in its own hemisphere? As an American, Louis Marshall defended the autonomous rights of the blacks of Port-au-Prince because it was the right thing to do and because it was good for the Jews of Warsaw and the Jews of New York City.

The day after the Carnegie Hall rally for Haiti, Marshall wrote enthusiastically to Senator Robert Owen about its "remarkable success."[132] The hall was filled to capacity; Marshall ripped straight into the secretary of state's description of the brief as one-sided and inadequate, and had the audience with him "from start to finish." Concurrently, Marshall tried to pull strings at the *New York Times* to obtain publicity for the Haitian independence campaign. In a personal letter to Ochs,[133] Marshall recounted the unhappy meeting with Hughes and implored the publisher to print the brief in the Sunday edition of the *New York Times.* After he detailed stages and events in America's occupation of Haiti, the last lines of Marshall's pitch to the *New York Times* publisher furnished hints suggesting that the moral outrage in the Caribbean also had negative implications for Jewish life. The minority treaties would benefit the Jews of Eastern Europe only in a world that was educated to respect national and minority rights. "There is no subject on which the public needs education more at this time than it does on that of the rights of weak nations and of minorities," Marshall wrote to Ochs.

The day after Marshall delivered his personal letter to Ochs, the *New York Times* editorialized in favor of Hughes's position. Dismissing Borah's Carnegie Hall accusations, the newspaper opined that the "United States has a good record for resisting imperialism." America's policies had been implemented on the island since 1915 to "bring order out of chaos," it claimed. When the paper affirmed Hughes's pledge that the United States is "considering all that is essential for Haiti's well-being and tranquility," the editorial virtually mocked Marshall and his twenty-three colleagues, teasingly referring to them as "Mr. Borah's associates in moral indignation."[134] In the Caribbean, there was no open door for lobbying on behalf of small nation rights.

Fittingly, Marshall's final words on this misadventure in Haitian advocacy were written to Moorfield Storey, an attorney of Puritan descent who had served as president of the Anti-Imperialist League until its dissolution the year before, and whose long career had started with a stint as personal secretary to the famed antislavery politician, Charles Sumner. Storey, his biographer notes, had sponsored with the NAACP in 1918 a private investigation of circumstances in Haiti, owing to concerns about the implications of overseas American rule over blacks.[135] In early May 1922, Storey implored Marshall to write another brief on Haiti, but the Jewish leader doubted that a second petition could have effect.[136] Marshall surmised that some "undisclosed cause" must have been behind Secretary of State Hughes's dismissive behavior. Fourscore and seven years before the United States, under the leadership of an African American president in an era of multicultural politics, would rally impressively in support of the Caribbean island convulsed by a horrific earthquake, it was a mystery to Marshall in 1922 that anyone in his country could claim that the United States was doing "all that is essential for Haiti's well-being and tranquility."

PART FOUR

Marshall Law

8

Ford

The term "Marshall law" was the English Jewish playwright Israel Zangwill's epigrammatic tribute to the extraordinary authority enjoyed by Louis Marshall in American Jewish affairs, particularly in the 1920s, following the death of Jacob Schiff in 1920 and the termination of Louis Brandeis's presidency of the Zionist Organization of America the following year.[1] The final part of this biography, "Marshall Law," probes the determinants, contents, and limits of Marshall's emblematic status in American Jewish affairs and his country's ethnic history.

Because Marshall's peak period of activity was the 1920s, this concluding part of the book focuses on that decade, but its sections do not always follow a linear chronological sequence, and some of its passages encroach upon earlier periods of his life. A few of Marshall's endeavors in this period of his life were systematically pursued or represent cohesively distinct and important challenges in his career; accordingly, such cases are treated here in separate, full chapters of Part Four. Specifically, the present chapter analyzes Marshall's opposition to Henry Ford's anti-Semitic campaign, and the book's concluding chapter (chapter 11) probes his efforts on behalf of overseas Jewish colonization projects in Crimea and Eretz Israel.

One topic in Part Four, Marshall's (and his sons') devotion to environmental protection (chapter 9), stretches chronologically from the late nineteenth century to his last days, and so is not completely rooted in the last decade of his life. However, Marshall's environmentalism gained firm institutional footing, largely through the establishment of the New York State College of Forestry at Syracuse University, in the later part of his life. Moreover, Marshall's commitments to wilderness protection belong to a survey of the peak ("Marshall law") phase of his life for reasons connected to the meaning of his career, rather than the dates of his endeavors. Thematically, Marshall's work to protect the wilderness gained momentum as a liberalized extension of his ethnic advocacy on behalf of Jewish rights. In his phase of greatest activity and achievement, Marshall conceptualized the protection of Jewish minority rights in America (and elsewhere) as part of an overall commitment to the rights of acutely vulnerable groups and to public interests.

If the unusual level of authority commanded by one leader of an ethnic group not vested with powers of taxation or coercive enforcement constitutes the most intriguing aspect of this Marshall law phase, Marshall's courageous insistence that Jewish experience and interests dictate the defense of his country's most helpless or downtrodden communities and resources represents its most inspiring feature. As an expression of the belief that Jewish welfare ultimately depended upon modern society's ever-expanding commitment to rights and the protection of the vulnerable, Marshall's environmental crusades are linked to his labors in the 1920s on behalf of African Americans and Native Americans, and are therefore most suitably surveyed as part of the culminating phase of his activity.

Because Marshall's labors barely eased in intensity and scope up to the days of his sudden illness and death in Zurich in September 1929, it is difficult to impute a genuine sense of closure to some objects of his labors. That is, Marshall died, but various forms of discrimination and exclusion persisted to the detriment of Jews and other groups in the United States. Thus, in addition to chapters centered on issues where Marshall's work and impact attained a noticeable degree of finality, chapter 10 offers a kaleidoscopic view of an array of Marshall's ongoing, unfinished projects and concerns in the 1920s, along with glimpses of how he was perceived in public and within his own family circle throughout his period of peak prominence.

While Marshall's work addressed a dizzyingly wide variety of Jewish and non-Jewish topics after World War I, readers will find that a common, optimistic hue binds the images in this kaleidoscopic chapter 10. Time after time, Marshall responded to the xenophobic or racist symbols and trends of the Tribal Twenties—from the alarming resurgence of the Ku Klux Klan to the ominous closure of America's doors to immigrants—by intensifying his commitment to constitutional rights and freedoms, and by extending them to neglected or abused groups and public interests. In this sense, Marshall law was a declaration that the Constitution would not just survive the passing threats posed in post–World War I America but would become ever more inclusively empowering.

Always a staunch advocate of American constitutionalism, Marshall's late idealism was, to some extent, a throwback to earlier phrases of his career. However, Marshall preached about constitutional virtues to Downtown Jews at the end of the nineteenth century in a vein that appears static, abstract, and evasive when compared to his 1920s vision of ever-expanding rights and protections. Whether Marshall's late, expansive perception of American constitutionalism was influenced by the buoyant posturing about prosperity and abundance that characterized American society generally in the 1920s (despite the country's nativist and racist trends) is debatable. As we shall see, Marshall's social outlook during the last decade of his life was rife with nostalgia for the simpler, less mechanized, rhythms of late nineteenth-century life in Upstate, and Uptown, New York.

More surely, the surging liberalism that characterized much of Marshall's work in the last decade of his life reflected an ethnic trend. Though he remained, nominally, a Republican, his affiliation with a dazzling diversity of civil rights causes symbolized a communal transition in an interwar period when American Jews found cause to express their internal sense of being "at home in America" (in Deborah Dash Moore's phrase) by committing themselves outwardly, as liberals, to the welfare of all the country's groups, typically by affiliation in the Democratic Party.[2]

The late, Marshall law, period of his life is a study in contrasts. The consolidation of Jewish self-defense activities in the labors of one individual contrasts with the necessarily pluralistic, diffuse patterns of community life in a country governed by norms of religion-state separation. Marshall's persona as a stern business lawyer chained to Manhattan offices contrasts with the rambling outdoors passion of his environmental commitment. The American Jewish community's general sense of prospering opportunity in the interwar period strikes a contrast with the growing peril of Jewish life overseas. The identity terms of Marshall's Uptown crowd, which reduced Jewish identity to religious issues and shunned Jewish nationalist formulas, contrast with fundamental self-understandings of the European Zionists, led by Chaim Weizmann.

Of all possible contrasts, one links Marshall's prodigious communal World War I activities, in the previous phase of his career, to his work in this "Marshall law" pinnacle. That is the contrast between Henry Ford the anti-Semite and Louis Marshall the champion of American Jewish rights. To what extent did the mass circulation of the scurrilously anti-Jewish *Protocols of the Elders of Zion* by America's folk hero, automobile manufacturer Henry Ford, vindicate Marshall's dark wartime forebodings about the prospect of an explosion of anti-Semitism? Conversely, to what extent did the most inspiring triumph of Marshall's communal defense work, the formal cessation of Ford's anti-Semitic campaign and the obtainment of an apology from the manufacturer, vindicate his lifelong belief in the just virtues of American democracy? Our examination of the final phase of Marshall's life begins with such questions, all posed by the contrast between the enigma of Ford's personality and the steadfast Jewish advocacy of Louis Marshall.

The Protocols of the Elders of Zion

The anti-Semitic *Protocols of the Elders of Zion* were brought to America in February 1918 by a military intelligence officer, Dr. Harris Ayres Houghton, who had developed obsessive suspicions about Jewish subversion of America' war effort. Believing that Jacob Schiff was implicated in America's failure to produce serviceable warplanes, Houghton made a translation of the *Protocols* available to Charles Evans Hughes who (it will be recalled) headed an official government investigation of the aircraft production scandal.[3] A year later, as suspicions about Bolshevism and its influences gripped the country during the Red Scare,[4] the *Protocols* were endorsed on Capitol Hill in testimony given to a Senate subcommittee headed by Senator Lee S. Overman. The recommendation was given by Reverend George S. Simons, superintendent of the Methodist Episcopal Church's Russian Mission, who had been in Petrograd during the 1917 revolutions. Simons, an old church friend of Houghton's, reported to this subcommittee that Bolshevism would never have taken hold in Russia had not radical, Yiddish-speaking Jews from New York's East Side been brought to Moscow and Petrograd to topple Kerensky's government in 1917. Regarding the *Protocols,* Simons testified solemnly that the document "shows what this secret Jewish society has been doing in order to make a conquest of the world."[5]

The Protocols had circulated during the peace talks in Paris, and Jewish diplomats such as Lucien Wolf had mulled over various possible responses to the libel.[6] After his return to New York from Paris, Marshall deflected offers to purchase the text for $50,000; he was pleased to have avoided this extortionist trap and to have acquired the *Protocols* for nothing.[7] He was, of course, concerned about anti-Semitic aspersions about conspiracies hatched by the "international Jew." Jewish lobbying efforts in Paris had been mired by infighting between nationalists and nonnationalists, but the overall image of an international group of Jewish organizational leaders pressuring hard to acquire minority rights for their brethren in Eastern Europe made a striking statement about Jewish mutuality and assertive self-confidence. Within weeks, anti-Semitism stood that image upside down. Nothing in the *Protocols* was true, but their calumnies about international Jewish conspiracies nonetheless pried deeply into the emotional vulnerability of internationally active Jews. Marshall himself was uncomfortably aware of how quickly anti-Semitism was turning the tide. Nothing like the Jewish diplomatic effort at Paris would happen again in the interwar world. That sort of activism was toppled by sucker punches thrown out by the *Protocols*' invective.

Within a year, American-based caution replaced the internationalist advocacy of Paris. In spring 1920, Marshall insisted that organizing a sequel to the Paris delegation would play into the hand of the anti-Semites—the opposite might have been just as true, and Marshall's maneuvers combined shrewd tactics and concessions to Jew-hatred. The submissive part of this formula was uncharacteristic and bore witness to the confusion and anxieties ushered in by anti-Semitism at the start of the 1920s.

In April 1920, colleagues from the Paris delegation lobbied with the Joint Distribution Committee in New York, hoping to secure American Jewish support for an international Jewish relief conference. Marshall grasped the urgency of their request, having received reports earlier in the year about the apparent massacre of tens of thousands of Jews in the Ukraine and about how some thirty Jews a day were perishing due to hunger and depredation in locales such as Lvov.[8] He left the desperate delegates from Europe high and dry, however. "To hold a Jewish conference of any kind at this time would only be playing into the hands of our enemies," Marshall explained.[9] Propaganda about international Jewish conspiracies had seeped into "every country of Europe," and was also spreading in the United States. "We must not give color to these infamous falsehoods by making it appear that at a time when the whole world is in a hubbub of nationalism, the Jews are engaged in international propaganda,"[10] he concluded.

Taking this position, Marshall felt acutely compromised. It made sense to avoid appearances that might be exploited by inveterate haters of the Jews, but Marshall knew that he was communicating with delegates from embattled East European Jewish communities who lacked the luxury of exercising caution. Marshall's pleading to them sounded pathetic; thus, in the new decade, it provided a measure of the gap between American Jewish concern about antidefamation tactics and European Jewish concern about survival. "My European friends know that I am not a coward, and that the interests of Jewry are my greatest concern," moaned Marshall. "But there is a time when the most courageous men must be discreet, and not add fuel to the flames of suspicion."[11]

Initial Responses to Ford

When considering responses in America to the *Protocols'* libelous allegations, Marshall initially did not favor the same technique of cautious discretion that he recommended to these European Jewish leaders. Automobile tycoon Henry Ford launched his anti-Semitic campaign in his *Dearborn Independent* precisely at this time,[12] and Marshall's gut reaction was in favor of an aggressive rebuttal. This time, docility was dictated not by his own fears of the agile hatred of anti-Semitism but rather by Jacob Schiff's. Ten days after Ford's weekly printed the premiere in its "The International Jew" series, Marshall wrote boldly to Sears Roebuck executive Julius Rosenwald, promising strong action against the automobile manufacturer. "I am getting together my heavy guns," declared

Marshall.[13] That same day, June 3, 1920, Marshall rifled off a telegram to Ford, forthrightly condemning the "insidious and pernicious" anti-Semitism of the preceding two editions of the *Dearborn Independent.*[14]

Throughout the twentieth century, Henry Ford remained an American icon (*Fortune* magazine crowned him, and not Bill Gates, "Businessman of the Century[15]). Though his reputation had been tarnished by an ill-managed pacifist journey on a peace ship during World War I, Ford's name had surfaced as a write-in candidate for the Republican nomination for president in 1916, and in 1918, Ford came within a whisker of being elected to the Senate from Michigan even though he had never campaigned for the office.[16] Marshall's telegram showed little deference to this imposing reputation. He informed Ford that his journal was propagating "a libel upon an entire people." Writing on behalf of 3 million fellow American Jews, Marshall asked Ford whether he had personally given sanction to "the echoes from the dark middle ages" that sounded in the *Independent.*

From the start, Marshall framed his opposition to Ford's publications around the contention that they were un-American. Marshall reasoned that his defense of constitutional liberties would take precedence over any sympathy Ford evoked as a self-made millionaire and as a living emblem of American ingenuity. A Jew fighting for his rights could tell any apostle of hatred, even the heroic Henry Ford, that his anti-Semitism had no place in America. Moreover, Marshall interpreted his efforts against Ford not as a mere exercise in Jewish self-protection but rather as a fight about the meaning of America. All Jews in the United States, Marshall wrote in his telegram to Ford, "had hoped that at least in America they might be spared the insult and the humiliation and the obloquy" that was being disseminated by the *Dearborn Independent.* Stipulating that discussion in the country about a Jewish problem was un-American, Marshall was taking the moral high ground.[17]

This forthright response contrasted with conciliatory tactics adopted by local Jewish leaders who were entranced or intimidated by Ford's heroic mystique. Most notably, Reform rabbi Leo Franklin, who had held the pulpit at Detroit's Temple Beth El since 1899 and who, at his Edison Avenue home, had maintained cordial neighborly relations with Ford for several years, believed that simple persuasion could dislodge the automobile tycoon from the *Independent*'s anti-Semitic rants. With some twenty other Detroit-area Jewish professionals and businessmen, Franklin belonged to a Wednesday night social club and was delegated by it to approach Ford; the club's working premise, which Franklin shared, was that Henry Ford had no knowledge of the *Independent*'s anti-Semitism and would immediately penalize his underlings once he was informed about it.[18]

As it happened, the Reform rabbi was in the middle of his diplomatic errand, conferring with his friend Henry Ford and with Ford's associates W. J. Cameron and E. G. Liebold, on June 3, when Marshall's angry telegram arrived. Franklin claimed that Ford had been on the verge of drafting a retraction before Marshall's peremptory demands made him think again. After reading the telegram, Ford's "face flushed," and he immediately adjourned for lunch, Franklin informed Marshall. After the meal, Franklin suggested that they proceed to compose the retraction, but Ford flatly declared, "I am not going to sign it."[19] Franklin's version of events received backing from B'nai B'rith president Adolf Kraus, who, it will be recalled, had since 1905 been entangled with Marshall in a number of organizational turf wars and ego battles.[20]

Marshall totally rejected Franklin's efforts and interpretations. Deflecting the rabbi's idea that Ford was a humanitarian who had been misled by hateful underlings, Marshall insisted that the automobile manufacturer was a limelight-seeking, dangerous "ignoramus." Ford has unlimited means, Marshall explained to Franklin a few days after the telegram incident, and "can poison the minds of those who form their opinions from headlines." Conciliatory approaches were foolish, Marshall pointedly told the rabbi, because they created "the impression that there are Jews who will excuse this kind of publication." Speculating that Stanford University president David Starr Jordan, a eugenicist and peace activist, had brought the theory of an international Jewish conspiracy to Ford's attention during their World War I peace ship odyssey, Marshall declared that a "vigorous attack" and "heroic remedies," not friendly approaches, were needed to disjoin anti-Semitism from the all-powerful apparatus of the Ford Motor Company.[21]

Just ten days after the telegram incident, Franklin grasped that he had underestimated the depth and intents of Ford's anti-Semitism, and he returned his latest customized Model T to the manufacturer.[22] Over the summer, the rabbi and Marshall engaged in "heart-to-heart" talks,[23] and Franklin eventually apologized for having implied that Marshall's initial response to Ford had backfired calamitously; but Marshall clearly felt that his leadership credentials had been impugned by the Reform rabbi, and the two never established close relations.[24]

Marshall's counter-campaign against Ford's anti-Semitic crusade in the *Dearborn Independent* became personalized on other levels. He felt that Ford was a wartime profiteer who had pulled strings to enable his son Edsel to bypass his patriotic obligations. The contrast between Ford's wartime track record and Marshall's own record of service highlighted the truly galling nature of the *Independent*'s aspersions about the un-American behavior of the Jews. During the war, it will be recalled, Marshall had worked arduously on the New York Draft Board of Appeals, hearing 175,000 cases, and his son James had served overseas.[25] Ford's staff aggravated Marshall's sense of personal insult: two days after Marshall sent his telegram to Ford, he received from "The Dearborn Publishing Company" a grossly rude reply. Ford's journalists ridiculed the American Jewish leader, dismissing him as a "Bolshevik orator" who lacked restraint and language skills required for civilized discourse in America. The "International Jew" articles will continue, proclaimed this June 5 telegram. It added, offensively, "You cruelly overwork your most useful term which is 'antizamitism.'"[26]

Marshall fumed, but throughout the summer of 1920, he delayed his response to the taunting hatred of the Ford Motor Company. Ironically, he hoped that the antidefamation efforts of his rival from the Jewish diplomatic effort at the peace conference, Lucien Wolf, might undermine the *Independent*'s innuendo. At Paris, Wolf had demurred when delegation colleagues like Maxim Vinaver urged him to expose the *Protocols'* mendacity. Tensions were running too high about the Russian Revolution, and Wolf, who believed that Jewish involvement in the Bolshevik ranks was significant, doubted the efficacy of a forthright rebuttal to anti-Semitic aspersions about Jewish conspiracies to undermine world stability.[27] In mid-June 1920, the experienced English Jewish activist shed this inhibition and published in the *London Spectator* an impressive exposé of aspects of *Protocols'* forgery.[28] Despite his low opinion of Wolf's activities at Paris,[29] Marshall felt that Wolf's publishing effort made headway toward unplugging Ford's anti-Semitism. His optimism seemed rooted in the hopeful rationalism of the prewar era and also in the fair play procedures of an orderly courtroom. As far as Marshall was concerned, a sound factual rebuttal of a share of the *Protocols'* allegations would deflate much of Ford's efforts, and a full refutation would fully stop the *Independent.* Well-argued truth was the antidote to anti-Semitism.

Hence, at the start of July 1920, Marshall informed Cyrus Adler that he would employ an East European Jew with literary talent to finish the fact-finding exposé of the *Protocols* that Wolf had started.[30] Marshall then set out for a vigorous summer vacation in the West with his nature-loving sons. For the first time in a quarter century, he totally cut himself off from his New York law office. His dithyrambic descriptions of horseback riding and bird-watching in magnificent sites such as Yellowstone reflect the enthusiasm and emotional renewal of a desk-bound city professional who genuinely loved the outdoors—in Glacier Park, Marshall and his son Bob hiked thirty-seven miles in one day, and at Yellowstone, Marshall reported seeing a herd of buffalo, six grizzly and black bears, deer, and eagles.[31] These descriptions can also be interpreted as, at least, a semiconscious private reply to the Americanized twist that Henry Ford's *Dearborn Independent* put to the *Protocols.* Here was America's foremost industrial hero saying that the

Jew was a foreign subversive who had no authentic roots in the country's soil; and there was Marshall, a devoted environmentalist, with his sons, both of them nature lovers and one a future figure of fame in the environmental movement, communing with the raw earth of the American West, hiking and climbing to express their love for a land that also belonged to them.

The depth of the crisis stirred by the continuing outburst of anti-Semitism in Ford's weekly was difficult to gauge in the summer of 1920, and it continues to puzzle scholars. One scholar who mulled the question sixty years after the *Independent*'s first publication of the "International Jew" series found it difficult to decide whether a third of the 260,000 voters polled in 1923 by *Collier's* favored Ford for president because of his anti-Semitism, or in spite of it.[32] Ambiguities and inconsistencies in Marshall's responses to the challenge should be seen in this context: then, as now, it was impossible to know whether the fact that an extremely popular and powerful American was summoning his resources to disseminate extremely deprecatory and false information about the Jews ought to be regarded as a passing nuisance or as a mortal threat.

The *Dearborn Independent* affair should be seen not as a transformative moment for American Jewish leadership but rather as a challenge that tested the staying power of its proven approaches. Partially, but not wholly, it validated its efficacy in a volatile environment charged by ethnic and racial tensions between the world wars.

Inherent within Marshall's wavering—assertive and passive—attitudes in his initial response to Ford was his emotional and practical indebtedness to political "neutralism," the preference for quiet diplomacy adopted by the German Jewish elite in America, as well as his own activist temperament and private doubts about the applicability of old approaches in a newly dangerous world. Trying to articulate a practically useful response to Ford's widely circulating hatred, Marshall equivocated with conflicting impulses, and this struggle ultimately yielded a curiously productive result. Marshall ended up perpetuating the quiet approach dictated by Jacob Schiff, whose suitability to the Ford assault he initially discounted.

Schiff passed away just four months after the start of the *Independent* juggernaut. During the final stretch of his life, Schiff insisted that the American Jewish Committee refrain from public remonstration against Ford's anti-Semitism. As Marshall urged bold action, the aging banker cautioned, "if we get into a controversy we shall light a fire." Schiff averred that if American Jewry ignored the *Independent*, its "attack will soon be forgotten."[33]

This cautiousness incensed Marshall. In mid-September 1920, he poured out his heart to David Brown, a Detroit-based fund-raiser for emergency Jewish relief overseas who had been ringing alarm bells about Ford's anti-Semitism. "I have insisted from the beginning that we should carry on an aggressive fight," Marshall wrote. Meaning Schiff, he confessed he was "credulous" about the position of those who shunned publicity in the Ford matter. Jew-hatred appeared to be spreading fast, he noted ("Documents have been relayed to various members of Congress, and are being sent to newspaper offices in the country").[34] A day before Schiff's death on September 25, 1920, Marshall was still hoping that he could energize his old ally for a fight against Detroit's Flivver King. "I wish that I could get the members of the American Jewish Committee to get their heads out of the sand," Marshall wrote to his son-in-law Jacob Billikopf.[35] It seemed that Marshall's restiveness was not tempered by the poignant solemnity of Schiff's funeral, during which thousands of mourners, along with 350 policemen, lined the blocks from Schiff's Fifth Avenue home to Temple Emanu-El on 43rd Street.[36] Two weeks after this moving tribute to Schiff, Marshall steered the American Jewish Committee's Executive Committee toward an activist orientation directly at odds with Schiff's circumspect instructions on the Ford issue. The committee decided to "deal very aggressively with the Ford matter."[37]

Soon enough, Marshall clamped limits upon this resolution to fight Ford. Holding back his own feelings of personal affront, he used whatever authority and rhetorical energy he could muster to dissuade other American Jewish spokespeople and activists from sparring directly against Ford in public. He rejected proposals favoring some form of public debate or duel with the manufacturer as being "cheap, vulgar and yellow."[38] One such proposal was forwarded by Rabbi Isaac Landman, editor of the *American Hebrew* whose anti-Zionist lobbying in spring 1919 had, Marshall believed, distracted the diplomatic effort to attain minority rights accords for Jews in Eastern Europe. In November 1920, Marshall peremptorily lectured Landman about the folly of "grandiose" proposals whose enactment would provide Ford the publicity he craved.[39]

Marshall's doubts about the efficacy of direct, public challenges to Ford would underpin his reserved response toward libel suits submitted against the manufacturer by aggrieved Jews later in the decade. His reservations did not always hold sway in the larger American Jewish community or even in Marshall's elite Uptown circle. In late 1926, Macy's Department Store co-owner Nathan Straus, the distinguished patron of pasteurized milk campaigns and a veteran supporter of Zionist and other Jewish organizational causes, issued a challenge to the *Dearborn Independent,* proposing that an independent jury of ten Christian clerics be convened to determine the credibility of Ford's assertions in the "International

Jew" series. Nonplussed, Ford's journal mocked Straus, mentioning insidiously that "his department stores operated under the Christian name of R. H. Macy."[40]

Organized Defense: *The History of a Lie*, John Spargo, and "An Address to Fellow Citizens by American Jewish Organizations"

In lieu of flamboyant public challenges, Marshall favored "carefully prepared and reasoned" responses to the *Independent*'s allegations. His lawyerly habits overtook all other impulses provoked by the Ford issue, but since Marshall had qualms about jurisdictional and other legal issues attendant to the prosecution of group libel cases in courtrooms,[41] he decided to take meticulously researched and prepared responses to Ford to the court of public opinion. Marshall arranged a three-pronged action against the *Independent*'s anti-Semitic campaign. Each prong was predicated on the assumption that accurate information about Jewish circumstances delivered by authoritative sources would suffice to stifle the scourge of Jew-hatred in America.

First, Marshall sponsored a journalistic exposé of the scurrilous lies in the *Protocols.* Some advised him to turn to a famed muckraker for this task, such as Ida Tarbell.[42] Marshall, however, preferred a newspaperman familiar with the language and the sociopolitical circumstances of czarist Russia out of which the *Protocols'* forgery emerged. He tapped for the task Herman Bernstein, the American Jewish journalist who in 1893 had emigrated to the United States from Eastern Europe at the age of seventeen and who had made his mark during the Russian Revolution as a foreign correspondent for the *New York Herald,* thanks to his discovery of the secret "Willie-Nicky" correspondence between Wilhem II and Nicholas II in years before World War I. Assembling information for public presentation in the abrogation campaign, Marshall (as mentioned) had worked closely with Bernstein before the war, and the latter had met Ford during the ill-fated peace ship adventure. (In fact, conflicting interpretations of what the journalist told Ford aboard the *Oskar II* constituted the basis of a libel suit that Bernstein filed against the industrialist later in the decade.[43])

In his impressive *History of a Lie,* published in 1921,[44] Bernstein elaborated upon the exposé of the *Protocols'* forgery that Lucien Wolf had contributed some months earlier. While Wolf had placed the shady German novelist Herman Goedsche at the center of the forgery, Bernstein uncovered documents at the US Library of Congress that revealed how and why Russian Jew haters, such as Hippolytus Lutostansky and Sergius Nilus, had expanded upon the lies.[45] "The protocols came into the world with the trademark 'made in Germany,'" wrote Bernstein, "and they were elaborated under the auspices of the Russian Black

Hundreds, in their efforts to save the dying Russian autocracy." Bernstein capped his diligent detective work with lines affirming Marshall's conviction that truth was stronger than anti-Semitism. "A lie shuns the sunlight. It thrives in darkness. It cannot survive analysis," declared Bernstein.

Beyond this enlightened optimism, the format of Bernstein's text as a kind of legal brief submitted to the court of public opinion bore Marshall's imprint. The AJC president worked hard drafting revisions of the *History of a Lie;* not surprisingly, Marshall considered Bernstein's book "the most valuable thing that has yet been written on the *Protocols*."[46] Nevertheless, he doubted whether the booklet alone could muzzle the *Independent*'s screed.

The problem was partly evidentiary. Frustratingly, not all of Marshall's efforts to authenticate reports about how the anti-Semitic forgery had been crafted by senior figures in the czar's administration were consummated: the complicity of figures such as the head of the Okhrana secret police service's foreign operations, Pyotr Rachkovsky, would be proven subsequently by the historian Norman Cohn.[47] In January 1921, when Bernstein's manuscript was already at the printer, a mysterious Russian princess, Katarina Radziwill, contacted Marshall and promised information implicating high officials in the czar's court.[48] Marshall secured the cooperation of the *New York Times* publisher Adolph Ochs, and the princess's revelations were en route to publication when rumors surfaced that Radziwill had been detained twenty-five years earlier in South Africa and charged with currency forgery. The princess explained that seventeen women circled the globe using her name under dubious pretenses. Ochs's concerns about Princess Radziwill's credibility were somewhat allayed, and the publisher and Marshall agreed that her sensational revelations would appear in the *New York Times* in an indirect report about a public lecture. The princess, however, wanted a newspaper exclusive and impulsively sold her story to Rabbi Landman at the *American Hebrew*. Marshall fumed. He believed that the effect of the princess's telling disclosures had been wasted upon a limited Jewish audience. (Subsequent historical research, it bears mention, confirms the veracity of Princess Radziwill's story.[49])

However incomplete it might have been, evidence for the disproof of the *Protocols*' indictment was hardly lacking in 1920–21. Marshall realized that the identity of the party making the case against the *Independent*'s libels was as important as the contents of the defense, and as a second prong of his strategy toward Ford, he cooperated closely with a Gentile activist and writer, John Spargo. In some ways, this was a surprising alliance, since Spargo had been deeply engaged with socialist causes and organizations since his arrival in the United States from England early in the twentieth century. During the First World War, Spargo had broken away from the pacifist neutralism of socialist colleagues and formed the pro-war Social Democratic League of America, as an analogue to pro-war labor associations in England; impressed by Spargo's stand during the war, Marshall was able to overlook his radicalism (for his part, Spargo would steadily shed his socialism during the 1920s and ended up joining the Republican Party and opposing Roosevelt's New Deal policies in the 1930s).[50]

After the eruption of the *Independent* attacks, Marshall and Spargo engaged in an ongoing discussion about the possible motives and implications of Ford's anti-Semitism.[51] The AJC president wholeheartedly encouraged Spargo, the socialist son of a Methodist minister, to prepare a booklet refuting the *Independent*'s allegation, but he felt it important that Spargo's work retain a veneer of independence. The two agreed that Spargo must not receive reimbursement for his work from any Jewish source,[52] and Spargo opened his 1921 publication, *The Jew and American Ideals,*[53] with a disingenuous disclaimer: "This little book was written without the knowledge of any Jew. It is not a defense of the Jew."[54]

Throughout the booklet, Spargo insisted that his aim was not to prepare a defense of the Jewish race, or of Judaism, but rather to uphold the "democratic, humanitarian principles of America."[55] Calling on Americans to disavow Ford's campaign in the name of "Christian civilization and American ideals," Spargo warned darkly that there was no reason to believe that the United States had special immunity protecting it against the scourge of anti-Semitism. The text's rejection of the *Independent*'s innuendo about Jewish Bolshevism reflected its author's orientation—socialism, Spargo insisted, was not a Jewish conspiracy but rather a vision of freedom consonant with the bedrock articles of Anglo-American democracy, the Magna Carta and the Declaration of Independence.[56] Quoting Louis Marshall,[57] Spargo disputed charges about self-interested Jewish orchestration of the Soviet revolution by pointing to abundant evidence of Jewish hardship and suffering since the Bolsheviks' rise to power in Russia. Upon the book's publication, Spargo sent Marshall a specially signed copy; grateful, Marshall thanked the writer for his "courage in attacking forces of darkness" and added effusively that Spargo's "deed will perpetually be enshrined in the grateful hearts of your Jewish fellow citizens."[58]

The third and final prong of Marshall's strategy, the dissemination of a self-defense statement on "The Protocols, Bolshevism and the Jews" signed by a coalition of American Jewish organizations and dated December 1, 1920, constitutes an extraordinary event in his own biography and in the history of American Jewry. A product not just of the fear engendered by vicious attacks leveled by the American hero, Henry Ford, but of the general confusion swirling in postwar America as a result of the Red Scare, this acutely apologetic document rubs against the grain of Jewish experience in America, a land distinctively bereft of medieval libels and inquisitorial traditions of polemical debate about Jewish worthiness.

The document, "The Protocols, Bolshevism and the Jews: An Address to Their Fellow Citizens by American Jewish Organizations,"[59] was drafted by Marshall's own hand, and he made sure that 250,000 copies were distributed across America in early December 1920, to educators, politicians, and opinion brokers.[60] Fear of Ford uniquely unified American Jewry; Marshall's apologetic manifesto was signed across the board by American Jewish organizations.[61]

Descending to a level of apologetic discourse, he had believed, would never be required of a Jew in democratic America, Marshall noted in this pamphlet that for six months Jews felt that it would be "beneath their dignity" to reply to the "recrudescence of medieval bigotry and stupidity" published by the *Independent.* However, since Ford was "employing his great wealth" in the dissemination of his fulminations, the Jews in America were forced to reply to the libels, however humiliating it was to do so. Jews of the world, Marshall pointed out, constituted less than 1 percent of its total population, and more than one-half of them were "on the verge of starvation." The suggestion that world Jewry was "planning in secret enclave to seize absolute power" was therefore a paranoiac, "ridiculous invention." Forgers of the *Protocols,* Marshall explained, were reactionary "protagonists of autocracy" who concocted crackpot theories about the Jews to cloak their inveterate hostility toward democracy.

Fully aware of Ford's iconic status in American society, Marshall chose not to write at length about the auto manufacturer's circumstances and possible motives. Ford's "puerile and venomous drivel," the pamphlet stated, "derives from the concoctions of professional agitators." It added succinctly that Ford "is merely a dupe." Noting that only two members of the Bolshevik cabinet, the People's Commissars, were Jewish, Marshall disputed Ford's allegations about Jewish domination of the Russian Revolution. As he rejected the image of Jews as incorrigible political radicals, Marshall depicted an alternative model of Jews as conservative upholders of democratic stability that reflected his own life philosophy ("The Jew has traditionally stood for religion, law, order, the family and the right of property"). Marshall's apologetic erased from reality the left-wing radicalism of many Downtown New York Jews and of well-known Jewish individuals and movements in postwar Europe. In the most explicit antidefamation exercise of his career, Marshall projected his own personal values onto world Jewry as a whole, as though to say that Henry Ford could not be right because Jews everywhere were just like Louis Marshall. In this way, he personalized the contest with

Henry Ford and suggested that his own course in life was the only one which guaranteed survival and prosperity for the modern Jew.

American opinion makers received Marshall's apologetic with great sympathy. By the end of 1920, the American Jewish Committee reported, thousands of newspaper editorials denounced Ford's campaign as a danger to American principles.[62] Marshall's relief was enormous—the state of tense expectation following the apologetic's release was unlike anything he had felt in his career. The pamphlet's directness closed off options in ways that grated against a trained lawyer's penchant for argumentative finesse. After all, what would have happened had reputable US newspapers engaged debate about the pros and cons of Ford's point of view vis-à-vis refutations newly published by an umbrella coalition of American Jewish organizations? The gambit relied entirely on what Marshall understood to be America's true spirit. A week after the apologetic's publication, when the Federation of Churches of Christ in America adopted forthright resolutions denouncing the attacks on the Jews,[63] Marshall knew that the truth would win.

By the end of January 1921, Marshall viewed media responses to the apologetic as more than a strong blow to Ford. Writing to Maxim Vinaver, a moderate proponent of constitutional development known sometimes as the "Louis Marshall of Russia," Marshall interpreted the media's condemnation of Ford's anti-Semitism as proof that America really is different. Whereas foreign "dark forces of autocracy," be they "Russian bureaucrats" or "Polish fanatics," had attempted to plant European anti-Semitism, via Ford, on New World soil, the "magnificent" response of the country's media proved that "such a foreign growth cannot gain a foothold on our soil."[64]

Not just the media vindicated this premise about America's immunity to virulent anti-Semitism. In mid-January 1921, a group of 119 distinguished Americans signed a petition that condemned Ford's *Independent* series as an "infringement" of the rules of citizenship in the country.[65] Ford's effort to divide Americans along lines of race and religion was at variance with the country's democratic system, this august group of Americans declared. This enlightened conclusion might not have been entirely true—in this period, Congress was legislating divisions of race via the adoption of restrictive immigration measures—but more than its contents, the imprimatur in this denunciation of Ford's anti-Semitism inspired hope. Among others, the document was signed by two US presidents, Taft and Wilson, the poet Robert Frost, attorney Clarence Darrow, muckraker Ida Tarbell, and the historian Charles Beard. The indefatigable Ford antagonist, John Spargo, organized the group and its petition.[66]

This 119 petition, and other responses to the three-pronged rebuttal to the *Independent*'s Jew-hatred, provided relief, but they were not necessarily a warrant for inaction. Henry Ford did not desist from his attacks on the Jews until 1927, and Marshall could therefore not ignore the issue throughout the decade. He concluded, however, that since opinion makers in mainstream America had roundly denounced Ford's anti-Semitism, the *Independent* could not pose an existential threat. Because, Marshall reasoned, Ford's hatred was fueled by a craving for publicity, ignoring the *Independent*'s scurrilous innuendo was the wisest course of action. Thus, the proactive phase in his response to Ford ended with this triple-edged effort in 1920–21. Thereafter, Marshall nestled securely in the shadow of Schiff's legacy of caution, and he forthrightly opposed Jewish colleagues who struck the same attitude of activist defiance toward Ford's insulting campaign that Marshall had championed before Schiff's passing.

The "King's Gambit" with President Harding

Toward the end of 1921, Ford's underlings nastily badgered Marshall in print, publishing an article entitled "America's Jewish Enigma, Louis Marshall."[67] Stifling his personal feeling of outrage toward the Flivver King, Marshall chose not to engage in a mud fight, since nothing more really needed to be said in public to discredit Ford. The American intellectual and political elite had already gone on record, saying that the *Independent*'s anti-Semitism was a crank crusade abusive to the country's democratic traditions.

Marshall did not ignore passing opportunities to stifle the *Independent* or damage the credibility of its famous backer, but he did not really seek these openings, nor did he seriously analyze the efficacy of actions taken on their basis. Most notably, in summer 1921, Marshall dispatched a petition to President Harding, turning to him as *parens patriae* and asking that he exert his "potent influence" to stop Ford's "sowing of the seeds of hatred, whose consequences may become tragic."[68] This appeal came after newspapers around the country reported that the president had relaxed on a summer vacation with Ford, along with Thomas Edison and Harvey Firestone.

"At first, I was shocked" by these reports, Marshall explained to Cyrus Adler. Upon reflection, however, he decided to use Harding's relationship with the auto manufacturer as a "blessed opportunity to accomplish something." Two years later, Marshall corresponded with Harding's former speechwriter Judson Welliver[69] and received cryptic hints that his "King's Gambit" maneuver with Harding had paid dividends. Welliver implied that when he had traveled to Detroit to prepare a long magazine article about Ford, he came with instructions from

President Harding to see if anything could be done to change the manufacturer's attitude on Jewish questions. Welliver announced to Ford that his Jew-hatred was "unworthy of a man of his position and importance"; and he "permit[ted] Mr. Ford to understand that I was sure that the President would agree with my sentiments." Welliver's account left much ground on the causal path uncovered. Just as it was not certain that the president sent the journalist-speechwriter to Detroit because an American Jewish organizational leader, Marshall, had demanded action against Ford, so too is Welliver's assessment that Ford "dropped" his anti-Jewish activity after he was informed that his friend Warren Harding disapproved of it far from the whole truth. Marshall was not overly concerned about loose ends left by tactical maneuvers such as his summer 1921 petition to Harding. No matter what was done, Ford's incorrigible Jew-hatred could never be absolutely muzzled.[70] The effects of various antidefamation approaches on this issue could never be precisely predicted or measured, since the source of the *Independent*'s publications was a violently irrational side of Ford's enigmatic character.

Aaron Sapiro's Million-Dollar Suit

In a felicitously unexpected sequence, Ford ended up delivering to Marshall in 1927 a great career triumph. Though Ford's renouncement of the *Independent*'s anti-Semitic series—"Statement by Henry Ford to Louis Marshall," June 30 1927[71]—was dictated by Marshall himself, it was the product of maneuvers and calculations that Marshall either opposed or knew nothing about. The circumstances of Ford's about-face appeared mysterious at the time, and commentators such as the leftist writer Upton Sinclair indulged in wild speculation about what had caused the Flivver King's abrupt apology. (Sinclair speculated that a Jewish movie producer had "instructed hundreds of cameramen all over the country" to collect footage of crashes involving Ford automobiles; the threat that such clips would be screened in a newsreel caused the famed car manufacturer to abjure the *Independent*, Sinclair fancifully wrote in his novel about Ford.[72]) While Ford ate humble pie, mechanically signing his name to a list of retractions and apologies composed by Marshall, something within the whole spectacle of an all-powerful automobile manufacturer surrendering to a Jewish communal leader possibly conveyed a perverse sort of appeal to anti-Semites. For them, the episode was not a demonstration of the rectitude of Jewish objections to their outlook but rather more fodder for their paranoia about Jewish power. Looked at practically, Ford's defeat paid tribute not to the perspicacity of particular responses Marshall adopted (there was never a way for him to know what really was driving the automobile maker) but rather to his stature and stamina as a Jewish leader. When

Henry Ford finally decided that attacking the Jews had become a hindrance, he had only one place to turn. Louis Marshall turned the lock and threw away the key, sentencing America's ugliest ever eruption of anti-Semitism to oblivion.

The catalyst in Ford's demise was Aaron Sapiro, a spirited advocate of farm cooperatives. Raised as an orphan in California, Sapiro (1854–1959) briefly undertook rabbinical studies at the Reform movement's Hebrew Union College and apprenticed as a young attorney under the tutelage of Progressive California governor Hiram Johnson.[73] By 1923, Sapiro had organized sixty-six farm cooperatives whose annual trade volume reached $400 million. A tough leader of the cooperative movement, Sapiro became known as an uncompromising champion of the ironclad contract, under which a farmer was obligated to market his products to a cooperative for a defined period.

In the mid-1920s, the popularity of the cooperative movement started to wane. Critics, including officials in the US Department of Agriculture, questioned some of Sapiro's methods. In twenty-one articles published by the *Dearborn Independent,* this criticism transmogrified as an allegation about Sapiro's part in a worldwide Jewish conspiracy to monopolize food markets. Sapiro's law practice had been doing reasonably well before the *Independent* publications (the attorney's salary peaked at $60,000); Sapiro charged that Ford's attacks irreparably harmed his reputation and his ability to make a living. He filed a civil damage claim of $1 million against Ford. That sum was tailor-made for sensational media reports about the lawsuit.

Sapiro's "million-dollar suit" against Ford proceeded in March 1927. Sapiro's attorney, William Gallagher, toughly questioned Ford's subordinates on the stand, whereas Sapiro was subjected to tiring questioning by Ford's lawyer, Missouri senator James Reed. Before Ford himself could take the stand, he was injured in a mysterious car accident and taken to a Detroit hospital that bore his name.[74] Ford's company announced that he was unfit to take the stand; meantime, the judge had to declare the proceeding to be a mistrial after one of the jurors spoke in public, denying that she had been offered a bribe. Ford biographers speculate that while the Sapiro case was taking these turns, the manufacturer decided to settle the matter once and for all, partly because he was plagued by bitter memories of the humiliations he endured during another libel suit, which Ford himself initiated in May 1919 against the *Chicago Tribune* and which had ridiculed his pacifist idealism.[75] Ford eventually settled with Sapiro out of court, paying the plaintiff's court costs and attorney fees to the tune of $140,000, and arranging a scholarship fund for a needy orphan.

As he did with two other libel actions against Ford,[76] Marshall kept his distance from Sapiro's "million-dollar" litigation.[77] Yet, circumstances in the unfolding of the Sapiro suit strongly suggest that Marshall's skepticism concerning the efficacy of libel action against Ford was not warranted. Marshall insisted that such courtroom procedures merely satiated Ford's craving for attention, but he failed to consider that Ford's business hunger could never be fully fed by bad publicity.

Ford's Apology: "A Staggering Blow to the Anti-Semites"

In the end, business calculations, no less than defensive actions taken by the Jews, appear to have dissuaded Ford from his anti-Jewish publications. In 1927, Ford reached a momentous decision to transition from his signature Model T line to a new vehicle, the Model A. For six months during the year, the fate of Ford's life work was suspended in doubt, as production lines were changed to manufacture the Model A. Thousands of workers were laid off as the company changed machinery and invested over $250 million in the new model. During this period of high tension for Ford Motor Company, writes Neil Baldwin, not the Jewish Question but rather the Model A Question[78] troubled the manufacturer; Ford invested heavily in a public relations campaign for the new car. His fortune resting with the popularity of the Model A, Ford appears to have decided to remove any stains from his reputation that might have accumulated as a result of the *Independent*'s Jew-baiting.

In mid-June 1927, Marshall was contacted by an Episcopalian clergyman who hinted about Ford's readiness to negotiate a retraction of the "International Jew" allegations. Marshall replied that his door would be open to any of Ford's representatives but that he would not himself initiate any contact with the manufacturer.[79] Former US congressman Nathan Perlman, who was active with the American Jewish Congress, also brought news of Ford's about-face to Marshall.[80] Within days, Earl David, a former US assistant attorney general, and Joseph Palma, from the US Secret Service, came to Marshall on Ford's behalf, claiming that the manufacturer "had no idea" of the real character of the publications which appeared in the *Dearborn Independent*.[81] Marshall explained that he was "interested merely in protecting the good name of the Jews, and in procuring from Ford a document which would be acceptable to the Jews"; if he wanted to clear the air with the Jews, Marshall added, Ford would also have to settle the libel actions on terms satisfactory to the plaintiffs in the two actions, Bernstein and Sapiro.[82] The two Ford delegates returned to Marshall about ten days later, announcing that the manufacturer accepted these terms; Marshall drafted the terms of Ford's retraction from Knollwood. The "Statement by Henry Ford to Louis Marshall," signed by Henry Ford at Dearborn, stated:

> I deem it to be my duty as an honorable man to make amends for the wrong done to the Jews as fellow-men and brothers, by asking their forgiveness for the harm that I have unintentionally committed, by retracting so far as lies within my power the offensive charges laid at their door by these publications, and by giving them the unqualified assurance that henceforth they may look to me for friendship and good will.[83]

Ford artlessly pled that "in the multitude of my activities" it had been impossible for him to be apprised of the contents of the *Independent*'s articles.

Marshall admitted that his aim in dictating the letter was to make Ford "an object for ridicule."[84] He explained to Julius Rosenwald, "I deemed it important to show the world the kind of man he was, willing to indulge in a series of criminal attacks upon a whole people, and capable at the same time to resort to the most infantile of excuses."[85] The retraction, Marshall exulted, was a "staggering blow to the anti-Semites." The Jews were "vindicated and absolved" by Ford's apology, and he looked "puny compared to them."[86]

Marshall had earned this sense of triumph through hard work and prudent handling of the final phase of the Ford affair, but he was not entirely gleeful. Any happy ending to the Ford crisis applied to the United States alone. Five weeks after Ford published his apology, Marshall sternly lectured a newspaperman from the *New York Sun,* who had referred to Ford's anti-Semitism as though it had been one long joke. "There are some subjects that may not with decency be treated jocularly," Marshall declared.[87] Looking back on the seven-year ordeal, he affirmed that any threat of physical danger had abated in the early phase, when the defense Marshall authored in the name of American Jewish organizations drew wall-to-wall sympathy. "We Jews of the US were not put in jeopardy . . . largely because the American press paid no attention to his vaporings," Marshall explained to the *Sun* journalist. However, in Central and Eastern Europe, the libels Ford disseminated could prove deadly to "desperate and harried" Jewish inhabitants, Marshall warned, ominously.[88]

In the 1920s, Arthur Brisbane's syndicated "Today" column, probably the most influential daily media artifact in the Roaring Twenties, served as a significant counterweight to Henry Ford's anti-Semitic crusade. Brisbane opposed Ford's Jew-hatred from the start, responding to the *Dearborn Independent* vituperative libels by claiming that "every other successful name you see in a city today is a Jewish name," and that Jews were responsible for 50 percent of the world's commercial success.[89] The *Independent* responded by ridiculing Brisbane's appeal for toleration, insinuating that the editor's view on Jewish issues had been co-opted by his professional reliance on Jewish bankers and advisers.[90] Not intimidated,

Brisbane persisted for the first seven years of the decade to oppose the *Dearborn Independent*'s hate campaign—his stand on this issue can be seen in the wider context of Hearst newspapers' fine track record in exposing anti-Semitism. (The historian Rafael Medoff has argued that in contrast to newspapers like the *New York Times,* Hearst's newspapers gave prominent coverage during the Holocaust to the mass murder of Jews.[91])

On May 11, 1927, Ford called in Brisbane for a secret meeting. The two conferred for five hours, and the industrialist indicated that he might bring the *Independent*'s anti-Semitic campaign to a halt. "No one can charge that I am an enemy of the Jewish people," Ford told Brisbane. "I employ thousands of them."[92] He subsequently stipulated that the Marshall-dictated retraction be published exclusively by Brisbane's newspapers, with the proviso that Brisbane's name not be cited in the apology.[93] Marshall appreciated Brisbane's work contesting Ford's campaign throughout the decade. Marshall knew that the Hearst journalist had unselfishly helped him attain the crowning accomplishment of his career in Jewish advocacy: as the champion of his people whose words and towering devotion clinched the deal, in a process that brought America's most dangerous anti-Semite to his knees. That said, Marshall chose to overlook the supreme irony of his life, the fact that the same journalist had, seventeen years earlier, unfairly stifled any hopes of his accomplishing his most fervent professional ambition. At the end of the *Dearborn Independent* affair, Marshall wrote to Brisbane, relating that when Palma informed him that Ford had signed the apology and requested only that his recantation be communicated via Brisbane, "it afforded me delight to acquiesce." Nobly, Marshall added, "It never occurred to me that you would act otherwise than in the high-minded way."[94]

9

Jews and Birds

Protecting the Rights of Migratory Birds

In 1913, Congress enacted a statute protecting migratory birds from hunters. In Arkansas and Kansas, federal courts ruled the statute to be unconstitutional, holding that the Constitution does not ascribe to the federal government powers to regulate game hunting.[1] The Justice Department acknowledged that these rulings had some measure of validity and feared that the Supreme Court would uphold them; obviating this obstacle, the US government negotiated a treaty with Great Britain stipulating that closed hunting seasons in the United States and Canada would be arranged by reciprocal legislation. Subsequently, in 1918, Congress passed a statute to bring the treaty into effect, but the state of Missouri objected to this statute and brought action to prevent a federal game warden, named Ray P. Holland, from enforcing it. This was the background to *Missouri v. Holland,* a landmark case whose resolution by the Supreme Court continues to provoke debate among legal scholars as to whether foreign treaties can effectively expand the authority of Congress by devolving upon it powers not specifically mandated by the Constitution.[2] Louis Marshall's role in what one authoritative scholar calls the "most famous and discussed case in the constitutional law of foreign affairs"[3] was central.

Marshall began to ponder the constitutionality of game protection in the period after his mourning for Florence when, as he confessed to Israel Zangwill, he threw himself "into hard work, in order to forget myself."[4] Beyond this psychological consideration of work as therapy, his engagement on the Migratory Bird Treaty Act stemmed from his longstanding enthusiasm for nature; an examination of this enthusiasm and its expression in environmental advocacy suggests intriguing connections to Marshall's lobbying for Jewish minority rights.

Jews were politically powerless, "migratory" people who required special forms of legal protection. When it came to Jews and birds, Marshall tended to think in preservationist terms, trying to protect an idyllic way of life from the predations of modernity. However awkward and demeaning it sounds, this analogy between migratory bird treaty protection and postwar Jewish minority rights treaty protection points to Marshall's evolving methodology.

In the World War I era, both objects of Marshall's advocacy urgently needed legal protection, but no certain framework existed to provide safeguards. European Jews, like birds, were domiciled in an array of legal jurisdictions, each with its own local laws and traditions; in both cases, it was not clear whether a central governing power had the legal authority, or practical enforcement power, to protect these defenseless objects. In his work on the migratory bird laws of North America and then during his diplomacy in Paris for minority rights for East European Jews, Marshall developed an approach blending conservatism and legal activism that would define the last, signature phase of his career, when the lifelong Republican and affluent business lawyer emerged on the cutting edge of campaigns for empowerment and minority rights; moving beyond Jews and birds, he championed the rights of Haitians and African Americans and Native Americans. His concern about the provision of legal protection to defenseless groups trumped his conservative penchant for narrow interpretations of constitutional provisions and for states rights.

Starting with the Migratory Bird Treaty Act, he thought creatively about how the powers of a central authority could be broadened for the purpose of minority protection. In the international arena, with regard to Jewish minority rights in Europe, such protection could be afforded only via the establishment of a new international mechanism, the League of Nations. Thus, in the name of preserving vulnerable groups, Jews and birds, Marshall's conservatism essentially had to take flight—he had to surrender his conservative preferences for local authority, along with his suspiciously conservative tendency to regard federal governance as organized mob rule, and vest new powers to an authoritative central government.

In America, Marshall's legal creativity and his moral concerns for the protection of the legally unempowered were most keenly appreciated on the Supreme Court bench by Oliver Wendell Holmes. Just as Holmes converted into law Marshall's arguments in the Leo Frank case about mob trials being inimical to the rights of an accused, he ruled in the *Missouri* case that the expansion of congressional power via a treaty for the protections for birds does not violate Tenth Amendment states rights standards.[5] I have remarked elsewhere on ways in which Marshall's philosophy overlapped with Holmes's skeptical liberalism—in a chaotic modern world, both were drawn to creative interpretations of the Constitution for the protection of groups that would have been safeguarded theoretically in earlier eras by God or nature.[6] Here, it suffices to point out how Marshall's specific concerns, as a nature lover and as a lifelong steward of Jewish interests, drew him to an alliance with Holmes that significantly modified the constitutional fabric of American democracy in terms of conceptions of due process of law, the powers of Congress relative to the states, and the realm of treaties and foreign affairs.

Preparing his 1916 brief on the migratory bird law, Marshall reasoned that environmental protectionists had defended Congress's contested 1913 statute, both in the 1914 Arkansas action, *United States v. Shauver*, and in the 1915 Kansas case, *United States v. McCullagh*, on a faulty theory.[7] They had been unable to prove that legal protection could be afforded to the birds as US property—the problem, it seemed to Marshall, was the way property had been conceptualized in this litigation. He decided to defend Congress's authority to regulate bird hunting in terms of its power to protect the public domain. Marshall reviewed precedents and interpretations regarding Article IV, Section 3 of the Constitution, vesting Congress with the right to make rules and regulations respecting US property, and concluded that Congress had something akin to "police power" in the protection of US property from trespassers.

Marshall's notes and letters on the migratory birds issue indicate that a single, striking phrase coined by famed ornithologist Henry Wetherbee Henshaw sparked his legal line of thought. In a discussion of how birds protect nature by eliminating insects, Henshaw had spoken of birds as the "policemen of the air."[8] While migratory birds might not be US property, their insectivorous function is crucial to the preservation of national forests and the public domain, Marshall concluded. This was a Eureka moment.

The value of the 265,000 square miles (excluding Alaska) of natural forests in the public domain was worth billions of dollars, Marshall calculated. Anything utilized to protect these assets, including the safeguarding provided by their aviary policemen, fell within the scope of Article IV, Section 3. As he explained to the director of the Bronx Zoo, who took an actively supportive interest in Marshall's advocacy on this issue, bird protection regulation was supported by a wealth of legal precedent that sanctioned measures to prevent trespass of the public domain or forest fire.[9] In colorful terms depicting bird preying on insects in national forests as police protection for plants and trees, Marshall referred in his brief to "the police agency provided by the Almighty as a safeguard against the continuous trespass of the innumerable hosts of noxious enemies."[10]

Marshall needed evidence to substantiate such rhetorical flourish for the birds. In late autumn 1916, alongside his review of Magnes's report on the disbursement of overseas relief for European Jews and the ongoing quibbling about proposed election procedures for the American Jewish Congress, he sent letters of inquiry to important naturalists in the country, trying to pinpoint the extent to which game birds such as wild geese and wild ducks destroyed insects that damaged vegetation. Among others, he questioned N. L. Britton of the New York Botanical Garden,[11] and W. T. Hornaday from the Bronx Zoo. Since the coot had been the bird in issue during the Arkansas *Shauver* case, he studied observations of that bird in a 1912 history of game birds, wildfowl and shorebirds published by the state ornithologist of Massachusetts[12] (it would have been better, he decided, had the environmentalists based their action in Arkansas on a more "predominately insectivorous" bird[13]). Waldo Lee McAtee, head of the government's Section of Economic Ornithology, informed Marshall that insects constituted 10 percent of the food of ducks and geese.[14]

Marshall's brief did not pertain specifically to the issue of whether treaties can expand congressional powers, but otherwise his argument conceptualizing bird protection as part of Congress's right to regulate the public domain and his thorough empirical demonstration of birds' insectivorous contribution provided the basis for Holmes's landmark formulations in the majority opinion in *Missouri v. Holland*. Exactly as he would do three years later after Holmes incorporated in the majority opinion in *Frank v. Magnum* his impassioned argument in the Frank appeal, characterizing mob trial as an unconstitutional infringement of due process,[15] Marshall expressed his "great satisfaction" in 1920 after Holmes ratified in *Missouri* Marshall's migratory bird brief, holding that "there was nothing in the Constitution that compelled the Government to sit by while a food supply is cut off and the protectors of our forests and our crops are destroyed."[16]

Environmentalism and Modern Jewish Identity

Jews have expressed their love of the land of America in manifold ways during more than 350 years of settlement in North America. Some contributed songs and images that became in American culture iconic emblems whose familiarity far outweighs anything that has been known regarding what Louis Marshall, a creature of Manhattan's business law offices, did for the rivers, mountains, and forests of a country he loved. For example, the contrast between Marshall's obscure lobbying for the "forever wild" amendment at New York's 1894 Constitutional Convention and the fame of Irving Berlin's "God Bless America" is telling.

In fact, Marshall's contributions in this sphere were significant, because they were an initial and a highly influential part of a process by which the environment has come to be seen as needful of public advocacy and legal protection; while various biographical treatments of Marshall have commented in passing on this continuing passion in his life,[17] this aspect of his career has, curiously, remained virtually unknown. In general, the surging interest of historiography in environmental issues would make this omission problematic were Marshall's concerns about migratory birds, his love for the Adirondacks and Knollwood, and his affiliation with the New York State College of Forestry at Syracuse University to have been ongoing extracurricular pursuits in his life. However, the need to correct this imbalance in our understanding of the meaning of Marshall's life is peremptory because environmental matters were, for him, more than a mere sidelight among many other pursuits.

When Marshall's work regarding the Adirondacks and national conservation issues is taken together with its perpetuation and creative expansion in the life of his son, Robert (Bob) Marshall, he becomes more than an asterisk in the environmental history of the United States. The Marshalls were, in fact, premier figures in the history of the environmental movement through the Great Depression. A compelling biography of Bob Marshall regards him as a "founding father of the modern environmental movement";[18] and Bob himself, one can safely say, would not have separated his activities, such as the establishment of the Wilderness Society, from the example his father set (though he was conscious of obvious ways in which his own radicalized outlook and unbounded outdoors lifestyle differed from his father's legacy[19]). The reasons for reexamining this aspect of Marshall's career, however, go beyond the fact that he bequeathed his love for nature to all his children and that one of them turned into an influential environmentalist.

It is in this environmental sphere where Marshall's Romantic vision of organic preservation is most palpable. As in various social frameworks, he believed that significant or radical alteration of any one part of the ecological system could set off an apocalyptic chain reaction. This organic view of reality was not a particularly original form of Romanticism (Marshall, after all, virtually nursed on his mother's recitations of German Romantic poetry), but it is too often overlooked in assessments of his impact in other contexts, particularly Jewish ones. The following passage, excerpted from a lobbying letter for the establishment of the Syracuse forestry school that Marshall rifled off to Al Smith, who was in 1911 a New York assemblyman, can be read intelligibly at face value, as a vaguely prophetic citation of twenty-first-century ecological concerns, such as climate change. I would, however, also encourage a reader of this particular passage and of Marshall's writings on environmental matters generally to insert, imaginatively, the terms "Jewish life" or "Judaism" in every place where Marshall refers to forests or other symbols and essentials of the environment:

> There is no subject which demands more serious attention on the part of American statesmen. If our forest lands are to be denuded in the future as they have been in the past, there will not only be a lumber famine, but there will be a change in climate of a most serious nature, a diminution of our sources of water

> supply, and at certain seasons of the year destructive freshets. In time our country would suffer all of the evils which are now felt in those European and Asiatic countries in which the forests have disappeared.[20]

The uniqueness of America's landscape was its capacity to preserve unadulterated images of God's work. Similarly, Judaism's distinctive contribution to human civilization was in its pure conveyance of God's will. In neither case did Marshall have any patience for an anthropomorphized or radicalized vision of America, or Judaism, being special in terms of the opportunity it provides for human adaptation. A realist, he understood the practical arguments in favor of modifications of environments, either natural ones or Jewish ones. Yet, the environment and Judaism were the two spheres where Marshall's idealistic instincts for total preservation were least restrained. In ecological matters, they produced, for example, a fundamental ambiguity in a project that engaged an extraordinary amount of Marshall's time during the last two decades of his life, the Syracuse forestry school. Many supporters and teachers involved with this institution viewed its objectives in terms of rationalized lumber management and cultivation of other Adirondack resources, and they sometimes scoffed at the "wilderness doctrine" of pure preservation that they attributed to the Marshalls (Bob completed his undergraduate study at the New York State College of Forestry between 1920 and 1924).[21] This criticism was not entirely fair (Louis Marshall had a keen interest in reforesting, and in his programmatic statements about the State College he was careful to insert sympathetic allusions to "scientific lumbering enterprises"[22]), but it legitimately underscored the Marshalls' Romantic preference for preservation more than anything else.

The main thrust of Louis Marshall's orientation toward the environment colored his work on Jewish affairs. He tended to treat the Zionists as crude lumberjacks who denuded Judaism and who dangerously proposed radical alteration in the natural environments of Jewish life. His non-Zionism was essentially a compromise bred by recognition that there was no stopping change in the allocation of Jewish resources and energy, given world realities; Marshall more or less regarded courses in lumber management at the forestry school in the same spirit.

Marshall always responded to the major changes in his own life by looking for new institutional anchors that would preserve something pure in the two worlds he cherished more than anything, besides his family. The year he left Syracuse for New York City—a major personal and professional transition for a prospering small-city lawyer who had lived for thirty-eight years with his parents—Marshall was instrumental in drafting a landmark conservationist ("forever wild") Catskills and Adirondacks amendment to the New York State Constitution.

Something would remain rustic and pristine in the region where he had passed the first half of his life. This yearning for the untouched past sometimes found semicomic expression in New York City, as in the case of his famous aversion for automobiles,[23] but it was also earnestly articulated in the relentless and vigilant legal measures he applied for the next thirty-five years to prevent abusive modification of the 1894 conservation measure by commercial interests. Even more to the point, the Marshall family's multigenerational love for the Knollwood retreat in the Adirondacks, attested to in the 2009 memoir produced by a journalist grandson that begins with an exclamation about Saranac Lake, "I am probably the only person alive who beat Albert Einstein in sailing races,"[24] affirms to the power of this instinct for nature preservation. Whenever Marshall was rattled by the character or pace of developments in his professional work, he retreated to Knollwood, or at least dreamed about it. Knollwood was a vision of everlasting, almost divine, beauty.

As part of the same dynamic, at times of deep personal struggle, Marshall found it impossible to move ahead in Jewish affairs without seeking some institutional anchor to preserve something true and essential in the Jewish past. His wife's passing in 1916 occurred at a time when Marshall was turbulently engaged in a dispute about the American Jewish Congress plan, an idea he regarded as a threatening and completely unnecessary novelty but one he knew could not be staved off forever. In a moment of setback, it will be recalled, Marshall established in his late wife's name a memorial fund for the religious education of young Jewish women, couching its purposes in noticeably traditionalist language. A similar analysis could be applied to Marshall's skillful handling of the reorganization of the Jewish Theological Seminary and recruitment of his future friend Solomon Schechter at the turn of the twentieth century; unnerved by rough-and-tumble dealings with Downtown Jewry and never enamored by the modernizing thrust of Emanu-El-style Reform Judaism, Marshall tended to regard JTS, and Schechter in particular, as agents for the orderly preservation of Jewish authenticity in chaotic New York, as a kind of Yavneh-like saving remnant.[25]

Broadly, Marshall's environmentalism can be compared to *volkish* land Romanticism important to successive generations of German Jews in the nineteenth and twentieth centuries and even to the *yediat haaretz* cult of land settlement and appreciation important in the pioneering traditions of Zionism. Finding creative and sophisticated ways of expressing their attachment to their lands of settlement, modern Jews hoped to articulate a sense of rooted belonging, be it in Germany, America, or Zionism. There were, admittedly, major variations in this theme running between the Black Forest tales of Berthold Auerbach in mid-nineteenth-century Central Europe, the agricultural explorations of Aaron Aaronsohn in late Ottoman Palestine, and Marshall's Adirondack reveries at Knollwood during the first decades of the twentieth century. However, no less striking than the differences of time period, Jewish personality, manner of expression, and outlying non-Jewish society is the common thread running between these experiences: an emphatic modern flight from the concept of the "wandering Jew."

Marshall's enthusiasm can be looked at through this kaleidoscope of modern Jewish history and should not be seen merely as a part of a straightforward, landlocked process of Americanization. One piece in the puzzle of modern Jewish identity is the way Jews in an array of national locales converted their love of the land into an existential statement. Generally part of a secularization process, the love of the new land of settlement became a source of authority hedging against a complete loss of order and faith. In the case of the Marshalls, Bob, who died young at the age of thirty-eight, personified this transition—having attended Manhattan's Ethical Culture School, he never appears to have drawn inspiration from any organized Jewish institution and instead conceptualized the American outdoors as his synagogue. More than anything, Marshall and his environmentalist son went to nature in search of the sacred.

From Conservatism to Conservation: The Outdoors and Marshall's Changing Outlook

Little is known about the origins of Marshall's love of the outdoors. At least by his late twenties, he engaged in outdoor hikes in the Adirondacks.[26] Marshall can first be identified as an environmentalist precisely at the moment he became a New York City lawyer, in 1894. Years later, Marshall recalled the 1894 Constitutional Convention's adoption of Article VII, Section 7, preserving the Adirondack and Catskill forests in their wild state, as its most important measure.[27] At the convention, Marshall stood out as a persuasive advocate and patron of Article VII, but the measure was proposed by New York City Democrat David McClure, who acted on the request of businessmen who were interested in watershed protection—forest destruction in the Adirondacks, they feared, would harm the headwaters of the Hudson River.[28] The act protected 600,000 acres of Adirondacks land. "Every word in the provision was carefully weighed," Marshall recalled. The legislators rejected elastic formulations that might have opened the Adirondacks doors to developers; they concluded that a "rigid" preservation law "should be laid down and rigidly enforced."[29]

The 1894 measure, Marshall believed, closed the New York State frontier to a century-long policy of "giving away our forest lands." During the first decades of the nineteenth century, New York State had sold millions of forest acres for a trifle five cents per acre, so by 1872 the state owned just 40,000 acres of forest land. A few months before the 1894 convention took session, a 400,000-acre tract of virgin forest was sold at a price of $1.50 per acre.[30]

Marshall vigilantly guarded against any legal efforts to trespass and violate this rule of full protection of the Adirondack and Catskill forests. A month before his death, he recalled that "almost annually," after 1894, "somebody has been trying to take the backbone out of this constitutional provision."[31] He provided his most impassioned defense of this "rigid," total preservation approach as a participant in the 1915 Constitutional Convention in lively debate parries with fellow delegates whom (it will be recalled) Marshall believed to be on the payroll of lumber companies. Though the 1915 proposed constitution was not approved by state voters, Marshall believed that his adamant preservation stand at the convention was a turning point stifling the momentum of commercial developers who sought to lower the environmental bar that had been raised in 1894.[32]

One year into the Great War, Marshall spoke with impassioned zeal at the 1915 convention, berating attempts to modify the rigid preservation rule in language that anticipated the mix of emotion and empiricism in subsequent Green movements for environmental protection:

> And it is certain as anything on earth can be that if we in any way relax the limitations which we are now seeking to place upon the Adirondacks, our waterways are doomed and our agricultural lands are doomed. The value of these forest preserves lies in the fact that they constitute great reservoirs for our water. They are, as it were, huge sponges which hold the water as it flows and allow it to flow away as it is required. We have been guilty of the grossest carelessness and neglect in our past history.[33]

This was the convention when Marshall stood on the floor and exposed rival delegates' commercial affiliations: Mr. Angell as the counsel of a large syndicate that held lands for lumbering purposes, Mr. Meigs as the president of the Santa Clara Lumber Company.[34] Mercilessly, he attacked delegates who claimed their proposed revisions of the 1894 policy would have minimal environmental effect. Refuting rivals' suggestion that they simply wanted license to cut down diseased trees, Marshall relied on the expertise of the Syracuse College of Forestry. Enraged, he scolded his opponents:

> It has been suggested in the Committee that [at question] are trees which are diseased, but I am informed by the Dean of the College of Forestry that under such a contract, or under such a term, eighty percent of all the trees in

> the Adirondacks could be cut down. What would you have left after you have adopted a provision of this character? Nothing but a howling wilderness of trees. Not a wilderness of trees—wild forest trees—but of stumps, enough to make one's heart sick to behold them.[35]

In this heated debate, as in far more tranquil reveries at Knollwood at Saranac Lake, the Adirondacks symbolized in Marshall's mind everything that was natural in the New World. An assault on them would eliminate the refreshing and revitalizing power of North America; his opponents in this debate proposed no more or no less than the disfiguration of the United States and its horrifying conversion into one of the planet's old, wasted lands:

> It is only a few years, if that policy should be adopted in section 2 of this article before we will have to chew the bitter cud of reflection, and future generations will find themselves precisely where today are found the people of China, Mesopotamia, of Syria, of Northern Africa, and in those nations where the foolish policy which is sought to be incorporated in this amendment has been observed.[36]

After World War I, Marshall hit his stride as the guardian of the Adirondack forests. The 1894 measure was inviolable. Marshall never hinted that the objects of his advocacy mingled in his mind, but it is difficult in retrospect to review the vehemence of his Adirondack custodianship without suspecting that his complete success in this environmental sphere compensated in his mind for the imperfect results of other protective agreements he negotiated on behalf of defenseless clients. By the early 1920s, the minority rights agreements collapsed under the weight of evolving sociopolitical realities in Eastern Europe. It was in this period when Marshall pungently boxed off any unnatural development in the Adirondacks, as though to prove that there was one place in the world where it was agreed that the depredations of modernity had no business. If it could not be fully protected in all Jewish communities around the globe, the idea of eternity would be kept sacred in the Adirondack forests.

Year after year, Marshall's defense of the Adirondacks never slackened. In 1923, he successfully petitioned New York governor Al Smith, calling for opposition to an amendment proposed by Senator Woodbridge Nathan Ferris for the development of waterpower sources in the Adirondacks (Marshall decried the proposal as a "golden opportunity to those interests which are seeking to absorb for themselves the water powers of the state"[37]) and for opposition to a proposal by a self-interested private group to establish a Raquette River Regulating District.[38] At the polls, New York State residents resoundingly defeated the Ferris and

Raquette River proposals by half a million votes. A year later, in 1924, Marshall published in the *New York Times* an extraordinary environmental "Declaration of Principles,"[39] which, he proposed, ought to bind all candidates for state office. All New York elected officials were to take a pledge of total allegiance to the 1894 measure for the Adirondack forests. In hyperbolic, pejorative idiom, this declaration described developers who sought private profit from large-scale waterpower projects as "cunning enemies." The language of the "Environmental Declaration" was noticeably similar to radicalized discourses, either to socialist philippic about class enemies or even to anti-Semitic invective about Jewish machinations; and its tone, in Marshall's writing, is atypical. In environmental matters, Marshall transformed as a Romantic employed by the forces of right in battle against the forces of wrong. "The enemies of the waters and forests of the state are ever vigilant and expect to compass their ends by concocting their cunning schemes in secret while the public sleeps," Marshall warned in his declaration.

In late 1926, four of the five members of the New York State Water Power Control Commission favored an eleventh-hour conferral of a development license to private corporations. Judging these waterpower concessions to be "very favorable to the corporate interests and very injurious to the State," Marshall led a concerted lobbying campaign with Governor Smith and in leading newspapers (which tended generally throughout the decade to side with Marshall's "green" positions in such disputes) to block the conferral of this license before the commission's dispersal on January 1. He happily reported to his son Bob that this lobbying produced a "sweeping victory" (his old law partner, Samuel Untermyer, a Democrat with connections to the Smith administration in Albany, allied closely with Marshall in this effort).[40]

In a fashion recapitulated in his late advocacy for African Americans and Native Americans, Marshall's lobbying for the environment in Upstate New York in the final years of his life recognizably anticipated terms and conceptualization of the great liberal causes of the 1960s and after. Despite his continuing, nominal affiliation with the conservative Republican Party, at the end of his life, Marshall was the country's prominent liberal lawyer.

However, in this last, liberal phase of his career there was a shift of emphasis in Marshall's Romantic idealism. Earlier, his environmentalism was predicated on a nostalgic desire to perpetuate a mid-nineteenth-century preurban landscape remembered from his Syracuse youth; this environmentalism was tempered by the conservative outlooks of Orthodox Jewish parents and, in all probability, by his mother's love of the German idealists. By the end of his life, Marshall surely realized that this rural skyline was forever lost; and so, no matter how impressively vast his or others' accomplishments might have been in zoning national parks and wilderness lands, these were not really alternatives to the urban realities of the Jazz Age. They were, instead, becoming "green" toy boxes.

In 1921, when Marshall plotted with the sympathetic New York City commissioner of parks (Francis Gallatin) for increased budgetary allocation and care of Central Park, his recitation of its species of plants was almost camp in its pedantry (his son Bob inherited and creatively developed this mania for long lists). Marshall wrote in praise of Central Park's "Kentucky coffee-tree, the sassafras, the Paulownia Imperialis, the Indian bean-tree, the bald cypress, the red, black and willow oaks, the European cut-leaved beech, the Chinese golden larch, the red and paper mulberry, the Chinese cork-tree, the Nordmann silver fir, and the persimmon trees."[41] Vaguely tongue-in-cheek (Marshall closed this letter to the parks commissioner with an understated apology for "this rather lengthy letter"), the letter reflects a transition in Marshall's environmentalism: once conceptualized in Romantic terms of idyllic reverie, it was becoming literal. Much of what he loved was already lost, and so he felt it better to be as specific as possible about what might possibly be saved. His concluding admonition in this letter to Gallatin refers to Central Park, but it reflects broader issues in his thinking about conservation in the 1920s:

> Those of the species that are now in the Park are getting old, some of them have passed beyond the stage of maturity, and we must therefore prepare against the day when the present giants have gone. I am anxious that my children and grandchildren shall have the same opportunity for enjoyment in beholding these noble trees that I have had.[42]

By the end of the turbulent, modern decade, Marshall had ceased to conceptualize environmentalism in terms of throwback communion with the rural past. That past was too long gone. Instead, his efforts turned into a last ditch battle to fend off the total conquest of modernity.

It is not too much to say that Marshall spoke out against the shattered nerves of city life in cadences resembling the complaints of 1960s flower children. Were it not for the conspicuously countercultural environmentalism and lifestyle of his son Robert (Bob) Marshall, a free spirit who modeled himself after this naturalist side of his father and who was remembered by his nephews as a "glamour figure" who had romantic affairs with Eskimo women and backpacks full of amazing stories about being treed by bears,[43] this judgment would seem like too speculative of a leap into a distant future of radical American Jewish politics.

In many ways, Marshall was a transitional figure in American Jewish politics. Before the relatively recent Neoconservative movement, Marshall loomed as one of the last diehard Republicans of American Jewish politics. However, his children and grandchildren ignored this party affiliation; arguably, Marshall's dogmatism in this respect gave them little choice, as evidenced by a letter he wrote to his youngest son George days after Herbert Hoover's election in 1928, in which the proud Republican father opined, "I am sure that Hoover, with all his broad experience, his ability to think scientifically and in an orderly manner, his appreciation of the problems which call for solution, will be equal to any emergency that may arise."[44] Instead, Marshall's children and grandchildren inherited from him a passion for underdogs and minority rights, remembering him as a liberal confined to conservative corporate dress. In fact, the late phase of Marshall's career can legitimately be associated with subsequent liberal and even radical phases of American Jewish culture from the 1930s to the 1970s, because Marshall came to fight for unpopular or unrepresented causes in an ardent, combative way that was destined to capture the idealistic imagination of his children and their cultural peers.

Admittedly, there is something counterintuitive about hints of antiestablishment influences exerted posthumously by the avowedly conservative Marshall, who remained a Harding-Coolidge-Hoover Republican until his death and who left an inheritance of millions to his four children accrued through business law in Manhattan's corporate offices, stock investments, and years of real estate transactions in Syracuse. Nevertheless, much in his late life, and nothing more than his crusading environmentalism, reflected a courageous dissent from the rules of modernity, and his actions could be taken (manifestly so, in Bob Marshall's case), as an antiestablishment call to create a new sort of future based on glimpses of a pure past. Always nostalgic, the environmentalism of this last period also seems rebellious.

The antiestablishment tenor of this late environmentalism rings loudly in a November 1927 complaint published by Marshall in the *New York Times,* protesting a proposed amendment to the New York Constitution that envisioned the construction of a highway up to the peak of White Face Mountain in Essex County.[45] As soon as Marshall heard from New York State senator Elwood Rabenold about this highway construction plan, he wrote to his son Bob, the young environmentalist who was stationed at the Northern Rocky Mountain Forest Experiment Station in Montana.[46] "Some of the northern New York sharks are trying to swallow the land," valued at $500,000, "for the purpose of filling their insatiable maw," Marshall told his son. Rabenold had hinted that there had "been a great deal of political conniving" to build the road, but Marshall was looking forward to exposing the highway as an act of naked greed. "If I can get a good chance to bump their heads, I shall take extreme pleasure in doing it," he promised Bob. This head butt was soon printed in the *New York Times.*

In this published complaint, Marshall noted that in terms of road construction, the only breach allowed in thirty-three years of rigid enforcement of the 1894 measure was the building of a single state highway from Saranac Lake, allowing the "general public the opportunity to travel on a continuous highway through the Forest Preserve." The White Face Mountain road, Marshall protested, would turn the region into a polluted junkyard. With some fine-tuning, Marshall's angry phrases could have sounded like those in the 1960s. He bemoaned "the intrusion of the automobile and all the commotion and danger, the disfigurement of the beautiful mountain, the strewing of the roadside with tin cans and the ballyhooing attendant upon the hustle and bustle that accompany such an invasion."

Supplementing their proposal, the backers of the White Face Mountain highway proposed that it lead to a World War I memorial to slain New Yorkers that would be built in the future. Marshall's dismissive rejection of this memorial idea as a "mere pretext" and an "insult" constituted a departure from his limitless patriotism of the World War I era; in fact, it articulated suspiciousness about the exploitation of patriotic symbols by corporate interests that had been absent in earlier phases of Marshall's life and was to become a trademark on the cultural horizon of subsequent generations of American Jewish liberals. Ending this fascinating document, Marshall's plea expressed his own lifelong love for the Adirondacks as the "most perfect mountain region in the world" and also previewed the spirit of commune movements that animated later generations of alienated or radicalized American Jews and non-Jews:

> Let us preserve some of the simple things. Let us know that there is somewhere in our State a region which is not commercialized and citified, and to which those may repair who yearn for a restoration of their shattered nerves amid the vast silences of the eternal mountains and the primeval forests. . . . The very laying out of such a highway would necessitate the destruction of thousands of trees centuries old. The very act of building the road is likely to be followed by further destruction following the inroad of the tourist roaring on his way like a prairie fire. Let us beware while there is still time. Let us not jeopardize this fine heritage. Let us not make a beginning which in time would be certain to make a barren waste of the most perfect mountain region of the world.[47]

8. Knollwood country home, facade. Courtesy of the Adirondack Museum.

Knollwood

The Adirondacks were the "most perfect mountain region in the world" owing to their natural beauty, and because they offered proof of the Jews' permanent place on the majestic continent. On broad levels, environmentalism for the Jew can be an exercise in antidefamation because it establishes a pure attachment to land untainted by any material motives. In this regard, the Adirondacks had compellingly specific charms. The Saranac Lake area where Marshall built his family's alluring country home had in American culture an incomparable reputation as a stimulus to reflection and spiritual restoration. Immediately before the Civil War, Ralph Waldo Emerson, James Russell Lowell, and Louis Agassiz set up their "Philosophers' Camp" on Follensby Pond west of the Saranac area. In Emerson's rapturous description of the region's "sacred mountains," the Adirondacks thrilled generations of Americans as a stretch of nature untainted by civilization, as an area where, the influential transcendentalist wrote, "nothing was ploughed, or reaped, or bought or sold."[48] Miracles happened in the Adirondacks, as exemplified famously by the career of Dr. Edward Livingston Trudeau, who came to the area to die of tuberculosis in 1873 but recovered and established his Saranac Lake village sanatorium a decade later.[49]

9. Knollwood country home, interior. Courtesy of the Adirondack Museum.

As memorialized in William James Stillman's striking painting of Emerson and fellow philosophers in their wilderness camp, the Adirondacks symbolized New World purity and the determination of a gifted new nation to glory in its bounty. Anti-Semitism in the area, therefore, excluded elite Jews from America's Garden of Eden, from the promise of the country's finest natural rewards. Marshall's predecessors and peers in America's Jewish elite were in no mood to be excluded from the Adirondacks: to acquiesce to anti-Semitism in the area was to condone the consignment of the Jew to urban ghettos and to admit that the Jew could never be at home in the country's most placidly natural setting. Some thirty years before the Jews had a constituted, organized body to combat anti-Semitism, they responded in a noticeably concerted, emphatic fashion to an anti-Semitic slur in the Adirondacks, protesting discrimination against the banker Joseph Seligman at the Grand Hotel in Saratoga during summer 1877. And, it will be recalled, on the eve of the establishment of the Jewish American Committee, Marshall and powerful Uptown confederates mobilized for action against anti-Semitism at Melvil Dewey's Lake Placid Club. The vehemence of these responses reflected a Jewish sense that anti-defamation battles in the Adirondacks targeted something more than insulting social slurs. They related as well to the Jew's rightful place in all that was pure and good about America.

In the Adirondacks, Jews followed the tracks of railroads that were never built. After facing demeaning social exclusion in East Coast resort areas operated by Gentiles, they seized opportunities facilitated by William West Durant, a developer of famed Adirondack camps (some of which remain as National Historic Landmarks) who had in the early 1880s purchased thousands of acres in the Adirondacks anticipating future railroad construction in the region.[50] After the railroad plans failed to materialize, Durant started selling his holdings in the early 1890s. This precipitated what one scholar describes as the "Adirondack land rush" of 1895–1910; Jews, including Marshall's Knollwood group, purchased lots around the Upper and Lower Saranac lakes and built camps, and many wealthy non-Jews also participated in this trend.[51] William L. Coulter, an architect who came to the Adirondacks at the age of thirty in 1896 hoping to cure his tuberculosis, gave this land rush its rustic visual imprint; by 1900, when he modeled Knollwood, he had reportedly already drafted plans for work worth a hefty $600,000 and had an army of workmen building Adirondack camps along the Saranac lakes.

The Knollwood consortium of six families commissioned Coulter to build the camp on Lower Saranac Lake's northeast shore in 1899, a time when the architect was busily engaged in other projects, including the building of philanthropist Alfred Vanderbilt's Great Camp Sagamore on Raquette Lake. Marshall, who handled a sprawling array of legal and lobbying matters connected to the construction of the consortium's camp, was joined by Daniel Guggenheim, Elias Ashel, George Blumenthal, Abram Stein, and Max Nathan. Marshall organized the six Knollwood families as a capital stock corporation in 1899. Under the agreements, transfer of stock required consent of all the partners; there were rental restrictions and shared operating expenses paid for a cook, groundskeeper, and housekeeper.[52] Patterned after older Adirondack camps, Knollwood featured six identical two-and-a-half-story Victorian shingle homes with a "casino" dining and recreation building at its center.[53] From the start, a rectangular log-frame boathouse was the focal point of Knollwood's daily summer activities; a two-story building, its lower level featured boat slips, and the upper half served as a game room; walkways radiated out from the boathouse along the shoreline. Linked by a wooden boardwalk, the six cottages were mostly hidden by trees. The six families drew straws to determine ownership of each unit. The cabins appeared as "soaring log gables," and their "thrilling" design featured "sunburst panels, with geometric patterns on the six side-by-side buildings. . . . Dark shadows created by the deeply set porches, especially by the wooden screens, [gave] to each camp an oddly light and skeletal appearance, as if nothing but the framework existed and the interior were a hollow space."[54]

In spring 1900, Marshall had two worries: the preservation and unity of Judaism in America and the construction of Knollwood. After the death of American Reform patriarch Isaac Mayer Wise, Marshall headed the campaign for a Wise memorial fund to strengthen the Hebrew Union College. His solicitation letters for this campaign conveyed a sense of the new century as a threat. Though American Jews enjoyed incomparable economic opportunity in the new era, it was far from certain that they would preserve their own religious traditions and learning:

10. Marshall resting with Adirondack guide Herb Clark. Courtesy of the Adirondack Museum.

> What a commentary it would be upon our people, who have acquired wealth and position, to have it said of them that, while the feeblest of religious sects in our nation is able to maintain a theological seminary in which its doctrines are taught, Judaism, the mother of all religions, has, in its American home, so degenerated and become so indifferent to its mission, as to allow this noble work to perish from the earth.[55]

Knollwood was also a Romantic response to the promises and perils posed by the new century. The core values and circumstances of human identity seemed set to unravel in the motorized whirlwind of the twentieth century; the purpose of moral striving in the new century was to overcome false social and spiritual divisions enforced by the mechanical artifices of modernity. With religion, as with nature, Marshall was at this moment deeply immersed in a nostalgic myth of past unity and purity. At Knollwood, he fulfilled a private quest for utopia, but this Romantic idealism colored his public affairs as well. In retrospect, it seems surprising that as late as spring 1900 Louis Marshall believed that concord and union could be achieved among the evolving branches of American Judaism. Yet, what might appear today as a naïvely irenic view of Jewish religious unity expressed a broad mood, the new century's hope that the best in the past could be perfectly restored. In religious affairs, by the end of April 1900 Marshall insisted that the Reform HUC could, and should, be amalgamated with the more traditional Jewish Theological Seminary, because the differences between the two "kindred" Jewish seminaries were nothing more than "matters of form."[56] The new century's sensational demonstrations of change were, in actual fact, superficial, and there was nothing to stop the harmonious reunion of modernizing and traditional Jewish religious forms.

Marshall's Romanticism in the religious sphere received a compelling posthumous tribute, when Julius Rosenwald donated half a million dollars to create a Louis Marshall Memorial Fund for the Jewish Theological Seminary in response to a long letter Marshall composed aboard the SS *Majestic* in August 1929, en route to the Zurich conference to establish the expanded Jewish Agency, just days before his death.[57] This moving final act attests to the persistence of Marshall's dream of Jewish learning unsullied by the divisions and distractions of Jewish life—just as he had insisted in 1900 that differences between Judaism's branches were superficial matters of form, he wrote three decades later to Julius Rosenwald that his work forging a Jewish Agency pact between Zionists and non-Zionists ought to have an analogue in the realm of the Jewish spirit. Weeks before his death, Marshall was still dreaming about accomplishing his utopian "objective": "bringing about unity among the forces of Israel, and of eliminating false conceptions and substituting sound and practicable ideas."[58] As it turned out, in the realm of religious affairs, that dream of unity could not keep pace with processes of differentiation and change in Jewish life.

In the life of a very practical Jewish leader and American lawyer, Knollwood remained as the only palpable demonstration of utopia, the only abiding proof that something essential about human experience could be preserved whole and protected against the senseless and divisive encroachments of the mechanical age.

From New York City in 1900, Marshall worried constantly about the camp's construction. He virtually hounded Coulter, imploring him to "watch the movements of any person who might enter our premises," because timber thieves were always on the prowl.[59] When he learned that the state had plans for a dam project on Saranac River, he launched an all-out lobbying effort for a $6,000 allocation of state funds for the addition of a lock to prevent the Saranac River and Lake from becoming inaccessible to one another. All spring, New York State politicians—William Wheeler, J. P. Allds, Elon Brown, John Raines—drowned in Marshall's petitions about the lock.[60] Soon enough, his lobbying for Knollwood bridged across elemental areas of earth, fire, and water. For instance, he petitioned New York's Forest, Fish and Game Commission, demanding that it stock Lower Saranac Lake with 500,000 bass fry. "This magnificent sheet of water is practically destitute of game fish," Marshall complained.[61]

Coulter's team worked at record speed. In July 1900, Marshall booked rooms for Florence and his two young children, James and Ruth, at the Lake Saranac resort Hotel Ampersand and could not believe his eyes when he walked into the camp and found Knollwood finished. Breathlessly, he wrote to one of his camp partners, "I had my money's worth from the sensations of agreeable surprise when the magnificent forest and cosy building burst upon my view. It seems as though the Magician's wand has been employed in the creation of Knollwood!"[62]

Apart from young Ruth's whooping cough, the first summer season at Knollwood was perfect, and Marshall spent winter and spring months the following year coaxing relatives and friends to spend some summer days in 1901 at their lake home. He convinced his brother Benjamin to reroute their parents for a summer rest in the Adirondacks instead of Philadelphia.[63] When one invited guest asked Marshall what he should wear at the much-vaunted Knollwood, his host replied that the camp was paradise but that its users did not have to "appear in the garb of the original inhabitants" of Eden. Yet, no fancy dress "indicative of civilization" was allowed. As he would be whenever he referred to Knollwood for the rest of his life, Marshall was smiling when he added, "You will be summarily turned out of the camp should you insult us by venturing to appear otherwise as a plain everyday woodsman. No frills are allowed. We are children of nature and must be natural."[64]

This last endearing description aptly described the Marshall family's methods of transport to and from Knollwood. Louis never purchased an automobile, and he vigilantly combated plans to cut down forest trees and build roads in the Adirondacks. These facts meant that the family traveled by train from New York City to Saranac village and then traveled a mile and a half by rowboat across Lake Saranac to reach the Knollwood camp (four-mile surrey rides around the lake were also an option). Often Bob and George would run the miles from the camp to Saranac village to greet their father when he arrived by train.[65]

Inside the house, Marshall stuffed bookshelves with classics from world literature, as well as Adirondack travel reports and almanacs. The Adirondack books shaped the lives of his children. At one point, Bob—the naturalist whose life story is largely framed around Knollwood and its surrounding area (during his first summer at the camp, in 1901, he was half a year old)—discovered on these bookshelves a dusty four-volume collection authored by Verplanck Colvin, *Report of the Topographical Survey of the Adirondack Wilderness.* The books' florid descriptions of the local mountains entranced Bob and his younger brother George;[66] by their teenage years, the boys spent the Knollwood summers scampering up mountain peaks in the Adirondacks, an activity that reached its zenith in 1921, the year when the two announced that they had climbed all forty-two of the Adirondack's 4,000-foot mountain peaks.[67] "Bob Marshall very simply laid the foundation for the modern hiker, and elevated the pursuit to something resembling cult status,"[68] writes the author of an entertaining, well-researched history of hiking in the Adirondacks. The feat of climbing all the 4,000-foot peaks, subsequently upgraded to forty-six in number, became in the last decades of the twentieth century a hiker's goal of considerable renown. Today, the "46ers" meet socially and drink an Adirondacks-brewed beer named after the hiking accomplishment whose origins were to be found on the bookshelf and outdoor summer discoveries of young Bob and George Marshall at Knollwood.

Most summers, Marshall spent four to six weeks at Knollwood and commuted to the camp from Manhattan on weekends during the other summer weeks. A quarter century after his death, Marshall's oldest child James authored a vivid portrait of his father at Knollwood, relaxed in his shirtsleeves:

> I still see him, at home in our camp at Saranac Lake, vest open, reading a newspaper or writing a letter; in his office, piles of unanswered mail on his desk, law books barricading him on the floor, dictating briefs and opinions and letters which enunciated rights which required defending; on the porch, in summer

reading aloud to us from Dickens, the Bible; walking through the woods or angling a boat for a fish that rarely touched his hook. In all of these memories, my father comes back to me, in shirt sleeves.[69]

On summer nights, dressed in his suspenders and shirtsleeves, Marshall would swat flies while reading to his children chapters from Dickens or James Fenimore Cooper. After cheering heroic triumphs in these tales, the excited Marshall children would have trouble falling asleep.[70] Two all-American traditions distinguished these happy summers. On July 4, Louis had the family read the Bible first thing in the morning; later he would lead the family around the cabin, each member carrying a flag, all merrily singing patriotic songs.[71] Throughout the summer, baseball was the afternoon pastime. Bob, who had a happy mania for keeping records, compiled a history of the "Knollwood League, 1916–1923" and estimated that baseball was played on some 5,000 afternoons in that interval.[72] Louis took part until his very last years, though as an older man he played a limited role as a pinch hitter who did not run the bases (through the 1920s, when Bob, a lifetime Pittsburgh Pirates fan, left the nest to work, among other places in forestry on the Montana-Idaho border, Louis regularly sent him updates about standings and World Series games[73]).

Louis and Bob: The Family Poetics of Environmental Advocacy

Before the establishment of the New York State College of Forestry in 1911, Marshall lacked an institutional base from which to articulate his concerns about environmental waste and ruin. After the establishment of the Knollwood camp, he spent the first decade of the century as a one-man Adirondacks environmental protection agency, rifling off letters of complaint to the Forest, Fish and Game commissioner and other state authorities about the lack of fire protection in the region and about other environmental subjects. Mixing biting humor and naturalist passions, these letters are minor stylistic masterpieces, and they launched a Marshall environmentalist style, which Bob perfected and which remains insufficiently appreciated outside of aficionados of the history of America's naturalist movement.[74]

It is difficult to identity which of the dust-covered nineteenth-century nature volumes encouraged Louis, and then Bob, to write with such a compelling mix of facetious irony and moral outrage about the environment (certainly, Dickens was one influence), but it is doubtful that Louis's style was entirely self-developed because the hyperbolic critique was unlike his writing on any other subject. Surely a contributing factor to this endearing facet of his career was that he operated in this sphere with, at least, rolled-up shirtsleeves, unconstrained by the formal procedures of courtroom litigation and argumentative precedent to which he was beholden as a lawyer. When it came to the Adirondacks and other environmental matters, the only precedent worth worrying about was God's munificence at the Creation. Any argument for the preservation of natural beauty, Louis and then his son Bob seemed to grasp, relied ultimately on truths known to the emotions.

Even though Bob's personality transformed in the 1920s and his 1933 volume *Arctic Village* thrilled thousands of Depression-era readers as the portrait of a genuine outdoorsman domiciled in the forbiddingly cold rough-and-tumble of Wiseman, Alaska,[75] both father and son seem to have been acutely cognizant of social differences separating them, as well-to-do New York Jews, from the working-class firefighters and lumbermen they encountered in the Adirondacks and other wilderness stretches around the country. In this respect, humor served them as a defense mechanism; they seemed aware that the professional environmental standards they were trying to uphold in fire protection and nature preservation were legitimate and necessary, but also that their formal articulation appeared arcane to rugged men of very different social background who lived hard lives, often with meager appreciation and compensation.

Louis probably inwardly knew that some measure of his posturing on environmental issues was hypocritical. He projected his work as sheer altruism, but at Knollwood, his own family and friends were beneficiaries of nature protection measures he himself helped legislate in 1894 and upheld thereafter; also, toward the end of his career, it was a bit disingenuous for him to hurl unqualified imprecation at developers given his investment decades earlier in power utility enterprises in Westchester County, if not elsewhere.[76] In other words, Marshall took rhetorical license in writing about the environment to highlight the contrast between the fallibility and foibles of all people and the innocent purity of nature.

Finally, by developing a high style of ironic sophistication in their writings on the environment, Marshall and his son set themselves apart, consciously or not, from the shrill moralistic rhetoric of the contemporary Temperance movement, as well as from the overweening utopian enthusiasms of radical religious and social movements that sprouted in Upstate New York throughout the nineteenth century. No advocate of any reform crusade could have put legwork into his or her cause comparable to the mileage Bob Marshall covered in his peripatetic wanderings through the Adirondacks, the Rocky Mountains, and the Koyukuk River region—no less than moralists of other stripes in this era, he "walked the talk." Yet the ironic humor he and his father packed into their environmental writings and petitions was rather unlike the intemperate preaching of the prohibitionists and other early twentieth-century reformers, and, in retrospect, it is one of the inviting qualities of their impassioned environmentalism.

In autumn 1908, Marshall wrote, as "a lover of the woods," to New York State's Forest, Fish and Game commissioner to articulate his despair about weeks of forest fires in the Adirondacks. He accused New York State of allowing railroads to run through the forests as "instruments of arson." His complaint appeared to draw rhetorical power from a Dickens novel he had read recently on summer nights to his children at Knollwood. This was not the way he wrote while filing litigation for a client in a civil suit:

> There is a continuous panorama of forest grave-yards, strewn with the blackened corpses of once noble trees, with dreary and desolate wastes, where the eye once reveled in verdure, with the spectacle of death, death on every hand, where but a few years ago the weary traveler beheld the beckoning finger of life. Locomotives of the volcanic type are still permitted to scatter ruin, locomotive engineers are still permitted to destroy the inadequate spark arresters, which are provided as a mere sham.[77]

Marshall then launched into a tirade about inadequate firefighting services in the Adirondacks. Carried away by his love of the local forests, he was in no mood to consider whether his plea for first-responder allocations and professionalization might have been at variance with early twentieth-century Republican Party reservations concerning taxation and government size. "What system of patrolling them [the Adirondack forests], especially in dry seasons, is resorted to?" Marshall asked. "What has ever been done to bring to justice those wretched criminals, who reward the hospitality of the State, by leaving behind them blazing forests to perpetuate the memory of their neglected camp fires?" He lamented how "it has apparently never occurred to those in charge of the forests to buy a pump, or hose, or other suitable apparatus with which to fight fire!"[78] Here, for the purpose of environmental protection, Marshall spoke in the language of professional urban discipline to castigate the "lackadaisical" rhythms of country life:

> When men are dragooned into fire service, they are permitted to work without supervision, every man on his own hook, with nobody in authority to direct him or to spur him on, with the usual result: happy-go-lucky, lackadaisical ineptitude and crass indifference.[79]

When remarking upon existing services of nature protection, Marshall hid behind a mix of professionally spirited criticism and indignant humor, but his son

Robert, who was not tied down by his father's array of professional concerns and ideological interests, was at liberty to investigate systematically and personally the paradoxes inherent in calls for professional management in environmental protection. Did a creature of corporate boardrooms in Manhattan really have the right to tell outdoors people how to work in the vicinity of their own homes? Was not the "happy-go-lucky spirit" of outdoors enthusiasts the product of a more natural way of life? From a preservationist standpoint, could it be self-defeating to bring the terms and values of industrial management ("authority," "supervision") to the forest?

In spring 1924, as Bob completed his studies at the New York State College of Forestry, he consulted with his father about possible career options in what would today be called environmental affairs. There was some discussion of Bob continuing postgraduate studies at Harvard; and though Louis spent years prodding his children to read more and to improve their spelling and writing skills (he was far from satisfied with the early education his children received at the Ethical Culture School[80]), he basically encouraged his third child to pursue his own zeal for the woods and to leave the books aside, at least for the time being. Bob had been collating facts and figures to support various environmental measures, but his father politely found a way to tell him that statistics would never save a tree in Jazz Age America:

> George showed me your statistical letter, which is quite striking in its presentation of facts. The American people, however, will not appreciate the data which you have gathered until the last tree has been cut. Then they will get up on their hind legs, in accordance with their usual custom, and howl, somebody will have to be condemned and made a scapegoat and then they will relapse into their wonted indifference.[81]

Robert finished summa cum laude at the Forestry College and thrilled his father by finishing sixth out of eighty-four candidates who took the US Civil Service examination in forestry (some of the competitors were graduate students from Harvard and Yale).[82]

Much to his father's dismay, red tape delayed field placement for Bob; the son did not seem to mind and spent the summer of 1924 at the Wind River Forest Experiment Station near Carson, Washington, merrily keeping meticulous records of how many pancakes each of the rangers ate for breakfast. Bob then worked on a master's thesis at the Harvard Forest in north-central Massachusetts, more on a holding pattern than with serious academic intent. (The few months seemed to have as much high jinks as study, with Bob winning a bet by sliding down a 600-foot dirt path on the seat of his pants and behaving perversely during automobile driving lessons, displaying his father's genetic or attitudinal legacy.[83]) Finally, in April 1925, the government invitation came: Robert was summoned to work at the Northern Rocky Mountain Forest Experiment Station, in Missoula, Montana. He arrived in June, and spent three years there.

His father had never seen this Rocky Mountain region but had heard much of its beauty, and he promptly boasted to Senator William Borah, the independent-spirited Republican "Lion of Idaho," about his son's whereabouts, close to the Idaho border.[84] Louis and Bob wrote hundreds of letters to one another in the 1920s, and both the father and son gloried in reading aloud passages from this correspondence to any hapless passerby who happened to be in the area.[85] As his son Bob traveled out west to embark on his first professional experience, Louis's letters unconsciously accentuated the dilemmas and challenges faced by a son who was becoming a full-time environmentalist and who would, by dint of his background and education, necessarily feel like an insider-outsider wherever he went in the wilderness.

Louis in his life moved from the half-rural Syracuse milieu to high business and social circles in New York City. A conspicuous limit to his highly assertive work style resulted from this transition; as in the Leo Frank case, Marshall sometimes allowed a New Yorker's view of country roughness to preclude options of personal involvement in difficult advocacy cases. In his warm, encouraging correspondence with Bob, Marshall did little to disguise his own reservations about the rural culture that was about to envelope his son's career. In one letter, for instance, he wrote about how Bob's residence in Missoula reminded him of a business trip he had made thirty years earlier to Rapid City, South Dakota. Possessor of something akin to a photographic memory, Louis recalled patronizingly the two advertisements published in the daily newspaper "of that flourishing town: the Tom Sweeney Hose company was to have a dance at the engine house, and the Bulwer Lytton Theosophical Society was planning a séance at the home of a town notable."[86]

Twenty-four years old, Bob had been at work on his first permanent job for one month when he was dispatched to Mount Watson to help put out one of sixty-one forest blazes that had been ignited by a July lightning storm.[87] Suddenly, he was in the middle of the sort of situation of first-responder service neglect that had, in the Adirondacks, been the object of his father's detached consternation for many years. Bob faced, in his words, a "red-hot Hades . . . a ghostlike picture showing the unconquerable, awful power of Nature." He reported for duty and was informally commissioned as "chief of commissary, chief of motor transportation, camp boss and general handy man." He quickly learned the names and circumstances of all 109 firefighters, who were badly outmatched in their battle against the "lurid, shifting, molten, fiery vapor, [that was] like the burning gases of a nebulous planet."[88]

These were the sort of people whose "flourishing" culture his father sometimes wrote sarcastically about, ensconced in the comfort of his Manhattan law office. The 109 firefighters, Bob noted, were "from the lowest and toughest element in the exceedingly tough town of Spokane." He carefully studied the crew's level of experience, finding that 97 of the 109 had been recruited on the spur of the moment. Many had criminal backgrounds; some were drunks or drug addicts; others "had evidently been half starved." For Bob, this was baptism under fire.

The personification of his father's World War I patriotism and concerns about Jewish honor, James Marshall had encountered unknown sides of human society while on duty with the Mount Sinai medical unit in France. The personification and elaboration of his father's environmental enthusiasms, Bob was, during this summer 1925 experience, seeing these same social sides during a Rocky Mountain forest fire. As had happened with James, the Victorian edge to the family's idealism was tested by rough reality, and Bob's documentation of this encounter poignantly reflects how hard it must have been for these young men to balance their father's penchant for fighting honorably for principles with the fact that they had been brought up as good Jewish boys. It was not easy growing up under the influence of the puritanical ruggedness of late nineteenth-century Republican environmentalists; the hard knocks James and Robert sometimes endured were a few steps short of the ordeals faced by the children of Theodore Roosevelt. Discernibly, however, Marshall bequeathed to his children a flexibility of character that helped them survive. Just as the key to Louis Marshall's success in mediation circumstances with Downtown workers during the International Ladies' Garment Workers' Union strike or with the European Jewish advocates on the Jewish delegation at the Paris Peace Conference was his ability to listen and to modify his preexisting orientations, so too did his son Robert find the inner resources needed to relate meaningfully to the miseries of the 109 firefighters on Mount Watson. "I used to like to talk with them while checking upon a line," Bob recorded after this experience. "Once I learned their names, they became more confidential. . . . They were much more appealing alone on the fire line than in the evening around the camp fire, with their smutty talk and grumbling."[89]

Learning Yiddish, rolling up his sleeves, and sweating profusely at stormy public meetings about the Jewish congress or the expanded Jewish Agency, or publishing a newspaper, Louis Marshall labored arduously with Downtown Jews for the purpose of protecting shared Jewish interests. Learning forestry, rolling up his sleeves, and sweating profusely at the fire line at Mount Watson, Bob Marshall labored arduously with western outdoorsmen for the shared purpose of protecting the wilds. In his Jewish advocacy, Louis articulated his own vision of Jewish well-being, but he was also transformed in ways he could only half understand—among many other things, he was drawn increasingly closer to the Zionists' nationalist conceptions of Jewish identity. In his environmental work, Robert applied methods he had learned at the New York College of Forestry, but he was also transformed by the work. He ended up advocating principles of government involvement and social change that were implicit in his father's discussions of the need for professional environmental management in the Adirondacks but underdeveloped owing to Louis's lifelong formal adherence to Republican Party conservatism.

Bob learned on Mount Watson that better firefighting would only be done by those who had an improved stake in their country's social system. More in the field than his father ever was in any sphere, apart from Jewish matters, Bob became partly radicalized (just as his father was partly radicalized in Jewish work). Robert Marshall's biographer well summarizes the impact of this Rocky Mountain experience: Bob "became convinced that the human misery he saw on the Mount Watson fire line was largely the result of an exploitative economic system, a system that destroyed lives not only in the slums of Spokane but also in the copper mines of Montana, the sawmills of the Appalachians."[90]

Robert (and his younger brother George) became interested in liberal-left causes and ideas, but he was far too high spirited and engaged with his environmental work to put much stock in rigid ideological categories. Here again, the comparison with his father's Jewish advocacy is apt. Both men were much too empirically and emotionally curious about the details of issues they loved to be carried away by detached doctrines. The ideal of the preservation of Jewish life, as in the case of the environment, was motivated by love; and at the heart of his father's Jewish lobbying was a genuine fascination with the small details of Jewish life.

When Louis allowed this empirical curiosity to become political, as (we will see) in the case of the Palestine Survey Commission that was taxingly organized at the end of the 1920s, he reached low ebbs in his Jewish work, the most distinguished aspect of his career. In fact, an arresting contrast between the son's cheerful naturalist empiricism in this late 1920s period and the sententious fact-finding Marshall organized as a precondition of his non-Zionist group's participation in the building up of the Yishuv through the Jewish Agency merits reflection—as it turned out in the Marshall family, it was easier not to take the Roaring Twenties too seriously when you were twenty-six years old, as opposed to seventy.

In 1927, Bob published in the *Nation* a wonderfully wry tribute to environmental determinism, entitled "Precipitation and the Presidents," claiming

11. Bob Marshall in his element. Courtesy of the Adirondack Museum.

that below average rainfall years had ushered new political parties into power in Washington throughout the nineteenth century. Bob's article concluded musingly: "Historians have so emphasized the petty actions of puny politicians that it seems worthwhile stressing one factor which even the largest campaign fund cannot alter—the ancient Roman politicians may have been wise when they chose Jupiter as their highest deity."[91] Exactly at the time when Bob was composing this comic put-down of politics by saying that the successive administrations of Republican administrations in the 1920s were all wet, his father was testily haggling with Chaim Weizmann about whether a Harvard epidemiologist and expert on milk pasteurization was too Zionistic for inclusion on the Palestine Survey Commission, whose findings would determine whether wealthy American Jews would agree to support systematically nonpolitical Zionist projects.

In general, father and son shared a burning passion, almost a mania, for collecting facts about the subjects they loved. The root of Louis's work on Jewish affairs and of Bob's career in forestry was engaged curiosity.

Marshall's lively spirited sister-in-law, Beatrice Lowenstein Magnes, highlighted that impassioned curiosity in a key passage of her memoir describing how she met her husband, Judah Magnes.[92] In 1907, Beatrice recalled, Jacob Schiff had caused a ruckus in American Jewish life by publishing an attack in the *American Hebrew* on Jewish Theological Seminary leader Solomon Schechter's Zionist enthusiasms. "Despite the fact that he was a Reform Jew," Beatrice recalled, Marshall reconnoitered at Knollwood to write a defense of Schechter's Zionism. Since Louis's handwriting was virtually undecipherable, Beatrice, who was visiting her sister's family at the Adirondack camp, offered to transcribe Marshall's reply, which she still recalled, six decades later, as a "magnificent exposition" opening with the phrase, "Although I am not a Zionist, and never expect to be a Zionist, still. . . ." Soon after the article was completed, Dr. Magnes, then a rabbi at Temple Emanu-El, came to the camp, and Beatrice's introduction to her charismatic future husband came when she followed her brother-in-law and the young rabbi around Knollwood, forgoing "tennis, golf, boating and fishing" (not easy sacrifices for the energetic young woman) to listen to the two men debate and educate one another about every conceivable Jewish topic of the day.[93] Reflecting how strong Jewish chemistry bonded these two rather incompatible personalities, Louis Marshall and Judah Magnes, this memoir's images suggest that Marshall's love for all things Jewish became virtually an aphrodisiac in the romance between Judah Magnes and Beatrice Lowenstein.

As in many other instances, Knollwood stands out in this recollection as the creative focal point in the Romantic attachments of the extended Marshall family. In fact, Beatrice's perceptive recollection about Marshall's attraction to Zionism stemming from an unbounded curiosity regarding all aspects of Jewish life, bears a very close resemblance to published and oral history accounts of the way his son Robert (often with his brother George) became fixated with environmental topics by hanging around the Knollwood camp,[94] meeting local Adirondack guides, particularly Herb Clark, collecting facts about mountains and plant life in the area, and eventually turning a summer romance into a lifelong career. The key to understanding the relentless energy and occasional humor that defined family members' efforts on the environment and other matters is Knollwood's fountain of idyllic curiosity.

In Louis Marshall's furious, funny 1908 letters to the New York commissioner of Forest, Fish and Game, based on the premise that 90 percent of forest destruction by fire would be spared were locomotives to use fuel instead of coal,[95] Marshall launched into a Monty Pythonesque disquisition of his attempts, against the backdrop of raging fires in the Adirondacks, to convince the Saranac Lake fire warden of the advantages of purchasing a fire pump:

> I asked him to buy a pump and five hundred feet of hose and said that I would pay for them, if the State did not. He subsequently notified me that he could not procure the necessary apparatus in the Village. . . . There are but few places, especially in the Adirondack Lake regions, where water cannot be easily found in sufficient qualities to be conveyed by a line of two inch hose of reasonable length, to the locality where fires have been ignited, especially in the early stages, to entirely extinguish them, and in more advanced stages to check the progress of the flames. And yet, it has apparently never occurred to those in responsible charge of the forests to buy a pump, or hose, or other suitable apparatus with which to fight fire! Must not this be a source of pride to our citizens?[96]

More reluctant than his father about exhibiting a sense of intellectual or social superiority, Bob Marshall channeled his empirical energies on environmental matters into humorous commentary that was zanily camp rather than bitingly sarcastic. His "Contribution to the Life History of the Northwestern Lumberjack," published in *Social Forces* during the last year of his father's life (1929) and apparently a cult classic among environmentalists, diligently recorded loggers' table habits and use of profanity. The "average woodchopper," Bob recorded, "spends just 35 minutes a day in food assimilation. . . . There is in each camp a fastest man or group of men who waste but 21 minutes diurnally in the mad dash for sustenance." During an hour of speech, Bob added, the average "hardy hewer of wood" uttered 136 words that were "unmentionable at church sociables. . . . Profane woods were overwhelmingly in the majority, for they constituted 96 of the 136 maledictions. Of the remaining 40, 31 were of sexual import and 9 were excretory in nature."[97] Logically enough, the well-educated, disciplined Marshall family's love of the outdoors had led to this, the most environmentally gifted son counting curses in the forests.

The New York State College of Forestry at Syracuse University

Bob's counting the loggers' curses was a humorous demonstration of the Marshall family's leaning toward a civilized approach to forestry. Even in the abandon of the wilderness, Bob could not stop learning. This perception of the forest as an object of study was brought to life in one of the most sustained and impressive efforts in his father's career, the establishment of the New York State College of Forestry at Syracuse University in 1911.

Delicately stroking egos in the New York State government in Albany and cultivating leaders and administrators at Syracuse University, Marshall invested considerable time and energy in this project throughout the last two decades of his life. His vision and contributions to environmental study in the state were memorialized a year after his death, when then New York governor Franklin Roosevelt arranged funds for the establishment of the Louis Marshall Memorial Building at the College of Forestry.[98] Exhibiting considerable negotiation ingenuity, Marshall sent letter after letter to New York State politicians and to Syracuse University officials, convincing the state that it had an interest in investing sums from its treasury for forestry study at an institution it only partly controlled, located on the grounds of Syracuse University, while persuading the university that its best chance of maximizing advantages and enhancing environmental study on its campus would be to surrender a portion of administrative control of the forestry school to the state and thereby receive a substantive amount of state funds.[99] While walking this tightrope between the state and the university, Marshall continually had to fend off the encroachments of Cornell University, which at the end of the nineteenth century attempted to open the nation's first college of forestry, in cooperation with New York State, in an experiment that had ended with controversy and ill feeling. Marshall had reason to believe that Cornell resentfully watched the cooperative agreements he forged between state officials in Albany and Syracuse University, and hoped to reestablish its own forestry college after the lamentable experience with Dr. Bernhard Fernow.

Colonel William Fox, superintendent of New York State's forests in the last years of the nineteenth century, conceived of the idea of a Cornell forestry school. The idea seemed promising and innovative, because forestry education at the time was limited to Europe and nowhere to be found in America throughout the decade that passed after the closing of the Western frontier. Fox opposed the 1894 constitutional measure for wilderness preservation in the Adirondacks and Catskills; he believed in rationalized forest management, not in eternal preservation of wilderness areas. Joining forces with Cornell University's president, Jacob Gould Schurman, Fox convinced the New York State legislature to appropriate funds for a state-funded forestry college at Cornell. Accompanying the establishment of this institution, the state exempted a forest area in the Adirondacks from the 1894 "forever wild" measure, allowing the Cornell forestry school to use it for instruction and experiments for a thirty-year period.

Cornell appointed as dean of the new school Dr. Fernow, a German-trained forestry expert who was the top official in the Department of Agriculture's Forestry Division. Moving quickly, Fernow acquired 30,000 acres of wild land at Axton, in Franklin Country, and negotiated a contract with the Brooklyn

Cooperage Company for conversion of the forest's logs and cordwood into barrels, methanol, and charcoal. Axton (originally, Axe-Town) was an old lumber settlement. As though drawing inspiration from this local precedent, Fernow's team began an aggressive campaign of tree chopping, ostensibly for scientific purposes.[100] The tree cutting alienated environmentalists and landowners in the Adirondacks; among other ills, wafts of smoke rose up from Fernow's experiments, irritating the lungs of articulate summer campers at Saranac Lake, who were convinced that the Cornell College of Forestry was partly responsible for the waves of fires that destroyed thousands of trees in the Adirondacks. Landowners in the area brought suit against the Brooklyn Cooperage Company.[101]

In Albany, state politicians got cold feet about the project and by 1903 choked off state allocations for the forestry college. Cornell immediately took the cue, shutting down the first-of-its-kind institution in 1903, after President Schurman informed the university's trustees that "not a cent of state money has inured to the benefit of Cornell University."[102]

Marshall thereafter remained an inveterate opponent of what Cornell had tried to do at Axton. Not really doing justice to the New York court's opinion in its ruling in the *People v. the Brooklyn Cooperage Company,* Marshall ridiculed the Cornell experiment, along with the very notion that scientific forestry could mean the cutting of thousands of trees, in his impassioned, principled defense of the "forever wild" measure at the 1915 New York Constitutional Convention. "I hold before me the decision in his [Brooklyn Cooperage Company Case]," which established that Cornell's forestry experiment was designed so that

> this tremendous tract of thirty thousand acres was to be cut down flat from one end of it to the other, in order that the scientific foresters might start a new forest which might mature a hundred years from the time that the contract was entered into. That is scientific forestry.[103]

Here, as elsewhere, Marshall failed to consider how his "forever wild" wilderness doctrine might be at variance with scientific requirements of experimentation.[104] He was an extremist on this environmental issue; not everyone accepted his association of pure preservation and scientific forestry. Certainly the majority opinion in the Brooklyn Cooperage decision he cited did not, since it stated:

> No expert in this case has questioned that the experiment of reforestation involves of necessity the cutting down of any standing forest, either under the selective system or the clear cutting system. The state purchased 30,000 acres for

> the experiment. It is immaterial whether or not this experiment could have been carried out with a smaller acreage.[105]

In Marshall's view, Cornell was responsible for an act of environmental ruin at Axton, and he believed that this fact put Syracuse University securely on the high road in the rivalry for state funds for its forestry college. Nevertheless, he periodically remained wary that Cornell might be trying to muscle its way in Albany with hopes of reviving its forestry experiments and education.[106] (Incidentally, for years, football games between Cornell and Syracuse universities were played amidst raucous heckles stemming from this forestry school conflict.[107])

Marshall's campaigning for the establishment of the New York College of Forestry featured a direct appeal to then governor Charles Evans Hughes in June 1910.[108] This early letter in Marshall's two decades of lobbying for the school indicates that he was, from the start, thinking about "forest protection" (a term used repeatedly in the letter) rather than forest management. He explained that "an intelligent system of forest protection" has been in operation in France, Germany, and Switzerland for many years, whereas "practically nothing" had been done in this field in the United States. Interestingly, as he pitched Syracuse University's appropriateness as a home for the proposed state college, Marshall emphasized the rural backgrounds of most of its 3,200 students, as though city youths were not really fit for forestry study (a principle his son Bob would disprove). He asked Hughes to steward the allocation of $55,000 to acquire property needed for the new school.

The College of Forestry establishment bill reached the desk of Hughes's successor, John Dix, in summer 1911, and Marshall left no rhetorical stone unturned as he coaxed the governor to sign the measure.[109] "The time has come for forest reconstruction," Marshall declared. "Our virgin forests are disappearing." Due to the ravages of the "inexorable axe," within "a few generations our mountainsides and our valleys will be as barren of trees as those of Palestine, Spain and Italy." $55,000 was not too much to ask to save everything that was natural in America and to prevent "the extermination of one of the greatest gifts that God in his bounty bestowed upon us." The arguments for the forestry college were irrefutable: "not a thinking man in this commonwealth could oppose them."

After the forestry college establishment bill became law in 1911, Marshall spent the years before World War I brokering between Syracuse University and the state legislature, explaining to each side how it needed to give leverage to the other. This was one of the great acts of finesse in Marshall's career. To secure a building for the forestry school, he convinced Syracuse University officials to

12. Louis Marshall Memorial Hall, State University of New York College of Environmental Science and Forestry. Courtesy of Fred Wellner.

cede a substantial tract of land, behind its sports stadium, to the state, because the politicians in Albany would never allocate funds for a state institution erected on a plot whose title was not owned by New York State.[110] Just as soon as the deed was transferred, he knocked on the doors of state senators, explaining why New York should allocate a quarter million dollars for a forestry college building that fortuitously happened to be next to Syracuse University. Forestry college students would be able to utilize the library, gymnasium, and other university facilities—and their institution would also happen to be on New York State land![111] Once again, the forestry college's fate was in the hands of New York's governor, now William Sulzer. Just weeks before Tammany launched impeachment proceedings against Sulzer, Marshall petitioned the governor, imploring him to "disregard every other consideration," make forestry education his top priority, and sign the allocation bill for the construction of the college's building.[112] "The state has no higher duty" than to rectify "the sins of our fathers" who "destroyed, recklessly and wastefully, our magnificent natural forests," Marshall wrote, adding that every college graduate "will be a missionary in the cause of conservation."

After one year of instruction, the forestry college expanded rapidly, enrolling 160 students from forty-six New York counties. It fielded 800 applications from admission candidates. No rational argument could be marshaled in Albany against the college's proven potential for growth, but Marshall invested weeks of effort untangling a skein of unfounded objections (some of which were raised, he suspected, by Cornell University supporters[113]) and also adjusting composition criteria of the board of trustees in a way that enabled both the New York State politicians and Syracuse University officials to believe that they controlled the institution. No, he explained to Governor Sulzer, it was not reasonable to maintain that the forestry college was ineligible for state budgetary allocations because Syracuse University was founded by Methodists ("I am the President" of the Forestry College's Board of Trustees, he pointed out; "nobody has ever questioned my Judaism, or charged me with sectarianism").[114] As to board control, he persuaded Syracuse University to accept an arrangement whereby three-quarters of the members would be appointed by the governor, provided the state completed legislation of a $250,000 bill for the construction of the forestry college building.[115] To obtain state authorization for the forestry college and then to put the institution on the ground in a proper building, Marshall necessarily created ambiguity about control in this prewar period, allowing the project's partners to harbor differing understandings about lines of authority.

He had barely returned from his peacemaking diplomacy after the war before squabbles about control issues forced him to clarify this creative confusion. An official from the New York Department of Education questioned whether Syracuse University officials could rightfully continue to confer degrees at the college's graduation ceremony. Marshall explained at length why the honor of degree conferral at graduation ceremonies was legitimately bestowed to Chancellor James Day of Syracuse University.[116] "While the New York State College of Forestry is, I repeat, a State institution, it was nevertheless intended that the relations between it and Syracuse University were to be of an intimate character," Marshall explained. As president of the board of trustees of the forestry college, Marshall conferred with the university's chancellor and the college's staff about an array of issues, including procedures for the development of postgraduate study.[117] His immersion in the everyday administrative details was characteristically thorough, but a review of the dozens of pages of correspondence in Marshall's archive relating to the forestry college indicates that his engagement with the institution went well beyond managerial conscientiousness. His characterization of a forestry college graduate as a "missionary in the cause of conservation" is striking, not only because it foreshadowed his own son's self-perception.

Here again, the comparison to the still greater passion in Marshall's life, Judaism, is apposite. As in the case of his labors in a comparable administrative position at the Jewish Theological Seminary, Marshall was in his work with the forestry seminary intrigued and excited by the project of training a cadre of experts committed to the conservation of something sacred. The administrators of JTS judged that they should be relatively forthcoming and generous in the recruitment of Downtown Jewish youths from poor immigrant families because these were candidates who had grown up close to religion, who were aware of the dangers modernity posed to it, and who had the potential to become the most industrious and committed preservers of Jewish tradition. Similarly, the administrators of the New York State College of Forestry understood that they should be forthcoming and generous in the recruitment of country youths because these were candidates who had grown up closer to the wilderness, who had watched the cutting of its trees and the ravaging of its wonders, and who had the potential to become the most creative and hearty preservers of forest lands that remained.

Thus, just months before his death, in a consultation with the dean of the forestry college, Marshall concurred that "it is advisable to have a more elastic yardstick" in the admission of country youths, as compared to the "city-trained boy."[118] The former had a more appropriate "background of heredity and environment" for forestry study and work. To substantiate this point, Marshall dipped into a well of sweet summer night memories from Knollwood and cited a revealing literary example, one that underscored the character of his family's engagement with environmentalism as an adaptation in the Jewish Adirondacks of classic nineteenth-century Romanticism. Were Marshall and his associates not to wield a creatively "elastic yardstick" in the administration of the forestry college, they would turn the institution into a mechanical outgrowth of precisely the detestable urban and industrial disciplines that had destroyed the wilderness. Not allowing rural youth some latitude in the admission process, Marshall wrote, would be akin to an episode in Dickens's *Hard Times:*

> A little boy who had never seen a horse and who was able to state from memory that it was a quadruped of a certain genus and species was highly approved, while a little boy who was the son of a circus-rider and who was less glib in his explanation as to what a horse was but had all his life been accustomed to horses,

> was sent to the foot of the class because he did not conform with the theories of Mr. Gradgrind, a typical, I was almost about to say college professor, but I will say, educator.[119]

The selection of this example said much about its chooser. Something of a Gradgrind-pedant himself, Marshall had taken resolute steps in his adult life to allow creative space at Knollwood and elsewhere for his own children ("we generally did as we wished," his eldest son recalled, thinking mostly about the freedom of the Knollwood summers[120]). He clearly attributed great remedial, even transformative, value to the environmentalist education of country youths (just as he had long believed in the power of education with regard to Jewish immigrant youths). True, Marshall's own career owed much to Gradgrind-like recitation of case law, but his mother had taught him to memorize by exposing him to the passionate verse of Romantic poets, and their idealistic principles and values were

13. Marshall with grandchildren Florence Billikopf and David Billikopf. Courtesy of Peter Schweitzer.

always layered within his mechanical methodology as a lawyer. In the ongoing battle between Facts, Facts, Facts and the idyllic forests of the Adirondacks, Marshall long envisioned the forestry college as a place where systematic education would not subvert the romantic curiosity that made true learning possible. This intriguing vision gave rise to America's first successful higher education institute for environmental study, a profoundly underappreciated contribution of Louis Marshall's career.

Organizing to Address the "Wilderness Problem": An American Jewish Committee for the Environment

Louis Marshall's environmentalism was an expression of a nostalgic impulse that was laden within an array of Jewish endeavors in the nineteenth and early twentieth centuries. As a Jewish communal leader, Marshall shared an attribute important in the lives and outlooks of European counterparts; between the French Revolution and World War I, a striking number of such Jewish communal leaders spent their adult lives in cities but had been born in villages and had intimate memories of rural settings and traditional routines.[121] Often their creative work as Jewish leaders was driven by a desire to restore some sense of unity that had, presumably, been lost. The scholar Richard Cohen's comment on an appreciable dynamic among modern Jewish artists seems to apply well to Marshall's environmentalism: "One outcome of the urbanization process which has attracted little attention is the need of individuals to transform their feelings of displacement, of a lost childhood experience . . . into a newly integrated whole."[122]

As is typically the case with nostalgia, the Marshall family's environmentalism was, to some extent, pining for something that was never exactly known nor never really could have ever been. Marshall's father Jacob never really met verdant wilderness in Upstate New York and instead became part and parcel of its industrial development, starting out as a trackhand for railroad construction in the Finger Lakes region. The argument could even be made that Marshall's impassioned attacks on railroad developers in the Adirondacks was not nostalgia for something lost that his family had once loved but rather a form of generational revenge, since his father had been cheated out of his pay by the manager of the Northern Central Railroad line around Canandaigua.[123]

In any case, nostalgic impulses need not breed passive inaction. By looking closely at Marshall's environmentalism, we find cause to be a bit less metaphorical and vague in the use of the well-worn generalization about the Jews' "love affair with America." We are encouraged to see Jewish experience in America in a new way: not as the passive enjoyment of a country that provided unique opportunity and freedom to an immigrant group fleeing from Old World persecution but rather as the contributory, sometimes proactive, participation of immigrants and their descendants in the establishment and refinement of ideals that help all Americans understand what their country is about. The Marshall family experience shows ways in which Jews really meant it when they said they loved their new land.

The Marshalls were pioneers in the legislation of precedent-setting environmental measures (e.g., Marshall's involvement in the 1894 "forever wild" Adirondacks rule) and in the monitoring of the enforcement of environmental rules in an industrial country that restlessly looked for things to do with its natural resources other than preserve them. Bob Marshall, contemporary environmental writers tell us, virtually invented the modern recreation of hiking. As the Syracuse University/New York State College of Forestry exemplifies, the Marshalls were pioneers in the development of first-of-their-kind educational programs designed to train generations of environmental professionals in conservation ethics and in the rational, prudent use of natural resources. They appear to have been the first Americans to have conceptualized the environment as a minority interest eligible for constitutional protections afforded by the law. Louis's work on the Migratory Bird Treaty Act, girding the *Missouri v. Holland* ruling, is a luminous demonstration of creative professionalism whereby a concerned expert stretches the limits of his experience and training to find a way to afford one defenseless, unrepresented group legal protection. Marshall's tour de force in *Missouri v. Holland* had significant repercussions in constitutional law whose pros and cons continue to be debated passionately by legal experts today (sometimes with an eye toward topics, such as the constitutionality of treaty agreements forged during the post–September 11, 2001, War on Terror, that appear to be at dizzying remove from the coots and geese that occupied Marshall's attention a century ago). Taking cues from his father, Bob Marshall indelibly perpetuated his family's contribution in this respect, defending this constitutional orientation toward conservation in his suggestively titled 1928 article "Wilderness as a Minority Right."[124] Finally, the Marshalls contributed decisively to the idea that a committed environmental vanguard, an advocacy group for trees and mountains, would be necessary in America to promote the cause of conservation and to protect the wilderness as a minority interest. These were all major contributions toward a sphere whose import has become palpably urgent to Americans in the twenty-first century, and as this chapter has tried to demonstrate, they drew upon many of the methods, sensibilities, and instincts that defined Louis Marshall's indefatigable labors for Jewish interests.

The hard core of the Marshall family's environmentalism was nostalgic emotion, but father and son searched continually for a method to make wilderness protection rationally persuasive. Bob, in fact, elevated the pining for purely unified nature to the level of scientific truth in an influential article, "The Problem of the Wilderness," published by the *Scientific Monthly* in 1930,[125] months after his father's death.

Aspects of Bob's odyssey departed from his father's sensibilities and wishes. Most noticeably, nature worship for Bob basically came to replace religious belief; his relatively explicit self-identification as an agnostic, nonpracticing Jew during the period of his doctoral studies at Johns Hopkins University, taken up during the last months of Louis's life, appears to have been a discretely avoided topic in correspondence between father and son. For years, after Bob left for undergraduate study and then worked as a forester, his father entreated him during the High Holy Days to fast on Yom Kippur and keep other observances,[126] but this prodding seemed to disappear as the 1920s advanced and Bob's passion for the outdoors became all-consuming.

In other ways, father and son remained profoundly connected, even energetically synchronized. Like his father, Bob was apparently a late bloomer in relationships with women; even though Louis kept indoors, in law offices, while his son could never leave the forests, patterns in the son's intimate and working life recapitulated his father's youthful history (tragically, Bob died unexpectedly while asleep on a train, at precisely the age—thirty-eight—when his father made the one major transformation of his life, leaving provincial Syracuse for the big city and a Manhattan law firm). The continuity in their environmental passion is obvious. Thus, it is reasonable to regard Bob's major statement on "The Problem of the Wilderness" as a Marshall manifesto, as his father's own last word as well on a topic of overwhelming importance to the entire family.

"Within the next few years the fate of the wilderness will be decided," Bob declared in this article. "This is a problem to be settled by deliberate rationality and not by personal prejudice." He argued for wilderness protection on physical, mental, and aesthetic grounds. Wilderness endeavor was an irreplaceable experience for the body. "Toting a fifty pound pack over an abominable trail, snowshoeing across a blizzard plateau or scaling some jagged pinnacle," he declared in muscular prose, "develop[s] a body distinguished by the soundness, stamina and élan unknown in normal surroundings." He praised the wilderness as a spur to "independent cogitation" and reminded the reader of the long list of distinguished American thinkers and writers and politicians who "felt the compulsion of periodical retirement in the solitudes." The wilderness afforded "withdrawal from the contaminating notions of neighbors" and encouraged nonprejudiced, purely constructive thought.

The part of this article that apparently stirred the most discussion was Marshall's argument for nature conservation from an aesthetic standpoint.[127] Cutting in the woods, he implied, could be tantamount to slashing great paintings. As his father's language sometimes was, the author's prose in this key passage was lofty and a little pompous ("The sheer stupendousness of the wilderness gives it a quality of intangibility which is unknown in ordinary manifestations of ocular beauty"), but his point was thought-provoking and effective. In public discussions, Bob defended it with Marshall family spunk: when a skeptic asked at one occasion, "how much wilderness do we really need?" Bob replied, without missing a beat, "how many Brahms symphonies do we need?"[128]

This landmark article in the history of American environmentalism ended with an effective public appeal for the formation of a conservation vanguard, for what in fact became the Wilderness Society.[129] "To carry out this program," Bob concluded, "it is exigent that all friends of the wilderness ideal should unite."

A quarter century earlier, Louis Marshall and his wealthy Jewish friends, who called themselves the "Wanderers" during their private meetings, spoke about how "something in the air" necessitated their organizing together as an elite vanguard to protect Jewish well-being, largely in response to the horrific depredation wrought by the pogroms in czarist Russia. Now Bob Marshall was mobilizing his resources and energy to form an elite vanguard of outdoor enthusiasts, to protect what remained of the wilderness from the relentless encroachment of urban modernity. In effect, he was calling for an American Jewish Committee for the environment, thereby showing how the vicissitudes and ideals of Jewish advocacy and self-defense could be translated in causes designed for the good of the earth. Many decades later, these causes remain at the forefront of progressive politics in America and beyond.

10

Ethnic Affairs in the 1920s

Images of Marshall

It is time to take a look at the man. Marshall had a bespectacled, studious but kindly face. Being noticeably rounder around the hips, his short, stocky frame contoured as a bowling pin. His dress was formal and deliberately obsolete. Marshall's old-style starched shirts, made of fine linen, attracted attention, but one had to look down to see the most striking part of his work uniform. At the time of his death, Marshall was one of the few men in the United States who still wore Victorian-style Congress gaiters[1]—these soft boots, devoid of hooks, eyes, or laces and attached to the feet via a simple pull-on strap at the back, must have reminded Marshall of simpler times in Syracuse, when he would stop at his uncle Jacob's shoe store on the way to school and read the newspaper aloud.

The space around him was cluttered and intellectually engaged. Wherever he went, the tangle of papers and books on his work desk reflected the extraordinary range of his Jewish and American activities. Writing three decades after Marshall's death, his oldest child James recalled the scene in his father's study at the Knollwood summer home—"I still see him," James recalled, with his vest open, reading a book or newspaper, "piles of unanswered mail on his desk, law books barricading him on the floor."[2] On the centennial of Marshall's birth, a journalist from the *Forward* recalled visiting his law office and "finding his desk covered in Yiddish newspapers published in the US and foreign countries." The office, this reporter remembered, "was crowded with Jews who had come to him for help. There were Jews with beards and skullcaps, rabbinical delegations, new arrivals to the country."[3]

His work stamina stunned all observers. Amazed commentators in the Yiddish press noted that Marshall dictated forty letters a day in connection with his public work (such reports added, approvingly, that 90 percent of these letters pertained to Jewish matters).[4] From the start, Marshall's professional discipline awed peers and clients; his assistant at the Syracuse law firm recalled that Marshall would work steadily in the office from nine in the morning until midnight, the only short interruptions being walks home for lunch and dinner.[5] A century after Marshall's birth, Marshall's youngest son George recalled that his father would work fourteen-hour days and enjoy every minute of them (George also made mention of Louis' favorite old hat).[6] Small, eccentric aberrations in Marshall's work routine drew notice. Among other things, he had a mania for collecting and reusing stamps. Marshall had a temper, and its expression was known not only in the workplace (James confessed that his father's "quick temper was not always easy to bear"[7]). Friends, associates, and even part-time antagonists overlooked these passing volcanic eruptions, because they understood that their source was earnest compassion and commitment. Marshall's temper was also offset by his sense of humor. James put these splenetic and happy antic aspects of his father's temperament in perspective, writing:

> I think of him as a man of great laughter. He never told bawdy jokes, but he laughed at his own absent-mindedness. Short and rotund, he virtually rolled when he laughed. He had a quick temper that was not always easy to bear, but that too was generally dissolved in humor and rarely did bitterness remain. His capacity for invective was astounding, but there were limits to this. When ladies or children were present, he would splutter, "He's a, He's a"—these became known as Heezas. The best known Heezas were Theodore Roosevelt and Stephen Wise.[8]

Contemporaries pointed to the same range of moods and traits in Marshall's personality, though their depictions relied on loftier and less intimate references. "In his kindliness he was as sweet as the gentle Hillel; in his just wrath he was as direct in his denunciations as Nathan before King David, or Savonarola," wrote Horace Stern months after Marshall's death.[9] Everyone who knew Marshall appreciated that gentleness was at his personality's rock core. In summer 1941, Jacob Billikopf worriedly prepared for a radio broadcast memorial in honor of his father-in-law; Billikopf consulted with James Rosenberg, who provided a touching story about Marshall and a helpful tip:

> He [Marshall] and I traveled from Paris to Switzerland in 1929 for the big meeting which created the Agency. We shared a compartment on the train. I had a headache and dear old Marshall, smiling, forced me to take the lower berth. The thing you should emphasize is that little story of mine—his quality of tenderness, of warmth, of thoughtfulness.[10]

Marshall collected art and had a special fondness for American landscape paintings. At the end of the nineteenth century, Marshall had time and resources to purchase well-respected paintings, such as George Inness's *End of the Rain,*[11] at auctions; one of his favorite possessions, Homer Martin's *Sun Worshippers,*[12] was exhibited on loan at New York City venues. By 1902, Marshall's growing collection had about ten paintings insured in the $2,000–$6,000 range.[13]

The flip side of Marshall's prodigious investment of time (and, not infrequently, his own money) in various Jewish and other charities was a peculiar frugality. He had the habit of moving about New York City with only a few dollars in his wallet and sometimes had to borrow funds from friends. Loudly, and at length, he protested what he regarded as excessive charges; in 1909, he fired off a six-page letter to the New York Central Railroad, demanding a sixty-cent refund for a ticket price enforced by a conductor. The same year, he found a seven-year-old, unused ticket for the New York Central and Hudson stuffed into a suit pocket and requested a refund and that the statute of limitations be waived.[14] Marshall's frugality sometimes dovetailed with his famous dislike for technological contrivances. He hated the telephone and seldom used it at work (happily, from the researcher's point of view, he preferred written correspondence, leaving a record of his dealings). In 1921, some twenty years after he first had a telephone installed, he berated the New York Telephone Company for faulty billing. His diatribe served up Luddite parsimony. "I shall not pay and if you desire to take out my telephone that would not be an unmixed evil," Marshall exclaimed. "There is scarcely an evening when I am not called to the telephone and informed that a wrong number was given. . . . Of course, all these calls are charged to me and paid for under the terms of your most 'efficient' contract."[15] Marshall never owned a car, and he kept mental notes of automobile accidents in which friends or acquaintances were involved.[16] Displaying his contempt for automobiles and his nostalgic fondness for the simpler patterns of late nineteenth-century New York City, he wrote to Mayor James Walker in 1926, complaining about the way Fifth Avenue sidewalks were being narrowed, to the detriment of the thoroughfare's "beauty and dignity," in order to accommodate cars.[17] Downtown Jews were fascinated by Marshall's apparent disdain for the glittering symbols of New York modernity. "In his whole life, Louis Marshall saw a movie but once or twice," gushed the Yiddish *Forward.*[18] The newspaper correctly noted that these few film viewings happened solely for professional reasons (as in 1927, when Marshall arranged with William Fox, of Twentieth Century Fox studios, a special screening to assess the potential offensiveness of scenes in a film about Jesus[19]).

Toward the end of Marshall's life, the Downtown press appeared to forget or forgive past contentious disputes, such as the World War I brawling about the

American Jewish Congress, and depicted the lawyer and his family circle as an image of Jewish unity. Of the various ways of looking at the man during this late phase of his career, these portraits of Marshall as a study in harmonious Jewish reconciliation had to have pleased him more than any other conceivable depiction. While Marshall stood in the center spotlight in these reports, the Lower East Side commentators were apt to shine side beams on their own, Downtown, figures who had forged constructive alliances with the American Jewish Committee president. A key personality in this respect was Jacob Billikopf, a Vilna-born professional in Jewish charity work who had lectured in sociology at the University of Missouri and worked as the superintendent of Jewish Charities in Kansas City before he was recruited during World War I to head the monumental campaign for overseas Jewish relief.[20] His productive labors for the $10 million wartime drive were highly appreciated by Uptown Jews such as Nathan Straus, Henry Morgenthau, and Jacob Schiff, who rewarded him with a $50,000 bonus in spring 1919.[21] Billikopf married Marshall's daughter Ruth. His relationship with members of the Marshall family had ups and downs, but Louis was not loath to show affection for "Billie," as exemplified by doggerel he penned during World War I in reply to Billikopf's query about whether a dress suit was required for Knollwood, where the weary fund-raiser was invited to relax in summer 1918. "In these diggings, you know, them togs is taboo / who smuggles them in, surely gets ballyhoo!" replied Marshall.[22] Billikopf and Marshall's brother-in-law Judah Magnes were present at Marshall's Zurich bedside on September 11, 1929, when he passed away.

One fascinating 1927 article in the *Forward* depicted Marshall's relations with his brother-in-law Judah Magnes and with his son-in-law Jacob Billikopf as a successful "mixture of Jewish generations, cultures, concepts and ideas: what an interesting chapter in fifty years of Jewish history!"[23] These "three Jewish boys, of distinctly different Jewish antecedents, born and raised in different periods and environs, in Syracuse, San Francisco [Magnes] and Wilna [Billikopf]," came together in Marshall's family, each finding deeply meaningful ways to serve the Jewish people.

This *Forward* piece suggested that the "war days" of fighting between the Downtown Yiddish Jews and the Uptown Yahudim had drawn to a close and that the Marshall family trio symbolized a new era of Jewish rapprochement and solidarity. The report surveyed ways Schiff and Marshall impeded efforts to ostracize the pacifist Magnes during World War I, and it noted how Magnes had transported his Jewish idealism to Mandatory Palestine ("Soul and mind he [Magnes] is now wrapped up in a new dream woven of old sacred values and modern Jewish demands"). Billikopf, a renowned fund-raiser for overseas Jewish relief, the article explained, had grown up in Wilna, near the family of *Forward* editor Abraham Cahan; he immigrated to Richmond, Virginia, at the age of fourteen. His inclusion in the family as the husband of Marshall's daughter Ruth occurred in years when "Jewishness became more and more rooted in the Marshall household," this Downtown report claimed. "Non-kosher sea food is never served in the Marshall home. Unleavened bread does not appear during the whole Passover week. Marshall fasts on Yom Kippur." Billikopf told the *Forward* about Marshall's fame among communities of European Jews. "While passing through cities and towns in Poland, Lithuania and Galicia on a recent visit, rabbis who saw him [Billikopf] specifically said they were happy to meet Louis Marshall's son-in-law," the report relayed. It concluded by presenting the shifting Syracuse, San Francisco, and Wilna scenes in the lives of Marshall and his two relatives as a "panorama" of Jewish union and striving.

After the Guillotine's Cut: Addressing Anti-Immigration Laws in the 1920s

The decade of postwar prosperity afforded tremendous opportunity to thousands of individual Jews, who moved forward rapidly in educational, professional, and residential spheres, finding a way to skirt by explicit or unstated quotas that were enforced in universities, or discriminatory housing agreements maintained in many neighborhoods. If Jews in this Jazz Age period began to feel "at home in America," they also suffered serious setbacks in key areas, several of them spheres in which Marshall and Jewish organizational colleagues had been active for a number of years. Simultaneously, the phrase "Marshall law" attaches itself to a period that many individual Jews today mark as the starting point of their own family's American success story and to an era disfigured by ugly trends of Nativism and racism and by serious setbacks to Jewish interests, just years before untold catastrophe descended upon Jewish life in Europe.

The harshest limit to the reach of Marshall law in the 1920s was posed by the country's increasingly restrictive immigration laws. On the eve of World War I, Marshall had wondered when the "guillotine" of immigration restriction might fall; before he left for the Paris Peace Conference, he could already sense the blade. "There is a great danger of our country becoming chauvinistic," Marshall lamented in a letter to Congressman Isaac Siegel in early 1919. Since the country had made tremendous sacrifices in the war "for the cause of humanity," it would be cruelly ironic for Americans to "become an insular people and slam our doors in the faces of those who seek to bring to us their strength and their helpful devotion."[24]

"Politically speaking, there is every reason to believe that there will be legislation that will prevent, if not wholly, at least to a very great extent, immigration of all kinds," Marshall dourly predicted in September 1919.[25] Throughout the next year, he lobbied unsuccessfully in the Republican Party for an accommodating attitude on immigration. "This is not the time for drastic changes in our immigration laws," he declared in correspondence with higher-ups from the National Republican Club.[26] He lobbied for Herbert Hoover's nomination as the Republican candidate for president, thinking that Hoover's record of international engagement with the American Relief Administration could be a counterweight to rising forces of Nativism in the party and in American society as a whole.[27] Meantime, the party's platform writers were busy drafting loosely worded statements on immigration to give the Nativists something to clutch. "Our immigration plank is unsatisfactory," Marshall complained in June. "The statement that 'the number of foreigners shall not exceed those that can be assimilated with reasonable rapidity' is extremely vague."[28] Harding's impending nomination by the party troubled him greatly, primarily because it reinforced prorestriction terms in the Republican platform. "The standards of Marion, Ohio, are not those of the entire US," declared Marshall, as Harding's candidacy took hold.[29]

Usually an astute observer of the American political scene, Marshall's assessments in this period were clouded by his lifelong appreciation of the Republican Party as a force of reasonable moderation. As the 1920s opened, he was slow to grasp how rigidly conservative his party had become and what Harding's "normalcy" slogans really meant for causes he had ardently championed for months or years. Harding's landslide victory, Marshall promised Oscar Straus after election day in November 1920, would "not make it impossible to create a League [of Nations] on reasonable, moderate lines."[30] Regrouping after the elections, some pro-immigration activists recommended temporary concessions, in the hope that short-term measures would quench the Nativists' appetites. Marshall's immigration advocacy partner Max Kohler leaned toward this idea. Marshall remonstrated. "It would be a sorry day in our history if immigration should be arbitrarily suspended even for an hour," Marshall declared in January 1921.[31]

As the American Jewish Committee president clung to America's passing tradition of immigration idealism, the blades of the guillotine for more restriction were quickly sharpening. On Capitol Hill, both houses passed H.R. 14461, proposing to reduce entry rights for fifteen months so that newcomers from any country could not exceed more than 3 percent of persons of that nationality who were recorded as dwelling in the United States by the 1910 Census. "There is no just reason for such restriction," Marshall pled to lame-duck president Woodrow Wilson.[32] "The underlying theory of this legislation is opposed to the historic policy of our country, that has in the past welcomed the immigrant," Marshall argued. Technically, it would be almost impossible to determine on the basis of the 1910 Census how many Jews would be admissible under the proposed bill, and an arbitrary restrictive policy toward the Jews would mean that "those who have suffered more from the war than any other people in Eastern Europe will be apt to find the doors of opportunity closed upon them." Marshall wrote to thank Wilson for administering a pocket veto on H.R. 14461,[33] but he braced for a legislative onslaught for restriction under the new Harding administration.

At the start of the mass East European Jewish immigration in the early 1880s, settled Jews in America had evinced a variety of attitudes toward the newcomers, some of them tinged with ambivalence, or even hostility.[34] Now, as the era of mass Jewish resettlement in the United States was rapidly drawing to a close, some Jewish spokespeople jumped aboard the Nativist bandwagon and endorsed immigration restriction legislation on various grounds. Outraged, Marshall hurled imprecation at these Jewish restrictionists. When Baltimore rabbi Morris Lazaron wrote to Secretary of State Hughes that "we have no right as American citizens to let down the bars entirely," Marshall lividly decried fellow American Jews who were "taking up the cudgels in favor of the policy of Know-Nothingism." Incredulous, he wrote to Lazaron: "At a time when the Jews of Eastern Europe are suffering hardships that are unprecedented, you are ready to slam the doors in their faces?" He attributed renegade pronouncements on immigration to false pride. "The only interpretation I can give to your action is that you regard yourself as better than your own people," he wrote to this rabbi.[35]

The Emergency Immigration Act of 1921, based on the 3 percent and 1910 Census formula, raced its way through the legislative and executive branches in spring 1921 and became law as a stopgap closure to immigration on May 19, 1921. A week before President Harding affixed his signature to the bill, Marshall asked for a hearing; "there was no opportunity afforded to the opponents of this measure to be heard before the Congressional committee with respect to its present features," he explained to the president.[36] Harding, however, refused to receive Marshall. Boxed out by both branches, Marshall filed a pro-immigration brief with the president as a forlorn protest. In retrospect, the concluding words of Marshall's brief appear as a cogent commentary on racist trends of the Tribal Twenties, but as advocacy of an alternative policy, they had no effect:

> This measure [1921 immigration restriction act, H.R. Bill 4075] casts an undeserved slur upon our foreign-born citizens. It tells them that they are men and women of an inferior race, that they are not assimilable, that they are undesirable, that even though they are citizens and have performed the duties of

> citizenship, they are not wanted. This is an unfortunate manifestation of a spirit of arrogance and of racial prejudice that bodes ill for the future if it is to be at all encouraged. It tends to destroy the feeling of brotherhood and of equality which in the past constituted so valuable a force in the creation of unity and harmony of which America has hitherto been the embodiment.[37]

There was not "the slightest likelihood" that the president would try to "override the practical unanimity of both houses of Congress" in favor of the bill, Marshall explained to Simon Wolf. "In order to keep our flag flying, however, I filed a brief."[38] Thus, by spring 1921, Marshall's work on immigration matters transformed in character. What had been advocacy was now protest and sheer affirmation of ethnic pride. In this immigration sphere, the only practical work left to Marshall in the 1920s would be to forward to responsible officials humanitarian appeals regarding individual cases of unbearable hardship and to contest in the courts the constitutionality of specific provisions of the restrictive legislation.

In winter–spring 1924, Congress moved to toughen and regularize the 1921 restriction law, which had been framed as a temporary, emergency measure. As Marshall recognized, by lowering the threshold figure to 2 percent and by using the 1890 Census as the new standard, the Nativists aimed at "minimizing the number of immigrants coming from Southern and Eastern Europe." It would be wrong to consent to a reduction of the quota rate from 3 percent to 2 percent, Marshall wrote to New York congressman Fiorella H. LaGuardia, since the change was seen as "an entering wedge to absolute prohibition."[39] Marshall opposed immigration restriction on principle, but the 1924 Johnson-Reed Act was particularly objectionable since it enshrined discrimination against particular nationalities. "If I were assured that the 1890 Census provision would be eliminated and the near relatives of immigrants who are new residents of the US might be admitted as non-quota immigrants," Marshall explained to LaGuardia, "I would [then] be reconciled to the 2% basis, if nothing better could be accomplished."

As weeks passed by in spring 1924, Marshall realized that conjuring alternative formulas to reconfigure the country's isolationist, antiforeigner mood along more rational lines was pointless. By essentially prohibiting immigration from Southern and Eastern Europe, he adamantly declared, Congress was moving "to write upon our statute book the infamous doctrines of the Ku Klux Klan." There is "no appreciable difference," he added, "between the pronouncements of the [Ku Klux Klan] Imperial Wizard, who opposes all who are not white, Protestant and Anglo-Saxon" and the newly legislated bill.[40] In April 1924, Marshall prayed that there was "a glimmer of hope" for a Coolidge veto of the restrictive bill, because possibly the president might "feel a serious embarrassment because of provisions of the bill relating to the exclusion of the Japanese."[41]

The impending legislation instigated racist-laced public discussion about whether certain types of immigrants, including Asiatic Jews, could successfully "assimilate" in America. In April 1924, Marshall composed an important letter to influential attorney William Guthrie[42] in an effort to clarify key terms in this discussion and to expose its racist premises. Marshall was a principled and uncompromising opponent of immigration restriction, and (as we will see) he became involved in the 1920s in litigation aimed at protecting the rights of immigrants from all minority groups. His words in this Guthrie letter are interesting because they suggest that he, too, had nonetheless sublimated some of the era's racial assumptions, or at least stooped and utilized them for tactical reasons.[43]

"It is only because of the Ku Klux Klan–Henry Ford insanity," Marshall explained to Guthrie, "that the question as to whether a Jew may be naturalized is worthy of even a moment's consideration."[44] If by denying that Jews could be "assimilated" in the American melting pot the Nativists were trying to "convey the idea of [an immigrant] being totally absorbed and losing his identity," Marshall wrote, "then I am frank to say that I hope the Jews will never be assimilated. They have retained their identity for fifty centuries." Returning to opposition of melting pot theories he had articulated a quarter century earlier, Marshall explained that "I have no patience with the idea that all men must be alike and that the dead level of uniformity must take the place of that variety created by the Almighty." Marshall added a new twist to this argument, implying that melting pot mechanics would degrade Jewish immigrants by wedding them to racial inferiors: "Would the world be any better if the Jews and Jewesses were to intermarry with those who are their intellectual inferiors as some of the assimilationists would have them do? I answer, a thousand times, No!" If, however, "assimilation" referred not to intermarriage and religious apostasy but to citizenship criteria, then Jewish immigrants were uniquely adaptable newcomers. "If by assimilation is meant the adjustment of the Jews to the laws and standards of living prevailing in the countries in which they live, then any careful observer would be compelled to say that there are no people on earth who are more ready to assimilate than the Jews."

For an ethnic leader and renowned lawyer whose career had been devoted to principles of equal opportunity and democratic freedom incorporated in the Constitution, the defeat of years of advocacy for open immigration at the hands of blatantly racist forces was an acutely confusing and demoralizing experience. "The country seems to have grown daft in its attitude toward immigration," Marshall blurted, weeks before the Johnson-Reed proposals became law. "It will be very difficult to undo the evil that is now threatening the country as a result of this hostile legislation."[45] In retrospect, what was happening on Capitol Hill in April–May 1924 appears as the most lugubrious event ever to occur in the United States from the standpoint of world Jewish interests; had they had such hindsight, America's Jewish organization leaders would surely have raised howls of protest, even if their effect could only have been symbolic in light of the country's xenophobic mood. At the time, the perspicacious Marshall entertained the raw outlines of this thought. On a note of moderate contrition, the AJC president regretted his organization's inactivity at this fateful moment. "I am sorry that we did not have a number of meetings of the American Jewish Committee in order to consider phases of the immigration legislation," Marshall wrote to Cyrus Adler at the end of April.[46] "I had in mind particularly a campaign of publicity. I do not think it would have made any difference, but perhaps some of the members of Congress might have been made to recognize the fact that they were riding for a fall and may have been stricken with madness." A very practical man, Marshall was confessing here not really to a mistake but rather to the limit of his powers in ethnic politics. Such politics is largely about symbols and emotions, and America's Jewish community, under his leadership, remained too inhibited in the mid-1920s to develop the right signs and slogans, and to articulate powerfully its sense of insult, even horror, when the "guillotine" of sustained immigration restriction finally hit in May 1924.

Marshall spent several days in mid-May in frustrating communication with presidential secretary C. B. Slemp,[47] trying to arrange a hearing with Coolidge to advocate a veto of the Johnson-Reed bill. His correspondence reflects a poignant state of self-denial, in which the combative Jewish champion could not quite get his lips around words acknowledging the truth that there was no place left to fight. Congress, he noted, "has worked in an atmosphere of prejudice, and I might almost say, of insanity. Its part of the fight is over. That of the public has now begun. It is regrettable that the public is only taking a very feeble interest in this great question."[48] As he had done in 1921 with Harding, Marshall ended up sending to President Coolidge an eloquently worded, and entirely ineffectual, brief in opposition of the Johnson-Reed Act.[49] Once again, he warned about the racist implications of restrictive legislation: "What we regard as the danger lurking in this legislation is, that it stimulates racial, national and religious hatreds and jealousies, that it encourages one part of our population to arrogate to itself a sense of superiority, and to classify another as one of inferiority."[50] Marshall professed not to be surprised when the Republican president signed drastic immigration restriction into law. "Before he [President Coolidge] came into office he had been impressed with the New England idea that restrictive immigration laws were desirable," a melancholy Marshall wanly observed.[51]

Before the 1920s, Marshall had drawn satisfaction from his advocacy on immigration matters from an inward sense that he was vindicating his own family's generational experience on the national stage. Open immigration validated his understandings of America—any hard-working, upstanding newcomer ought to have the opportunity to seek the freedoms and quality of life his own family had attained. The restriction setbacks in 1921 and 1924 belied these perceptions, as though America had decided to recapitulate the traumatic hardship of his parents' life experiences and to exorcize their positive meanings and results. With these familial understandings in mind, Marshall responded to the embittering dénouement of the 1924 restrictive legislation in outbursts whose fury had no parallel in other tempestuous spheres of his career.

14. A New York delegation that testified to a House committee in favor of a bill to unite separated families. Marshall is seated between Bernard Richards, executive secretary of the American Jewish Congress, and Max Hollander, grand secretary of the Independent Order Brith Abraham; standing are Representatives Samuel Dickstein and Nathan Perlman. Courtesy of Jacob Rader Marcus Center of the American Jewish Archives.

After the Johnson-Reed law's enactment, Marshall tirelessly attended to the fates of 8,000 Jews who were marooned overseas as a result of the newly toughened standards of entry to the United States.[52] These were Jews who had secured the required visa documentation for immigration but discovered that their hopes and dreams had been shattered by America's new law. On the eve of World War I, it will be recalled, Marshall had a premonition that future restrictive laws in the United States might shipwreck Jewish and other immigrants in this fashion ("a man sells his household goods in Russia or in Hungary," Marshall forecasted in his 1914 address to the New York University forum, and then when he reaches Ellis Island "the books are opened, and it is found that he is too late or too early. . . ."). Now, advocating for the 8,000 marooned Jews, he argued for special entry rights on the grounds that members of the group had invested in obtaining passports and visas on the valid assumption that they were eligible for immigration. Marshall pressed the point in correspondence with one of the cosponsors of the 1924 act, Pennsylvania senator David Reed. Rebuffing Marshall's arguments, Reed sarcastically offered each of the would-be Jewish newcomers a $10 reimbursement for passport expenditures. "Literally stunned" by this cynical and apathetic reply, Marshall erupted in one of his career's angriest tirades:

> Here I was trying to picture to you the wreckage of 8000 lives, broken hearts, despairing fathers and mothers—8000 tragedies—and all that you were willing to do was to offer a resolution, which has never yet been offered, to pay them back their $10. I have practiced law for nearly fifty years and in many states, I have been a member of three Constitutional Conventions, I have had all kinds of experiences, pleasant and unpleasant, but the one that will haunt me to my dying day is your mocking remark: "We will pay them back their $10."[53]

Replying to this apoplectic letter, Reed denied that his offer for the $10 reimbursement had a mocking intent.[54] Marshall subsequently explained to the prorestriction legislator that his advocacy of the 8,000 marooned Jews had foundations in "the sufferings of my parents when they came to this country as immigrants." The year 1926, he explained, was the centennial of the birth of his mother, "the best American I have ever known."[55] His mother, Marshall continued, arrived in the United States on a sailing vessel in 1853, after a sixty-three-day journey from Halifax. "The ship was brought to the port by mutineers. She finally succeeded in reaching Syracuse, New York, with her brother and sister, after going through indescribable experiences." Such memories of his parents' immigration hardships, he added, rendered him "sensitive" with regard to those "worthy people who possess the pioneer spirit and who seek to better their lot by coming to this country."

A tragedy for the Jews and other immigrant peoples, the closure of America's doors in the 1920s constituted, for Marshall, a capsized birthright and a turbulent, troubling conclusion to one of his most significant arenas of operation.

The final recourse was to litigate procedural or constitutional questions in the courts in an attempt to open leaks of opportunity for a few individual immigrants whose entry would otherwise be excluded by the flood of restrictive legislation. In fact, Marshall managed to pry open an entry route for thousands of marooned Jews by taking to the Supreme Court in 1924 the case of a hapless Jerusalem woman, Gittel Gottlieb.

Gottlieb left Jerusalem with her son Israel in 1922 to join her husband Solomon Gottlieb, a rabbi who had settled and found work in New York City fourteen months earlier, and had filed for citizenship.[56] His wife and son's entry was originally barred under terms of the 1922 Cable Act, which held that the wives of persons with special immigration status (ministers, actors, artists, etc.) were no longer guaranteed entry; since the 1922 quota of Palestine immigrants was filled, Gittel and Israel were denied entry. They appealed this decision; acting on long-standing sentiments and precedents in American society and jurisprudence in favor of family reunification, a New York appellate court held that it was unconscionable to allow husbands entry to the country, while blocking their spouses (the relevant case law for this decision appeared to involve the wives of Chinese merchants). Not wasting any time, as soon as the appellate court announced its decision, steamship companies marketed junkets to wives and minor children of resident aliens who had made their way to the United States by virtue of their privileged immigration status. Thousands of wives and children had already entered the United States by the time the New York immigration commissioner's appeal in the Gottlieb case reached the Supreme Court (1924). Marshall was joined by Max Kohler in his defense of Gittel Gottlieb's right to reunification with her husband. The language of the Cable Act left him virtually no leverage, and he basically relied on the accumulation of legal and public sentiment holding it "absurd" to deny reunification rights to spouses. The Supreme Court held that the relevant 1920s immigration law left no room for such humanitarianism. "The words of the statute leave no room for construction, no matter how harsh the consequence," the court found, rejecting Marshall's Gottlieb brief. The only thing gained by this hapless litigation effort was a reprieve for thousands of family members who had rushed into the country from overseas as Gittel's fate was being adjudicated—Congress granted them special entry rights.

Even after the Johnson-Reed Act became law, Marshall was able to notch small victories for immigrant protection in court appeals. One 1925 legal victory was particularly gratifying, since it related to a subject of long-standing concern to him. In *Tuton v. United States*,[57] Marshall brought to the Supreme Court his claim that aliens deserved a fair and complete legal process, including rights to appeal, in their pursuit of citizenship. Teaming with Eugene Untermyer, he argued in the Supreme Court that an alien had a right to appeal a decision reached by a US district court regarding his or her naturalization proceedings. The right to become a citizen is of "utmost moment" to petitioners, Marshall argued in an impassioned brief. As an alien, the petitioner lacked voting rights in most states and could be debarred from property ownership or from employment in public work projects. A procedure rendering decisions about naturalization, in addition to the concomitant conferral of such fundamental rights, to the sole prerogative of one district court judge was untenable, he claimed. Writing for the Supreme Court, Justice Brandeis upheld Marshall's arguments, holding that "neither precedent nor the history of the [relevant] legislation . . . leads to a denial of the appellate review." In an era when pro-immigration forces suffered overwhelmingly broad defeat, this was a small but not meaningless victory.

Marshall's most assertive court challenges to Nativist dynamics in 1920s America were three California land cases involving Asian immigrants. From the standpoint of pro-immigration advocacy, the outcome of this litigation was far from encouraging. The cases, however, warrant passing mention as evidence of the way Marshall's activities in the defense of Jewish interests in this complicated decade were propelling him toward a recognizably liberal orientation on minority rights.

One case, *Porterfield v. Webb*,[58] involved the owner (Porterfield) of an eighty-acre farm in Los Angeles County who desired to lease his land to a Japanese alien (Mizuno) and sought an injunction blocking the application of provisions in the California state acts of 1913 and 1920 that barred one class of aliens from acquiring realty interests. Porterfield argued that these provisions were unconstitutional infringements of equal protection standards. Marshall identified the racist basis of California's treatment of aliens, powerfully decrying the way the 1913 and 1920 acts allowed property rights to one class of aliens because they are "white or black," and denied them to another class of "red, yellow or brown" aliens. Euphemistically calling racism "arbitrary selection," he argued forcefully that the discrimination against Japanese and Chinese aliens had absolutely no basis in constructive, rational criteria of citizenship. The distinction between property acquisition rights of the two classes of aliens, he wrote,

> is not made dependent upon character, morals, economic position, intellectual or physical capacity, ability to increase the wealth of the State or the value of its taxable property, or a willingness to serve the State. It is merely the result of arbitrary selection. . . . Can this be said to constitute the equal protection of the laws?[59]

California argued that Chinese and Japanese immigrants were "unassimilated and unassimilable" for political and economic reasons. They were subjects of Asian monarchies that would always call them home "when the call to arms comes." Also, in socioeconomic terms, Asian aliens were unfit for California farming. Chills must have gone down Marshall's spine in the Supreme Court hearing as he listened to California's US attorney general Webb rehearse arguments about Asian incapacity for American agriculture at a time when Henry Ford's *Dearborn Independent* was saying the same thing about Jews. "It is a question of recognizing the obvious fact that the American farm, with its historical associations of cultivation and environment," California argued, "cannot exist in competition with a farm developed by Orientals with their totally different standards and ideas of cultivation of the soil, of living and social conditions."[60] The Supreme Court upheld California's arguments, holding that with regard to alien classification, "the States have wide discretion. Each has its own problems, depending on circumstances there."

In *Webb v. O'Brien*,[61] the second of three Asian land cases argued in the Supreme Court on April 23–24, 1923, Marshall argued that California's 1913 and 1920 acts ought not to prohibit a cropping arrangement negotiated by an Asian alien farmer (Inouye) with a Santa Clara landowner (O'Brien) because it did not involve the acquisition or leasing of property. California might have had its reasons for banning Japanese or Chinese aliens from acquiring or leasing land, but the cropping arrangement in question in this case, Marshall argued, "is in its essence a contract of employment. . . . It does not convey or transfer any land to Inouye; it does not provide for the payment by him of any rent."[62] California argued that the cropping arrangement offered the Japanese alien "practical dominion of the soil," and once again its US attorney general Webb regaled the Supreme Court with doomsday visions of foreigners turning the state's soil into an Asian fiefdom.[63] The Supreme Court rejected Marshall's argument that the cropping arrangement was a mere employment measure—the cropper's right to have housing for himself, to have employees live on the land, and to receive one-half of the crops as his return rendered this essentially a leasing arrangement, which California could legitimately ban under its alien laws.

In the third of these cases, *Frick v. Webb*,[64] Marshall defended the right of Japanese aliens to acquire stock in a California corporation that owned land titles, arguing that stock purchases could be distinguished from realty acquisition and that his client's Fourteenth Amendment equality rights had been violated. This was strike three on the West Coast. Once again, the court upheld California's restrictive measures, finding that it had the right to ban a class of aliens from "indirect as well as direct ownership and control of agricultural land," and the stock sales in question constituted indirect acquisition of realty.

The Red Scare

The ascendance of anti-alien forces in America's social and political arenas yielded negative, sometimes devastating results for Jewish causes. The Tribal Twenties had undeniably gloomy aspects, but they stand out as an exemplary phase in Marshall's career due to the way he reconceptualized his setbacks in Jewish advocacy as issues of concern to all Americans. Once he reached a dead end as a proponent of Jewish minority rights overseas and of open immigration policy in the United States, he refused to stand still as the frustrated ethnic advocate of a particular interest. Instead, he broadened the focus by championing the causes of colonized Haitians and those of disempowered Asian laborers in California. The conceptual leap in his thinking can be elucidated. Marshall's point was that Americans would never take the rights of East European minorities seriously until they learned to be respectful of the rights of vulnerable small nations in their own hemisphere; his point was that the right of Jewish immigration to America would not be revived until a new spirit of toleration and accommodation was furnished to alien laborers of various nationalities and backgrounds who were trying to make ends meet, from one coast to the other in the United States. Before World War I, Marshall's brand of ethnic activism had been triggered by a dialogue between elite and immigrant Jewish groups in Uptown and Downtown New York, and by responses to crises faced by Jews in Eastern Europe. In contrast, in the 1920s, Jewish politics stewarded by Marshall was taking on a noticeably liberal cast in the United States, but not primarily in response to events in Jewish communities overseas. Marshall's identity as an impassioned defender of American constitutional democracy reconsolidated in defiance of blatantly discriminatory processes in postwar American society. He was finding that there was little he could do at the moment for key Jewish interests other than to fight for America's preservation as an openly tolerant society.

This pattern by which the stalled advocacy of particular Jewish interests revitalized in a broadly liberal campaign for constitutional rights emerged right at the start of the postwar period. In early 1919, Marshall was cognizant that the image of "Jewish Bolshevism" was becoming a staple accusation in the Red Scare—Russian Jews in New York were thought of as subversive elements, allied in spirit or in actual underground networks with Jewish revolutionaries who (it was believed) predominantly filled the Bolshevik ranks. "There is a grave misunderstanding as to the attitude of the Jews toward Bolshevism," Marshall insisted in a letter to Senator Lee Overman,[65] whose subcommittee (it will be recalled) investigated radical subversion in this period. "The residents of the East Side of New York are, as a whole, as reputable and patriotic a body of people as are to be found in any other part of the country," Marshall explained to Overman. Marshall kept complaining about the Jewish Bolshevism stereotype. "What I greatly deplore is the fact that whenever anyone discusses Bolshevism, the first thing that comes to his lips is that Jews are to be found among the Bolsheviki," groused Marshall.[66] He developed empirical arguments to deflate the myth of Jewish Bolshevism. "The fact that Trotsky was born a Jew and that other apostate Jews have been associated with Bolshevism has been much made of," wrote Marshall in October 1919. "But it is forgotten that Lenin, the brains of Bolshevism, and the rank and file of his followers are not Jews."[67] Repeatedly, he insisted that Jewish radicals such as Emma Goldman were not representative of their community and were themselves "utterly devoid of Jewish interests and commitments."[68] "I am as well acquainted with the Jews in the US as any man in America," Marshall boasted to the counsel for the US Steel Corporation. And, based on that expertise, he could say authoritatively that "the Jew is not by disposition radical. He is essentially conservative, and has been wedded to the ideals of his forefathers for more than thirty centuries."[69]

Weeks of such pleading led nowhere, and in spring 1920, Henry Ford began to utilize his company's powerful resources to reproduce the Jewish Bolshevism canard on a frighteningly large scale. Marshall's powerfully expressed, and informed, argumentation had not backfired. However, as in the case of the pro-immigration briefs he later filed with successive Republican presidents, Marshall discovered that a level-headed presentation of reliable information about Jewish-related topics sometimes made little headway in a public climate suffused with mythic stereotype and intolerance. As happened with immigration advocacy, he had to realign the focus of his argument in keeping with the spirit of the times.

Marshall, of course, found Bolshevik radicalism repugnant, but by the start of 1920, he realized that his advocacy efforts ought to be directed against the Red Scare's unconstitutional prosecution of Bolshevism per se. The amalgam of ignorance, fear, and xenophobia that gave rise to the Red Scare and to its hysterical prosecution of perceived Bolsheviks and other revolutionaries represented a grave threat to Jews and all other Americans, Marshall judged. The "Jewish Bolshevism" myth was a symptom of broader trends of thought and policy inimical to the ideal of an open, democratic society; his most effective way of deflating the myth was to wage a general defense of the ideal of constitutional liberty, because it was the foundation of all forms of Jewish success in America.

Marshall opposed the Red Scare's antiradical crackdown enforced by Attorney General A. Mitchell Palmer. "While I am fundamentally opposed to everything that savors of Bolshevism and revolution, I am nevertheless greatly in doubt as to the wisdom of the procedure being followed by the Attorney General," Marshall wrote to Simon Wolf, referring to the Palmer Raids.[70]

In early January 1920, Palmer's methods had percolated to the state level, and in the most egregious local instance of an antiradical crackdown, the newly convened New York State Assembly removed on January 7 five freely elected socialist delegates. With Charles Evans Hughes, Marshall headed a small group of lawyers who protested the legality of this expulsion, an act that effectively disenfranchised the 60,000 constituents who had sent the five assemblymen to Albany. All but one of the five members of this group were conservative Republicans; its protest was commissioned by the Association of the Bar of the City of New York, though some distinguished bar members, including William Guthrie, defended the expulsion of the five assemblymen on the grounds that the Socialist Party's 1919 platform subversively advocated the overthrow of organized governments.[71] Marshall's forty-page brief was framed around the fundamental premise of representative government: no elected delegate can be denied a seat due to his political opinions. Marshall furnished an array of precedents in support of various technical objections, such as the claim that the assembly had failed in its duty to hold a hearing before the elected delegates took an oath of office. Apart from specific points of law, Marshall's brief rested on the theory that such persecutory acts undertaken in the Red Scare spirit were invariably counterproductive. "Nothing tends so greatly to give vitality even to a worthless cause as persecution," Marshall's brief declared.[72]

"Though I am unalterably opposed to socialist doctrines, I regard the suspension by the Assembly of socialist members as a dangerous attack upon our constitutional system of government," Marshall wrote in the *Syracuse Journal*.[73] He wrote to state assemblymen that the expulsion was the "most disheartening episode in the history of our state," and wondered, "how can men be so blind as to invite the very evils they have pretended to attack."[74] When the *American Israelite* attacked Marshall's defense of socialists, the AJC president replied emotionally: "Let it be said when I am gone that I never feared to do what was right merely because it was momentarily unpopular among people who have become crazed by their hatreds and their prejudices and their stupidity."[75] Repeatedly, he charged that fighting Bolshevism by using undemocratic, Bolshevik-like (or czarist) methods could only backfire. He drove home this point pungently to the *New*

York Times, a newspaper that had supported the expulsion of the five socialists from the assembly. "When people are kept away from the ballot box by Czaristic methods. . . . the forces of discontent may be tempted to resort to force," Marshall warned the *Times.*[76] The assembly, however, ignored such arguments. On April 1, it upheld the expulsion of the five delegates.

The Ku Klux Klan

In 1924, staggeringly high membership figures for the Ku Klux Klan (KKK), estimated at 4 million, symbolized the decade's high tide of hateful intolerance. Based around the slogan of "one hundred percent Americanism," the Klan targeted Catholics, blacks, Jews, and foreigners.[77] The precise hierarchy of the organization's targets depended upon the region—outside of the South, Catholics appeared to be the focus of Klan animosity. Everywhere, Jews appeared on KKK hate lists. Relying on the ancient accusation of Jews as Christ killers and borrowing from Ford's *Dearborn Independent,* the KKK circulated anti-Semitic materials; Klan-affiliated media outlets headlined paranoiac accusations about the Jewish instigation of "war between blacks and whites to overthrow all the gentile governments of the world," and about the "Jews' invisible government in New York, the Ke-hil-lah."[78] Such anti-Semitic screed was probably most voluminous among Klan publicists and members in northern locales, but it was Jews of small southern and western communities who seemed most vulnerable to Klan intimidation. From Little Rock, Arkansas, a local Jewish leader described his community to Louis Marshall as a "hopeless minority" in a town "cursed with a half-baked, illiterate Protestant pulpit."[79]

Marshall collected data regarding the Klan's anti-Jewish activities. Henry Fry, the son of a Confederate officer who had worked briefly as an organizer for the Klan in Tennessee before resigning in disgust and authoring a series of exposés about the KKK in the *New York World* in September 1921, informed Marshall that Klan members and officers conducted propaganda activities against Jews "as viciously as against the Catholics."[80]

Marshall appreciated Fry's writings about the Klan and kept contact with the whistle-blower. "I wish to congratulate you for all you have done to drag the KKK into [the] open and to inform the American people of the danger that threatens them from that unspeakable organization," Marshall wrote to Fry in late 1922.[81] Most importantly, Marshall agreed with Fry's conclusion that Catholics and Jews would only add fuel to the Klan's fires by actively opposing the organization. "I have always regarded it [the Klan issue] as one in which the Protestant majority of this country is especially concerned," he wrote to Fry. "The very fact that

Catholics or Jews are attacking the KKK will add to the latter thousands of weak-minded persons."[82]

Marshall reiterated this premise in dozens of communications in the early 1920s. The Protestant churches had to take the lead in public showdowns against the Klan. "I have communicated with non-Jews of high standing who have studied this subject carefully, and they insist that it would be a tremendous blunder for the Jews to accept the gauge of battle," Marshall wrote to one inquirer at the end of 1922.[83] A few months later, he scolded Rabbi Joseph Silverman for associating with a public organization, the American Unity League, that fought the KKK. "The policy of ignoring the [KKK] movement is the sound attitude for us to take," Marshall lectured Rabbi Silverman.[84] Other Jewish organizational leaders basically concurred with this strategy. Stephen Wise, for instance, also held that Protestants should carry the democratic torch, leading any public campaign against the Klan. However, as Morton Rosenstock commented, Marshall's response to the Klan was somewhat more cautious and obsessively reliant upon Protestant leadership than reactions of other Jewish organizational heads. Wise's American Jewish Congress, for instance, publicly disclosed an anti-Klan resolution.[85] The American Jewish Committee, in contrast, took the opposite tack. At a late December 1922 meeting of the AJC Executive Committee, Marshall reported that Judge Aaron Levy, grandmaster of the Independent Order of Brith Abraham, had issued a public statement declaring that his organization would make an open fight against the KKK. Marshall, the AJC decided, "should advise heads of other Jewish organizations and editors of Jewish newspapers against making a Jewish issue out of the KKK movement."[86]

Marshall himself issued just one public statement against the Klan, in the *World*, in late October 1923. He jousted lightly with the Klan's claims of Anglo-Saxon superiority ("It is difficult to know what Anglo-Saxon patriotism means") and pointed to ways the Klan's imperial wizard "preaches a violation of the Constitution." Even in this public denunciation of the KKK, Marshall reiterated the thesis that the Protestants had to take the antidefamation helm on this issue. He declared, "It is for the American people as a whole, it is for the Protestant churches, as many of them have spontaneously done, to repudiate so iniquitous a program."[87]

Marshall nullified schemes proposing that American Jewish resources be used to oppose Klan-affiliated candidates in local elections around the country. In a confidential letter to Paul Warburg,[88] he explained that Texas personalities, including oilman J. S. Cullinan, had approached him in fall 1922, asking him to support the candidacy of independent candidate George Peddy, who was running in the senate race against Democrat Earle Bradford Mayfield and who was known as the "Klan candidate." Marshall was perturbed by the blustering tough talk of Peddy's backers, who referred to any Jewish merchants in Texas who did not side with them as "cowards"; more importantly, he was deterred by the thought that Jewish involvement in such a state election could badly misfire and merely reinforce paranoid prejudices about Jewish cabals. Marshall alerted these Texan politicos "to the fact that the Jews from whom they expected financial assistance were largely men from . . . Wall Street." Were it to be publicized that their candidate "secured its funds from Jews and Wall Street interests," that nominee would be immediately "condemned to obloquy" and defeated, Marshall explained.

Marshall's responses to KKK hatred encapsulate the pattern of his leadership on ethnic affairs in the 1920s. From the start, he refused to regard the Klan's activities, even its anti-Semitism propaganda, as a specifically Jewish issue; any confrontation with the Klan could have effect only if the organization's prejudice was perceived as a threat to all Americans. Through a chain of coincidences, a promising opportunity to join an umbrella coalition of various religious groups in an anti-Klan battle arose in Oregon. Marshall's part in *Pierce v. Society of Sisters* proved to be an inspiring example of ecumenical mobilization against forces of bigotry in the Tribal Twenties.

In 1922, a Democratic candidate for governor, Walter Pierce, who had the Klan's backing, swept the Republic incumbent out of office, winning by the largest margin in the state's electoral history. Not long thereafter, Oregon's legislature passed a law making it a misdemeanor for any parent of a child between the ages of eight and sixteen to fail or neglect to send the youngster to a public school in the state. This public school law was a full frontal attack on private school education. A product of religious prejudice and patriotic fervor in postwar America, the Oregon law was widely seen at the time as the handiwork of the Ku Klux Klan.[89]

Marshall was drawn into the public school law controversy by his relationship with a local Oregon Jewish leader, Jesse Winburn, who was a fervent backer of Governor Pierce. Winburn originally hailed from Syracuse, and Marshall had known his family in the city. He searched incredulously for an explanation of how any Jewish figure could become a committed supporter of a Klan politician and eventually decided that Winburn must have foolishly been swayed by flatterers. Marshall entreated him to abjure his Klan connections and oppose the public school law, lest his behavior eventually contribute to the "annihilation of your own people and of all other minorities."[90] As a result of this correspondence, Winburn denounced the public school law, and Marshall became engaged in litigation against it.[91]

The Oregon public school law was seen as an assault on Catholic parochial schools, and so, naturally, Catholic clergy and laypeople from around the country emerged as some of its most vocal antagonists. Casting the law as an outright violation of civil rights, particularly of the cherished principle of parents' right to educate their children as they see fit, these Catholic spokespeople returned repeatedly to a perception of Oregon's measure as an un-American, Soviet-style intrusion. Austin Dowling, archbishop of St. Paul and a leader of education work for the National Catholic Welfare Conference, derided Oregon's measure as a "Soviet claim to invade the home and substitute communal for parental claim." The same motif appeared in the critique of Baltimore archbishop Michael Curley, who likened Oregon's law to state socialism and associated it with the principles of Karl Marx.[92]

Identifying Oregon's law as a dangerous attempt to curtail any cultural group's right to educate children in line with its value system, a number of American religious groups filed amici curiae briefs with the Supreme Court, supporting the 1925 effort in *Pierce v. Society of Sisters*[93] to overturn the Oregon law. These included the Domestic and Foreign Missionary Society of the Protestant Episcopal Church, the North Pacific Union Conference of Seventh Day Adventists, and the American Jewish Committee.[94]

Writing for the AJC, Marshall joined the chorus of critics who regarded Oregon's law as a Bolshevik-tempered measure.[95] "If private, parochial and denominational schools are to be deprived of the right to educate children . . . then we shall be in precisely the same situation that now exists in Russia," claimed Marshall. He added other contexts to the critique. Oregon's effort dovetailed with a trend of social conformism in the 1920s. Disabling the educational apparatuses of ethnoreligious groups would turn America into a nation of "mechanical robots and standardized Babbits," he commented. His experience with immigrant matters taught Marshall that private schools were prime agents of Americanization. He therefore rejected the assumption of the Oregon statute writers, who held that "the assimilation and education" of immigrants "is best secured through attendance in public schools." Not true, concluded Marshall: "the assimilation, so-called, of our foreign born citizens is advanced rather than retarded by the private, parochial and religious schools."

Early in the 1920s, American Jewish educators at Columbia University had assembled evidence and arguments that cast doubt on the wisdom of the aggressive Americanization of immigrant groups and provided implicit or explicit support for the development of autonomous cultural and educational institutions by the country's ethnoreligious groups.[96] In his brief on the Oregon public education law, Marshall underscored this retreat from the melting pot ideology. He seemed to be articulating cultural autonomy as an official American Jewish position:

> There is no such thing as a melting pot, anthropologically speaking. If there were, it would be a misfortune. However much iron and copper and zinc and gold may be mixed, the net result is a product which possesses none of the virtues of the original metals and is utterly useless. Far better would it be to purify and refine the original metals, for then their individual values would be enhanced.[97]

"The child is not the mere creature of the state," ruled the Supreme Court in its ruling on the *Pierce v. Society of Sisters* case. Overturning the Oregon law, the court regarded it as "unreasonable interference with the liberty of parents and guardians to direct the upbringing and education of children under their control."[98] Within a few days, the decision was hailed as a triumph for toleration by 490 major editorials published in forty-four states, including southern states where KKK influence was, in this period, particularly strong.[99]

Prohibition

Prohibition—the Eighteenth Amendment and the Volstead Act—became law in mid-January 1919. Within a month, Marshall, a teetotaler, pronounced his position. "I consider the Prohibition amendment absurd, and in many ways unjust," he declared. "Prohibition does not prohibit," he said. Marshall correctly anticipated that the law would merely "stimulate the excessive use of rotgut whiskey, and other dangerous concoctions."[100] Five years after the last round of drinks was formally served in the United States and Prohibition took effect, Marshall still rankled about the Eighteenth Amendment, criticizing it as an unworthy encroachment upon state sovereignty.[101] Yet, so long as the Eighteenth Amendment was not repealed, Marshall heeded Prohibition, not just because he himself never drank but because of his lifelong fear of mob anarchy. That Prohibition was clumsily enforced did not warrant expressions of public disrespect for the law. As far as he was concerned, responsible public figures, such as Columbia University president Nicholas Murray Butler, were speaking too dismissively about the law's lack of enforceability. As long as it was law, Prohibition had to be taken seriously; other approaches to the circumstances it had created could lead to the "destruction of constitutional government."[102]

Not long after Prohibition took effect, Marshall engaged contacts with the Internal Revenue Department for the purpose of ironing out rules to make wine available for Jewish sacramental purposes. He approached the Union of Orthodox Rabbis, as well as rabbis "representing various [non-Orthodox] shades of thought." These discussions culminated in a plan for the allowance and distribution of wine for sacramental purposes; "had this plan been adopted," Marshall lamented as early as September 1920, "it would have pre-empted abuses."[103] The problem was that the Internal Revenue commissioner overlooked these consultations and issued regulations on the ignorant assumption that all Jews in America were Orthodox.[104] Equally troubling, the regulations tapped rabbis as the distributing agents for wine, a cumbersome task entailing the collection of money and the actual transport of the sacramental drinks to each congregant's home. The procedure somehow seemed profane; undeniably, it was impractical. "I did not approve of the thought that the rabbinate should be drawn into the business of distributing wine," reflected Marshall.[105]

Abuses fermented rapidly as a result of the imprudently devised Prohibition regulations regarding sacramental wine. In New York City, during fiscal year 1924, an unholy and staggering amount of wine (3 million gallons), was requisitioned and supposedly imbibed under the sacramental wine provision.[106] Heedless exploitation of the sacramental wine provision was quickly made by "wine rabbis." Ford's *Dearborn Independent* quickly made capital out of an association of illegal booze and crooked Jews. In December 1921, Ford's anti-Semitic outlet ascribed 95 percent of the country's bootlegging to Jews.[107] Ironically, in its allegations about Jewish criminality under Prohibition, the *Independent* used as leverage Ford's former friend Rabbi Leo Franklin, who at the time served as president of the Central Conference of American Rabbis (CCAR); Franklin asserted that many of the Jews who sought licenses to distribute sacramental wine were not, in fact, rabbis.[108] In 1922, the CCAR's Executive Committee petitioned the Internal Revenue commissioner for the revocation of Article 7 of the Volstead Act, the exemption for sacramental wine.[109]

Frustrated by the complications connected to rabbinical distribution of sacramental wine, Marshall wondered aloud in March 1920 about possible remedies. Were the regulations to be liberalized to expedite distribution of the wine, the changes "might lead to unpleasant insinuations against the Jews by the newspapers," Marshall feared.[110] His consultations with several rabbis produced one possible creative solution to the predicaments of Prohibition—these rabbis suggested that Jewish law allowed the use of unfermented wine for ritualistic purposes.[111] As months passed, the question of fermented or unfermented wine was referred to Professor Louis Ginzberg of the Jewish Theological Seminary, a Jewish law authority of, Marshall hoped, requisite stature; in late 1922, the American Jewish Committee published Ginzberg's responsum, holding that grape juice had equal value in sacramental ritual.[112] For months, Marshall tried to persuade all corners of American Jewry of the wisdom and utility of Professor Ginzberg's finding. "There are those of the ultra-Orthodox wing who may not accept Prof. Ginzberg's judgment," Marshall noted in June 1923. "I have challenged them over and over again to produce a responsum which would indicate that their avowed belief that fermented wine is necessary is correct, but thus far they have failed to do so."[113]

Marshall coaxed and cajoled rabbis from Orthodox and Reform branches, but was unable to forge a unified approach to the sacramental wine issue. In the middle of the decade, members of the Uptown elite were scratching their heads about whether Orthodox and non-Orthodox leaders might possibly hold a constructive meeting about the fermented/unfermented wine issue, "to thrash it out among themselves" and to reach a constructive solution. Meantime the anti-Semites kept spinning yarns about criminal Jewish inebriation of the nation; the facts actually suggested that Prohibition gave a boost to Jewish criminality (between 1924 and 1932, when Jews composed 3 percent of the country's population, 12 percent of persons indicted for bootlegging were Jewish[114]). Prohibition's perplexities remained beyond the reach of Marshall law.

The Character, Impact, and Limits of "Marshall Law"

The twenties, then, were far from a period of unmitigated triumph for Marshall and Jewish organizational effort. "Marshall law" was very much in effect: at key points in the decade, events of critical importance to Jewish life—from the continuation or cessation of Henry Ford's anti-Semitic campaign to the funding of the Yishuv's effort to create a Jewish national home or state in Eretz Israel—seemed to revolve around the disposition and continuing efforts of an extremely energetic and unusually experienced ethnic communal leader, Louis Marshall. Yet, his ability to reform or adjust inconvenient or devastating realities, from the wine rabbis and Jewish bootleggers who flourished illicitly under Prohibition to the termination of America's tradition of open immigration, was manifestly limited. His responses to patterns of isolationist bigotry and xenophobia in the Roaring Twenties may seem exemplary to subsequent generations of Jews and non-Jews, but his courageously liberal defenses of ostracized socialist New York assemblymen, powerless Asian farmers in California, and worthy parochial school educators in Oregon really did little in his own day to rectify everyday problems of discrimination, intimidation, and humiliation faced by the country's Jews in rural and city locales.

Depending on one's circumstances, there was room in this decade to wonder dispassionately, without the Downtown-Uptown partisan pyrotechnics that characterized communal Jewish discussions in prewar America, whether Marshall law was really good for the Jews. When Marshall articulately added his voice to an umbrella coalition campaign against a Klan-spirited school law in Oregon, did it really make a difference to Jews harassed by KKK hooligans in Little Rock? Did his impassioned defense of free speech rights in the New York State Assembly really help Jewish leftists on the Lower East Side of New York, or in Milwaukee, feel more secure as they promoted their visions of a utopian future? Though Marshall held faint hopes that exposure of iniquitous and hypocritical policies toward Asian aliens on the West Coast might embarrass President Coolidge and encourage him to modify his attitude toward immigrant restriction, did Marshall's litigation in these California land cases really do anything to increase the survival chances of European Jews in the 1930s?

This last question regarding immigration might be especially unfair to ask (what could any advocate of open immigration have done in the early 1920s, given the onslaught of Nativist feeling?), but it points to an acutely significant issue of priorities in ethnic leadership in an era like the isolationist 1920s, when "one hundred percent American" societal conceptualizations provided obvious incentive to a figure like Marshall to downplay his own ethnic identity and to craft his pronouncements as directed to all Americans, of all creeds. Marshall himself, along with a prevailing majority of American Jews who (unlike Marshall) joined the Democratic Party in the interwar period, clearly came to believe that a liberal attitude toward minority rights in America was "good for the Jews." Though the "Jewish" motivations of his work for other minority groups are traceable, how could an ethnic leader in his position have possibly judged whether higher priority should be given to persistent struggle, no matter how futile, on behalf of specifically defined Jewish issues, or to causes such as NAACP legal battles that involved non-Jewish groups and whose successful prosecution would hopefully reinforce America's status as a free and open society? When Marshall wrote to his son Bob in April 28, 1923, that "I finally finished the argument of the Japanese cases [in California], which are very interesting and important,"[115] his circumstances appear ennobling to Americans of any era who care about the country's commitment to constitutional ideals of fairness and rights. But was his orientation good for the Jews?

These ongoing dilemmas are never easily resolvable, and a precociously intelligent figure like Marshall was hardly unaware of them. In fact, the first and best focus for any assessment of the meaning of Marshall law in the 1920s is its promulgator. Did Marshall himself become embittered by legislative victories won by Nativists and his own inability to forge a happy ending on an issue such as immigration rights, to which he devoted a quarter century of effort? And how exactly did he prioritize or synthesize his indefatigable efforts for "American" and for "Jewish" causes?

At every phase of his life, Marshall had passing moments of splenetic anger, and we have noted low points in the 1920s, such as his lugubrious attestation that an insensitive remark by restrictionist Senator Reed would "haunt me to my dying day." He was not, however, emotionally derailed by any major setback in the 1920s, and the respect, even adulation, of his contemporary peers, coupled with his important successes (most famously, the Ford apology) in this decade of troubling prosperity, buoyed his spirits. His compelling habit of forgiving enemies, on practical if not moral grounds, attained almost celestial dimensions during this time.

An incredible exemplification of Marshall's equanimity was a visit to his offices in January 1928 by Henry Ford, an event that could have only happened in America. In his report to his son Bob about the visit, Marshall referred to the automobile manufacturer, not really ironically, as "Henry."[116] Ford told Marshall that he had "relieved his mind of the great mistake and blunder he had made in his anti-Jewish publications." Naïvely, Marshall wrote that Ford "showed he had sincerely repented." The Flivver King stroked Marshall's ego, saying he was "ready to do anything" that Marshall "might at any time suggest to enable him to minimize the evil that had been done." Marshall forthrightly demanded that Ford take steps to stop the translation and dissemination of *Dearborn Independent* screed about the Jews in European countries. Marshall's description of the end of the interview is priceless:

> Henry invited me to see his new car and asked me to select any of his products that I might desire. I respectfully declined, informing him of my devotion to pedestrian locomotion. The office was in an uproar of excitement. As he left, he was waylaid by newspapermen.[117]

Marshall was not a young man when he passed away, but his death did not result from any chronic, threatening illness, so his voluminous personal archive does not include documents saturated by a testamentary desire to address broad questions about the meaning of his life and its final years. Because he did not anticipate its abrupt end in Zurich, Marshall had no reason to wonder whether the period of his unprecedented stature in American Jewish affairs ought really to be regarded as a triumphant one for his people. Still, some of his papers betray oblique hints about his frame of mind toward the end of his life.

Marshall's will, drawn eight years before his death, has touching turns of phrase that could only have been written by a man justifiably proud of his family's accomplishments. Hoping to bequeath to his children and grandchildren a vision of peace and serenity, he urged them to keep the Knollwood cabin in the family as a summer home, where they would "foster the spirit of unity and harmony that has always prevailed in my family."[118]

That Marshall composed a handwritten fund-raising appeal for the Jewish Theological Seminary to Julius Rosenwald while sailing aboard the SS *Majestic* for Europe,[119] weeks before his death in Zurich, says something about his untainted faith in the JTS after almost three decades of close affiliation with this unique institution. "The Jewish Theological Seminary has performed miracles," wrote Marshall, not solely in the vein of fund-raising hype. Broadly, such attestations reflected this Jewish leader's confident appreciation that his own decades of labor had yielded spiritual dividends for his people. In this letter, Marshall wrote sentences like "we have been compelled to make bricks without straw" without any trace of bitterness; objectively, opulently endowed philanthropists like Schiff or Rosenwald never provided resources to make his work managing a project like JTS a simple affair, but Marshall derived tremendous inward satisfaction from the arduous labors he invested in meaningful institutions such as the seminary, the protectory, and (of course) the American Jewish Committee.

Despite the bigoted tribalism of groups like the KKK in the 1920s, Marshall did not feel at the end of the decade that his people faced any special threat from Christian America. As far as he was concerned, the relationship between the two great monotheistic faiths, Judaism and Christianity, was more or less on the same footing as it had been in the Syracuse days of his youth. In a revealing letter written weeks before his death to Alfred W. Anthony, of the Federal Council of the Churches of Christ in America,[120] Marshall dismissed missionary efforts to convert Jews in the same pungent terms that appear in his discussions of missionary work, or related topics, at all phases of his career. "Before you begin to convert us, it might be in order first to convert the Christians to the recognition of those elements of Christianity which have been derived from Judaism," Marshall defiantly wrote. As he had always done, he stressed the need for ecumenical toleration: "I have the utmost respect for all religions . . . I refer not only to Judaism and Christianity, but also to Mohammedanism, Buddhism and Confucianism, and to many other faiths which have shaped the lives of the vast majority of mankind throughout the centuries."

As a leader of a small minority group, Marshall recognized that a certain degree of vigilance was constantly required to protect Jewish rights, even in America. This requirement was everlasting—nothing in the 1920s had upgraded or eliminated it. In this June 1929 letter to Anthony, Marshall referred to this duty as a kind of family inheritance; his unusually lengthy recollection of his father's experiences and the implied burden they had cast on his own life deserve quotation:

> You will ask me why it is that I so greatly mistrust the philosophy of conversionism which you have so eloquently voiced. My father came to this country in 1849 from Germany as a boy of nineteen. What drove him to our shores was the hope of enjoying genuine religious liberty. While in his native land, engaged in earning a livelihood, he had occasion to go on errands from one town to another through a forest. It frequently happened that he was waylaid by gangs of zealous Christians, who seized him and thundered at him: "Jew, say Christ!" Failure to yield prompt obedience brought brutal beatings and shameful insults. That was but one type of conversionists. There were others whose methods were more subtle, the kind which the late Solomon Schechter aptly termed the "higher anti-Semitism."
>
> The memory of these facts is engraved deeply in my heart. Years ago it led me to make to myself a vow that I would contest to the bitter end any infraction of liberty of conscience. Since then, in whatever form attempted, I have fought as earnestly for those of other faiths or no faiths as I have for those of my own.[121]

Whatever setbacks Marshall and the Jews suffered during the turbulent 1920s, or any other decade, his confidence in the future of his people in America was embedded ineradicably in personal experiences of religious cordiality and respect, dating from his Syracuse childhood and early manhood. Neither Henry Ford nor the KKK in the 1920s could appear in his eyes as representative Christian Americans. Marshall always had in his view the daily amiability experienced by persons of different faiths in his first law firm in Syracuse. "Good will was as natural as it was to breathe," recalled Marshall. Marshall took another breath from that Syracuse source in this 1929 letter:

> When I first began to practice law my four associates were, respectively, an Episcopalian, a Unitarian, a Methodist and a Presbyterian. We accepted one another, as we were. There arose no religious differences, there was no desire to change one another's faith, there prevailed mutual respect and esteem. Had anybody ventured to suggest religious propaganda he would have been laughed out of court—and yet each of us remained loyal to his faith. Good will was as natural as it was to breathe.[122]

Late in his life, when Marshall faced realities and recognized that Jews had endured serious setbacks in America after World War I, he insisted that these were not mortal blows. He spoke realistically and affirmed that America's Jewish community had already accumulated resources sufficient to ensure a flourishing cultural and spiritual life for decades to come. He had fought long and valiantly against the "guillotine" of immigration restriction; when the blade fell, he did not lose his head. His late comments about the future of American Jewry were pragmatically confident:

> I cannot see how new immigration laws, however objectionable they are, will or can prevent the development of Judaism in America. . . . There are over 3.5 million Jews in this country, every one of whom has in himself the power to assist in its development. The circumstance that, for a time, at least, the number of Jews who can come from outside the U.S. will be limited cannot prevent the development of Judaism among those who are in the U.S. In fact, it should stimulate those who are here to maintain our great traditions of the past, and adapt them to the American environment.[123]

Perhaps because he was so daringly ahead of his time in his advocacy of rights for African Americans, Native Americans, Asian Americans, and the environment, Marshall did not seem irritated or befuddled by ways in which he was more than one step behind the pace of the 1920s. In fact, he seemed to enjoy becoming obsolete about many things. He was his own Romantic late nineteenth-century environment that needed to be preserved, unchanged.

On Marshall's seventieth birthday in December 1926, the *New York Times Magazine* published a profile of the Jewish leader as an endearingly old-fashioned individualist.[124] The piece vividly showed that the man's constitutional viewpoint remained rock solid and that he viewed definitive symbols of the Roaring Twenties as passing excrescences. Thirty years before, in his discussion about whether "ours is a Christian government," Marshall had expressed himself in rigidly patriotic constitutional terms. "Sustain your constitutions, state and national, as they have been framed by the fathers of the Republic. Do not permit them to be disturbed one jot," coached Marshall in 1896.[125] The events of past years—World War I, Henry Ford's anti-Semitism, the KKK, the closure of immigration doors—had not dislodged Marshall from this fundamental constitutional faith. The seventy-year-old told the *New York Times* that the Constitution would be as applicable in 2076 as it was in 1926:

> It is the enduring document of all time. Its application in another century and a half will be as fresh as it is today. Fundamentally it embraces the natural rights of man, and these will never change.[126]

Respect for the Constitution remained for Marshall an article of quasi-religious faith. In 1924, two years before these seventieth birthday celebration remarks, he officiated a debate on capital punishment between Judge Alfred J. Talley and

Clarence Darrow at the Manhattan Opera House. Marshall confessed afterward to his son Bob that while his sympathies were aligned with Darrow's opposition to capital punishment, Darrow's methods "disgusted" him. Clarence Darrow had "no respect for the law and the Constitution," Marshall believed; he went so far as to step out of his role as impartial referee at the debate and to "speak some very plain truths" about the Constitution, in opposition to Darrow's apparent cynicism on the subject.[127]

The main problem posed by 1920s life to America's constitutional democracy, Marshall opined in the *New York Times* seventieth birthday profile, was "haste." In this connection, he hazarded criticism of Prohibition, saying, "our experience with the 18th amendment has shown that we acted too hastily." Prohibition was one of a few modern encroachments of centralized power that offended Marshall's enthusiasm for states rights. "When I was a young man, the privileges of the States were strongly defined," he commented, nostalgically. At points in this seventieth birthday profile, Marshall gloried in this nostalgic pining for his Syracuse youth, when "men discussed public matters with reverence."[128] He said he abhorred the way new media technologies were not purveying serious information. When he was a boy, Marshall said, "the radio and movies had not been created to bring us the latest football scores." In the 1920s, people seemed to be moving around too fast to sustain deeply meaningful discussions about important issues. "This national haste takes our mind away from public affairs," Marshall complained. "Newspapers have become so big that we cannot possibly read them. We merely look at their headlines during a twenty minute ride every morning." The nation was crowded with opinionated citizens who formed their views from such perfunctory headline perusal and who paid attention to story details only when they were about personal income tax.

Toward the end of the 1920s, his was a mixed vision. In the seventieth birthday interview, Marshall also waxed nostalgic about states rights and small town debates about big issues as though the country's democracy was best protected when its traditions remained isolated; simultaneously, he criticized the country's isolationist policies and called on Americans to engage more vigorously in international affairs. This was an oblique way of commenting on the tragedy that was engulfing his work on minority rights in Eastern Europe, partly as a result of America's decision not to join the League of Nations; Marshall's remarks also implied that Americans of any particular ancestry owed a debt of assistance to their overseas brethren comparable to the responsibility Marshall had incurred as an American Jewish leader who worked diligently to support overseas Jews. "What shall we say if a World Court is created in which we have no part, and some day we find ourselves hauled before that court?" Marshall wondered. "Every principle of American doctrines bids us to join the court, and assist the League. It is impossible for us to remain apart from the affairs of the Old World." Throughout this candid, charming seventieth birthday piece, Marshall had humorously chastised American citizens for their hastiness; yet, at the article's conclusion, when he was asked to state his birthday wish, Marshall essentially delivered a message that was the opposite of telling Americans to slow down. He urged Americans to become more robustly engaged in the world. "If I have any wish to express on my 70th birthday it is to see a spirit of indulgence among nations," Marshall said. "Let us extend the benefits of our institutions whenever possible. I do not believe it is in our moral fiber to be selfish or narrow."[129]

Eclecticism is an overlooked aspect of Marshall's outlook, and it became particularly pronounced in the 1920s, a period when idealistic figures on the American landscape eschewed grand theories of meaning.[130] Marshall was too moralistic a character to identify wholeheartedly with the ethical relativism of contemporary figures like Oliver Wendell Holmes;[131] but like these counterparts, he appears in the 1920s to have articulated positions on issues of Jewish and American concern on the basis of his pragmatic instincts rather than all-embracing moral theories. Trying to identify Marshall's attitude regarding Jewish self-preservation or integration in America, scholars have ascribed forms of "religious pluralism" to him, suggesting that he favored the cultivation of religiously distinctive elements while trying to minimize ethnically Jewish identity components.[132]

This classification is helpful, but an examination of Marshall's papers and pronouncements, particularly in the 1920s, cannot fully validate it. Just as Marshall occasionally voiced reservations about institutions designed with an intent to strengthen Judaism, he periodically supported the cultivation of symbols or institutions that reinforced American Jews' ethnic identities. Even before the 1920s, Marshall's decision as to whether a Jewish "religious" or "ethnic" project warranted support depended on a complex array of factors, including prevailing moods in Downtown-Uptown affairs and in the American public, and the character of the project's prominent personality. Was, for instance, Marshall being a "religious pluralist" when he decided to throw his support before World War I to the New York City Kehillah project, an experiment that promoted semiautonomous Jewish activities in religious and nonreligious areas (from Jewish education to a kind of Jewish police agency) and also provided an innovative representation formula germane to Marshall's ongoing interest in the question of communal democratization? Throughout his career, no rigid ideology guided Marshall's thinking on issues of Jewish continuity and American integration; by the 1920s, he can most reasonably be identified as a pragmatic *behaviorist.* His judgment in favor of autonomy or integration in any particular instance depended primarily on utilitarian standards: would acting in one way or another strengthen Jewish roots in America's democracy and also strengthen the Jews' ties to their own religion?

In the 1920s, Marshall often condemned separatist-spirited Jewish projects and proposals on the grounds that their implementation would re-create a "ghetto." Hence, in January 1924, Marshall caustically outlined his "unqualified objections" to an unassuming correspondent from Brooklyn who had floated plans for the establishment of a Jewish university in the city. Melting pot dynamics in higher education, Marshall wrote, foster "mutual understanding, American solidarity, and the elimination of prejudices." Resolutely, Marshall referred to higher education as a vehicle of social empowerment and cultural integration. "Those Jews who have had the opportunity of mingling with non-Jews," he proclaimed, "and especially with older American stock, know what it means to touch shoulders with their fellow students." He added: "A Jewish university would be a glorified ghetto."[133]

This was a forcefully presented defense of the melting pot, and its integrationist spirit appeared to rub against the grain of earlier orientations in Marshall's career, including his support of the Kehillah project. However, Marshall knew that in an era when quotas were in effect on prestigious campuses, the American university was actually a defective melting pot.[134] Tellingly, Marshall admitted in late 1927 that the ideal of fraternal Americanization on the college campus remained elusive.[135] "The sad fact remains that Jewish students at Cornell and at other universities are treated unkindly and uncharitably, sometimes brutally, and always with reserve, by their classmates," he declared. "What is now occurring in the universities of Rumania and Hungary," he added darkly, "is only a more disgraceful form of animosity than that which prevails in our American colleges."[136]

Marshall opposed Jewish integration in public American institutions that had a clear denominational character. He scolded Jews who frequented YMCA (Young Men's Christian Association) facilities.[137] "The YMCA is avowedly evangelical," he declared in May 1920. Any Jew who joined a YMCA facility, he opined, "is lacking in self-respect."[138] This position, some Jewish commentators objected, exaggerated missionary threats and discouraged Jewish integration in the American melting pot. Marshall stood his ground in the YMCA debate, rebuffing suggestions that he had become a Jewish separatist. "I have probably had more association with non-Jews in the course of my life than most Jews in the country," he declared in a 1920 letter. "Anyone who says I don't associate with Gentiles does not know my theories of life."[139] Here, he offered a loose defense of a religious pluralist viewpoint: "There should be no difference between Jew and Gentile in all matters which pertain to good citizenship and public welfare. Each, however, should be free to live his own life socially."[140]

Marshall denied the legitimacy of split political identities, and he consistently affirmed that American Jews owed full political loyalty to their own country. Yet, he acknowledged that non-American political symbols could have powerful emotional resonance among his community of Jews, and he did not disavow the display of Zionist emblems in the American public square. An ambivalent letter to Edwin Kaufman of the Central Jewish Institute reflects Marshall's inward wrestling with this issue of symbols.[141] In principle, ethnic groups in America could not expect the display of their own separate symbols in the public square. "When Abraham Hewitt was mayor of New York, he refused to allow the Irish flag to be displayed at City Hall. He was criticized, but his principle was sound, in principle," reflected Marshall. Moreover, he questioned the historical validity of Jewish symbols. "If we, as Jews, ever had a flag, or a symbol other than the Mogen David," he asserted, "it has disappeared." Despite these reservations stemming from principle and from understandings of historical usage, Marshall gave surprising leeway to symbolic Jewish displays of multiple loyalties. He wrote, "I would have no objection to its [the Jewish flag] being displayed anywhere, so long as it is in juxtaposition with the American flag."[142]

In America's open, rapidly developing society, Jewish leadership has never been doctrinaire, and it is interesting to note that this rule of ideological flexibility applies even to the 1920s period of Marshall law, a period when organized Jewish efforts in the United States were supervised by a uniquely authoritative and moralistic personality. As in the preceding phases of Marshall's career, in the 1920s, there were setbacks and successes for Jewish causes, but he proceeded with an inner sense of satisfaction about the worthiness of the efforts and their long-term contribution toward a viable, flourishing way of life for Jews in America. On all sides of the Jewish community, and also among Gentile Americans who cared deeply about their country's treatment of minority groups, there was little doubt about the vitality of Marshall law: its prosecution, thousands of admirers believed, was good for the Jews and good for Americans. This appreciation was warmly displayed on Marshall's seventieth birthday in December 1926. Over 8,000 colleagues and prominent admirers, from some 350 cities and representing organizations in France, Denmark, Russia, Hungary, Argentina, Canada, and Cuba, signed a moving tribute to Marshall, which was presented to him at his home of 47 East 72nd Street by Cyrus Adler, Julius Rosenwald, David Brown, Herbert and Irving Lehman, Cyrus Sulzberger, and Felix Warburg.[143]

It seemed symbolically appropriate that Samuel Untermyer was not present at this seventieth birthday ceremony but nonetheless made his presence felt in Marshall's home. Fittingly, Untermyer busied himself in his written congratulations to his former law partner with ambivalent words about making money. "His [Marshall's] professional life has not been devoted solely to money-getting," Untermyer wrote. "He has given himself freely to great public causes, without compensation and, at times, [at] his own cost."[144]

The family circle lavished Marshall with affection on this wonderful occasion. As was her knack, Marshall's sister-in-law Beatrice Lowenstein Magnes won everyone's heart at the seventieth birthday celebrations with her high-spirited verse about his career. The comic lines displayed deep insight about the key transitions and moods in Marshall's life, about how rapidly and unexpectedly a Jewish small town lawyer from Syracuse emerged as a national Jewish leader in Manhattan, about his impassioned crusades against anti-Semites, and about the unique mix of Americana and Jewish solidarity that intertwined creatively in Marshall's life work. "Life was simple, life was sweet," penned Beatrice, recalling his Syracuse days, "when Louis lived on Cedar Street." Then he went to New York City:

> Not a single indication, as they pulled out from the station,
> Of the coming agitation, on behalf of immigration;
> Not a hint of aggravation, over Russian abrogation. . . .
> Have you heard how Louis had a scrap with Mr. Dewey?
> How he threw him in Lake Placid, after burning him with acid
> in a vitriolic document whose words reverberate around the state?. . . .
> He bunts and bats and slams and socks
> the ball sails on for blocks and blocks
> it bring home Schiff and Adolph Ochs, and Felix [Warburg] beaming from
> the box.
> Thus at one grand jamboree was formed the mighty JDC.[145]

Marshall's Advocacy and the Rise of Jewish Ethnicity in America

In the politics of Marshall law, he saved the best for last.

Throughout the 1920s, Marshall debated politics with his children, who wondered how his impassioned defenses of disadvantaged minorities and his advocacy of the League of Nations and his opposition to isolationism could remain hinged to the conservative policies of the Republican Party. Often, he matched wits with his son George, the youngest child who for years in the 1920s remained home on 72nd Street while his two older siblings married and started families, and Robert roamed the wilderness lands of America. Marshall enjoyed George's company tremendously; for him, it was bittersweet to watch his and Florence's baby boy become a twenty-one-year-old adult in February 1925. "George certainly is most industrious and conscientious and has stick-to-itiveness which in the long run yields results," the proud father reflected on that occasion.[146]

George had also become the family's outspoken proponent of left-wing causes. "George is a rebel and he questions many existing tendencies and policies," his brother-in-law Jacob Billikopf observed. Referring to the radical pacifism of Judah Magnes, Billikopf believed that George's attitude on social, economic, and political questions is "one which would powerfully appeal to his uncle in Jerusalem."[147] Providing glimpses of the politics of the Marshall household, Billikopf described George debating with his father iconic 1920s events such as the Sacco and Vanzetti case. "The interesting thing about George is that at the dinner table he will express himself pretty freely and carry on arguments with his father quite boldly."[148] Such personal observations convey hints about how Marshall was engaged with youthful liberal idealists of the 1920s, either in agreeable disagreement or in a mode of formal disagreement wherein shared internal values were more important than contrary outward labels of affiliation.

Marshall remained a Republican because a party crossover would have been anathema to his personal code of values. On matters such as party loyalty, he was fixed to ideas of honor that were imbued with nineteenth-century Romanticism. In practical effect, however, decades of give-and-take with New York's Downtown Jews irrevocably altered the brand of patrician conservatism he had transported from Syracuse to Manhattan. Marshall sensed that due to many years of accountability to the Jewish masses of the Lower East Side he had become quite unlike Republican figures of national prominence, long-standing associates like Charles Evans Hughes, who tended to view political matters from a standpoint of aristocratic detachment. As Marshall saw it, Republican leaders like Hughes related to American political matters in the 1920s the way he and his Uptown peers had related to Jewish issues at the turn of the century—although keenly interested in the moral betterment of the masses, their patrician approach too often lacked a ground-level, empathetic grasp of their constituents' needs and desires.

In April 1926, a few months ahead of his seventieth birthday, Marshall spoke on the radio at an occasion honoring the fiftieth anniversary of the founding of the Legal Aid Society. Charles Evans Hughes, who had recently completed his stint as secretary of state, was one of the other speakers, and Marshall privately confessed to consternation about Hughes's "total lack of appreciation of how the work of the Legal Aid Society ought to be carried on." Marshall flinched when Hughes "kept emphasizing the necessity of strong men in the community"; Hughes spoke in a "somewhat patronizing way, for the purpose of preventing the weak from rising against their makers." Appalled, Marshall set aside prepared remarks on "Social Aspects of the Legal Aid Society" and launched into an eloquent disquisition that essentially projected the lessons of his lifetime in Jewish affairs onto the broader landscape of American society and politics. As though he were recalling the gist of his own experiences for Jewish moral reform during the first phase of his New York City career, Marshall insisted that politics was never just about the good works and lofty intentions of well-to-do stewards. Instead, in a democracy, local or national prosperity depended on mutual understanding and constructive give-and-take between the fortunate classes and the hard-working masses. Rejecting the patrician politics of superiority, he advocated the equality of brotherhood. His broadcasted words revealed how liberalism had leavened in a lifetime of diverse experience whose focus had been earnest mediation between Jewish Uptown and Downtown communities. "I called attention" to some facts, Marshall declared in this summary of his impromptu radio rebuttal to Charles Evans Hughes. He listed the facts:

> That in all the centuries there had appeared strong men, but the history of the world indicated that they had made a mess of it . . . that the greatness of a country was not to be measured by the strength and power of fortunate individuals, and that the attitude of the public toward those who were poor and weak should not be that of superiors looking down on inferiors. I expressed the opinion that nothing had ever been said on the subject which carried a greater truth than the words of Leviticus—"If thy brother be waxen poor and his means fail with thee, then thou shalt uphold him." I regarded that the proper spirit was that of brotherhood, not of superiority but of equality, and that the objective that was to be obtained was for brother to help brother through the operation of the principles of justice.[149]

Sixteen years earlier, Hughes had won a seat on the Supreme Court bench that Marshall had coveted (and Hughes would return to the court as chief justice in 1930), but Marshall's impassioned attack on Hughes's "patronizing" brand of Republican politics in this 1926 radio broadcast was not really motivated by personal resentment. Over Haiti, Marshall parted ways with mainstream Republican politics. At the Paris Peace Conference, Marshall read between the lines of sophistic argumentation about national versus individual rights, and drew the simple conclusion that guided his staggeringly devoted work for ethnic minorities in America during the 1920s: treaty provisions or political pronouncements about public policy meant absolutely nothing if they were not rooted in earnest compassion for the downtrodden. When Marshall described to his son Bob why he lashed out against Hughes in the 1926 radio broadcast, he marked the map of his emotional, though not formal, departure from conservative Republican politics at Haiti:

> Incidentally, I felt rather pleased to have had this opportunity to make these comments on the remarks of Judge Hughes, because I had in mind an occasion, several years ago, when as the head of a delegation, I called upon him in Washington, when he was Secretary of State, on behalf of the Haitians, who had been subjected to outrageous treatment by our marines and our government. He was very much irritated at the time and did not have the good sense to conceal the fact. . . . I thought this might possibly be another occasion when I could show to him that lack of warmth and human feeling on the part of a man, however big he may be, is an element of weakness.[150]

In Jewish affairs, the unique reach of Marshall's activities in the last phases of his career is almost self-evident. Largely disorganized before his journey from upstate to Uptown, Jewish affairs organized with increasing differentiation after his death, and today it is impossible to imagine a single American Jewish leader acting as the prime mover, communal spokesman, or key mediator connected concurrently to an urgent matter of communal self-defense (such as the Ford crisis), to the development of a Diaspora welfare organization (the Joint) and of a seminal religious institution (the Jewish Theological Seminary), to the consolidation of relations between American Jewry and Israel, and to many other matters. However, Marshall's unusual position in the 1920s should be seen not only in this context of Jewish affairs but as a thought-provoking event in the ethnic history of the United States.

Examples of intrafaith collaboration and of bridge-building between leaderships of various ethnic communities are hardly lacking in America's past and present. Yet, how often has it happened that a figure who has both titular and substantive prominence in one ethnic community simultaneously becomes the leader of campaigns precious to the lives of other ethnic communities and public interests? Are there parallels to Marshall's situation as an official head of American Jewish affairs in the 1920s who simultaneously took the lead in causes crucial to the future of African Americans, Native Americans, and the environment? How many Americans before or since Louis Marshall have campaigned so energetically within institutions of power for such a richly diverse cluster of minority rights as he did (specifically, in the years stretching between his work on the Jewish delegation of Versailles and his final journey to clinch the Pact of Glory for the Jewish Agency in Switzerland)?

Pondering these questions, we are encouraged to frame Marshall's life as part of a communal process more powerful than his own bountiful personal energy. We should, in fact, see Marshall's late liberalism for what it was: the product of a cohesive historical experience, that is, the rise of Jewish ethnicity in the United States.

Marshall's idealism was bereft of the expedient motivations or a sense of separate detachment that scholars have imposed retroactively on Jewish experience in 1920s America. Marshall did not really fight for African American rights to validate Jewish sociopolitical gains in the country, as Hasia Diner suggested in her groundbreaking study.[151] Nor did he relate to environmental protection or minority rights from a position of affluent nostalgia or patronizing noblesse oblige, as Michael Alexander implied in his study of Jazz Age Jews.[152] Nor was his monumental labor for the protection of human liberty and natural wilderness motored by a need to prove, beyond a shadow of doubt, that Jews were white, as other scholars have argued, in a strained attempt to integrate, anachronistically, various axioms of late twentieth-century America in the country's interwar, 1920s landscape.[153] Finally, in contradistinction to the neoconservative theories of Norman Podhoretz,[154] it is unreasonably tendentious to represent Marshall's evolving liberalism as though it were the fallacious transport of European Jewish concerns to America. Can a lawyer who fought tooth and nail for twenty years to keep the door open to Jewish immigrants, who witnessed his labors for Leo Frank being hoisted up a tree, and who watched millions read anti-Semitic screed in the *Dearborn Independent* be legitimately accused of atavistically importing nineteenth-century European Jewish concerns about anti-Semitism and sociopolitical emancipation to the free landscape of the New World?

Marshall law was about Jewish peoplehood, and it was about America. Rooted ultimately in an emotional sense of Jewish solidarity, Marshall's brand of ethnic politics clearly transcended his own class loyalties as a wealthy Uptown Jewish lawyer affiliated with bankers and manufacturers and his partisan commitments as a Republican in a period when that party's pro-business, isolationist, conservative dynamics became irretrievably entrenched. Louis Marshall fought for minority liberties because he had come to understand that Jews, and all people, could only live where rights were honored. As the decade wore on, so too did distinctions between Jewish rights, black rights, Asian rights, and even the rights of birds and trees appear to wear down. Neither noblesse oblige nor a yearning for whiteness pushed him forward; instead, he was propelled by a vision of the United States, and perhaps the world, as a community of subgroups united by a common commitment to constitutional rights. The experience of Jewish ethnicity drove him to that vision, and American democratic reality enabled him to pursue it. His activity ought not to be seen speculatively, in terms of some supposed psychological motivation such as a search for whiteness, but rather as an expression of what his own personal history, and American Jewish experience generally, had brought him to do. Louis Marshall fought for rights, everywhere. So too did Jews in America for decades to come.

The National Association for the Advancement of Colored People

Charles Edward Russell, a muckraker journalist and one of the five cofounders of the National Association for the Advancement of Colored People (NAACP), took part in the delegation Marshall headed to protest the oppression of Haiti and was inspired by the "power and dignity" of the AJC president's brief for freedom on the Caribbean island. In November 1928, writing as "a humble and inefficient servitor of the NAACP," Russell sent a letter of "profound gratitude" to Marshall. "The services you have contributed to befriend poor colored men driven to death by the madness of racial hatred have been so great and useful that we can never tell you all we owe to you," gushed Russell. "No man has done more for them. I hope the knowledge of that fact is with you."[155]

During the first years of the 1920s, the NAACP worked hard on Arkansas riot litigation, stemming from violent occurrences in that state when African Americans were gunned down, first by white men in a church (on September 30, 1919) and then the following day by another group of white men. This spree of violence continued with the killing of one white man, Clinton Lee; Lee's death was followed by the conviction of five African Americans for murder. Moorfield Storey of Beacon Hill, the head of the NAACP Board of Directors who (it will be recalled) began his career as personal secretary to abolitionist senator Charles Sumner, brought the appeal of the five men, who faced death sentences, to the Supreme Court. Issuing the Supreme Court's ruling in *Moore v. Dempsey*,[156] Oliver Wendell Holmes relied on Marshall's mob rule arguments regarding the Leo Frank affair in *Frank v. Mangum*;[157] quoting from this earlier case, Holmes opined that "if the State, supplying no corrective process, carries into execution a judgment of death or imprisonment based upon a verdict thus produced by mob domination, the State deprives the accused of his life or liberty without due process of law."[158] The Supreme Court upheld Storey's petition for a new trial.

Impressed by this *Moore v. Dempsey* litigation, Marshall congratulated the NAACP. The organization, which had been in contact with Marshall for several years, welcomed his interest and quickly placed him on its board.[159] "I shall be very content to serve," Marshall wrote to Storey in November 1923, accepting the NAACP's invitation. "I agree with you that, now that the Ku Klux Klan is sowing the seeds of discord throughout the country, it is the duty of those who believe in the maintenance of America's best traditions to unite in counteracting that influence."[160]

For the next several years, Marshall became the pivotal figure in NAACP litigation. Between 1913 and 1927, oral arguments in all five NAACP cases heard by the Supreme Court were made by Storey or Marshall, or by the two men together. By the mid-1920s, however, the octogenarian Storey gladly allowed his Jewish counterpart to take the lead in NAACP litigation. In an informative study of white-black attorney cooperation in NAACP work in this pre–Depression era, August Meier and Elliot Rudwick commented that Marshall and Storey were "essentially conservative men" who were driven by "concern with due process, law and order, and the protection of an individual's constitutional rights."[161]

NAACP work in this Storey-Marshall era concentrated on housing discrimination enforced by private agreements and on disenfranchisement issues. On the first issue, residential covenants, hopes had soared during World War I, when the Supreme Court unanimously ruled, in *Buchanan v. Warley*,[162] that a Louisville, Kentucky, ordinance mandating residential segregation violated the Fourteenth Amendment. Storey won what was the first of a "half century of landmark constitutional victories" for the NAACP;[163] the ruling ended residential segregation enforced by municipal or state laws.[164] The expectation of increased housing opportunity for African Americans wrought by court litigation was not easily and quickly met, however. The main stumbling block was that the scope of the Buchanan ruling was limited to legislative segregation, whereas African Americans in the early 1920s were finding themselves excluded from middle-class urban neighborhoods due to privately negotiated residential covenants.

In one case, surveyed in riveting detail by the historian Kevin Boyle, a doctor in Detroit, Ossian Sweet, camped in a newly acquired home in summer 1925 with ten other African Americans to defend his purchase against an enraged white mob; somebody fired shots from Sweet's porch, and Sweet and his confederates faced charges for murder.[165] The Sweet trial became a mid-1920s spectacle, partly because the defense of the accused men was taken up by famed lawyer Clarence Darrow, along with a talented American Jewish associate, Arthur Garfield Hays.

In January 1926, the NAACP tried to use the Sweet case as a lever to persuade the Supreme Court to expand the scope of the ban on housing discrimination. Chief Justice William Howard Taft gaveled the courtroom into session; after giving a brief introduction, Storey surrendered the podium to Marshall. This was a logical succession—Storey was eighty and ill, and Marshall had over twenty years of experience with high-profile public campaigns crafted creatively to challenge exclusion of minorities in private social spheres, dating from the petition he had drafted against Melvil Dewey. This time, however, attacking the constitutionality of private exclusion pacts proved difficult. In what the historian of the Sweet case calls a "flanking attack"[166] (in fact, a tactic structurally similar to the Dewey petition argument), Marshall argued that individuals could do whatever they wanted privately to exclude and segregate, but judges had no authority to enforce these residential covenants because to do so would violate the standard set by the 1917 Buchanan ruling. "The legislature may not segregate," Marshall argued. "The governing body of a city or village may not do so. Can a court, acting as a branch of government, by its mandate bring about segregation without running foul of the [Buchanan] decision? I think not."

The court thought differently. Colleagues, including James Cobb, an African American professor of law at Howard University who had shepherded this case through lower courts, thought that Marshall seemed hesitant in his delivery of arguments about the rectitude of banning private exclusion agreements; also, in a message to NAACP's James Weldon Johnson, Storey correctly prognosticated that the justices would "find some way of dodging the questions on the ground that the court has no jurisdiction in this case."[167]

When such NAACP litigation against residential covenants stalled in the mid-1920s, it seemed that its only tangible, beneficial effects would be the consolidation of resources and work procedures at the civil rights association. Working closely together on housing discrimination issues, Storey and Marshall discussed whether litigation against exclusion covenants in Washington, DC, posed jurisdiction issues or could reasonably fall within the scope of the Buchanan ruling.[168]

Marshall also developed a strong relationship with Cobb, who was a Howard University graduate and had worked for eight years before America's entry in World War I as a special assistant to the US attorney general. Starting in 1923, Cobb worked on housing discrimination cases in the nation's capital; magnanimously, when the time came to persuade the Supreme Court to rule on the litigation, he announced, "I shall be pleased to let Marshall take it."[169] With Storey nominally affiliated with this DC case, *Corrigan and Curtis v. Buckley,* the NAACP announced in 1926 that "two of the most prominent lawyers in the US" would present arguments to the Supreme Court against discriminatory residential covenants in the government's backyard. The court, however, refused to take the case.

On Capitol Hill, some congressmen grumbled about the NAACP's challenge to segregation in Washington, DC. Branding the civil rights association's effort an "invasion," Mississippi senator Byron P. Harrison wondered, "why the business people and the residents of the District remain silent I cannot understand."[170] Withstanding pressures, Marshall and Cobb remained allied. Marshall endorsed

Cobb's nomination as a municipal court judge in Washington, DC (when he took the bench, Cobb was replaced at the NAACP by George E. C. Hayes); both Marshall and Cobb endured racist slurs by legislators like Harrison, who moaned about the pro-integration invasion in Washington by those who "endorse for high office men of the colored race." In a coyly understated refutation of racist allegations concerning NAACP's work on Corrigan and Curtis, and the Cobb nomination, Marshall wrote to Senator William Borah in spring 1926, describing the NAACP's honorable intents and affirming that "it would be most deplorable if the color line were drawn with respect to the holding of office. It would result in infinite harm, besides being fundamentally unjust."[171]

The deferential arrangement whereby the NAACP's black attorneys handled litigation in the lower courts and then prominent white attorneys delivered the same arguments in Supreme Court hearings did not survive after Marshall and Storey passed from the scene. A turning point in the evolution of ethnic politics at the NAACP occurred during the Sweet trial, when the organization's Walter White arrived in Detroit, branded the three black defense attorneys who had been working on the case "shysters," and replaced them with Darrow and Hays, acting in what many regarded a high-handed fashion.[172] After Marshall's death, a new generation of African American attorneys in the 1930s started to wonder why the NAACP should not be organized as a self-defense organization with an ethnic profile comparable to that of the American Jewish Committee. Jesse Heslipwell articulated the thought in an address to a black lawyers convention in 1932:

> It is more apparent each day that men of the type of Moorfield Storey, Louis Marshall, Clarence Darrow and Arthur Garfield Hays are rapidly fading away. They extend to us, negro lawyers, the torch of service, and only we, negro lawyers, can accept it and carry on the battle for justice.[173]

Because of the problem of applying Fourteenth Amendment standards to private agreements, the NAACP's work on residential covenants yielded frustratingly meager results in the 1920s, but Marshall worked hard with the association to protect the breakthrough 1917 Buchanan decision and to continue to challenge residential covenants. Especially in the south, localities sought creative ways to bypass Buchanan in the legislation of racist segregation codes. The city of Richmond, for instance, issued an ordinance making it illegal for a person to take residence in a building occupied by a majority of residents with whom he or she would not be allowed to intermarry. The city disingenuously argued that its segregation ordinance was based not on race or color, but on intermarriage. Part of a biracial NAACP team, Marshall wrote the brief challenging Richmond's ordinance[174] but died before the case reached the Supreme Court. The Supreme Court order in *City of Richmond v. Deans*[175] (May 1930) affirming a lower court's decision to void the city's ordinance was, for Marshall, a posthumous triumph.

The jewel in the NAACP's crown in the 1920s was its litigation challenging black disenfranchisement, and it owed its key victory to Marshall. The organization's litigation challenged white-only primaries in Texas.[176] The NAACP's El Paso branch selected a white title lawyer, Fred Knollenberg, to handle the case, because he was held in esteem by the local African American community. Knollenberg, however, ignored Cobb's briefings on the case, and Storey was too infirm to make it to the Supreme Court hearing; the outcome was disastrous, but fortunately the court granted the NAACP a second chance to state its arguments in *Nixon v. Herndon*.[177] Cobb turned to Marshall for help; scholars of NAACP litigation in the interwar period conclude that Marshall's "masterful presentation" in the Nixon case "probably did much to account for the [Supreme Court's] unanimous decision in March 1927 against the Texas law."[178]

Louis Marshall never exactly shared Oliver Wendell Holmes's faith that modern governance ought to be left to the representative legislative mechanisms of the masses, but their constitutional outlooks dovetailed on key points of twentieth-century law, and Marshall's brief[179] and Holmes's affirmation in *Nixon v. Herndon* represent a particularly stirring note in an ongoing legal duet. Marshall's high-spirited, preachy, and verbosely detailed brief was serenaded into law by Holmes's taciturn, pungently sarcastic opinion.

The 1923 Texas statute prohibiting African Americans from voting in the state's Democratic Party primaries blatantly violated the Fourteenth and Fifteenth Amendments, Marshall argued.[180] Texas claimed that the Fifteenth Amendment's ban on debarring persons the "right to vote" based on race or color applied not to primaries but rather to general elections. Marshall pointed out that racism fueled the Lone Star State's semantic wrangling, since precisely the same language relating to the "right to vote" was utilized in the Nineteenth Amendment, and nobody in Texas or anywhere else was challenging white women's right to vote in party primaries. In 1870, when the Fifteenth Amendment was drafted, primary elections had yet to be instituted in the political landscape, nor were voting machines, the initiative, and the referendum in use. Does anyone really have the "hardihood" to claim that the amendment's reference of the "right to vote" must be limited solely to electoral procedures in use at the time of its adoption? Marshall asked. Obviously enjoying himself, he pointed out that when the words were written for Article I of the Constitution vesting Congress with the right to regulate interstate commerce, "our instrumentalities of commerce were limited to stage coaches and wagons on land, and to sloops, rafts and rowboats on water." The application of Texans' reasoning in the primary election matter to the relevant section in Article I would prohibit Congress from regulating commerce transacted via "steamboats, railroads, aeroplanes, the telegraph, the telephone and the radio."

Using extensive demographic and political data culled from the 1927 *New York World Almanac* regarding gubernatorial and presidential elections in Texas, Marshall showed that politics in the state were decided, for all intents and purposes, in the Democratic Party primaries. General elections in Texas were a mere ritualistic ratification of whichever candidate the Democrats nominated. In this respect, Marshall caustically noted, Texas' argument that the Fifteenth Amendment was being honored because blacks could vote, not in primaries, but in general elections, was a "tragic joke." The offer of a right to vote solely in general elections was a "useless toy, a Dead Sea Apple." For African Americans, the Fifteenth Amendment right to vote and Fourteenth Amendment guarantees of equal protection were being grossly violated in Texas, concluded Marshall. This was the sort of classic, spirited brief that spilled amply from his pen when he knew that common sense, constitutional formulations, and case precedents were on his side.

Holmes issued a savagely curt rebuttal of Texas' arguments. The state had argued that the NAACP's challenge was "political"; Holmes dismissed this objection as "little more than a play upon words." His sarcasm lavished indirect praise upon Marshall's brief and vindicated the NAACP. His resounding two final sentences clinched this litigation as a highlight of the organization's litigation in the 1920s:[181]

> The statute of Texas in the teeth of the prohibitions referred to assumes to forbid negroes to take part in a primary election the importance of which we have indicated, discriminating against them by the distinction of color alone. States may do a great deal of classifying that it is difficult to believe is rational, but there are limits, and it is too clear for extended argument that color cannot be made the basis of a statutory classification affecting the right set up in this case.[182]

The NAACP appreciated this result and also the prodigious voluntary labor Marshall had invested in its work over the decade. In 1930, the civil rights organization launched the Moorfield Storey–Louis Marshall Memorial Campaign. The campaign's literature praised Marshall's work on the "famous Texas White Primary case," and "innumerable other cases testing, affirming, and safeguarding the basic citizenship of the Negro." The NAACP declared, "It is safe to say that in the past few years, not a single case of any constitutional importance has been undertaken that was not either prepared by Mr. Marshall, or else carefully supervised and directed by him."[183]

Native American Rights

Exactly as the history-changing African American rights organization the NAACP was organizing its memorial to Marshall, Native American affairs organizations issued in January 1930 stirring tributes to the "heartiness, passion of determination and swiftness of action" Marshall had displayed for Indian welfare in the country.[184] Marshall's "great service to the Indians' cause was rendered in the final two years of his life," the *American Indian Life Bulletin* recorded. Marshall's briefs and testimony before congressional committees on behalf of Native American causes, this outlet added, "had the quality of a trumpet challenge to the imagination and conscience." In his advocacy, Marshall saw an "oppressed minority, an ancient culture, proscribed yet living on"; he defended members of an "ancient religion" who were "without defined constitutional rights."[185]

In Native American affairs in the 1920s, John Collier represented perhaps the closest counterpart to Marshall's situation as president of the American Jewish Committee. A Columbia University–educated social reformer, Collier founded the American Indian Defense Association in 1923. Five years later, Marshall and his son George met with Collier in Washington and reviewed papers concerning the Middle Rio Grande Conservatory District in New Mexico; Marshall and Collier agreed that the implementation of plans for this district would entail confiscation of property belonging to six Pueblo tribes. Marshall received power of attorney to represent the Pueblo tribes in negotiations with the secretary of the interior.[186] In May 1928, Marshall addressed the commissioner of Indian Affairs and his staff for 180 minutes, and spent ensuing weeks preparing a brief on this issue.[187] "To Mr. Marshall the situation in New Mexico compressed a century of history," the *American Indian Life Bulletin* later noted. "The Pueblos, struggling for life, reminded him of a hundred other tribes which have perished." According to this Native American journal, Marshall "poured time and strength, literally for weeks," on the Pueblo case, in the year before he died.[188]

11

Crimea and Eretz Israel

On May 26, 1924, President Coolidge signed into law the Johnson-Reed immigration act, effectively closing the country's doors to newcomers from Southern and Eastern Europe. Three weeks after America's exit as a haven for indigent or persecuted East European Jews, the Joint Distribution Committee's Executive Committee opted to support Jewish colonization in the Soviet Union.[1] The decision proved to be highly controversial, particularly among Zionists who believed that American Jewish philanthropy ought to give utmost priority to Jewish colonization in Eretz Israel, but the Soviet colonization decision's intrinsic rationale, along with the energetic backing Louis Marshall himself gave to it, has to be seen through the narrowing prism of life options available to world Jewry in the 1920s. The procession of Marshall and Uptown peers from Capitol Hill to Crimea was guided by their own instincts of Jewish solidarity and by the objective circumstances of their time. Once Eastern European Jews could no longer make new lives for themselves in New York City, America's Jewish elite had to think creatively about how to help them survive and make the best of their days somewhere else.

Debates in the 1920s about priorities given to Jewish colonization in one place or the other, the Soviet Union or Eretz Israel, were intricately connected to ongoing issues in global Jewish politics and to Marshall's own orientation toward Zionism and international Jewish issues. Partisans in these debates had their eyes on complex developments in Mandatory Palestine and Soviet Communism that were unlike issues of religion, education, and popular culture relevant to Jewish communal affairs in 1920s America.

Jewish Farm Colonies in the Soviet Union: Origins and Dynamics

The 1918 Constitution of the Russian Republic disenfranchised an entire class of acutely vulnerable persons, the *lishentsy.* Regarded as nonproductive, petit bourgeois elements, the *lishentsy* faced discrimination in spheres of employment, housing, and education. Rights and positive class status could be regained via five years of productive agricultural or industrial labor.[2] Out of some 3 million persons classified as *lishentsy,* Soviet Jews appear to have constituted from one-third[3] to one-half[4] of the total; compared to other ethnonational groups in the new Soviet Union, this was an extraordinarily high figure, and it contributed to the sense that a special "Jewish problem" persisted in Russia after the consolidation of the Soviet Communist regime.

Jewish colonies were on the ground in the Soviet Union before the JDC adopted its "Agro-Joint" project in the mid-1920s. A mixture of miserable overcrowding in the shtetls, anti-Semitism, and privation during the civil war years, and Zionist recruitment and activity in the Hehalutz youth movement had led dozens of Soviet Jews to colonies in Kherson and the Crimean steppe.[5] JDC officials were introduced to conditions in the Soviet Union in 1921 through participation with Herbert Hoover's American Relief Administration (ARA), which responded to calamitous famine in the Ukraine and other regions.[6] James Rosen gained in-the-field experience as a JDC man contracted by the ARA in the Soviet Union.

Rosen had a long life history in Russia. Born into an elite Jewish family in Moscow in 1877, he fled czarist Russia in his mid-twenties due to suspicions of radical activity. In the 1920s, he was an agronomist, with a PhD from the University of Michigan and an international reputation, owing partly to his development of an improved type of rye.[7] In his work with the ARA, Rosen encountered Jewish farmers at Kherson, and from that point his enthusiasm for Jewish farm colonization proved irrepressible.

Rosen's own retrospective understanding of the prodigious JDC farm colonization and relief effort he spearheaded in the Soviet Union remains a mystery, because after World War II he burned a memoir devoted to the subject.[8] Influenced perhaps by the highly divisive arguments sparked by the JDC's Soviet colonization project within American Jewish circles for years after the mid-1920s, historians have reached little agreement about the net benefits and costs of an endeavor indelibly associated with the energies of this one man,[9] but Jonathan Dekel-Chen, the author of the latest, most thorough, survey of the subject, sets the broad parameters of any assessment. Up to the JDC's withdrawal from the project, in 1937–38, more than 150,000 Jews left shtetls to settle on 250 new colonies spread over about 1 million acres of land in Crimea and southern Ukraine.[10] The Joint invested a hefty $17 million in this project, though much of that sum came in the form of loans that were, in fact, repaid.[11]

The Soviet colonization project agitated an ugly dispute with the American Zionists and embroiled the JDC businessmen in an extremely complicated relationship with the Communist regime in the Soviet Union. Memories of the Red Scare had far from receded when Marshall and his group adopted the colonization project, and that left them vulnerable to the charge that they were abetting a revolutionary enemy of American's socioeconomic system. Henry Ford and his *Dearborn Independent* had been trumpeting scurrilous charges about "Jewish Bolshevism" for years, and the JDC embraced the Soviet work *before* Ford publicly recanted, withdrawing his allegations about how an international Jewish conspiracy manipulated the Soviet revolution. In this extremely volatile atmosphere, what exactly were Marshall and his associates expecting in terms of gains that might offset anti-Semitic innuendo and intramural Jewish contentiousness attendant to their policy?

Mainly, Marshall and his JDC peers were motivated by humanitarianism and honor. Nobody on the JDC believed that the colonization work could fully alleviate the suffering of Soviet Jews;[12] at most, it could affect perhaps 10 percent of this population. Nevertheless, such a fraction translated to a rough but constructive life for many thousands of Soviet Jews who faced extinction. As it became clear that other world Jewish organizations, such as the Paris-based Jewish Colonization Association, were not prepared to underwrite large-scale Jewish colonization in the USSR, Marshall grasped that American Jewish honor was at stake. Consistently, he argued that dodging what was, admittedly, a gamble would cost his community its honor. Just months before his death he reiterated this understanding; his strong words gain poignancy when considered in light of developments subsequent to 1929:

> Whenever the fate of hundreds of thousands of our brethren is at stake I shall always be found ready and willing to take the gambler's chance for their sake so long as no better alternative exists. Do not for a moment believe that I am over-optimistic as to the future of Russia. My mind is not blinded. I would rather die fighting to take a chance with Jews than sit in sack cloth and ashes waiting for the blow to descend.[13]

Other motives, expectations, and dynamics supplemented this perception of humanitarian honor. With Rosen taking the lead, the JDC group was able to exploit confusion in the relevant branch of the Soviet bureaucracy, the Committee for the Settlement of Jewish Laborers on the Land (Komzet). Rosen appears to have persuaded Soviet bureaucrats in Moscow that the JDC was the world's leading Jewish organization.[14] At phases, Moscow showed interest in showcasing the Jewish colonies as proof of Communism's creative handling of Jewish issues; JDC executives were aware that such Soviet sensitivity about charges of anti-Semitism provided leverage.[15] In the years before the Great Depression, these Soviet bureaucrats sometimes harbored significantly exaggerated estimates of American Jewry's economic power; disavowals of such estimates made by Agro-Joint delegates could be somewhat cagey.[16] Conversely, Rosen sometimes soft-pedaled discussions in his reports to JDC managers about hardships faced by the Jewish colonists and problems in their relations with neighbors.[17] It remains unclear whether Rosen's affirmations entirely persuaded the JDC men that the promises and signatures of Komzet officials could be trusted—Marshall's letters are open to interpretation on this point.[18] In other words, misinformation on various levels influenced operative decisions in the JDC's Crimea venture.

Yet the JDC decision makers displayed due diligence in efforts to stay as close as possible to the colonies. As happened many times in the 1920s with regard to on-site reviews of an array of aspects of the Soviet Revolution, visitors who saw the Jewish colonists in the Crimea and the Ukraine sent back positive, sometimes glowing, reviews to Marshall and his associates.[19] These reports reinforced JDC inclinations as the colonization policy took shape, and they also validated the impact of investments once they were made; in Marshall's case, these two related functions are exemplified by a laudatory report about the colonization project made to him in 1925 by Henry Moskowitz,[20] a respected social worker, and also by affirmations sent to him in 1929 by his own son James, a lawyer, who had been personally dispatched to Russia by Marshall.[21]

Marshall and his associates hoped that colonies of hard-working, self-sufficient Jewish farmers would impress Soviet officials and Gentile villagers, and thereby ameliorate anti-Semitism in Russia.[22] Whether it was the Jewish colonists' labor or the revolutionary efficiency of the tractors Rosen brought to the project, there is, in fact, evidence that the Jewish colonies "became an example of farming unlike anything else in the USSR."[23] Occasionally, JDC men wondered whether success in the Crimean colonies might even serve an important antidefamation function in the United States. For instance, James Rosenberg's 1927 travelogue, *On the Steppes,* which Marshall edited, indulged in some wishful thinking: "I wish Ford might see the Jewish boys running Ford tractors."[24]

This example of antidefamation hopes being affixed, even in a hypothetically detached way, to the Soviet colonies hints that laden within the JDC work were expectations that somewhat exceeded the purely practical considerations of humanitarian relief. On some levels, it paralleled Zionism in that its backers hoped that its success would remove the onus of the so-called Jewish question. Occasionally, JDC managers were excited by its social engineering potential, implying that the Soviet farm project work would make a new Jewish prototype comparable to the *halutz* pioneer touted by the Zionists as the object of their labors in Eretz Israel. The same James Rosenberg wrote in his travel notebook: "As I look at these bronzed young Jews, the hygienic and eugenic aspect of the work is one of its weightiest assets."[25]

In addition to these social engineering expectations, political implications of the Jewish colonies sometimes excited the JDC men. Before the 1924–25 decision to adopt Rosen's plan, some Soviet officials flirted with ideas of establishing an autonomous Jewish republic near the Black Sea. In fact, Jewish autonomy schemes stirred continuing interest in the Politburo between 1924 and 1926, and some Soviet officials championed such plans through the early 1930s.[26] Marshall did not entirely discount the possibility that the colonies might eventually become the foundation of an autonomous Jewish republic,[27] though this dream cannot be considered a prime motivating factor in his own, or the JDC's, work.[28]

Louis Marshall in the 1920s represented a German-Jewish elite in America that had been keenly interested in Russian affairs for decades. Stretching from Schiff's funding of Japan in its 1905 war with czarist Russia to the famous AJC abrogation campaign, the range of this elite's activities concerning the Jewish situation in the Russian empire and the USSR is remarkable. These two examples, the Russo-Japanese War and abrogation, reflect maneuvers that were designed to change political, economic, and social realities in Russia and in the United States in response to the persecution of Jews in Eastern Europe. Of course, political realities in Russia transformed dramatically in 1917, but both before and after the Bolshevik Revolution, the American Jewish elite experimented with ideas and policies that reflected endless variations of radical confrontation or pragmatic accommodation regarding the Jewish situation in Russia.

The common denominator in all these responses was that, while the opposition to Russian discrimination was authentically and viscerally felt by men like Schiff and Marshall, their actions on the issue were never entirely altruistic. In Jewish parts of New York City, the bridge between Downtown and Uptown typically crossed over Moscow. In the 1920s, Marshall inherited Schiff's situation prior to World War I in the sense that the foremost test of his leadership credibility in the eyes of masses of American Jews, themselves immigrants from Eastern Europe, was his handling of the Russian question.

This being the case, Marshall closely followed developments in Soviet Russia during the first half of the 1920s. His own political sympathies veered toward the liberals who campaigned for the establishment of an orderly constitutional democracy in postwar Russia. During the violent, chaotic civil war of 1919–20, Marshall felt that a White Russian victory would be the best outcome for the Jews of Russia.[29] Yet, as early as November 1920, Marshall confided to his cousin Benjamin Stolz that America's refusal to recognize the Red regime would be counterproductive.[30] At the beginning of the decade, Marshall regularly received appeals from leaders of the Constitutional Democratic Party (Kadets) and the Socialist-Revolutionary Party (SR), which addressed him as the "leader of American Jewry" and insisted that "only the ascendancy of democracy can prevent a wave of White terror and bloody anti-Jewish pogroms in Russia."[31] When Marshall and his JDC associates adopted the Agro-Joint project in the mid-1920s, they implicitly rejected that premise and acknowledged that millions of Jews would have to find the best way to live under Communist rule. This level of adjustment with Soviet realities was stimulated by the fact that Downtown Jews harbored a variety of attitudes toward the Bolshevik Revolution, many of them antagonistic to the grim analyses and forecasts forwarded by constitutional moderates, or monarchists, from the White camp in Russia's civil war.

In 1917, as waves of revolution convulsed Russia, Marshall complied with a request to join the Russian Information Bureau, which circulated anti-Bolshevik materials and campaigned in the name of Russian constitutional democracy. This bureau eventually quartered in the Woolworth Building in Lower Manhattan and recruited, along with Marshall, a number of prominent American "honorary advisers." By June 1922, it closed shop in the absence of any tangible result or hope of having an effect on an entrenched Soviet regime that was surviving Lenin's incapacitation. The most that its director, A. J. Sack, could do in the bureau's farewell to Marshall, and to fellow advisers like Theodore Roosevelt and George Kennan, was to thank them for their "moral help."[32] From Marshall's standpoint of Jewish leadership, millions of Jews in Eastern Europe needed rather more than moral help. And, by the middle of the decade, Marshall knew that history was not on the side of Kadets like Professor Pavel Milyukov, no matter that they remained, in his eyes, sympathetic figures.

To the extent that they were able, world Jewish organizations kept an eye on the humanitarian distress faced by Jews who endured years of political, social, and economic upheaval of civil war and shifting Bolshevik policy in the new USSR.

In the period when the JDC's executive leadership was giving the go-ahead to the Agro-Joint project, this international review effort produced extremely bleak forecasts regarding the future of Jewish life under Soviet rule. Essentially, Marshall and the JDC adopted the Soviet colonization plan after having received, since the end of World War I, a ceaseless stream of information about mass Jewish death and deprivation in Eastern Europe. In retrospect, some details in this stream appear overblown, even hysterical; for instance, at the second Jewish World Relief Conference, held in late August 1924 in Carlsbad, delegates reported that cocaine use had become an "extremely prevalent social calamity" among Jewish children in the Ukraine.[33] However Marshall assessed this or that detail, he could not have ignored the gist of this August 1924 meeting's reports about Jewish children in the Ukraine, which grimly detailed the incidence of tuberculosis, overcrowding, constant malnutrition, and homelessness. This was not information to be received with equanimity. Delegates at this Jewish World Relief Conference spoke apocalyptically about circumstances that "have brought Russian Jewry face to face with the danger of extermination." In Marshall's mind, when the Zionists spoke with great conviction about the need to build up the Yishuv, they were not directly addressing the issues raised by this conference's doomsday report about Soviet Jewish life.

The Zionist–Agro-Joint Dispute

Marshall did not attend the JDC Executive Committee meeting on June 17, 1924, that concluded with a decision to adopt the Soviet Jewish colonization plan.[34] Taking the lead for the project's prospective patrons, Felix Warburg posed broad, leading questions; tackling these queries with detailed, optimistic replies, Rosen dispelled misgivings harbored by the American Jewish elite. He spoke rapturously about how lands in the Ukraine and Crimea are the "best black soil of Russia. . . . There are no more fertile lands anywhere in the US." One-quarter of the 6 million arable acres in the Crimea were available to the Jewish colonization project, Rosen promised. Such descriptions whetted the curiosity of the JDC board, but Warburg spoke for his colleagues when he wondered whether Russian Jews were really fit for farming. "Is it not a fact that if we send people into these colonies who have no experience, we are not helping the situation?" he asked Rosen. The champion of the Soviet Jewish colonies laid such doubts to rest. Jews in Russia, he assured the JDC, had "learned a good deal about farming" in the eleven years that had elapsed since the eruption of World War I. They had no choice because the Soviet Revolution had "driven them out of business."

Experienced reviewers of business propositions, the JDC heads may not have fully shared Rosen's boundless optimism about the likelihood of Jewish farm colonies becoming a genuine success story in Communist Russia. Nevertheless, they clearly viewed his proposition as the most sensible course to take regarding Russian Jewry. America's portals were newly closed to Jewish immigrants. JDC board members generally kept anxieties about the Zionist formula of Jewish statehood to themselves, but they openly distrusted American and world Zionist officials and simply disliked working with them. Jews were not encouraged to run small businesses in what the Soviets fashioned to be a communist idyll, and the businessmen and bankers in America's Jewish elite could not endorse, practically or emotionally, proactive Russian Jewish political or cultural work on behalf of that Marxian idyll. As far as they could see, the only thing left for the Russian Jews was to head to farm colonies. James Rosenberg articulated this lesser-of-all-evils position at the June 1924 JDC meeting, saying "there is no economic outlook for the Jews in Russia, so far as I am aware, unless we can do something along the agricultural lines which Dr. Rosen has recommended." Warburg agreed with this assessment, though he conditioned JDC support to "Dr. Rosen's being on the spot."

By committing a sizeable share of its resources to the Jewish colonies in the Soviet Union, the JDC brushed against the spirit of American foreign policy, since the United States had not diplomatically recognized the Soviet regime, and also challenged Zionist claims about the prerogative of Jewish settlement in Eretz Israel.

As it turned out, the mid-1920s was a time of ideological assertion and improvisation not just for the JDC. Less than a year before the JDC board received Rosen's Crimea pitch with sympathy, the Zionist movement had adopted a resolution that went against the grain of fundamental Jewish nationalist principles. Meeting in Carlsbad in August 1923, the Zionist Congress decided formally that "the Jewish Agency shall, at the earliest possible moment, be extended by the inclusion of those Jewish organizations and associations who are in sympathy with the Palestine Mandate."[35] This was a plan to secure the funds of wealthy "non-Zionist" American Jews who opposed the Jewish statehood formula but who might furnish support for nonpolitical projects in the Yishuv in exchange for some form of involvement in the Jewish Agency, an organization that was formed under the terms of the Mandate to represent the Yishuv in its dealings with the British administration in the country and that the Zionists regarded as the pillar of their Jewish state-in-the-making.

The expanded Jewish Agency plan was, in Zionist terms, a concession of fundamental principles. Years before Theodor Herzl appeared on the scene, Jews in the Pale of Settlement responded in the early 1880s to the convulsive shock of anti-Semitic pogroms by dreaming of a day of secure Jewish autonomy, of what was to become known as "auto-emancipation." Pioneers on the first aliyah waves in the late Ottoman period drew a line in the sand of the Holy Land to distinguish themselves from early groups of pre-Zionist, religious inhabitants whose existence dependent on *halukah,* charity funds provided to them by Jewish communities in the Diaspora. The "New" Yishuv of Zionist colonization would be fully self-sufficient: liberating capable pioneers in the farm communes and new towns of Eretz Israel from humiliating dependence upon foreign largesse was a core tenet of Zionist ideology.[36] By proposing to institutionalize the receipt of American Jewish funds via non-Zionist inclusion on an expanded Jewish Agency, the Zionist movement was stamping a secularized veneer upon what was, in some ways, a revived *halukah* system.

A conservative-minded figure like Marshall might have sensed that lurking beneath the revolutionary bravura of the Zionist movement, the New Yishuv had needs and concerns qualitatively similar to those of pre-Zionist communities in Eretz Israel and of contemporary Jewish communities and colonists outside of Mandatory Palestine. Zionist officials and activists, however, could never have concurred with such an assessment—animated by a singular sense of purpose, they knew that by building the infrastructure of a Jewish state they were doing something Jews had not done in close to 2,000 years.

For all these reasons, none of the parties in the Agro-Joint–Zionist dispute could ever be in a comfort zone. American Jewish capitalists who opposed Soviet Communism on principle decided to fund projects within it; Zionists expanded the Jewish Agency as a way of securing American funds, even though they were opposed on principle to the receipt of Diaspora philanthropy. On both sides of the debate, pragmatism trumped principle, and each side operated out of a deep sense of duty to a needful, deserving Jewish community. With neither side standing on high ideological ground, however, the best each could do was to complain about the other's lowly methods.

Ahead of the Carlsbad conference, Zionist officials drafted plans with the aim of minimizing the political influence non-Zionists might exercise on an expanded Jewish Agency. In late June 1923, Zionist officials in London who were thinking about a half-and-half split between sixty-eight Zionist and non-Zionist members, pointedly tried to narrow the involvement of American Jews. Their proposal offered room to four non-Zionist delegates from Britain, six non-Zionists from the United States, three from Germany, and so on; the plan was to keep American involvement to a minimum.[37]

In the mid-1920s, impassioned Zionists around the world objected that the inclusion of Marshall and his associates on the Jewish Agency was tantamount to an abdication of Zionist self-government. How could a movement dedicated to the ideology of building up an independent Jewish nation in Eretz Israel offer a 50 percent share in its key decision-making processes to Diaspora Jews who harbored fundamental objections to the ideology of Jewish nationalism? Objections to the Jewish Agency expansion plan stemmed from a complicated array of circumstances and motivations, including power politics and ego in the Zionist leadership, anti-capitalist outlooks, and the natural sense of insult felt by various Jewish subgroups. The gist of the objections, however, was accepted, to some extent, by everyone in the Zionist movement (Weizmann included). Why should members of a movement committed to the principle that Jews ought to control their own historical destiny share power with outsiders who disrespected their yearning for national autonomy? The affront threatened the Zionists' cherished sense of independence, and that resource was considered more valuable than any medical clinic or classroom which might be funded by American non-Zionists' money.

In 1924, Jews fleeing anti-Semitism in Poland and Hungary began to stream into the Yishuv, on the fourth aliyah wave of immigration. Unemployment mounted, and Zionist organizations' coffers were emptying. Weizmann pitched the expanded Jewish Agency plan, declaring that the building of Eretz Israel depended on non-Zionist support. Precisely at this moment, Polish Zionist leader Yitzhak Gruenbaum put this chapter of Louis Marshall's career in historical perspective by formulating his objection to the agency in a memorable phrase. "Eretz Israel can wait," Gruenbaum reportedly exclaimed at a spring 1924 Zionist Inner Actions Committee meeting.[38] The rapid development of the Yishuv was not desirable, this phrase implied, if such progress enjoined disavowal of what the Zionists most ardently desired—independent self-sufficiency.

As a leader of the "radical" faction in interwar Polish Zionist politics, Gruenbaum had practical reasons for opposing the agency plan. Reflecting power realities rather than demographics, proposals for non-Zionist participation on the Jewish Agency were blatantly undemocratic. With its population of 3.6 million souls, American Jewry was to receive thirty delegates, whereas Polish Jewry, with a population of 3.7 million, was to receive just ten delegates.[39] In the mid-1920s, some Zionist factions, therefore, opposed Weizmann's expanded agency proposal in the name of democracy; they even floated a more democratic-sounding mechanism, a World Jewish Congress, as a possible alternative to a partnership between Zionists and non-Zionists in an expanded Jewish Agency.

At key points in the mid-1920s, the controversial proposal to partner with Marshall's group dominated worldwide Zionist discussions. The agency plan was the central plank on the agenda of the Thirteenth Zionist Congress in Carlsbad in August 1923, and delegates passionately reviewed alternatives. This gathering concluded with a compromise formula by which a world congress was to convene within three years, but in the meantime, Weizmann was authorized to continue to solicit American non-Zionist funds and participation on various interim councils.[40] From May 1923 onward, a number of Zionist factions, including the Labor Zionists and the religious Mizrahi party, followed a routine of pointedly objecting in principle to the expanded agency plan while proposing alternatives (like the world congress) that everyone knew to be unfeasible. This response pattern implied tacit acceptance of partnership with Marshall's non-Zionists as a necessary evil.

Weizmann, who was embroiled in this period in a legal dispute about his scientific work and also in a marital crisis, had little energy for these debates. Instead of coalition building and patiently proving to Zionist subgroups that nobody really had a better plan to raise crucial funds for the Yishuv, he repeatedly threatened to resign were his proposal for non-Zionist partnership to be rejected. The plan for cooperation with the non-Zionists proved to be a continuing test of Weizmann's leadership in the 1920s; to the end, decisive votes on the issue went Weizmann's way, usually resoundingly, but they never enhanced his credibility and popularity as a leader. While Weizmann spoke eloquently about the benefits to be reaped via an expanded agency, everyone else in the movement seemed to regard doing business with Marshall and his American colleagues as a Faustian bargain. In a critical, late vote on the agency plan conducted by the Zionist Inner Actions Committee in summer 1928, forty-one delegates voted with Weizmann, and only four (two from the revisionist faction, and two from the radical faction) opposed his plan. Yet, the vehemence of complaints about the plan, articulated both during this meeting and in contemporary media outlets, stunned and depressed Weizmann. "Almost everyone is against the Jewish Agency," Weizmann wrote to his wife Vera.[41]

Half a year after the Zionist Congress endorsed at Carlsbad the Jewish Agency expansion plan, Marshall chaired at the Astor Hotel a "non-partisan conference to consider Palestinian problems." This meeting ended with a decision to appoint a committee to study possibilities of non-Zionist involvement in the agency and to confer with the WZO.[42] That committee convened a few months later, on May 4, 1924, at Marshall's home. His old business partner and Keren Hayesod (Palestine Foundation Fund) president Samuel Untermyer took part in the meeting, as did Judge Horace Stern and Lee Frankel, an insurance executive and innovator in areas of Jewish social service; Weizmann was on hand, as was American Zionist leader Louis Lipsky. This gathering corrected any Zionist expectation that wealthy American non-Zionists might surrender funds without demanding a proportional share of representation on an expanded Jewish Agency. The committee recommended that the new agency have 150 members; the split between Zionists and non-Zionists was to be half and half, and 40 percent of the non-Zionist delegates were to be American Jews.

Almost a year passed before Marshall chaired, again at the Astor Hotel (on March 1, 1925) a second "Non-Partisan Conference" on Palestine issues. While he was in no hurry to finalize arrangements for the expanded Jewish Agency, Marshall endeavored in the twelve-month period to win the approval of "prominent men" in Jewish America for the expanded agency scheme, and he also helped promote the Palestine Economic Corporation.[43] Generally suspicious in dealings with Weizmann's associates, Marshall wrangled mildly with Zionist officials about the precise sequence by which the expanded Jewish Agency would take shape.[44]

Nothing in this period softened Marshall's dislike of Soviet Communism (indeed, in early 1925, he castigated Soviet Communism as a "tyranny of absolutism . . . as abhorrent to me as Tsarism"[45]), but he remained drawn to the Crimea colonization project's humanitarian relief potential. During these months, Marshall managed to compartmentalize support for the Soviet Jewish colonization plan and the expanded Jewish Agency scheme. Interestingly, in this interval, nobody noticed any contradiction between the two efforts.

Before the end of 1924, Agro-Joint, represented by Joseph Rosen, ironed out an agreement with Soviet authorities to "Settle Toiling Jews on Land of the Presidium of Nationalities." Under this pact with the Soviet Komzet, the JDC agreed to invest no less than $400,000 during 1924–25 on the Agro-Joint project in the Crimea and Ukraine.[46] Through spring 1925, Marshall and his JDC colleagues received highly optimistic reports about the Jewish colonies' prospects in the USSR. Louis Fischer, an idealistic American Jewish journalist from Philadelphia who had observed Zionist communes firsthand while serving in Palestine with the Jewish Legion during World War I, argued vociferously that Jewish communal farming would work as well in Soviet Russia. In his lengthy report on the "Soil Movement of Jews in Soviet Russia," Fischer recorded that, between 1924 and autumn 1925, 2,000 families would settle in the Jewish colonies at a cost of $500,000 to the JDC. Ten times that amount, or some 100,000 individuals, were motivated to take part in the Jewish colonies, Fischer reported.[47] Marshall himself received Fischer's enthusiastic analysis somewhat coolly.[48] The report is "well written and interesting," Marshall wrote to James Rosenberg, but Fischer had operated on the assumption that political conditions in Russia were settled. In fact, Marshall wrote, "Russian life is constantly on the brink of a volcano." Meantime, American Jews, Marshall believed, had become "completely exhausted by their efforts for the relief of their European brethren from 1914–1922." Marshall at this point professed to being "skeptical" about the advisability of assertively supporting the Soviet colonies project, but his JDC peers were less cautious. In mid-May 1925, JDC members were assured that Fischer's validation of Agro-Joint activity in the USSR "bears the unqualified approval of Dr. Rosen" and is "authoritative."[49]

Dr. Bernard Kahn, the JDC's European director, declared in a report on a summer 1925 visit to the Soviet Union that "the success of the Jewish settlements is real."[50] Thanks to JDC efforts, "the Jewish problem in Russia will be tremendously relieved," he added. Kahn wrote that, together with Rosen, he had engaged in serious discussions with Soviet officials and found them agreeably disposed toward Agro-Joint's work. "With the movement of the Jews into the heretofore little known to them occupation, the land, a historical moment has come of much promise," he declared.

By spring–summer 1925, JDC investment in the Agro-Joint's Soviet venture was significant, reaching $1.3 million for the purchase of farming implements and livestock, and for related expenses.[51] Kahn circulated a confidential memorandum to JDC Executive Committee members in the summer, indicating that the Soviet colonization work for the next three years would require funding of $8.5 million, out of a total investment of $14 million for Jews in Europe. After this mammoth three-year effort, he promised, "Russia and east Europe will have been brought to a point where further help will be needed only to the same degree that it was before the war; further large collections . . . will no longer be necessary."[52]

Meantime, trying to enlist the support of influential, wealthy American Jews for the expanded Jewish Agency plan, Marshall acted as though this ambitious JDC plan for Soviet Jewish colonization did not exist. At the second Non-Partisan Conference (March 1, 1925), he spoke as if Zionism offered an especially compelling solution to the socioeconomic afflictions of European Jewry.[53] "Unfortunately the condition of the Jews in Eastern Europe has not improved," Marshall explained at this second Astor Hotel meeting. On account of the impending Immigration Act of 1924, the Jews of Europe could no longer "look on the US as a haven of refuge." In contrast, in "Palestine the doors have been opened wide," and 2,000 Jews were making new homes in the Yishuv each month. For all its disclaimer references to "those who are unwilling to deal with the [Zionist] subject from a political aspect," Marshall's address was steeped in effusive commitment, as though the inclusion of prominent American Jews on an expanded Jewish Agency would be the fulfillment of an age-old dream.[54] In words that would soon prove to be bitingly ironic, Marshall recalled that "it was for lack of unity that Palestine was destroyed centuries ago" and praised his listeners for their ability to "sink differences for the benefit of a great cause."

After this soaring address, Marshall worked in May 1925 on the minutiae of American Jewish membership on the expanded agency with Weizmann's trusted delegate Leonard Stein. Then, the Fourteenth Zionist Congress, meeting in Vienna, approved the formula of a 150-member Jewish Agency, with 40 percent of the seventy-five non-Zionist seats to be reserved for the Jewish community of the United States.[55] Marshall, however, felt that the Zionist Congress resolutions infringed specific understandings that had arisen in his contacts with Stein, relating (among other things) to the length of delegate terms to the agency.[56] This objection was personal—Marshall's ego was routinely bruised by the Zionists who treated him, he thought, as an "errand boy." It riled Marshall that he had been in Geneva in summer 1925 (to monitor compliance with the Paris peace treaty's minority rights accords), and nobody at the Zionist Congress thought to summon him for consultation about adjustments in the expanded agency plan. Much more significantly, the Zionist Congress at Vienna set the stage for rancorous collision between JDC backers of the Soviet colonization project and American Zionists. Rabbi Stephen Wise fired the first salvo, displaying in his Vienna speech to the congress "unmistakable hostility" to the Agro-Joint project.[57]

Wise's maneuver could not have completely surprised Marshall. As the historian Mark Raider has observed, Marshall and Wise—one the proponent of a cautious, patrician style, the other a free-swinging idealist who "seems to have been constitutionally incapable of accepting the status quo"—were locked in a decades-long contest for leadership of the American Jewish community, dating from the late 1905 dispute about pulpit freedom at Temple Emanu-El.[58] Yet, while he was more than familiar with the capacity of American Jewish leaders to become embroiled in disputes that combined ego and principle, Marshall had believed up to summer 1925 that the Soviet colonization work would be granted immunity by the Zionist rhetoricians, largely because Weizmann, who knew that the largesse of wealthy American Jewish philanthropists was at stake, would hold his associates in line. Two days before his July 4, 1925, voyage to Europe, Marshall wrote a mollifying letter to Weizmann, surveying progress in work on the expanded agency.[59] Despite its accommodating tone, this letter conveyed a clear warning. Commending the American Zionists for not challenging the JDC's Soviet work during the ZOA's twenty-eighth annual convention, held in Washington DC, Marshall added that "it would have been a serious mistake" had the American Zionists attacked Marshall's group for supporting Jewish colonization in the USSR. Were American non-Zionists to garner an impression that the WZO "is indifferent to the fate of Jews in other countries," their "reaction would be deplorable," Marshall explained, threateningly, to Weizmann.

Wise knew about the JDC's plans for the Soviet colonies for weeks and did not murmur a word of criticism about them. On May 18, 1925, Marshall wrote to him that the JDC Executive Committee had voted unanimously to raise approximately $5 million a year for Jewish agricultural work in Soviet Russia.[60] To make matters worse, Marshall met briefly with Wise in Geneva, before the Vienna surprise, and the Free Synagogue rabbi had, to Marshall's mind, agreed "that there was enough money in the US to help all good causes."[61] This discussion had been held in the presence of Judah Magnes, who found himself positioned, as he had in the Emanu-El dispute two decades earlier, somewhere between Marshall's understanding of communal discipline and Wise's independent insistence upon the right to act according to his own sense of right. Magnes's peace-oriented, inclusive Zionist vision was not representative of the Jewish nationalist movement as a whole;[62] in Geneva, Marshall mistakenly believed that his having Magnes by his side, concurring with the JDC position that "the desire to help the Russian people to go upon the land would not injure the Palestinian program,"[63] would broaden Wise's thinking on the matter. Wise's subsequent behavior in Vienna, openly challenging the JDC's investment in Soviet colonization, implied a self-perception that he was a more loyal Zionist than Magnes, even though the latter had resided for several years in Mandatory Palestine and was managing the birth of the Hebrew University of Jerusalem. Wise's self-image as a better Zionist than Magnes, who in 1905 had won the post of Reform rabbi at Emanu-El, would become much more explicit a few months after Marshall's death, when the Free Synagogue rabbi publicly mocked Magnes as an aider and abettor of terrorists for having advocated the formation of a joint Arab-Jewish parliament as a response to the 1929 riots.[64]

In mid-September 1925, the JDC organized in Philadelphia the National Conference of the United Jewish Campaign to finalize arrangements for a three-year $15 million campaign, a third of which would go to the Soviet project. No dissension was anticipated, but from the moment it was convened, Marshall recalled, a "cloudburst" of "violent antagonism" erupted. Philadelphia Zionists had packed the hall.[65] Months later, Marshall still bristled about the "demagogical methods" employed by the Zionist "tricksters" at this Philadelphia meeting.[66] Marshall was harangued. Critics castigated him as a Bolshevik or as the potential murderer of unsuspecting Jews who would be wiped out by pogroms on Soviet farmlands. Others objected that the JDC was investing funds in a country unrecognized by the United States.[67]

This September meeting was held on a sweltering hot day, and Marshall, almost seventy years old, dripped perspiration from head to foot. After minutes of tense banter, he noted that the Fischer report had been sponsored by the American Jewish Congress, under Wise's tutelage and that its contents justified the JDC's investment in the Agro-Joint project. This reference was taken as an insinuation that Wise had suppressed discussion of Fischer's report because its spirit and recommendations ran contrary to the Zionist bid for control of American Jewish philanthropy. Wise challenged Marshall on this point, causing "great excitement."[68] With the meeting reaching a corrosive impasse, Jewish labor leader Joseph Barondess stepped in, acting as (in Marshall's description) a "dove of peace." Under Barondess's direction, the dispute was referred to a committee whose main members were Wise, Felix Warburg, Nathan Straus, and Marshall. On Marshall's invitation, Wise drafted a resolution endorsing the JDC plan for the Soviet Jewish colonies; the resolution's final paragraph, which subsequently spawned more ill feeling, loosely promised that the non-Zionists in Marshall's group would consider the Yishuv's needs in due course. The resolution was adopted by the conference, with just a handful of Zionist diehards, such as Jacob De Haas, voting against it. Marshall, exhausted, left Philadelphia with the belief that the Zionists had been routed, "horse, foot and dragoons."[69]

By and large, the American Jewish community shared Marshall's assessment. For a few weeks, Marshall sparred with the reborn American Jewish Congress about whether the conference resolutions expressly endorsed Jewish "colonization" in the Soviet Union, but this appeared to be mostly semantic quibbling, and Marshall assured the Zionists in the congress that the JDC supported an array of activities in the Yishuv, having disbursed over the years more than $7 million for Palestine.[70] After the Philadelphia conference, the Yiddish press supported Marshall and the JDC. The socialist-inclined *Forward* wrote on September 15 that the JDC plan offering Russian Jews "the opportunity of becoming farmers is not only a material but also a moral gain." This influential Yiddish newspaper predicted that the Agro-Joint work "will be supported by all classes and factions of American Jewry."[71] Elsewhere in the Yiddish press, editorialists opined that Marshall had conceded too much to the Zionists. Whereas Marshall had admitted that there is a "certain element of gambling" in any colonization venture, the risk laden within the Soviet Jewish farm work is "unusually small," insisted *Die Warheit*.[72]

The American Zionists disagreed. Their opposition to the Agro-Joint work reflected American-based rivalries, because Zionists outside of the United States were not uniformly opposed to the JDC venture. Chaim Weizmann kept a relatively mild tone when discussing the Crimean colonies (his own brother Shmuel was deputy chairman of Ozet, the Society for the Settlement of Jewish Toilers on the Land, which worked in concert with Komzet in the Soviet bureaucracy[73]). Also, Arthur Ruppin, a patriarch of Zionist settlement in Eretz Israel, spoke in favor of the Soviet colonies in practical words that bore a resemblance to Marshall's explications on the subject.[74] American Zionists, however, had their reasons to avoid displaying such nonpartisan latitude on the issue. In America, after the 1921 rift between Weizmann and Brandeis, Zionist leaders like Louis Lipsky who remained loyal to Weizmann's mainstream camp were routinely berated for their alleged lack of expertise and discipline and for corrupt, Tammany Hall–type mismanagement.[75] They sought in this mid-1920s debate to turn the tables and to portray the non-Zionists as gamblers who were unwisely investing American Jewish philanthropic funds on the margins, in the unproven Crimea colonization venture. Moreover, they charged, the non-Zionists instantly reneged on promises they made in Philadelphia.

Just weeks after the Philadelphia meeting, American Zionists pointed their arrows at David Brown, a Jewish communal leader from Detroit who after World War I branched out from a lucrative family coal and ice distribution business and emerged as a talented fund-raiser for relief causes relating to Jews and non-Jews in Europe and Asia. Brown had chaired the JDC's national $14 million campaign in 1921, and in 1925 he was tapped to lead the new JDC $15 million initiative. Indignant American Zionists charged that under Brown's watch, the new fund-raising initiative latched exclusively onto the Soviet project; they charged that JDC's publicity materials omitted the last paragraph of the Philadelphia accord, which delineated the non-Zionists' commitment to take the Yishuv's needs into account. Accused of "treason, bad faith and dishonesty,"[76] Brown was pilloried by the American Zionists.

Marshall probably understood that the Zionists' accusations about Brown's double-dealing were emotional payback for years of exaggerated allegations about Zionist duplicity leveled by a triumvirate of anti-Zionists, non-Zionists, and disaffected Zionists in the Brandeis camp. He overlooked the fact that Brown was a caustic individual who enjoyed baiting Zionists like Weizmann and Wise.[77] Pointing to the main moral flaw in American Zionist posturing in this Crimea controversy, Marshall trenchantly observed that the players in his non-Zionist camp had generously supported Yishuv projects over the years, despite their reservations about political Zionism, whereas the Zionists had paid ideological lip service to *gegenwartsarbeit* notions of bolstering Diaspora Jewish life, here and now, but had in practical terms done nothing in support of JDC work for Jewish life outside of Palestine. Marshall was troubled by the way this double standard masked rank ingratitude. His lambasted Detroit friend David Brown, he complained angrily to Chaim Weizmann, had been the state of Michigan's largest contributor to the Zionist Keren Hayesod drive. Only "blackguards" could accuse him of betraying the Yishuv.[78]

A decade after Marshall was put on the defensive during the American Jewish Congress debate by Zionist claims that his Uptown German group was stifling the democratic development of American Jewry, the Zionists in the mid-1920s once again collared him, claiming this time that the Uptown Jews were recklessly redirecting philanthropic funds and jeopardizing the best chance that had been offered in two millennia for the Jews' national revival in their ancestral homeland. In his complicated relationship with Zionism, Marshall repeatedly found himself roped uncomfortably by highly publicized accusations about his alleged abandonment of trusts held sacred by the Downtown masses: the Jews' democratic growth in America and their national rebirth in Eretz Israel.

As he had a decade earlier, Marshall fought back aggressively. He had his own public reputation and private sense of honor to protect, but he also sparred with the Zionists at the insistence of his JDC associates, who complained for months about the Zionists' attacks and at points formally designated Marshall "to hit back" against the them, as a "one-man" JDC committee.[79] Tapping into his lawyerly argumentative skills, Marshall rifled off strongly worded letters to American Zionist leaders. Put on the defensive by the charge that his group was ignoring the Yishuv's development needs, Marshall produced a dizzying list of countercharges.

For instance, in early September 1925, Marshall clarified to ZOA's New England region president, Elihu Stone, that the JDC drive promised no more than $5 million to the Soviet Jewish colonies. The ZOA, wrote Marshall, "overlooks the fact that the Jews of Russia are human beings who have a right to live" and who "have a right to say whether they will live in the lands in which they were born rather than to be subjected to the process of transportation to lands to which they do not desire to be removed."[80] Whipped up in a polemical counteroffensive, Marshall relied on rumors about land speculation in Mandatory Palestine that he had overheard during his summer 1925 trip to Europe and basically accused Zionists of being Holy Land real estate shysters. "A number of very ambitious Zionists are speculating in land in Palestine, with the result that they are driving up prices . . . the spirit of Miami and of Far Rockaway has been introduced upon the sacred soil of Palestine by men whom I can only speak of as traitors to a great cause."[81] Such advocacy was not Marshall's most judicious moment. It led him to endorsements of putative Soviet munificence (the Russians were offering 3 million acres of free land to the Jews, in contrast to the "Far Rockaway" fleecing of colonization work in the Yishuv) that were ill-suited to his general point of view.

These polemics reached a low point when Marshall accused one rabbi, George Fox, of Chicago's South Shore Temple, of being a *moser,* a disloyal miscreant who betrayed Jewish well-being. Fox's letter to Secretary of State Frank Kellogg, written just before the Philadelphia conference, shocked Marshall, not without reason. The letter was not just an innocent inquiry about the legal propriety of supporting a Jewish project in a country with which the United States had not established diplomatic relations. Fox appeared to be counseling the US State Department about a folly undertaken by Marshall and his group. "I feel that should 15 million US dollars be invested in this agricultural experiment, that a great benefit would redound to the Soviet Republics," Fox opined, adding that it was "both unwise and inexpedient" for the JDC to conduct negotiations with the Soviet Union.[82] Kellogg replied to Fox a week later, saying neutrally that the

State Department would not comment on the propriety of any American Jewish undertaking in the Soviet Union.[83]

This response satisfactorily established that the JDC project was not in violation of any American law or policy, but Marshall was absolutely livid about the rabbi's action. Not yet finished wiping the sweat from his brow after the scorching Philadelphia meeting, Marshall fired off a letter to Rabbi Fox on September 18 that compared him to Iago, Henry Ford, and a *moser*. Marshall emphasized that the JDC had never taken a step in Russia in the absence of coordination with responsible US officials. Marshall himself had met frequently with Kellogg and his predecessor, Charles Evans Hughes, and ascertained that they "saw no impropriety in trying to help the unfortunate people of Russia." He accused Fox of harboring a self-defeating double standard: what sort of morality could endorse a situation whereby "American citizens may engage in trade in Russia, but American Jews may not come to the rescue of their Russian brethren who for ten years have been undergoing the tortures of hell?" Not a dollar of JDC money was to go into the coffers of the Soviet government, Marshall explained; the philanthropy's exclusive target was the Jewish colonies. By suggesting to the secretary of state that Marshall and the JDC were doing anything but rightfully supporting Soviet Jews, Rabbi Fox had "committed an offense against your [Fox's] people which can never be pardoned."[84]

Marshall did not pull punches, but by the end of the decade, he and the JDC implicitly acknowledged that this public showdown with the Zionists over Crimea was counterproductive. To put an end to the mudslinging as well as to the unpredictability and instability of fund-raising campaigns that depended upon hundreds of small donors, the JDC group formed the American Society for Jewish Farm Settlements in Russia (ASJFSR). In view of the acrimony of the mid-decade debates, this strategic Uptown fund-raising decision to rely on large, multiyear donations from a few select donors seemed sensible.[85] Marshall himself donated $100,000 to the ASJFSR; Felix Warburg gave $1 million.[86] By the end of the 1920s, Rosenwald had taken the lead in the Soviet colonization philanthropy, subscribing $5 million to the project on the condition that an equivalent, matching sum be raised in a ten-million-dollar drive. Rosen kept pressuring the JDC, declaring that even Rosenwald's bountiful offer was not enough; "we could accomplish a great deal more, with adequate means," Rosen affirmed.[87]

The Marshall-Weizmann Negotiations

The ASJFSR was an ingenious, late application of Uptown Jewry's traditional preference to carry out good works discreetly, behind the scenes, but the mid-1920s debate about Agro-Joint work in the Ukraine and Crimea could never have been stifled by artful fund-raising techniques or by other public debate avoidance devices. The daily welfare of hundreds of thousands of Jews was at stake, but in the end, the debate was not about practicalities and reflected instead the differing emotional priorities of Jewish groups. Though historians have routinely detached the Crimea colonization controversy from the raucous Brandeis-Weizmann split that occurred within the Zionist movement at the beginning of the decade, the itemized lists of demands, proposals, and conditions that circulated in these debates (consolidation or pluralism in fund-raising procedures, the use of expert commissions to validate various action proposals, the participation of wealthy or influential Jews who rejected political Zionist formulas) are strikingly similar. Links between them derived from one abiding emotional dilemma: ought endeavors in Eretz Israel be the central prerogative in modern Jewish experience?

In his clashes with Louis Brandeis and Louis Marshall during the decade, Weizmann astutely came to realize that the formal affiliations of these two rivals as Zionists or non-Zionists were essentially meaningless. Whatever they called themselves, American Jews would never unconditionally affirm the centrality of Eretz Israel endeavors. This being the case, Weizmann gravitated naturally throughout the decade toward an alliance with the non-Zionist Marshall, because it was simply too confusing to deal with important American Jews like Brandeis who called themselves Zionists but who shared their community's conviction about the bountiful uniqueness of Jewish experience in America. In a later period, it bears mention, Weizmann's successor and Israel's first prime minister, David Ben-Gurion, traversed the same ideological journey after the state's establishment in 1948, deciding that it was more usefully expedient to deal with Marshall's successors, leaders of the traditionally "non-Zionist" American Jewish Committee, than to deal with blue-blooded American Zionists like Abba Hillel Silver.[88]

At the height of the Crimean controversy, Weizmann dodged the mudslinging. In May 1926, he attested that during the past year he had not made a single public utterance about the Agro-Joint work.[89] Yet when he informed Marshall that he kept a "perfectly unbiased and open mind" about JDC's priorities, Weizmann was prevaricating. Privately, he accused Marshall of acting on behalf of the Soviet colonization venture on the basis of incorrect information. "I am in a position to get news about this [Crimea] experiment very often," the Zionist leader wrote to Marshall, adding that the empirical evidence about Jewish farm colonies in the Soviet Union does not warrant "the excessive optimism" of Rosen, Brown, and other advocates of the enterprise.[90] Weizmann chided Marshall for his and his JDC colleagues' "apparent indifference . . . with regard to Palestine." Lauding the virtues of town and country Zionist settlement efforts in Mandatory

Palestine, Weizmann highlighted the Petach Tikvah colony, where 8,000 residents were leading a "clean, healthy open-air Jewish life, in peace with themselves and their neighbors." Opportunities to acquire 120,000 dunams of land in the Petach Tikvah district were being lost, Weizmann charged. His point was clear. Instead of harnessing American Jewish resources to develop this hinterland in a way that "would place Jaffa and Tel Aviv on an unshakeable foundation," Marshall was gambling precious funds on a dubious Soviet scheme. Beneath the diplomatic varnish of his dealings with American Jewry's most powerful figure in the Roaring Twenties, Weizmann was never able to conceal genuinely felt consternation about Marshall's decision to sanction the Soviet excursion at a time when the Zionist movement was "on the road to establishing a productive, great Jewish community in Palestine."[91]

Marshall obviously discerned that Weizmann's attitude toward the Crimean work was fundamentally negative and laced with antagonistic propositions about Jewish duty and responsibility. Now that there was no American solution for the settlement of disadvantaged or persecuted overseas Jewish communities, Marshall could no longer imagine that debates about Jewish settlement initiatives around the world had a moot academic dimension—hundreds of thousands of Jewish immigrants would no longer stream into New York at a time when Zionists and Bundists and Marxists argued about the alternative merits of minority rights in Eastern Europe or in autonomous colonies in that region or in Palestine. Thus, for Marshall, the Agro-Joint debate combined honor and substance, and he locked horns with his Zionist interlocutors with a vehemence unusual even when measured by his own most scalding standards. He felt that his lifelong commitment to Jewish welfare was not regarded by the Zionists for what it was; instead, the Zionists regarded his lifework instrumentally, as a component to be exploited for its fund-raising potential.

Weizmann had betrayed him by allowing his Zionist epigones to treat his and the JDC's work with such rank disrespect. "I may say, but this is in confidence, that I feel very much disappointed by Dr. Weizmann's failure to assert his authority and prevent these outrages," Marshall fumed in a revealing personal letter to his brother-in-law, Judah Magnes.[92] In an indicting, long letter to Weizmann, Marshall was scarcely more circumspect.[93] After reviewing both his own years of work on behalf of broad Zionist causes, starting with his having induced the American Jewish Committee to support the Balfour Declaration, and the sequence of events and mishaps in his dealings with Zionists about fund-raising procedures that exploded in the miserable turbulence of the Philadelphia conference for the United Jewish Campaign, Marshall testified that "in my long experience I have never listened to such manifestations of violent hatred, such imputations upon the honor and good faith of men who had gathered for benevolent purposes," as those expressed at the ill-fated meeting in the city of brotherly love. Citing his grievances about the insults endured by himself and JDC colleagues like Brown and Rosenwald, Marshall was essentially objecting to how the American Zionist movement had co-opted Downtown Jewish populism, transposing familiar rhetoric about the cultural worthlessness of fabulously wealthy Uptown philanthropists onto what should have been a substantive and practical discussion about Jewish settlement initiatives.

Marshall could never forgive Stephen Wise for enhancing his popularity by rehashing demagogically familiar Downtown sentiments at the expense of the welfare, or even survival, of many thousands of Soviet Jews. "Dr. Wise, in a speech made at Springfield, Mass., said that one Bialik was worth more than a thousand Felix Warburgs, amid tumultuous applause from the audience," Marshall recounted to Weizmann as part of his copious roster of "slanderous and libelous charges" leveled by the Zionists.[94]

Marshall's indictment of the Zionists concentrated on their loose regard for scrupulous professional business procedures. Here, at the incendiary apex of the Agro-Joint controversy, Marshall was saying precisely what Brandeis had said during his calamitous clash with Weizmann a few years before: with their "Eastern" mentality, the Zionists preyed upon Jewish emotional attachments to Eretz Israel in a manner that belied the professional standards and internalized sense of public accountability characteristic of the "Western" experience of American Jews. As part of his blistering list of Zionist abuses at the time of the Crimea controversy, Marshall ridiculed a Zionist Organization of America campaign to raise funds for a 70,000-tree forest in Palestine at a cost of $1.50 a tree. He explained to Weizmann that he asked his son Robert, then an employee of the US Forest Service, to investigate how much it would really cost to transport and grow trees in Palestine. The answer was one cent or one and a half cents per tree. "Just let that fact sink in," Marshall berated Weizmann and his fellow Zionists. "It affords an illustration of the methods resorted to for the exploitation of the public."[95]

In actual fact, Marshall jousted with the Zionists on the Crimean battlefield out of burning personal resentment. For twenty years, since the formation of the American Jewish Committee was sparked by lively debate about community stewardship versus community democratization, Marshall had given considerable thought to the issue of to what extent power of the purse could legitimately mandate forms of control or influence in the Jewish world. As his comments at the time of the AJC's formation suggest, Marshall was more of a moderate about perceived choices between stewardship and democratization than his Uptown reputation indicates. More than had ever happened before or could conceivably occur again, American Jewish communal power was concentrated in the hands of one man during the period of Marshall law in the 1920s. Perhaps paradoxically, that leader was a democratic realist who understood that authority and power in the community must ultimately rest with all its members. Marshall believed that the transition from stewardship to other models of community power would be gradual and orderly. The Crimean controversy and the concurrent discussions of non-Zionist involvement on an expanded Jewish Agency alarmed him, because they appeared to convert this gradual, orderly transition into a complete farce.

As far as Marshall was concerned, the blatant disrespect exhibited by the Zionists toward JDC members involved in the Agro-Joint project was unpardonable. It betokened the Zionists' unwillingness to regard the non-Zionists as full and equal members on the Jewish Agency. "In plain language, the non-Zionists now believe that all that is desired of them is to raise money, and that in all other respects they will be totally ignored," Marshall candidly explained to Weizmann.[96] Marshall's elaboration of this point in a confidential, July 1926 letter to Magnes[97] throws historical perspective on the status of Zionist activity in America in the interwar period.

At the end of the decade, torturously labyrinthine negotiations led to the inclusion of Marshall's non-Zionist camp on the Jewish Agency under the terms of an agreement called at the time, with tremendous euphemistic flourish, the Pact of Glory (the sobriquet reflects a pattern in Jewish experience by which loftiness in the naming of a Jewish institution or agreement stands in inverse proportion to the intensity of the bickering that precedes its establishment). Analyzing sporadic American Jewish responses to the crisis of Arab rioting and uprising in Mandatory Palestine immediately after Marshall's death, historians such as Naomi Cohen have upbraided elite American Jewish stewards for apathy that accompanied, and presumably preceded, the 1929 troubles.[98] However, it was not really disinterest but rather long-standing dilemmas about community control and power that precluded a more effective consolidation of American Jewish energy and resources, heading toward the new era of Jewish experience that was heralded by the late summer 1929 riots in Palestine and the subsequent Great Depression.

The Pact of Glory was never anything of the sort. No viable wedding of non-Zionist and Zionist orientations could ever have been arranged in the 1920s. Marshall never understood the pact as anything other than a marriage to minimize the inconvenience of continued public rankling with the Zionists. His group operated on principles of Jewish duty and noblesse oblige, believing that its considerable assets imposed a writ for, and the burden of, responsible communal leadership. In contrast, the Zionists (at least as Marshall understood it) wanted to take Uptown Jewry's money and run. Marshall understood the Jewish Agency partnership negotiations as a ruse, and he acutely resented playing in them the role of the fall guy. In fact, it is difficult to find in Marshall's career a more emotionally inglorious moment than the lead up to his endorsement of the Pact of Glory. The rancor of the Jews' Crimean War soiled everything. Marshall revealed his feelings to Magnes:

> So far as the Jewish Agency is concerned, I am satisfied that there was never any intention on the part of the Zionist organization to do anything else but to fool us into the belief that they would lay aside their alleged monopoly of Palestine. God knows that I have never had the slightest desire of being a member of the Agency. I have enough to do without wasting time in discussion with a lot of impractical theorists or tricky politicians. But I did hope, for the sake of Palestine, that the Zionist Organization, which I regard as an incubus, would lose its hold. They, however, thought that they could commit us at once into joining the Agency, selecting our representative, and readily accepting any conditions that they might impose, [on us] in the meantime collecting for them money which they preferred not to collect.[99]

Marshall's anger at the Zionists in this period seemed unlikely to be tamed. Judge Julian Mack, possessor of a cordial and judicious character, and also of substantive experience mediating stormy disputes connected to the Zionist movement, offered in the summer of 1926 to play peacemaker between Marshall and Weizmann. Marshall demurred, telling Mack that the controversy was not a "squabble between two men" but rather "a matter relating to great principles." As a leading member of the Brandeis group, which five years earlier had marched out of the Zionist movement as a result of disagreements with Weizmann, Mack had heard this refrain before. Marshall, for his part, felt that the American Zionist leadership had intimidated even authoritative figures like Mack during the Crimea controversy. Privately, Mack conceded to Marshall that he accepted the facts conveyed in Louis Fischer's report about the Soviet colonies and hinted that he supported the Agro-Joint venture. Marshall was "hurt" by Mack's reticence about this perspective in public.[100]

After fielding Marshall's adamant, detailed complaints, Weizmann feared that any engaged response to them would merely prompt further rounds of rhetorical pyrotechnics. In May 1926, he consulted with Marshall's associate Cyrus Adler and sent Marshall perfunctory replies, pledging to "use whatever influence I possess to straighten things out" and affirming that "we have reached a stage now where none of us can afford to indulge in recriminations."[101] These wan utterances had little effect. Marshall demanded public apologies for insults hurled at the JDC and effective steps to stop the damage that, in his view, the American Zionists had caused to the United Jewish Campaign. "Those who were prepared wholeheartedly to participate in the Jewish Agency have had cold water dashed upon their enthusiasm," he scolded Weizmann. An attitude of contrition was owed toward "those who, without the slightest self-interest, have been seeking to help eight million Jews of Eastern Europe."[102] Marshall was unyielding; Felix Warburg and Irving Lehman interceded and attempted to persuade him to appear with Weizmann in public,[103] but Marshall insisted that no cooperation with the Zionists would be possible without an apology.

Weizmann, whose spirits rose in this period after a visit to Eretz Israel and the successful settlement of a worrisome legal action about his research contribution to the production of acetone, was understandably annoyed and humiliated by Marshall's demand. By casting Weizmann and his fellow Zionists in the role of antagonists who obstructed the JDC's campaign for the welfare of masses of East European Jews, Marshall contributed in these low moments toward an ugly process of polarization in Jewish politics. It is no tribute to the fractiousness of this JDC-Zionist debate about Crimea that half a year before Marshall arranged Henry Ford's historic apology for his *Dearborn Independent*'s anti-Semitic campaign, he presided over a sackcloth and ashes apology tendered by the head of the World Zionist Organization. In summer 1927, Marshall dictated Ford's apology to the car manufacturer's proxies; half a year earlier, Weizmann conferred with Marshall about the wording of the Zionist apology and then finalized the document in consultation with heads of the New York UPA (United Palestine Appeal) campaign, Judge Otto Rosalsky and Judge Henry Dannenbaum.[104] Strained and inelegant on some levels, this comparison to the Ford apology underscores the substantive authority commanded by Marshall law in the 1920s—both the Zionists and the anti-Semites had to reckon with the Jewish interests and sensitivities that Louis Marshall represented.

Seen in historical perspective, an equally striking aspect of Marshall law is that in the Israel-America context, it long outlasted its namesake. The way in which Chaim Weizmann was forced to swallow his pride and to soft-pedal his movement's deeply felt objections to the Agro-Joint work in the Soviet Union in order to obtain precious funds from non-Zionist American Jews adumbrates the well-known 1950 episode in which Israel's prime minister David Ben-Gurion was forced to recant publicly his deeply felt belief that thousands of young American Jews ought to make their lives in the new Jewish state and to issue declarative statements to a later-day American Jewish Committee head, Jacob Blaustein, about how American Jews do not live in *galut* (exile) in order to obtain precious American Jewish funds for Israel.[105] In his 1927 consultation and correspondence with Marshall, Weizmann's ideological retreats centered on Zionist recognition of American Jews' right not to accord absolute primacy to Jewish colonization in Eretz Israel; this ideological surrender parallels Ben-Gurion's concessions in the 1950 Blaustein correspondence. The enactment of Marshall law in this context followed a clear pattern: for generations, elite American Jews withheld their much-sought-after resources until they were satisfied that the founders of the Jewish state in Eretz Israel fully recognized the vitality of Jewish experience on other continents. The power of the purse was used by American Jewish leaders to ensure that Zion would never be rebuilt unless its makers paid tribute to a pluralism that was never part of their own pioneering ideology.

The Joint Palestine Survey Commission

Eventually Weizmann came up with a device that brought an end to a dispute that had left the Zionists and non-Zionists emotionally exhausted and that had jeopardized the credibility of their fund-raising efforts. In late 1926, in a meeting with Felix Warburg, Marshall, Irving Lehman, and Herbert Lehman, Weizmann improvised, knowing that Warburg had proposed at a recent JDC meeting that Joseph Rosen be sent to Eretz Israel to survey possibilities for American Jewish investment via the Palestine Economic Corporation.[106] Weizmann suggested that an impartial commission of laypeople and experts be established to compose a ten-year development plan for the Yishuv. Such a commission would "satisfy the world at large that conservative, constructive ideas are the only guiding principles for Palestine."[107] Meeting participants received this proposal with sympathy. Weizmann asked Warburg to serve as one of the commissioners, but this appeal was politely rejected. Marshall agreed to work with Weizmann to sort out guidelines for the commission.

From the inception of its involvement with the Yishuv in the Mandatory period, American Jews had believed that Eretz Israel required expert scrutiny. Reliance on professional, expert research and management was an article of faith in American Progressive politics, and the most authoritative Progressive figure on the American Zionist landscape, Louis Brandeis, conceptualized the present and future well-being of the Jewish national home in terms of scientific understanding and effort. For European Zionists who focused on spiritual and cultural aspects of the nationalist movement, Brandeis's fixation on mosquitoes, quinine, and malaria was somewhat notorious. From the start of the 1920s, however, Yishuv-based and European Zionists were forced to humor the American Zionist's predilection for expert surveys of agricultural, educational, and economic aspects of Mandatory Palestine. Typically, the Zionist movement extracted useful technical information conveyed in reports produced by committees of experts and ignored the reports' underlying social philosophy, which typically favored free markets, individual ownership of agricultural resources, and other tenets of American capitalism.[108]

By the late 1920s, Marshall, a meticulous researcher of evidence in any case he adopted and advocated, might have been able to discern that the dynamics generated by the application of rational expert surveys on the infinitely emotive landscape of Eretz Israel were inconclusive. The most important precedent was a three-man panel of experts commissioned in autumn 1920 to review the desirability of the financial and administrative "reorganization" of the quasi-governmental body (the Zionist Commission) in operation in the Yishuv at the time.[109] After it arrived in Palestine in November 1920, this reorganization committee, which included a competent American Zionist (Robert Szold, an attorney who had worked for the US government during WWI), transmitted a mixed message. It accused the acting Zionist Commission officials, especially the forceful Russian Zionist leader Menachem Ussischkin, of impetuous and reckless economic management; for Brandeis and his followers, the Zionist movement's purchase at this time of 60,000 dunams of farmland in the Jezreel Valley exemplified a hazardous tendency to act on *halutz* pioneering dreams in the absence of actual budgetary resources. Instead of imposing a kind of scientific sovereignty on the ideologically contentious nationalist movement, the activity of this 1920 reorganization panel actually aggravated intramural squabbling in the Zionist movement after Brandeis and others incorporated the reorganization panel's findings in their fateful attack on perceived mismanagement wrought by Weizmann and his "East" European camp.

The 1920 reorganization committee's work pointed to the difficulty of maintaining a consistent scientific viewpoint under the emotionally stormy and objectively challenging circumstances connected to the absorption of thousands of Jewish immigrants in an underdeveloped and war-scarred locale. The reorganization group raised hackles in the Yishuv when it proposed slashing its education budget in half. Concurrently, undermining their reputation as "Western" advocates of careful, thrifty management, these 1920 visiting experts frantically sent cables to Zionist colleagues in London, importuning them to send urgently whatever cash reserves were at hand to stave off ruin in the embryonic Jewish national home.[110]

In view of such precedents, Marshall could not realistically have perceived an experts' survey as a substantive cure for the ideological tensions and power struggles that had been surfacing on the road to an expanded Jewish Agency. Far from that, the survey idea was an expedient palliative whose purpose was to reduce temporarily the feverishness of the Crimea or Eretz Israel colonization debate in the mid-1920s. Practically, Marshall understood that his fellow non-Zionists in the 1920s tended to project principles of business investment into the domain of philanthropy, and so it made sense to them that the fund-raising responsibilities incurred under a newly arranged and expanded Jewish Agency should be supported by a thorough examination of what needed to be done and prioritized in the Yishuv. Overlooking past examples of the politicization of scientific survey and management in Palestine, they headed toward the Pact of Glory thinking about Zionist colonization as an investment dossier in need of sound presentation.

The acceptance of the expert commission mechanism formally brought the Crimean controversy to a close. On behalf of the United Jewish Campaign, David Brown issued a statement in January 1927 hailing a "momentous exchange of letters" between Marshall and Weizmann.[111] He was referring to a missive sent by Weizmann on January 13, which underscored that the "most imperative need just now is for Sholom, peace, among all the forces of American Jewry."[112] Weizmann pledged respect for pluralism in the Jewish world ("I am urging upon all Zionists the importance of realizing that every Jew has the right to his own opinions as to what is needful for the good of Jewry"). In his reply to Weizmann, Marshall observed that "bitter partisanship" of the preceding year and a half had "threatened serious impairment to those outstanding causes cherished by all of us."[113] He accepted Weizmann's olive branch, viewing it as "convincing proof that strife has ceased in the ranks of American Jewry."

"I am ready to forget the past," Marshall declared to Sears Roebuck magnate Julius Rosenwald.[114] The rancor, he hoped, was gone, and it was time to reinforce the credibility of partnership on the Jewish Agency in the eyes of powerful non-Zionists like Rosenwald, whose objections to Jewish nationalism combined critical perceptions of the character of Zionist leaders and deeply rooted fears about the political implications of their cause. Some members of the Zionist organization were guilty of "fanaticism," Marshall explained to Rosenwald, but "the rank and file of the Zionists are worthy, honorable and conscientious." By sitting on the Jewish Agency with the Zionists, Marshall and his comrades would not be acknowledging that history was on their side. "There is not the slightest chance that there will ever be a Jewish state," Marshall declared in this 1927 letter. He asked Rosenwald to contribute to the UPA campaign in Chicago, headed by Judge Harry Fisher.

Rosenwald was never an easy target for fund-raising solicitations regarding the Yishuv. At this interval, Marshall was willing to appeal to such skeptical philanthropists due to dire reports he had received about swelling unemployment in Eretz Israel. During the first half of 1927, about one-third of the workers in the country were looking for jobs; construction was the most decimated branch.[115] Early in the year, Marshall confided in a private letter that he had known about unemployment conditions for some time. "Should a collapse occur," he reflected, the Jewish colonists in the Holy Land "would never be able to survive the consequences of the disillusionment that would follow."[116]

Though the situation in Palestine was alarming, Marshall insisted that until the fact-finding survey and all other procedures inherent in the establishment of the Jewish Agency were completed, he could not go full throttle in a campaign to support the Yishuv. Desperate for funds, Weizmann prodded Marshall and Felix Warburg for months in 1927, asking them to expedite all the survey's organizational details so that a full-blown philanthropic campaign could be launched. Marshall balked. Until the survey was completed and reviewed, his colleagues would not respond freely to such a campaign, fearing that they were being duped.[117]

Marshall lobbied in spring 1927 for suitable American participation on the commission of experts. Hardly concealing his suspicions, he negotiated with Weizmann's assistant Leonard Stein; haplessly, Stein tried to mediate between Marshall's perspective and that of Sir Alfred Mond, the British industrialist and president of Haifa's Technion, who insisted that German representation on the expert panel was crucial.[118] Marshall demanded that Mond not be awarded full chairmanship of the commission; under a compromise formula, Lee Frankel, whose professional pedigree featured a stint on the Ellis Island Commission and, more recently, chairmanship of the National Health Council, was appointed in March 1927 as American co-chairman of the Palestine commission.[119] Even the name of the survey team was negotiated, with Marshall accepting Stein's suggestion that Non-Partisan Palestine Commission be replaced by Joint Palestine Survey Commission.[120] Bearing in mind past controversies generated by the activity of visiting experts, Weizmann and Stein implored Marshall to keep the Yishuv's educational system outside the jurisdiction of the survey. Proposals for fields to be surveyed focused on technical, or bread-and-butter issues—climate, demography, labor wages and working conditions, public finance, the public debt, and taxation.

Throughout these discussions, none of the sides evinced a desire to examine Arab-Jewish relations and their potential to disrupt Zionist settlement work in Mandatory Palestine. Poignantly, the issue that (after the 1929 unrest) came to dominate all discussion of Zionism and pre-state Israel was submerged murkily in the documents that outlined the parameters and focal points of the survey (these documents referred generically to "social and race problems—charities and social services, dependency and delinquency, insurance, races and the race problem, anthropometry").[121]

As far as Marshall was concerned, financial management, not Arab hostility, posed the main challenge to Zionist viability in Eretz Israel. When he wrote to Weizmann in May 1927,[122] the Zionist leader undoubtedly heard echoes of the perspective Brandeis had articulated seven years before. Far from an ideologically complex matter of national revival, Marshall presented Palestine colonization as a purely technical enterprise. "There is nothing Zionistic or non-Zionistic about agriculture, commerce, industry, finance, health or education," Marshall explained to Weizmann. "The subjects must be approached without prejudice or prepossessions." Finance was the key issue. Marshall offered to bury past allegations of economic mismanagement in the Yishuv, but he demanded that "reliable, certified" accountants, perhaps from Price, Waterhouse, participate in the survey to examine the make-or-break topic of financial accountability.

As though to reinforce the proposition that American Jews, unlike European Zionists, knew how to balance budgets, Marshall reminded Weizmann that his non-Zionist group had raised its share, $50,000, of the funds needed to accomplish the expert survey, and he wondered in May 1927 whether the Zionists had collected their share.[123] Mostly, Marshall acquiesced to names suggested by the Zionists as experts in various fields to be covered in the survey; he red-penciled one poultry expert slated for participation in the agricultural delegation, but that was unusual.[124] Lobbying for the inclusion of a Harvard epidemiologist, Milton Rosenau, as the head of the sanitary and hygiene team, Marshall assured Weizmann that Rosenau, an authority on milk pasteurization, was not an inveterate anti-Zionist.[125] Marshall was relieved when his son James declined an offer to serve as secretary of the survey ("you would have learned what it is to be in the thick of a college football game," he wrote to James, "the pulling and hauling would have been insufferable"[126]).

The most contentious negotiation item related to the authority of the survey's findings. In April, when Weizmann's group hastily patched together survey guidelines, its agenda was to guarantee that no matter what was found, the commission's findings would not jeopardize the establishment of the Jewish Agency. Frankel remonstrated, claiming that the Zionist guidelines rendered the survey moot, ensuring that its findings would not exert any influence on the future of colonization work in the Yishuv. Moreover, the proposed guidelines precluded the commission from examining financial management in Eretz Israel.[127] Marshall eventually assented to this critique. If the Zionists think that the survey is a "hurrah boys affair," they "will find themselves woefully mistaken," Marshall swore in a private communication.[128] Rather than revising the Zionists' guidelines, Marshall drafted a supplemental "specifications" document. Mond refused to accept the non-Zionists' specifications and threatened to resign from the commission should they be added formally to the original guidelines document. Stein held his breath as this late flare-up ignited without any lasting damage. In London, Weizmann told Zionist executives that the dowry to be won in the marriage with the non-Zionists was worth the exhausting and emotionally draining matchmaking. "America will indeed build Eretz Israel, but it is imperative to first gain its trust," Weizmann declared.[129]

Commission member departures for Palestine were staggered. Frankel and Rosenau left on May 14, 1927; the last team, led by agricultural expert Elwood Mead, left in August.[130] Frankel arrived in Palestine at the end of the first week of July 1927, just as Marshall, in Knollwood, was finalizing the triumphant Ford apology. Frankel and Maurice Hexter, a social worker and future Yishuv-based member of the Jewish Agency Executive, met with the Yishuv's communal government, the Va'ad Leumi (National Council), industrialists, and bankers in Tel Aviv, and also made efforts to "obtain the Arab political view from representative Arabs."[131] Frankel decided during the visit not to become entangled in ideological questions raised by Labor Zionist communal methods in kibbutz and moshav farm efforts. He declared in a meeting with Colonel Kisch and other members of the Palestine Zionist Executive that "whether the development of the colonies shall be the [socialistic] kvuzah or whether it shall be along the lines of individual ownership is, I believe, something that neither you nor I can determine."[132] (In August, commission member Dr. Elwood Mead, commissioner of reclamation in the US Department of Interior, headed an agricultural survey and produced what Ilan Troen has described as an antisocialist "brief against the growing commitment of Zionist settlement authorities to the kibbutz."[133]) Trying to get a grasp of Yishuv expectations regarding the future of the Jewish national home, Frankel prodded senior members of the Palestine Zionist Executive: could 250,000 Jewish immigrants be absorbed over the next decade were sufficient capital and credit to be afforded? Kisch's deputies affirmed generally that everything was possible but also did not soft-pedal their financial demands. "We need 25 million pounds," the Zionist Executive told Frankel and Hexter.[134]

Frankel came away feeling satisfied about his involvement in this survey project.[135] Sailing home on the Mediterranean in July 1927, he described to Marshall the placid water and the cloudless sky—perhaps, he added, "these are auguries of what the Agency may accomplish for Palestine" should the facts and fundamentals compiled by the commission be reviewed "dispassionately and sanely." Frankel judged that the main challenge to Jewish colonization in Palestine was the land's limited water supply. "Why did the God of Israel place the Sea of Galilee 800 feet below sea level, instead of 800 feet above sea level," he wondered. He noted, with concern, that 9,000 Yishuv workers were unemployed. Developments in the revisionist Zionist camp caused some worry. Referring to right-wing revisionists, Frankel wrote that the "extremists will need to be restrained." Overall, the American chairman of the expert commission denied that the Yishuv might face an Arab problem. "Relations between Jews and Arabs are improving," Frankel wrote, two years before events cruelly belied this aspect of his observations.

Buoyant on the heels of Henry Ford's defeat, Marshall welcomed Frankel's reports. In September, he circulated them to associates like Felix Warburg, saying that Frankel "points out the stupendous difficulties that must be overcome" but also "does not regard the outlook as hopeless, provided conservative counsels are permitted to prevail."[136] He flattered Frankel: "your report is a masterpiece of analysis and statesmanship."[137]

Wrangling about full disclosure of the Joint Palestine Survey continued through the first months of 1928, due in part to disclosures inserted in a chapter on Jewish settlement ventures by John Cambell, who served on the commission in a semiofficial capacity as representative of the British government. Cambell, who had recently served as a deputy chairman for a committee on Greek refugee resettlement, alluded to sexual permissiveness on the communal *kvutzoth* (the reference was eventually expurgated from the published report).[138] The Zionists and non-Zionists agreed to confer formally in early June 1928 to review the survey findings and to discuss the manner of their public presentation. Marshall blew optimism into the sails as he set off for London, declaring that the upcoming conference would be a turning point for Jewish life in Eretz Israel.[139]

Mond, Weizmann, Frankel, and Marshall took part in the London conference. The Zionists proposed withholding disclosure of the individual experts' reports and incorporating their basic findings in one summary report; Marshall demurred, but agreed, that several sensitive or problematic passages be expunged from the individual surveys before their public release. He defused tensions by declaring that he agreed with the Zionists' general perspective about the survey; its purpose, all were agreed, was not to criticize destructively the Yishuv's past efforts but rather to contribute to the formulation of a positive development program for the future.[140] Though gaps remained between Weizmann's preference to withhold the experts' reports and Marshall's insistence that the next non-Zionist conference would not be assembled until they were made public, the Zionist leader left these London meetings feeling that his side had accomplished as much as it could, under the circumstances. At least the non-Zionists agreed to delay the reports' publication, and they agreed to the Zionists' proposal of an annual budget of 1 million pounds.[141]

In fact, the survey report became public by the end of the month, causing an immediate uproar. In Warsaw, Gruenbaum decried the survey as a scurrilous attack on the Zionist soul, and in the Yishuv's Labor Zionist newspaper *Davar*, Berl Katznelson berated the "insulting document."[142] The radicals and revisionists, long-standing critics of the expanded agency plan, hoped that the commission's overtly procapitalist preferences for private farming and land acquisition would push the Labor Zionists toward them in the formation of a united opposition to overthrow Weizmann. As it turned out, the Labor Zionists vented their outrage about the survey's findings regarding methods of Jewish settlement in Eretz Israel but voted with Weizmann. The expanded agency plan won by a resounding majority in the July 1928 Inner Actions Committee vote.

Despite this result, Marshall continued to grumble about Zionist orientations. He wrote to Magnes on July 30, 1928, that the Actions Committee's behavior "disturbed" him. The Zionists "intend to compel the Agency to adopt the doctrinaire theories of the labor unions, the iniquities and indecencies of the *kvusooths,* and to relegate the Agency into a mere collecting machine." Comparing Zionist ideologues to doctrinaire Soviet revolutionaries, Marshall added, acidly, that "Zionists who do not know the difference between a spade and a hoe are ready to determine the most important questions of agricultural science. The only thing they understand is on which side their bread is buttered."[143]

As far as Marshall was concerned, nothing in these dealings with the Zionists was spiritually uplifting. When an American rabbi wrote to Marshall saying he was devoting his energies toward helping the agency, the non-Zionist leader quickly replied, in a deflating tone ("the Agency will be conducted on business lines. I do not see how you as a rabbi could in any way help with it").[144] Marshall eventually assented to the arrangement of a non-Zionist conference in New York to adopt the survey recommendations and the agency expansion plan; his request that Weizmann take part in the meeting delayed matters, since the Zionist leader could not free himself for the trip until October 20. Meantime, the Zionists fastidiously fretted about possible disclosure of Cambell's report, and Marshall ridiculed them as self-styled champions of democracy who hide factual information from the masses.[145] Mond arrived in New York and promptly compromised the fragile truce between Marshall and Weizmann. Mond told the Jewish press that he had reservations about joining an expanded agency, and, he added, should such an entity arise, it ought to deal with diplomatic matters and not interfere with the substantive settlement work undertaken by the Zionist organization (he later retracted these comments).[146]

These inauspicious preludes did not preempt the success of the non-Zionist conference at the Biltmore Hotel, on October 20–21.[147] The 400 delegates unanimously embraced the survey report as the proper foundation for the labors of non-Zionist members of the Jewish Agency. These Biltmore resolutions recognized that changing future circumstances in the Yishuv might legitimately cause the agency to overlook various recommendations forwarded in the survey report; this writ for elasticity was designed as an overture to the Zionists, who were determined to minimize the report's programmatic impact.[148] Marshall loomed as the commanding figure at this event, and he was pleased by its orderly character.[149]

The laborious survey process was resolved essentially because the business-oriented American Jews in Marshall's group decided to sidestep the fact that the character of Jewish colonization in Palestine was increasingly colored by the socialistic orientation of the Labor Zionist movement. Marshall insisted that ultimate authority to decide the socioeconomic character of the Jewish national home must rest with the Jewish Agency. Lurking within Marshall's turgid explication of this point in a November 1928 message to Weizmann ("without intending to determine the form of land settlement that shall hereafter be pursued in Palestine, Moshav, Kvuzah or otherwise, it is to be understood that it shall be left to the judgment of the Jewish Agency to determine the economic soundness and practicability of any proposed plan of settlements"[150]) was the reincarnation of the basic issue that dominated his career as a Jewish steward and leader. With the agreement to create an enlarged Jewish Agency signed and sealed at the October 1928 New York conference, the problem of communal control was now, in some measure, being transplanted to the hallowed soil of Eretz Israel. Who would determine whether the Jewish work in progress there would be founded on capitalist principles of rugged individualism and open markets, which Marshall and his American non-Zionist colleagues considered the essence of American democracy, or whether it would enshrine socialist methods of communal ownership, which appealed to Berl Katznelson, David Ben-Gurion, and other Labor Zionist activists who were in this period powerfully asserting their presence on the ground in the Yishuv?

"Downtown" in this new Jewish politics no longer meant the teeming urban tenements of Hester Street. Instead, a new sort of Downtown was taking root in the rustic communal countryside of Eretz Israel, in the kibbutz and moshav settlements. That Marshall's Uptown group continued to exercise power of the purse carried some measure of control, but the Jewish Agency expansion plan was noticeably difficult for Marshall to negotiate because this time he was far from his home field.

The sense of shared Jewish responsibility that ultimately brought the non-Zionists and Zionists together on the agency was genuine, but it also seemed distantly abstract, compared to the palpable feelings of common destiny experienced by Uptown and Downtown New York Jews in episodes mediated by Marshall, such as the 1910 cloakmakers strike and the American Jewish Congress debates during World War I. The New York Jews, after all, were making their lives and homes in the same city.

Marshall expended considerable emotional energy in the 1920s accusing Weizmann, Lipsky, and other Zionist leaders of bad faith and double-dealing, but such excoriation was ultimately beside the point. Tacitly, he understood that the problem of control in this Zionist context had dimensions that went well beyond the caliber of the nationalist movement's leadership. His energies as a Jewish leader in affluent and working neighborhoods of New York continually revitalized because of his familiarity and love for the turf. When he negotiated a Protocol of Peace among workers and bosses in a Jewish neighborhood of New York, Marshall brought to the arbitration incomparable expertise regarding the dispute's legal aspects, along with deep familiarity with differing work roles and opportunities

15. Marshall in the mid-1920s. Courtesy of Jacob Rader Marcus Center of the American Jewish Archives.

in local Jewish life, stemming from his personal history and his professional experience. But how was he to judge whether his group's philanthropic resources ought to support the Histadrut labor organization, the Hamashbir cooperative, and other new, emblematic institutions of the Labor Zionist movement? When it came to the Yishuv's development, the outcome of a contest between the outlooks of Marshall's experts and the endeavors of the *halutz* pioneers themselves was predetermined. On the American side of the expanded Jewish Agency initiative, Marshall had the most lines in the 1920s, but he never could become a major player in the drama that was unfolding in Eretz Israel.

The Labor Zionist *halutzim* did not seem to be of the exact same stock as Asser Levy, the New Amsterdam Jewish pioneer revered by Marshall as his historical forefather. Or, phrased another way, the problem was that the Zionist *halutzim* projected the same rough-and-ready pioneering mentality as Asser Levy, but they were flexing their Jewish muscles under social and political conditions far less malleably accommodating to Marshall's view than semi-mythologized memories of old New York. Unable to truly understand the Zionist pioneers, Marshall had no hope of entering with them into an intelligible update of the New York Downtown-Uptown negotiation about stewardship models versus democratization. He had power as a non-Zionist leader instrumental in the drafting and signing of the much-ballyhooed Pact of Glory for the expanded Jewish Agency, but he was never really in the game. Marshall had always returned from negotiations with Downtown New York Jews hungry for more Jewish work, but the dealings with the Zionists were wearying, not only because Marshall was aging. In the end, he fell ill and passed away in Zurich in August 1929, just as the Jewish world was celebrating there the consummation of the Pact of Glory. Some sad poetic truth could be gleaned from the fact that, out of all the items on Marshall's dizzyingly long list of Jewish labors, his work for the Jewish Agency proved to be the most exhausting, and last, endeavor.

12

Epilogue

Massena, Zurich, Emanu-El

By the end of the 1920s, the added weight of advancing years encumbered Marshall's dealings with the distant Holy Land. Before his death, the end of his term of high influence in communal affairs was perceptible in his difficulty traversing physical space and ideological gaps in dealings with the Zionists. Yet the effects of age and the liabilities of the consolidation of communal power in one leader made their heaviest showing not in Mandatory Palestine but rather in Massena, New York.

While Marshall remained at the nerve center of Jewish affairs and was widely appreciated to the very end, isolation was inevitably brought on by exhaustion, stress, and age. This solitude was most cruelly felt not as a function of his physical distance from other significant loci of Jewish experience, such as the Zionists' state-in-the-making. Toward the end of the 1920s, the Upstate New York idyll of his childhood memories sometimes also seemed remote. In autumn 1928, exactly when Marshall clinched the expanded Jewish Agency deal, he was compelled to do communal defense work in opposition to the most primitive of anti-Jewish insults in, of all places, Upstate New York.

Marshall's journey from upstate to Uptown was never deliberately one way. He had always tried to leave part of himself in Syracuse. Toward the end of his life, however, he seemed further from the tranquil reality of his own nineteenth-century upstate youth than he intended to be and perhaps not at the infinite remove from the lachrymose medieval circumstances of the Jews' collective past that he, and generations of Jewish activists and thinkers in the United States, imagined themselves to be.

The Massena Blood Libel

On September 22, 1928, a day before Yom Kippur eve, four-year-old Barbara Griffiths disappeared in marshy land outlying Massena, New York, an upstate township of some 12,000 residents located just below the Canadian border in Saint Lawrence County.[1] Massena was a conservative, Republican town whose Anglo-Saxon Protestant population mixed placidly with immigrant Poles, Italians, Lithuanians, Yugoslavs, and Greeks. The town's nineteen Jewish families had all arrived after 1898. They prayed in an old Congregational church, which had been renamed Adath Israel, and fared fairly well economically, operating clothing, furniture, and jewelry stores.

On the whole, the town had not dipped very deeply into the wells of Roaring Twenties' prosperity. In the last years of the 1800s, health spas featuring the sulfurous water of the Raquette River had generated some income, whereas in the first decades of the twentieth century, the main employer in town was the Aluminum Company of America, Alcoa, where little Barbara's struggling middle-class father, Dave, earned $35 a week as a shipping clerk.

After the girl failed to return from the swampy "Nightingale Section," Dave alerted local fire and police authorities, and a large search team was formed under the supervision of Company B state troopers from nearby Malone, New York, whose head was Corporal Harry "Mickey" McCann, an Irish Catholic World War I veteran with a high school degree. The police and volunteer search team worked in close cooperation with Massena's mayor, W. Gilbert Hawes, a native of Tarrytown, New York, who had little education but had married well, monopolized the town's bottled milk trade, and, surprisingly, won election as mayor in 1922, running as a Democrat in the Republican town (townsfolk surmised that voters confused this rather undistinguished candidate with members of another Hawes family, which ran a well-respected lumber business). After searchers came up empty handed, it was this impulsive former dairy manager who ordered McCann to focus the investigation on the possibility that local Jews had abducted Barbara Griffiths to use her blood for nefarious ritual purposes.

The cue for the blood libel was apparently given by a Greek immigrant, Albert Comnas, who operated the Crystal Palace ice cream parlor in town. Troopers who took a soda break in Comnas's establishment reportedly gleaned the theory that "the Jews are having a holiday, maybe they need blood," from this Salonika native. As the weary and nervous troopers and the embittered proprietor mulled this age-old canard, they found an easy target for corroboration: Willie Shulkin, the mentally ill twenty-two-year son of Jacob Shulkin, the prospering owner of a few furniture and appliance stores in Upstate New York and the president of Massena's Adath Israel congregation, had wandered into the parlor for an ice cream that Saturday night and had no real idea about what its agitated patrons and owner were asking him. Hapless Willie was dragged to the town police station for questioning. His interrogators concluded in their report that the "officers realized the boy was of low mentality, and sent him home." Nevertheless, whatever Willie said persuaded Mayor Hawes that it would be a good idea for McCann and his comrades to summon Adath Israel's rabbi, Berel Brennglass, the next day for questioning about the possibility that the Griffiths girl had been abducted by Jews for their own religious purposes.

Before the rabbi was subjected to this ordeal, the town's leading Jews, including Jacob Shulkin, conferred urgently late Saturday night about possible responses to the developing blood libel. When they decided to phone Louis Marshall, the Massena Jews were personally frightened about the prospect of a pogrom in their hometown and were also, as Jacob Shulkin later attested, "strong in our opinion that it was a national affair, *k'lol yisroel*."[2] The conversation with Marshall lasted until 11:00 PM.

The first excrescence of blood libel harassment of Jews in North America was occurring painfully close to Marshall's native grounds (Massena is some 200 miles from Syracuse). Concerned that a full report of this ugly affair be disclosed to the world, Marshall immediately phoned a Ukrainian-born reporter for the Jewish Telegraphic Agency, Boris Smolar, and asked that he take the first train to Massena. This journey on the night milk train through the Adirondacks seemed to last forever; Smolar arrived in Massena at noon on Sunday, a few hours before the traditional Kol Nidre service on Yom Kippur eve. Almost exactly at this moment, Corporal Mickey McCann was summoning Rabbi Brennglass to police headquarters to "have a conversation and obtain important information."[3]

Brennglass, who had arrived in America at the age of forty in 1913, after having studied at the Slobodka Yeshiva in Kovno, trudged the 300 yards to headquarters from his dwelling on East Orvis Street. A short, thin man with a graying beard, the rabbi passed some 300–400 agitated townsfolk who congregated outside of city hall. Asked by McCann whether his people in the Old Country participated in human sacrifices, Brennglass indignantly noted his surprise that an officer in the world's most enlightened country could pose such a "foolish and ridiculous" question. The rabbi rose up from this extraordinary interrogation, castigating it as "*rehkiles,* a slander against the entire Jewish people"; courageously, as he left the premises, he upbraided the crowd for "insinuating such things against your Jewish neighbors."[4] The rabbi was determined to proceed with Kol Nidre services.

Still in a panic, members of his congregation decided in mid-afternoon to send out additional distress calls, this time to Rabbi Stephen Wise of the American Jewish Congress. Smolar was in Rabbi Brennglass's study at 3:00 PM, taking notes on the surreal police investigation, when somebody burst in and announced triumphantly that the girl had been found, alive and unharmed.

Jew-baiting in the town outlasted the worrisome disappearance and happy discovery of the four-year-old girl. Townspeople recalled that adults in Massena argued for weeks about the merits of the accusation against the Jews and that Jewish and Gentile schoolchildren fought. Some claimed that Mayor Hawes proactively led a local boycott against Jewish merchants.[5] Still, on Tuesday, September 25, McCann's superior, Lieutenant Edward Heim of the State Highway Patrol, rounded up the Massena officials and escorted them to a special meeting in Adath Israel. For two hours, Heim and others apologized to Rabbi Brennglass, Jacob Shulkin, and other local Jews, but their contrition seemed lost among self-serving explanations about the urgency of the Barbara Griffiths search and the obligation to chase all possible leads.

The offended Jewish townsfolk may also have perceived that the apology was politically motivated. National elections were just weeks away. Republican functionaries in Upstate New York sensed (correctly, as it turned out) that the national presidential candidate, Herbert Hoover, stood a strong chance of sensationally snatching New York's electoral votes from his Democratic rival, Al Smith, governor of the Empire State. In a state where 2 million Jews cast ballots, the image of a recalcitrant, Jew-hating Massena—a town known as a Republican stronghold—was a political liability for the Republicans. Not swayed by their visitors' explanations and apologies, the congregation's members told Lieutenant Heim and his subordinates that they had already referred the matter to a prominent attorney in New York and that his recommendations would govern their actions.

That attorney formulated an aggressive response.[6] After a delay of a week and a half, Marshall wrote to Mayor Hawes, decrying "one of the most shocking exhibitions of bigotry that has ever occurred in this country." It was "inexpressibly horrible" that a blood libel would be perpetrated "in this state of ours" by public officers; Hawes and McCann had perpetrated a transgression that "does not merely affect the Jews of Massena, whose very lives were placed in jeopardy, but the entire Jewish population of this country and of the world." The president of the American Jewish Committee demanded that the Massena mayor offer an apology, whose terms Marshall would have to approve, and also resign from his office; should Hawes dodge both of these courses, Marshall threatened that he would file a demand in the appellate division of the state supreme court, calling for the mayor's removal from office on the ground of official misconduct.[7]

These were firmly stated demands and threats, and Marshall's dramatic premise (what had happened in Massena was fraught with implications for the world) made headway in global media. Sections of Marshall's letter to the mayor were cited sympathetically in the *London Times.* All of the New York papers conveyed Marshall's outrage; the *Sun,* for example, noted that while "American common sense" had long prevented anti-Semitic blood libels from taking root in the country, the Massena outrage was like "fire in the stubble, easily stamped out at first, but hard to control once it gains headway."[8]

Marshall's antidefamation work regarding Massena yielded public relations returns, but it was late in coming. His long-time rival, Stephen Wise, outmaneuvered him on the Massena incident. Wise acted faster and took advantage of his access to Albany's Democratic Party machinery in Governor Al Smith's administration. Two or three days before Marshall's letter to Hawes, Wise fired off apology demands to all the culprits in the Massena libel; in the first days of October, while Marshall was working the media, Wise managed to wrest from Governor Al Smith a message (whose words were formulated by Belle Moskowitz) denouncing the "absurd" ritual murder charge and promising that "the state of New York would thoroughly investigate the matter."[9] When Wise received from Mayor Hawes a clarification letter that sounded more like a threat than an apology ("I hold no ill feeling against the Jewish people of this community," Hawes wrote, "and I hope that the exceedingly pleasant relations which have prevailed here in the past may continue without interruption"), Wise pressed on, arranging a closed meeting at the capitol building in Albany. The meeting, held on October 4, involved members of Massena's Jewish community, Hawes and other town officials, top officers from the New York State Police, and Wise and select colleagues from the American Jewish Congress. This meeting ended with an effusively self-excoriating statement from the Massena mayor, attesting to his own "serious error of judgment" and saying that just as there would have been absolutely no warrant to question a Protestant minister or Catholic bishop about ritual murder suspicions, it was grievously wrong to question a local rabbi in a way that gave credence to a "cruel libel."[10]

Whatever their sincerity, the mayor's words exhausted all possible lexicon entries for apology, and everyone involved in the Massena affair was at this stage resolved to put to rest a libel that had caused no physical damage to anything or anyone. Strangely, Marshall continued to prosecute charges in the incident well after his presumed clients, the aggrieved Jews of Massena, explicitly told him to stop. When Wise was shepherding the closed meeting in Albany on October 4, Marshall hosted in his Manhattan office two Massena Jewish delegates, who had made their way to the big city without knowledge of the conciliation meeting upstate. Marshall exploded with rage when he discovered he had been upstaged in Albany. He expressed "surprise" in an October 6 letter to Jacob Shulkin about not having been invited to the Albany meeting. Livid, Marshall wrote that in fifty years of activity in Jewish affairs, he had never encountered anything like the "cavalier manner" by which Massena Jews had effectively dismissed him from the case.[11] Reiterating that the blood libel affair was a matter of interest to every Jew in the world, Marshall seemed to lose hold of logic, stating in one section of his letter to Shulkin that advocacy in the matter related to "an important proposition" that "in no manner concern[ed]" the Jews of Massena themselves.[12]

This, as Saul Friedman has pointed out, was rather self-involved rhetoric that callously disregarded the night of terror and subsequent harassment and boycotts endured by the Massena Jews.[13] At the end of the first week of October, public opinion was decidedly in favor of closing the case in Massena. The interfaith Permanent Commission on Better Understanding between Christians and Jews urged this conclusion, and the Jewish mayor of Ogdensburg, New York, Julius Frank, contacted Marshall, asking him to cease pressure on Massena officials. Marshall, however, persisted for days with his claim that Mayor Hawes's apology was inadequate and that redress for the Massena wrong had not been collected.

Theoretically, he could (and did) claim that his antidefamation work proceeded on the assumption that national and global calculations, not the passing sensitivities of any local community, had the prerogative. This explanation, however, does not appear persuasive in light of the circumstances of autumn 1928. Marshall had his own partisan political reasons to make sure that the Democrats would not appear on the presidential ballot as the antidefamation party of choice. No less, considerations of personal prestige and Jewish organizational rivalry dictated and strained Marshall's advocacy in Massena.

Ten years before, in the turbulent debates about the formation of an American Jewish Congress, Uptown and Downtown leaders had drawn swords about procedures, tone, and style of advocacy on behalf of the personal and communal rights of millions of Jews in East Europe. At the end of the decade, the same distrust and rivalry persisted between the Democratic Downtown leader of the American Jewish Congress, Stephen Wise, and the Republican president of the American Jewish Committee, Louis Marshall, but with the reference point in their rivalry having reduced from the Jewish masses of Eastern Europe to the nineteen Jewish families of a quiet Saint Lawrence County township, it appeared that the largest lasting motivator in their debate was personal ego.

The Massena affair does not recapitulate the character of antidefamation work undertaken by Marshall in the 1920s in cases relating to possible or actual anti-Semitic libels. For instance, in an underappreciated effort, Marshall worked hard, and successfully, for the dismissal of a murder indictment against Captain Robert Rosenbluth, a graduate of the Yale School of Forestry and a former Joint Distribution Committee worker in Siberia who was falsely implicated in the death of Major Alexander Pennington Cronkhite in Washington State in October 1918.[14] Years later, when charges against Rosenbluth were finally dropped,

Marshall justifiably complained to Adolph Ochs of the *New York Times*[15] about the little interest shown by the media in the exoneration of the Jewish US army captain, the so-called American Dreyfus.[16]

"I think at least ten diatribes were published in the *Dearborn Independent*" about the Rosenbluth case, Marshall reminded Ochs in this 1924 letter. Major Cronkhite's father was a major general, and Ford's pundits had depicted Rosenbluth as a "dirty Jewish spy" who had killed Major Cronkhite to divert his father from his duties as a divisional commander of the American Expeditionary Forces in France. Aroused by the *Independent*'s scurrilous accusations, the Harding administration's Justice Department aggressively prosecuted Rosenbluth and a comrade (Sergeant Potheir). Marshall personally arranged for expert witnesses, such as L. L. Thompson, a former Washington State attorney general, to testify on Rosenbluth's behalf,[17] and, understandably, the acquittal provided considerable satisfaction to Marshall as a counterexample to the tragic end of the Leo Frank affair and also, as Marshall explained to Ochs, as a strong blow delivered against Ford's hateful hypocrisy. "I am looking to take advantage of an opportunity which I have long looked for, to smite this scoundrel [Ford] hip and thigh, and at the same time rehabilitate a man who has deserved well of this country. He risked his life in the army, while Ford was profiteering and his son was evading service,"[18] Marshall noted, as he vented his frustration about how the Rosenbluth defense lost effect as an antidefamation campaign against Ford due to media apathy. While the public learned a few truths about Rosenbluth and his deserved exoneration, one thing it never knew was a postacquittal development attesting to the character of the lawyer who had provided crucial assistance in the captain's defense. For months, Marshall and his son Bob helped Rosenbluth rebuild his life by finding work and gaining some economic stability—in spring 1925, Bob reported to his father about his visit to Potter County, Pennsylvania, scouting for some property that would help Rosenbluth make a fresh start.[19]

Thus, the Massena blood libel affair in 1928 cannot be regarded as a miniature representation of Marshall's antidefamation endeavors in the 1920s. Yet, it pointed to the final limits of the reach of "Marshall law." As Marshall grew older, it finally seemed to be happening: however energetic and impassioned his Jewish advocacy remained, there were unmistakable signs in the Massena sequence pointing to his difficulty keeping pace with events. His old rival, Stephen Wise, seemed to maneuver faster than Marshall, and months before his death, the American Jewish Committee president did not seem entirely adept at proportioning the use of 1920s information media to the level of the challenge faced by a particular community of Jews. He even seemed somewhat out of touch with the needs and desires of Jewish individuals who dwelled in his beloved native region of Upstate New York.

More broadly, with America's power system reconfiguring on the eve of the Great Depression in terms of party loyalties, class structure, and professional differentiation, many Jews, including Marshall's devoted admirers, must have understood that it could be precarious to face future challenges with communal authority remaining largely in the hands of any one leader, no matter how intelligent, experienced, industrious, and talented that person might be. That individual was liable to bring his own political party preferences and his own old way of doing things to situations in the 1930s characterized by changing communal political preferences and new ways of doing things in America.

Zurich: Final Bow

Marshall died in Zurich, on September 11, 1929. Hospitalized, he fought for several days, and the deferral allowed his son James, along with Judah Magnes and Jacob Billikopf, to gather by his bedside and to give comfort in his final hours.[20] Inevitably, Marshall's participation days before at the Zurich meetings held to finalize and celebrate the expanded Jewish Agency arrangement was viewed as the final, crowning public moment of his career. "World Jewry was meeting in assembly in Zurich, to devise a solemn compact for united action," one writer of a Marshall memorial recorded. "Dress ranged from Oriental looking caftans to the most modern western styles." Paying a "supreme compliment," Chaim Weizmann simply announced, "Louis Marshall," knowing there was no need to review credentials when introducing a figure whose decades of effort for Jewish causes were well known to everyone in the meeting hall. As Marshall stood up, so too did the audience, wrote Horace Stern. "If ever there was a spontaneous surge of respect, of admiration, of love, of devotion for a fellow being, it rose from those men and women like the foam from an ocean wave."[21]

Funeral

Funeral services were held at the new Temple Emanu-El building in New York City on 65th Street and 5th Avenue, at 10:00 AM, September 24.[22] For days, craftsmen had speedily put the final touches on the Italian-tinted marble, golden mosaic, and other synagogue features to open the facility ten days ahead of schedule and to accommodate the funeral of a Jewish leader who had done so much for the congregation over the years. Awed visitors who came the night before the funeral to the Beth'el chapel where Marshall's body lay in state described the Reform temple as the "most luxurious place of worship in America." The 3,000 tickets for the funeral service were issued by Marshall's law firm; prompt arrival was required, and newspaper reports cited names of invited mourners who were tardy and not allowed entry into Emanu-El.

Handel's *Largo* was played during the short, twenty-five-minute ceremony. Outside the synagogue, 25,000 grieving admirers thronged the streets. "Such an outpouring has not been witnessed in New York at the funeral of a private citizen," newspaper reports announced. Police revised arrangements, and eventually 250 of New York's Finest lined the crowded streets. One perceptive reporter noted that the man who had led the investigation of the Rabbi Jacob Joseph funeral riots and exposed the "complete lack of sympathy between the police and the people of the East Side" in 1902 had an honor guard of 100 policemen at his own funeral. Honorary pallbearers included Cyrus Adler, Benjamin Cardozo, William Guthrie, Charles Evans Hughes, Adolph Ochs, and Nathan Straus. One honorary pallbearer, NAACP secretary James Weldon Johnson, headed a delegation of black mourners. James Marshall wrote to his uncle Judah Magnes, who had returned to riot-afflicted Jerusalem, that his father's coffin looked "simple and humble, an oaken box with a black cover spotted with red roses and one small wreath."[23]

Marshall was brought to rest in Salem Fields Cemetery, on Jamaica Avenue in Brooklyn. That afternoon and evening, 250 memorial services were held; the main memorial was conducted at the Washington Heights YMHA. For weeks, Marshall family members were flooded with "tributes and resolutions and letters." His father's son, James discussed ways of achieving unity in the mourning, lest any local Jewish or non-Jewish leader refer to Marshall's memory in an unduly self-interested or ineffectual manner.[24]

Acknowledgments

Notes

Bibliography

Index

Acknowledgments

Thanks are due first of all to Prof. Henry Feingold, Modern Jewish History series editor, Syracuse University Press. From the moment this project was conceived, his support was constant, encouraging, and informed. I am fortunate to have benefited from his experience and knowledge of American Jewish history, and this book owes much to him.

Louis Marshall's papers are a sprawling component in the remarkable documentary collection of the Jacob Rader Marcus Center of the American Jewish Archives (AJA), located in Cincinnati, Ohio. I enjoyed and profited from every minute of innumerable research trips to the archive, starting with the receipt of a Loewenstein-Wiener Research Fellowship in 2006. Under Dr. Gary Zola's direction, the American Jewish Archives are a researcher's paradise. I have had the pleasure of working closely at the AJA with Senior Archivist Kevin Proffitt, and I thank him for his help. Thanks also to Frederic Krome and his successor, Dana Herman, along with Camille Servizzi and everyone else on the AJA staff.

I first began to organize thoughts and information about Marshall in response to an invitation sent by Prof. Mark Raider to participate in a scholarly symposium held in conjunction with the 150th anniversary of Marshall's birth. For some years, I have appreciated Mark's collegial professionalism and scholarly dedication, and these traits played a catalyst role in this project. Thanks also to Prof. Eric Goldstein, who, with Prof. Raider, edited and published an article about Marshall that I contributed to a special 2008 issue of the *American Jewish History* journal, which emerged out of the Marshall symposium.

I was fortunate to discuss Marshall family history with one of Louis's grandchildren, Roger Marshall. Roger arranged a memorable visit to Saranac Lake and to the Marshall family summer home at Knollwood. This visit to the Adirondacks provided invaluable insight about the Marshall family in general and was particularly germane to the "Jews and Birds" chapter. In addition to Roger Marshall and his wife Barbara, I thank other hosts and discussion partners during this visit: Mary Hotaling and Amy Catania of the Saranac Laboratory Museum, Caroline Welsh and Angela Nye of the Adirondack Museum, and the kind proprietors of the Adirondack Motel.

A key research stretch for this project, during the academic year 2009–10, was made possible by funding for a visiting professorship in Israel studies provided by the Charles and Lynn Schusterman Family Foundation and the American-Israeli Cooperative Enterprise (AICE), with assistance from the Columbus Jewish Foundation, the Columbus

Jewish Federation, Judy and Merom Brachman and Anna and Danny Robins. I am happy to acknowledge specifically in this connection the help of AICE's indefatigable executive director, Dr. Mitchell Bard.

The Ohio State University's Melton Center for Jewish Studies graciously invited me to work as a visiting professor during the same 2009–10 year, and I profited tremendously from the stimulating, warm atmosphere this teaching stint provided, conveniently in the vicinity of the Louis Marshall papers. Prof. Matt Goldish, Melton Center director, displayed exceptional patience regarding the oddity of a visiting professor in Israel studies investing much research time in the area of American Jewish history; I thank him for this friendly exhibition of scholarly látitude. I am also happy to thank Melton Center administrator Lori Fireman for her help. I thank also Professors Carole Fink, Alan Beyerchen, Robin Judd, and other faculty members associated with the Melton Center for their support and interest in my work.

Friendship with Robin Judd and Ken Steinman and family, of Columbus, Ohio, was much appreciated during this research year, and its highlights, including the thrills and spills of my initiation in the international association of researchers of Jewish history who cannot ski, are fondly recalled by members of my own family. Thanks also go to community *shaliach* Avi Kagan and family, as well as to my Ohio relatives Seth Young and Lois Rosow, and Julie Zavon.

I acknowledge the collegial interest and encouragement of members of the Ohio State University's History Department: Profs. Peter Hahn, Kevin Boyle, James Bartholomew, Mansel Blackford, Nicholas Breyfogle, Steven Conn, Jane Hathaway, Christopher Reed, Jennifer Siegel, David Stebenne.

In Syracuse, I enjoyed the hospitality of Marshall enthusiast and author Herbert Alpert—I thank Herb especially for the tour of Marshall's native grounds. Thanks also to Pamela Priest, archivist at the Onondaga Historical Association.

I acknowledge gratefully the following: the staff of the American Jewish Historical Society at the Center for Jewish History; Charlotte Bonelli, director of the American Jewish Committee Archives; staff at the Joint Distribution Committee; Barbara Niss, archivist at the Levy Library, Mount Sinai Medical Center; staff at the Manuscripts Division, New York Public Library; staff at the Manuscript Division, Library of Congress.

I thank the following scholars: Prof. Jonathan Sarna, for sharing insights about Marshall and points of commonality and divergence between his career and Louis Brandeis's career; Dr. Richard Hawkins, of the University of Wolverhampton, for sharing information about Marshall's law partner, Samuel Untermyer; and Dr. Ofer Schiff, for his invitation to speak about Marshall.

Rabbi Peter Schweitzer, a great-grandson of Louis Marshall and leader of the City Congregation for Humanistic Judaism, generously provided photographs for this volume.

With much gratitude, I acknowledge the support and work of the entire staff of Syracuse University Press. At Syracuse University Press, very special thanks are due to

Editorial and Production folks Kay Steinmetz, Marcia Hough, Ruthnie Angrand, and Fred Wellner for their herculean efforts on the production of this long book.

My students and colleagues at the Max Stern College of Emek Yezreel never cease to inspire me. I am especially indebted to my friend and boss, the college's president Prof. Aliza Shenhar.

My children—Eitan, Galit, Lior and Talia—contributed to this work in ways that are too multifarious to acknowledge properly, so I will have to be content here to allude to the energizing impact of their visits to Ohio during the academic year when I was absent from the Galilee.

I grew up deeply captivated by the mesmerizing influence of colorful, talented American Jewish lawyers, and the memory of their character traits lent insight as I researched facets of Louis Marshall's career. Joseph Becker, my childhood friend Robert Becker's father, warrants mention in this respect, as do many colleagues of my father, David Silver, himself an attorney and also a lifelong student of history. While writing this volume, I was happily conscious of ways it consolidated as a creative meeting ground between roads taken and not taken in my own family history. More than anything, I am indebted to my father's help in its production, starting with the cash-for-clunkers trade-in he negotiated to enable my own weekly journeys on Ohio's long flat roads. This book is dedicated to him.

Notes

Introduction

1. NAACP: Moorfield Story–Louis Marshall Memorial Campaign, Spring 1930, LM Papers, Box 20/7.

2. *American Indian Bulletin,* no. 15 (Jan. 1930), LM Papers, Box 20/7.

3. These terms "German" and "Russian" are widely known cultural demarcations, but they are imprecise geographic markers of two waves of Jewish immigration to the United States—the arrival of 200,000–250,000 Jews from Central European lands in the mid–nineteenth century and the immigration of ten times that number of Jews from Eastern European countries in a forty-year period starting in the early 1880s and ending a few years after World War I. For a discussion of the problematic nature of categories such as "German" Jewish immigration to the United States: Hasia Diner, *A Time for Gathering: The Second Migration, 1820–1880* (Baltimore: Johns Hopkins Univ. Press, 1992), 6–35.

German-Russian/Uptown-Downtown demarcations in American Jewish history belong to a wider phenomenon of polarized and mythologized West-East categorization that can be found in many contexts, from the "Ostjuden" debates in pre–Holocaust Germany and the work of the French-based Alliance Israelite Universelle among Jews of Asian and African lands, to ongoing oppositions between Ashkenazi elites and masses of Mizrahi immigrants and their descendants in Israel. That is, the Uptown-Downtown mediation that became the focus of Marshall's career in Jewish politics represents an American part of a dynamic that is becoming increasingly appreciated by scholars as a key, if not dominant, axis of modern Jewish history. To date, highly suggestive discussions of this axis tend to ignore or downplay the North American theater of Marshall's activity (see, e.g., Aziza Khazzoom, "The Great Chain of Orientalism: Jewish Identity, Stigma Management and Ethnic Exclusion in Israel," *American Sociological Review* 68, no. 4, 481–510).

4. See, for instance, Benny Kraut, "American Jewish Leaders: The Great, Greater, and Greatest," *American Jewish History* 78 (Dec. 1988), 201–36.

1. Syracuse

1. *Proceedings: Democratic Republican State Convention* in Syracuse, July 24, 1856 (Albany, 1856), 6, 13.

2. Jonathan Sarna, "Two Jewish Lawyers Named Louis," *American Jewish History* 94, no. 1–2 (Mar.–June 2008), 1–19.

3. Marshall to Edward Friton, Apr. 24, 1929, in Charles Reznikoff, *Louis Marshall: Champion of Liberty: Selected Papers and Addresses* (Philadelphia: Jewish Publication Society of America, 1957), 1:6.

4. Marshall to Charles Sedgwick, Apr. 13, 1914, in Reznikoff, *Louis Marshall,* 1:4–5. Jacob was employed in Cuylerville by the father of a prominent New York City attorney, Hamilton Odell, with whom Louis was friendly.

5. B. G. Rudolph, *From a Minyan to a Community: A History of the Jews of Syracuse* (Syracuse: Syracuse University Press, 1970), 17.

6. For Leeser's description, see ibid. 39–42. The push and pull of tradition and change in Syracuse's Jewish community can be discerned in prayer arrangements incorporated in the new building. As a nod to the Reform modernists, the Temple of Concord directors agreed to move the *bimah* (reader's desk) from the center of the prayer floor to the front platform, in front of the Ark. In deference to traditional, Orthodox sensibilities, balconies for female worshippers were built around three sides of the new temple building. Ibid., 38.

7. Ibid., 192.

8. A Syracuse native, Herbert Alpert, located this *Syracuse Daily Standard* report, from Dec. 16, 1856. He also received corroboration of the odd windstorm incident from George Marshall, Louis's youngest son, in a 1987 letter. Herbert Alpert, *Louis Marshall, 1856–1929: A Life Devoted to Justice and Judaism* (Bloomington: iUniverse, 2008), 4. I thank Herbert for the clarification of this point and his hospitable presentation of Marshall's native grounds.

9. Rudolph, *From a Minyan to a Community,* 192.

10. In 1924, Marshall wrote that his father Jacob was "a man of the highest integrity," who had the "unqualified respect and confidence of every man with whom he ever did business." Marshall to Charles Sedgwick, Apr. 13, 1924.

11. Marshall to Charles Schwager, Dec. 17, 1928, in Reznikoff, *Louis Marshall,* 1:5.

12. Marshall to David Reed, Apr. 14, 1926, in Reznikoff, *Louis Marshall,* 1:235. That Marshall evoked cherished memories of his mother in this correspondence with Reed is interesting. Marshall wrote to the senator in protest of the US officials' callous disregard for 8,000 immigrant Jews, who had invested in the journey to America but were marooned overseas after the passage of the restrictionist Immigration Act of 1924. In a series of letters to Reed, he inveighed against the fateful closure of America's doors to Jewish and other immigrants, going as far as to claim that Senator Reed's "mocking" insensitivity to the plight of the marooned 8,000 Jews was the most harrowing attitude he had experienced in fifty years of professional work. By bringing his adored mother into this discussion, the woman "responsible for all that I have ever accomplished in life," Marshall was saying that the anti-immigration nativists had struck against what was most precious and sacred to him. Matthew Silver, "Louis Marshall and the Democratization of Jewish Identity," *American Jewish History* 94, no. 1–2 (Mar.–June 2008), 66.

13. Marshall to Charles Schwager, Dec. 17, 1928.

14. Interview with John Mumford, cited in Jerome Rosenthal, "The Public Life of Louis Marshall" (Ph.D. diss., Univ. of Cincinnati, 1983), 3.

15. Marshall to Mrs. Eldridge, Feb. 5 and 7, 1916, Louis Marshall Papers, Jacob Rader Marcus Center of the American Jewish Archives, Cincinnati (hereafter, LM Papers), Box 1585.

16. The donation of Marshall's family home to the Syracuse Jewish community is discussed in chapter 4. For reports on the deed ceremony for the Marshall home, Nov. 24, 1910, see LM Papers, Box 20/3; see also Rudolph, *From a Minyan to a Community,* 17. Syracuse Jewish youths in the

1930s Depression years played ping-pong and shot pool in this Cedar Street facility, which had become the YWHA. One recalled seeing a photograph in the foyer of a "paunchy . . . unsmiling" lawyer, Louis Marshall. Alpert, *Louis Marshall, 1856–1929,* 1–3.

17. Marshall to Charles Flint, Sept. 6, 1928, in Reznikoff, *Louis Marshall,* 1:6.

18. Ibid.

19. Louis Marshall, "Rabbi Meir of Rothenburg," Jewish Theological Seminary, Mar. 29, 1906, LM Papers, Box 1619.

20. Ibid.

21. Ibid.

22. Rudolph, *From a Minyan to a Community,* 53–54; David Stolz file, Onondaga Historical Association Museum and Research Center (hereafter, OHAMRC).

23. Rudolph, *From a Minyan to a Community,* 119.

24. Marshall to Benjamin Stolz, Nov. 21, 1922, in Reznikoff, *Louis Marshall,* 2:967.

25. Alpert, *Louis Marshall, 1856–1929,* 8.

26. High school diploma certificate, Apr. 14–15, 1874, LM Papers, Box 20/3.

27. Alpert, *Louis Marshall, 1856–1929,* 8.

28. Rudolph, *From a Minyan to a Community,* 112–13.

29. Alpert, *Louis Marshall, 1856–1929,* 7. Marshall participated in debate frameworks after his high school graduation. Through 1876, he belonged in Syracuse to the Andrew White Debating Society and contributed to publications issued by it. LM Papers, Box 20/3.

30. Marshall's recollection is from a *New York Times Magazine* article published on Dec. 12, 1926, and cited in Rosenthal, "The Public Life of Louis Marshall," 3.

31. Marshall to George Brown, May 19, 1870, LM Papers 15/2.

32. John K. Mumford, "Louis Marshall: Leader of American Israel. An Appreciation," *New York Tribune,* June 15, 1924.

33. Cyrus Adler, "Louis Marshall: A Biographical Sketch," *American Jewish Year Book* 32 (1930–31), 23.

34. Adler, "Louis Marshall," 24; Rosenthal, "The Public Life of Louis Marshall," 5–6.

35. Marshall to Harold Medina, Mar. 9, 1929, in Reznikoff, *Louis Marshall,* 1:8.

36. Adler, "Louis Marshall," 23–24.

37. Rosenthal, "The Public Life of Louis Marshall," 5; Alpert, *Louis Marshall, 1856–1929,* 10; Sarna, "Two Jewish Lawyers Named Louis," 3.

38. Marshall to Robert Marshall, Dec. 10, 1926, in Reznikoff, *Louis Marshall,* 2:1046.

39. Marshall to A. J. Northrup, Jan. 29, 1917, LM Papers, Box 1587.

40. Sarna, "Two Jewish Lawyers Named Louis."

41. Robert Stevens, *Law School: Legal Education in America from the 1850s to the 1980s* (Chapel Hill: Univ. of North Carolina Press, 1983), 22. I thank Prof. David Stebenne for his assistance regarding this reference, and the history of American law education in general.

42. Ibid., 21

43. Julius Goebel (ed.), *A History of the School of Law, Columbia University* (New York: Columbia Univ. Press, 1955), 42.

44. Ibid., 35.

45. Ibid., 34.

46. Ibid., 37.

47. Goebel, *History of the School of Law,* 51.

48. Stevens, *Law School,* 26.

49. Goebel, *History of the School of Law,* 52.

50. Ibid., *History of the School of Law,* 76.

51. Stevens, *Law School,* 25. By 1890, 23 of 39 jurisdictions in the country required some period of study or formal apprenticeship for admission to the bar.

52. For a discussion of the transformation of legal instruction at Harvard, see Stevens, *Law School,* 35–42.

53. Brandeis enrolled in Harvard Law School in autumn 1875. For his experiences there, see Melvin Urofsky, *Louis D. Brandeis: A Life* (New York: Pantheon Books, 2009), 25–45.

54. Stevens, *Law School,* 38.

55. Goebel, *History of the School of Law,* 80.

56. Ibid., 42.

57. Ibid., 40. Dwight received public attention in 1886 for his defense of five professors at Andover Theological Seminary whose jobs were in danger due to their heterodox outlooks.

58. Ibid.

59. Information in this section draws from Richard Hawkins, "Lynchburg's Swabian Jewish Entrepreneurs in War and Peace," *Southern Jewish History* 4 (Oct. 2001), 44–82.

60. Rosenthal, "The Public Life of Louis Marshall," 6.

61. William C. Ruger file, OHAMRC. The canal ring was an alleged conspiracy to defraud New York State in canal construction projects.

62. Ibid.

63. William S. Jenney to Samuel Untermyer, Sept. 25, 1929, in Reznikoff, *Louis Marshall,* 1:8–9.

64. James Byron Brooks file, OHAMRC.

65. Marshall's tribute to Brooks, who passed away in 1914 at the age of 75, was published in the *Syracuse Herald,* Feb. 7, 1915. OHAMRC.

66. Rosenthal, "The Public Life of Louis Marshall," 7.

67. Jenney to Untermyer, Sept. 25, 1929.

68. Ibid.

69. *Syracuse Post Standard,* Mar. 1, 1891, OHAMRC.

70. *Syracuse Herald,* Sept. 11, 1929, OHAMRC.

71. *Syracuse Post Standard,* Jan. 15, 1888, OHAMRC.

72. Syracuse Water Company v. City of Syracuse, 116 N.Y. 167 (1889).

73. Charles River Bridge v. Warren Bridge 36 U.S. 420 (1837).

74. Rudolph, *From a Minyan to a Community,* 104.

75. Sarna, "Two Jewish Lawyers Named Louis," 5; Rosenthal, "The Public Life of Louis Marshall," 7–8; Oscar Handlin, introduction to Reznikoff, *Louis Marshall,* 1:xiii.

76. For a well-known survey of the Uptown world, see Stephen Birmingham, *Our Crowd: The Great Jewish Families of New York* (New York: Harper and Row, 1967).

77. Ibid., 167–68.

78. *Syracuse Herald,* Sept. 27, 1929, OHAMRC.

79. Here is a detailed, though not comprehensive, list of Marshall's real estate sales in Syracuse, cited by deed and page number; for example, 292/490 refers to Syracuse deed 292, page 490. Sale prices are not indicated on the deeds, nor are there reliable tax stamp indications of transaction prices. Marshall also accrued revenue from stock investments. All are from Syracuse County Clerks Office, Real Property Division.

• Marshall to S. Elizabeth Arnow, Dec. 1886; 259/203.
• Marshall and Henry Elsner to Henry Rosenbloom, May 1893; 292/490.
• Marshall to Clara Williams, Jan. 1894; 297/195.
• Marshall to Maurice Rosenberg, Oct. 1898 (the sale price, $3,100, is cited in this deed); 328/177.
• Marshall and Henry Elsner to Henry Kord, Apr. 1912; 416/312.
• Marshall to Murray Realty, Dec. 1911; 418/129.
• Marshall to Celia Greenberg, Oct. 1911; 415/247.
• Marshall and Elsner to Mary Hamlin, Apr. 1909; 393/130.
• Marshall and Elsner to William Quincy, May 1907; 380/90.
• Marshall to Fannie Bigelow, June 1916; 457/62.
• Marshall to Abe Tompkin, July 1920; 492/202.
• Marshall to Carl Kallfelz, 1920; 490/405.
• Marshall to Giovanni Fiori, 1921; 497/435.
• Marshall to Mary Donfee Hosler, 1922; 518/301.
• Marshall to Leo Kirchner, July 1923; 525/278.
• Marshall to Patrick Lavelle, June 1923; 525/139.
• Marshall to Lawrence Wakefield, Apr. 1923; 525/102.
• Marshall to Kirchner Realty, May 1923; 525/105.

80. Marshall to Rebekah Kohut, Apr. 16, 1925, in Reznikoff, *Louis Marshall,* 2:922.

81. Information about Simson is drawn from Myer Isaacs, "Sampson Simson," *Publications of the American Jewish Historical* 10 (1902), 109–17.

82. Lance Sussman, *Isaac Leeser and the Making of American Judaism* (Detroit: Wayne Univ. Press, 1995), 207.

83. Israel Bartal, "Old Yishuv and New Yishuv: Image and Reality," *Jerusalem Cathedra* 1981, 222.

84. For Touro and his will, see Max Kohler, "Judah Touro, Merchant and Philanthropist," *Publications of the American Jewish Historical Society* 13 (1905).

85. A. Schischa, "The Saga of 1855: A Study in Depth," in Sonia Lipman and V. D. Lipman (eds.), *The Century of Moses Montefiore* (New York: Oxford Univ. Press, 1985), 271–72, 325–26.

86. Isaacs, "Sampson Simson," 114.

87. From Marshall's brief, "The Jewish Concepts of Charity," submitted for the North American Relief Society in Riker v. Leo 133 N.Y. 519 (1892), in Reznikoff, *Louis Marshall,* 2:913–22.

88. Deut. xxiv, 19–21; Lev. xxiv, 35–37.

89. Marshall, "Jewish Concepts of Charity," 921.

90. Marshall to Rebekah Kohut, Apr. 16, 1925.

91. "Sampson Simson's Bequest," *New York Times,* Apr. 13, 1892.

92. Rosenthal, "The Public Life of Louis Marshall," 11–12.

2. Manhattan and Moral Reform

1. Rosenthal, "The Public Life of Louis Marshall," 14. For background regarding New York Jewry in this period, the standard works are Moses Rischin, *The Promised City: New York's Jews, 1870–1914* (New York: Corinth, 1964), and Irving Howe, *The World of Our Fathers: The Journey*

of the East European Jews to America and the Life They Found and Made (New York: Simon and Schuster, 1974).

2. Quotes in these paragraphs are from Samuel Untermyer to Louis Marshall, Dec. 20, 1894; Samuel Untermyer to Louis Marshall, Sept. 29, 1895, LM Papers, Box 79.

3. Untermyer to Marshall, Dec. 20, 1894; Untermyer to Marshall, Sept. 29, 1895.

4. Untermyer to Marshall, Dec. 20, 1894; Untermyer to Marshall, Sept. 29, 1895.

5. Untermyer to Marshall, Dec. 20, 1894; Untermyer to Marshall, Sept. 29, 1895.

6. For a description of Marshall's activities at this convention, see Rosenthal, "The Public Life of Louis Marshall," 16, and also chapter 9 of this biography. Marshall served on the Judiciary Committee at the Constitutional Convention, and he was largely responsible for the inclusion of the "forever wild" clause protecting the Adirondacks in the convention's final work.

7. Marshall to William McKinley, Mar. 14, 1900, LM Papers, Box 1571.

8. For Smith's anti-Semitism: Alan Mendelson, *Exiles from Nowhere: The Jews and the Canadian Elite* (Montreal: RBS, 2008), 11–54.

9. Marshall to Oscar Straus, Mar. 14, 1900, LM Papers, Box 1571.

10. Louis Marshall, "Is Ours a Christian Government?" *Menorah* (Jan. 1896), in Reznikoff, *Louis Marshall,* 2:936–49.

11. In 1892, Justice Brewer commented that "this is a Christian nation," in Church of the Holy Trinity v. the United States, 143 U.S. 457 (1892).

12. Lilian Handlin, *George Bancroft: The Intellectual as Democrat* (New York: Harpercollins, 1984).

13. Ibid., 949.

14. People of the State of New York ex rel. George Tyroler v. Warden of City Prison of New York, 157 N.Y. 116 (1898).

15. Rosenthal, "The Public Life of Louis Marshall," 27–30.

16. People of the State of New York ex rel. George Tyroler v. Warden of City Prison of New York 157 N.Y. 116 (1898).

17. Biographical information about Florence relies on Beatrice Magnes, *Episodes: A Memoir* (Berkeley: J. L. Magnes Memorial Museum, 1977), 17–20.

18. Emanu-El confirmation event, Sunday, June 5, 1887, officiated by Dr. Gottheil; LM Papers, Box 14/7.

19. Magnes, *Episodes,* 19–20.

20. Marshall to Florence, Mar. 7, 1895, LM Papers, Box 10/4.

21. Marshall to Florence, Mar. 13, 1895, LM Papers, Box 10/4.

22. Marshall to Florence, Mar. 28, 1895, LM Papers, Box 10/4.

23. Florence to Marshall, Apr. 30, 1895, LM Papers, Box 10/4.

24. Florence Marshall diary, LM Papers, Box 14/3.

25. Marshall to Florence, May 6, 1895, LM Papers, Box 10/4.

26. Florence Marshall diary, LM Papers, Box 10/4.

27. Mark Bevir, "British Socialism and American Romanticism," *English Historical Review* 110, no. 438 (Sept. 1995), 883. The quotation is from an article Davidson published in 1900.

28. Ibid., 884.

29. Morris Raphael Cohen, *A Dreamer's Journey: The Autobiography of Morris Raphael Cohen* (Boston: Beacon Press, 1949), 103. Cohen said that correspondence with Davidson in mid-1899

"transformed my life plans" (105). See also James Good, "The Development of Thomas Davidson's Religious and Social Thought" (2004), http://www.autodidactproject.org/other/TD.html.

30. Marshall to Morris Cohen, Dec. 22, 1904, LM Papers, Box 1573.

31. Allen Davis, *Spearheads for Reform: The Social Settlements and the Progressive Movement, 1880–1914* (New York: Oxford Univ. Press, 1967).

32. Bevir, "British Socialism," 878.

33. For Gordin's satire: Lucy Dawidowicz, "Louis Marshall's Yiddish Newspaper, *The Jewish World*," *Jewish Social Studies* 25, no. 2 (Apr. 1963), 109–10; Gerald Sorin, *A Time for Building: The Third Migration, 1880–1920* (Baltimore: Johns Hopkins Univ. Press, 1992), 88. For Gordin: Beth Kaplan, *Finding the Jewish Shakespeare: The Life and Legacy of Jacob Gordin* (Syracuse: Syracuse Univ. Press, 2007).

34. Deborah Dash Moore, *B'nai B'rith and the Challenge of Ethnic Leadership* (Albany: State Univ. of New York Press, 1981), 64.

35. In spirit, Schiff's activities in opposition to the czarist regime, including the floating of loan support to Japan during the 1904–5 war and supporting the AJC's abrogation campaign (analyzed in chapter 4), seem tantamount to a one-man war. For Schiff's calculations and activities in this respect, see Naomi Cohen, *Jacob H. Schiff: A Study in American Jewish Leadership* (Hanover: Brandeis Univ. Press, 1999), 33–34, 134–37, 144–52.

36. This biographical information is drawn from Miriam Blaustein, ed., *Memoirs of David Blaustein, Educator and Communal Worker* (1913) (facsimile edition, New York: Arno Press, 1975), 3–34.

37. This description draws from S. P. Rudens, "A Half Century of Community Service: The Story of the Educational Alliance," *American Jewish Year Book, 5707* (Philadelphia: The Jewish Publication Society of America, 1944), 73–86.

38. Blaustein, *Memoirs of David Blaustein,* 54.

39. Isidor Straus to Marshall, June 15, 1897, LM Papers, Box 91.

40. Marshall to Albert Hochstadter, Mar. 7, 1899, LM Papers, Box 124.

41. Jerold Auerbach, *Rabbis and Lawyers: The Journey from Torah to Constitution* (Bloomington: Indiana Univ. Press, 1990), 93.

42. In 1919, years after the end of the reform phase analyzed here, Marshall identified Uptown paternalism as the key impediment in the alliance's work. Referring to the alliance's detached patrons and social workers, Marshall wrote, "They held themselves aloof from the people. They did not associate with them, socially, religiously or otherwise. They acted as Lords and Ladies Bountiful bringing gifts to people who did not seek for gifts. They frankly avowed the purpose of bettering those among whom they labored and of dealing with them as a problem." Marshall to Samuel Greenbaum, Jan. 27, 1919, cited in Morton Rosenstock, *Louis Marshall: Defender of Jewish Rights* (Detroit: Wayne Univ. Press, 1965), 48.

43. Committee on Moral Culture, Annual Report, Nov. 8, 1899, LM Papers, Box 124.

44. Ibid.

45. Committee on Moral Culture, [Annual Report], 1900–1901, LM Papers, Box 124.

46. Ibid.

47. Davis, *Spearheads for Reform.*

48. Louis Lipsky, *A Gallery of Zionist Profiles* (New York: Farrar, Straus and Cudahy, 1956), 193–95; Lucy Dawidowicz, "Louis Marshall's Yiddish Newspaper," 103.

49. Marshall to David Blaustein, Jan. 4, 1900, LM Papers, Box 124.

50. David Blaustein to Marshall, Feb. 12, 1900, LM Papers, Box 124.

51. Marshall correspondence, LM Papers, Box 124.

52. Gerald Kurland, *Seth Low: The Reformer in an Urban and Industrial Age* (New York: Twayne, 1971), 57.

53. Ibid., 73.

54. Lawrence Fuchs, ed., *American Ethnic Politics* (New York: Harper and Row, 1968), 53.

55. Kurland, *Seth Low,* 121.

56. Ibid., 117–20.

57. Marshall to Felix Adler, Nov. 19, 1900, LM Papers, Box 1571.

58. David Blaustein to Marshall, Nov. 11, 1901, LM Papers, Box 124.

59. The offering of nonkosher food at the July 1883 celebration in Cincinnati for the HUC's initial class of four graduating rabbis scandalized some traditional-minded rabbis and catalyzed a search for new frameworks for Judaism in America; this search accelerated after the Reform movement promulgated its Pittsburgh Platform commanding the observance of only Jewish laws and customs that "elevate and sanctify our lives." Jonathan Sarna, *American Judaism: A History* (New Haven: Yale Univ. Press, 2004), 144–51.

60. Jeffrey Gurock, *The Men and Women of Yeshiva: Higher Education, Orthodoxy and American Judaism* (New York: Columbia Univ. Press, 1988), 11; Hasia Diner, "Like the Antelope and the Badger: The Founding and Early Years of the Jewish Theological Seminary, 1886–1902," in *Tradition Renewed: A History of the Jewish Theological Seminary,* ed. Jack Wertheimer (New York: Jewish Theological Seminary of America, 1997), 1:13.

61. Sarna, *American Judaism,* 184–85.

62. Diner, "Like the Antelope and the Badger," 1:7–14.

63. Mel Scult, "Schechter's Seminary," in Wertheimer, *Tradition Renewed,* 1:85–89.

64. Ibid., 1:47. Scult argues that the Schiff-Marshall-Adler group and scholars sympathetic to its actions are guilty of a "deliberate distortion of the actual events."

65. Ibid., 1:50.

66. Diner, "Like the Antelope and the Badger," 1:17.

67. Sarna, *American Judaism,* 185.

68. Diner, "Like the Antelope and the Badger," 1:35.

69. Sarna, *American Judaism,* 185.

70. Abraham Karp, "Solomon Schechter Comes to America," *American Jewish Historical Quarterly* 53, no. 1 (Sept. 1963), 55–56.

71. Ibid., 45.

72. This short biographical account of Schechter draws from Sarna, *American Judaism,* 188; and Jerold Auerbach, *Rabbis and Lawyers,* 100–101.

73. Auerbach, *Rabbis and Lawyers,* 101.

74. Ibid.

75. Karp, "Solomon Schechter," 48.

76. Ibid., 57.

77. Sarna, *American Judaism,* 98.

78. Marshall correspondence, Apr. 1900, LM Papers, Box 1571.

79. Marshall to Joseph Stolz, May 9, 1900, LM Papers, Box 1571.

80. Jenna Weissman Joselit, "By Design: Building the Campus of the Jewish Theological Seminary," in Wertheimer, *Tradition Renewed,* 1:273.

81. Auerbach, *Rabbis and Lawyers,* 97–98.

82. Marshall to Mayer Sulzberger, Apr. 9, 1901, LM Papers, Box 1581.

83. Ibid.

84. Ibid.

85. This description is based on Marshall's recounting of events in the JTS reorganization's initial phase, in April 1901. Other descriptions increase the sums—Auerbach describes a 1901 meeting in Schiff's home where the host pledged $100,000, Leonard Lewisohn donated $100,000, Daniel Guggenheim and his brothers added $50,000, and Mayer Sulzberger offered his fine library. Auerbach, *Rabbis and Lawyers,* 97.

86. Marshall to Julius Rosenwald, Aug. 6, 1929, in Reznikoff, *Louis Marshall,* 2:889–94.

87. Marshall to Philip Cowan, Apr. 30, 1900, LM Papers, Box 1571; Moshe Davis, *The Emergence of Conservative Judaism: The Historical School in Nineteenth Century America* (Philadelphia: The Jewish Publication Society of America, 1965), 321.

88. Marshall to Philip Cowan, Apr. 30, 1900.

89. Marshall to Leonard Lewisohn, May 16, 1901, LM Papers, Box 1571.

90. Marshall to Hebrew Union College, June 15, 1903, LM Papers, Box 1572.

91. Marshall to Joseph Stolz, June 7, 1904, LM Papers, Box 1573.

92. Marshall to Edgar Nathan, June 11, 1907, LM Papers, Box 1576.

93. Marshall to David Blaustein, June 11, 1907, LM Papers, Box 1576.

94. Marshall to Solomon Schechter, June 13, 1907, LM Papers, Box 1576.

95. Marshall to Solomon Schechter, June 20, 1907, LM Papers, Box 1576.

96. Marshall to editor of *Jewish Daily News,* June 28, 1907, LM Papers, Box 1576.

97. Ibid.

98. Marshall to Jacob Schiff, Jan. 11, 1902, LM Papers, Box 1572.

99. Ibid.; Marshall to Jacob Schiff, May 9, 1903, LM Papers, Box 1572.

100. Scult, "Schechter's Seminary," 1:52.

101. Marshall to N. A. Elsberg, Jan. 14, 1902, LM Papers, Box 1572.

102. Ibid.

103. Scult, "Schechter's Seminary," 1:52–53.

104. Ibid.

105. Marshall to Jacob Schiff, Mar. 29, 1902, LM Papers, Box 1572; Scult, "Schechter's Seminary," 1:53

106. Moses Ottinger to Marshall, Dec. 15, 1902, cited in Scult, "Schechter's Seminary," 1:54–55.

107. Marshall to Jacob Schiff, Mar. 29, 1902.

108. Marshall to Jacob Schiff, Dec. 9, 1902, LM Papers, Box 1572.

109. Marshall to Jacob Schiff, Dec. 29, 1902, LM Papers, Box 1572.

110. Marshall to Rayner Frank, Apr. 22, 1908, LM Papers, Box 1577.

111. Marshall to Julius Rosenwald, Aug. 6, 1919.

112. Marshall to Leonard Lewisohn, May 16, 1901.

113. Sarna, *American Judaism,* 188.

114. Scult, "Schechter's Seminary," 1:58.

115. Marshall to A. S. Solomons, May 15, 1902, LM Papers, Box 1572.

116. Auerbach, *Rabbis and Lawyers,* 105; Scult, "Schechter's Seminary," 1:73.

117. Auerbach, *Rabbis and Lawyers,* 106–7.

118. Scult, "Schechter's Seminary," 1:74.

119. The student was Herman Rubenovitz, JTS class of 1908, Scult, "Schechter's Seminary," 1:74.

120. Magnes, *Episodes,* 32–35.

121. Marshall to Mayer Sulzberger, Mar. 30, 1903; Marshall to Cyrus Adler, Apr. 3, 1903, LM Papers, Box 1572. There appears to be a discrepancy in Marshall's papers as to whether Schechter was offered an initial annual salary of $4,000 or $5,000 (Scult, "Schechter's Seminary," 1:55, suggests the former figure). Schechter was underpaid at Cambridge and relied on loans from friends to get by—his sensitivity about the JTS salary should be seen in this light. The mixture of rivalry and cooperation in his relationship with his HUC counterpart, Kaufmann Kohler, is discussed in Sarna, *American Judaism,* 189–91.

122. Marshall to Cyrus Adler, June 16, 1902, LM Papers, Box 1572.

123. Marshall to Isidor Lewi, Oct. 25, 1904, LM Papers, Box 1573.

124. Lehman eventually left the JTS and joined Stephen Wise's Free Synagogue, where he experienced another tumultuous tenure. "E. H. Lehman Put Out of Free Synagogue," *New York Times,* Oct. 8, 1912.

125. Marshall to Eugene Lehman, Feb. 28, 1905, LM Papers, Box 1574.

126. Ibid.

127. Marshall to Eugene Lehman, Mar. 11, 1905, LM Papers, Box 1574.

128. Marshall to Isidor Lewi, Oct. 25, 1904.

129. Marshall to Eugene Lehman, Mar. 11, 1905.

130. *Syracuse Herald,* Sept. 27, 1929, OHAMRC.

131. Dawidowicz, "Louis Marshall's Yiddish Newspaper," 102–32.

132. Mordecai Soltes, *The Yiddish Press: An Americanizing Agency* (New York: Teachers College, Columbia Univ., 1925), 176.

133. The AJC monitored and supported Mordecai Soltes's research about the Yiddish press as an Americanizing force. American Jewish Committee Archives, AJC Executive Committee Minutes, vol. 5, Nov. 17, 1923.

134. Marshall correspondence, June 5, 1902, LM Papers, Box 1572.

135. Marshall to Cyrus Sulzberger, June 14, 1902, in Dawidowicz, "Louis Marshall's Yiddish Newspaper," 104.

136. Information in this paragraph draws from Soltes, *The Yiddish Press,* 14–29.

137. Marshall to Edward Lauterbach, Sept. 16, 1904, LM Papers, Box 1573. Marshall explains that in 1900 *Daily News* editor Ezekiel Sarasohn favored the reelection bid of incumbent president William McKinley until the last days of the race, when he switched colors and endorsed William Jennings Bryan. Schiff and Marshall "severely took to task" the Yiddish editor for this betrayal of the Republican cause.

138. Marshall to Adolph Ochs, Jan. 21, 1902, LM Papers, Box 1572.

139. Dawidowicz, "Louis Marshall's Yiddish Newspaper," 104.

140. Ibid.

141. Marshall correspondence, June 5, 1902, LM Papers, Box 1572.

142. For the *Jewish World* investment tally: Dawidowicz, "Louis Marshall's Yiddish Newspaper," 105; Marshall to Isidor Straus, June 7, 1902, LM Papers, Box 1572. Marshall personally raised $14,000 for the newspaper.

143. Marshall to Adolph Ochs, June 7, 1902, LM Papers, Box 1572.

144. Marshall to Isidor Lewi, July 14, 1902, LM Papers, Box 1572.

145. Marshall to Jacob Schiff, June 18, 1902, LM Papers, Box 1572.

146. For Rubinow's career: J. Lee Kreader, "Isaac Max Rubinow: America's Prophet for Social Security" (PhD diss., University of Chicago, 1988). Ironically, fifteen years after he penned penetrating journalistic criticism of heavy-handed *Yahudim* moral posturing on the East Side, Rubinow would metaphorically cross over from Downtown to Uptown roles—he was excoriated by Zionist pioneers in newly British Palestine as a paternalistic American director of the Hadassah medical unit. See Matthew Silver, *First Contact: Origins of the American-Israeli Connection, Halutzim from America During the Palestine Mandate* (West Hartford: Graduate Group, 2006), 71–132.

147. Isaac Max Rubinow, "The Jewish Question in New York City, 1902–1903," *American Jewish Historical Society Publications* 49 (Sept. 1959–June 1960), 112.

148. Ibid., 113.

149. Ibid., 116.

150. Ibid.

151. Dawidowicz, "Louis Marshall's Yiddish Newspaper," 110; Rubinow, "The Jewish Question in New York City," 119.

152. Dawidowicz, "Louis Marshall's Yiddish Newspaper," 110.

153. *American Hebrew,* Mar. 6, 1903, cited in Dawidowicz, "Louis Marshall's Yiddish Newspaper," 110.

154. Marshall to David Blaustein, June 19, 1902, LM Papers, Box 1572.

155. Marshall to John McDonough, Aug. 21, 1902 LM Papers, Box 1572.

156. Marshall to Max Bucans, Aug. 14, 1902, LM Papers, Box 1572.

157. Dawidowicz, "Louis Marshall's Yiddish Newspaper," 111.

158. Marshall to Max Bucans, Aug. 19, 1902, LM Papers, Box 1572.

159. Ibid.

160. Marshall to Max Bucans, Sept. 12, 1902, LM Papers, Box 1572.

161. "Investigating the Rioting," *New York Times,* Aug. 2, 1902, 2.

162. Marshall to Max Bucans, Sept. 12, 1902.

163. Dawidowicz, "Louis Marshall's Yiddish Newspaper," 119–20.

164. Marshall to Joseph Jacobs, Oct. 31, 1902, LM Papers, Box 1572.

165. Dawidowicz, "Louis Marshall's Yiddish Newspaper," 106.

166. Ibid., 116.

167. Ibid., 118–19; Marshall to H. H. Rogers, Aug. 24, 1903, LM Papers, Box 1572. Marshall warned the Republican financier that other Yiddish newspapers had a "tendency in the direction of socialism and anarchy."

168. Dawidowicz, "Louis Marshall's Yiddish Newspaper," 121.

169. Marshall to Z. H. Masliansky, Oct. 4, 1902, LM Papers, Box 1572.

170. Marshall to D. M. Hermalin, Dec. 12, 1903, LM Papers, Box 1572.

171. Marshall to Z. H. Masliansky, Dec. 12, 1903, in Dawidowicz, "Louis Marshall's Yiddish Newspaper," 115.

172. Eli Lederhendler, *Jewish Immigrants and American Capitalism, 1880–1920: From Caste to Class* (Cambridge: Cambridge Univ. Press, 2009).

173. Marshall to Max Bucans, Aug. 25, 1902, LM Papers, Box 1572.

174. Marshall to Max Bucans, Oct. 23, 1902, LM Papers, Box 1572.

175. Ibid.

176. Dawidowicz, "Louis Marshall's Yiddish Newspaper," 103.

177. Ibid., 106.

178. Ibid., 112.

179. Marshall to Max Bucans, Sept. 9, 1902, LM Papers, Box 1572.

180. Ibid. Marshall refers to the involvement of Schiff and Mayer Sulzberger with the Baron de Hirsch fund.

181. In the 1902 elections, for instance, the *World* aggressively lobbied for Republican candidate Charles Adler, who was routed by Democratic rival Henry Mayer Goldfogle in the race for a seat in Congress from the Ninth District. "Every patriotic Jew" ought to vote for Adler, declared the *World,* but by a margin of two to one, Jews on the East Side cast ballots for the Democratic candidate. Dawidowicz, "Louis Marshall's Jewish Newspaper," 119–20.

182. Hutchins Hapgood, *The Spirit of the Ghetto* (1902) (Cambridge, MA: Harvard College, 1967).

183. Marshall to Adolph Ochs, Apr. 9, 1904, LM Papers, Box 1619.

184. Adolph Ochs to Marshall, Apr. 12, 1904, LM Papers, Box 1619. Neither man in this correspondence seemed troubled by the inconsistency of their belonging to an elite Jewish discussion club named, half-facetiously, by its own members, "the Wanderers."

185. Marshall to Adolph Ochs, Sept. 13, 1902, LM Papers, Box 1572.

186. Marshall to D. M. Hermalin, Apr. 15, 1904, LM Papers, Box 1573.

187. Marshall to Paul Herzog, May 9, 1904, LM Papers, Box 1573; Dawidowicz, "Louis Marshall's Yiddish Newspaper," 123.

188. Dawidowicz, "Louis Marshall's Yiddish Newspaper," 123.

189. Marshall to D. M. Hermalin, May 28, 1904, LM Papers, Box 1573.

190. Marshall to Ezekiel Sarasohn, June 2, 1904, LM Papers, Box 1573.

191. Marshall to Edward Lauterbach, Sept. 16, 1904, LM Papers, Box 1573.

192. Ibid.

193. Ibid.

194. Jenna Weissman Joselit, *Our Gang: Jewish Crime and the New York Jewish Community, 1900–1940* (Bloomington: Indiana Univ. Press, 1983), 14.

195. For the context of the New York Kehillah's emergence, see chapter 3.

196. Joselit, *Our Gang,* 15.

197. Marshall to Seth Low, Mar. 25, 1902, LM Papers, Box 1572.

198. Marshall to Jacob Schiff, Apr. 7, 1902, LM Papers, Box 1572.

199. Ibid.

200. Marshall to George McClellan, Mar. 26, 1904, LM Papers, Box 1572.

201. Marshall correspondence, Feb. 24, 1904, LM Papers, Box 1572.

202. Ibid.

203. Marshall to Isaac Guggenheim, Oct. 31, 1906, in Rosenthal, "The Public Life of Louis Marshall," 73.

204. Marshall to Isidor Straus, Mar. 5, 1904, LM Papers, Box 1573.

205. Marshall correspondence, Nov. 19, 1904, LM Papers, Box 1573.

206. Ibid.

207. Marshall to Abraham L. Wolbarst, Dec. 1, 1904, LM Papers, Box 1573.

208. Marshall to Jacob Schiff, Dec. 7, 1904, LM Papers, Box 1573.

209. For the protectory's redesignation as the Hawthorne School: Rosenthal, "The Public Life of Louis Marshall," 79.

210. Joselit, *Our Gang,* 16.

211. Rosenthal, "The Public Life of Louis Marshall," 76.

212. Marshall to Samuel Hamburger, June 22, 1907, in Rosenthal, "The Public Life of Louis Marshall," 75.

213. Joselit, *Our Gang,* 20.

214. Ibid.

215. Ibid., 22.

3. The Origins of Organized Activism

1. Sorin, *A Time for Building,* 176–77.

2. Descriptions in this section are drawn from Leonard Dinnerstein, *Uneasy at Home: Antisemitism and the American Jewish Experience* (New York: Columbia Univ. Press, 1987), 149–77.

3. Ibid., 161.

4. Ibid.

5. Ibid., 167.

6. Ibid., 168.

7. "Report of the Mayor's Committee," *American Hebrew* (Sept. 19, 1902); Dinnerstein, *Uneasy at Home,* 168.

8. "Report of the Mayor's Committee."

9. Marshall to Max Bucans, Sept. 12, 1902, LM Papers, Box 1572.

10. Ibid.

11. Marshall to editors of *Jewish Gazette,* Dec. 29, 1902, LM Papers, Box 1572; Reznikoff, *Louis Marshall,* 1:11–12.

12. Information in this section draws from Shlomo Lambroza, "The Pogroms of 1903–1906," in *Pogroms: Anti-Jewish Violence in Modern Russian History,* ed. Shlomo Lambroza and John Klier (New York: Cambridge Univ. Press, 1992), 195–248.

13. Ibid., 221.

14. Ibid., 207.

15. The extent to which Jacob Schiff's underwriting of multimillion-dollar loans to the Japanese fueled Russian allegations of worldwide Jewish collusion with the Japanese enemy remains unclear. For accounts of the Schiff loan and its possible motivations and effects: Cohen, *Jacob H. Schiff,* 134–37; Daniel Gutwein, "Jacob H. Schiff and the Financing of the Russo-Japanese War" [in Hebrew], *Zion* 54 (1989), 321–50. In this context, it bears mention that the Rothschild family financed Russia's war effort.

16. Lambroza, "The Pogroms of 1903–1906," 234.

17. Jonathan Frankel, *Crisis, Revolution and Russian Jews* (Cambridge: Cambridge Univ. Press, 2009), 6. 71.

18. Marshall to D. M. Hermalin, Dec. 12, 1903, LM Papers, Box 1572.

19. For the Saratoga incident: Birmingham, *Our Crowd,* 143–47; Diner, *A Time for Gathering,* 191–92.

20. This section draws from Wayne Wiegand, *Irrepressible Reformer: A Biography of Melvil Dewey* (Chicago: American Library Association, 1996).

21. Ibid., 372.

22. Ibid., 252.

23. Ibid.

24. Ibid., 264.

25. Ibid., 266.

26. "A Petition to the Regents of the University of the State of New York," in Reznikoff, *Louis Marshall,* 1:12–14.

27. Ibid.

28. Wiegand, *Irrepressible Reformer,* 269.

29. Marshall to Bernard Lowenstein, Jan. 27, 1905, LM Papers, Box 1574.

30. Marshall to H. W. Rosenbaum, Jan. 25, 1905, LM Papers, Box 1574.

31. Information in this section draws from Shuly Rubin Schwartz, *The Emergence of Jewish Scholarship in America: The Publication of the Jewish Encyclopedia* (Cincinnati: Hebrew Union College Press, 1991).

32. Ibid., 20–21.

33. Isidore Singer, *Russia at the Bar of the American People: A Memorial of Kishinef* (New York: Funk and Wagnalls, 1904).

34. Schwartz, *The Emergence of Jewish Scholarship,* 97.

35. See, in this connection, Marshall's Feb. 11, 1905, letter to I. K. Funk, in Reznikoff, *Louis Marshall,* 1:15–18.

36. Schwartz, *The Emergence of Jewish Scholarship,* 277–79.

37. Ibid.

38. Marshall to I. K. Funk, Feb. 11, 1905, in Reznikoff, *Louis Marshall,* 1:15–18.

39. Ibid., 17.

40. Library Committee of New York University meeting, Feb. 2, 1905, Melvil Dewey Papers, Columbia University Libraries Archival Collection, Box 70; Schwartz, *The Emergence of Jewish Scholarship,* 270–74.

41. Schwartz, *The Emergence of Jewish Scholarship,* 280–85.

42. Regents of the University of the State of New York meeting, Feb. 15, 1905, LM Papers, Box 151; Schwartz, *The Emergence of Jewish Scholarship,* 280.

43. Marshall to Whitelaw Reid, undated, LM Papers, Box 1574.

44. Marshall to Bernard Lowenstein, undated, LM Papers, Box 1574.

45. Ibid.

46. Marshall to Edward Lauterbach, May 17, 1905, June 1, 1905, June 17, 1905, LM Papers, Box 1574.

47. Schwartz, *The Emergence of Jewish Scholarship,* 287.

48. Rosenthal, "The Public Life of Louis Marshall," 38.

49. Marshall to Arthur Brisbane, Nov. 4, 1915, in Reznikoff, *Louis Marshall,* 2:1155–160.

50. Sarna, "Two Jewish Lawyers Named Louis." For Brandeis's emergence as an attorney for the people, see Urofsky, *Louis D. Brandeis,* 201–27.

51. The Israeli scholar Allon Gal emphasized Brandeis's incomplete integration in Boston's Wasp elite circles as a factor motivating his conversion as a Zionist, relatively late in a life that lacked strong previous commitments to Jewish life. This is not the sole interpretation of an ultimately irresoluble question of personal motivation, but Gal's biography provides, nonetheless, an impressive collection of evidence of Brandeis as a Brahmin outsider. Allon Gal, *Brandeis of Boston* (Cambridge, MA: Harvard Univ. Press, 1980).

52. Brandeis closely followed Untermyer's work on the Pujo investigation, calling it "admirable," and met with Marshall's partner in mid-March 1913. He then composed his series of articles in favor of breaking up the money trust; they were published by his friend Norman Hapgood in *Harper's Weekly* and then released as a collection: Louis Brandeis, *Other People's Money, and How the Bankers Use It* (New York: F. A. Stokes, 1914). Brandeis was reticent about Jewish dimensions of banking controversies, but readers of his articles were, of course, conscious of anti-Semitic innuendo concerning Jewish domination of the money trust, a perspective that had in late nineteenth-century America influenced rural progressive politics in the Populist movement. That Brandeis's interest in banking questions was most pointedly articulated in the period when he became an American Zionist leader has a vague circumstantial suggestiveness, but no proof has been furnished regarding a "Jewish" motivation of his famous call to break up the money trust. For a recent, thoughtful essay implying that it is naïve to dismiss the possibility of such a motivation, see Jerry Muller, "The Long Shadow of Usury," in *Capitalism and the Jews* (Princeton: Princeton Univ. Press, 2010), 1–72.

53. Rosenthal, "The Public Life of Louis Marshall," 36.

54. Metropolitan Street Railway Company v. New York State Board of Tax Commissioners, 199 U.S. 1 (1904).

55. Jerold Auerbach, *Unequal Justice: Lawyers and Social Change in Modern America* (New York: Oxford Univ. Press, 1976), 25. In 1910, it bears mention, Root publicly supported income tax proposals that became the Sixteenth Amendment.

56. Ibid.

57. Rosenthal, "The Public Life of Louis Marshall," 36.

58. Metropolitan Street Railway Company v. New York State Board of Tax Commissioners, 199 U.S. 1 (1904).

59. Rosenthal, "The Public Life of Louis Marshall," 39–40.

60. Marshall to W. W. Armstrong, Apr. 23, 1907, in Rosenthal, "The Public Life of Louis Marshall," 40–41. Armstrong was a New York State senator.

61. Rosenthal carefully studied the correspondence relating to Marshall's work on this case but was unable to determine whether a $5,000 payment to him was understood as an installment or a total fee. Rosenthal, "The Public Life of Louis Marshall," 41.

62. Arthur Goren, *The Politics and Public Culture of American Jews* (Bloomington: Indiana Univ. Press, 1999), 38. In this general connection, see also Judith Friedman Rosen, "Earlier American Jewish Anniversary Celebrations: 1905 and 1954," *American Jewish History* (December 2004), 481–97.

63. Lambroza, "The Pogroms of 1903–1906," 229.

64. Goren, *The Politics and Public Culture,* 39.

65. For a survey of Schiff's shifting ideas about opportunities posed by the Russo-Japanese War and the rationale of his financial support of the Japanese, see Cohen, *Jacob H. Schiff,* 134–37.

Toward the end of the war, Marshall believed that the "utter annihilation" of Russian forces at Vladivostok would do more to mollify Jewish suffering in Russia than any proposed political reform. Marshall to Solomon Schechter, Aug. 24, 1905, LM Papers, Box 1574.

66. Marshall to Gustavus Rogers, July 25, 1905, LM Papers, Box 1574.

67. Goren, *The Politics and Public Culture,* 37.

68. Louis Marshall, *Executive Committee in Charge of the Celebration of the 250th Anniversary of the Settlement of Jews in the U.S.,* 26; Rosen, "Earlier American Jewish Anniversary Celebrations," 482.

69. Marshall to Mayer Sulzberger, Apr. 29, 1905, LM Papers, Box 1574.

70. Marshall to Jacob Schiff, May 22, 1905, LM Papers, Box 1574.

71. Marshall to G. M. Hyams, Sept. 14, 1905, LM Papers, Box 1574.

72. Marshall to Simon Wolf, May 23, Nov. 1, 1905, LM Papers, Box 1574.

73. Marshall to Jacob Schiff, Apr. 13, 1905, LM Papers, Box 1574.

74. Goren, *The Politics and Public Culture,* 37.

75. Rosen, "Earlier American Jewish Anniversary Celebrations," 484.

76. Marshall to David Blaustein, Oct. 7, 1905, LM Papers, Box 1574.

77. Marshall to H. Pereira Mendes, Nov. 16 1905, LM Papers, Box 1574.

78. Goren, *The Politics and Public Culture,* 39.

79. Marshall to Max Kohler, Nov. 10, 1905, LM Papers, Box 1574.

80. Rosen, "Earlier American Jewish Anniversary Celebrations," 483–84.

81. This description draws from Goren, *The Politics and Public Culture,* 39–40.

82. Ibid., 41.

83. Ibid.

84. Ibid., 39.

85. Marshall to Nathan Straus, Dec. 1, 1905, LM Papers, Box 1574.

86. Ibid.

87. Marshall, "The Jew as an American Citizen," Congregation Rodeph Shalom, Philadelphia, Apr. 17, 1906, LM Papers, Box 151.

88. Naomi Cohen, *Not Free to Desist: A History of the American Jewish Committee, 1906–1966* (Philadelphia: The Jewish Publication Society of America, 1972), 4.

89. Matthew Silver, "Louis Marshall and the Democratization of Jewish Identity," 42.

90. Cohen, *Jacob H. Schiff,* 138.

91. Ibid.

92. Ibid., 139.

93. Marshall to Solomon Schechter, Aug. 24, 1905, LM Papers, Box 1574.

94. Marshall to Adolph Ochs, Dec. 1, 1905, LM Papers, Box 1574.

95. For accounts of the Emanu-El affair: Melvin Urofsky, *A Voice That Spoke for Justice: The Life and Times of Stephen S. Wise* (Albany: State University of New York Press, 1982); Mark Raider, "The Aristocrat and the Democrat: Louis Marshall, Stephen S. Wise and the Challenge of American Jewish Leadership," *American Jewish History* 94, nos. 1–2 (Mar.–June 2008), 95–98; Reznikoff, *Louis Marshall,* 2:831–38.

96. Sarna, *American Judaism,* 251.

97. Raider, "The Aristocrat and the Democrat," 97.

98. Marshall to Stephen S. Wise, Dec. 1, 1905, in Reznikoff, *Louis Marshall,* 2:831–33.

99. Reznikoff, *Louis Marshall,* 2:832–36.

100. *New York Times,* Jan. 8, 1906, 5, in Reznikoff, *Louis Marshall,* 2:836.

101. Adolph Ochs, "Pulpit and Pews," *New York Times,* Jan. 11, 1906, 8, in Reznikoff, *Louis Marshall,* 2:836–37.

102. Arthur Goren, ed., *Dissenter in Zion: From the Writings of Judah L. Magnes* (Cambridge, MA: Harvard Univ. Press, 1982), 3–13; Daniel Kotzin, *Judah Magnes: An American Jewish Nonconformist* (Syracuse: Syracuse Univ. Press, 2010).

103. Marshall to Judah Magnes, Nov. 29, 1905, LM Papers, Box 1574.

104. Marshall to Magnes, Dec. 1, 1905, LM Papers, Box 1574.

105. Marshall to Joseph Stolz, Dec. 6, 1905, LM Papers, Box 1574.

106. Ibid.

107. Evyatar Friesal, "Magnes: Zionism in Judaism," in *Like All the Nations? The Life and Legacy of Judah L. Magnes,* ed. Moses Rischin and William Brinner (Albany: State Univ. of New York Press, 1987), 69–81.

108. Marshall to Judah Magnes, Dec. 6, 1905, LM Papers, Box 1574. So powerful was Magnes's charm that he convinced Marshall and his board associates at Emanu-El to regard his mid-December sermon as a guest appearance rather than as a tryout. He was hired without a hitch. Marshall to Joseph Silverman, Dec. 12, 1905, LM Papers, Box 1574.

109. Marshall to Jacob Saperstein, Dec. 9, 1905, LM Papers, Box 1574.

110. Ibid.

111. Marshall to Joseph Stolz, Dec. 15, 1905, LM Papers, Box 1574.

112. Marshall's comment that the idea of a national Jewish organization was "in the air" during this period was used by Naomi Cohen as the title of her chapter on AJC's founding: Cohen, *Not Free to Desist,* 8.

113. Marshall to Joseph Stolz, Dec. 15, 1905, LM Papers, Box 1574.

114. Ibid.

115. Moore, *B'nai B'rith,* 70.

116. Cohen, *Jacob H. Schiff,* 159–68; Meri-Jane Rochelson, *A Jew in the Public Arena: The Career of Israel Zangwill* (Detroit: Wayne Univ. Press, 2008), 152–53.

117. Esther Panitz, *Simon Wolf: Private Conscience and Public Image* (Rutherford, NJ: Fairleigh Dickinson Univ. Press, 1987), 176.

118. Ibid., 97.

119. Ibid., 136.

120. Marshall to Adolf Kraus, Dec. 26, 1905, LM Papers, Box 1574.

121. Ibid.

122. Ibid.; Silver, "Louis Marshall and the Democratization of Jewish Identity," 46.

123. Marshall to Cyrus Adler, Dec. 30, 1905, LM Papers, Box 1574; Reznikoff, *Louis Marshall,* 1:20–21; Silver, "Louis Marshall and the Democratization of Jewish Identity," 46.

124. Marshall to Mayer Sulzberger, Dec. 29, 1905, LM Papers, Box 1574.

125. Marshall to Adler, Dec. 30, 1905.

126. Invitation to AJC General Meeting, Jan. 8, 1906, LM Papers, Box 1575. The invitation was signed by Marshall, Samuel Greenbaum, Nathan Bijur, and Joseph Jacobs (secretary).

127. Marshall to Joseph Stolz, Jan. 12, 1906, LM Papers, Box 1575; Marshall correspondence, Jan. 1906, LM Papers, Box 1575.

128. Marshall to Joseph Stolz, Jan. 12, 1906.

129. This section is based on Protocol of Meetings, Feb. 3–4, 1906, American Jewish Committee Minutes, vol. 1, American Jewish Committee Archives.

130. Ibid.

131. Jonathan Woocher, "The Democratization of the American Jewish Polity," in *Authority, Power and Leadership in the Jewish Polity,* ed. Daniel Elazar (New York: Univ. Press of America, 1991), 168.

132. Protocol of Meetings, Feb. 3–4, 1906, American Jewish Committee Minutes, vol. 1, American Jewish Committee Archives.

133. Ibid.

134. Ibid.

135. Marshall to Judah Magnes, Mar. 24, 1906, LM Papers, Box 1575.

136. Report of Mar. 18 meeting (addressed to Mayer Sulzberger), LM Papers, Box 1575.

137. Marshall to Cyrus Adler, Mar. 24, 1906, LM Papers, Box 1575.

138. Marshall to Simon Wolf, Adolf Kraus, and Emil Hirsch, May 15, 1906, LM Papers, Box 1575.

139. Marshall to Simon Rosendale, May 16, 1906, LM Papers, Box 1575.

140. May 12 letter to Mayer Sulzberger, from Emil Hirsch, Adolf Kraus, J. L. Leucht, and Josiah Cohen. Minutes of May 19, 1906, meeting, American Jewish Committee Minutes, vol. 1, American Jewish Committee Archives.

141. Minutes of May 19, 1906, meeting, AJC Minutes, vol. 1, American Jewish Committee Archives.

142. David Dalin, "The Patriarch, The Life and Legacy of Mayer Sulzberger," in *When Philadelphia Was the Capital of Jewish America,* ed. Murray Friedman (Philadelphia: Balch Institute Press, 1993), 60.

143. Ibid.

144. Ibid.

145. Sulzberger, to be fair, also criticized the "assumed superiority" of settled American Jews in his summation remarks at the end of the AJC constituent conferences. In her 1972 study, Naomi Cohen described Sulzberger's remarks as "eloquent": Cohen, *Not Free to Desist,* 15.

146. Murray Friedman, "The Philadelphia Group—A Collective Portrait," in Friedman, ed., *When Philadelphia Was the Capital of Jewish America,* 9–22.

147. Ibid., 15.

148. Marshall to Jacob Saperstein, May 23, 1906, LM Papers, Box 1575.

149. Marshall to Henry Stix, Jan. 16, 1907, LM Papers, Box 1576.

150. Judith Goldstein, *The Politics of Ethnic Pressure: The American Jewish Committee Fight Against Immigrant Restriction, 1906–1917* (New York: Garland Publishers, 1990), 71. The figures cited, drawn from the *Report of the Commissioner-General of Immigration,* are from July 1905 to June 1906, a period ending a few weeks after the submission of the Dillingham bill.

151. Goldstein, *The Politics of Ethnic Pressure,* 90.

152. Ibid., 91.

153. John Higham, *Strangers in the Land: Patterns of American Nativism, 1860–1925,* 2nd ed. (New Brunswick: Rutgers Univ. Press, 2002), 158.

154. Edward Bemis, "Restriction of Immigration," *Andover Review* 9 (Mar. 1888), 251–63.

155. Ibid., 261–63.

156. Goldstein, *The Politics of Ethnic Pressure,* 72–73.

157. Ibid., 76–77.

158. Ibid., 77.

159. Ibid., 79. For a thought-provokingly long list of academics connected to the league, see Barbara Miller Solomon, *Ancestors and Immigrants: A Changing New England Tradition* (Cambridge, MA: Harvard Univ. Press, 1956), 123.

160. Solomon, *Ancestors and Immigrants,* 124.

161. Ibid.

162. Goldstein, *The Politics of Ethnic Pressure,* 105–6.

163. Marshall correspondence, Aug. 1902, LM Papers, Box 1572.

164. Marshall to Nissim Behar, June 6, 1905, LM Papers, Box 1574.

165. Ibid., 87.

166. Solomon, *Ancestors and Immigrants,* 167.

167. Ibid., 168.

168. Ibid.

169. Goldstein, *The Politics of Ethnic Pressure,* 95.

170. Ibid., 97.

171. Solomon, *Ancestors and Immigrants,* 125.

172. Goldstein, *The Politics of Ethnic Pressure,* 102–3.

173. Ibid., 110.

174. Ibid., 94.

175. Marshall to Jacob Ruppert, Jan. 21, 1907, LM Papers, Box 1576.

176. Marshall to Jacob Wertheim, Feb. 2, 1907, LM Papers, Box 1576.

177. Marshall to Carrol S. Page, Jan. 28, 1907, Louis Marshall Collection P–24, Center for Jewish History [CJH].

178. William Dillingham to Carrol S. Page, Feb. 1, 1907, LM Collection P–24, CJH.

179. Marshall to Carrol S. Page, Feb. 6, 1907, LM Papers, Box 1576.

180. Marshall to William Dillingham, Feb. 7, 1907, LM Collection P–24, CJH.

181. Marshall to Daniel Guggenheim, Feb. 9, 1907, LM Collection P–24, CJH.

182. Goldstein, *The Politics of Ethnic Pressure,* 123.

183. Ibid., 124.

184. Ibid., 125.

185. Marshall to Edward Lauterbach Feb. 9, 1907, LM Papers, Box 1576.

186. Marshall to Cyrus Adler, Feb. 6, 1907, LM Papers, Box 1576.

187. Marshall to Edward Lauterbach, Feb. 9, 1907.

188. Marshall to Jacob Schiff, Feb. 13, 1907, LM Papers, Box 1576.

189. Goldstein, *The Politics of Ethnic Pressure,* 120.

190. Ibid., 126–27. See, generally, Charles Neu, *An Uncertain Friendship: Theodore Roosevelt and Japan, 1906–1909* (Cambridge, MA: Harvard Univ. Press, 1967).

191. Marshall to Mayer Sulzberger, Feb. 18, 1907, LM Papers, Box 1576.

4. Abrogation

1. Clifford Egan, "Pressure Groups, the Department of State, and the Abrogation of the Russian-American Treaty of 1832," *Proceedings of the American Philosophical Society* 115, no. 4 (Aug. 1971), 328–34.

2. Naomi Cohen, "The Abrogation of the Russo-American Treaty of 1832," *Jewish Social Studies* 25, no. 1 (Jan. 1963), 38.

3. Ibid., 7.

4. J. J. Goldberg, *Jewish Power: Inside the American Jewish Establishment* (Reading, 1996), 338–44.

5. For an insightful argument holding that this Uptown disavowal of Jewish politics in America was essentially rhetorical, see David Dalin, "Louis Marshall, the Jewish Vote, and the Republican Party," *Jewish Political Studies Review* 4 (Spring 1992), 55–84.

6. Marshall to Adolph Lewisohn, Nov. 11, 1907, LM Papers, Box 1576.

7. American Jewish Committee Executive Committee Minutes, vol. 1, Apr. 21, 1907, American Jewish Committee Archives.

8. Panitz, *Simon Wolf,* 95–96.

9. Marshall to Mayer Sulzberger, Oct. 14, 1908, LM Papers, Box 1577.

10. Marshall to Elihu Root, Feb. 1, 1908, LM Papers, Box 1577, in Reznikoff, *Louis Marshall,* 1:50–52.

11. Marshall to Herbert Friedenwald, Feb. 4, 1908, LM Papers, Box 1577; Reznikoff, *Louis Marshall,* 1:52–53.

12. Ibid.

13. Marshall to Elihu Root, Feb. 13, 1908, LM Papers, Box 1577; Reznikoff, *Louis Marshall,* 1:53–55.

14. Marshall to Henry Goldfogle, Feb. 14, 1908, LM Papers, Box 1577.

15. Marshall to Henry Goldfogle, Feb. 24, 1908, LM Papers, Box 1577.

16. Marshall to Julius Rosenwald, Mar. 5, 1908, LM Papers, Box 1577. In this period, Marshall made use of the circulars' withdrawal in AJC fund-raising pitches to other notables, including Isidor Straus.

17. Cohen, "Abrogation," 3.

18. Ibid., 3–4.

19. Egan, "Pressure Groups," 329, 331.

20. Cohen, "Abrogation," 4.

21. Ibid., 3–8.

22. Spencer Klaw, "The World's Tallest Building," *American Heritage* 28, no. 2 (Feb. 1977), http://www.americanheritage.com/content/world%E2%80%99s-tallest-building?page=3.

23. Marshall to Mayer Sulzberger, May 13, 1908, LM Papers, Box 1577.

24. Ibid.

25. Ibid.

26. Cohen, "Abrogation," 6, 8. Cohen notes that this May 1908 memorandum called also for the abrogation of America's 1887 extradition agreement with Russia, but this demand was subsequently dropped as a result of objections raised in 1911 by Congressman Herbert Parsons in discussions with Marshall.

27. Marshall to Judah Magnes, Apr. 4, 1908, LM Papers, Box 1577.

28. Marshall to Benno Lewinson, May 12, 1908, LM Papers, Box 1577; Reznikoff, *Louis Marshall,* 2:894–97.

29. Ibid.

30. Ibid.

31. Israel Zangwill's play of this name, *The Melting Pot,* was first produced in this year. Rochelson, *A Jew in the Public Arena,* 180–87; David Biale, "The Melting Pot and Beyond: Jews and the

Politics of American Identity," in *Insider/Outsider: American Jews and Multiculturalism,* David Biale, Michael Galchinsky, and Susannah Heschel (Berkeley: Univ. of California Press, 1992), 17–33.

32. Marshall to Benno Lewinson, May 12, 1908.

33. *Report of the Commission of Immigration of the State of New York,* Apr. 5, 1909, LM Papers, Box 1. Members of the commission were Marshall (chairman), Frances Kellor (secretary), Philip Danahy, Charles Larmon, Marcus Marks, James Reynolds, Gino Speranza, Lillian Wald, Edward Whitney.

34. Marshall to Charles Taft, Aug. 21, 1908, LM Papers, Box 1577.

35. Marshall to Henry Wollman, Aug. 27, 1908, LM Papers, Box 1577.

36. Marshall to Mayer Sulzberger, Aug. 28, 1908, LM Papers, Box 1577.

37. Marshall to *Cincinnati Times-Star,* Sept. 16, 1908, LM Papers, Box 1577.

38. Arthur Goren, *New York Jews and the Quest for Community: The Kehillah Experiment, 1908–1922* (New York: Columbia Univ. Press, 1970); Theodore A. Bingham, "Foreign Criminals in New York," *North American Review* 188 (Sept. 1908), 384–94.

39. Information and allegations about Jewish or other ethnic crime were obviously exploitable by Nativists in the immigration discussions of the Dillingham Commission pre-WWI era, a period when government studies on "immigration and crime" were published. This issue weighed heavily on the thoughts of Marshall and other communal leaders, and was recognized implicitly by scholars like Goren, who in his classic study *New York Jews* (148) cited the government publications on immigrant crime alongside a quotation of Marshall's lament, "Jewish criminality is a cancer gnawing at our vitals."

40. For a discussion of concerns and responses to allegations about Jews and white slavery: Linda Kuzmack, *Woman's Cause: The Jewish Woman's Movement in England and the United States 1881–1933* (Columbus: Ohio State Univ. Press, 1990).

41. Marshall to Adolph Radin, Sept. 8, 1908, LM Papers, Box 1577.

42. Ibid.

43. Rosenthal, "The Public Life of Louis Marshall," 145.

44. Goren, *New York Jews,* 28.

45. Ibid.; Rosenthal, "The Public Life of Louis Marshall," 144.

46. Rosenthal, "The Public Life of Louis Marshall," 145.

47. Marshall to Arthur Woods, Sept. 15, 1908, LM Papers, Box 1577.

48. "Wrong about Jews, Bingham Admits," *New York Times,* Sept. 17, 1908.

49. In the wake of his controversial WWI pacifism, Magnes submitted his resignation from the Kehillah in 1920 and finally left the organization two years later; an organizational remnant of the Kehillah apparently functioned until 1925. Goren, *New York Jews,* 242–44. Goren (25–43) discusses the Kehillah's establishment and its relationship to the Bingham allegation.

50. Marshall worked hard in this period to legislate a "Civil Rights Act" in the Adirondacks to mitigate the ill effects of anti-Semitic hotel owners who posted insulting advertisements such as "Hebrews, consumptives, dogs not taken." Marshall's proposed bill, based on the theory that private property owners lacked a right to enforce discrimination in perniciously demeaning public language, imposed short jail terms or fines on offenders. The *New York Times* publisher Adolph Ochs collaborated with Marshall, editorializing for the bill, which was eventually legislated in New York in 1913. See Louis Marshall to Martin Saxe, June 3, 1907, LM Papers, Box 1576; Louis Marshall to Martin Saxe, May 22, 1907, in Reznikoff, *Louis Marshall,* 1:249–50; Marshall to Adolph

Ochs, May 23, 1907, LM Papers, Box 1576; "Bill to Protect Jews in Hotels," *New York Times,* May 23, 1907; Rosenstock, *Louis Marshall,* 69.

51. All of the facets mentioned here, research, education and more, are surveyed in Goren, *New York Jews.* The colorful experiment in internal communal law enforcement is also discussed in Joselit, *Our Gang.*

52. Marshall to the *Jewish Daily News,* Sept. 16, 1908, LM Papers, Box 1577.

53. In addition to the Rochelson and Biale references cited above, see, in this connection, Philip Gleason, *Speaking of Diversity: Language and Ethnicity in Twentieth-Century America* (Baltimore: Johns Hopkins Univ. Press, 1992), 3–46.

54. "Louis Stern Out as Emanu-El Trustee," *New York Times,* Jan. 30, 1908.

55. The trustees included A. J. Dittenhoefer, M. H. Moses, James Seligman, Daniel Guggenheim, Marshall, Samuel Schafer, and David Levintritt. The consistent opponents of Marshall's position were Moses and Seligman.

56. "Louis Stern Out as Emanu-El Trustee," *The New York Times,* Jan. 30, 1908.

57. Marshall to Jacob Schiff, Feb. 14, 1908, LM Papers, Box 1577.

58. Marshall to Solomon Schechter, Mar. 24, 1908, LM Papers, Box 1577. Marshall notes that Schiff's observations in Ottoman Palestine were "by no means hostile to the Zionists"; the banker hinted that their success depended upon ending Jerusalem Jews' reliance on foreign charity *halukah* funds.

59. Marshall to Jacob Schiff, Feb. 14, 1908.

60. Maurice Wohlgelernter, *Israel Zangwill: A Study* (New York: Columbia Univ. Press, 1964), 20–30.

61. Marshall to Adolphus S. Solomons, Oct. 21, 1905, LM Papers, Box 1574.

62. Ibid.

63. Cohen, *Jacob H. Schiff,* 159.

64. Marshall to Mayer Sulzberger, Oct. 22, 1908, LM Papers, Box 1577.

65. Marshall to Solomon Schechter, Sept. 14, 1909, LM Papers, Box 1578.

66. Ibid.

67. Goren, *Dissenter in Zion,* 103–6.

68. Ibid.

69. *New York Times,* Apr. 8, 1918, cited in Reznikoff, *Louis Marshall,* 2:809.

70. Goren, *New York Jews,* 4–5.

71. Marshall to Judah Magnes, Oct. 10, 1908, LM Papers, Box 1577.

72. Ibid.

73. Silver, "Louis Marshall and the Democratization of Jewish Identity."

74. Marshall interview in the *Jewish Daily News,* Oct. 28, 1908.

75. Ibid.

76. Marshall statement, Oct. 22, 1908, LM Papers, Box 1577. The case of the Latvian refugee Pouren was often cited by Marshall and other AJC spokesmen in this period. Secretary of State Root, who was soon to become a US senator, informed Schiff on Oct. 19, 1908, that the United States "had communicated" to Russia "an expression of its desire" for a "complete revision" of the 1832 treaty (see "Jan Pouren's Case Reopened by Root," *New York Times,* Oct. 22, 1908), http://query.nytimes.com/mem/archive-free/pdf?res=F00C11FA3B5A17738DDDAB0A94D8415B888CF1D3. The State Department's expression was pro forma and was, in all probability,

manipulated by the Republican office seekers a week before the elections to cultivate Jewish voters. Despite Marshall's touting of it as an unprecedented event in international politics, Root's letter to Schiff had no impact on subsequent Taft administration policy and was thus mentioned only in passing by Cohen in her "Abrogation" article (9) and not at all in her biography of Schiff.

77. Cohen, "Abrogation," 10.

78. Marshall to Solomon Schechter, Nov. 1, 1908, LM Papers, Box 1577.

79. Marshall to Oscar Straus, Mar. 4, 1909, LM Papers, Box 1578.

80. The contested Lowenstein will saga continued for years, and many folders in Marshall's papers sag with documents relating to it for a stretch of years beginning in Apr. 1907. Background to the affair can be found in "Lowenstein Will Contest: Petitioners Allege That Testator Was of Unsound Mind," *New York Times,* Apr. 29, 1907.

81. Marshall to Samuel Rabinowitz, Jan. 10, 1909, LM Papers, Box 1578.

82. Marshall to Solomon Schechter, Mar. 4, 1909, LM Papers, Box 1578.

83. Marshall to Adolph Ochs, Mar. 2, 1909, LM Papers, Box 1578.

84. When Marshall collected evidence in 1905 for his petition against Melvil Dewey, Butler's name appeared on lists connected to the exclusive Lake Placid Club. The petitioners debated among themselves whether to challenge Butler publicly about his association with the anti-Semitic resort but decided that the evidence was insufficiently conclusive. Marshall correspondence, Feb. 1905, LM Papers, Box 1574.

85. Cohen, *Jacob H. Schiff,* 73–74.

86. Cohen, *Jacob H. Schiff* (75) writes that Schiff "embraced a novel legal solution," leaving Marshall's authorship anonymous.

87. Marshall to Thomas Gray, Mar. 2, 1909, LM Papers, Box 1578.

88. Cohen, *Jacob H. Schiff,* 75.

89. Marshall to J. Allds, Apr. 9, 1909, LM Papers, Box 1578.

90. Wald's Henry Street Settlement was one of Jacob Schiff's favored projects on the Lower East Side (Cohen, *Jacob H. Schiff,* 91). The relationship between the banker and settlement house worker was positive and complex, and despite the obvious differences, including gender and Wald's situation as a leftist-oriented field worker, it can be compared to the Schiff-Marshall connection, particularly with regard to the way both Wald and Marshall depended upon Schiff's largesse to promote their visions of Jewish immigrant adaptation in America. An interesting (and overlooked) examination of the Schiff-Wald relationship can be found in Beatrice Siegel, *Lillian Wald of Henry Street* (New York: Macmillan, 1983).

91. *Report of the Commission of Immigration,* 140.

92. Marshall to *Jewish Daily News,* Apr. 24, 1909, LM Papers, Box 1578.

93. *Report of the Commission of Immigration,* 140.

94. Marshall to Samuel Straus, *Globe,* Apr. 17, 1909, LM Papers, Box 1578.

95. Brandeis, *Other People's Money and How the Bankers Use It.* For the Pujo hearings' impact on Brandeis: Urofsky, *Louis D. Brandeis,* 321.

96. See the summary in Engel v. O'Malley, 219 U.S. 128 (1910).

97. "Immigrant Banks," *New York Times,* Apr. 30, 1909.

98. Marshall to Charles Evans Hughes, May 1, 1909, LM Papers, Box 1578.

99. For a description of this cooperation on the Foley bill: Marshall to Lillian Wald, Jan. 7, 1911, LM Papers, Box 1580.

100. Marshall to James Foley, Nov. 16, 1909, LM Papers, Box 1578.

101. Marshall to Israel Zangwill, Feb. 2, 1910, Marshall to Philip Danahy, Feb. 15, 1910, Marshall to Charles Evans Hughes, Feb. 24, 1910, LM Papers, Box 1579. Williams was by this time state comptroller.

102. Marshall to E. A. Merritt, Apr. 26, 1910, LM Papers, Box 1579.

103. Marshall to John Williams, May 27, 1910, LM Papers, Box 1579.

104. Lobbying for the Parker and Foley bills could not be supported out of the immigration commission's budget after the commission was disbanded. By early 1910, Marshall had invested $1,000 of his own money in the lobbying and turned to friends and acquaintances for funds. Marshall to Paul Warburg, Jan. 13, 1910, LM Papers, Box 1579.

105. Engel v. O'Malley, 219 U.S. 128 (1910).

106. Ibid.

107. Marshall to Lillian Wald, Aug. 31, 1910, LM Papers, Box 1579.

108. Marshall to Nathan Bijur, Oct. 14, 1909; Marshall to Jacob Saperstein, Oct. 25, 1909, LM Papers, Box 1578.

109. Marshall to Adolph Ochs, Oct. 14, 1910, LM Papers, Box 1579.

110. Engel v. O'Malley, 219 U.S. 128 (1910).

111. Marshall to Lillian Wald, Jan. 7, 1911, LM Papers, Box 1580.

112. Rosenthal, "The Public Life of Louis Marshall," 165.

113. Henry Greenberg, "Louis Marshall: Attorney General of the Jewish People," in *Noble Purposes: Nine Champions of the Rule of Law,* ed. Norman Gross (Athens, OH: Ohio Univ. Press, 2007), 113.

114. Ibid., 112.

115. Rosenthal, "The Public Life of Louis Marshall," 261–63; Lloyd Gartner, "The Correspondence of Mayer Sulzberger and William Howard Taft," *Proceedings of the American Academy for Jewish Research* 46 (1978–79), 130–32; Stephen Wise, *Challenging Years: The Autobiography of Stephen Wise* (New York: Putnam's Sons, 1949), 145–46; David Dalin, "Louis Marshall, The Jewish Vote and the Republican Party," 69–74; Sarna, "Two Jewish Lawyers Named Louis," 16.

116. Rosenthal, "The Public Life of Louis Marshall," 262–63.

117. Surveyors of this failed Supreme Court nomination bid mentioned in note 115 allude to Taft's preference for Hughes. The most extreme account of this preference was provided by Marshall's long-standing rival Stephen Wise, whose memoir (145–46) claims that President Taft already had in his pocket a letter from Governor Hughes accepting the Supreme Court offer when Schiff, Mayer Sulzberger, and Isaac Ullman came to meet with him in the White House and lobby for Marshall on Apr 7, 1910. Wise's factual claim is not supported by Taft's correspondence.

118. Gartner, "Correspondence of Mayer Sulzberger," 132; Wise, *Challenging Years,* 145.

119. The Guggenheimer, Untermyer, and Marshall law firm destroyed most of its records when it was dissolved, and the surviving documents do not reflect the dynamics in Marshall's relationship with Samuel Untermyer. Some of Untermyer's personal papers made their way to a grandson, but according to Dr. Richard Hawkins, who has conducted extensive research on Samuel Untermyer's activities, these documents also convey little information about the Marshall-Untermyer connection. I thank Dr. Hawkins for providing information about Untermyer.

120. Marshall to Arthur Brisbane, Nov. 1, 1915, LM Papers, Box 1584.

121. Reznikoff, *Louis Marshall,* 2:1155–60.

122. Information in this section draws from Cynthia Connolly, *Saving Sickly Children: The Tuberculosis Preventorium in American Life, 1909–1970* (New Brunswick: Rutgers Univ. Press, 2008).

123. Ibid., 54.

124. Ibid., 56.

125. *Evening Sun,* Nov. 10, 1909, Nathan Straus Collection, New York Public Library, Box 16.

126. *New York American,* Nov. 10, 1909, Nathan Straus Collection, Box 16.

127. Connolly, *Saving Sickly Children,* 56.

128. *New York Herald,* Nov. 19, 1909, Nathan Straus Collection, Box 16.

129. *Lakewood Times and Journal,* Nov. 19, 1909, Nathan Straus Collection, Box 16.

130. Connolly, *Saving Sickly Children,* 56.

131. John Franklin Fort to Marcus Marks, Nov. 27, 1909; *New York Tribune,* Nov. 28, 1909, Nathan Straus Collection, Box 16.

132. *New York Herald,* Nov. 23, 1909; *Jersey City Journal,* Dec. 7, 1909; Nathan Straus Collection, Box 16.

133. Rosenthal, "The Public Life of Louis Marshall," 31.

134. Samuel Untermyer to Nathan Straus, Dec. 10, 1909, Nathan Straus Collection, Box 16.

135. "Max Nathan Asks Straus to Move Preventorium," *New York Times,* Dec. 13, 1909, http://query.nytimes.com/mem/archive-free/pdf?res=F30E16FE385A12738DDDAA0994DA415B898CF1D3.

136. *New York Evening Journal,* Dec. 16, 1909, Nathan Straus Collection, Box 16.

137. *New York Times,* Dec. 17, 1909.

138. *New York World,* Jan. 10, 1910, Nathan Straus Collection, Box 16.

139. Ibid.

140. Samuel Untermyer to Nathan Straus, Jan. 10, 1910, Nathan Straus Collection, Box 16.

141. Max Nathan to Nathan Straus, Jan. 10, 1910; *New York Times,* Jan. 10, 1910; Nathan Straus Collection, Box 16.

142. Nathan Straus to Samuel Untermyer, Jan. 11, 1910; *New York Times,* Jan. 11, 1910; Nathan Straus Collection, Box 16.

143. *New York Evening Journal,* Jan. 17, 1910, press clippings in Nathan Straus Collection, Box 16.

144. *New York Evening Journal,* Feb. 1, 1910, Nathan Straus Collection, Box 16.

145. Ibid.

146. "We protest against this unnecessary destruction of our property," Marshall wrote to the White Plains Board of Supervisors on Oct. 5, 1912. "The establishment of a [tuberculosis] hospital would nullify every possibility of devoting the property to residential purposes. . . . and thus destroy investments made in good faith for development," Marshall argued. "I am familiar with tuberculosis hospitals," he added. "In each instance they have been constructed at points remote from usual lines of travel, on wild land, in forest regions." LM Papers, Box 1581.

147. Marshall to Marcus Marks, Dec. 29, 1909, Nathan Straus Collection, Box 8.

148. Samuel Untermyer memorandum to Marshall, Mar. 7, 1910, LM Papers, Box 10.

149. Oliver Carlson, *Brisbane: A Candid Biography* (New York: Stackpole Sons, 1937), 256.

150. Ibid., 98.

151. Ibid., 180.

152. Ibid., 179.

153. Ibid., 182.

154. Ibid., 129.

155. Arthur Brisbane to Marcus Marks, Feb. 4, 1910, Nathan Straus Collection, Box 8.

156. Ibid.

157. *Newark Star,* Mar. 10, 1910, Nathan Straus Collection, Box 16.

158. Arthur Brisbane to Marcus Marks, Feb. 4, 1910.

159. Marshall to Jacob Schiff, Nov. 16, 1909, LM Papers, Box 1578.

160. Gartner, "Correspondence of Mayer Sulzberger," 130.

161. Jacob Schiff to Mayer Sulzberger, Mar. 30, 1910, in Gartner, "Correspondence of Mayer Sulzberger," 130–31.

162. Ibid., 125.

163. Mayer Sulzberger to William Howard Taft, Mar. 30, 1910, Taft Papers Series 5, Reel 349, Library of Congress Manuscript Collections. Sulzberger mentions in this note that he wrote to Taft about Marshall's worthiness for the Supreme Court bench at the time of Justice Peckham's death.

164. Gartner, "Correspondence of Mayer Sulzberger," 132.

165. William Howard Taft to Arthur Brisbane, Apr. 8, 1910, Taft Papers Series 8, Reel 501.

166. Ibid.

167. William Howard Taft to Charles Evans Hughes, Apr. 22, 1910, Taft Papers Series 8, Reel 501.

168. See, for instance, F. E. Warren to William Howard Taft, Apr. 8, 1910, and William Howard Taft to Charles Menderson, Apr. 11, 1910, Taft Papers Series 8, Reel 501.

169. *New York Evening Journal, Chicago American, San Francisco Examiner,* Apr. 11, 1910, Nathan Straus Collection, Box 8.

170. Marshall to Benjamin Tuska, Apr. 7, 1910, LM Papers, Box 1579.

171. Ibid.

172. Marshall to Thomas Mulry, Apr. 29, 1910, LM Papers, Box 1579.

173. William Howard Taft to Samuel Koenig, Apr. 8, 1910, Taft Papers Series 8, Reel 501.

174. Ibid.

175. Marshall to E. R. A. Seligman, Oct. 14, 1909, LM Papers, Box 1578.

176. For Aaronsohn: Eliezer Livneh, *Aaron Aaronsohn: Haish u'zemano* [in Hebrew] (Jerusalem: Mosad Bialik, 1969); Ronald Florence, *T. E. Lawrence, Aaron Aaronsohn and the Seeds of the Arab-Israeli Conflict* (London: Viking, 2007).

177. Marshall to Cyrus Adler, Nov. 10, 1909, LM Papers, Box 1578.

178. Marshall to Adolph Lewisohn, Nov. 20, 1909; Marshall to Daniel Guggenheim, Nov. 24, 1909, LM Papers, Box 1578.

179. In 1897, Baron Edmond de Rothschild pled with the impetuous twenty-one-year-old Aaronsohn, declaiming "at your age, a person should be more modest." Livneh, *Aaron Aaronsohn,* 26–27.

180. Marshall to Aaron Aaronsohn, Jan. 13, 1910, LM Papers, Box 1579.

181. Marshall to Cyrus Adler, Jan. 18, 1910, LM Papers, Box 1579.

182. Marshall to Isaac Seligman, Feb. 21, 1910, and Marshall to Aaron Aaronsohn, Mar. 8, 1910, LM Papers, Box 1579. Other subscribers were Paul Warburg and Isaac Seligman, each at $1,000.

183. Marshall to Jacob Schiff, Mar. 22, 1910, LM Papers, Box 1579.

184. Marshall to Aaron Aaronsohn, Mar. 26, 1910, LM Papers, Box 1579.

185. Marshall to Jacob Schiff, Mar. 26, 1910, LM Papers, Box 1579.

186. Marshall to Aaron Aaronsohn, Apr. 6, 1910, LM Papers, Box 1579.

187. Marshall to Aaron Aaronsohn, Apr. 2, 1910, LM Papers, Box 1579.

188. Ibid.

189. Ibid.

190. Ibid.

191. Marshall to Morris Loeb, June 20, 1911, LM Papers, Box 1580.

192. Eric Goldstein, "Contesting the Categories: Jews and Government Racial Classification in the United States," *Jewish History* 19 (2005), 91.

193. Bernard Richards, "Jews Against Race," *Hebrew Standard,* Jan. 7, 1910.

194. Mack's biographer suggests that the traumatically ineffective testimony to the Dillingham Commission was a turning point in his Jewish career, ushering in his Zionist commitments. Harry Barnard, *The Forging of an American Jew: The Life and Times of Judge Julian W. Mack* (New York: Harzl Press, 1974).

195. Marshall to Judah Magnes, Mar. 10, 1910, LM Papers, Box 1579.

196. Goren, *New York Jews,* 41–42.

197. Marshall to Judah Magnes, Mar. 10, 1910.

198. Ibid.

199. Goldstein, "Contesting the Categories," 89.

200. Marshall to Henry Goldfogle, May 10, 1910, and Marshall to Solomon Schechter, Sept. 9, 1910, LM Papers, Box 1579.

201. Marshall to Judah Magnes, Mar. 10, 1910.

202. Protocol of Executive Committee Meetings, Feb. 20, 1910, American Jewish Committee Minutes, vol. 1, American Jewish Committee Archives.

203. Ibid.

204. Ibid.

205. Marshall to Israel Friedlander, Mar. 19, 1910, LM Papers, Box 1579.

206. Ibid.

207. Marshall to Clara Bronner, Oct. 6, 1910, LM Papers, Box 1579.

208. Alpert, *Louis Marshall, 1856–1929,* 2.

209. Marshall to Jacob Marshall, Oct. 7, 1910, LM Papers, Box 20/3.

210. Newspaper clippings, LM Papers, Box 20.

211. Ibid.

212. Alpert, *Louis Marshall, 1856–1929,* 3.

213. Ibid, 1.

214. Marshall to Charles Evans Hughes, June 8, 1910, in Reznikoff, *Louis Marshall,* 2:1080–82; Marshall to James Day, June 17, 1910, LM Papers, Box 1579.

215. Marshall to Samuel Untermyer, June 1910, LM Papers, Box 1579.

216. Marshall to Henrietta Szold, Aug. 12, 1910, LM Papers, Box 1579.

217. Richard Greenwald, *The Triangle Fire, the Protocols of Peace and Industrial Democracy in Progressive Era New York* (Philadelphia: Temple Univ. Press, 2005), 57–75; Leon Stein, ed., *Out of the Sweatshop: The Struggle for Industrial Democracy* (New York: Quadrangle, 1977), 87–175.

218. This section draws from Stein, *Out of the Sweatshop.*

219. Greenwald, *Triangle Fire,* 59.

220. Ibid.; Urofsky, *Louis D. Brandeis,* 243–53.

221. Greenwald, *Triangle Fire,* 61.

222. Ibid., 62.

223. Ibid., 64.

224. Stein, *Out of the Sweatshop,* 112.

225. Urofsky, *Louis D. Brandeis,* 251–52.

226. In his authoritative biography, *Louis D. Brandeis,* Urofsky refers repeatedly to Brandeis's conservatism on industry and labor matters. Greenwald, who offers a nuanced, convincing description of this 1910 strike, recognizes Brandeis's contributions toward the betterment of industrial relations, while also calling attention to pro-management aspects of his thinking and efforts. Brandeis's influence on the protocol, Greenwald writes, was felt in "the attempt to rationalize, standardize and Taylorize the garment industry. All work stoppages would be eliminated. Work would continue as grievances were arbitrated." Greenwald, *Triangle Fire,* 74.

227. For a survey of the Brandeis-Marshall relationship: Sarna, "Two Jewish Lawyers Named Louis."

228. Greenwald, *Triangle Fire,* 65.

229. Ibid., 67–69.

230. Ibid., 6.

231. Ibid., 70.

232. Ibid.

233. Ibid. The phrasing of Marshall's compromise was altered somewhat in the final signed agreement, whose wording is published in Greenwald, *Triangle Fire,* 74.

234. Marshall to Meyer London, Sept. 1, 1910, LM Papers, Box 1579, in Reznikoff, *Louis Marshall,* 2:1129.

235. Greenwald, *Triangle Fire,* 72–73.

236. Ibid., 73–74.

237. Ibid.

238. Stein, *Out of the Sweatshop,* 114.

239. Marshall to Gertrude Barnum, Nov. 29, 1912, in Reznikoff, *Louis Marshall,* 2:1127; Mark Raider, "Introduction," *American Jewish History* 94, nos. 1–2 (Mar.–June 2008), x. The newly discovered protocol document bears the signature of all the consenting parties.

240. Rosenthal, "The Public Life of Louis Marshall," 244.

241. Marshall to Gertrude Barnum, Nov. 29, 1912.

242. Marshall to Solomon Schechter, Sept. 9, 1910, LM Papers, Box 1579.

243. Ibid. Marshall estimated that 70,000 workers had been out of work during the strike.

244. Goren, *New York Jews,* 96–104.

245. Marshall to William Popper, LM Papers, Box 1579.

246. Judah Magnes, sermon delivered at Temple Emanu-El, Apr. 24, 1910, in Goren, *Dissenter in Zion,* 108.

247. Marshall to Solomon Schechter, Nov. 8, 1910.

248. Marshall to Isaac Ullman, Dec. 19, 1910, LM Papers, Box 1579.

249. Marshall to Jacob Schiff, Dec. 24, 1910; Reznikoff, *Louis Marshall,* 1:57–59.

250. Marshall to Mayer Sulzberger, Jan. 20, 1911, LM Papers, Box 1580; Reznikoff, *Louis Marshall,* 1:59.

251. Marshall to Julian Mack, Jan. 20, 1911, LM Papers, Box 1580.

252. Cohen, "Abrogation," 14.

253. Marshall, "Russia and the American Passport," address to UAHC meeting, Jan. 19, 1911, in Reznikoff, *Louis Marshall,* 1:60.

254. Ibid.

255. Cohen, "Abrogation," 4–5.

256. Marshall, "Russia and the American Passport," 62.

257. Cohen, "Abrogation," 17.

258. This section relies on Cohen, "Abrogation," 15–16.

259. Ibid., 38.

260. Ibid., 19.

261. Ibid., 19–20.

262. Marshall to Julian Mack, Jan. 25, 1911, LM Papers, Box 1580.

263. Marshall to Louis Ehrich, Jan. 23, 1911, LM Papers, Box 1580.

264. Marshall to Simon Guggenheim, Jan. 26, 1911, LM Papers, Box 1580.

265. Ibid.

266. Cohen, "Abrogation," 21–22.

267. Marshall to Herbert Parsons, Jan. 28, 1911, LM Papers, Box 1580.

268. Ibid.

269. Marshall to Solomon Schechter, Feb. 8, 1911, LM Papers, Box 1580.

270. Cohen, "Abrogation," 20.

271. Marshall to Simon Wolf, Oct. 18, 1916, in Reznikoff, *Louis Marshall,* 1:78.

272. Marshall to Jacob Schiff, Feb. 9, 1911.

273. Ibid.

274. This account synthesizes the description Marshall relayed to Simon Wolf more than five years after the meeting (Marshall to Simon Wolf, Oct. 18, 1916, in Reznikoff, *Louis Marshall,* 1:78–87) and a shorter but somewhat more reliable report given by Marshall to the AJC on Feb. 19, 1911 (AJC Executive Committee Minutes, Vol. 1, American Jewish Committee Archives). The main differences between these sources are that the Wolf letter conveys a transcript of President Taft's statement, and Marshall's contemporary record indicates that his and Schiff's direct, agitated appeals to the president were interrupted by Taft's request that his Jewish guests peruse Ambassador Rockhill's dispatch.

A few weeks after the White House meeting, the AJC men debated making a public record of its happenings. Wolf had prepared a transcript of events preceding the adjournment but before Marshall and Schiff argued the question with President Taft. B'nai B'rith leaders opposed publication of Wolf's statement. By the end of Mar. 1911, Schiff decided against publicizing events in the meeting because he thought it impolitic to draw attention to Taft's reservations (see Marshall to Adler, Mar. 31, 1911, LM Papers, Box 1580.)

275. Cohen, *Jacob H. Schiff,* 199.

276. Horace Stern, *Louis Marshall: An Appreciation* (Feb. 1930), in Reznikoff, *Louis Marshall,* 87.

277. Marshall to Thomas Slicer, Feb. 17, 1911, LM Papers, Box 1580.

278. Ibid.

279. Marshall to Simon Wolf, Oct. 18, 1916, in Reznikoff, *Louis Marshall,* 1:81.

280. Marshall to Thomas Slicer, Feb. 17, 1911.

281. Cohen, "Abrogation," 21.

282. Marshall to Herbert Parsons, Mar. 1, 1911, LM Papers, Box 1580.

283. Marshall to Henry Goldfogle, Mar. 2, 1911, LM Papers, Box 1580, in Reznikoff, *Louis Marshall,* 1:89–90.

284. This section relies on J. Alexis Friedman, *The Impeachment of Governor William Sulzer* (New York: Columbia Univ. Press, 1939), 15–25.

285. Ibid., 22.

286. Marshall to William Sulzer, Apr. 11, 1911, LM Papers, Box 1580.

287. Ives v. South Buffalo Railway Company, 201 N.Y. 271 (1911).

288. Price Fishback and Shawn Everett Kantor, *A Prelude to the Welfare State: The Origins of Workers' Compensation* (Chicago: Univ. of Chicago Press, 2000), 1–6.

289. The discussion here relies on Commission appointed under Chapter 518 of the Laws of 1909 to inquire into the question of employers' liability, *Report to the Legislature of the State of New York* (Albany, 1910)

290. Ives v. South Buffalo Railway Company, 201 N.Y. 271 (1911).

291. Urofsky, *Louis D. Brandeis,* 211–12, 477–78.

292. Marshall to James Day, Mar. 30, 1911, LM Papers, Box 1580.

293. Marshall to William Werner, Apr. 1, 1911, LM Papers, Box 1580.

294. Adler, "Louis Marshall," 28.

295. Cohen, "Abrogation," 22.

296. Ibid., 22–23.

297. Marshall to Jacob Schiff, Mar. 20, 1911, LM Papers, Box 1580.

298. Marshall to Simon Guggenheim, Mar. 21, 1911, LM Papers, Box 1580.

299. Marshall to J. Walter Freiberg, Mar. 23, 1911, LM Papers, Box 1580.

300. Marshall to Clara Bronner, Oct. 6, 1910, LM Papers, Box 1579.

301. In early 1914, Schiff berated Marshall at an AJC Executive Committee meeting regarding public disclosures about a language and policy debate concerning the Haifa technical school, the Technion (then Technikum). Ill feeling between the two men peaked during this incident, which is connected fascinatingly to debates about Yishuv culture and to relations between the American Jewish organizational elite and the German Hilfsverein; however, because this was a passing blow-up between Marshall and Schiff and because of Marshall's relatively loose connection to the Technion project, this episode is not analyzed here. For details, see Rosenthal, "The Public Life of Louis Marshall," 277–81; and Cohen, *Jacob H. Schiff,* 183–87.

302. Rosenstock, *Louis Marshall,* 268.

303. Marshall to Henry Bronner, Oct. 29, 1910, LM Papers, Box 1580.

304. Cohen, "Abrogation," 27.

305. Hasia Diner, *In the Almost Promised Land: American Jews and Blacks, 1915–1935* (Baltimore: Johns Hopkins Univ. Press, 1977), 166–68.

306. Marshall to Julius Rosenwald, May 11, 1911, LM Papers, Box 1580.

307. Marshall to Julius Rosenwald, May 5, 1911, LM Papers, Box 1580.

308. Marshall to John Hanchett, May 18, 1911, LM Papers, Box 1580.

309. Marshall to Ida Marshall, May 6, 1911, LM Papers, Box 1580.

310. Marshall to Judah Magnes, Nov. 29, 1905, Dec. 4, 1905, LM Papers, Box 1574.

311. Cohen, "Abrogation," 25–26.

312. Marshall to F. B. Harrison, May 29, 1911, LM Papers, Box 1580.

313. Cohen, "Abrogation," 31.

314. Marshall to Morris Loeb, May 31, 1911, LM Papers, Box 1580.

315. Isaac A. Hourwich, *Immigration and Labor* (New York: Arno Press, 1912/1969).

316. Ibid., 11.

317. Ibid., 6.

318. Ibid., 7.

319. The AJC member who pointed to this defect was Cyrus Adler. Eric L. Goldstein, *The Price of Whiteness: Jews, Race, and American Identity* (Princeton: Princeton Univ. Press, 2006), 198–99.

320. Marshall to Herbert Friedenwald, June 14, 1911, LM Papers, Box 1580.

321. Marshall to Beatrice Magnes, July 20, 1911, LM Papers, Box 1580.

322. "The Other Side of the Passport Question," *New York Times,* July 9, 1911.

323. Cohen, "Abrogation," 24–25.

324. "Jews' Real Charge Against the Czar; Veteran Diplomat Misunderstands Passport Question, Writes Louis Marshall," *New York Times,* July 16, 1911.

325. "American Passport in Russia," *American Jewish Year Book, 5665,* 283–305.

326. Marshall to Judah Magnes, July 29, 1911, LM Papers, Box 1580.

327. Marshall to Moses Weinman, Aug. 16, 1911, LM Papers, Box 1580.

328. Marshall to Frances Kellor, July 29, 1911; Marshall to John D. Rockefeller, Aug. 28. 1911; Marshall to Jacob Schiff, Aug. 28, 1911, LM Papers, Box 1580.

329. Marshall to Samuel Stiefel, Aug. 28, 1911, LM Papers, Box 1580.

330. Marshall to Charles Jacobson, Aug. 16, 1911; Marshall to V. H. Kriegshaber, Aug. 17, 1911; LM Papers, Box 1580.

331. Marshall to Simon Wolf, July 20, 1911, LM Papers, Box 1580.

332. Naomi Cohen, *A Dual Heritage: The Public Career of Oscar Straus* (Philadelphia: Jewish Publication Society of America, 1969), 100–107.

333. Cohen, "Abrogation," 31.

334. Marshall to Oscar Straus, Oct. 16, 1911, LM Papers, Box 1580.

335. Marshall to the editors of *Outlook,* Oct. 13, 1911, in Reznikoff, *Louis Marshall,* 1:97–99.

336. Marshall to Jacob Schiff, Oct. 17, 1911, LM Papers, Box 1580. Schiff showed a passing curiosity about the arbitration idea.

337. Marshall to Mayer Sulzberger, Oct. 19, 1911, LM Papers, Box 1580.

338. Marshall to Julian Mack, Oct. 20, 1911, LM Papers, Box 1580.

339. Ibid.

340. Marshall to Jacob Schiff, Nov. 1, 1911, LM Papers, Box 1580.

341. Marshall to Elihu Root, Nov. 8, 1911; Marshall to James A. O'Gorman, Nov. 3, 1911; Marshall to Nathaniel Schlamm, LM Papers, Box 1580.

342. Marshall to Mayer Sulzberger, Nov. 17, 1911, LM Papers, Box 1580.

343. Ibid.

344. Cohen, "Abrogation," 33.

345. Marshall to Mayer Sulzberger, Nov. 17, 1911.

346. Marshall to Simon Wolf, Nov. 18, 1911, LM Papers, Box 1580.

347. Cohen, "Abrogation," 34–35.

348. Marshall to William Sulzer, Dec. 7, 1911, LM Papers, Box 1580.

349. Marshall correspondence, Dec. 7, 1911, LM Papers, Box 1580.

350. Cohen, "Abrogation," 35.

351. Ibid., 37.

352. Ibid., 38.

353. Marshall to Isaac Ullman, Dec. 8, 1911, LM Papers, Box 1580.

354. Marshall to Henry Green, Feb. 2, 1912, LM Papers, Box 1581.

355. Marshall to Benjamin Stolz, Dec. 22, 1911, in Reznikoff, *Louis Marshall,* 1:103; Marshall to Joseph Stolz, Jan. 13, 1912, LM Papers, Box 1581.

356. Marshall to Joseph Stolz, Jan. 13, 1912.

5. Avoiding the Guillotine of Immigration Restriction

1. Marshall to Jacob Marshall, Jan. 6, 1912, LM Papers, Box 1581.

2. Ron Chernow, *The House of Morgan: An American Banking Dynasty and the Rise of Modern Finance* (New York: Macmillan, 1990), 150–59.

3. Marshall to Mr. Phillips, Oct. 27, 1908, LM Papers, Box 1577.

4. For Untermyer's connection to the Keren Hayesod (Palestine Foundation Fund) and his other Zionist activities, see Richard Hawkins, "Hitler's Bitterest Foe: Samuel Untermyer and the Boycott of Nazi Germany, 1933–1938," *American Jewish History* 93, no. 1 (Mar. 2007), 21–50; Richard Hawkins, "Samuel Untermyer and the Zionist Project: An Attempt to Reconcile the American 'Melting Pot' with Zionism," *Australian Journal of Jewish Studies* 21 (2007), 114–54.

5. Marshall to Max Nathan, Mar. 13, 1911, LM Papers, Box 1580.

6. Marshall to Edward Lauterbach, Apr. 29, 1912, LM Papers, Box 1581; Goldstein, *Politics of Ethnic Pressure,* 202.

7. Minutes, Conference on Immigration, Dec. 30, 1911, CJH, LM Papers, Box 1.

8. Goldstein, *Politics of Ethnic Pressure,* 200–201.

9. Ibid., 236.

10. Max Kohler to Charles Nagel, Jan. 21, 1911, CJH, Max Kohler Papers, Box 12.

11. Marshall to Max Kohler, Dec. 14, 1914; Jacob Schiff to Max Kohler, May 2, 1912, CJH, Max Kohler Papers, Box 12.

12. Max Kohler, *The Injustice of a Literacy Test for Immigrants* (New York: Max Kohler, 1912).

13. Marshall to Henry Cabot Lodge, Jan. 26, 1912, LM Papers, Box 1581.

14. Marshall to Isidor Raynor, Feb. 16, 1912, LM Papers, Box 1581.

15. Goldstein, *Politics of Ethnic Pressure,* 203.

16. Marshall to Max Kohler, Apr. 23, 1912, LM Papers, Box 1581.

17. Goldstein, *Politics of Ethnic Pressure,* 208–11.

18. Ibid., 212.

19. Marshall to Joseph Stolz, Apr. 29, 1912, LM Papers, Box 1581.

20. Isaac A. Hourwich to Marshall, Apr. 30, 1912, CJH, Marshall Papers, Box 1; Marshall to Isaac A. Hourwich, May 21, 1912, LM Papers, Box 1581; Goldstein, *Politics of Ethnic Pressure,* 225–26.

21. Goldstein, *Politics of Ethnic Pressure,* 216–17.

22. Marshall to John L. Burnett, May 21, 1912, LM Papers, Box 1581.

23. Marshall to John L. Burnett, May 28, 1912, LM Papers, Box 1581; Reznikoff, *Louis Marshall,* 1:118–19.

24. Goldstein, *Politics of Ethnic Pressure,* 219.

25. Ibid., 220.

26. Marshall to Jacob Schiff, June 15, 1912; Marshall to Isidor Raynor, June 21, 1912, LM Papers, Box 1581.

27. Goldstein, *Politics of Ethnic Pressure,* 222.

28. Marshall (and Julius Rosenwald and Harry Cutler) to William Howard Taft, Oct. 23, 1912, in Reznikoff, *Louis Marshall,* 1:119–21.

29. Goldstein, *Politics of Ethnic Pressure,* 223.

30. Marshall to Ida Marshall, Apr. 20, 1912, LM Papers, Box 1581.

31. Marshall to Oscar Straus, Apr. 22, 1912, LM Papers, Box 1581. Hollywood kept the Straus couple in mind in its 1958 reenactment of the Titanic tragedy, *A Night to Remember,* whereas the 1997 blockbuster, *Titanic,* barely glanced at the Straus story.

32. Ibid.

33. Marshall to Jacob Marshall, Apr. 12, 1912, LM Papers, Box 1581.

34. Marshall to Benjamin Stolz, Apr. 23, 1912, LM Papers, Box 1581.

35. Marshall correspondence, Apr. 1912, LM Papers, Box 1581.

36. Marshall to Ida Marshall, Apr. 20, 1912.

37. "Oppose Dr. Magnes for Ritual Changes; Orthodox Reforms at B'nai Jeshurun Synagogue Not Pleasing to Part of the Congregation," *New York Times,* Dec. 20, 1911; Marshall to B'nai Jeshurun, Mar. 1, 1912, LM Papers, Box 1581.

38. "Tribute to Straus," *New York Times,* May 12, 1912; Marshall to Ida Marshall, Apr. 27, 1912, LM Papers, Box 1581.

39. "Tribute to Straus," *New York Times,* May 12, 1912.

40. Marshall to Isaac Untermyer, May 20, 1912, LM Papers, Box 1581.

41. Marshall to Joseph Stolz, June 17, 1912, LM Papers, Box 1581.

42. Marshall to Isaac Untermyer, July 10, 1912, LM Papers, Box 1581.

43. Marshall to Jacob Schiff, Aug. 9, 1912, Aug. 13, 1912, LM Papers, Box 1581; Reznikoff, *Louis Marshall,* 2:1152–55.

44. Marshall to Jacob Schiff, Aug. 13, 1912, in Reznikoff, *Louis Marshall,* 2:1154.

45. Marshall to Jacob Schiff, Aug. 19, 1912, LM Papers, Box 1581.

46. Marshall to William Sulzer, Oct. 3, 1912, LM Papers, Box 1581.

47. Marshall to Benjamin Stolz, Oct. 3, 1912, LM Papers, Box 1581.

48. Cohen, *A Dual Heritage,* 214; Friedman, *The Impeachment,* 15–37.

49. Marshall to Jacob Schiff, Oct. 17, 1912, LM Papers, Box 1581.

50. Friedman, *The Impeachment,* 27.

51. Cohen, *A Dual Heritage,* 218.

52. Ibid.

53. Marshall to *Die Warheit,* Oct. 18, 1912, LM Papers, Box 1581.

54. Dalin, "Louis Marshall, the Jewish Vote, and the Republican Party," 55–84.

55. Marshall to *Die Warheit,* Oct. 18, 1912.

56. Marshall to *New York Herald,* Oct. 29, 1912, LM Papers, Box 1581.

57. Cohen, *A Dual Heritage,* 219.

58. Marshall to Judah Magnes, Nov. 1, 1912, LM Papers, Box 1581.

59. Ibid.

60. Marshall to L. E. Miller, Nov. 2, 1912, LM Papers, Box 1581.

61. Ibid.

62. Friedman, *The Impeachment,* 33.

63. Marshall to William Howard Taft, Nov. 6, 1912, LM Papers, Box 1581.

64. Friedman, *The Impeachment,* 34.

65. Marshall to William Dillingham, Jan. 1, 1913, in Reznikoff, *Louis Marshall,* 1:123–25; Marshall to Isidor Raynor, Feb. 16, 1912.

66. Goldstein, *The Politics of Ethnic Pressure,* 229.

67. Ibid., 229–334.

68. "Memorandum in Opposition to Senate Bill," Louis Marshall, Feb. 6, 1913, CJH, Marshall Papers, Box 1.

69. Ibid.

70. Marshall to Jacob Schiff, Feb. 7, 1913, in Goldstein, *The Politics of Ethnic Pressure,* 240.

71. Goldstein, *The Politics of Ethnic Pressure,* 241.

72. Ibid., 243.

73. Ibid., 274.

74. President Wilson vetoed yet another literacy test bill in 1917, but this time his action was overridden by Congress and the test was incorporated in the Immigration Act of 1917. Rosenstock, *Louis Marshall,* 86.

75. Marshall to Cyrus Adler, Dec. 9, 1913, in Goldstein, *The Politics of Ethnic Pressure,* 247.

76. Marshall to Fulton Brylawski, Jan. 24, 26, 31, 1914, Feb. 1, 1914; Marshall to A. H. Sabbath, Jan. 27, 1914, CJH, Marshall Papers, Box 1.

77. Luria v. United States, 231 U.S. 9 (1913).

78. Friedman, *The Impeachment,* 32–33.

79. Ibid., 64.

80. Ibid., 77.

81. Ibid., 96.

82. Ibid., 104–5.

83. Ibid., 138.

84. Ibid., 143.

85. Ibid., 243.

86. Ibid., 244.

87. Ibid., 185.

88. Ibid., 194.

89. Ibid., 218.

90. Ibid., 221.

91. Ibid., 259.

92. See, in this connection, Rosenthal, "The Public Life of Louis Marshall," 297–98.

93. Marshall and Herrick received the largest fees, $10,000 apiece. Ibid.

94. Marshall, "Address on Immigration," New York University Forum, Feb. 20, 1914, CJH, Marshall Papers, Box 1, in Reznikoff, *Louis Marshall,* 1:131–46.

95. Ibid., 1:142.

96. Ibid., 1:145.

6. World War I

1. Marshall to Mrs. Bernard Marshall [Ida], Sept. 1, 1914, LM Papers, Box 1583.

2. Marshall to Joe Stolz, Aug. 4, 1914, LM Papers, Box 1583.

3. Zosa Szajkowski, *Jews, Wars, and Communism: The Attitude of American Jews to World War I, the Russian Revolutions of 1917 and Communism (1914–1945)* (New York: Ktav Publishing House, 1972), 1:3.

4. Ibid., 4.

5. Ibid., 5.

6. Joel Rappaport, "The American Yiddish Press and the European Conflict in 1914," *Jewish Social Studies* 19 (1957), 117.

7. Ibid.

8. Marshall to Jacob Schiff, Oct. 30, 1914, LM Papers, Box 1583.

9. Marshall to Cyrus Adler, Aug. 5, 1914, LM Papers, Box 1583.

10. Marshall to the editor of the *American Hebrew,* Sept. 8, 1914, Box 1583.

11. Marshall to Jacob Schiff, Aug. 25, 1914, LM Papers, Box 1583.

12. Marshall to the editor of the *American Hebrew,* Sept. 8, 1914, LM Papers, Box 1583.

13. Marshall to Jacob Schiff, Oct. 9, 1914, LM Papers, Box 1583.

14. For differing assessments of the "neutrality" standard in this German Jewish context in the United States, see Naomi Cohen, *Encounter with Emancipation: The German Jews in the United States, 1830–1914* (Philadelphia: Jewish Publication Society of America, 1984), 129–58; David Dalin, "Louis Marshall, the Jewish Vote, and the Republican Party," *Jewish Political Studies Review* 4, no. 1 (Spring 1992), 55–84.

15. Marshall to David Philipson, Nov. 18, 1918, LM Papers, Box 1583.

16. Marshall to Jacob Schiff, Sept. 14, 1914, LM Papers, Box 1583.

17. Marshall to Jacob Schiff, Dec. 11, 1914, LM Papers, Box 1583.

18. Louis Marshall, "War and the Jewish Question," *American Hebrew,* Apr. 30, 1915.

19. Louis Marshall to Walter Rothschild, Sept. 14, 1914, LM Papers, Box 1583.

20. Marshall to Elihu Root, Dec. 12, 1914, LM Papers, Box 1583.

21. Marshall to Joseph Krimsky, Nov. 18, 1914, LM Papers, Box 1583.

22. General information here on the Frank case draws from Steve Oney, *And the Dead Shall Rise: The Murder of Mary Phagan and the Lynching of Leo Frank* (New York: Random House, 2003); Leonard Dinnerstein, *The Leo Frank Case* (New York: Columbia Univ. Press, 1968).

23. Dinnerstein, *The Leo Frank Case,* 74–76; Oney, *And the Dead Shall Rise,* 345–48.

24. Marshall letters to Henry Alexander, Dec. 1, 4, 1914, LM Papers, Box 1583.

25. Marshall to Albert D. Lasker, Dec. 3, 1914, LM Papers, Box 1583.

26. Marshall to Harry Friedenwald, Dec. 9, 1914, LM Papers, Box 1583.

27. Marshall to Leonard Hass, Dec. 9, 1914, LM Papers, Box 1583.

28. Marshall to Charles Tuck, Dec. 15, 1914, LM Papers, Box 1583.

29. Marshall to Harry Friedenwald, Dec. 9, 1914.

30. Two accounts of American Zionism in its early periods that vary somewhat in emphasis and detail, but reach the same broad conclusions, are Evyatar Friesal, *The Zionist Movement in the United States, 1897–1914* [in Hebrew] (Tel Aviv: Hakibutz Hameuchad, 1970); Melvin Urofsky, *American Zionism from Herzl to the Holocaust* (Garden City, NY: Anchor Press, 1975).

31. The literature on Brandeis's contribution to American Zionism in this period is extensive. Two important accounts are Melvin Urofsky, *Louis D. Brandeis: A Life* (New York: Pantheon Books, 2009), 515–44; Ben Halpern, *A Clash of Heroes: Brandeis, Weizmann, and American Zionism* (New York: Oxford Univ. Press, 1987).

32. Jonathan Frankel, "The Jewish Socialists and the American Jewish Congress Movement," *Yivo Annual of Jewish Social Science* 16 (1976), 203.

33. Yonathan Shapiro, *Leadership of the American Zionist Organization, 1897–1930* (Urbana: Univ. of Illinois Press, 1971).

34. Marshall to Adolf Kraus, Sept. 8, 1914, LM Papers, Box 1583.

35. Marshall to William Jennings Bryan, Aug. 28, 1914, LM Papers, Box 1583.

36. Zosa Szajkowski, "Concord and Discord in American Jewish Overseas Relief, 1914–1924," *Yivo Annual of Jewish Social Science* 14 (1969), 101–2.

37. Except where noted, the discussion in the remainder of this paragraph relies on the analysis in Nathan Efrati, *The Jewish Community in Eretz Israel During World War I* [in Hebrew] (Jerusalem: Yad Izhak Ben Zvi, 1991), 88–115.

38. Marshall to Adolf Kraus, Sept. 8, 1914, LM Papers, Box 1583.

39. The Standard Oil intermediaries asked for a negligible commission in the transfer of this relief money to the Yishuv. Wryly, the pro-business Marshall wrote to Morgenthau, "this shows that there may be some good even in hated monopolies." Marshall to Henry Morgenthau, Oct. 15, 1914, LM Papers, Box 1583.

40. Rumors about Cohen's role as an anti-Zionist informant to Ottoman empires were planted by Isaac Straus, a Jewish banker from Germany who carried out propaganda work for the Central powers in America, particularly in the period of American neutrality. Straus was a Zionist and an adamant opponent of the Hilfsverein. Szajkowski, *Jews, Wars, and Communism,* 1:39–41.

41. Marshall to Louis Brandeis, Aug. 31, 1914, LM Papers, Box 1583.

42. Marshall to Cyrus Adler, Sept. 2, 1914, LM Papers, Box 1583.

43. Marshall to Jacob Schiff, Sept. 14, 1914, LM Papers, Box 1583.

44. Marshall to Judah Magnes, Sept. 16, 1914, LM Papers, Box 1583.

45. In summer 1914, the AJC controlled funds of $100,000 that had been collected just less than a decade earlier for pogrom victims in Russia. Szajkowski, "Concord and Discord," 99.

46. Marshall to Jacob Schiff, Sept. 22, 1914, LM Papers, Box 1583.

47. Yehuda Bauer, *My Brother's Keeper: A History of the American Joint Distribution Committee, 1929–1939* (Philadelphia: Jewish Publication Society of America, 1974), 6.

48. Marshall to Harry Fischel, Oct. 14, 1914; Marshall to Leon Kamaiky, Oct. 22, 1914; LM Papers, Box 1583.

49. Harry Fischel to Marshall, Oct. 15, 1914, cited in Szajkowski, "Concord and Discord," 107.

50. Szajkowski, "Concord and Discord," 106.

51. Marshall to Simon Wolf, Nov. 9, 1914, LM Papers, Box 1583.

52. Marshall to Jacob Schiff, Oct. 26, 1914, LM Papers, Box 1583. Oscar Straus, who joined the AJC in this period, was also appointed to this organizing committee for what became the JDC.

53. Bauer, *My Brother's Keeper,* 3–18.

54. Ibid.

55. Szajkowski, "Concord and Discord," 113.

56. Ibid., 129.

57. Ibid., 130.

58. Ibid., 112.

59. Marshall to Bernard Drachman, Oct. 5, 1914, cited in Szajkowski, "Concord and Discord," 107.

60. Szajkowski, "Concord and Discord," 120.

61. Ibid.

62. Ibid., 157.

63. Cited in Szajkowski, "Concord and Discord," 108.

64. Ibid., 131–32.

65. Ibid., 101.

66. Ibid., 156.

67. A revealing article about Marshall, Billikopf, and Magnes, written by Harry Lang in the *Forward* on Nov. 27, 1927, is discussed in Part Four.

68. Szajkowski, "Concord and Discord," 133.

69. Oscar Janowsky, *The Jews and Minority Rights, 1898–1919* (New York: AMS Press, 1966), 91.

70. Ibid., 91–92.

71. See Aaron Alperin's contribution in Lawton Kessler, Aaron Alperin, and Jack Diamond, "American Jews and the Paris Peace Conference," *YIVO Annual of Jewish Social Science* 2–3 (1948), 232. For specific examples of congress movements in Diaspora communities, see Janowsky, *The Jews and Minority Rights,* 190–92, 203; Joseph Tennenbaum, *Between War and Peace* [in Hebrew] (Jerusalem: World Jewish Congress, 1960), 13–14, 16. See also Silver, "Louis Marshall and the Democratization of Jewish Identity," 43.

72. Frankel, "Jewish Socialists and the American Jewish Congress Movement," 209.

73. Cited in Frankel, "Jewish Socialists and the American Jewish Congress Movement," 207. Syrkin's 1915 pamphlet was entitled *Yidisher kongres in Amerike.*

74. Ibid.

75. Ibid, 211.

76. Marshall to Solomon Schechter, Feb. 19, 1915, LM Papers, Box 1584.

77. Jerold Auerbach, *Rabbis and Lawyers: The Journey from Torah to Constitution* (Bloomington: Indiana Univ. Press, 1990).

78. For the general background to this comparison relating to Marshall's work in international Jewish diplomacy, see Carole Fink, *Defending the Rights of Others: The Great Powers, the Jews, and International Minority Protection, 1878–1938* (New York: Cambridge Univ. Press, 2004). For Lucien Wolf, see Mark Levene, *War, Jews and the New Europe: the Diplomacy of Lucien Wolf, 1914–1919* (London: Littman Library of Jewish Civilization, 2009).

79. In his Supreme Court "Argument for the Appellant, Leo Frank" (237 U.S. 309), Marshall described Frank's trial in Atlanta as a "judicial lynching, where the mob triumphantly intervened and was permitted to control and dominate the instrumentalities of juridical procedure" (Reznikoff, *Louis Marshall,* 1:306). By a margin of seven to two, the Supreme Court on Apr. 19, 1915, rejected Marshall's argument that mob rule circumstances in such a case infringed due process. The two dissenters, Oliver Wendell Holmes and Charles Evans Hughes, argued that "mob law does not become due process of law by securing the assent of a terrorized jury." This dissent recapitulated Marshall's argument and formed the basis of the Supreme Court's 1923 ruling in Moore v. Dempsey, a result that Marshall found "exceedingly grateful." See his letter to Walter White of the NAACP, Mar. 12, 1923, in Reznikoff, *Louis Marshall,* 1:316–17.

80. C. Vann Woodward, *Tom Watson: Agrarian Rebel* (New York: Macmillan, 1938).

81. Marshall to Leo Frank, Jan. 30, 1915, LM Papers, Box 1584.

82. Marshall to Martin Glynn, Feb. 1, 1915, LM Papers, Box 1584.

83. Marshall to John Slaton, June 21, 1914, LM Papers, Box 1584.

84. Marshall to Woodrow Wilson, Jan. 30, 1915, LM Papers, Box 1584.

85. Marshall to William Barnes, Feb. 1, 1915, LM Papers, Box 1584.

86. Marshall letters to Jacob Schiff, Daniel Guggenheim, and Meyer London, May 10, 1915, LM Papers, Box 1584.

87. Marshall to Leonard Haas, May 28, 1915, LM Papers, Box 1584.

88. It bears repeating that Congress overrode Wilson's veto in 1917 and incorporated literacy tests in the 1917 Immigration Act (see chapter 5, n85).

89. Marshall to Leonard Haas, June 21, 1915, LM Papers, Box 1584.

90. Marshall to Jacob Wertheim, Sept. 21, 1915, LM Papers, Box 1584.

91. Marshall to Simon Wolf, Feb. 19, 1915, LM Papers, Box 1584.

92. John Higham, *Strangers in the Land: Patterns of American Nativism, 1860–1925,* 2nd ed. (New Brunswick: Rutgers Univ. Press, 2002), 264–99.

93. Marshall to Leonard Haas, May 28, 1915, LM Papers, Box 1584.

94. Marshall and Leo Frank corresponded about this subject in late January 1915, and Marshall's contacts with the Rolands Feature Film Company continued through February. LM Papers, Box 1584.

Retrospective dramatizations of the Frank trial have been extensive. Starting with a silent film in 1921, director Oscar Micheaux devoted three movies to the trial. In a 1937 film, *They Won't Forget,* Leo Frank's Jewish identity was expurgated. Governor Slaton's decision was depicted in the 1964 television series *Profiles in Courage.* Jack Lemmon and Kevin Spacey appeared in a 1988 made-for-TV production about the trial. The 1998 Broadway musical about the case, *Parade,* won a Tony. *The People vs. Leo Frank* film appeared on PBS in 2009.

95. See Dalin's article "Louis Marshall, the Jewish Vote and the Republican Party" for a strong demonstration of this point.

96. Marshall to William Barnes, Feb. 1, 1915.

97. Marshall to Salmon O. Levinson, Jan. 8, 1915, LM Papers, Box 1584; Reznikoff, *Louis Marshall,* 1:245–46.

98. Marshall to Isadore Levy, Jan. 22, 1916, LM Papers, Box 1585. In a powerfully phrased letter to the *New York Times* (Jan. 17, 1916), Marshall replied to Root's accusation, pointing out that three judges of the Court of Appeals in New York, nineteen of the Supreme Court justices of the first and second judicial districts and twelve of the officers and directors of the New York County Lawyers Association belonged to the 30 percent category slurred by Root's remark. "Mr Root does not understand the feelings of those who learned at their mother's knee, to cherish the gift of liberty conferred upon them by America and its institutions," concluded Marshall. Reznikoff, *Louis Marshall,* 1:275.

99. Marshall to Salmon O. Levinson, Jan. 8, 1915.

100. Marshall to editor of *Jewish Chronicle,* Feb. 27, 1915, LM Papers, Box 1584.

101. Marshall to Solomon Schechter, Feb. 19, 1915, LM Papers, Box 1584.

102. Time will tell whether a single-volume study of global Jewish leadership and politics during WWI can be written. For a study of the wartime Jewish leadership of a nonnationalist European analogue to Marshall, see Levene, *War, Jews and the New Europe.* For the figures cited in the text, see Jehuda Reinharz, *Chaim Weizmann: The Making of a Zionist Leader* (New York: Oxford Univ. Press, 1985); Vladimir Jabotinsky, *The Story of the Jewish Legion* (New York: B. Ackerman, 1945); Eli Shaltiel, *Pinhas Rutenberg* [in Hebrew] (Tel Aviv: Am Oved, 1990); Eliezer Livneh, *Aaron Aaronsohn: Haish u'zemano* (Jerusalem: Mosad Bialik, 1969); Michael Bar-Zohar,

Ben-Gurion: A Biography (New York: Adama Books, 1986). Pro-congress lobbying by Zhitlovsky and Syrkin are discussed in Frankel, "Jewish Socialists and the American Jewish Congress Movement." For background regarding Jewish political outlooks through World War One, see Jonathan Frankel, *Prophecy and Politics: Socialism, Nationalism and the Russian Jews, 1862–1917* (Cambridge: Cambridge Univ. Press, 1981).

103. Marshall to Mortimer Schiff, Mar. 15, 1915, LM Papers, Box 1584. (Szajkowski, in *Jews, Wars, and Communism,* 14, mistakenly attributes this letter to Jacob Schiff.)

104. Marshall, "War and the Jewish Question," 732.

105. The discussion in this paragraph relies on Szajkowski, *Jews, Wars, and Communism,* 1:5–9.

106. Frankel, "Jewish Socialists and the American Jewish Congress Movement," 218.

107. Ibid.

108. Marshall, "War and the Jewish Question."

109. Quotes and information in this paragraph are culled from Marshall, "War and the Jewish Question."

110. Frankel, "Jewish Socialists and the American Jewish Congress Movement," 219.

111. Ibid., 220.

112. Ibid., 221.

113. Marshall to Solomon Schechter, Mar. 8, 1915, LM Papers, Box 1584.

114. Marshall to Joseph Barondess, Feb. 19, 1915, LM Papers, Box 1584.

115. Marshall and Hourwich subsequently traded punches on the congress issue in the Yiddish press. Frankel, "Jewish Socialists and the American Jewish Congress Movement," 220, 328.

116. Marshall to Felix Warburg, May 1, 1915, LM Papers, Box 1584.

117. Frankel, "Jewish Socialists and the American Jewish Congress Movement," 221.

118. Ibid., 222.

119. Marshall to Cyrus Adler, May 24, 1915, LM Papers, Box 1584.

120. Marshall to Judge Mayer Sulzberger, May 24, 1915, LM Papers, Box 1584.

121. Marshall to Cyrus Adler, May 24, 1915.

122. Marshall to Cyrus Adler, May 10, 1915, LM Papers, Box 1584.

123. Marshall to Judah Magnes, May 21, 1915, LM Papers, Box 1584.

124. Marshall's letters to family, May 24, 1915, LM Papers, Box 1584.

125. Marshall letter to Julian Mack, June 14, 1915, LM Papers, Box 1584.

126. Ibid.; Marshall letter to Solomon Schechter, July 26, 1915, LM Papers, Box 1584. For Straus, see chapter 6, n40.

127. Rosenthal, "The Public Life of Louis Marshall," 330.

128. Marshall to James A. Foley, Mar. 17, 1914, cited in Rosenthal, "The Public Life of Louis Marshall," 330.

129. Rosenthal, "The Public Life of Louis Marshall," 331.

130. On the funding issue, Marshall was conscious that Protestant groups sometimes blocked the allocation of public funds to Catholic and Jewish institutions. Marshall to Joseph Jacobs, Feb. 11, 1915, LM Papers, Box 1584.

131. Marshall to Jacob Schiff, Sept. 21, 1915, LM Papers, Box 1584; Rosenthal, "The Public Life of Louis Marshall," 332.

132. Rosenthal, "The Public Life of Louis Marshall," 334. Marshall insisted that the convention was fair to labor, because it adopted reforms such as the recognition of compensation benefits

for occupational diseases, on par with benefits awarded to industrial accidents. Marshall to Dix Smith, Oct. 8, 1915, LM Papers, Box 1584.

133. For discussion of the Marshall family's work on environmental matters and its connection to Louis's work on Jewish affairs and minority rights, see Part Four.

134. Rosenthal, "The Public Life of Louis Marshall," 332.

135. Marshall letters to Judah Magnes and Mayer Sulzerger, Sept. 21–22, 1915, LM Papers, Box 1584; Rosenthal, "The Public Life of Louis Marshall," 332–33.

136. Marshall jabbed his rival Elihu Root in this verse he shared with an associate: "Why gloat with diabolic glee / And fill all space with clatter? / 'Tis evident you do not see / The real Root of the matter." Rosenthal, "The Public Life of Louis Marshall," 336.

137. Marshall to Judah Magnes, Sept. 22, 1915, LM Papers, Box 1584.

138. Ibid.

139. Frankel, "Jewish Socialists and the American Jewish Congress Movement," 223.

140. For an extended discussion of the Brandeis-Marshall comparison: Jonathan Sarna, "Two Jewish Lawyers Named Louis," *American Jewish History* 94, nos. 1–2 (Mar.–June 2008), 1–20.

141. Frankel, "Jewish Socialists and the American Jewish Congress Movement," 225.

142. Ibid.

143. "Conference Versus Congress," *American Hebrew*, Aug. 13, 1915.

144. Ibid., 226.

145. Marshall's postwar negotiations with the Zionists for an expanded Jewish Agency are analyzed in Part Four.

146. Marshall to Cyrus Adler, Sept. 22, 1915, LM Papers, Box 1584.

147. Marshall to Harry Friedenwald, Aug. 2, 1915, LM Papers, Box 1584.

148. For a discussion of the pair's contrasting orientations toward Judaism, see Sarna, "Two Jewish Lawyers Named Louis," 2–3.

149. Marshall to Friedenwald, Aug. 2, 1916.

150. Marshall to Jacob Schiff, Jan. 7, 1916, LM Papers, Box 1585.

151. Marshall to Louis Brandeis, Jan. 29, 1916, LM Papers, Box 1585.

152. Marshall to Louis Brandeis, Feb. 14, 1916, LM Papers, Box 1585.

153. Frankel, "Jewish Socialists and the American Jewish Congress Movement," 259.

154. Ibid.

155. Marshall to Bernard Richards, Mar. 16, 1916; Reznikoff, Louis Marshall, 2:514–17.

156. Frankel, "Jewish Socialists and the American Jewish Congress Movement," 262–63.

157. Marshall to John Slicher (editor of *Leslie's Weekly*), Feb. 18, 1916, LM Papers, Box 1585.

158. Frankel, "Jewish Socialists and the American Jewish Congress Movement," 273.

159. Ibid., 264.

160. Marshall to Henry Elsner, Dec. 9, 1915, LM Papers, Box 1584.

161. Marshall to Esther Rieser, Mar. 31, 1916, LM Papers, Box 1585.

162. Alpert, *Louis Marshall, 1856–1929,* 43.

163. Marshall eloquently eulogized Dr. Elsner, his friend of half a century, in the *Syracuse Post-Standard* on Feb. 18, 1916: "There are few whose departure from earth is capable of arousing such genuine sorrow and such precious memories." Elsner and Marshall were occasional partners in real estate dealings in Upstate New York.

164. Marshall to Esther Rieser, Mar. 31, 1916, LM Papers, Box 1585.

165. Marshall to Esther Rieser, May 15, 1916, LM Papers, Box 1585.

166. Alpert, *Louis Marshall, 1856–1929,* 52.

167. Ibid., 45–48. (As I understand it, the Bible is now in the possession of a Marshall grandson, Roger [George's son]; interview with Roger Marshall, Apr. 30, 2010.)

168. Marshall to Jacob Schiff, June 10, 1916, LM Papers, Box 1585; correspondence in LM Papers, Box 1585.

169. Unpublished verse, LM Papers, Box 20.

170. Dr. Gustav Gottheil presided over the confirmation ceremony of Florence Lowenstein at Temple Emanu-El on June 5, 1887. LM Papers, Box 14.

171. LM Papers, Box 14. See also Alpert, *Louis Marshall, 1856–1929,* 49.

172. The trustees of the fund were trusted associates and valued educators—Cyrus Adler, Israel Friedlander, Irving Lehman, Judah Magnes, Felix Warburg. LM Papers, Box 14.

173. Marshall to Abraham Freedlander (editor of Chicago *Jewish Sentinel*), Aug. 10, 1916, LM Papers, Box 1586.

174. Marshall to Joe Stolz, Aug. 4, 1916, LM Papers, Box 1586.

175. Alpert, *Louis Marshall, 1856–1929,* 45.

176. Marshall to children, Aug. 3, 1916, LM Papers, Box 1586.

177. Marshall to daughter Ruth, Aug. 30, 1916, LM Papers, Box 1586.

178. Marshall to sons Robert and George, Oct. 5, 1916, LM Papers, Box 1586.

179. Marshall to sister Ida, Oct. 13, 1916, LM Papers, Box 1586.

180. James Marshall to Marshall, Dec. 19, 1916, James Marshall Collection (157), AJA, Box 38.

181. Marshall to son James, Dec. 24, 1916, James Marshall Collection, Box 38.

182. Urofsky, *Louis D. Brandeis,* 519–20; Selig Adler, "The Palestine Question in the Wilson Era," *Jewish Social Studies* 10 (Oct. 1948), 303–34; Richard Ned Lebow, "Woodrow Wilson and the Balfour Declaration," *The Journal of Modern History* 40, no. 4 (Dec. 1968), 501–23.

183. In this connection, see Professor Mark Raider's suggestive comments about why Marshall, in contrast to a long list of other modern Jewish individuals, never received systematic biographical treatment in the twentieth century: Mark Raider, "Introduction," x–xii.

184. Reznikoff, *Louis Marshall,* 1:153–54.

185. Ibid. Marshall erroneously cited 1906 as the year of the Immigration Commission's founding.

186. Marshall to editor of *Harper's Weekly,* Apr. 15, 1916, LM Papers, Box 1585. These were *Harper's* final days as a weekly.

187. Marshall to William Dillingham, May 26, 1916, LM Papers, Box 1585.

188. Jacob Schiff to Marshall, Mar. 10, 1916; Frankel, "Jewish Socialists and the American Jewish Congress Movement," 271–72.

189. Marshall to Max Goldfarb, May 16, 1916, LM Papers, Box 1585.

190. Frankel, "Jewish Socialists and the American Jewish Congress Movement," 273.

191. Marshall to Leon Sanders, Grand Master, Independent Order of Brith Abraham, May 20, 1916, LM Papers, Box 1585.

192. Frankel, "Jewish Socialists and the American Jewish Congress Movement," 276.

193. Ibid., 277.

194. Ibid., 278.

195. Marshall to Cyrus Sulzberger, Aug. 1, 1916, LM Papers, Box 1586.

196. Marshall to Louis Brandeis, July 24, 1916, Reznikoff, *Louis Marshall,* 2:517–18.

197. Marshall to Cyrus Sulzberger, Aug. 1, 1916.

198. Sarna, "Two Jewish Lawyers Named Louis," 18–19. Brandeis did not attend Marshall's funeral.

199. Marshall to Adolf Kraus, Aug. 18, 1916.

200. Marshall to Julian Mack, Aug. 4, 1916.

201. Frankel, "Jewish Socialists and the American Jewish Congress Movement," 280.

202. Ibid.

203. Marshall to Israel Zangwill, Aug. 30, 1916; Reznikoff, *Louis Marshall*, 2:519.

204. Marshall to Esther Reisser, Dec. 2, 1916, LM Papers, Box 1586.

205. Marshall to Judge Mack, Sept. 1, 1916, LM Papers, Box 1586.

206. Marshall to William Wilcox, Sept. 11, 1916, LM Papers, Box 1586.

207. Marshall to George Blumenthal, Oct. 5, 1916, LM Papers, Box 1586.

208. Marshall to editor of *Der Tag*, Nov. 1, 1916, LM Papers, Box 1586.

209. Marshall to Herbert Parsons, Oct. 26, 1916, LM Papers, Box 1586.

210. Marshall to William Wilcox, Sept. 15, 1916, LM Papers, Box 1586.

211. Marshall correspondence, Nov. 1916, LM Papers, Box 1586.

212. As late as Jan. 1919, Marshall articulated isolationist objections to the League of Nations plan, telling William Guthrie that Wilson's scheme was "fraught with infinite peril to our institutions." He revised this position as a result of his minority rights lobbying at the Paris conference. See Silver, "Louis Marshall and the Democratization of Jewish Identity," 52.

213. Cong. Rec. (Senate), Dec. 11, 1916, 157–58.

214. About a month after the exchange in Congress, Marshall and Gallinger wrote relatively conciliatory letters, and Marshall praised the senator's work on school reform in Washington, DC. (Gallinger was genuinely interested in the progress of African American pupils in the public schools of the nation's capital.) Marshall to Jacob Gallinger, Jan. 4, 1917, LM Papers, Box 1587.

215. Ibid.

216. Marshall to James Reed, Dec. 20, 1916, LM Papers, Box 1586.

217. For a discussion of Marshall and claims of Jewish whiteness and racial particularity, see Goldstein, *The Price of Whiteness*, 167, 176.

218. Cong. Rec. (Senate), Dec. 11, 1916, 157.

219. Goldstein, *The Price of Whiteness;* Karen Brodkin, *How Jews Became White Folks and What That Says about Race in America* (New Brunswick, NJ: Rutgers Univ. Press, 1998).

220. Marshall to James Reed, Dec. 20, 1916.

221. Cong. Rec. (Senate), Dec. 11. 1916, 159.

222. Marshall to Henry Cabot Lodge, Dec. 21, 1916, LM Papers, Box 1586.

223. Marshall to Adolph Ochs, Jan. 19, 1917, LM Papers, Box 1587.

224. Laurel Leff, *Buried by the Times: The Holocaust and America's Most Important Newspaper* (Cambridge: Cambridge Univ. Press, 2005).

225. Marshall to Thaddeus Sweet, Mar. 17, 1917, LM Papers, Box 1587.

226. Marshall to Adolph Ochs, Sept. 1, 1916, LM Papers, Box 1586.

227. Marshall to Beatrice Magnes, Aug. 23, 1916, LM Papers, Box 1586.

228. Marshall to Herman Bernstein (report on meeting with Syromyatnikov), Aug. 14, 1916, LM Papers, Box 1586.

229. Frankel, "Jewish Socialists and the American Jewish Congress Movement," 281–84.

230. Marshall to Jacob Schiff, Aug. 21, 1916, LM Papers, Box 1586.

231. Frankel, "Jewish Socialists and the American Jewish Congress Movement," 285.

232. Ibid.

233. Ibid., 297.

234. Ibid., 300–301.

235. For a suggestion that secular Jewish culture reached its acme in America during this wartime period, before being attenuated internally by assimilation and externally by the restrictionist legislation of the early 1920s, see Henry Feingold, *Lest Memory Cease: Finding Meaning in the American Jewish Past* (Syracuse: Syracuse Univ. Press, 1996) 175–76.

236. Lebow, "Woodrow Wilson and the Balfour Declaration," 501–23.

237. Marshall to Cyrus Adler, Jan. 3 and Jan. 6, 1917, LM Papers, Box 1587.

238. With Marshall managing the overseas donor group (Henrietta Szold served as its secretary), Rosenwald and others funded Aaronsohn's experimental station on the assumption that the project would have nothing to do with Zionist politics; thus, they were subsequently mortified when the Nili spy activities embroiled Atlit, an American-incorporated scientific station, deeply in wartime politics in contravention of America's official policy of neutrality toward the Ottoman Empire. A theory holding that this embittering sequence produced Rosenwald's reluctance to continue funding projects in the Yishuv is a kind of scholarly urban legend alluded to frequently in discussions of the Yishuv period. It is hard to substantiate. A matter-of-fact memoirist like Jewish educator Alexander Dushkin, troubled by the Zionist indifference of Rosenwald (a prodigious, liberal-minded donor, some of whose family became avowed anti-Zionists), referred to the Atlit catastrophe as a possible determinant of Rosenwald's attitude ("some said that it all started when Rosenwald was shocked that Aaron Aaronsohn . . . was discovered during World War I as the leader of the Nili ring") but concluded that the Sears Roebuck magnate mostly withdrew support from the Zionists because "he was convinced that the Arabs would slaughter all Jews in Palestine" (Alexander Dushkin, *Living Bridges* [Jerusalem: Keter, 1975], 96–97). In his admirably fair-minded and thorough biography of Rosenwald, his own grandfather, Peter Ascoli, lends some credence to the legend ("angered by the news of Aaronsohn's activities, JR vowed to cut-off his support") but also notes that the persuasive agronomist from Atlit managed to "patch up his differences" with the Chicago businessman and philanthropist just before a mysterious plane crash claimed Aaronsohn's life (Peter Ascoli, *Julius Rosenwald* [Bloomington: Indiana Univ. Press, 2006], 185, 202). However inconclusive, this subject deserves mention in light of chapter 11 here, which relates to Marshall's stewardship of the JDC Crimean colonization project, in which he, Rosenwald, and others seemed myopically to view another agricultural development specialist, Joseph Rosen, as a kind of Aaronsohn-Atlit substitute, without the entangling political dross.

239. Anecdotal evidence of this fissure, caused by the blatantly pro-German attitudes of some members of the Uptown elite, is conveyed in Birmingham, *Our Crowd,* 317–23.

240. Marshall to M. F. Seidmann (editor of *Jewish Correspondent*), Feb. 5, 1917, LM Papers, Box 1587.

241. Marshall to US Civil Service Commission, Feb. 20, 1917, LM Papers, Box 1587.

242. Marshall to Leon Gomberg, Mar. 24, 1917, LM Papers, Box 1587.

243. Marshall to Cyrus Adler, Mar. 19, 1917, LM Papers, Box 1587.

244. Marshall to Herman Bernstein, Apr. 16, 1917, LM Papers, Box 1587.

245. Marshall to Robert Lansing, Apr. 9, 1917, LM Papers, Box 1587.

246. Marshall to Jacob Schiff, Apr. 25, 1917, LM Papers, Box 1587.

247. Marshall correspondence, Apr. 1917, LM Papers. Box 1587.

248. Marshall to Jacob Schiff, Nov. 13, 1917, LM Papers, Box 1587.

249. Marshall to Cyrus Adler, Mar. 19, 1917, LM Papers, Box 1587.

250. See chapter 6, n233.

251. Zosa Szajkowski, "The Pacifism of Judah Magnes," *Conservative Judaism* 22, no. 3 (1968), 36–55.

252. Yohai Goell, "Aliyah in the Zionism of an American Oleh: Judah L. Magnes," *American Jewish Historical Quarterly* 65 (1975–76), 99–120.

253. Silver, *First Contact,* 199–201.

254. Background information here is drawn from *The Mount Sinai Unit in the World War: With Scenes at Base Hospital # 3 A.E.F. at Vauclaire, Dordogne, France,* a publication found in the archives of Mount Sinai Hospital, New York.

255. Marshall to George Blumenthal, Oct. 5, 1916; Reznikoff, *Louis Marshall,* 2:810.

256. Marshall correspondence, June 1917, LM Papers, Box 1587.

257. Marshall to Joe Stolz, Nov. 26, 1917, LM Papers, Box 1587.

258. James's departure occurred abruptly, and his father was not able to see him off. Marshall to Joe Stolz, Feb. 16, 1918, LM Papers, Box 1588.

259. "A Native American" [Louis Marshall], "Laws of Citizenship," *New York Times,* June 30, 1917.

260. Marshall to Theodore Roosevelt, June 30, 1917, LM Papers, Box 1587.

261. Marshall to Herman Bernstein, Mar. 31, 1917, LM Papers, Box 1587.

262. Marshall to Jacob Schiff, Apr. 20, 1917, LM Papers, Box 1587.

263. Lucy Dawidowicz, "Louis Marshall and the *Jewish Daily Forward:* An Episode in Wartime Censorship, 1917–1918," in *For Max Weinrich on His Seventieth Birthday: Studies in Jewish Languages, Literature and Society* (London: VG & Mouton, 1964), 31–44.

264. Frankel, "Jewish Socialists and the American Jewish Congress Movement."

265. For the schneider controversy and extreme responses to it: Jabotinsky, *Story of the Jewish Legion,* 72–73; Yigal Elam, *The Jewish Legion in World War I* [in Hebrew] (Tel Aviv: Defense Ministry, 1973), 240.

266. "Treason to Advise Men Against Draft; Marshall Says Those Who Urge Eligibles Not to Register Are Liable to Death Penalty," *New York Times,* June 3, 1917.

267. Marshall to Jacob Schiff, June 1, 1917, LM Papers, Box 1587.

268. Marshall to Judah Magnes, June 1, 1917, LM Papers, Box 1587; Reznikoff, *Louis Marshall,* 2:972.

269. Marshall to Beatrice Magnes, June 1, 1917, LM Papers, Box 1587.

270. Marshall to his children, Aug. 6, 9, 1917, LM Papers, Box 1587.

271. Marshall to Richard Gottheil, Aug. 6, 9, 1917, LM Papers, Box 1587.

272. Marshall to children, Aug. 16, 1917, LM Papers, Box 1587.

273. Marshall correspondence, July 1917, LM Papers, Box 1587.

274. Marshall to Cyrus Sulzberger, Aug. 16, 1917, LM Papers, Box 1587.

275. Dawidowicz, "Louis Marshall and the *Jewish Daily Forward,*" 43.

276. Background information here is drawn from Dawidowicz's "Louis Marshall and the *Jewish Daily Forward*" and from Soltes, *The Yiddish Press.*

277. Leon Trotsky, *My Life* (New York: Pathfinder Press, 1970), 275–76.

278. Marshall to Abraham Cahan, Oct. 8, 1917, LM Papers, Box 1587; Reznikoff, *Louis Marshall,* 2:974–75.

279. Ibid.

280. Dawidowicz, "Louis Marshall and the *Jewish Daily Forward*," 38.

281. Norma Fain Pratt, *Morris Hillquit: A Political History of an American Jewish Socialist* (Westport: Greenwood Press, 1979), 139.

282. Ibid., 87.

283. Hillquit's candidacy in the 1917 New York mayoral race was, from Marshall's standpoint, nightmarishly successful, but scholars have never been able to determine what share of his 20 percent of the vote came from the city's Jews. His biographer (Pratt, Morris Hillquit, 158) writes that this question "has still to be determined," and a detailed article specifically devoted to the 1917 election doubts whether Hillquit's impressive showing can be regarded as the result of a "Jewish vote" (Zosa Szajkowski, "The Jews and New York City's Mayoralty Election of 1917," 300.

284. Pratt, *Morris Hillquit,* 156.

285. Hillquit disagreed with the Haywood-IWW syndicalist position, upholding that trade union activity ought to be a fulcrum for socialist organization; as a lawyer he was also more inclined than Haywood to use arbitration rather than strikes to deal with labor issues.

286. Pratt, *Morris Hillquit,* 27.

287. Ibid., 116.

288. Theodore Draper, *The Roots of American Communism* (New York: Viking, 1957), 92.

289. Pratt, *Morris Hillquit,* 124–26.

290. Ibid.

291. Marshall to Jewish daily newspapers, Oct. 29, 1917, LM Papers, Box 1587.

292. Marshall's Nov. 4, 1915, letter to Brisbane is printed in Reznikoff, *Louis Marshall,* 2:1155–60.

293. Marshall to Henry Morgenthau, Oct. 31, 1917, LM Papers, Box 1587.

294. Marshall to Judge Mack, Oct. 31, 1917, LM Papers, Box 1587.

295. Pratt, *Morris Hillquit,* 155.

296. Szajkowski, "The Jews and New York City's Mayoralty Election of 1917," 289.

297. Ibid., 287–88.

298. Ibid., 291–92.

299. Ibid., 296.

300. Ibid., 292.

301. Marshall to Abraham Cahan, Nov. 3, 1917, LM Papers, Box 1587.

302. Marshall to Judge Mack, Oct, 31, 1917, LM Papers, Box 1587.

303. See chapter 6, n283.

304. Szajkowski, "The Jews and New York City's Mayoralty Election of 1917," 304.

305. Marshall to Mrs. Julius Beer, Nov. 13, 1917, LM Papers, Box 1587.

306. Ibid.

307. Dawidowicz, "Louis Marshall and the *Jewish Daily Forward*," 41.

308. Marshall to children, Sept. 13, 1917, LM Papers, Box 1587.

309. Ibid. Edmond Guggenheim was part of a "quiet generation" in his prominent family's history. John Davis, *The Guggenheims: An American Epic,* 2nd ed. (New York, 1994), 313.

310. Marshall to Provost Marshal, Major General Enoch Crowder, June 8, 1918, LM Papers, Box 1587.

311. Marshall to daughter Ruth, June 15, 1918, LM Papers, Box 1588.

312. Marshall to son James, May 18, 1918, LM Papers, Box 1588.

313. Marshall to Herbert Friedenwald, May 20, 1918, LM Papers, Box 1588.

314. Foster Hirsch, *The Boys from Syracuse: The Shuberts' Theatrical Empire* (Carbondale: Southern Illinois University Press, 1998), 9–13.

315. Rudolph, *From a Minyan to a Community,* 159.

316. See, e.g., Louis Marshall to Lee Schubert, Aug. 16, 1905, LM Papers, Box 1574.

317. Hirsch, *The Boys from Syracuse,* 120.

318. Marshall to Lee Shubert, Mar. 13, 15, 1918, LM Papers, Box 1588.

319. Marshall to Newton D. Baker, Mar. 4, 1918, LM Papers, Box 1588.

320. Marshall correspondence, Mar. 1918, LM Papers, Box 1588.

321. Marshall to son James, Mar. 9, 1918, LM Papers, Box 1588.

322. Marshall to Baker, Mar. 4, 1918.

323. See also Marshall to Newton Baker, Nov. 14, 1917; Reznikoff, *Louis Marshall,* 1:257.

324. Marshall to Jacob Schiff, Mar. 8, 1918, LM Papers, Box 1588.

325. Marshall to Jacob Schiff, Apr. 4, 1918, LM Papers, Box 1588.

326. Ibid.

327. Marshall to son James, Apr. 27, 1918, LM Papers, Box 1588.

328. Marshall to Cyrus Adler, June 1, 1918, LM Papers, Box 1588.

329. The information in this paragraph draws from Stephen Frese, "Divided by a Common Language: The Babel Proclamation and its Influence in Iowa History," *History Teacher* 39, no. 1 (Nov. 2005).

330. Marshall to Charles Silberman, June 13, 1918, LM Papers, Box 1588.

331. Marshall to William L. Harding, June 13, 1918, LM Papers, Box 1588.

332. Marshall to William L. Harding, July 9, 1918; Reznikoff, *Louis Marshall,* 2:988–93.

333. Marshall to Paul Lee Ellerbe, Aug. 6, 1918, LM Papers, Box 1588.

334. Lafayette Young, *New York Times,* July 30, 1918.

335. Frese, "Divided by a Common Language."

336. Dawidowicz, "Louis Marshall and the *Jewish Daily Forward,*" 43.

337. Marshall to Jacob Newman, Dec. 7, 1917, LM Papers, Box 1587.

338. Marshall to Jacob Schiff, Jan. 22, 1918, LM Papers, Box 1588.

339. Cohen, *Jacob H. Schiff,* 206.

340. Marshall to Jacob Newman, Jan. 11, 1918, LM Papers, Box 1588.

341. Marshall to William Lamar, Sept. 18, 1918, LM Papers, Box 1588.

342. Marshall to Abraham Cahan, Oct. 17, 1918, LM Papers, Box 1588.

343. Marshall to Abraham Cahan, Oct. 26, 1918; Marshall to editor of *New York Tribune,* Oct. 28, 1918, LM Papers, Box 1588.

344. Marshall to Abraham Cahan, Oct. 31, 1918, LM Papers, Box 1588.

345. Ibid.

346. Marshall to Bennie Stolz, Apr. 4, 1918, LM Papers, Box 1588.

347. Marshall to son James, Mar. 18, 1918, LM Papers, Box 1588.

348. Marshall correspondence, May 1918; Marshall to son James, May 18, 1918, LM Papers, Box 1588.

349. Marshall to son James, May 25, 1918, LM Papers, Box 1588.

350. James Marshall to Marshall, May 5, 1918, James Marshall Collection 157, Box 38.

351. Marshall to son James, May 25, 1918, LM Papers, Box 1588.

352. Marshall to son James, June 8, 1918, LM Papers, Box 1588.

353. James Marshall to Marshall, July 12, 1918, James Marshall Collection 157, Box 38.

354. Marshall to Mayer Sulzberger, Aug. 20, 1918, LM Papers, Box 1588.

355. *The Mount Sinai Unit in the World War,* Mount Sinai Hospital Archive.

356. Marshall to son James, Sept. 4, 1918, LM Papers, Box 1588.

357. Marshall to children, Sept. 9, 1918, LM Papers, Box 1588.

358. Marshall to James, Sept. 21, 1918, LM Papers, Box 1588.

359. Marshall to James, Sept. 25, 1918, LM Papers, Box 1588.

360. Marshall to James, Nov. 11, 1918, LM Papers, Box 1588.

361. Marshall to Jacob Schiff, Nov. 14, 1917, LM Papers, Box 1587. For Marshall's full explanation of meanings of "nation," see the copy of this letter in Reznikoff, *Louis Marshall,* 2:710–14.

362. Ibid.

363. Marshall to Cyrus Adler, Dec. 26, 1917, LM Papers, Box 1587.

364. Melech Epstein, *Profiles of Eleven* (Detroit: Wayne State Univ. Press, 1965), 180–83.

365. Marshall to Jacob Schiff, Apr. 8, 1918, LM Papers, Box 1588.

366. Reznikoff, *Louis Marshall,* 2:714.

367. Menahem Kaufman, *An Ambiguous Partnership: Non-Zionists and Zionists in America 1939–1948* (Detroit: Wayne State Univ. Press, 1991), 73–95, 275–311.

368. Zvi Ganin, *An Uneasy Relationship: American Jewish Leadership and Israel, 1948–1957* (Syracuse: Syracuse Univ. Press, 2005), 9–11.

369. Ibid., 92–94.

370. Reznikoff, *Louis Marshall,* 2:715–16.

371. Marshall to son James, Apr. 27, 1918, LM Papers, Box 1588.

372. Ibid.

373. Marshall to Adolph Ochs, Apr. 29, 1918, LM Papers, Box 1588.

374. Marshall to Lionel de Rothschild, July 12, 1918, LM Papers, Box 1588.

375. Marshall to David Philipson, Sept. 5 1918, LM Papers, Box 1588.

376. Marshall's relationship with Schechter and their work together in the consolidation of the Jewish Theological Seminary is discussed in chapter 2.

377. Marshall to Julian Mack, Sept. 30, 1918, LM Papers, Box 1588.

378. Ibid.

379. Marshall to son James, Nov. 8, 1918, LM Papers, Box 1588.

380. Marshall to Louis Brandeis, Nov. 9, 1918, LM Papers, Box 1588.

381. Marshall to Woodrow Wilson, Nov. 7, 1918, LM Papers, Box 1588.

7. Paris and Haiti

1. Kessler, Alperin, and Diamond, "American Jews and the Paris Peace Conference," 231.

2. Ibid., 232.

3. Ibid., 232–33.

4. Louis Marshall, "Jewish Rights in Eastern Europe," in Reznikoff, *Louis Marshall,* 2:526–36.

5. Ibid., 534.

6. Marshall to Mayer Sulzberger, Dec. 21, 1918, in Reznikoff, *Louis Marshall,* 2:538.

7. Kessler, Alperin, and Diamond, "American Jews and the Paris Peace Conference," 234.

8. Ibid., 237.

9. Ibid., 234.

10. Naomi Cohen, "An American Jew at the Paris Peace Conference of 1919: Excerpts from the Diary of Oscar S. Straus," in *Essays on Jewish Life and Thought,* ed. Joseph Blau (New York: Columbia Univ. Press, 1959), 162.

11. Marshall to Isaac Landman, Dec. 19, 1918, in Reznikoff, *Louis Marshall,* 2:536.

12. Kessler, Alperin, and Diamond, "American Jews and the Paris Peace Conference," 234.

13. Moshe Davis, "The Human Record: Cyrus Adler at the Peace Conference, 1919," in *Essays in American Jewish History,* American Jewish Archives (Cincinnati: American Jewish Archives, 1958), 461.

14. Kessler, Alperin, and Diamond, "American Jews and the Paris Peace Conference," 235. Zionist lobbying at the Paris conference was highly dramatic. Though this division of labor was basically honored, American Zionist delegates such as Felix Frankfurter, who worked on drafts of the British Mandate proposal and lobbied vociferously against the staging of a Wilsonian-type plebiscite in Syria—via a group of missionaries, oil men, and Progressives that came to be known as the King-Crane commission—did not work in complete detachment from Marshall's minority rights' group. For the American Zionist diplomacy in Paris, see Frank Manuel, *The Realities of American Palestine Relations* (Washington, DC: Public Affairs Press, 1949), 232; Adler, "The Palestine Question in the Wilson Era," 303–34; Harry Howard, *The King-Crane Commission: An American Inquiry in the Middle East* (Beirut: Khayats, 1963).

15. Marshall to Manley O. Hudson, Jan. 1, 1921, in Reznikoff, *Louis Marshall,* 2:554; Kessler, Alperin, and Diamond, "American Jews and the Paris Peace Conference," 235–37.

16. Marshall to Manley O. Hudson, Jan. 1, 1921, in Reznikoff, *Louis Marshall,* 2:554. The Joint Foreign Committee and the alliance submitted their separate memorandums on Feb. 21; Lucien Wolf subsequently boasted about his being the "first to champion before the Peace Conference of 1919 the cause of Civil and Religious Liberty." Fink, *Defending the Rights of Others,* 195.

17. Marshall to Edward Lauterbach, Feb. 11, 1919, LM Papers, Box 1589.

18. Marshall to Mayer Sulzberger, Dec. 21, 1918.

19. Marshall correspondence, Mar. 1919, LM Papers, Box 1589; Silver, "Louis Marshall and the Democratization of Jewish Identity," 49.

20. Davis, "The Human Record," 462. Adler noted that he traveled to Paris only because Marshall and Schiff insisted he should.

21. Marshall to Mayer Sulzberger, Dec. 21, 1918.

22. Marshall to William D. Guthrie, Jan. 20, 1919, LM Papers, Box 1589; Silver, "Louis Marshall and the Democratization of Jewish Identity," 52.

23. Marshall to James Marshall, Feb. 15, 1919.

24. Marshall to Manley O. Hudson, Jan. 21, 1921.

25. Marshall to Woodrow Wilson, Nov. 14, 16, 1918, in Reznikoff, *Louis Marshall,* 2:595–98.

26. Woodrow Wilson to Marshall, Nov. 16, 1918, in Reznikoff, *Louis Marshall,* 2:596.

27. Marshall to Ida Marshall, Mar. 7, 1919, LM Papers, Box 1589. Close to two years after this meeting with Wilson, Marshall described it similarly as having been "very satisfactory." Marshall to Manley O. Hudson, Jan. 21, 1921.

28. Marshall to children, Mar. 22, 1919, LM Papers, Box 82.

29. Davis, "The Human Record," 468 [Mar. 30, 1919, diary entry].

30. Marshall to children, Apr. 7, 1919, LM Papers, Box 82.

31. Ibid.

32. Cohen, "An American Jew at the Paris Peace Conference," 166–68.

33. Ibid., 167.

34. "A Conversation between Roman Dmowski and Louis Marshall," New York City, Oct. 6, 1918, in Reznikoff, *Louis Marshall,* 2:586–87.

35. Cohen, "An American Jew at the Paris Peace Conference," 168.

36. Carole Fink, "Louis Marshall: An American Jewish Diplomat in Paris, 1919," *American Jewish History* 94, nos. 1–2 (Mar.–June 2008), 29–30.

37. Fink, *Defending the Rights of Others,* 199.

38. Ibid.

39. Ibid. Fink's analysis of the meeting is based on Minutes, Apr. 5–6, 1919, CZA A405/77/1B.

40. Fink, *Defending the Rights of Others,* 200. For Marshall's claim about the delegation's tardiness in submitting its proposal, see Marshall to B. Zuckerman, June 6, 1923.

41. Marshall to his children, Apr. 7, 1919.

42. Davis, "The Human Record," 472 [Apr. 8, 1919, diary entry].

43. Marshall chaired the committee, whose membership was split between nonnationalists (Adler, Jacques Bigart, and Lucien Wolf) and nationalists (Sokolow, Menachem Ussischkin, and Yehoshua Thon). Fink, *Defending the Rights of Others,* 199.

44. Marshall to his children, Apr. 7, 1919.

45. Davis, "The Human Record," 472 [Apr. 8, 1919 diary entry].

46. This criticism is raised explicitly in Kessler, Alperin, and Diamond, "American Jews and the Paris Peace Conference," 241–42, and it is implied by the analysis in Auerbach, *Rabbis and Lawyers.*

47. Fink, *Defending the Rights of Others,* 201.

48. Tennenbaum, *Ben milhamah ve-shalom,* 45 (my translation).

49. Davis, "The Human Record," 486 [May 27, 1919, diary entry].

50. Ibid. Strauss's comment was made in 1954.

51. Marshall to children, Apr. 18, 1919, LM Papers, Box 82.

52. Ibid.

53. Fink, *Defending the Rights of Others,* 204.

54. Ibid., 205.

55. Fink, "Louis Marshall," 31.

56. Marshall to children, Apr. 18, 1919. As hinted in the text, Marshall negotiated with House's team and continued to lobby for a minority rights treaty, on his own initiative, without waiting for the Jewish delegation's appointed committee to finish its draft of a proposed treaty.

57. Fink, "Louis Marshall," 30.

58. Davis, "The Human Record," 471 [Apr. 7, 1919, diary entry].

59. Marshall to children, Apr. 18, 1919; Davis, "The Human Record," 474 [Apr. 16, 1919, diary entry].

60. Marshall to children, Apr. 18, 1919.

61. Fink, *Defending the Rights of Others,* 174–76. The ensuing discussion of the diplomacy of the Beit Am relies on Fink's engaging account.

62. Marshall to children, Apr. 18, 1919.

63. Marshall to children, Apr. 28, 1919, LM Papers, Box 82.

64. Fink, *Defending the Rights of Others,* 183.

65. Ibid., 185.

66. Fink, "Louis Marshall," 30.

67. Marshall to children, Apr. 28, 1919, May 3, 1919.

68. Fink, "Louis Marshall," 39.

69. Ibid.

70. Ibid., 28. The impact of Japan's demand upon diplomacy for minority rights is discussed in fascinating detail in Fink, *Defending the Rights of Others,* 154–60.

71. Felix Frankfurter to Woodrow Wilson, May 8, 1919, CZA A 264/7.

72. In this connection, it bears mention that neither Wolf nor any of the alliance delegates really had access to Lloyd George and Clemenceau.

73. Fink, "Louis Marshall," 33.

74. Levene, *War, Jews and the New Europe,* 293–94; Silver, "Louis Marshall and the Democratization of Jewish Identity," 53.

75. Ibid.

76. Marshall to Dr. Blank, Sept. 10, 1925, LM Papers, Box 1597; Silver, "Louis Marshall and the Democratization of Jewish Identity," 53.

77. Marshall to Israel Zangwill, Nov. 10, 1919, LM Papers, Box 1589; Reznikoff, *Louis Marshall,* 2:676–77.

78. Marshall to Samuel Koenig, June 5, 1920, in Reznikoff, *Louis Marshall,* 2:683–84.

79. Fink, *Defending the Rights of Others,* 233.

80. Ibid., 235.

81. This summary relies on Fink, "Louis Marshall," 33–34. For extended discussion of the Committee on New States, see Fink, *Defending the Rights of Others,* 211–19.

82. Marshall to children, May 18, 1919, LM Papers, Box 82.

83. Fink, "Louis Marshall," 33–34.

84. Alpert, *Louis Marshall, 1856–1929,* 97–100.

85. Marshall's estimate of the meeting, cited in the text, is quite similar in tone and phrasing to Adler's May 26 diary entry. Davis, "The Human Record," 485.

86. Marshall to children, May 27, 1919, LM Papers, Box 82.

87. Marshall to Hudson, Jan. 21, 1921.

88. Marshall to children, May 27, 1919.

89. Davis, "The Human Record," 485.

90. Ibid.

91. Marshall to children, May 27, 1919.

92. Fink's basis for calling this a "discouraging" interview is unclear. *Defending the Rights of Others,* 225.

93. Fink, "Louis Marshall," 35.

94. Ibid., 34.

95. Fink, *Defending the Rights of Others,* 250–51.

96. Marshall to Julian Mack, Oct. 24, 1919, in Reznikoff, *Louis Marshall,* 2:611.

97. Fink, "Louis Marshall," 36.

98. Marshall to children, June 28, 1919, LM Papers, Box 82.

99. Ibid.

100. The survey that follows in the text relies on Fink, *Defending the Rights of Others,* 257–60.

101. Silver, "Louis Marshall and the Democratization of Jewish Identity," 55.

102. Fink, "Louis Marshall," 37.

103. Ezra Mendelsohn, *The Jews of Central Europe Between the World Wars* (Bloomington: Indiana Univ. Press, 1983), 35.

104. Manuel, *Realities of American Palestine Relations,* 232.

105. E. P. Thompson, *The Making of the English Working Class* (New York: Viking, 1963/1966), 12.

106. Fink, "Louis Marshall," 39.

107. Ibid., 23.

108. Silver, "Louis Marshall and the Democratization of Jewish Identity," 57–58.

109. This summary of Marshall's diplomatic endeavors and its Jewish significance is taken from Silver, "Louis Marshall and the Democratization of Jewish Identity," 51–52, 59.

110. Marshall to his children, July 28, 1919, LM Papers, Box 1589.

111. Ibid. See also Marshall to his children, July 31, 1919, LM Papers, Box 1589.

112. "Mass Welcome to Louis Marshall," July 28, 1919, LM Papers, Box 151.

113. Ibid.

114. Marshall to Meir Berlin, Feb. 18, 1924, Feb. 21, 1924, LM Papers, Box 1595.

115. Michael André Bernstein, *Foregone Conclusions: Against Apocalyptic History* (Berkeley: Univ. of California Press, 1994).

116. This description of the Marshall-Filderman connection draws from Silver, "Louis Marshall and the Democratization of Jewish Identity," 59.

117. For Article 44, see Fink, *Defending the Rights of Others,* 29.

118. Marshall to William Howard Taft, Jan. 14, 1913, in Reznikoff, *Louis Marshall,* 2:502–3.

119. See, for instance, Marshall to M. Nicholas Titulesco, Jan. 5, 1926, LM Papers, Box 1598.

120. Marshall to Robert Marshall, Mar. 9, 1926, LM Papers, Box 1598.

121. Marshall to Herbert Lehman, Apr. 15, 1926, LM Papers, Box 1598.

122. Marshall to Wilhelm Filderman, May 12, 1928, LM Papers, Box 1600. For Filderman's recollection of his work with Marshall and a general description of his activities during this period, see his *Memories and Diaries, 1900–1940* (Jerusalem: Goldstein-Goren Diaspora Research Center, 2000), 1:211–12 passim.

123. "Borah Sees Haiti Prey of Our Greed," *New York Times,* May 2, 1922.

124. Ibid.

125. Information in this section is drawn from Hans Schmidt, *The United States Occupation of Haiti, 1915–1934* (New Brunswick: Rutgers Univ. Press, 1971).

126. Foreign Policy Association, *The Seizure of Haiti by the United States: A Report on the Military Occupation of the Republic of Haiti and the History of the Treaty Forced upon Her* (New York: Foreign Policy Association, 1922).

127. Ibid., 13.

128. This account relies on Marshall to Adolph Ochs, May 2, 1922, LM Papers, Box 1593; Marshall to Charles Evans Hughes, May 2, 1922, in Reznikoff, *Louis Marshall,* 2:998–1002.

129. Marshall to Charles Evans Hughes, in Reznikoff, *Louis Marshall,* 2:1001.

130. Marshall to Charles Evans Hughes, May 2, 1922, LM Papers, Box 1593.

131. For varying interpretations of the roots and motivations of American Jewish alliances with African Americans in the period of Marshall's activity, see Diner, *In the Almost Promised Land;* Michael Alexander, *Jazz Age Jews* (Princeton: Princeton Univ. Press, 2001), 127–83; Goldstein, *The Price of Whiteness.*

132. Marshall to Robert Owen, May 2, 1922, LM Papers, Box 1593.

133. Marshall to Adolph Ochs, May 2, 1922.

134. *New York Times,* May 3, 1922; Marshall to Adolph Ochs, May 3, 1922, LM Papers, Box 1593.

135. William Hixson, *Moorfield Storey and the Abolitionist Tradition* (New York: Oxford Univ. Press, 1972).

136. Marshall to Moorfield Storey, May 11, 1922, LM Papers, Box 1593.

8. Ford

1. Dawidowicz, "Louis Marshall's Yiddish Newspaper," 103; Silver, "Louis Marshall and the Democratization of Jewish Identity," 41.

2. Moore, *At Home in America: Second Generation New York Jews* (New York: Columbia University Press, 1981), 201–32.

3. Robert Singerman, "The American Career of the *Protocols of the Elders of Zion,*" *American Jewish History* 71 (1980), 49–50.

4. For background about the Red Scare: Robert K. Murray, *Red Scare: A Study in National Hysteria, 1919–1920* (Minneapolis: Univ. of Minnesota Press, 1955). For possible connections between anti-Semitism and crackdowns in this Red Scare period against Jewish radicals: Szajkowski, *Jews, Wars, and Communism.*

5. Robert Singerman, "The American Career of the Protocols of the Elders of Zion," *American Jewish History* 71 (1980), 51–52.

6. Levene, *War, Jews and the New Europe,* 246–47.

7. Marshall to Cyrus Adler, Sept. 18, 1919, LM Papers, Box 1589. The sale offer for the *Protocols* was made by Casimir Pilenas, formerly a spy employed in the czar's secret service by Pyotr Rachkovsky.

8. Marshall correspondence, Apr. 1920, LM Papers, Box 1590.

9. Marshall to Dr. Salkind, Apr. 20, 1920, LM Papers, Box 1590.

10. Ibid.

11. Ibid.

12. The editorial staff at Ford's *Dearborn Independent* had planned the anti-Semitic campaign for many weeks in early 1920 and inaugurated it with blazing headlines—"The International Jew: The World's Problem"—in the weekly's May 22, 1920, edition. The journal's first editor, E. G. Pipp, a liberal Catholic, resigned from the *Independent* and started to publish a weekly rebuttal to Ford's anti-Semitism. These events are discussed in Neil Baldwin, *Henry Ford and the Jews: The Mass Production of Hate* (New York: Public Affairs, 2003), 132–33. For discussion of the roots and character of Ford's anti-Semitic animus, see Leo Ribuffo, "Henry Ford and the American Jew," *American Jewish History* 69, no. 4 (June 1980), 437–77; Steven Watts, *The People's Tycoon: Henry Ford and the American Century* (New York: A. A. Knopf, 2005), 376–97; Rosenstock, *Louis Marshall,* 128–48; Robert Rifkind, "Confronting Anti-Semitism in America: Louis Marshall and Henry Ford," *American Jewish History* 94, nos. 1–2 (Mar.–June 2008), 72.

13. Marshall to Julius Rosenwald, Mar. 6, 1920, LM Papers, Box 1590.

14. Marshall to Henry Ford, June 3, 1920, in Reznikoff, *Louis Marshall,* 1:329.

15. Watts, *The People's Tycoon,* xiv.

16. Ibid., 240–48.

17. Marshall to Henry Ford, June 3 1920.

18. Baldwin, *Henry Ford,* 121–22, 127.

19. Ibid., 122–23.

20. See Marshall's letter to Joseph Krauskopf, Oct. 28, 1920, LM Papers, Box 1590.

21. Marshall to Leo Franklin, June 7, 1920, LM Papers, Box 1590.

22. Ford feigned incomprehension regarding the rabbi's decision to return the car. He phoned the rabbi and asked, "What's wrong, Dr. Franklin? Has something come between us?" Baldwin, *Henry Ford,* 132.

23. Marshall to David Brown, Sept. 17, 1920, LM Papers, Box 1590.

24. Baldwin, *Henry Ford,* 123.

25. Silver, "Louis Marshall and the Democratization of Jewish Identity," 68.

26. Reznikoff, *Louis Marshall,* 1:329.

27. Levene, *War, Jews and the New Europe,* 247.

28. Lucien Wolf, "Documents Forged to Defame a People," *London Spectator,* June 12, 1920. Wolf correctly traced an important interim point in the *Protocols'* forgery, a fictional discussion in a Jewish graveyard in Prague incorporated in an 1868 novel, *Biarritz,* written by a Prussian postal clerk, but he was unable to pinpoint the origins of the anti-Semitic lie, the 1863 text *Dialogue aux enfers entre Montesquieu et Machiavel.* For a detailed discussion of the serpentine history of the *Protocols'* forgery, see Norman Cohn, *Warrant for Genocide: the Myth of the Jewish World-Wide Conspiracy and the Protocols of the Elders of Zion* (Harmondsworth: Penguin Books, 1970).

29. Marshall to Dr. Blank, Sept. 10, 1925, LM Papers, Box 1597; Silver, "Louis Marshall and the Democratization of Jewish Identity," 53.

30. Marshall to Cyrus Adler, July 1, 1920, LM Papers, Box 1590.

31. Marshall's letters, July–Aug. 1920, LM Papers, Box 1590. For Marshall's love of the outdoors, see the next chapter of this study.

32. Ribuffo, "Henry Ford," 477.

33. Cohen, *Jacob H. Schiff,* 245.

34. Marshall to David Brown, Sept. 17, 1920, LM Papers, Box 1590.

35. Marshall to Jacob Billikopf, Sept. 24, 1920, LM Papers, Box 1590.

36. Cohen, *Jacob H. Schiff,* 246.

37. Marshall to Julius Rosenwald, Oct. 10, 1920, LM Papers, Box 1590.

38. Marshall to Jules Levy, Dec. 3, 1920, LM Papers, Box 1590.

39. Marshall to Isaac Landman, Nov. 8, 1920, LM Papers, Box 1590.

40. Baldwin, 215

41. One scholar published a provocative article challenging the prudence of Marshall's skepticism about group libel actions against Ford: Victoria Saker Woeste, "Insecure Equality: Louis Marshall, Henry Ford, and the Problem of Defamatory Antisemitism, 1920–1929," *Journal of American History* (Dec. 2004), 877–905. Woeste's early research developed a curious allegation about breach of professional liability that is contradicted by its own internal evidence regarding the status of Marshall's professional relationship with Samuel Untermyer. For criticism of this article: Rifkind, "Confronting Anti-Semitism in America," 71–90. As this book was prepared for publication, Woeste released an extended version of her argument: Victoria Saker Woeste, *Henry Ford's War on Jews and the Legal Battle Against Hate Speech* (Stanford: Stanford University Press, 2012).

42. Marshall to Leo Weil, Dec. 3, 1920, LM Papers, Box 1590.

43. Bernstein embarked on the *Oskar II* as the founder and editor of the Yiddish newspaper the *Day*. *The Dearborn Independent* subsequently implied that Bernstein was the inspiration for its "International Jew" series, since he had told Ford that Jews used their control of gold to manipulate world politics and wars. Ford repeated the *Independent*'s allegation against Bernstein in an interview. Outraged, the journalist filed suit for libel; Marshall refused to handle the case and urged his former partner, Samuel Untermyer, not to handle it either (Untermyer ignored this advice). See Woeste, "Insecure Equality," 889; Baldwin, *Henry Ford,* 236–37; "Statement by Herman Bernstein in Answer to Henry Ford's Accusation," Jan. 1922, LM Papers, Box 63.

44. Bernstein, *History of a Lie.*

45. Bernstein lacked corroboration of leads indicating that Nilus was a leading instigator of the libel. Subsequently, in May 1921, these were published by Frenchman Alexandre du Chayla. Stephen Bronner, *A Rumor about the Jews: Antisemitism, Conspiracy and the Protocols of Zion* (New York: St. Martin's Press, 2000), 76.

46. Marshall to Julius Rosenwald, Mar. 26, 1921, LM Papers, Box 1591.

47. Cohn, *Warrant for Genocide.*

48. For the Radziwill affair, see Marshall's letter in Jan.–Feb. 1921, LM Papers, Box 1591.

49. Bronner, *Rumor about the Jews,* 78.

50. For Spargo: Markuu Routsila, *John Spargo and American Socialism* (New York: Palgrave Macmillan, 2006).

51. At the end of 1920, Marshall and Spargo discussed David Starr Jordan's possible relation to Ford's anti-Semitism (Marshall to Spargo, Dec. 31, 1920, LM Papers, Box 1590), and in the early weeks of 1921, the two discussed new developments in the Ford affair, including Princess Radziwill's promising disclosures (Marshall to Spargo, Jan. 7, Feb. 4, Feb. 7, 1921, LM Papers, Box 1591).

52. Marshall to Spargo, Feb. 4, 1921, LM Papers, Box 1591.

53. John Spargo, *The Jew and American Ideals* (New York: Harper and Brothers, 1921).

54. Ibid., Foreword.

55. Ibid., 124.

56. Ibid., 54.

57. Ibid., 91–92.

58. Marshall to Spargo, Mar. 8, 1921, LM Papers, Box 1591.

59. Louis Marshall et al., "The Protocols, Bolshevism and the Jews: An Address to Their Fellow Citizens by American Jewish Organizations," *The American Jewish Year Book, 5682* (Philadelphia: Jewish Publication Center of America, 1921, 367–77.

60. Ibid., 308.

61. Signatories included: American Jewish Committee, Zionist Organization of America, Union of Orthodox Jewish Congregations, United Synagogue of America, B'nai B'rith and the Anti-Defamation League, Central Conference of American Rabbis, Rabbinical Assembly of the Jewish Theological Seminary, and Union of Orthodox Rabbis of the United States and Canada.

62. *American Jewish Year Book, 5683* (Philadelphia: Jewish Publication Center of America, 1922), 330–44.

63. Marshall to Henry Butzel, Dec. 8, 1920, LM Papers, Box 1590.

64. Marshall to Maxim Vinaver, Jan. 25, 1921, LM Papers, Box 1591.

65. *American Jewish Year Book, 5683,* 340.

66. Ibid.

67. "America's Jewish Enigma: Louis Marshall," *Dearborn Independent* (Nov. 1921); reprinted in *Aspects of Jewish Power in the United States,* vol. 4, *International Jew* (Dearborn: Dearborn Publishing, 1921), 179–92.

68. Marshall to President Warren G. Harding, July 25, 1921, in Reznikoff, *Louis Marshall,* 1:361–63.

69. Marshall letter to Albert D. Lasker, Sept. 7, 1923; Judson Welliver letter to Marshall, Sept. 12, 1923, in Reznikoff, *Louis Marshall,* 1:363–64.

70. Over a decade after Ford's famous 1927 renunciation of his anti-Semitism, he saw fit to receive the Grand Service Cross of the Supreme Order of the German Eagle, the highest honor given by Hitler's Germany to distinguished foreigners. Baldwin, *Henry Ford,* 283–84.

71. "Statement by Henry Ford to Louis Marshall," June 30, 1927, in Reznikoff, *Louis Marshall,* 1:376–79.

72. Upton Sinclair, *The Flivver King: A Story of Ford-America* (1937) (Chicago: Labor Classics, 1999), 58.

73. Grace Larsen and Henry Erdman, "Aaron Sapiro: Genius of Farm Cooperative Promotion," *Mississippi Valley Historical Review* 49 (1962), 242–68; Baldwin, *Henry Ford,* 204–18; Woeste, *Insecure Equality,* 890–91.

74. Baldwin, *Henry Ford,* 222. There were no reliable witnesses of Ford's accident.

75. Watts, *The People's Tycoon,* 265–71; Baldwin, *Henry Ford,* 233.

76. In addition to Bernstein's libel action, Morris Gest in early 1921 sought $5 million in damages from Ford because the *Independent* accused him of producing perverse plays. Ribuffo, "Henry Ford," 465.

77. Baldwin, *Henry Ford,* 222.

78. Ibid., 230–32.

79. Marshall to Samuel Untermyer, July 1, 1927, in Reznikoff, *Louis Marshall,* 1:374.

80. Baldwin, *Henry Ford,* 235. Marshall and Perlman subsequently squabbled about the sequence of events in the Ford retraction; organizational and personal prestige was at stake. On July 18, 1927, Marshall wrote to Perlman: "I feel aggrieved by your suggestion that you participated in these negotiations as a Vice President of the American Jewish Congress." LM Papers, Box 1599.

81. Marshall to Untermyer, July 1, 1927.

82. Ibid.

83. "Statement by Henry Ford to Louis Marshall," June 30, 1927, in Reznikoff, *Louis Marshall,* 1:379.

84. Marshall to Julius Rosenwald, July 27, 1927, LM Papers, Box 1599.

85. Ibid.

86. Ibid.

87. Marshall to H. I. Phillips, Aug. 4, 1927, LM Papers, Box 1599.

88. Ibid.

89. Baldwin, *Henry Ford,* 233–35.

90. See "Arthur Brisbane to the Help of Jewry," *International Jew* (July 3, 1920), 77–84.

91. Rafael Medoff, "Hearst and the Holocaust," *Jerusalem Post* (Jan. 1, 2001), http://www.jpost.com/Opinion/Op-EdContributors/Article.aspx?id=139929.

92. Baldwin, *Henry Ford,* 235.

93. Ibid., 237.

94. Marshall to Arthur Brisbane, July 19, 1927, LM Papers, Box 1599.

9. Jews and Birds

1. The description in this paragraph draws from Louis Henkin, *Foreign Affairs and the United States Constitution* (Oxford: Oxford Univ. Press, 1996), 190–94; Nicholas Rosenkranz, "Executing the Treaty Power," *Harvard Law Review* 118 (2005), 1876; Arthur Sutherland, "Restricting the Treaty Power," *Harvard Law Review* 65, no. 8 (June 1952), 1318.

2. Rosenkranz's article "Executing the Treaty Power" defends the claim that Justice Holmes's opinion in the case, upholding Marshall's argument, is "wrong" and that the Supreme Court ruling in *Missouri* should be overruled. Another critical attempt to reexamine the logic of the Holmes-Marshall position is Thomas Healy, "Is *Missouri v. Holland* Still Good Law? Federalism and the Treaty Power," *Columbia Law Review* 8, no. 7 (Nov. 1998), 1726–56. See also David M. Golove, "Treaty-Making and the Nation: The Historical Foundations of the Nationalist Conception of the Treaty Power," 98 *Michigan Law Review* 1075 (2000), 1314.

3. Henkin, *Foreign Affairs and the Constitution,* 190.

4. Marshall to Israel Zangwill, Aug. 30, 1916, in Reznikoff, *Louis Marshall,* 2:519.

5. Holmes held that a treaty can be valid if it implies powers not specifically vested to the states by the Constitution so long as it "does not contravene any prohibitory words to be found in the Constitution." Holmes's eloquent ruling was phrased in highly emotive language that transformed Marshall's desire to protect birds into a spirited discussion about the character and limits of constitutional democracy. Modern developments (presumably, the effort to protect the environment) "could not have been foreseen completely" by the framers of the Constitution, wrote Holmes. "It was enough for them to realize or to hope that they had created an organism; it has taken a century and has cost their successors much sweat and blood to prove that they created a nation." More to the point, Holmes argued that an expansion of government power via treaty agreement can be valid so long as "it is [not] forbidden by some invisible radiation from the general terms of the Tenth Amendment." Henkin, *Foreign Affairs and the Constitution,* 191.

6. Silver, "Louis Marshall and the Democratization of Jewish Identity," 61.

7. See Marshall's 1916 brief on the Migratory Birds Act, "To the Chief Justice of the United States Supreme Court, Edward D. White," in Reznikoff, *Louis Marshall,* 2:1068–74.

8. See, for instance, Marshall's use of this phrase in his letter to W. T. Hornaday, Nov. 10, 1916, in Reznikoff, *Louis Marshall,* 2:1075.

9. Ibid.

10. Marshall, "To the Chief Justice," in Reznikoff, *Louis Marshall,* 2:1074.

11. Marshall to N. L. Britton, Oct. 26, 1916, LM Papers, Box 1586.

12. Edward Howe Forbush, *A History of the Game Birds, Wild-Fowl and Shore Birds of Massachusetts and Adjacent States* (Boston: Doubleday, 1912).

13. Marshall to Hornaday, Nov. 10, 1916.

14. Ibid.

15. Marshall to William White, Mar. 12, 1923, in Reznikoff, *Louis Marshall,* 1:316–17.

16. Marshall to John Agar, Apr. 20, 1920, in Reznikoff, *Louis Marshall,* 2:1078.

17. The most extensive discussion of the topic can be found in the Rosenthal dissertation, "The Public Life of Louis Marshall," 30–35, 324–29, 462–79. Interestingly, in 1957, years ahead of the environmental movement, Charles Reznikoff published in his two-volume collection of Marshall's writing an ample and extremely useful section on the environment (2:1013–124), its only drawback being occasional repetition of secondary issues, such as three letters and seven pages (2:1061–68) of

discussion about whether a bobsled run on Lake Placid could reasonably be regarded as an exception to the 1894 New York State constitutional amendment preserving the Adirondack and Catskill forests.

An *American Jewish History* special edition on Marshall, published in sync with the 150th anniversary of his birth, featured engaging articles on legal, diplomatic, political, and Jewish aspects of Marshall's life, yet devoted precisely one picture—an inviting picture of "Louis Marshall, man in shirtsleeves" (as his son James recalled his father's outdoors presence at their beloved mountain home, Knollwood, on Lake Saranac in the Adirondacks), showing the fruits of a fishing expedition—to this topic. *American Jewish History* 94, nos. 1–2 (Mar.–June 2008).

18. James Glover, *A Wilderness Original: The Life of Bob Marshall* (Seattle: Mountaineers Books, 1986) 273.

19. Bob Marshall's biography points out that the son was more athletic and less intellectual than his father, and that Louis's social and political philosophy was more conservative. Both men had a highly developed sense of humor, though Bob's was more ostentatious. Bob, James Glover concludes, drew two main traits from his father: "extraordinary energy and a deep commitment to perceived humanitarian ideals" (ibid., 111). One prosaic point might be added to this sensible assessment: Louis Marshall left much wealth to his four children, and Bob applied part of this inheritance to the Wilderness Society—in other words, there is tangible organizational continuity on environmental matters. Bob Marshall wrote with extraordinary eloquence about his father; obviously moved by it, Reznikoff appended Bob's posthumous tribute to his father as the final words in the extensive, two-volume collection (2:1173–74).

20. Marshall to Alfred Smith, Mar. 30, 1911, in Reznikoff, *Louis Marshall,* 2:1082.

21. Glover, *A Wilderness Original,* 52.

22. See, for instance, the Alfred Smith, Mar. 30, 1911, letter.

23. Silver, "Louis Marshall and the Democratization of Jewish Identity," 66.

24. Jonathan Marshall, *Dateline History: The Life of Journalist Jonathan Marshall* (Phoenix: Acacia, 2009), i.

25. Auerbach, *Rabbis and Lawyers,* 109.

26. Rosenthal, "The Public Life of Louis Marshall," 30, alludes to a trip in 1885 to the Adirondacks north of Syracuse; one environmental writer notes that Marshall first visited Saranac Lake in 1885 (Jim Glover, "Louis Marshall: A Visionary Who Helped Preserve the Adirondacks," *Adirondack Life* (May–June 1985).

27. See Marshall's remarks at the 1915 Constitutional Convention in Reznikoff, *Louis Marshall,* 2:1020.

28. Glover, *A Wilderness Original,* 12.

29. Marshall to Arnold Knauth, July 30, 1929, in Reznikoff, *Louis Marshall,* 2:1062.

30. Marshall's 1915 remarks, in Reznikoff, *Louis Marshall,* 2:1020.

31. Ibid.

32. Marshall to Alfred Donaldson, June 3, 1921, in Reznikoff, *Louis Marshall,* 2:1026.

33. Marshall's 1915 remarks, in Reznikoff, *Louis Marshall,* 2:1020.

34. Ibid., 1021.

35. Ibid., 1023.

36. Ibid., 1025.

37. Marshall to Alfred Smith, Aug. 14, 1923, in Reznikoff, *Louis Marshall,* 2:1037.

38. Ibid., 2:1039.

39. Marshall, "A Declaration of Principles," *New York Times,* Oct. 22, 1924.

40. For a description of this environmental campaign: Marshall to son Robert, Dec. 10, 1926, in Reznikoff, *Louis Marshall,* 2:1046–47.

41. Marshall to Francis Gallatin, June 27, 1921, in Reznikoff, *Louis Marshall,* 2:1028.

42. Ibid., 2:1028–29.

43. Jonathan Marshall, *Dateline History,* 22–23.

44. Marshall to George Marshall, Nov. 13, 1928, LM Papers, Box 14/8. George Marshall became a staunch liberal who defied McCarthyism on principle, at considerable personal inconvenience.

45. Discussion in this paragraph refers to Marshall, "To the Editor of *The New York Times,*" Nov. 3, 1927, in Reznikoff, *Louis Marshall,* 2:1047–50.

46. Marshall to son Robert, Feb. 24, 1926, Robert Marshall Papers Collection 204, Box 1, Jacob Rader Marcus Center of the American Jewish Archives.

47. Marshall, "To the Editor of *The New York Times,*" Nov. 3, 1927.

48. Harvey Kaiser, *Great Camps of the Adirondacks* (Boston: Godine, 1982), 131–32.

49. Ibid.

50. Ibid., 132–36.

51. Ibid., 136, 140–53.

52. Rosenthal, "The Public Life of Louis Marshall," 31.

53. This description is drawn from Godine, 140–44.

54. Ibid., 141.

55. Marshall letter for Isaac Mayer Wise memorial campaign, Apr. 20, 1900, LM Papers, Box 1571; Marshall to Joseph Stolz, May 9, 1900, LM Papers, Box 1571.

56. Marshall to Philip Cowen, Apr. 30, 1900, LM Papers, Box 1571. See chapter 2.

57. For Rosenwald's gift to create the Louis Marshall Memorial Fund at the Jewish Theological Seminary: *American Hebrew,* Sept. 27, 1929; Reznikoff, *Louis Marshall,* 2:894.

58. Marshall to Julius Rosenwald, Aug. 6, 1929, in Reznikoff, *Louis Marshall,* 2:889–94.

59. Marshall to William L. Coulter, Mar. 9, 1900, LM Papers, Box 1571.

60. Marshall correspondence, Mar.–Apr. 1900, LM Papers, Box 1571.

61. Marshall to Forest, Fish and Game Commission, Aug, 21, 1901, LM Papers, Box 1571.

62. Marshall to Abram Stein, July 23, 1900, LM Papers, Box 1571.

63. Marshall to brother Benjamin, June 27, 1901, LM Papers, Box 1571.

64. Marshall to Simon Rosendale, Aug. 9, 1901, LM Papers, Box 1571.

65. Glover, *A Wilderness Original,* 20; interview with Roger Marshall, May 28, 2010.

66. Glover, *A Wilderness Original,* 29–30.

67. A few years later, the boys climbed four more peaks that were discovered to be the requisite height; high peaks in the Adirondacks were subsequently known as the "46." The naming of one or more of these peaks after the Marshall boys became embroiled in an inane controversy that was resolved many years later, in 1972, with a mountain in the MacIntyre Range being named for Robert. Ibid., 88–91.

68. Tim Rowland, *High Peaks: A History of Hiking the Adirondacks, from Noah to Neoprene* (Charleston: History Press, 2008), 105.

69. Marshall, "Louis Marshall: Man in Shirt Sleeves," 12–13.

70. Glover, "Louis Marshall," *Adirondack Life.*

71. Ibid.

72. Glover, *A Wilderness Original,* 21. Bob Marshall's baseball records are kept today at the Saranac village library.

73. See Robert Marshall Collection (hereafter RM Collection), American Jewish Archives, 204, Box 1. Love for baseball spread throughout the Marshall family. After Judah Magnes settled in Jerusalem in the early 1920s, Marshall sometimes referred teasingly to his brother-in-law's distance from the Major Leagues.

74. An engaging collection of Robert Marshall's environmental writings has been published by Phil Brown, *Bob Marshall in the Adirondacks: Writings of a Pioneering Peak Bagger, Pond-Hopper and Wilderness Preservationist* (Elizabethtown: Lost Pond Press, 2006).

75. Robert Marshall, *Arctic Village: A 1930s Portrait of Wiseman, Alaska* (New York: Literary Guild, 1933). Bob sent copies of this book and royalty shares to natives of the Koyukuk region.

76. In spring 1900, Marshall bought most available shares of the White Plains Suburban Water Company, with the aim of acquiring a controlling interest and then reselling (see Marshall correspondence, Feb.–Apr. 1900, LM Papers, Box 1571). Though he does not appear to have been acting on behalf of any ecologically dubious development scheme in Westchester County, his tendency late in his life to refer to developers as a completely different class of men can be considered in view of these earlier business projects. Marshall expressed genuine outrage and concern in his environmental work, but his words were sometimes also rhetorical and not completely realistic.

77. Marshall to J. S. Whipple (Forest, Fish and Game commissioner of New York), Sept. 25, 1908, in Reznikoff, *Louis Marshall,* 2:1015.

78. Ibid., 1016–17.

79. Ibid., 1017.

80. On Jan. 29, 1915, Marshall sent the following diatribe to the principal of the Manhattan Ethical Culture School, which his children attended:

> I find that but very few of the pupils of your school are able to spell properly. Neither are they able to write well. Neither are they proficient in mental arithmetic. The reason is obvious: modern pedagogy seems to abhor discipline and drill. It is feared that the brain is injured by memorizing, or by close application. In the early and impressionable years of childhood, it is believed that children must not work, but must merely play. The consequence is that their minds are flabby, and that the present generation cannot compare with preceding ones in [the] grasp of fundamentals of education. The most stupid boy of 40 years ago was able to spell correctly, use multiplication tables and make something about the geography of the work, while today the brightest children make ducks and drakes of the three R's. . . . In your highest grades not a single one of your pupils would be able to spell correctly 75% of the words in this precious document. (LM Papers, Box 1584)

81. Marshall to son Robert, Feb. 6, 1924, RM Collection 204, Box 1.

82. Marshall to son Robert, June 7, 1924, RM Collection, Box 1.

83. Glover, *A Wilderness Original,* 62.

84. Marshall to son Robert, Apr. 23, 1925, RM Collection, Box 1.

85. Glover, *A Wilderness Original,* 7.

86. Marshall to son Robert, Feb. 24, 1926, RM Collection, Box 1.

87. The description here draws from the account in Glover, *A Wilderness Original,* 69–72.

88. Ibid., 69.

89. Ibid., 71.

90. Ibid., 72.

91. Ibid., 66.

92. Magnes, *Episodes,* 33–38.

93. Ibid., 36.

94. Herb Clark was the guide who coached and cultivated the two Marshall boys' love of nature. For an account of their introduction to Adirondack environmentalism, see Glover, *A Wilderness Original,* 25–36.

95. Marshall to J. S. Whipple, Oct. 1, 1908, in Reznikoff, *Louis Marshall,* 2:1018.

96. Marshall to J. S. Whipple, Sept. 28, 1905, in Reznikoff, *Louis Marshall,* 2:1017.

97. Glover, *A Wilderness Original,* 93.

98. For a timeline of the New York State College of Forestry: Reznikoff, *Louis Marshall,* 2:1123. Today, the building is Marshall Hall, and the school is named State University of New York–College of Environmental Science and Forestry. The building's main hall has plaques with likenesses of Louis Marshall and Robert Marshall, and inscriptions about their lives.

99. These petitions and letters can be found in Reznikoff, *Louis Marshall,* 2:1080–124.

100. Alfred Donaldson, *A History of the Adirondacks,* vol. 2 (New York: Purple Mountain Press, 1921), 202–5.

101. The suit was filed by Eric Swenson, president of the Association of Residents on Upper Saranac Lake (ibid., 206). On one account, plaintiffs in the suit objected to the fact that the Cornell foresters "denuded the area, leaving behind a mess of slash and bleak landscapes." Christopher Angus, *The Extraordinary Adirondack Journey of Clarence Petty* (Syracuse: Syracuse Univ. Press, 2002).

102. "Cornell School of Forestry Suspended," *New York Times,* June 18, 1903, 5.

103. Marshall, "The New York State Forest Preserve," New York State Constitutional Convention 1915, in Reznikoff, *Louis Marshall,* 2:1022.

104. One 1962 dissertation, submitted to the New York College of Forestry at Syracuse, discussed the Marshall's wilderness doctrine and commented critically on its fundamental ambivalence. The author described Louis Marshall as an "individual responsible to a large degree for the growth of the forestry profession on the one hand," and as "the prime mover behind the force denying its public practice on the other." Roger Thompson, "The Doctrine of the Wilderness: A Study of the Policy and Politics of the Adirondacks Preserve-Park" (PhD diss., Syracuse University, 1962), 157; see Glover, *A Wilderness Original,* 52.

Thinking of Louis Marshall's environmentalism, Thompson observed that "it is not unusual to find a sort of ambivalence contained within one individual"—he probably did not realize that this sentence applies aptly to an array of Marshall's pursuits, most particularly his lifelong activity in Jewish politics, a term whose reality he on many levels denied.

105. People v. the Brooklyn Cooperage Company, 131 N.Y.S. 957 (App. Div. 3d Dept., Nov. 15, 1911).

106. See Marshall's letter of Feb. 5, 1916, to Raphael Zon, a leading forester at the US Department of Agriculture (who at the end of the 1920s allied with Bob Marshall in wilderness protection efforts). Marshall describes Cornell's experiments under "Dr. Furnow" (*sic*) as a "fiasco" and implies that in its aftermath, Syracuse University rightfully became the front-runner in forestry education in New York State (Reznikoff, *Louis Marshall,* 2:1096). Yet he sometimes warned his Syracuse University associates to watch Cornell carefully, as a potential rival in forestry: "Cornell is on the warpath," he informed Syracuse University chancellor James R. Day on Sept. 29, 1917 (Reznikoff, *Louis Marshall,* 2:1096).

107. Angus, *Extraordinary Adirondack Journey,* 32.

108. Marshall to Charles E. Hughes, June 8, 1910, in Reznikoff, *Louis Marshall,* 2:1080–82.

109. Marshall to John A. Dix, July 25, 1911, in Reznikoff, *Louis Marshall,* 2:1083–85.

110. Marshall to James R. Day, Jan. 6, 1913, in Reznikoff, *Louis Marshall,* 2:1086.

111. Marshall to J. Henry Walters, Jan. 15, 1913, in Reznikoff, *Louis Marshall,* 2:1086.

112. Marshall to William Sulzer, Feb. 8, 1913, in Reznikoff, *Louis Marshall,* 2:1087.

113. Marshall to William Sulzer, Feb. 11, 1913, in Reznikoff, *Louis Marshall,* 2:1091–92.

114. Ibid.

115. Marshall to Syracuse University Committee, Mar. 5, 1913, in Reznikoff, *Louis Marshall,* 2:1095.

116. Marshall to Augustus S. Downing, Dec. 26, 1919, in Reznikoff, *Louis Marshall,* 2:1101–4.

117. Marshall to James R. Day, Sept. 29, 1917, in Reznikoff, *Louis Marshall,* 1096.

118. Marshall to Franklin Moon, Feb. 16, 1929, in Reznikoff, *Louis Marshall,* 2:1122.

119. Ibid.

120. James Marshall, "Louis Marshall: Man in Shirt Sleeves."

121. Paula Hyman, "Traditionalism and Village Jews," in *The Uses of Tradition,* ed. Jack Wertheimer (New York: Jewish Theological Seminary of America, 1992), 187–202.

122. Richard I. Cohen, *Jewish Icons: Art and Society in Modern Europe* (Berkeley: Univ. of California Press, 1998), 178.

123. Marshall to Charles Sedgwick, Apr. 13, 1914, in Reznikoff, *Louis Marshall.*

124. Robert Marshall, "Wilderness as a Minority Right," *Service Bulletin* (Aug. 27, 1928); Glover, *A Wilderness Original,* 95–97.

125. Robert Marshall, "The Problem of the Wilderness," *Scientific Monthly* 30, no. 2 (Feb. 1930), 141–48.

126. See, for instance, Marshall to son Bob, Sept. 18, 1920, RM Collection, Box 1 ("I expect you will spend the better part of the day at Temple on Wednesday. Be careful when you break your fast not to overeat").

127. Glover, *A Wilderness Original,* 116.

128. Ibid.

129. Ibid.

10. Ethnic Affairs in the 1920s

1. *Syracuse Herald,* Sept. 24, 1929, OHAMRC.

2. Marshall, "Louis Marshall: Man in Shirt Sleeves," 12–13.

3. N. Zalowitz, *Jewish Forward,* Dec. 22, 1956.

4. Harry Lang, "Louis Marshall," *Jewish Forward,* Nov. 27, 1927.

5. William Jenney to Samuel Untermyer, Sept. 25, 1929, in Reznikoff, *Louis Marshall,* 2:9.

6. George Marshall letter, Dec. 14, 1956, LM Papers, Box 21/1.

7. Marshall, "Man in Shirt Sleeves," 12.

8. Ibid. On Marshall's seventieth birthday in 1926, his children produced a similar depiction, producing a skit called "A Day at Knollwood." They imagined their father complaining to a train conductor—"A lower! I want an upper, you blankety, blank, blank"; while the imaginary Louis cursed and stomped in this play, his daughter Ruth sat on stage with her fingers in her ears. LM Papers, 21/1.

9. Horace Stern, "Louis Marshall: An Appreciation," Feb. 1930, LM Papers, Box 21/3.

10. James Rosenberg to Jacob Billikopf, July 1941, Jacob Billikopf Papers, MS Collection 13, Box 19, American Jewish Archives.

11. LM Papers, Box 1572. Marshall purchased the Inness painting for $1,550. "The Clarke Picture Sale," *New York Times,* Feb. 16, 1899, 7.

12. Samuel Untermyer also collected Homer Martin paintings. LM Papers, Box 1572. For the *Sun Worshippers:* "A Room Full of Color," *New York Times,* Dec. 12, 1903, 2.

13. These included *Shepherd Playing with a Goat,* Jean Baptiste Camille Corot ($6,000); *Valley of the Touques,* Constant Troyon ($3,000); *In the Catskills,* Alexander H. Wyant; *Sun Worshippers;* and *End of the Rain.* LM Papers, Box 1572.

14. These anecdotes are relayed by Rosenthal, "The Public Life of Louis Marshall," 227, based on Marshall correspondence to New York Central, Feb. 26, Mar. 4, 1909.

15. Marshall to New York Telephone Company, Dec. 17, 1921, in Rosenthal, "The Public Life of Louis Marshall," 24.

16. Silver, "Louis Marshall and the Democratization of Jewish Identity," 66.

17. Marshall to James Walker, Apr. 12, 1926, in Silver, "Louis Marshall and the Democratization of Jewish Identity."

18. Lang, "Louis Marshall."

19. Marshall to William Fox, Dec. 2, 1927, cited in Silver, "Louis Marshall and the Democratization of Jewish Identity," 66.

20. Jacob Billikopf Papers, MS Collection 13, Box 35, American Jewish Archives.

21. *Jewish World,* Mar. 17, 1919, Billikopf Papers, Box 35.

22. Marshall to Jacob Billikopf, July 15, 1918, Billikopf Papers Box 19.

23. Lang, "Louis Marshall."

24. Marshall to Isaac Siegel, Jan. 9, 1919, LM Papers, Box 1589.

25. Marshall to Reuben Fink, Sept. 4, 1919, LM Papers, Box 1589.

26. Marshall to William Williams, Feb. 10, 1920, LM Papers, Box 1590.

27. Marshall correspondence, May 1920; Marshall to Samuel Koenig, June 5, 1920, LM Papers, Box 1590.

28. Marshall to Ogden Mills, June 10, 1920, LM Papers, Box 1590.

29. Marshall correspondence, Aug. 1920, LM Papers, Box 1590.

30. Marshall to Oscar Straus, Nov. 4, 1920, LM Papers, Box 1590.

31. Marshall to Felix Warburg, Jan. 22, 1921, LM Papers, Box 1590.

32. Marshall to Woodrow Wilson, Feb. 26, 1921, LM Papers, Box 1590; Reznikoff, *Louis Marshall,* 1:166–69.

33. Marshall to Woodrow Wilson, Mar. 5, 1921, LM Papers, Box 1590.

34. Esther Panitz, "The Polarity of American Jewish Attitudes Towards Immigration, 1870–1891," in *The Jewish Experience in America,* vol. 4, *The Era of Immigration,* ed. Abraham Karp (New York: Ktav, 1969), 31–62; Zosa Szajkowski, "The Attitude of American Jews to East European Jewish Immigration, 1881–1893," *Publications of the American Jewish Historical Society* 40, no. 3 (Mar. 1951), 149–82.

35. Marshall to Morris Lazaron, Apr. 26, 1921, LM Papers, Box 1590.

36. Marshall to Warren G. Harding, May 11, 1921, LM Papers, Box 1590.

37. Marshall to Warren G. Harding, May 17, 1921, in Reznikoff, *Louis Marshall,* 1:190.

38. Marshall to Simon Wolf, May 23, 1921, LM Papers, Box 1590.

39. Marshall to Fiorello H. LaGuardia, Feb. 11, 1924, LM Papers, Box 1595.

40. Marshall to Leopold Plaut, Mar. 21, 1924, LM Papers, Box 1595.

41. Marshall to Herbert Lehman, Apr. 22, 1924, LM Papers, Box 1595.

42. Marshall to William Guthrie, Apr. 9, 1924, LM Papers, Box 1595.

43. For discussion of Marshall's occasional resort to claims of Jewish racial particularity, see Eric Goldstein, *The Price of Whiteness,* 167, 176; Silver, "Louis Marshall and the Democratization of Jewish Identity," 65.

44. Marshall to Guthrie, Apr. 9, 1924.

45. Marshall to A. J. Sabath, Apr. 25, 1924, LM Papers, Box 1595.

46. Marshall to Cyrus Adler, Apr. 29, 1924, LM Papers, Box 1595.

47. Marshall to C. B. Slemp, May 17, May 19, 1924, LM Papers, Box 1595.

48. Marshall to Samuel Dickstein, May 19, 1924, LM Papers, Box 1595.

49. Marshall to Calvin Coolidge, May 22, 1924, in Reznikoff, *Louis Marshall,* 1:208–14.

50. Ibid., 211.

51. Marshall correspondence, May 27–28, 1924, LM Papers, Box 1595.

52. This section draws on Silver, "Louis Marshall and the Democratization of Jewish Identity," 66–67.

53. Marshall to David A. Reed, Apr. 10, 1926, in Reznikoff, *Louis Marshall,* 1:232.

54. David Reed to Marshall, Apr. 12, 1926, in Reznikoff, *Louis Marshall,* 1:234.

55. Marshall to David Reed, Apr. 14, 1926, Marshall Papers, Box 2, CJH; Reznikoff, *Louis Marshall,* 1:235–36.

56. Commissioner of Immigration of the Port of New York v. Gottlieb, 265 U.S. 310 (1924). The ensuing description draws from Martha Gardner, *The Qualities of a Citizen: Women, Immigration and Citizenship, 1870–1965* (Princeton: Princeton Univ. Press, 2005), 122–30.

57. Tuton v. United States, 270 U.S. 568 (1925).

58. Porterfield v. Webb, 263 U.S. 231 (1923). For Marshall's brief, "The Rights of Japanese": Reznikoff, *Louis Marshall,* 1:466–500.

59. Marshall, "The Rights of Japanese," in Reznikoff, *Louis Marshall,* 1:226.

60. Ibid., 1:229.

61. Webb v. O'Brien, 263 U.S. 313 (1923).

62. Ibid., 316.

63. "We should have practical dominion of the soil by this particular ineligible alien. His interests would demand that he cultivate the soil according to his own theories and impose therein living environments as would be most conducive to his own advantage, just as he would if he owned the land." Ibid., 314.

64. Frick v. Webb, 263 U.S. 326 (1923).

65. Marshall to Lee Overman, Feb. 15, 1919, LM Papers, Box 1589.

66. Marshall to James Young, Feb. 19, 1919, LM Papers, Box 1589.

67. Marshall to Richard Lindabury, Oct. 22, 1919, LM Papers, Box 1589.

68. Marshall to Richard Lindabury, Oct. 24, 1919, LM Papers, Box 1589.

69. Ibid.

70. Marshall to Simon Wolf, Jan. 6, 1920, LM Papers, Box 1590.

71. Rosenthal, "The Public Life of Louis Marshall," 574–75. Marshall and Hughes were joined on this committee by Ogden Mills, Morgan O'Brien, and Joseph Proskauer; all but Proskauer were Republicans.

72. Ibid., 575–77.

73. Marshall to *Syracuse Journal,* Jan. 13, 1920, LM Papers, Box 1590.

74. Marshall to William Pellet, Apr. 8, 1920, LM Papers, Box 1590.

75. Marshall to Leo Wise, Apr, 12, 1920, LM Papers, Box 1590, in Reznikoff, *Louis Marshall,* 2:981.

76. Marshall to Louis Wiley, Apr. 14, 1920, LM Papers, Box 1590.

77. This description relies on Rosenstock, *Louis Marshall,* 202–8.

78. Ibid., 204.

79. Charles Jacobson to Marshall, Mar. 20, 1923; Rosenstock, *Louis Marshall,* 206.

80. Rosenstock, *Louis Marshall,* 203.

81. Marshall to Henry Fry, Nov. 27, 1922, LM Papers, Box 56.

82. Ibid.

83. Marshall to M. E. Lubin, Dec. 21, 1922, LM Papers, Box 56.

84. Marshall to Joseph Silverman, Feb. 25, 1923, LM Papers, Box 1594.

85. Rosenstock, *Louis Marshall,* 210.

86. American Jewish Committee Executive Committee Minutes, vol., 4, part 2, Dec. 10, 1922, American Jewish Committee Archives.

87. Marshall, "Statement on the Ku Klux Klan," *World,* Oct. 28, 1923.

88. Marshall to Paul Warburg, Feb. 13, 1924, LM Papers, Box 1595.

89. Lloyd Jorgenson, "The Oregon School Law of 1922: Passage and Sequel," *Catholic History Review* 54, no. 3 (Oct. 1968), 455–66.

90. Marshall to Jesse Winburn, Oct. 21, 1922, LM Papers, Box 56; Rosenstock, *Louis Marshall,* 212.

91. Rosenstock, *Louis Marshall,* 212.

92. Jorgenson, "The Oregon School Law," 458.

93. Pierce v. Society of Sisters, etc., 268 U.S. 510 (1925).

94. Jorgenson, "The Oregon School Law," 463.

95. Marshall, "Toleration—The Fundamental Precept of Liberty," for the American Jewish Committee as amicus curiae for appellants in Pierce v. Society of Sisters, in Reznikoff, *Louis Marshall,* 2:957–67.

96. Isaac Berkson, *Theories of Americanization: A Critical Study with Special Reference to the Jewish Group* (New York: General Books, 1920); Alexander Dushkin, *Jewish Education in New York City* (New York: Bureau of Jewish Education, 1918).

97. Marshall, "Toleration—The Fundamental Precept of Liberty, in Reznikoff, *Louis Marshall,* 2:957–67.

98. Pierce v. Society of Sisters, etc., 268 U.S. 510 (1925).

99. Jorgenson, "The Oregon School Law," 463–64.

100. Marshall letter, Feb. 11, 1919, LM Papers, Box 1589. An extended study of Jews and Prohibition, released as this volume was being prepared for publication, offers background to the information presented in this section: Marni Davis, *Jews and Booze: Becoming American in the Age of Prohibition* (New York, New York University Press, 2012).

101. Marshall to Emanuel Celler, May 24, 1924, in Rosenthal, "The Public Life of Louis Marshall," 674.

102. Marshall to Harry Emerson Fosdick, Dec. 7, 1928, in Rosenthal, "The Public Life of Louis Marshall," 675.

103. Marshall to Martin Meyer, Sept. 16, 1920, LM Papers, Box 1590.

104. Rosenthal, "The Public Life of Louis Marshall," 675.

105. Marshall to Martin Meyer, Sept. 16, 1920.

106. Feingold, *A Time for Searching: Entering the Mainstream, 1920–1945* (Baltimore: Johns Hopkins Univ. Press, 1992), 49.

107. "The Jewish Element in Bootlegging," *International Jew* 4 (1921), 35.

108. *Central Conference of American Rabbis: 32nd Annual Convention* 31 (1921), 23.

109. Feingold, *A Time for Searching,* 50.

110. Marshall to M. S. Margolies, Mar. 20, 1920, in Reznikoff, *Louis Marshall,* 2:934.

111. Ibid.

112. "Report of the American Jewish Committee," Nov. 12, 1922, *American Jewish Year Book, 5684* (Philadelphia: The Jewish Publication Society of America, 1923–24), 379.

113. Marshall to Albert D. Lasker, June 7, 1923, in Reznikoff, *Louis Marshall,* 2:935.

114. Feingold, *A Time for Searching,* 49–50.

115. Marshall to Robert Marshall, Apr. 28, 1923, RM Papers, Collection 204, Box 1.

116. Marshall to Robert Marshall, Jan. 11, 1928, RM Papers, Collection 204, Box 1.

117. Ibid.

118. *Syracuse Herald,* Sept. 27, 1929, OHAMRC.

119. Marshall to Julius Rosenwald, Aug. 6, 1929, in Reznikoff, *Louis Marshall,* 2:889–94.

120. Marshall to Alfred W. Anthony, June 19, 1929, LM Papers, Box 1601.

121. Ibid.

122. Ibid.

123. Marshall to A. Sneider, Apr. 26, 1926, LM Papers, Box 1598; Silver, "Louis Marshall and the Democratization of Jewish Identity," 69.

124. James C. Young, "Louis Marshall Looks Back over 70 Years," *New York Times Magazine,* Dec. 12, 1926, 9–18.

125. Louis Marshall, "Is Ours a Christian Government?" in Reznikoff, *Louis Marshall,* 2:949.

126. Young, "Louis Marshall Looks Back over 70 Years."

127. Marshall to Robert Marshall, Oct. 28, 1924, RM Papers, Collection 204, Box 1. Not surprisingly, the letter conveys hints that Marshall objected as well to Darrow's skeptical views regarding organized religion.

128. Ibid.

129. Ibid.

130. This section on Marshall's views on social and religious issues in the 1920s draws from Silver, "Louis Marshall and the Democratization of Jewish Identity," 61–65. For a survey of rising skepticism about grand theories of meaning in American's intellectual culture: Louis Menand, *The Metaphysical Club* (New York: Farrar, Straus, 2001).

131. Edward White, *Justice Oliver Wendell Holmes: Law and the Inner Self* (New York: Oxford University Press, 1993).

132. Rosenstock, *Louis Marshall,* 35. Rosenthal's dissertation, "The Public Life of Louis Marshall," also ascribes "religious pluralism" to Marshall. Ezra Mendelsohn labels Marshall's brand of activism "integrationist," an approach that advocated acculturation without assimilation in 1920s America and in a variety of other modern sociopolitical contexts insightfully surveyed in this scholar's volume *On Modern Jewish Politics* (New York: Oxford University Press, 1993). His definition of the term integrationist ("What its adherents really wanted the Jews to do was to

integrate into the majority society without being entirely swallowed up by it" [16]) accords with the discussion in the text but is undeniably broad.

133. Marshall to M. F. Seidman, Jan. 8, 1924, LM Papers, Box 1595.

134. For Marshall's responses to quota developments at Harvard and elsewhere: Rosenstock, *Louis Marshall,* 243–55. For a general discussion of academic quotas in this period: Marcia Graham Synnott, *The Half-Opened Door: Discrimination and Admissions at Harvard, Yale and Princeton, 1900–1970* (Westport: Greenwood Press, 1979).

135. Marshall to Frank Hiscock, Nov. 29, 1927, LM Papers, Box 1599.

136. Ibid.

137. Marshall's positive connection to the Young Men's Hebrew Association is described in Adler, "Louis Marshall," 43–44.

138. Marshall to Louis Goldberg, May 10, 1920, LM Papers, Box 1590.

139. Ibid.

140. Ibid.

141. Marshall to Edwin Kaufman, May 8, 1920, LM Papers, Box 1590.

142. Ibid.

143. "8,112 Sign Tribute to Louis Marshall on his 70th," *New York Times,* Dec. 13, 1926.

144. Ibid.

145. Marshall Scrapbook, Dec. 14, 1926, LM Papers, Box 20/3.

146. Marshall to Robert Marshall, Feb. 11, 1925, RM Papers, Collection 204, Box 1.

147. Jacob Billikopf to Judah Magnes, May 12, 1927, Jacob Billikopf Papers, MS Collection 13, Box 18.

148. Ibid.

149. Marshall to Robert Marshall, Apr. 9, 1926, RM Papers, Collection 204, Box 1.

150. Ibid.

151. Diner, *In the Almost Promised Land.*

152. Alexander, *Jazz Age Jews.*

153. Goldstein, *The Price of Whiteness;* Karen Brodkin, *How Jews Became White Folks and What That Says about Race in America* (New Brunswick, 1998).

154. Norman Podhoretz, *Why Are Jews Liberals?* (New York: Doubleday, 2009).

155. Letter from Charles Edward Russell to Marshall, Nov. 21, 1928, RM Papers, Collection 204, Box 1.

156. Moore v. Dempsey, 261 U.S. 86 (1923).

157. Frank v. Mangum, 237 U.S. 309 (1914); Marshall brief, "A Judicial Lynching," in Reznikoff, *Louis Marshall,* 1:304–11. See chapter 6, n79.

158. M. Glenn Abernathy and Barbara Perry, *Civil Liberties under the Constitution* (Columbia, SC: Univ. of South Carolina Press, 1993), 116.

159. Subsequent discussion here draws from August Meier and Elliot Rudwick, "Attorneys Black and White: A Case Study of Race Relations Within the NAACP," *Journal of American History* 62, no. 4 (Mar. 1976), 913–46.

160. Marshall to Moorfield Storey, Nov. 30, 1923, in Reznikoff, *Louis Marshall,* 1:426.

161. Meir and Rudwick, "Attorneys Black and White," 920.

162. Buchanan v. Warley, 245 U.S. 60 (1917).

163. Kevin Boyle, *Arc of Justice: A Saga of Race, Civil Rights and Murder in the Jazz Age* (New York: Holt, 2004), 202.

164. Roger Rice, "Residential Segregation by Law, 1910–1917," *Journal of Southern History* 34, no. 2 (May 1968), 179.

165. Boyle, *Arc of Justice.* I thank Kevin Boyle for clarifying aspects of this case and of various ethnic matters in 1920s America.

166. Ibid., 308.

167. Ibid., 309.

168. Marshall to Moorfield Storey, Dec. 12, 1924, Sept. 24, 1925, in Reznikoff, *Louis Marshall,* 1:460–62.

169. Meier and Rudwick, "Attorneys Black and White," 928. Marshall never appears to have commented on ways this procedure paralleled the choices he himself had made, as a Jewish advocate, when (in matters like the abrogation campaign) he chose non-Jews to make final arguments in public tribunals.

170. Cong. Rec. 7337 (Apr. 15, 1926), in Reznikoff, *Louis Marshall,* 463.

171. Marshall to William E. Borah, Apr. 19, 1926, in Reznikoff, *Louis Marshall,* 1:462–64.

172. Boyle, *Arc of Justice,* 211–14; Meier and Rudwick, "Attorneys Black and White," 933–34. Boyle (309) hints that Cobb resented Marshall's handling of the Sweet litigation at the Supreme Court.

173. Meier and Rudwick, "Attorneys Black and White," 934.

174. Ibid., 927.

175. City of Richmond et al. v. Deans, 281 U.S. 704 (1929); 37 F.2d 712 (1930).

176. This account of the sequence of NAACP attorneys on the case is taken from Meier and Rudwick, "Attorneys Black and White," 929. The Supreme Court ruling lists Knollenberg and A. B. Spingarm (sic.), joined by Marshall, Storey, and Cobb on the briefs.

177. Nixon v. Herndon, 273 U.S. 536 (1927).

178. Meier and Rudwick, "Attorneys Black and White," 932.

179. Louis Marshall, "The Right to Vote" (1927), Brief for Plaintiff-in-Error, Nixon v. Herndon, in Reznikoff, *Louis Marshall,* 1:426–47.

180. Marshall, "The Right to Vote."

181. Marshall also counseled the NAACP in litigation challenging all-white primaries in Florida and Virginia. Meier and Rudwick, "Attorneys Black and White," 929.

182. Nixon v. Herndon, 273 U.S. 536 (1927), 541.

183. NAACP: Moorfield Story–Louis Marshall Memorial Campaign, spring 1930, LM Papers 20/7.

184. *American Indian Life Bulletin,* no. 15 (Jan. 1930), LM Papers, Box 20/7.

185. Ibid.

186. Marshall to Robert Marshall, May 5, 1928, RM Papers, Collection 204, Box 1.

187. Ibid.

188. *American Indian Life Bulletin,* no. 15 (Jan. 1930).

11. Crimea and Eretz Israel

1. JDC Executive Committee Meeting Minutes, June 17, 1924, LM Papers, Box 70. For background to this immigration legislation and Marshall's responses, see Feingold, *A Time for Searching,* 24–30.

2. Jonathan Dekel-Chen, *Farming the Red Land: Jewish Agricultural Colonization and Local Soviet Power, 1924–1941* (New Haven: Yale Univ. Press, 2005), 7–8.

3. Jerome Rosenthal, "Dealing with the Devil: Louis Marshall and the Partnership Between the Joint Distribution Committee and Soviet Russia," *American Jewish Archives* 32 (Apr. 1987), 9.

4. Dekel-Chen, *Farming the Red Land,* 7.

5. Ibid., 21–22.

6. Ibid., 29.

7. Ibid., 2, 26, 29.

8. Ibid., 1.

9. Dekel-Chen's assertive revisionist account of the Soviet colonies takes issue with largely negative assessments, including works by Zosa Szajkowski (*The Mirage of American Jewish Aid in Soviet Russia, 1917–1939* [New York: S. Frydman, 1977]) and Henry Feingold (*A Time for Searching,* 178–87). Writing before Dekel-Chen, Rosenthal ("Dealing with the Devil") generally lauded the effort undertaken by Marshall and the JDC. Partly because it refers to just one of many Jewish endeavors in Marshall's career, Rosenthal's opening assertion is food for thought: The colonization project "was probably the most constructive philanthropic plan ever attempted by private sources for adapting masses of Jews to new economic and political conditions in their native land" (1). By and large, Rosenthal followed Bauer's groundbreaking analysis of this JDC effort (*My Brother's Keeper*), though the Bauer survey keeps the effective results of this project within fairly circumscribed limits (12,000 Jewish families were saved from starvation, estimated Bauer [71–78]). Dekel-Chen offers one interesting, and debatably paradoxical, observation about the Zionist-JDC polemics in the mid-1920s (which other commentators believed to be mutually draining and debilitating): competition between the JDC and the Zionist Organization of America (ZOA) over colonization in Crimea or Palestine "probably strengthened both" organizations (Dekel-Chen, *Farming the Red Land,* 94).

10. Dekel-Chen, *Farming the Red Land,* 4.

11. Bauer, *My Brother's Keeper,* 97–98; Rosenthal, "Dealing with the Devil," 15.

12. Dekel-Chen, *Farming the Red Land,* 30.

13. Marshall letter to Dr. A. Margolen, Mar. 16, 1929, in Rosenthal, "Dealing with the Devil," 14.

14. Dekel-Chen, *Farming the Red Land,* 43.

15. This point is substantiated by contacts between Rosen and Felix Warburg, cited by Dekel-Chen, *Farming the Red Land,* 38.

16. Ibid.

17. In his sympathetic account of Rosen's work, Dekel-Chen notes that his "reports told JDC officials in New York more about the conflict surrounding the Left Opposition than about life in the colonies" (*Farming the Red Land,* 72).

18. Dekel-Chen (ibid., 44) cites Marshall's statement, "my observation [is] that the Soviet [Union] would scrupulously keep its contracts with citizens of other nations." But in the same year, 1928, Marshall worried about whether Agro-Joint agreements with the Soviets were ironclad, and showing suspicion about Soviet behavior, he contemplated demanding that they be renegotiated. Rosenthal, "Dealing with the Devil," 13.

19. On-site reports were so routinely positive that by the end of the 1920s, the JDC was subsidizing their dissemination as memoirs, films, and paintings. Dekel-Chen, *Farming the Red Land,* 92.

20. In Nov. 1925, Moskowitz told Marshall that the colonies were "worthwhile and impressive." Rosenthal, "Dealing with the Devil," 10.

21. James Marshall met with Komzet chief Peter Smidovich. Ibid., 13.

22. Dekel-Chen, *Farming the Red Land,* 47.

23. Ibid., 67.

24. James Rosenberg, *On the Steppes: A Russian Diary* (New York: Knopf, 1927), cited in Rosenthal, "Dealing with the Devil," 17.

25. Rosenberg, *On the Steppes,* cited in Dekel-Chen, *Farming the Red Land,* 27.

26. Ibid., 46–47.

27. Rosenthal, "Dealing with the Devil," 11–12.

28. Dekel-Chen, *Farming the Red Land,* 47.

29. Rosenthal, "Dealing with the Devil," 5.

30. Ibid., 6.

31. Letter from Pavel Milyukov and Nicholas Avksentiev to Marshall, Nov. 18, 1920, LM Papers, Box 1609.

32. A. J. Sack to Marshall, June 29, 1922, LM Papers, Box 64.

33. Report from the Jewish World Relief Conference, Carlsbad, Aug. 21–27, 1924, LM Papers, Box 1609.

34. JDC Executive Committee Meeting Minutes, June 17, 1924, LM Papers Box 70. All quotations and information in this paragraph are drawn from this record.

35. Chaim Weizmann, memorandum on the Jewish Agency, Dec. 18, 1923, LM Papers, Box 1605.

36. For a survey of personalities and processes in this transition from the Old Yishuv to the New Yishuv: Mordechai Eliav, *Erets-Yisrael ve-yishuva ba-meah ha-19, 1777–1917* (Jerusalem: Keter, 1978), 251–335. For myths and realities of this distinction drawn between the two Yishuv communities: Israel Bartal, "Old Yishuv and New Yishuv," 215–31.

37. Weizmann, memorandum on Jewish Agency, LM Papers, Box 1605.

38. Yigal Elam, *The Jewish Agency: Formative Years, 1919–1931* [in Hebrew] (Jerusalem: Hassifriya Haziyonit, 1990), 63, 427. The statement was reported in the *New Palestine;* Gruenbaum later denied the report.

39. Elam, *The Jewish Agency,* 67.

40. Ibid., 54.

41. Ibid., 118.

42. LM Papers, Box 1605. The Astor Hotel meeting was held on Feb. 17, 1924. Besides Marshall, committee members were to be Cyrus Adler, A. G. Becker, Jacob Billikopf, David Brown, Lee Frankel, Elisha Friedman, Horace Stern, Samuel Untermyer.

43. Marshall letter to Chaim Weizmann, May 28, 1926, in Reznikoff, *Louis Marshall,* 2:752.

44. Ibid.

45. Rosenthal, "Dealing with the Devil," 9.

46. Agreement between government of USSR and Agro-Joint, Nov. 29, 1924, LM Papers, Box 1609.

47. Louis Fischer, "To the Soil Movement of Jews in Soviet Russia," LM Papers, Box 1609; Matthew M. Silver, "Fighting for Palestine and Crimea: Two Jewish Friends from Philadelphia During the First World War and the 1920s," *Studies in Contemporary Jewry* 18 (2002), 201–16.

48. Marshall to James Rosenberg, Mar. 19, 1925, Joint Distribution Committee Archives (JDC Archives), Agro-Joint Collection, 21/32 Reel 508.

49. J. C. Hyman to Marshall, May 13, 1925, LM Papers, Box 1609.

50. Dr. B. Kahn, "My Trip to Russia, June–July 1925," LM Papers, Box 1609.

51. Ibid.

52. Bernard Kahn, Confidential Memorandum, Aug. 23, 1925, JDC Archives, 21/32 Reel 26.

53. *New Palestine,* Mar. 27, 1925, LM Papers, Box 1605.

54. "We will have an opportunity, such as no people has ever had, of helping to rebuild a land and of realizing the hope of those who have for centuries longed for such an opportunity." Ibid.

55. Chaim Weizmann letter to Marshall, Apr. 29, 1925, LM Papers, Box 154; Louis Lipsky letter to Marshall, May 4, 1925; Note of a Conversation Between Marshall and Leonard Stein, June 7, 1925, LM Papers, Box 154. Marshall and Stein agreed that the agency would eventually be based in Jerusalem; Marshall insisted on a proxy voting scheme for American delegates.

56. Marshall to Chaim Weizmann, May 28, 1926, in Reznikoff, *Louis Marshall,* 2:752.

57. Ibid., 2:753.

58. Raider, "The Aristocrat and the Democrat," 111.

59. Marshall to Chaim Weizmann, July 2, 1925, in Reznikoff, *Louis Marshall,* 2:747–48.

60. Marshall letter to Stephen Wise, May 18, 1925, LM Papers, Box 1609.

61. Marshall letter to Judah Magnes, July 2, 1926, LM Papers, Box 1605.

62. Silver, *First Contact,* 189–238.

63. Marshall to Judah Magnes, July 2, 1926.

64. Naomi Cohen, *The Year after the Riots: American Responses to the Palestine Crisis, 1929–1930* (Detroit: Wayne State Univ. Press, 1988), 231.

65. These descriptions are from Marshall's letter to Chaim Weizmann, May 28, 1926, in Reznikoff, *Louis Marshall,* 2:754.

66. Marshall to Magnes, July 2, 1926, JDC Archives, Agro-Joint Collection, 21/32 Reel 508.

67. Marshall to Weizmann, May 28, 1926, JDC Archives, Agro-Joint Collection, 21/32 Reel 508.

68. Marshall to Magnes, July 2, 1926, JDC Archives, Agro-Joint Collection, 21/32 Reel 508.

69. Ibid.

70. Joseph Hyman to Bernard Richards, Nov. 2, 1925; Marshall Statement on Behalf of the Joint Distribution Committee; Resolution Adopted by the American Jewish Congress in Relation to the JDC; JDC Archives, Agro-Joint Collection, 21/32 Reel 508.

71. *Forward,* Sept. 15, 1925, in LM Papers, Box 1609.

72. *Die Warheit,* Sept. 15, 1925, in LM Papers, Box 1609.

73. Dekel-Chen, *Farming the Red Land,* 78.

74. Ruppin stated that the Soviet colonization work should be seen as "a philanthropic act to assist the economic welfare of tens of thousands of Jewish families in Russia. As such, this effort should be supported." Ibid., 78.

75. Deborah Lipstadt, "The Zionist Career of Louis Lipsky" (PhD diss., Brandeis University, 1976).

76. Marshall to Chaim Weizmann, May 28, 1926, in Reznikoff, *Louis Marshall,* 2:754–55.

77. After one meeting with Brown, Weizmann reflected, "I would not want my enemy to go through this again. I was in bed the whole day after [the meeting]." Dekel-Chen, *Farming the Red Land,* 75.

78. Ibid.

79. At the JDC Executive Committee meeting on June 28, 1926, David Brown announced, "I think it is very important that we give answer to the propaganda of the Zionist organization. . . .

We have taken a lot of abuse and we have answered them back in a dignified manner but they have been fighting very bitterly, and it has not been a very happy situation." Brown submitted a motion that Marshall be appointed as a committee of one to "hit back" against the Zionists. The motion carried. JDC Archives, Agro-Joint Collection, 21/32 Reel 26.

80. Louis Marshall to Elihu Stone, Sept. 10, 1925, LM Papers, Box 1609.

81. Ibid.

82. Rabbi George Fox to Secretary of State Frank Kellogg, Sept. 3, 1925, LM Papers, Box 1609.

83. Secretary of State Frank Kellogg letter to Rabbi George Fox, Sept. 9, 1925, LM Papers, Box 1609.

84. Louis Marshall to Rabbi George Fox, Sept. 18, 1925, LM Papers, Box 1609.

85. Dekel-Chen, *Farming the Red Land,* 38–39.

86. Rosenthal, "Dealing with the Devil," 12.

87. Joseph Rosen to Cyrus Adler, May 11, 1928, JDC Archives, Agro-Joint Collection, 21/32 Reel 509.

88. Ariel Feldestein, *Ben-Gurion, Zionism and American Jewry, 1948–1963* (London: Routledge, 2006).

89. Chaim Weizmann letter to Marshall, May 13, 1926, LM Papers, Box 1605.

90. Ibid.

91. Ibid.

92. Marshall to Judah Magnes, July 2, 1926, LM Papers, Box 1605.

93. Marshall to Chaim Weizmann, May 28, 1926, in Reznikoff, *Louis Marshall,* 2:750–60.

94. Ibid.

95. Ibid.

96. Ibid.

97. Marshall to Judah Magnes, July 2, 1926.

98. Cohen, *The Year after the Riots.*

99. Marshall to Judah Magnes, July 2, 1926.

100. Marshall to Jacob Billikopf, LM Papers, Box 1598.

101. Chaim Weizmann to Marshall, May 28, 1926, LM Papers, Box 1605.

102. Marshall to Weizmann, Nov. 15, 1926, LM Papers, Box 1598.

103. Elam, *The Jewish Agency,* 91.

104. Ibid., 92–93.

105. Ganin, *An Uneasy Relationship;* see also chapter 6, n370, this volume.

106. Elam, *The Jewish Agency,* 91.

107. Felix Warburg memorandum, Dec. 23, 1926, LM Papers, Box 154.

108. S. Ilan Troen, "American Experts in the Design of Zionist Society," in *Envisioning Israel: The Changing Ideals and Images of American Jews,* ed. Allon Gal (Detroit: Wayne State Univ. Press, 1996), 200–204.

109. Evyatar Friesel, *Zionist Policy After the Balfour Declaration 1917–1922* [in Hebrew] (Tel Aviv: Kibbutz Hameuhad, 1977), 177–80.

110. Ibid., 177.

111. David Brown statement, Jan. 25, 1927, LM Papers, Box 154.

112. Chaim Weizmann to Marshall, Jan. 13, 1927, LM Papers, Box 154.

113. Marshall to Chaim Weizmann, Jan. 17, 1927, LM Papers, Box 154.

114. Marshall to Julius Rosenwald, Feb. 9, 1927, LM Papers, Box 1599.

115. Elam, *The Jewish Agency,* 98.

116. Marshall to Leon Lauterstein, Feb. 9, 1927, LM Papers, Box 1599.

117. Elam, *The Jewish Agency,* 105.

118. Correspondence between Marshall and Leonard Stein, Apr.–June 1927, LM Papers, Box 154. The figure mentioned in this respect was Oscar Wassermann (Elam, *The Jewish Agency,* 93).

119. Lee Frankel to Marshall, May 3, 1927, LM Papers, Box 154; Elam, *The Jewish Agency,* 94.

120. Elam, *The Jewish Agency,* 96.

121. "Outline of Palestine Survey," LM Papers, Box 154.

122. Marshall to Chaim Weizmann, May 11, 1927, LM Papers, Box 154.

123. Ibid. Subsequently, this joint $100,000 funding of the survey added to squabbling between the sides. Marshall, who paid $5,000 out of his own pocket, entrusted a share of the non-Zionist's contribution with Emmanuel Mohl, who was directing Palestine Economic Corporation efforts in the Yishuv. Mohl's reservations about depositing this sum in a joint account incensed Stein and other Zionists. Elam, *The Jewish Agency,* 106–7.

124. Marshall to Leonard Stein, May 7, 1927, LM Papers, Box 1599. The name of the proposed expert was Benjamin Brown.

125. Marshall to Weizmann, May 11, 1927, LM Papers, Box 1599.

126. Marshall to James Marshall, May 9, 1927, LM Papers, Box 1599.

127. Elam, *The Jewish Agency,* 95.

128. Marshall to James Marshall, May 9, 1927, LM Papers, Box 1599.

129. Elam, 97.

130. Ibid.

131. Summary of Meeting of Palestine Zionist Executive, June 26, 1927, LM Papers, Box 154.

132. Ibid.

133. Troen, "American Experts," 200.

134. Summary of Meeting of Palestine Zionist Executive, June 26, 1927.

135. Lee Frankel to Marshall, July 2, 1927, LM Papers, Box 154.

136. Marshall to Felix Warburg, Sept. 8, 1927, LM Papers, Box 1599.

137. Marshall to Lee Frankel, Sept. 8, 1927, LM Papers, Box 1599.

138. Elam, 110, 451.

139. Ibid., 112.

140. Ibid., 115.

141. Ibid., 116.

142. Ibid.

143. Marshall to Judah Magnes, July 30, 1928, LM Papers, Box 1600.

144. Marshall to Nahum Freidless, July 30, 1928, LM Papers, Box 1600.

145. Elam, 120.

146. Ibid., 121.

147. Jewish Agency memorandum on history of Jewish Agency, Jan. 10, 1929, LM Papers, Box 1605.

148. Elam, 122.

149. Marshall to Julian Mack, Oct. 27, 1928, LM Papers, Box 1600.

150. Marshall to Chaim Weizmann, Nov. 20, 1928, LM Papers, Box 1605.

12. Epilogue: Massena, Zurich, Emanu-El

1. Unless noted otherwise, information in this section draws from Saul Friedman, *The Incident at Massena: the Blood Libel in America* (New York: Stein and Day, 1978).

2. Ibid., 91.

3. Ibid., 109.

4. Ibid., 117–19.

5. Ibid., 146–47.

6. Marshall to W. G. Hawes, Oct. 1, 1928, LM Papers, Box 1600.

7. Ibid.

8. Friedman, *Incident at Massena,* 159–60.

9. Ibid., 155.

10. Ibid., 166–67.

11. Marshall to Jacob Shulkin, Oct. 6, 1928, LM Papers, Box 1600.

12. Ibid.

13. Friedman, *Incident at Massena,* 172.

14. For the Rosenbluth affair: Rosemary Davies, *The Rosenbluth Case: Federal Justice on Trial* (Ames: Iowa State Univ. Press, 1970); Alpert, *Louis Marshall, 1856–1929,* 119–45.

15. Marshall to Adolph Ochs, Oct. 16, 1924, LM Papers, Box 1596.

16. For public perceptions of Rosenbluth as an America Dreyfus: Gene Smith, "The American Dreyfus," *American Heritage Magazine* 45, no. 7 (Nov. 1994), 93–94.

17. Marshall correspondence, fall 1924, LM Papers, Box 1596. Arranging former attorney general Thompson's testimony cost Marshall $5,500.

18. Marshall to Adolph Ochs, Oct. 16, 1924.

19. Marshall to Robert Marshall, Mar. 4, 1925, RM Papers, Collection 204, Box 1. Rosenbluth eventually pursued a career in social work in Chicago, married, and had two children.

20. Jacob Billikopf correspondence, Sept. 29, 1929, Jacob Billikopf Papers, MS Collection 13, Box 18.

21. Horace Stern, "Louis Marshall: An Appreciation," Feb. 1930, LM Papers, Box 21/3.

22. This funeral description is drawn from the *Syracuse Herald,* Sept. 24, 1929, and newspaper clippings, OHAMRC.

23. James Marshall to Judah Magnes, Oct. 1929, James Marshall Papers, Collection 157, Box 38, American Jewish Archives.

24. James Marshall to Solomon Lowenstein, Oct. 2, 1929, James Marshall Papers, Collection 157, Box 38.

Bibliography

Archival Sources

American Jewish Committee Archives, New York, New York.
American Jewish Historical Society, Center for Jewish History (CJH), New York, New York.
Central Zionist Archives (CZA), Jerusalem
Columbia University Libraries Archival Collection, New York, New York
Jacob Rader Marcus Center of the American Jewish Archives, Cincinnati, Ohio
Joint Distribution Committee Archives, New York, New York
Manuscript Division, Library of Congress, Washington, DC
Archives and Manuscripts, New York Public Library, New York, New York
Mount Sinai Hospital Archives, The Gustave L. and Janet W. Levy Library, New York, New York
Onondaga Historical Association Museum and Research Center (OHAMRC) Archives, Syracuse, New York
Syracuse County Clerk's Office, Syracuse, New York.

Works Cited

Abernathy, M. Glenn, and Perry Barbara. *Civil Liberties under the Constitution*. 6th ed. Columbia, SC: Univ. of South Carolina Press, 1993.

Adler, Cyrus. "Louis Marshall: A Biographical Sketch." *American Jewish Year Book* 32 (1930–31), 21–55.

Adler, Selig. "The Palestine Question in the Wilson Era." *Jewish Social Studies* 10 (Oct. 1948), 303–34.

Alexander, Michael. *Jazz Age Jews*. Princeton: Princeton Univ. Press, 2001.

Alpert, Herbert. *Louis Marshall, 1856–1929: A Life Devoted to Justice and Judaism*. Bloomington: iUniverse, 2008.

Angus, Christopher. *The Extraordinary Adirondack Journey of Clarence Petty*. Syracuse: Syracuse Univ. Press, 2002.

Ascoli, Peter. *Julius Rosenwald*. Bloomington: Indiana Univ. Press, 2006.

Auerbach, Jerold. *Rabbis and Lawyers: The Journey from Torah to Constitution*. Bloomington: Indiana Univ. Press, 1990.

———. *Unequal Justice: Lawyers and Social Change in Modern America.* New York: Oxford Univ. Press, 1976.

Baldwin, Neil. *Henry Ford and the Jews: The Mass Production of Hate.* New York: Public Affairs, 2003.

Barnard, Harry. *The Forging of an American Jew: The Life and Times of Judge Julian W. Mack.* New York: Herzl Press, 1974.

Bartal, Israel. "Old Yishuv and New Yishuv: Image and Reality." *Jerusalem Cathedra* (1981), 215–31.

Bar-Zohar, Michael. *Ben-Gurion: A Biography.* 1978. New York: Adama Books, 1986.

Bauer, Yehuda. *My Brother's Keeper: A History of the American Joint Distribution Committee, 1929–1939.* Philadelphia: Jewish Publication Society of America, 1974.

Bemis, Edward. "Restriction of Immigration." *The Andover Review* 9 (Mar. 1888), 251–63.

Berkson, Isaac. *Theories of Americanization: A Critical Study with Special Reference to the Jewish Group.* New York: General Books, 1920.

Bernstein, Herman. *The History of a Lie: The Protocols of the Wise Men of Zion, a Study.* New York: Ogilvie, 1921.

Bernstein, Michael André. *Foregone Conclusions: Against Apocalyptic History.* Berkeley: Univ. of California Press, 1994.

Bevir, Mark. "British Socialism and American Romanticism." *English Historical Review* 110, no. 438 (Sept. 1995), 878–901.

Biale, David. "The Melting Pot and Beyond: Jews and the Politics of American Identity." In *Insider/Outsider: American Jews and Multiculturalism,* edited by David Biale, Michael Galchinsky, and Susannah Heschel, 17–33. Berkeley: Univ. of California Press, 1992.

Bingham, Theodore A. "Foreign Criminals in New York." *North American Review* 188 (Sept. 1908), 384–94.

Birmingham, Stephen. *Our Crowd: The Great Jewish Families of New York.* New York: Harper and Row, 1967.

Blaustein, Miriam, ed. *Memoirs of David Blaustein, Educator and Communal Worker.* 1913. Facsimile edition. New York: Arno Press, 1975.

Boyle, Kevin. *Arc of Justice: A Saga of Race, Civil Rights and Murder in the Jazz Age.* New York: Holt, 2004.

Brandeis, Louis. *Other People's Money, and How the Bankers Use It.* New York: F. A. Stokes, 1914.

Brodkin, Karen. *How Jews Became White Folks and What That Says about Race in America.* New Brunswick: Rutgers Univ. Press, 1998.

Bronner, Stephen. *A Rumor about the Jews: Antisemitism, Conspiracy and the Protocols of Zion.* New York: St. Martin's Press, 2000.

Brown, Phil. *Bob Marshall in the Adirondacks: Writings of a Pioneering Peak-Bagger, Pond-Hopper and Wilderness Preservationist.* (Elizabethtown: Lost Pond Press, 2006).

Carlson, Oliver. *Brisbane: A Candid Biography.* New York: Stackpole Sons, 1937.

Chernow, Ron. *The House of Morgan: An American Banking Dynasty and the Rise of Modern Finance.* New York: Macmillan, 1990.

Cohen, Morris Raphael. *A Dreamer's Journey: The Autobiography of Morris Raphael Cohen.* Boston: Beacon Press, 1949.

Cohen, Naomi. "The Abrogation of the Russo-American Treaty of 1832." *Jewish Social Studies* 25, no. 1 (Jan. 1963), 3–41.

———. "An American Jew at the Paris Peace Conference of 1919: Excerpts from the Diary of Oscar S. Straus." In *Essays on Jewish Life and Thought,* edited by Joseph Blau, 159–68. New York: Columbia Univ. Press, 1959.

———. *A Dual Heritage: The Public Career of Oscar Straus.* Philadelphia: Jewish Publication Society of America, 1969.

———. *Encounter with Emancipation: The German Jews in the United States, 1830–1914.* Philadelphia: Jewish Publication Society of America, 1984.

———. *Jacob H. Schiff: A Study in American Jewish Leadership.* Hanover: Brandeis Univ. Press, 1999.

———. *Not Free to Desist: A History of the American Jewish Committee, 1906–1966.* Philadelphia: Jewish Publication Society of America, 1972.

———. *The Year after the Riots: American Responses to the Palestine Crisis, 1929–1930.* Detroit: Wayne State Univ. Press, 1988.

Cohen, Richard. *Jewish Icons: Art and Society in Modern Europe.* Berkeley: Univ. of California Press, 1998.

Cohn, Norman. *Warrant for Genocide: The Myth of the Jewish World-Wide Conspiracy and the Protocols of the Elders of Zion.* Harmondsworth: Penguin Books, 1970.

Connolly, Cynthia. *Saving Sickly Children: The Tuberculosis Preventorium in American Life, 1909–1970.* New Brunswick: Rutgers Univ. Press, 2008.

Dalin, David. "Louis Marshall, the Jewish Vote, and the Republican Party." *Jewish Political Studies Review* 4 (Spring 1992), 55–84.

———. "The Patriarch: The Life and Legacy of Mayer Sulzberger." In *When Philadelphia Was the Capital of Jewish America,* edited by Murray Friedman, 58–74. Philadelphia: Balch Institute Press, 1993.

Davies, Rosemary. *The Rosenbluth Case: Federal Justice on Trial.* Ames: Iowa State Univ. Press, 1970.

Davis, Allen. *Spearheads for Reform: The Social Settlements and the Progressive Movement, 1880–1914.* New York: Oxford Univ. Press, 1967.

Davis, John H. *The Guggenheims: An American Epic.* 1978. 2nd ed. New York: S.P.I. Books, 1994.

Davis, Marni. *Jews and Booze: Becoming American in the Age of Prohibition.* New York: New York Univ. Press, 2012.

Davis, Moshe. *The Emergence of Conservative Judaism: The Historical School in Nineteenth Century America.* Philadelphia: Jewish Publication Society of America, 1965.

Davis, Moshe. "The Human Record: Cyrus Adler at the Peace Conference, 1919." In *Essays in American Jewish History,* American Jewish Archives, 457–91. Cincinnati: American Jewish Archives, 1958.

Dawidowicz, Lucy. "Louis Marshall and the *Jewish Daily Forward:* An Episode in Wartime Censorship, 1917–1918." In *For Max Weinreich on His Seventieth Birthday: Studies in Jewish Languages, Literature and Society,* 31–43. London: VG and Mouton, 1964.

———. "Louis Marshall's Yiddish Newspaper, *The Jewish World.*" *Jewish Social Studies* 25, no. 2 (Apr. 1963), 102–32.

Dearborn Independent. "America's Jewish Enigma: Louis Marshall." *Dearborn Independent* (Nov. 1921). Reprinted in *Aspects of Jewish Power in the United States,* 179–92. Vol. 4, *International Jew.* Dearborn, 1921.

Dekel-Chen, Jonathan. *Farming the Red Land: Jewish Agricultural Colonization and Local Soviet Power, 1924–1941.* New Haven: Yale Univ. Press, 2005.

Diner, Hasia. *In the Almost Promised Land: American Jews and Blacks, 1915–1935.* Baltimore: Johns Hopkins Univ. Press, 1977.

———. "Like the Antelope and the Badger: The Founding and Early Years of the Jewish Theological Seminary, 1886–1902." In *Tradition Renewed: A History of the Jewish Theological Seminary,* edited by Jack Wertheimer, 1:1–43. New York: Jewish Theological Seminary of America, 1997.

———. *A Time for Gathering: The Second Migration, 1820–1880.* Baltimore: Johns Hopkins Univ. Press, 1992.

Dinnerstein, Leonard. *The Leo Frank Case.* New York: Columbia Univ. Press, 1968.

———. *Uneasy at Home: Antisemitism and the American Jewish Experience.* New York: Columbia Univ. Press, 1987.

Donaldson, Alfred. *A History of the Adirondacks.* Vol. 2. New York: Purple Mountain Press, 1921.

Draper, Theodore. *The Roots of American Communism.* New York: Viking, 1957.

Dushkin, Alexander. *Jewish Education in New York City.* New York: Bureau of Jewish Education, 1918.

———. *Living Bridges.* Jerusalem: Keter, 1975.

Efrati, Nathan. *The Jewish Community in Eretz Israel During World War I.* [In Hebrew]. Jerusalem: Yad Izhak Ben Zvi, 1991.

Egan, Clifford. "Pressure Groups, the Department of State, and the Abrogation of the Russian-American Treaty of 1832." *Proceedings of the American Philosophical Society* 115, no. 4 (Aug. 1971), 328–34.

Elam, Yigal. *The Jewish Agency: Formative Years, 1919–1931.* [In Hebrew]. Jerusalem: Hassifriya Haziyonit, 1990.

———. *The Jewish Legion in WWI.* [In Hebrew]. Tel Aviv: Defense Ministry, 1973.

Eliav, Mordechai. *Erets-Yisrael ve-yishuva ba-meah ha–19, 1777–1917.* Jerusalem: Keter, 1978.

Epstein, Melech. *Profiles of Eleven.* Detroit: Wayne State Univ. Press, 1965.

Feingold, Henry. *Lest Memory Cease: Finding Meaning in the American Jewish Past.* Syracuse: Syracuse Univ. Press, 1996.

———. *A Time for Searching: Entering the Mainstream, 1920–1945.* Baltimore: Johns Hopkins Univ. Press, 1992.

Feldestein, Ariel. *Ben-Gurion, Zionism and American Jewry, 1948–1963.* London: Routledge, 2006.

Filderman, Wilhelm. *Memories and Diaries, 1900–1940.* Vol. 1. Jerusalem: Goldstein-Goren Diaspora Research Center, 2000.

Fink, Carole. *Defending the Rights of Others: The Great Powers, the Jews, and International Minority Protection, 1878–1938.* New York: Cambridge Univ. Press, 2004.

———. "Louis Marshall: An American Jewish Diplomat in Paris, 1919." *American Jewish History* 94, nos. 1–2 (Mar.–June 2008), 21–40.

Fishback, Price, and Shawn Everett Kantor. *A Prelude to the Welfare State: The Origins of Workers' Compensation.* Chicago: Univ. of Chicago Press, 2000.

Florence, Ronald. *T. E. Lawrence, Aaron Aaronsohn and the Seeds of the Arab-Israeli Conflict.* London: Viking, 2007.

Forbush, Edward Howe. *A History of the Game Birds, Wild-Fowl and Shore Birds of Massachusetts and Adjacent States.* Boston: Doubleday, 1912.

Foreign Policy Association. *The Seizure of Haiti by the United States: A Report on the Military Occupation of the Republic of Haiti and the History of the Treaty Forced upon Her.* New York: Foreign Policy Association, 1922.

Frankel, Jonathan. *Crisis, Revolution and Russian Jews.* Cambridge: Cambridge Univ. Press, 2009.

———. "The Jewish Socialists and the American Jewish Congress Movement." *Yivo Annual of Jewish Social Science* 16 (1976), 202–341.

———. *Prophecy and Politics: Socialism, Nationalism and the Russian Jews, 1862–1917.* Cambridge: Cambridge Univ. Press, 1981.

Frese, Stephen. "Divided by a Common Language: The Babel Proclamation and Its Influence in Iowa History." *History Teacher* 39, no. 1 (Nov. 2005), 59–88.

Friedman, J. Alexis. *The Impeachment of Governor William Sulzer.* New York: Columbia Univ. Press, 1939.

Friedman, Murray. "The Philadelphia Group: A Collective Portrait." In *When Philadelphia Was the Capital of Jewish America,* edited by Murray Friedman, 9–22. Philadelphia: Balch Institute Press, 1993.

Friedman, Saul. *The Incident at Massena: The Blood Libel in America.* New York: Stein and Day, 1978.

Friesal, Evyatar. "Magnes: Zionism in Judaism." In *Like All the Nations? The Life and Legacy of Judah L. Magnes,* edited by Moses Rischin and William Brinner, 69–81. Albany: State Univ. of New York Press, 1987.

———. *The Zionist Movement in the United States, 1897–1914.* [In Hebrew]. Tel Aviv: Hakibutz Hameuchad, 1970.

———. *Zionist Policy after the Balfour Declaration, 1917–1922.* [In Hebrew]. Tel Aviv: Kibbutz Hameuhad, 1977.

Fuchs, Lawrence, ed. *American Ethnic Politics.* New York: Harper and Row, 1968.

Gal, Allon. *Brandeis of Boston.* Cambridge, MA: Harvard Univ. Press 1980.

Ganin, Zvi. *An Uneasy Relationship: American Jewish Leadership and Israel, 1948–1957.* Syracuse: Syracuse Univ. Press, 2005.

Gardner, Martha. *The Qualities of a Citizen: Women, Immigration and Citizenship, 1870–1965.* Princeton: Princeton Univ. Press, 2005.

Gartner, Lloyd. "The Correspondence of Mayer Sulzberger and William Howard Taft." *Proceedings of the American Academy for Jewish Research* 46 (1978–79), 120–40.

Gleason, Philip. *Speaking of Diversity: Language and Ethnicity in Twentieth-Century America.* Baltimore: Johns Hopkins Univ. Press, 1992.

Glover, James. "Louis Marshall: A Visionary Who Helped Preserve the Adirondacks." *Adirondack Life* (May–June 1985).

———. *A Wilderness Original: The Life of Bob Marshall.* Seattle: Mountaineers, 1986.

Goebel, Julius, ed. *A History of the School of Law, Columbia University.* New York: Columbia Univ. Press, 1955.

Goell, Yohai. "Aliyah in the Zionism of an American Oleh: Judah L. Magnes." *American Jewish Historical Quarterly* 65 (1975–76), 99–120.

Goldberg, J. J. *Jewish Power: Inside the American Jewish Establishment.* Reading: Addison–Wesley, 1996.

Goldstein, Eric. "Contesting the Categories: Jews and Government Racial Classification in the United States." *Jewish History* 19 (2005), 79–107.

———. *The Price of Whiteness: Jews, Race, and American Identity.* Princeton: Princeton Univ. Press, 2006.

Goldstein, Judith. *The Politics of Ethnic Pressure: The American Jewish Committee Fight Against Immigrant Restriction, 1906–1917.* New York: Garland Publishers, 1990.

Golove, David M. "Treaty-Making and the Nation: The Historical Foundations of the Nationalist Conception of the Treaty Power." 98 *Michigan Law Review* 1075 (2000).

Good, James. "The Development of Thomas Davidson's Religious and Social Thought" (2004). Available at http://www.autodidactproject.org/other/TD.html.

Goren, Arthur, ed. *Dissenter in Zion: From the Writings of Judah L. Magnes.* Cambridge, MA: Harvard Univ. Press, 1982.

Goren, Arthur. *New York Jews and the Quest for Community: The Kehillah Experiment, 1908–1922.* New York: Columbia Univ. Press, 1970.

———. *The Politics and Public Culture of American Jews.* Bloomington: Indiana Univ. Press, 1999.

Greenberg, Henry. "Louis Marshall: Attorney General of the Jewish People." In *Noble Purposes: Nine Champions of the Rule of Law,* edited by Norman Gross, 111–25. Athens: Ohio Univ. Press, 2007.

Greenwald, Richard. *The Triangle Fire, the Protocols of Peace and Industrial Democracy in Progressive Era New York.* Philadelphia: Temple Univ. Press, 2005.

Gurock, Jeffrey. *The Men and Women of Yeshiva: Higher Education, Orthodoxy and American Judaism.* New York: Columbia Univ. Press, 1988.

Gutwein, Daniel. "Jacob H. Schiff and the Financing of the Russo–Japanese War." [In Hebrew]. *Zion* 54 (1989), 321–50.

Halpern, Ben. *A Clash of Heroes: Brandeis, Weizmann, and American Zionism.* New York: Oxford Univ. Press, 1987.

Handlin, Lilian. *George Bancroft: The Intellectual as Democrat.* New York: Harpercollins, 1984.

Handlin, Oscar. "Introduction." In *Louis Marshall: Champion of Liberty: Selected Papers and Addresses,* Charles Reznikoff. 2 vols. Philadelphia: Jewish Publication Society of America, 1957.

Hapgood, Hutchins. *The Spirit of the Ghetto.* 1902. Cambridge, MA: Harvard College, 1967.

Hawkins, Richard. "Hitler's Bitterest Foe: Samuel Untermyer and the Boycott of Nazi Germany, 1933–1938." *American Jewish History* 93, no. 1 (Mar. 2007), 21–50.

———. "Lynchburg's Swabian Jewish Entrepreneurs in War and Peace." *Southern Jewish History* 4 (Oct. 2001), 44–82.

———. "Samuel Untermyer and the Zionist Project: An Attempt to Reconcile the American 'Melting Pot' with Zionism." *Australian Journal of Jewish Studies* 21 (2007), 114–54.

Healy, Thomas. "Is *Missouri v. Holland* Still Good Law? Federalism and the Treaty Power." *Columbia Law Review* 8, no. 7 (Nov. 1998), 1726–56.

Henkin, Louis. *Foreign Affairs and the United States Constitution.* Oxford: Oxford Univ. Press, 1996.

Higham, John. *Strangers in the Land: Patterns of American Nativism, 1860–1925.* [1955]. 2nd ed. New Brunswick: Rutgers Univ. Press, 2002.

Hirsch, Foster. *The Boys from Syracuse: The Shuberts' Theatrical Empire.* Carbondale: Southern Illinois Univ. Press, 1998.

Hixson, William. *Moorefield Storey and the Abolitionist Tradition.* New York: Oxford Univ. Press, 1972.

Hourwich, Isaac A. *Immigration and Labor.* New York: G. P. Putnam's Sons, 1912; New York: Arno Press, 1969.

Howard, Harry. *The King-Crane Commission: An American Inquiry in the Middle East.* Beirut: Khayats, 1963.

Howe, Irving. *The World of Our Fathers: The Journey of the East European Jews to America and the Life They Found and Made.* New York: Simon and Schuster, 1974.

Hyman, Paula. "Traditionalism and Village Jews." In *The Uses of Tradition,* edited by Jack Wertheimer, 187–202. New York: Jewish Theological Seminary of America, 1992.

Isaacs, Myer. "Sampson Simson." *Publications of the American Jewish Historical Society* 10 (1902), 109–17.

Jabotinsky, Vladimir. *The Story of the Jewish Legion.* New York: B. Ackerman, 1945.

Janowsky, Oscar. *The Jews and Minority Rights, 1898–1919.* New York: AMS Press, 1966.

Jorgenson, Lloyd. "The Oregon School Law of 1922: Passage and Sequel." *Catholic History Review* 54, no. 3 (Oct. 1968), 455–66.

Joselit, Jenna Weissman. "By Design: Building the Campus of the Jewish Theological Seminary." In *Tradition Renewed: A History of the Jewish Theological Seminary,* edited by Jack Wertheimer, 1:273. New York: Jewish Theological Seminary of America, 1997.

———. *Our Gang: Jewish Crime and the New York Jewish Community, 1900–1940.* Bloomington: Indiana Univ. Press, 1983.

Kaiser, Harvey. *Great Camps of the Adirondacks.* Boston: Godine, 1982.

Kaplan, Beth. *Finding the Jewish Shakespeare: The Life and Legacy of Jacob Gordin.* Syracuse: Syracuse Univ. Press, 2007.

Karp, Abraham. "Solomon Schechter Comes to America." *American Jewish Historical Quarterly* 53, no. 1 (Sept. 1963). Reprinted in Abraham Karp, ed. *The Jewish Experience in America,* 111–30. Waltham: American Jewish Historical Society, 1969.

Kaufman, Menahem. *An Ambiguous Partnership: Non-Zionists and Zionists in America, 1939–1948.* Detroit: Wayne State Univ. Press, 1991.

Kessler, Lawton, Aaron Alperin, and Jack Diamond. "American Jews and the Paris Peace Conference." *YIVO Annual of Jewish Social Science* 2–3 (1948).

Klaw, Spencer. "The World's Tallest Building." *American Heritage* 28, no. 2 (Feb. 1977). Available at http://www.americanheritage.com/content/world%E2%80%99s-tallest-building?page=3.

Kohler, Max. *The Injustice of a Literacy Test for Immigrants.* New York: Max Kohler, 1912.

———. "Judah Touro, Merchant and Philanthropist." *Publications of the American Jewish Historical Society* 13 (1905), 96–103.

Kotzin, Daniel. *Judah Magnes: An American Jewish Nonconformist.* Syracuse: Syracuse Univ. Press, 2010.

Kraut, Benny. "American Jewish Leaders: The Great, Greater and Greatest." *American Jewish History* 78 (Dec. 1988), 201–36.

Kreader, J. Lee. "Isaac Max Rubinow: America's Prophet for Social Security." PhD diss., University of Chicago, 1988.

Kurland, Gerald. *Seth Low: The Reformer in an Urban and Industrial Age.* New York: Twayne, 1971.

Kuzmack, Linda. *Woman's Cause: The Jewish Woman's Movement in England and the United States, 1881–1933.* Columbus: Ohio State Univ. Press, 1990.

Lambroza, Shlomo. "The Pogroms of 1903–1906." In *Pogroms: Anti-Jewish Violence in Modern Russian History,* edited by Shlomo Lambroza and John Klier, 195–247. New York: Cambridge Univ. Press, 1992.

Larsen, Grace, and Henry Erdman. "Aaron Sapiro: Genius of Farm Cooperative Promotion." *Mississippi Valley Historical Review* 49 (1962), 242–68.

Lebow, Richard Ned. "Woodrow Wilson and the Balfour Declaration." *Journal of Modern History* 40, no. 4 (Dec. 1968), 501–23.

Lederhendler, Eli. *Jewish Immigrants and American Capitalism, 1880–1920: From Caste to Class*. Cambridge: Cambridge Univ. Press, 2009.

Leff, Laurel. *Buried by the Times: The Holocaust and America's Most Important Newspaper*. Cambridge: Cambridge Univ. Press, 2005.

Levene, Mark. *War, Jews and the New Europe: The Diplomacy of Lucien Wolf, 1914–1919*. London: Littman Library of Jewish Civilization, 2009.

Lipman, Sonia, and V. D. Lipman, eds. *The Century of Moses Montefiore*. New York: Oxford Univ. Press, 1985.

Lipsky, Louis. *A Gallery of Zionist Profiles*. New York: Farrar, Straus and Cudahy, 1956.

Lipstadt, Deborah. "The Zionist Career of Louis Lipsky." PhD diss., Brandeis University, 1976.

Livneh, Eliezer. *Aaron Aaronsohn: Haish u'zemano*. Jerusalem: Mosad Bialik, 1969.

Magnes, Beatrice. *Episodes: A Memoir*. Berkeley: J. L. Magnes Memorial Museum, 1977.

Manuel, Frank. *The Realities of American Palestine Relations*. Washington, DC: Public Affairs Press, 1949.

Marshall, James. "Louis Marshall: Man in Shirt Sleeves." *American Judaism* (Aug. 1956), 12–13.

Marshall, Jonathan. *Dateline History: The Life of Journalist Jonathan Marshall*. Phoenix: Acacia, 2009.

Marshall, Louis. "Address on Immigration." New York University Forum, Feb. 20, 1914. CJH, Marshall Papers, Box 1. Reprinted in Reznikoff, *Louis Marshall*, 1:131–46.

———. "Is Ours a Christian Government?" *The Menorah* (Jan. 1896). Reprinted in Reznikoff, *Louis Marshall*, 2:936–49.

———. "The Jew as an American Citizen." Congregation Rodeph Shalom, Philadelphia, 1906. LM Papers, Box 151.

———. "The Jewish Concepts of Charity." Submitted for the North American Relief Society in *Riker v. Leo* 133 N.Y. 519 (1892). Reprinted in Reznikoff, *Louis Marshall*, 2:913–22.

———. "Jewish Rights in Eastern Europe." Address at American Jewish Congress meeting, Dec. 15, 1918. Reprinted in Reznikoff, *Louis Marshall*, 2:526–36.

———. "Louis Marshall Looks Back over Seventy Years." *New York Times Magazine* (Dec. 12, 1926).

———. "Rabbi Meir of Rothenburg." Lecture at Jewish Theological Seminary, New York, Mar. 29, 1906. LM Papers, Box 1619.

———. "The Right to Vote." Brief for Plaintiff-in-Error, Nixon v. Herndon, 1927. Reprinted in Reznikoff, Louis *Marshall*, 1:426–47.

———. "Russia and the American Passport." Address to UAHC meeting, New York, Jan. 19, 1911. Reprinted in Reznikoff, *Louis Marshall*, 1:59–71.

———. "War and the Jewish Question." *American Hebrew* (Apr. 30, 1915).

Marshall, Louis, et al. "The British Declaration Concerning Palestine." Statement of American Jewish Committee, New York, 1918. Reprinted in Reznikoff, *Louis Marshall*, 2:715–16.

Marshall, Louis, et al. "The Protocols, Bolshevism and the Jews: An Address to their Fellow Citizens by American Jewish Organizations," Dec. 1, 1920. In *The American Jewish Year Book, 5682*. Philadelphia: Jewish Publication Center of America, 1921.

Marshall, Louis, et al. *Report of the Commission of Immigration of the State of New York*. New York, 1909. LM Papers, Box 1.

Marshall, Robert. *Arctic Village: A 1930s Portrait of Wiseman, Alaska*. New York: Literary Guild, 1933.

———. "The Problem of the Wilderness." *Scientific Monthly* 30, no. 2 (Feb. 1930), 141–48.

———. "Wilderness as a Minority Right." *Forest Service Bulletin* (Aug. 27, 1928).

Meier, August, and Elliot Rudwick. "Attorneys Black and White: A Case Study of Race Relations Within the NAACP." *Journal of American History* 62, no. 4 (Mar. 1976), 913–46.

Menand, Louis. *The Metaphysical Club*. New York: Farrar, Straus, 2001.

Mendelsohn, Ezra. *The Jews of Central Europe Between the World Wars*. Bloomington: Indiana Univ. Press, 1983.

———. *On Modern Jewish Politics*. New York: Oxford Univ. Press, 1993.

Mendelson, Alan. *Exiles from Nowhere: The Jews and the Canadian Elite*. Montreal: RBS, 2008.

Moore, Deborah Dash. *At Home in America: Second Generation New York Jews*. New York: Columbia Univ. Press, 1981.

———. *B'nai B'rith and the Challenge of Ethnic Leadership*. Albany: State Univ. of New York Press, 1981.

Mount Sinai. *Mount Sinai Unit in the World War: With Scenes at Base Hospital #3 A.E.F. at Vauclaire, Dordogne, France*. 1920. Mount Sinai Hospital Archives, New York.

Muller, Jerry. *Capitalism and the Jews*. Princeton: Princeton Univ. Press, 2010.

Murray, Robert K. *Red Scare: A Study in National Hysteria, 1919–1920*. Minneapolis: Univ. of Minnesota Press, 1955.

Neu, Charles. *An Uncertain Friendship: Theodore Roosevelt and Japan, 1906–1909*. Cambridge MA: Harvard Univ. Press, 1967.

Oney, Steve. *And the Dead Shall Rise: The Murder of Mary Phagan and the Lynching of Leo Frank*. New York: Random House, 2003.

Panitz, Esther. "The Polarity of American Jewish Attitudes Towards Immigration, 1870–1891." In Abraham Karp, *The Jewish Experience in America*, 31–62. Vol. 4, *The Era of Immigration*. New York: Ktav, 1969.

———. *Simon Wolf: Private Conscience and Public Image*. Rutherford, NJ: Fairleigh Dickinson Univ. Press, 1987.

Podhoretz, Norman. *Why Are Jews Liberals?* New York: Doubleday, 2009.

Pratt, Norma Fain. *Morris Hillquit: A Political History of an American Jewish Socialist*. Westport: Greenwood Press, 1979.

Proceedings: Democratic Republican State Convention. Syracuse, July 24. Albany, 1856.

Raider, Mark. "The Aristocrat and the Democrat: Louis Marshall, Stephen S. Wise and the Challenge of American Jewish Leadership." *American Jewish History* 94, nos. 1–2 (Mar.–June 2008), 91–114.

———. "Introduction." Special issue on Louis Marshall and American Jewish Leadership. *American Jewish History* 94 (Mar.–June 2008), ix–xiii.

Rappaport, Joel. "The American Yiddish Press and the European Conflict in 1914." *Jewish Social Studies* 19 (1957), 113–28.

Reinharz, Jehuda. *Chaim Weizmann: The Making of a Zionist Leader.* New York: Oxford Univ. Press, 1985.

Reznikoff, Charles. *Louis Marshall: Champion of Liberty: Selected Papers and Addresses.* 2 vols. Philadelphia: Jewish Publication Society of America, 1957.

Ribuffo, Leo. "Henry Ford and the American Jew." *American Jewish History* 69, no. 4 (June 1980), 437–77.

Rice, Roger. "Residential Segregation by Law, 1910–1917." *Journal of Southern History* 34, no. 2 (May 1968), 177–99.

Richards, Bernard. "Jews Against Race." *Hebrew Standard* (Jan. 7, 1910).

Rifkind, Robert. "Confronting Anti-Semitism in America: Louis Marshall and Henry Ford." *American Jewish History* 94, nos. 1–2 (Mar.–June 2008), 71–90.

Rischin, Moses. *The Promised City: New York's Jews, 1870–1914.* New York: Corinth, 1964.

Rochelson, Meri-Jane. *A Jew in the Public Arena: The Career of Israel Zangwill.* Detroit: Wayne State Univ. Press, 2008.

Routsila, Markuu. *John Spargo and American Socialism.* New York: Palgrave Macmillan, 2006.

Rosen, Judith Friedman. "Earlier American Jewish Anniversary Celebrations: 1905 and 1954." *American Jewish History* (Dec. 2004), 481–97.

Rosenkranz, Nicholas. "Executing the Treaty Power." *Harvard Law Review* 118 (2005), 1867–938.

Rosenstock, Morton. *Louis Marshall: Defender of Jewish Rights.* Detroit: Wayne State Univ. Press, 1965.

Rosenthal, Jerome. "Dealing with the Devil: Louis Marshall and the Partnership Between the Joint Distribution Committee and Soviet Russia." *American Jewish Archives* 32 (Apr. 1987), 1–22.

———. "The Public Life of Louis Marshall." PhD diss., University of Cincinnati, 1983.

Rowland, Tim. *High Peaks: A History of Hiking the Adirondacks, from Noah to Neoprene.* Charleston: History Press, 2008.

Rubinow, Isaac Max. "The Jewish Question in New York City, 1902–1903." *American Jewish Historical Society Publications* 49 (Sept. 1959–June 1960), 90–136.

Rudens, S. P. "A Half Century of Community Service: The Story of the Educational Alliance." *American Jewish Year Book, 5707* (Philadelphia: Jewish Publication Society of America, 1944), 73–86.

Rudolph, B. G. *From a Minyan to a Community: A History of the Jews of Syracuse.* Syracuse: Syracuse Univ. Press, 1970.

Sarna, Jonathan. *American Judaism: A History.* New Haven: Yale Univ. Press, 2004.

———. "Two Jewish Lawyers Named Louis." *American Jewish History* 94, nos. 1–2 (Mar.–June 2008), 1–19.

Schmidt, Hans. *The United States Occupation of Haiti, 1915–1934.* New Brunswick: Rutgers Univ. Press, 1971.

Schwartz, Shuly Rubin. *The Emergence of Jewish Scholarship in America: The Publication of the Jewish Encyclopedia.* Cincinnati: Hebrew Union College Press, 1991.

Scult, Mel. "Schechter's Seminary." In *Tradition Renewed: A History of the Jewish Theological Seminary*, edited by Jack Wertheimer, 45–61. Vol. 1. New York: Jewish Theological Seminary of America, 1997.

Shaltiel Eli. *Pinhas Rutenberg.* [In Hebrew]. Tel Aviv: Am Oved, 1990.

Shapiro, Yonathan. *Leadership in the American Zionist Organization, 1897–1930.* Urbana: Univ. of Illinois Press, 1971.

Siegel, Beatrice. *Lillian Wald of Henry Street.* New York: Macmillan, 1983.

Silver, Matthew. "Fighting for Palestine and Crimea: Two Jewish Friends from Philadelphia During the First World War and the 1920s." *Studies in Contemporary Jewry* 18 (2002), 201–16.

———. *First Contact: Origins of the American–Israeli Connection, Halutzim from America During the Palestine Mandate.* Hartford: Graduate Group, 2006.

———. "Louis Marshall and the Democratization of Jewish Identity." *American Jewish History* 94, nos. 1–2 (Mar.–June 2008), 41–70.

Sinclair, Upton. *The Flivver King: A Story of Ford-America.* 1937. Chicago: Labor Classics, 1999.

Singer, Isidore. *Russia at the Bar of the American People: A Memorial of Kishinef.* New York: Funk and Wagnalls, 1904.

Singerman, Robert. "The American Career of the *Protocols of the Elders of Zion.*" *American Jewish History* 71 (1980), 48–78.

Smith, Gene. "The American Dreyfus." *American Heritage Magazine* 45, no. 7 (Nov. 1994), 93–94.

Solomon, Barbara Miller. *Ancestors and Immigrants: A Changing New England Tradition.* Cambridge, MA: Harvard Univ. Press, 1956.

Soltes, Mordecai. *The Yiddish Press: An Americanizing Agency.* New York: Teachers College, Columbia University, 1925.

Sorin, Gerald. *A Time for Building: The Third Migration, 1880–1920.* Baltimore: Johns Hopkins Univ. Press, 1992.

Spargo, John. *The Jew and American Ideals.* New York: Harper and Brothers, 1921.

Stein, Leon, ed. *Out of the Sweatshop: The Struggle for Industrial Democracy.* New York: Quadrangle, 1977.

Stern, Horace. *Louis Marshall: An Appreciation.* Feb. 1930. Reprinted in Reznikoff, *Louis Marshall*, vol. 1.

Stevens, Robert. *Law School: Legal Education in America from the 1850s to the 1980s.* Chapel Hill: Univ. of North Carolina Press, 1983.

Sussman, Lance. *Isaac Leeser and the Making of American Judaism.* Detroit: Wayne State Univ. Press, 1995.

Sutherland, Arthur. "Restricting the Treaty Power." *Harvard Law Review* 65, no. 8 (June 1952), 1305–38.

Synnott, Marcia Graham. *The Half-Opened Door: Discrimination and Admissions at Harvard, Yale and Princeton, 1900–1970.* Westport: Greenwood Press, 1979.

Szajkowski, Zosa. "The Attitude of American Jews to East European Jewish Immigration, 1881–1893." *Publications of the American Jewish Historical Society* 40, no. 3 (Mar. 1951), 149–82.

———. "Concord and Discord in American Jewish Overseas Relief, 1914–1924." *Yivo Annual of Jewish Social Science* 14 (1969), 99–158.

———. "The Jews and New York City's Mayoralty Election of 1917." *Jewish Social Studies* 32, no. 4 (Oct. 1970), 286–306.

———. *Jews, Wars, and Communism: The Attitude of American Jews to World War I, the Russian Revolutions of 1917 and Communism (1914–1945).* Vol. 1. New York: Ktav, 1972.

———. *The Mirage of American Jewish Aid in Soviet Russia, 1917–1939.* New York: S. Frydman, 1977.

———. "The Pacifism of Judah Magnes." *Conservative Judaism* 22, no. 3 (1968), 36–55.

Tennenbaum, Joseph. *Ben milhamah ve-shalom* [Between War and Peace]. Jerusalem: World Jewish Congress, 1960.

Thompson, E. P. *The Making of the English Working Class.* 1963. New York: Viking, 1966.

Thompson, Roger. "The Doctrine of the Wilderness: A Study of the Policy and Politics of the Adirondacks Preserve-Park." PhD diss., Syracuse University, 1962.

Troen, S. Ilan. "American Experts in the Design of Zionist Society." In *Envisioning Israel: The Changing Ideals and Images of American Jews,* edited by Allon Gal, 193–218. Detroit: Wayne State Univ. Press, 1996.

Trotsky, Leon. *My Life.* New York: Pathfinder Press, 1970.

Urofsky, Melvin. *American Zionism from Herzl to the Holocaust.* Garden City, NY: Anchor Press, 1975.

———. *Louis D. Brandeis: A Life.* New York: Pantheon Books, 2009.

———. *A Voice That Spoke for Justice: The Life and Times of Stephen S. Wise.* Albany: State Univ. of New York Press, 1982.

Watts, Steven. *The People's Tycoon: Henry Ford and the American Century.* New York: A. A. Knopf, 2005.

Wertheimer, Jack, ed. *Tradition Renewed: A History of the Jewish Theological Seminary.* 2 vols. New York: Jewish Theological Seminary of America, 1997.

White, Edward. *Justice Oliver Wendell Holmes: Law and the Inner Self.* New York: Oxford Univ. Press, 1993.

Wiegand, Wayne. *Irrepressible Reformer: A Biography of Melvil Dewey.* Chicago: American Library Association, 1996.

Wise, Stephen. *Challenging Years: The Autobiography of Stephen Wise.* New York: Putnam's Sons, 1949.

Woeste, Victoria Saker. *Henry Ford's War on Jews and the Legal Battle Against Hate Speech.* Stanford: Stanford University Press, 2012.

Woeste, Victoria Saker. "Insecure Equality: Louis Marshall, Henry Ford, and the Problem of Defamatory Antisemitism, 1920–1929." *Journal of American History* (Dec. 2004), 877–905.

Wohlgelernter, Maurice. *Israel Zangwill: A Study.* New York: Columbia Univ. Press, 1964.

Woocher, Jonathan. "The Democratization of the American Jewish Polity." In *Authority, Power and Leadership in the Jewish Polity,* edited by Daniel Elazar. Lanham: Univ. Press of America, 1991.

Woodward, C. Vann. *Tom Watson: Agrarian Rebel.* New York: Macmillan, 1938.

Index

Aaronsohn, Aaron, 177–81, 186, 260, 274, 362, 408; Atlit experimental station, 178, 180–81, 306–7

Abrogation: background and historical context, 136–37, 141–42; early activities in abrogation campaign, 139–42, 183–84, 193–99; ethnic and political alliances, 204–5; meeting with President Taft, 199–204; national campaign, 208–9, 212–13, 215–21

Adirondacks, 5, 50, 89–90, 145, 169, 212, 215, 223, 282, 290, 292, 317, 406–12, 415–18, 421–25, 427, 429, 431–34, 438, 440, 528

Adler, Cyrus, 10–11, 43–44, 129, 132, 178–79, 208, 226, 339, 341, 388, 396, 453, 477, 513, 534; abrogation campaign, 154, 194, 306; AJC founding, 117, 121, 123–24, 139; World War I and Paris Peace Conference, 253, 279, 285–86, 309, 329, 349–50, 352–54, 356–58, 362–63, 367

Adler, Felix, 42

Agassiz, Louis, 416

Agnew, George B., 326

Agro-Joint. *See* Joint Distribution Committee

Albany, NY, 18, 24, 72, 100, 156, 158–59, 176, 215, 217, 239, 282–83, 285–86, 412, 433–37, 461, 530

Aldrich, Nelson, 132

Alexander, Henry, 256

Alexander, Michael, 482

Allenby, Edmund, 339

Alliance Israelite Universelle, 118, 127, 261, 349, 353, 360, 361

Alpert, Herb, 185

American Hebrew, 44, 109, 253, 285, 348, 390, 392, 431

American Indian Defense Association, 489

American Indian Life Bulletin, 489

American Israelite, 141, 461

American Jewish Committee (AJC), xii, 4, 7, 36, 79–81, 106, 145, 150, 229, 231, 254–56, 259–62, 316–17, 326, 334, 365–67, 389–90, 395, 417, 443, 447, 449, 453, 463, 465, 467, 486, 489, 509–11, 514, 529, 531–32; abrogation campaign, 136–37, 154, 194–98, 200, 203, 212–13, 215–16, 218–21, 234, 241, 307, 364; 494; background and historical import, 107–9; Balfour Declaration, 338–41; controversy, 258, 266, 275–80, 283–85, 297–300; Executive Committee of, 146–47, 183, 201–2, 280, 285, 390, 463; founding of, 109–10, 114, 116–24, 152; immigration lobbying, 129–34, 224, 226, 235; New York Kehillah, 147; search for action agenda, 138–40, 183–84

American Jewish Congress, 108, 120, 136, 152, 258–59, 264, 305, 339, 345–46, 349, 359–60, 365–66, 399, 408, 447, 463, 504–5, 528, 531; historical context of, 265–68; establishment controversy, 273–81, 283–88, 297–300, 506, 523

American Jewish Historical Society, 102

American Jewish Relief Committee. *See* Joint Distribution Committee

American Jewry 250th anniversary. *See* Marshall, Louis

American Relief Administration. *See* Hoover, Herbert
American Socialist, 318, 320
American Society for Jewish Farm Settlements in Russia, 508
Ames, James B., 14
Amherst College, 90
Anglo-Jewish Association. *See* Joint Foreign Committee
Anthony, Alfred W., 471
Anti-Defamation League, 257
Arbeter Ring (Workmen's Circle), 266
Ashel, Elias, 418
Associated Press, 213
Atlit. *See* Aaronsohn, Aaron
Auerbach, Berthold, 408
Auerbach, Jerold, 268
Axton, NY, 433–35

Babel Proclamation. *See* Marshall, Louis
Baker, Newton, 328
Bakhmetev, Boris, 219
Baldwin, Neil, 399
Baldwin, William, 84
Balfour Declaration, 274, 294, 306, 324, 338–42, 354, 510
Baron de Hirsch Fund, 38
Barondess, Joseph, 278, 324, 349, 504
Beard, Charles, 395
Beecher, Henry Ward, 110
Behar, Nissim, 127
Bemis, Edward, 125, 128
Benderly, Samson, 193
Benedict, Leopold, 349
Ben-Gurion, David, 274, 305, 340, 509, 514–15, 523
Bennett, William, 323
Ben-Zvi, Yitzhak, 274
Berlin (Bar-Ilan), Meir, 345, 369
Bernstein, Herman, 142, 208, 301, 308, 324, 391–92, 399
Bettman, Bernhard, 200, 202
Bialik, Haim Nahman, 87, 511
Bijur, Nathan, 84, 131–32, 160–61, 219
Billikopf, Jacob, 263, 265, 357, 390, 445, 447–48, 479, 533
Billikopf, Ruth Marshall (daughter of LM), 33, 290, 292, 327, 350, 357, 421, 447–48, 478
Bingham, Theodore A., 71; apology to Jews, 147; *North American Review* article about Jewish criminality, 145–46
Blaine, James, 145
Blaustein, David, 37–38, 41–42, 50, 62, 103–4
Blaustein, Jacob, 340, 514–15
Blaustein, Louis, 340
Bloomfield, Meyer, 187, 189
Blumenthal, George, 227, 311, 418
Blumenthal, Joseph, 43
B'nai B'rith, 36, 109, 114–16, 121, 128, 135, 138, 200, 202, 219, 223, 253, 262, 270, 300, 387
Board of Delegates on Civil and Religious Rights. *See* Union of American Hebrew Congregations
Borah, William, 371, 376–77, 427, 486
Boyle, Kevin, 484
Bradley, Richard M., 129
Brandeis, Louis, xiv, 5, 12, 14, 81, 158, 177, 207, 261–62, 268, 294, 301, 306, 338, 343–44, 381, 457, 509, 511, 513, 515–16, 519; American Jewish Congress controversy, 119–20, 258–59, 283–88, 297–300; cloakmakers strike and Protocol of Peace, 187–89, 192; compared to LM, 97–100, 188, 286, 299
Brennglass, Berel, 528–29
Brewer, David, 27, 162, 172
Brisbane, Albert, 170, 172
Brisbane, Arthur, 163, 233, 322, 400–401; biography, 170–71; and Henry Ford, 171; Lakewood controversy, 164, 167, 172–75
Britton, Nathaniel L., 405
Brooks, James Byron, 17–18
Brown, David, 263, 390, 477, 506, 509, 511, 517
Brown, Elon, 421
Brown University, 37

Bryan, William Jennings, 110, 153, 171, 229–30, 259
Brylawski, Fulton, 225, 236
Bublick, Gedalye, 265
Bucans, Max, 60, 62, 67
Buchanan v. Warley, 484–86
Buffalo News, 238
Bund, 87, 94–95, 297, 309, 510
Burleson, A. S., 319–20
Burnett, John, 225–26, 234, 269, 296
Butler, Nicholas Murray, 155, 466

Cahan, Abraham, 66, 109, 317–20, 323–25, 332–35, 448; Jacob Joseph funeral riot, 84
Cambell, John, 521–22
Cameron, William J., 387
Cannon, Joseph, 128–30, 134
Cardozo, Benjamin, 162, 534
Carnegie, Andrew, 65, 90, 127, 270
Carnegie Hall, 101–4, 220, 251, 287, 342–43, 368, 371, 375–76
Central Committee for Relief of Jews Suffering Through the War. *See* Joint Distribution Committee
Central Conference of American Rabbis, 114, 467
Central Jewish Institute, 477
Chaffee, Zechariah, 373
Chamberlain, Houston Stewart, 267, 274
Chamberlain, Joseph, 208
Charles River Bridge v. Warren Bridge, 19, 99
Chicago Tribune, 398
Cincinnati Times-Star, 144–45, 196
City College of New York, 34, 143–44, 302–3
City of Richmond v. Deans. See Marshall, Louis
Civil War, 4, 9, 12, 17, 202, 235, 242, 316, 375
Clark, Champ, 208
Clark, Herb, 212, 419, 431
Clemenceau, George, 359, 361
Cleveland, Frances, 165
Cleveland, Grover, 104, 125, 129, 145, 165, 224
Cloakmakers strike, 98, 186–92, 216, 347, 373, 428, 523; Protocol of Peace, 188–92, 233, 524
Cobb, James, 485–87
Cohen, Ephraim, 260
Cohen, Julius Henry, 187, 189, 192
Cohen, Morris Raphael, 34–35
Cohen, Naomi, 136–37, 141, 197–98, 211, 220, 512
Cohen, Richard, 440
Cohn, Norman, 392
Collier, John, 489
Collier's, 389
Columbia Law School, 10–15
Columbia University, 41, 46, 53–54, 91, 155, 177, 214, 290, 296, 465–66, 489
Colvin, Verplanck, 422
Committee for the Settlement of Jewish Laborers on the Land, 492–93, 501
Committee of Jewish Delegations, 349, 353–58, 360, 364–65, 481
Commons, John, 126
Comnas, Albert, 527
Congregation Rodeph Shalom, 104, 112
Conley, Jim, 256, 270
Conservative Judaism, 40, 43, 45, 47, 49–51, 58, 63, 137, 212
Constitutional Democratic Party (Kadet), 308, 495
Coolidge, Calvin, 414, 451, 453–54, 469, 490
Cornell, Robert C., 85
Cornell University, 27, 433–35, 437, 476
Corrigan and Curtis v. Buckley. See Marshall, Louis
Coulter, William L., 418, 421
Creelman, James, 208
Cresson, Warder, 22
Crimea. *See* Jewish farm colonies in Soviet Union; Marshall, Louis
Cronkhite, Alexander Pennington, 531–32
Crowder, Enoch, 327

Culberson, Charles Allen, 204
Cullen, Edgar Montgomery, 316
Cullinan, J. S., 463
Curley, Michael, 465
Cutler, Harry, 219, 226, 349
Czolgosz, Leon, 172

Dalin, David, 232
Danbury, CT, 21
Dannenbaum, Henry, 514
Darrow, Clarence, 395, 474, 484, 486
Dartiguenave, Philippe, 372
Davar, 522
David, Earl, 399
Davidson, Thomas, 33–35
Dawidowicz, Lucy, 60, 63, 313, 317, 333
Day, John, 437
Dearborn Independent. See Ford, Henry
de Graffenreid, Leo, 149
De Haas, Jacob, 68, 349, 505
Dekel-Chen, Jonathan, 491
Democratic Party, 132, 141–42, 196, 218, 221, 229, 290, 301, 383, 409, 412, 469, 488, 527, 529–31; and Tammany Hall, 171, 226, 240
de Rothschild, Edmond, 178
de Rothschild, James, 306
de Rothschild, Lionel, 341–42
Des Moines Capital, 332
Dewey, Annie, 90
Dewey, John, 344
Dewey, Melvil, 57, 89, 142, 147, 485; biography, 90; dispute with LM's group, 92–97; Lake Placid Club, 90–92, 417
Dickens, Charles, 423, 425, 438–39
Dickstein, Samuel, 454
Die Warheit, 232, 505
Dillingham, William, 124, 131, 134, 225, 234, 242–43, 297
Dillingham Commission. *See* Nativism
Diner, Hasia, 43, 482
Disraeli, Benjamin, 182
Dix, John, 435
Dluski, Casimir, 352–53
Dmowski, Roman, 346, 352–53, 364, 366
Domestic and Foreign Missionary Society, 465
Douglas, Charles Noel, 324
Douglas, Frederick, 5
Dowling, Austin, 465
Drachman, Bernard, 93
Draper, Theodore, 321
Durant, William West, 418
Dwight, Theodore William, 11–15; Dwight method, 11–14; law and philanthropy, 15; political outlook, 15

Edgerton, Charles, 126
Edison, Thomas, 396
Educational Alliance, 36, 41, 50–51, 53, 58, 60, 62–63, 68, 70, 74, 85, 110, 127, 137, 143, 176, 227–29, 314–15, 349, 366; ideological background, 33–35; moral culture committee, 38–40, 60, 91; organizational background, 37–38; People's Synagogue, 40
Einstein, Albert, 408
Eliot, Charles, 14
Elsner, Henry, 20, 289
Emerson, Ralph Waldo, 416–17
Enelow, Hyman G., 337
Engel v. O'Malley. See Marshall, Louis
Eretz Israel. *See* Palestine
Erie Canal, 5, 10
Ethical Culture Society, 42; Ethical Culture School 409, 426

Federal Council of the Churches of Christ in America, 471
Federation of American Zionists. *See* Zionism/Zionists
Federation of Churches of Christ in America, 395
Fernow, Bernhard, 433–34
Ferris, Woodbridge Nathan, 411
Filderman, Wilhelm, 370
Filene, Lincoln, 187, 189

Fink, Carole, 353, 358–61, 364–65
Firestone, Harvey, 396
Fischel, Harry, 261
Fischer, Louis, 501, 504, 513
Fisher, Harry, 517
Ford, Edsel, 387
Ford, Henry, xi, 90–91, 147, 171, 203, 371, 381, 383, 452, 460, 468, 472–73, 481, 493, 508; apology to Jews, 170, 399–401, 470, 514, 520–21, 532; biography, 386; *Dearborn Independent* anti-Semitism, 142, 273, 325, 385–96, 398, 400–401, 458, 462, 467, 470, 482, 492, 532; and Harding, 396–97; Sapiro suit, 397–99
Fort, John Franklin, 166–67
Fox, George, 507–8
Fox, John, 132
Fox, William, 433
Frank, Julius, 531
Frank, Leo, 236, 255–57, 268–71, 301, 403, 482, 532
Frank Case. *See* Marshall, Louis
Frankel, Jonathan, 88, 258, 277, 298, 313
Frankel, Lee, 500, 518, 520–21
Frankfurter, Felix, 285, 359–61, 366, 373
Franklin, Leo, 386–87, 467
Frank v. Magnum, 405, 483
Freiberg, J. Walter, 200
Fremont, John, 5
Frick v. Webb. See Marshall, Louis
Friedenwald, Harry, 257, 286
Friedenwald, Herbert, 140, 208, 213, 224–25, 234
Friedlander, Israel, 184, 194
Friedman, Saul, 531
Frost, Robert, 395
Fry, Henry, 462
Funk, Isaac K., 93–95
Furth, Jacob, 200

Gallagher, William, 398
Gallatin, Francis, 413
Gallinger, Jacob Harold, 302–3
George, Henry, 65, 170–71
Gibson, Hugh, 363
Ginzberg, Louis, 467
Glynn, Martin, 239, 269
Goedsche, Herman, 391
Goldfarb, Max, 297–98
Goldfogle, Henry, 140, 204, 208, 219
Goldman, Emma, 460
Goldstein, Eric, 182
Goldstein, Judith, 132
Gompers, Samuel, 38, 126–27, 319
Gordin, Jacob, 35, 62
Goren, Arthur, 101, 151
Gottheil, Richard, 24, 32, 274, 296, 316
Gottlieb, Gittel, 456
Grace, John, 373
Gray, Elbert, 270
Griffiths, Barbara, 526–29
Gruenbaum, Yitzhak, 499, 521
Guggenheim, Benjamin, 227
Guggenheim, Daniel, 44, 92, 132, 149–50, 178, 223, 270, 418
Guggenheim, Edwin, 326
Guggenheim, Isaac, 74
Guggenheim, Simon, 44, 199, 209
Guggenheimer, Nathaniel, 15
Guggenheimer, Randolph, 15, 24
Guggenheimer, Untermyer: and Marshall, 16, 25–26, 158, 169–70, 174–75, 222, 227
Guthrie, William D., 99, 351, 452, 461, 534

Haas, Herbert, 256
Haiti, 371–77
Hall, Prescott, 126
Hamilton College, 13
Hammond, John Hays, 219
Hapgood, Hutchins, 68
Harding, Warren, 372–74, 396–97, 414, 449–50, 453, 532
Harding, William L., 330–32
Harper's Weekly, 296–97
Harrison, Benjamin, 19
Harrison, Byron P., 485
Harvard Law School, 12, 14, 357

Harvard University, 37, 126, 426, 430
Hawes, W. Gilbert, 527–31
Hayes, George E. C., 486
Hays, Arthur Garfield, 484, 486
Haywood, William (Big Bill), 321
Hearst, William R., 171, 238
Hebrew Immigrant Aid Society (HIAS), 223, 287
Hebrew Standard, 182
Hebrew Union College (HUC), 40, 42, 45–46, 48–49, 55, 112, 398, 419–20
Hebrew University of Jerusalem, 310, 504
Hedges, Job E., 231, 233
Henry Street Settlement. *See* Wald, Lillian
Henshaw, Henry Wetherbee, 404
Herrick, Cady, 239
Herzl, Theodor, 497
Herzog, Paul, 61, 69
Heslipwell, Jesse, 486
Hess, Alfred, 166
Hewitt, Abraham, 477
Hexter, Maurice, 520
Higham, John, 125, 129, 270
Hilfsverein der deutschen Juden, 260
Hillquit, Morris, 186, 320–25, 338
Hirsch, Emil, 120–21
Hollander, Max, 454
Holly, William, 373
Holmes, Oliver Wendell, 14, 207, 301; judicial restraint outlook and LM, 161, 403–5, 475, 483, 487–88
Hoover, Herbert, 353, 357, 414, 449, 491, 529
Hornaday, William T., 405
Horowitz, Louis, 142
Houghton, Harris Ayres, 383–84
Hourwich, Isaac A., 214, 225, 243, 278–79, 347
House, Edward M., 357
Howard, University, 485
Hudson, Manley, 357
Hughes, Charles Evans, 144, 301–2, 316, 326–27, 362, 374–77, 384, 435, 450, 461, 479–81, 508, 534; banking regulation, 158–59; Supreme Court nomination, 162, 173–74, 206
Hylan, John, 323–25

Immigration, xi, 81, 101, 113–16, 124, 223–27, 242–44, 448–57; Asian debates and restrictions, 128, 133–34, 198, 224, 452, 457–59, 469; literacy test restrictions, 125–32, 223–26, 234–36, 242, 255, 268–70, 296, 302–4
Immigration Restriction League. *See* Nativism
Industrial Removal Office, 115, 128
Ingersoll, Robert, 18
Inness, George, 446
International Ladies' Garment Workers Union. *See* Cloakmakers strike
Isaacs, Myer, 23
Ives v. South Buffalo Railway Company. See Marshall, Louis

Jabotinsky, Vladimir, 274, 313
Jackson-Vanick amendment, 221
Jacobs, Joseph, 64–65, 68
Jacobson, Nathan, 9
Jenney, Brooks, Ruger, and Marshall (law firm), 9, 472
Jenney, William, 17–18
Jerusalem, 22–23
Jewish Agency for Palestine, 24, 48, 99, 181, 285, 294, 342–43, 368, 420, 428–29, 445, 481, 497–500, 502–16, 522–23, 526, 533
Jewish Board of Deputies. *See* Joint Foreign Committee
Jewish Chronicle, 273–74
Jewish Colonization Association, 178, 492
Jewish Congress Organization Committee. *See* American Jewish Congress
Jewish Daily Forward, 59–60, 66–67, 84, 104, 109, 187, 189, 266, 317–19, 322–26, 333–34, 444, 446–47, 505

Jewish Daily News, 148
Jewish Exponent, 44
Jewish farm colonies in Soviet Union, 490; American Jewish support and opposition, 501–14; background and rationale, 490–97
Jewish Gazette, 86
Jewish Messenger, 48
Jewish National Fund, 180
Jewish Protectory (Hawthorne School), 70–75, 85, 98, 137, 148, 281, 471
Jewish Socialist Federation, 266
Jewish Telegraphic Agency, 528
Jewish Theological Seminary (JTS), xii, 7–8, 33, 38, 40, 58, 60, 63, 71, 85, 98, 135–36, 151, 267, 366, 408, 420, 431, 438, 467, 471, 481; early development after reorganization, 55–57; fund-raising for, 53–54; recruitment of Schechter, 44–45, 49–50, 54–55; reorganization, 42–44, 46–49, 51–53; Zionism disputes, 54–55
Jewish Tribune, 11
Jewish Welfare Board, 358
Jewish World, 35, 41–42, 53, 57, 62, 71, 85, 89, 95, 110, 119, 137, 366; class divisions, 66–68; establishment, 60–61; finances, 65, 69–70; functions and significance, 63–64, 68–69; political slant, 64–65, 70; Yiddish press, 59–60; Zionism, 68
Jewish World Relief Conference, 495–96
Jezreel Valley, 516
Johns Hopkins University, 442
Johnson, Hiram, 398
Johnson, James Weldon, 485, 534
Joint Distribution Committee (JDC), xii, 301, 305, 358, 365, 370, 385, 481, 531; Agro-Joint and Jewish farm colonies in Soviet Union, 241, 490, 491–98, 501–11, 514; establishment of, 262–65, 478
Joint Foreign Committee, 349, 353, 360
Joint Palestine Survey Commission, 516–22
Jordan, David Starr, 126, 387
Joselit, Jenna Weissman, 71, 75
Joseph, Jacob, 41, 63–64; biography, 82; funeral riot, 82–86, 94, 160, 175, 534

Kahn, Bernard, 501–2
Kallen, Horace, 264
Kamaiky, Leon, 261
Katz, Mark, 146
Katznelson, Berl, 522–23
Kaufman, Eugene, 477
Kellog, Frank, 507–8
Kellor, Frances, 144, 159, 216
Kennan, George, 495
Keren Hayesod, 500, 506
Kerensky, Alexander, 309, 384
Kisch, F. H., 520
Kishinev pogrom, 36, 66, 82, 86–89, 93–94, 105–6, 112, 117, 141, 149, 254, 263
Knollenberg, Fred, 487
Knollwood, 50, 55, 90, 144–45, 166, 186, 212, 215, 223, 249, 290, 292, 301, 317, 399, 406, 408–9, 411, 416–24, 431, 438–39, 444, 470, 520
Knopf, Sigard Adolphus, 164
Knox, Philander, 197–98, 204, 219–20
Koenig, Samuel, 176
Kohler, Kaufmann, 55, 102
Kohler, Max, 102–3, 115, 223–24, 240, 308, 449, 456
Kohut, Alexander, 24
Komzet. *See* Committee for the Settlement of Jewish Laborers on the Land
Konti, Isidore, 103
Koufax, Sandy, xiv
Kraus, Adolf, 109, 114–18, 121, 200, 253, 270, 300, 387
Kuhn, Loeb and Company, 19
Ku Klux Klan, 382, 451–52, 462–66, 471–73, 483

La Follette, Robert, 234
LaGuardia, Fiorella H., 451
Lake Placid, 89–91, 94

Lakewood preventorium, 164–70, 172, 174–75
Lamar, William, 333–34
Landman, Isaac, 348–49, 390, 392
Langdell, Christopher Columbus, 14
Lansing, Robert, 308, 340–41, 348
Lasker, Albert D., 256, 270
Lauterbach, Edward, 91, 96, 132
Lazaron, Morris, 450
League for the Attainment of Equal Rights for the Jewish People in Russia, 265
League of Nations, 251, 302, 346, 348, 351–53, 355, 359, 361–63, 369, 403, 449, 474–75, 478
Lederhendler, Eli, 67
Leeser, Isaac, 6, 22
Legal education
Lehman, Eugene, 56–58
Lehman, Herbert, 370, 477, 515
Lehman, Irving, 189, 256, 291, 477, 514–15
Leipziger, Henry, 38, 91, 93
Lennon, John B., 187
Leslie's Weekly, 323
Levi, Leo N., 36, 115
Levinson, Salmon O., 272–73
Levinthal, Bernhard L., 349
Levy, Aaron, 463
Levy, Asser, 105–7, 112, 314, 525
Levy, Sylvan, 361
Lewi, Isidor, 58, 61
Lewinson, Benno, 143
Lewisohn, Adolph, 47, 60, 74, 92, 138, 178
Lewisohn, Leonard, 44, 47
Liebold, Ernest G., 387
Lipsky, Louis, 284, 299, 305, 500, 505, 524
Litchfield, CT, 13
Littauer, Lucius, 130
Lloyd George, David, 359, 361
Lodge, Henry Cabot, 125–26, 134, 181–82, 224–25, 234
Loeb, Morris, 181, 214
London, Meyer, 186–87, 189, 192, 262, 270, 331, 339
London Spectator, 388
London Times, 529
Low, Seth, 41–42, 64–65, 72–73, 82, 84–85, 155, 160
Lowell, Abbott Lawrence, 126
Lowenstein, Bernard, 154
Lueger, Karl, 267
Luria v. United States. See Marshall, Louis
Lurton, Horace, 173
Lusitania, 280
Lutostansky, Hippolytus, 391
Lynchburg, VA, 15–16

Maccabaean, 109, 146
Mack, Julian, 119, 138, 181–82, 185, 194–95, 199, 218, 262, 299–300, 323, 325, 338, 342–45, 349, 351–52, 362, 367, 513
Magnes, Beatrice Lowenstein, 30, 55, 143, 215, 228, 305, 316, 431, 478
Magnes, Judah, 30, 55, 88, 117–18, 121, 138, 143, 146–47, 183, 193–94, 213, 228, 260, 264–65, 282–83, 290, 305, 431, 447, 479, 503–4, 510, 512–13, 522, 533–34; American Jewish Congress controversy, 276–80, 285, 298–300; biography, 112; melting pot controversy, 149–51; New York Kehillah, 147–48, 153; Russian Jewish defense, 112–13, 116; World War I pacifism, 277, 300, 310, 314–17, 321, 323, 331–34
Marcus, Joseph, 189
Marks, Marcus, 109, 144, 165–66, 169, 172, 175
Marshall, Benjamin (brother of LM), 7, 216–17, 421
Marshall, Florence Lowenstein (wife of LM), 16, 25, 30–33, 186, 209, 222, 227, 249, 281, 287, 289–94, 300, 350, 363, 402, 408, 421, 478
Marshall, George (son of LM), 33, 212, 290, 292–93, 388–89, 414, 422, 426, 429, 431, 445, 478–79, 489
Marshall, Jacob (father of LM), 5–7, 19, 131, 185, 209, 216–17, 222, 440, 472–73

Marshall, James (son of LM), 33, 290, 293–94, 308, 310, 335–37, 341, 350–51, 387, 421–22, 428, 444–45, 478, 493, 519, 533–34

Marshall, Louis: Aaronsohn and Atlit station, 177–81, 186, 306–7; abrogation of 1832 treaty with Russia, 133, 139–42, 153, 184, 193–205; 208–9, 212–13, 215–21, 231, 273, 307, 364; African American affairs, xii, 371, 382, 403, 412, 473, 482–89; AJC founding, xii, 109–24; American Jewish Congress controversy, 152, 258, 267–68, 273–81, 283–88, 294, 297–300, 305–6; American Jewry 250th anniversary, 100–107, 142; anti-Semitism in US, 84, 94–95, 272–73, 317, 326, 471–73; attitude toward Soviet Union, 494–96, 501; Babel Proclamation, 330–32; bank regulation and Foley bill, 158–61, 186; birth, 4–6; Catholic and Jewish relations, 64, 157, 269, 326, 462, 464–66; *City of Richmond v. Deans,* 486–87; class relations and socialism, 66–68, 188, 207–8, 229–30, 232–33; cloakmakers strike and Protocol of Peace, 188–92, 233, 524; *Corrigan and Curtis v. Buckley,* 485–86; death of, 533–34; democratization of American Jewish organizations, 118–24, 152–54, 475, 511–12, 523, 525; Dewey dispute, 90–97, 485; early education and youth, 9–10; Educational Alliance, 33–41; *Engel v. O'Malley,* 159–61; environmental affairs, xii, 282, 402–42, 473, 482; family roots in Europe, 7–9; Ford's anti-Semitism, 383, 385–401; Frank (Leo) case, 236, 255–57, 268–71, 301, 403, 427; *Frick v. Webb,* 458–59; fund-raising, 47, 53–54, 74, 138, 141, 178–80, 211, 254, 257, 259–65, 471, 508, 517–18; ghetto semantics and realities, 68–69, 85, 155, 476; on Germany's history and future, 336–38, 472; Haiti and national rights, 371–77, 403, 480–81, 483; historical status of, xiv, 71–73, 81, 240–41, 294, 304, 468–70, 477–78, 482–83, 488–89, 499; immigration activism, 101–2, 105–6, 113–16, 127, 129–34, 144, 153–54, 156–57, 181–83, 213–15, 223–27, 234–37, 240–45, 255, 301–4, 448–59, 482; *Ives v. South Buffalo Railway Company,* 205, 207–8, 232–33; Jewish affairs in armed forces, 26–27; Jewish criminality, 71–72; Jewish farm colonies in Soviet Union, 492–97, 501–4; Jewish Protectory, 71–75; Jewish Theological Seminary, xii, 42–59, 211–12, 408, 471; *Jewish World,* 59–70; 117; Jacob Joseph funeral riot, 82–86; Judaism, unity, and streams, 47–51; Kishinev pogrom, 88–89; Lakewood preventorium dealings, 169–70; law apprenticeship, 10; law career, 17–21, 25–26, 29–30, 97–100, 222–23, 472; law school, 10–15; *Luria v. United States,* 236–37; and Judah Magnes, 112–13, 116–17, 121, 146–47, 149, 151–53, 155, 193–94, 278–79, 282, 298–300, 310, 314–17, 331–33; marriage to Florence Lowenstein, 30–33; Massena affair, 528–32; melting pot debates, 143–44, 149–51, 452, 465–66, 476; *Metropolitan Street Railway Company v. New York Board of Tax Commissioners,* 99–100; *Missouri v. Holland,* 402–5, 441; Native American affairs, xii, 371, 382, 403, 412, 473, 489; New York Kehillah, 147–48, 151–55, 182–83, 476; New York 1912 gubernatorial elections, 228–34; New York 1917 mayoral race, 320–25, 338; *Nixon v. Herndon,* 487–88; overseas Jewish minority rights, 47–48, 250–51, 294, 302, 342, 344, 346–71, 384–85, 403, 474, 478, 503; physical appearance and daily habits, 444–46; *Pierce v. Society of Sisters,* 464–66; Poland and Polish Jewry, 343–46, 351–52, 357–58, 362–65, 376; political affiliation and Republican Party, 15, 64–66, 70, 72, 230–32, 251, 301, 320, 359, 361, 375–76, 383, 403, 412, 414, 429, 449, 478–82, 531; *Porterfield v. Webb,* 457–58; real estate dealings, 19–21;

Marshall, Louis (*cont.*)
religious observance level of, 47, 448; Russian revolutions, 307–9; and Solomon Schechter, 45, 50, 54–55; and Jacob Schiff, 46–47, 155–56, 203, 209–12, 230, 250; Sampson Simson case, 21–24; Sulzer impeachment, 237–40; Supreme Court candidacy, 135, 161–64, 172–76, 183, 480; Tammany Hall, 41–42; *Titanic*, 227–28; *Tuton v. United States*, 457; *Tyroler v. Warden of City Prison of New York*, 29–30; *Webb v. O'Brien*, 458; and Stephen Wise, 110–12; World War I draft issues, 312–14, 316–17, 325–29, 387; World War I and global politics, 249, 252–55, 274; Yiddish press, 59–60, 252–53, 274, 315–19, 322–25, 332–35, 349; and Israel Zangwill, 150–51; Zionism, 55, 68, 177–81, 257–61, 285–88, 306–7, 338–43, 496, 498–500, 502–26
Marshall, Robert (Bob, son of LM), xii, 33, 212, 290, 292–93, 336, 370, 388–89, 406, 409, 412–15, 422–32, 441, 469–70, 474, 478, 480–81, 511; and wilderness doctrine, 440–43, 532
Marshall, Zilli Strauss (mother of LM), 5–7, 19, 183, 185–86, 209, 455
Martin, Homer, 446
Marx, David, 255
Masliansky, Zvi Hirsch, 38, 40–41; *Jewish World*, 60–62, 66, 68, 110
Massena, NY, 526–32
Masses, 318
Mayfield, Earle Bradford, 463
McAtee, Waldo Lee, 405
McCann, Harry, 527–29
McClellan, George, 73, 147, 155
McClure, David, 409
McCormick, Medill, 373
McDonald, James G., 374
McKinley, William, 26, 172
Mead, Elwood, 520
Medoff, Rafael, 401
Meir, August, 484
Meir of Rothenburg, 7–8
Mendelsohn, Ezra, 365
Metropolitan Street Railway Company v. New York Board of Tax Commissioners. See Marshall, Louis
Meyer, Edgar, 227
Meyer, Eugene, 227, 338
Meyer, Julius, 99–100
Miller, David Hunter, 357, 362, 365
Milyukov, Pavel, 308, 495
Missoula, MT, 427
Missouri v. Holland. See Marshall, Louis
Mitchel, John Purroy, 240, 323–25
Mond, Alfred, 518–19, 521–22
Montefiore, Moses, 22
Moore, Deborah Dash, 383
Moore v. Dempsey, 483
Morgan, J. P., 65, 222
Morgen Journal, 59, 70, 233
Morgenthau, Henry, 259, 261, 301, 322, 324, 348, 363, 447
Morias, Henry, 53
Morias, Sabato, 42–44, 53
Moskowitz, Belle, 530
Moskowitz, Henry, 493
Motzkin, Leo, 88, 353–54
Mount Sinai Hospital, 22, 46, 311, 335, 337, 428
Mulry, Thomas M., 64, 84, 175
Murphy, Charles, 234, 237

Nagel, Charles, 223, 235
Nathan, Max, 166–69, 223, 418
Nation, 429
National Association for the Advancement of Colored People (NAACP), xii, 144, 294, 303, 377, 469, 483–88
National Catholic Welfare Conference, 465
National Liberal Immigration League, 126–27
National Workmen's Committee on Jewish Rights in the Belligerent Lands, 266, 288, 297–98
Nativism, 88, 101, 115–16, 125–29, 134–35, 146, 157, 176, 216, 224, 234, 236–37,

240–42, 269, 297, 301–4, 308, 326, 448–52, 457, 469; Dillingham Commission, 134, 144, 153–54, 156, 181–83, 213–14, 242, 296; Immigration Restriction League, 126–27, 129
New York Constitutional Conventions, xiii, 26, 272, 281–82, 322, 405, 409–10, 434, 455
New York Evening Journal, 168
New York Herald, 232, 324, 391
New York Kehillah, 71, 155, 182, 193, 275–76, 298, 315, 332–33, 462, 475–76; American Jewish Congress controversy, 275–79; democratic representation and, 152–53; founding of, 147–48, 151
New York State College of Forestry at Syracuse University, xii, 21, 186, 215, 217, 381, 406–7, 410, 423, 426, 429, 432–41
New York Sun, 400, 529
New York Times, 24, 60, 85, 87, 93, 95, 104, 109, 111, 146–47, 149, 151, 155, 158, 160, 167–68, 189, 194, 208, 210, 213, 215, 256, 281, 291, 298–99, 304–5, 309, 311–12, 332, 337, 341, 371, 376, 392, 401, 412, 414–15, 462, 473–74, 532
New York Tribune, 334
New York World, 324, 462, 488
New York University, 91, 94, 242, 455; Board of Regents of New York University, 91–92, 95–97
Nilus, Sergius, 391
Nixon v. Herndon. See Marshall, Louis
North American Relief Society, 21–24
North American Review. See Bingham, Theodore A.
North Pacific Union Conference of Seventh Day Adventists, 465
Northrup, Ansel Judd, 12
Norton, Charles, 195

Ochs, Adolph, 60, 109, 111, 194, 208, 213, 215, 305, 309, 312, 376, 392, 478, 532, 534; bank regulation, 160–61; ghetto as term of use, 69, 85, 155; immigration advocacy, 304
O'Gorman, James, 218–19
Orlando, Vittorio, 359
Orthodox Central Committee. *See* Joint Distribution Committee
Orthodox Judaism, 42–43, 50–51, 139, 212, 261–62, 329, 412, 466–68
Ottinger, Albert, 7
Ottinger, Moses, 53
Outlook, 217–18
Overman, Lee S., 171, 384, 460
Owen, Cunliffe, 215
Owen, Robert, 374, 376
Ozet. *See* Society for the Settlement of Jewish Toilers on the Land

Paderewski, Ignace Jan, 344, 346, 353, 363–64
Page, Carrol S., 131
Palestine: British conquest and Mandate in, xi, 241, 306, 310, 338–43, 344, 354–55, 359, 365–66, 368, 429, 456, 490, 494, 497, 500, 502, 504, 506–7, 509–11, 514–18, 520–21, 523, 526; in Ottoman times, 22–24, 177–81, 259–60, 262, 283–85, 288, 300, 306, 409, 497
Palestine Economic Corporation, 500, 515
Palestine Foundation Fund. *See* Keren Hayesod
Palma, Joseph, 399
Palmer, Mitchell, 236, 461
Palmer raids. *See* Red Scare
Paris Peace Conference, 47–48, 250, 352–61, 448, 480–81
Parker, Alton, 132
Parsons, Herbert, 204
Partridge, John, 84–86
Passover, 19, 30, 86, 193, 209, 308, 358, 448
Peckham, Rufus W., 172
Peddy, George, 463–64
People's Council for Democracy and Peace, 321

People's Relief Committee. *See* Joint Distribution Committee
People v. the Brooklyn Cooperage Company, 434
Peretz, Isaac, 296
Perlman, Nathan, 399, 454
Petach Tikvah, 510
Philipson, David, 254, 298, 342
Phipps, Henry, 165
Pierce, Walter, 464
Pierce v. Society of Sisters. See Marshall, Louis
Pinsk, 358, 362
Pinsky, David, 288
Podhoretz, Norman, 482
Porterfield v. Webb. See Marshall, Louis
Pouren, Jan Janoff, 153
Prohibition, 466–68
Proskauer, Joseph, 340
Protocols of Peace. *See* Cloakmakers strike
Protocols of the Elders of Zion, 142, 367, 383–85, 388, 391–92, 394
Pujo Committee. *See* Untermyer, Samuel
Putnam, Herbert, 96

Rabenold, Elwood, 414
Rachkovsky, Pyotr, 392
Radziwill, Katarina, 392
Raider, Mark, 110, 503
Raines, John, 421
Raynor, Isidor, 224, 226
Red Cross, 253, 309, 311, 330
Red Scare, 171, 319, 325, 384, 394, 459–62, 492
Reed, David, 6, 455, 470
Reed, James, 302–3, 398
Reeve, Tapping, 13
Reform Judaism, 40, 42–43, 45–49, 57, 63, 112, 114–15, 120–21, 137, 149, 179, 182, 193, 199, 202, 212, 228, 254, 290, 315, 342, 387, 398, 420, 431, 468, 534
Reid, Whitelaw, 96
Reilly, John, 204
Republican Party, 5, 15, 42, 72, 144, 171, 173, 226, 230, 251, 281–82, 290, 301, 323, 325, 359, 361, 373, 375–76, 383, 393, 425, 427–28, 430, 449, 478–81, 527, 529, 531; abrogation campaign, 141–42, 153–54, 196, 202, 204, 218, 221; immigration issues, 132, 134; Yiddish press and, 59–60, 64–65, 70
Reznikoff, Charles, 163, 332
Richards, Bernard, 182–83, 185, 265, 287, 324, 454
Richman, Julia, 38
Riis, Jacob, 164–65
Ripley, William, 127–28
Rochester Herald, 238
Rockefeller, John D., 65, 216
Rockhill, William W., 154, 197–99, 201
Rogers, Henry H., 65
Romanian Jewry, 66, 138, 235, 296, 346–47, 355, 367, 370
Roosevelt, Franklin D., 7, 372, 393, 433
Roosevelt, Theodore, 26, 66–67, 89, 94, 102–3, 110, 113, 119, 126, 128–30, 133, 139, 142, 153, 217–18, 226, 229–30, 234–35, 238, 301, 311–12, 428, 445, 495
Root, Elihu, 133–34, 255, 324; abrogation struggle, 139–40, 153, 218–19; and anti-Semitism in America, 272; corporate law, 99
Rosalsky, Otto, 146, 514
Rosen, James, 491–94, 496–97, 501, 508–9, 515
Rosenau, Milton, 519–20
Rosenberg, Abraham, 192
Rosenberg, James, 445, 493–94, 497, 501
Rosenbluth, Robert, 531–32
Rosenfeld, Morris, 251
Rosenstock, Morton, 463
Rosenwald, Julius, 47, 177–78, 180, 211, 263, 307, 319, 346, 385, 400, 420, 471, 477, 508, 511, 517; abrogation campaign, 140–41, 219, 226
Ross, Edward, 126
Rothschild, Walter, 255
Rubinow, Isaac Max, 61
Rudwick, Eliot, 484

Ruger, Wallace, Brooks, and French (law firm), 17–18
Ruger, William, 17
Ruppert, Jacob, 130
Ruppin, Arthur, 260, 505
Russell, Charles Edward, 483
Russian Information Bureau, 495
Rutenberg, Pinchas, 274, 288

Sack, A. J., 495
Sanders, Leon, 223
Sanger, Adolph, 21
Saperstein, Jacob, 59, 70
Sapiro, Aaron, 397–99
Sarasohn, Ezekiel, 69–70
Sargent, Frank, 126
Sarna, Jonathan, 12
Schechter, Solomon, 62, 109, 151, 192, 211, 267, 274, 408, 472; biography, 44–45; recruitment to JTS, 43–44, 46, 49; relationship with LM, 50, 54–55, 155; Zionist attitude, 55–57, 343, 431
Schiff, Jacob, xi, 4, 19, 35–37, 41, 102, 104, 138, 155, 157, 164, 209–12, 215–16, 255, 270, 281, 287, 290, 338, 340, 346, 349, 362, 368, 381, 385, 389–90, 396, 431, 447, 471, 478; abrogation campaign, 136, 153, 183–84, 194–96, 200–203, 218–19, 268; AJC founding, 109, 118, 120; attitude and activity toward czarist Russia, 101, 109, 113, 141, 304, 307–9, 494; cloakmakers strike, 189; Dewey dispute, 92; Galveston project, 115, 128, 150, 223; immigration activism, 131–33, 214, 224; Jewish Protectory, 72–74; Jewish Theological Seminary, 43–49, 51–55, 211–12; *Jewish World,* 60–62, 65, 69; Lakewood preventorium, 165; melting pot controversy, 149–50; New York 1912 gubernatorial elections, 230–33, 238; as non-Zionist, 178–80; Supreme Court nominations and LM, 162, 172–74; World War I politics and disputes, 250, 253–54, 259–61, 263, 275, 279–80, 287–88, 297, 305, 307, 312, 315, 329, 333
Schiff, Mortimer, 275
Schiff, Otto, 255
Schmidt, Hans, 372–73
Schmitz, Eugene, 133
Schurman, Jacob Gould, 433–34
Schweinfurth, Georg, 178
Scientific Monthly, 442–43
Scult, Mel, 51
See, Eugene, 353
Seligman, Edwin, R. A., 177
Seligman, Isaac, 102, 109, 165
Seligman, Joseph, 20, 89, 417
She'arith Israel (synagogue), 22
Shubert, Lee, 327–28
Shubert, Sam, 327–28
Shulkin, Jacob, 527–31
Shulkin, Willie, 527
Siegel, Isaac, 448
Silver, Abba Hillel, 509
Silverman, Joseph, 111, 463
Simmons, Furnifold M., 125, 127
Simons, George S., 384
Simson, Sampson, 21–23; Simson case, 21–25, 98
Sinclair, Upton, 397
Singer, Isidore, 56, 93–95
Singer, Jacob, 223
Slaton, John, 257, 269–70
Slemp, C. B., 453
Smith, Al, 370, 406, 411–12, 529–30
Smith, Charles, 303
Smith, Ellison, 234, 269
Smith, Goldwin, 27
Smith, Nathaniel, 10
Smolar, Boris, 528
Society for the Settlement of Jewish Toilers on the Land, 505
Society of Concord. *See* Temple of Concord
Sokolow, Nahum, 353
Spargo, John, 319, 392–93, 395
Spencer, Nelson, 373
Spitzer, Eliot, 239
Stanford University, 126, 387

Stein, Abram, 418
Stein, Leonard, 502, 518, 520
Stein, Philip, 200
Stern, Horace, 202–3, 445, 500, 533
Stern, Irma, 149
Stern, Louis, 149
Stillman, William James, 417
Stolz, Benjamin (cousin of LM), 9, 20, 185, 221, 310, 494
Stolz, David (uncle of LM), 9
Stolz, Jacob (uncle of LM), 9
Stolz, Joseph (cousin of LM), 9, 46, 49, 113–14, 138, 221, 229
Stone, Elihu, 507
Storey, Moorfield, 303, 373, 377, 483–84, 486, 488
Straus, Ida, 227–28
Straus, Isaac, 281
Straus, Isidor, 37–38, 44, 74, 92, 94, 227–29
Straus, Jesse, 37
Straus, Julius, 280
Straus, Nathan, 104, 228, 259, 284, 305, 390–91, 447, 504, 534; Lakewood preventorium controversy, 164–70, 172, 175
Straus, Oscar, 104, 129, 227, 238, 280, 298, 313, 322, 324, 346, 348, 352–53, 449; abrogation campaign, 145, 194, 217–18; AJC founding, 109, 119–20, 122; immigration activism, 154; New York 1912 gubernatorial elections, 228–29, 231–33
Straus, Sarah, 352–53
Strauss, Lewis, 353, 357
Stuyvesant, Peter, 105, 314
Sulzberger, Cyrus, 119–20, 223, 226, 477
Sulzberger, Mayer, 24, 43–44, 46–47, 54, 121, 123, 131, 133, 145, 172–74, 194, 200, 202, 218–19, 223, 337, 347, 350
Sulzer, William, 204–5, 220, 436–37; impeachment, 237–40; New York 1912 gubernatorial elections, 229, 231–34
Sumner, Charles, 377, 483
Sun, 94–95, 139
Supreme Court, US, xi, 17, 81, 98–99, 158, 160–64, 172–76, 183, 186, 223, 234, 240, 256, 258, 286–87, 298–99, 301, 402–4, 456–58, 465–66, 480, 483–85, 487
Sweet, Ossian, 484, 486
Sweet, Thaddeus, 304
Syracuse, xi, 3–7, 9, 17–21, 38, 90, 185, 209, 217, 242, 253, 271, 327–28, 335, 407, 412, 414, 427, 442, 444, 447–48, 455, 464, 471–72, 474, 478–79, 526, 528; growth of, 5; Jewish community of, 5
Syracuse Daily Courier, 9
Syracuse Daily Standard, 6
Syracuse Journal, 461
Syracuse Post Standard, 18
Syracuse University, 9, 207, 217, 433, 435–37, 442; College of Law, 17; founding of, 5
Syracuse Water Company v. City of Syracuse, 19
Syrkin, Nahman, 265, 274, 347, 349
Szajkowski, Zosa, 263, 265
Szold, Henrietta, 186
Szold, Robert, 516

Taft, Charles, 144–45
Taft, William Howard, 129, 153, 226, 229–30, 234–35, 395, 484; abrogation struggle, 136, 145, 154, 183, 194–96, 198–203, 216, 219–20; Supreme Court nominations and LM, 162, 164, 173–76
Tageblatt, 59, 70, 104, 146, 278
Talley, Alfred J., 473
Tammany Hall, 15, 25, 41–42, 64–65, 171, 204, 231–32, 281–82, 284, 323, 325, 505; Jacob Joseph funeral riot, 82; and Sulzer impeachment, 234, 237–40, 436–37
Taney, Roger, 19
Tarbell, Ida, 391, 395
Tel Aviv, 520
Temple Emanu-El, 30, 32, 40, 49, 55, 110–13, 147, 261, 276, 290, 298, 337, 390, 408, 431, 503–4; Marshall funeral, 533–34; melting pot controversy, 149, 151, 193

Temple of Concord, 5–7, 9, 209
Tennenbaum, Joseph, 356
Thompson, E. P., 366
Thompson, L. L., 532
Titanic, 217–18
Titulesco, Nicolas, 370
Touro, Judah, 22
Troen, Ilan, 520
Trotsky, Leon, 318, 334, 460
Trudeau, Edward L., 166, 416
Tuton v. United States. See Marshall, Louis
Tyroler v. Warden of City Prison of New York. See Marshall, Louis

Ukraine. *See* Jewish farm colonies in Soviet Union; Marshall, Louis
Ullman, Isaac, 173, 194, 219, 221
Union of American Hebrew Congregations, 115, 120, 138, 193–95, 199, 200, 202; Board of Delegates on Civil and Religious Rights, 115, 135, 211, 223
Union of Orthodox Rabbis, 466
United Hebrew Trades, 266
United Palestine Appeal, 514, 517
United States v. McCullagh, 404
United States v. Shauver, 404–5
University of Michigan, 491
University of Missouri, 447
Untermyer, Eugene, 457
Untermyer, Isidor, 15
Untermyer, Samuel, 16, 29, 162, 186, 287, 312, 324, 412, 477, 500; birth and origins, 15; Lakewood preventorium controversy, 167–70, 173–74; Pujo Committee, 98, 158, 222; relations with LM, 25–26, 163, 169–70, 222–23
Ussischkin, Menachem, 516

Vanderbilt, Alfred, 418
Van Devanter, Willis, 237
Vann, Irving, 239
Villard, Oswald Garrison, 213
Vinaver, Maxim, 265, 388, 395

Wainwright, J. Mayhew, 206
Wald, Lillian, 144, 156, 159, 161, 164, 374
Waldman, Morris, 264
Walker, James, 446
Warburg, Felix, 20, 60–61, 193, 477–78, 496–97, 504, 508, 511, 514–15, 518, 521
Warburg, Paul, 463
Ward, Robert DeCourcy, 126, 133
Washington, Booker T., 211
Watson, Tom, 268–69
Webb v. O'Brien. See Marshall, Louis
Weinman, Moses, 227
Weizmann, Chaim, 259, 274, 285, 299, 342–43, 352, 383, 430, 499–502, 505–6, 509–24, 533
Weizmann, Shmuel, 505
Welliver, Judson, 396
Werner, William, 208
Wertheim, Maurice, 340
Wertheim, Morris, 260
Westchester County, NY, 20, 71, 74, 169, 424
Wheeler, William, 421
White, Andrew D., 127
White, Walter, 486
Whitman, Charles, 336
Whitney, Edward, 84, 144
Wiener, Leo, 296
Wilderness doctrine. *See* Marshall, Robert
Wilderness Society, 406, 443
Wilenkin, Gregory, 219
Williams, Clark, 158–59
Williams, John, 159
Williams, John Sharp, 132
Wilson, Woodrow, 127, 129, 226, 229–30, 233–35, 269–70, 283, 286, 294, 300–302, 306, 310, 316, 323, 329, 343–46, 395, 449–50; and Paris Peace conference, 348, 351–52, 357, 359, 361, 363
Winburn, Jesse, 464
Wise, Isaac Mayer, 45, 48–49, 57, 268, 419
Wise, Stephen, 344–45, 349, 351–52, 445, 463, 503–4, 506, 511, 528, 530; Emanu-El pulpit dispute, 110–12; rivalry with LM, 173–74, 299, 503, 531

Witte, Sergius, 109
Wolbarst, Abraham Leo, 74
Wolf, Lucien, 268, 360–62, 366, 384, 388, 391
Wolf, Simon, 102, 118, 131, 216, 461; immigration activism, 115–16, 135, 181–82, 451; rivalry with LM group, 116, 121, 138–39, 200, 219, 270, 288
Wollman, Henry, 11, 169
Woocher, Jonathan, 119
Woods, Arthur, 146–47
Woodward, C. Vann, 268
World War I. *See* Adler, Cyrus; Magnes, Judah; Marshall, Louis; Paris Peace Conference; Schiff, Jacob
Wynn, Ed, 328

Yale University, 56, 99, 426
Yiddish press, 59–60
Yishuv (Jewish community of Ottoman and British Mandatory Palestine), 22–24, 178–79, 241, 259–61, 285, 305–6, 338–39, 342–44, 368, 429, 468, 496–99, 502, 505–7, 509–10, 515–23, 525
Young Judea, 184–85
Young Men's Christian Association (YMCA), 476

Zangwill, Israel, 300, 361, 381, 402; melting pot ideology, 144, 149–51; territorialism, 115
Zhitlovsky, Chaim, 274, 345–47
Zichron Ya'akov, 177
Zionism/Zionists, xiv, 55, 68, 81, 216, 241, 306–7, 324, 338–43, 358, 368, 408, 429–31, 477; Aaron Aaronsohn and Atlit, 177–81; American, background and growth, 257–59; American, and immigration issues, 181–82; and American Jewish Congress dispute, 136, 258–59, 265–66, 278, 283–88, 294, 297–300, 305–6; Federation of American Zionists, 146, 283, 286, 296; and Jewish Agency negotiations, 508–25; and Jewish farm colonies in Soviet Union dispute, 490, 493, 496–508; at Paris Peace Conference, 348–50, 353, 358–59; response to Kishinev pogrom, 87
Zunz, Leopold, 57
Zurich, 24, 368, 382, 420, 447, 470–71, 525, 533